Client-centered therapy

By the same author
and published by Constable

Counseling and psychotherapy

On becoming a person:
a therapist's view of psychotherapy

Becoming partners:
marriage and its alternatives

Client-centered therapy

Its current practice, implications and theory

Carl R. Rogers Ph.D.

with special chapters by
Elaine Dorfman
Thomas Gordon
Nicholas Hobbs

Constable London

Published by Constable and Company Limited
3 The Lanchesters, 162 Fulham Palace Road, London W6 9ER

Reprinted 1965, 1973, 1976, 1981, 1984, 1986,
1987, 1989, 1990, 1991, 1992, 1993, 1994, 1995
ISBN 0 09 453990 1

Printed in Great Britain by
St Edmundsbury Press Ltd, Bury St Edmunds, Suffolk

WE MARK *with light in the memory the few interviews
we have had, in the dreary years of routine and of sin,
with souls that made our souls wiser; that spoke what we
thought; that told us what we knew; that gave us leave to
be what we inly were.*

— EMERSON, Divinity School Address, 1838

EDITOR'S INTRODUCTION

IN THE PRESENT VOLUME Dr. Carl Rogers and some of his associates have crystallized the great progress that has been made in the past decade in the development of the techniques and basic philosophy of counseling. In this book there is a clear exposition of procedures by means of which individuals who are being counseled may be assisted in achieving for themselves new and more effective personality adjustments. It deals with the nature of this important and subtle therapeutic process and with related counseling problems.

This is no static guidebook to monuments of past thinking. It is rather a current synthesis and a dynamic integration of successful techniques of general counseling and of counseling procedures in special situations. Its pages open up most attractive new lines of study in which further experimentation and investigation may be carried on with profit.

The point of view in regard to psychotherapy and counseling that is explained in this book is one which has from the first been hospitable to analysis of its results by scientific and experimental techniques. The amount of such research that is reported in the present volume may well surprise those whose field of specialization is not in this area of study. This attitude of open-mindedness and of welcome to valid new ideas that are developed by scientific techniques has by no means been characteristic of all previous psychotherapeutic systems.

The implications of the new and vital contributions of nondirective counseling to a number of novel and broad fields are presented in the book. The place of play therapy in work with children is explored in a special chapter. Group therapy is likewise given novel and interesting consideration. The importance of the therapeutic principles that are discussed in the book is treated in relation to problems of group leadership and administration. The application of a nondirective client-centered approach for teaching is evaluated. The special chapter which deals with the school situation cannot fail to be recognized as a significant challenge to the thinking of those who are interested in the improvement of all education that rises above the level of mere routine training. There is a chapter on the preparation of new professional workers in the field of counseling in which special insights are presented, dealing with some of the deepest aspects of the human personality as recognized by the author.

In every chapter of the book there are references to an active and growing theory of the nature of the personality and of the underlying mechanisms which determine human behavior. The final chapter of the book, however, presents a formal treatment of the psychological theory which is basic to the whole client-centered point of view not only in counseling but in all interpersonal relations. This theory concerns itself with a modern understanding of the psychology of the self. It gives a new point of view from which to consider the nature of the maladjustment of modern man in his physical and social environments. Here are outlined in detail therapeutic procedures which do not deal alone with obvious surface adjustments but which seek to reach deep aspects of the personality.

This book supplements, expands, and qualitatively enriches the views so well expressed previously in the author's *Counseling and Psychotherapy*. The present volume does not replace this earlier book. The student who is just becoming acquainted with this modern point of view in psychology may wish to use both books together. In some respects the older work still provides certain essential steps of introduction to the basic concepts of modern counseling which are not repeated in the same detail in this book.

Client-Centered Therapy is a mature presentation of the nondirective and related points of view in counseling and therapy. It seems to the editor that this new book will be of especial value to individuals who are professionally concerned with the problems of working with human maladjustment or with any aspect of the work of assisting other human beings to meet in an adequate and rewarding way the problems of modern living.

The volume is not a rigid presentation of a closed system. The author and his collaborators have captured the gift of making the reader feel as he turns its pages that he is already participating in the constructive and forward-looking thinking which characterizes the basic point of view of the book.

LEONARD CARMICHAEL

Tufts College

PREFACE

THIS BOOK is the product of many minds, and the result of a great deal of group interaction. First and foremost it is a product of the staff of the Counseling Center of the University of Chicago, and of the work there being done in psychotherapy and psychotherapeutic research. So deep has been the mingling of thought and experience in this group that any member of the staff would be bold indeed to regard any conceptualization of psychotherapy as strictly his own. The book is also a pooling of ideas and experiences from psychologists and other workers in the field of therapy scattered from coast to coast. The author would like to indicate something of his indebtedness to those who have influenced his thinking, by naming several who are most likely to find portions of their own thought included in this book. The list would include: Virginia M. Axline, Douglas D. Blocksma, Oliver H. Bown, John M. Butler, Arthur W. Combs, Paul E. Eiserer, Thomas Gordon, Donald L. Grummon, Gerard V. Haigh, Nicholas Hobbs, Richard A. Hogan, Bill L. Kell, E. H. Porter, Jr., Victor C. Raimy, Nathaniel J. Raskin, Esselyn C. Rudikoff, Elizabeth T. Sheerer, Jules Seeman, Arthur J. Shedlin, William U. Snyder, Donald Snygg, Bernard Steinzor, H. Walter Yoder. From this list are omitted many whose work is just as significant as that of those given here, but it includes, I believe, those whose thinking has most influenced the contents of this book. In addition, the author is deeply indebted to Elaine Dorfman, Nicholas Hobbs, and Thomas Gordon for their contributions of individual chapters in areas where he feels less competent.

In writing this book I have often thought of the idea expressed by a semanticist, that the true, the genuine, the real meaning of a word can never be expressed in words, because the real meaning would be the thing itself. If one wishes to give such a real meaning he should put his hand over his mouth and *point*. This is what I should most like to do. I would willingly throw away all the words of this manuscript if I could, somehow, effectively *point* to the experience which is therapy. It is a process, a thing-in-itself, an experience, a relationship, a dynamic. It is not what this book says about it, nor what another book says about it, any more than a flower is the botanist's description of it or the poet's ecstasy over it. If this book serves as a large signpost pointing to an

ix

experience which is open to our senses of hearing and sight and to our capacity for emotional experience, and if it captures the interest of some and causes them to explore more deeply this thing-in-itself, it will have accomplished its purpose. If, on the other hand, this book adds to the already staggering pile of words about words, if its readers get from it the notion that truth is words and that the printed page is all, then it will have sadly failed to achieve its purpose. And if it suffers that final degradation of becoming "classroom knowledge" — where the dead words of an author are dissected and poured into the minds of passive students, so that live individuals carry about the dead and dissected portions of what were once living thoughts and experiences, without even the awareness that they were once living — then better by far that the book had never been written. Therapy is of the essence of life, and is to be so understood. It is only the sad inadequacy of man's capacity for communication that makes it necessary to run the risk of trying to capture that living experience in words.

If then the purpose of this book is not simply to put dead words on paper, what is its purpose? What is it intended to convey? What is this book about? Let me try to give an answer which may, to some degree, convey the living experience that this book is intended to be.

This book is about the suffering and the hope, the anxiety and the satisfaction, with which each therapist's counseling room is filled. It is about the uniqueness of the relationship each therapist forms with each client, and equally about the common elements which we discover in all these relationships. This book is about the highly personal experiences of each one of us. It is about a client in my office who sits there by the corner of the desk, struggling to be himself, yet deathly afraid of being himself — striving to see his experience as it is, wanting to *be* that experience, and yet deeply fearful of the prospect. The book is about me, as I sit there with that client, facing him, participating in that struggle as deeply and sensitively as I am able. It is about me as I try to perceive his experience, and the meaning and the feeling and the taste and the flavor that it has for him. It is about me as I bemoan my very human fallibility in understanding that client, and the occasional failures to see life as it appears to him, failures which fall like heavy objects across the intricate, delicate web of growth which is taking place. It is about me as I rejoice at the privilege of being a midwife to a new personality — as I stand by with awe at the emergence of a self, a person, as I see a birth process in which I have had an important and facilitating part. It is about both the client and me as we regard with wonder the potent and orderly forces which are evident in this whole experience, forces which seem deeply rooted in the universe as a whole. The book is, I believe, about life, as life vividly reveals itself in the therapeutic process — with its blind power and its tremendous capacity for destruction, but with its overbalancing thrust toward growth, if the opportunity for growth is provided.

But the book is also about my colleagues and me as we undertake the beginnings of scientific analysis of this living, emotional experience. It is about our conflicts in this respect — our strong feeling that the therapeutic process is rich in shadings, complexities, and subtleties, and our equally strong feeling that the scientific finding, the generalization, is cold, lifeless, and lacking in the fullness of the experience. But the book also expresses, I trust, our growing conviction that though science can never make therapists, it can help therapy; that though the scientific finding is cold and abstract, it may assist us in releasing forces that are warm, personal, and complex; and that though science is slow and fumbling, it represents the best road we know to the truth, even in so delicately intricate an area as that of human relationships.

Again the book is about these others and me as we go about our daily tasks and find ourselves compellingly influenced by the therapeutic experience of which we have been a part. It is about each of us as we try to teach, to lead groups, to consult with industry, to serve as administrators and supervisors, and find that we can no longer function as we formerly did. It is about each of us as we try to face up to the internal revolution which therapy has meant for us: the fact that we can never teach a class, chair a committee, or raise a family without having our behavior profoundly influenced by a deep and moving experience which has elements of commonality for all of us.

Finally, the book is about all of us as we puzzle over this experience — as we endeavor to put it into some intellectual framework, as we try to build concepts which will contain it. It is most deeply about us as we realize the inadequacy of these words, forms, constructs, to contain all the elements of the vivid process which we have experienced with our clients. It is about our feeling of tentativeness as we advance these theories in the hope that they may strike here and there a spark which will aid in illuminating and advancing this whole area of endeavor.

Perhaps all this conveys some notion of what the book is about. But this prefatory note cannot be concluded without a word of thanks to the people who have really written it, who have, in the most genuine sense been its major contributors — the clients with whom we have worked. To these men, women, and children who have brought themselves and their struggles to us, who have with such natural grace permitted us to learn from them, who have laid bare for us the forces which operate in the mind and spirit of man — to them goes our deepest gratitude. We hope that the book will be worthy of them.

CARL R. ROGERS

Chicago, Illinois

CONTENTS

PART I *A Current View of Client-Centered Therapy*

1. The Developing Character of Client-Centered Therapy   3

2. The Attitude and Orientation of the Counselor   19

3. The Therapeutic Relationship as Experienced by the Client   65

4. The Process of Therapy   131

5. Three Questions Raised by Other Viewpoints: Transference, Diagnosis, Applicability   197

PART II *The Application of Client-Centered Therapy*

6. Play Therapy   235
   by Elaine Dorfman, M.A.

7. Group-Centered Psychotherapy   278
   by Nicholas Hobbs, Ph.D.

8. Group-Centered Leadership and Administration   320
   by Thomas Gordon, Ph.D.

9. Student-Centered Teaching   384

10. The Training of Counselors and Therapists   429

PART III *Implications for Psychological Theory*

11. A Theory of Personality and Behavior   481

REFERENCES   535

INDEX   549

PART I *A Current View of Client-Centered Therapy*

Chapter 1 · The Developing Character of Client-Centered Therapy

Professional interest in psychotherapy is in all likelihood the most rapidly growing area in the social sciences today. In clinical psychology and psychiatry the development of this field is proceeding with astonishing rapidity. Nearly twenty per cent of the members of the American Psychological Association give psychotherapy — or adjustment counseling or some similar term — as one of their major interests, whereas a decade ago this would have been true of only a handful. Programs of training in psychotherapy have been growing in number, scope, intensity, and we hope in effectiveness. Furthermore, we find educators who are eager to keep pace with the developments in therapy in order that they may adapt and use these findings through the work of school and college counselors and adjustment teachers. Ministers and religious workers are seeking training in counseling and psychotherapy in order to improve their skill in dealing with the personal problems of their parishioners. Sociologists and social psychologists have a keen interest in this field because of its possible adaptations to work with groups, and because it helps to shed light on the dynamics of groups as well as individuals. And last, but far from least, the average citizen is supporting the rapid extension of psychotherapeutic work to his children in school, to veterans by the thousands, to industrial workers, and to the students, parents, and other adults who wish psychological help.

In short, there appears to be a strong trend toward studying, developing, and utilizing those procedures which offer help in bringing to modern man an increased peace of mind. It would seem that as our culture has grown less homogeneous, it gives much less support to the individual. He cannot simply rest comfortably upon the ways and traditions of his society, but finds many of the basic issues and conflicts of life centering in himself. Each man must resolve within himself issues for which his society previously took full responsibility. Because psychotherapy holds promise of resolving some of those conflicts, of giving the individual a more satisfying adjustment within himself as well as a more satisfying relationship to others and to his environment, it has become a significant focal point of both public and professional interest.

In this broadening stream of interest in and development of psychotherapeutic procedures, nondirective or client-centered counseling has had its growth. It is a product of its time and its cultural setting. Its development would not have been possible without the appreciation of man's unconscious strivings and complex emotional nature which was Freud's contribution to our culture. Though it has developed along somewhat different paths than the psychotherapeutic views of Horney or Sullivan, or Alexander and French, yet there are many threads of interconnection with these modern formulations of psychoanalytic thinking. Especially are roots of client-centered therapy to be found in the therapy of Rank, and the Philadelphia group which has integrated his views into their own. Even more deeply, client-centered therapy has been influenced by psychology as it has developed in the United States, with its genius for operational definitions, for objective measurement, its insistence upon scientific method and the necessity of submitting all hypotheses to a process of objective verification or disproof. As will be evident to readers of this volume, it has also been indebted to Gestalt psychology, with its emphasis upon the wholeness and interrelatedness of the cluster of phenomena which we think of as the individual. Some of its roots stretch out even further into the educational and social and political philosophy which is at the heart of our American culture. So much is this true that paragraphs from a book such as Lilienthal's small volume on the TVA, if lifted from context, could equally well be regarded as an exposition of the basic orientation of the client-centered therapist.[1] Thus client-centered therapy has drawn, both consciously and unconsciously, upon many of the current streams of clinical, scientific, and philosophical thought which are present in our culture.

Yet it would perhaps be a mistake to view client-centered therapy as solely a product of cultural influences. Most deeply of all, it is built upon close, intimate, and specific observations of man's behavior in a relationship, observations which it is believed transcend to some degree the limitations or influences of a given culture. Likewise in its research attempts to discover the significant laws which operate in a therapeutic relationship it is endeavoring to cut through to invariances, to behavioral sequences which are true not only for a day or a culture, but which describe the way in which man's nature operates.

Though ten years ago neither "nondirective" nor "client-centered" had been coined as a label, interest in the point of view described by these terms has grown very rapidly. It has captured the attention of psychologists and others to a point where one cannot pick up a psychological journal or book without a considerable likelihood of finding some reference to it, whether negative or positive. There appears to be a need for some means of informing those who wish to know more fully of the development of this particular therapeutic approach to individual problems and human relationships. It is hoped that this book will to some extent satisfy such a need.

A Changing Approach

There has been a tendency to regard the nondirective or client-centered approach as something static — a method, a technique, a

[1] See for example the discussion of Democracy at the Grass Roots, and The Release of Human Energies, in *TVA — Democracy on the March*, by David E. Lilienthal.

rather rigid system. Nothing could be further from the truth. The group of professional workers in this field are working with dynamic concepts which they are constantly revising in the light of continuing clinical experience and in the light of research findings. The picture is one of fluid changes in a general approach to problems of human relationships, rather than a situation in which some relatively rigid technique is more or less mechanically applied.

In this flux of changing thinking there are some central hypotheses which give unity to the search for further knowledge. Perhaps one of the reasons for the high stimulus-value which client-centered therapy seems to have had is the fact that these hypotheses are testable, are capable of proof or disproof, and hence offer a hope of progress, rather than the stagnation of dogma. There appears to be more than a likelihood that psychotherapy is, by the efforts of various workers, being brought out of the realm of the mystical, the intuitive, the personal, the undefinable, into the full light of objective scrutiny. This inevitably means that change rather than rigidity becomes the characteristic of such a field. To those at work in client-centered therapy, this characteristic of development, of reformulation, of change, appears to be one of its most outstanding qualities.

The Aim of This Volume

The purpose, then, of this volume is to present, not a fixed and rigid point of view, but a current cross section of a developing field of therapy, with its practices and theory, indicating the changes and trends which are evident, making comparisons with earlier formulations and, to a limited extent, with viewpoints held by other therapeutic orientations.

In doing this, one aim will be to bring together the clinical thinking of those who are engaged in client-centered therapy. The hypotheses they have come to hold, the formulations they are making of the therapeutic process, will be presented. Illustrative material from electrically recorded interviews will, it is hoped, indicate something of the ways in which issues are dealt with in the counseling hour. Statements from clients [1] themselves about their experience will also be given, since such material has had definite influence on the thinking of the therapists. Thus it is hoped that the reader may gain an overview of the current thinking and practice of clinical therapists working from a similar orientation, with a wide range of individuals.

A further aim will be to review the research evidence which has been and is being gathered in respect to the hypotheses which are explicit or implicit in therapy. Little by little, objective evidence is accumulating in regard to various phases of therapy, and the results of this research endeavor will be analyzed and considered.

A newer aspect of this volume, and one which has been less covered in journal publications, is the presentation of a theory of therapy and a theory of personality. Both in the attempt to explain the process of therapy, and in the desire to understand the basic personality structure which makes therapy possible, theory is being continually formulated and revised, and the ramifications of this thinking will be presented, with stress upon its fluid quality.

Finally the effort will be made to pose some of the unanswered problems and perplexities which cry out for deeper understanding, for more adequate research, for new and more penetrating theory.

The Presentation of a "School of Thought"

It is clearly the purpose of these pages to present only one point of view, and to leave to others the development of other

---

[1] What term shall be used to indicate the person with whom the therapist is dealing? "Patient," "subject," "counselee," "analysand," are terms which have been used. We have increasingly used the term client, to the point where we have absorbed it into the label of "client-centered therapy." It has been chosen because, in spite of its imperfections of dictionary meaning and derivation, it seems to come closest to conveying the picture of this person as we see it. The client, as the term has acquired its meaning, is one who comes actively and voluntarily to gain help on a problem, but without any notion of surrendering his own responsibility for the situation. It is because the term has these connotations that we have chosen it, since it avoids the connotation that he is sick, or the object of an experiment, and so on. The term client does have certain legal connotations which are unfortunate, and if a better term emerges we shall be happy to use it. For the present, however, this seems the term most appropriately related to our concept of the person coming for help.

orientations. There will be no apology for this "one-sided" presentation. It appears to the writer that the somewhat critical attitude which is usually held toward anything which may be defined as a "school of thought" grows out of a lack of appreciation of the way in which science grows. In a new field of investigation which is being opened up to objective study, the school of thought is a necessary cultural step. Where objective evidence is limited, it is almost inevitable that markedly different hypotheses will be developed and offered to explain the phenomena which are observed. The corollaries and ramifications of any such hypothesis constitute a system which is a school of thought. These schools of thought will not be abolished by wishful thinking. The person who attempts to reconcile them by compromise will find himself left with a superficial eclecticism which does not increase objectivity, and which leads nowhere. Truth is not arrived at by concessions from differing schools of thought. The eventual disappearance of such rival formulations comes about either when the issues are settled by research evidence, or when both types of hypotheses are absorbed into some new and more penetrating view which sees the problems from a new vantage point, thus redefining the issues in a way not hitherto perceived.

There are disadvantages connected with the presentation of a single orientation, or a school of thought, but these are minimized if we are aware of them. There is the possibility that hypotheses will be presented as dogmas. There is the possibility that emotional involvement with a point of view may make the perception of contradictory evidence unlikely. Over against these disadvantages is the advantage of facilitation of progress. If we have a consistent system of hypotheses which we are testing, and if we are able to discard, revise, reformulate these hypotheses in the light of objective experience, we have a valuable tool, a "task force," by which new areas of knowledge may be opened up.

Consequently, one will find in this volume the development of a point of view, the statement of a related system of hypotheses, and no attempt to present other systems, since this is much better done by those who advocate them. Such objective research evidence as has been collected with relation to these hypotheses will be presented, as well as clinical evidence in its most objective form, the recorded interview. Efforts have been made to eliminate emotional bias, but the reader may well discover points at which this aim has not been achieved, and at which he will therefore have to make his own corrections. If a systematic body of hypotheses, with implications reaching into every type of interpersonal and group relationship, serves to stimulate more research, more critical evaluation of clinical practice, more adequate theoretical thinking, then this presentation will have served its purpose.

RECENT DEVELOPMENTS IN CLIENT-CENTERED THERAPY

It was in 1940 that the writer made a first attempt at crystallizing in written form [1] some of the principles and techniques of a newer approach to therapy, an approach which soon became labeled "nondirective counseling." Two years later *Counseling and Psychotherapy: Newer Concepts in Practice* (166) [2] was published. In that volume a presentation was given of the practice of those principles in the counseling field which were aimed at releasing the integrative capacities of the individual. It may be of service to the reader to review briefly some of the developments which have taken place in the decade or so since these ideas were first formulated. It will then be more evident why another presentation seems necessary at this time.

Developments in Range of Practice

At the time when *Counseling and Psychotherapy* was being written, a part of the work at the Psychological Clinic of Ohio State University was being carried on from the nondirective point of view, based on earlier work done by the staff of the Rochester Guidance Center under the author's direction. In addition, a

[1] In a paper entitled "Newer Concepts of Psychotherapy," delivered to the Minnesota chapter of Psi Chi in December, 1940. In a slightly revised form, this paper became Chapter II of the book *Counseling and Psychotherapy*, published in 1942.

[2] Numbers in parentheses refer to the list of references at the end of the book.

very similar point of view had been independently developed and put into practice by Roethlisberger, Dickson, and their colleagues in the Western Electric plant. A somewhat similar therapeutic approach, stemming directly from the work of Otto Rank (work which had also influenced the present writer) was being practiced by social workers, psychiatrists, and psychologists who received their training in the Philadelphia area under such workers as Jessie Taft, Frederick Allen, and Virginia Robinson. This was about the extent of any practical experience with a therapeutic orientation which relied primarily upon the capacity of the client.

At the present time several hundred counselors in colleges and in the Veterans Administration, psychologists in counseling centers, in mental hygiene clinics, and in psychiatric hospitals, as well as workers in schools, industry, social work, and religious work, are attempting, with varying degrees of training and skill, to test out for themselves the hypotheses of a nondirective approach. These widely spread professional workers have had experience with students, with other adults, with maladjusted children and their parents. They have dealt, in appropriate settings, with such specialized areas as marital problems, vocational problems, speech difficulties, psychosomatic conditions such as allergies, a wide range of neurotic problems, and to some extent with psychoses. There has not as yet been adequate time for research investigations of the process and outcomes in each of these groups, but the experience of these workers has been feeding back into the central stream of thinking about client-centered therapy.

During the decade, too, therapists experienced in this orientation have watched with interest as their cases grew longer and longer, involving an increasing degree of personality reorganization. Thus, where ten years ago a nondirective counselor found that his cases tended to average five or six interviews each, and rarely to run longer than fifteen, this same counselor finds that his cases now average fifteen to twenty interviews, and that fifty or one hundred interviews are not unusual. Has this development occurred because of the greater skill of the counselor in building an understanding relationship? Or because of the fact that as a counselor becomes well established more seriously maladjusted individuals turn to him? Or because some subtle change has taken place in viewpoint or technique? Whatever the cause, the thinking about client-centered therapy has been enriched by this range of intensity of experience.

Thus we may say that at the present time the clinical thinking in regard to client-centered therapy has been fed by the wide range of problems and the great variation of intensity of its work. From the mildly misbehaving child to the psychotic adult, and from the person who gains some help in two interviews to the individual who undergoes an extensive reorganization of personality in one hundred and fifty interviews — these mark some of the greatly extended boundaries of the present practice of client-centered therapy.

Development of a Variety of Activities

Ten years ago nondirective counseling was thought of as a process of verbal interchange, useful primarily in the counseling of adolescents and adults. Since that time the basic principles of such counseling have been thought to be applicable to a variety of activities, some of them very diverse indeed from psychotherapy itself. Some of these will be discussed at length later in this book, but a brief mention may be made here of certain directions in which client-centered therapy has been found to have implications.

Play therapy with problem children has been found effective when carried on from a client-centered point of view. Axline's book (14) gives a thorough and persuasive picture of the work which has been done in this field, where verbal interchange is often at a minimum or even lacking entirely.

Group therapy, both with children and adults, has been carried on effectively, operating on the same fundamental hypotheses as in individual counseling. Work has been done with maladjusted adults, with students who have problems, with students prior to examinations, with veterans, with interracial groups, with children, and with parents.

Out of the experience with group therapy came the desire to conduct college classes in a client-centered — or more appropriately, a student-centered — fashion. Some of our most significant learnings have come from the resounding failures and the glowing successes of our attempts to adapt the principles and procedures of successful psychotherapy to education.

These are the major fields in which the implications of client-centered therapy have been worked out. But equally significant contributions to our thinking have come from other attempts, less fully explored. Interesting experiences in using a client-centered approach in group situations of friction and poor morale have convinced us that this approach has a contribution to make to industrial, military, and other groups. Especially meaningful have been our attempts to apply client-centered principles to our own organizational administration, committee work, and problems of personnel selection and evaluation. There is still much to be learned in these fields, but enough progress has been made to be stimulating indeed.

Thus in a decade, we have seen client-centered therapy develop from a method of counseling to an approach to human relationships. We have come to feel that it has as much application to the problem of employing a new staff member, or the decision as to who is to get a raise, as it does to the client who is troubled by an inability to handle his social relationships.

Progress in Research

Nowhere are the advances in the field of psychotherapy indicated in such striking fashion as in the steady progress of research. Ten years ago there were no more than a handful of objective research studies which were in any way related to psychotherapy. During the past decade more than forty such studies have been published by workers with a client-centered orientation. In addition, there are a number of studies as yet unpublished, and more than a score of increasingly significant research projects under way. It is difficult to exaggerate the general effect that this work has had. Though the researches have had definite and often serious limitations, each one has used instruments of a known and stated degree of reliability, and the methods have been described in sufficient detail so that any competent worker can verify the findings, either by restudying the same case material or by using the same method on new material. Two of the early studies have already been confirmed by being repeated on current cases. All of this development has meant that it is becoming increasingly difficult to speak in purely dogmatic terms about any aspect of psychotherapy. Little by little it has become apparent that we can investigate objectively almost any phase of psychotherapy about which we wish to know, from the subtlest aspect of the counselor-client relationship to measures of behavioral change.

The basis for this development has been first and foremost the accumulation of complete electrically recorded case material. *Counseling and Psychotherapy* carried the first complete verbatim therapeutic case presented in published form. This was followed by the *Casebook of Non-directive Counseling* (199), in which five cases were given, with most of the interviews verbatim. At the present time the Counseling Center of the University of Chicago has nearly thirty cases completely recorded and transcribed, which are available to qualified research workers. It is hoped that at least fifty more will be added, for which the sound recording as well as the typescript will be available. This will give a mass of basic material for research investigation such as never has existed before. Successes and failures, cases carried by expert counselors and by those in training, short cases and long cases — all will be exemplified.

In the accumulation of recorded case material and in the prosecution of research in therapy, client-centered therapists have thus far carried the major burden. Yet there is encouraging evidence that workers with other views are now recording their cases, and it is only a question of time before research studies will be made by Freudian analysts, hypnotherapists, Adlerians, and eclectic therapists. It is these research studies of the future which will help to remove the labels and unify the field of psychotherapy.

The Development of Training Programs

When *Counseling and Psychotherapy* was being published in

1942, the publishers wished to know what market there would be for the book in university courses in adjustment counseling. The answer at that time seemed to be that there were no more than two or three such courses throughout the country. Due to a variety of recent influences upon the psychological profession, this picture has changed to an astonishing degree. More than a score of universities now offer some type of graduate training in psychotherapy, with varying degrees of emphasis being given to a client-centered point of view. In several of these universities a full-fledged sequence of training courses is available, with the practice of therapy under supervision a central portion of the experience. Such training in therapy is not simply a sporadic development. It is given formal approval by the American Psychological Association, which has stated that the training of the clinical psychologist is not complete without training in psychotherapy, and that to be given the highest level of American Psychological Association approval the graduate program in clinical psychology must include a well-planned program in this field (160). Much the same type of development has taken place in psychiatry, and in place of the sporadic on-the-job training in therapy which was once so prevalent, increasingly integrated programs are being built in various centers.

Against this general background of growth of training programs in therapy, there has been a constant evolution of training in client-centered therapy. So much have our methods and procedures changed that a later chapter in this volume is set aside to consider them. The principle of reliance upon the individual has found its implementation in the training program as well as in therapy itself. Our concern has shifted from counselor technique to counselor attitude and philosophy, with a new recognition of the importance of technique considered from a more sophisticated level. There has been the experience of slow and gradual training of Ph.D. candidates in clinical psychology. There has also been the extremely valuable experience of supplying, during 1946 and 1947, a short and intensive training experience for more than a hundred mature and qualified psychologists who were to become Personal Counselors for the Veterans Administration. In attempting to train for therapy, we have inevitably learned much about therapy.

The Development of Theory

As we have carried on the increasingly ramified work which is suggested in the preceding sections, the necessity for unifying theories has become strongly felt, and the formulation of theory has become one of the major preoccupations of the client-centered therapist. We have proven in our own experience Kurt Lewin's oft-quoted statement that "Nothing is so practical as a good theory." Much of our theory construction has revolved about the construct of the self, as will be evident in later pages. Attempts have been made, however, to phrase explanations in terms of learning theory, and in terms of the dynamics of an interpersonal relationship. In this whole process, theories have been discarded or greatly modified, as well as developed. Several years ago the theory of therapy seemed best phrased in terms of the development of verbalized insight. This type of formulation seems to us today to fall far short of explaining all the phenomena of therapy, and hence occupies a relatively small place in our current thinking.

Having viewed from inside the group the persistent and rapid flowering of theory, it has been a matter of interest to observe how frequently client-centered therapy has been criticized because "it proceeds from no coherent theory of personality." This criticism seems like such an odd distortion of the place of theory in scientific advance that a brief counter-statement seems in order.

There is no need for theory until and unless there are phenomena to explain. Limiting our consideration to psychotherapy, there is no reason for a theory of therapy until there are observable changes which call for explanation. Then a unifying theory is of help in explaining what has happened, and in providing testable hypotheses about future experiences. Thus, in the field of therapy the first requisite is a skill which produces an effective result. Through observation of the process and the result a parsimonious theory may be developed which is projected into new experiences in order to be tested as to its adequacy. The theory is revised and modified with the purpose — never fully attained — of providing a complete conceptual framework which can adequately contain all the observed phenomena. It is the phenomena which are basic, not the theory.

Elton Mayo gives a succinct statement of this point of view, first in his own words and then in the words of one of his colleagues. A quotation may give the gist of his thinking.

> Speaking historically, I think it can be asserted that a science has generally come into being as a product of well-developed technical skill in a given area of activity. Someone, some skilled worker, has in a reflective moment attempted to make explicit the assumptions that are implicit in the skill itself. This makes the beginning of logico-experimental method. The assumptions once made explicit can be logically developed; the development leads to experimental changes of practice and so to the beginning of a science. The point to be remarked is that scientific abstractions are not drawn from thin air or uncontrolled reflection: they are from the beginning rooted deeply in a pre-existent skill.
>
> At this point, a comment taken from the lectures of a colleague, the late Lawrence Henderson, eminent in chemistry, seems apposite: ". . . In the complex business of living, as in medicine, both theory and practice are necessary conditions of understanding, and the method of Hippocrates is the only method that has ever succeeded widely and generally. The first element of that method is hard, persistent, intelligent, responsible, unremitting labor in the sick room, not in the library: the complete adaptation of the doctor to his task, an adaptation that is far from being merely intellectual. The second element of that method is accurate observation of things and events, selection, guided by judgment born of familiarity and experience, of the salient and recurrent phenomena, and their classification and methodical exploitation. The third element of that method is the judicious construction of a theory — not a philosophical theory, nor a grand effort of the imagination, nor a quasi-religious dogma, but a modest pedestrian affair . . . a useful walking stick to help on the way. . . . All this may be summed up in a word: The physician must have, first, intimate, habitual, intuitive familiarity with things; secondly, systematic knowledge of things; and thirdly, an effective way of thinking about things." (130, pp. 17–18)

Operating from this point of view it has seemed to us that it is entirely natural that the fragile flower of theory has grown out of the solid soil of experience. A reversal of this natural order would seem unsound. Hence there will be found in this volume a ramified group of theoretical formulations which have a certain unity and which, it is felt, provide a fruitful way of thinking about therapeutic change, and also a conceptualization of the individual personality which is based on observation of personality change. But it cannot be too strongly stressed that the theories are changing and fluid. It is the phenomena that they endeavor to explain which remain as stubborn facts. Perhaps tomorrow or next year we shall perceive a much more comprehensive theoretical formulation which can contain a much wider range of these basic facts. If so, then this new theory will provide more and better hypotheses for testing, and more stimulation to a progressive search for truth.

An Overview

This introductory chapter has endeavored to provide something of an external overview of the factors which have influenced the course of thinking in client-centered therapy during the past eight or ten years. But what conclusions have counselors reached? How have they modified their approach as they have dealt with more varied and more serious cases? What do they regard as essential in being of help to the person with problems? What fresh understandings of the process of therapy have been achieved as they have listened, singly and in groups, to the recordings of significant interviews? How do they explain their failures, and what changes have entered into their thinking as they have tried to reduce the likelihood of failure? What have been the achievements and disappointments involved in the laborious research analysis of this mine of recorded material? What theories have these therapists come to hold, and why do they regard them as reasonable? Do they have any formulations which help to give meaning to the confused worlds of professional and personal experience? The pages which follow represent one individual's interpretation of the current answers which are being given to these questions — answers which will be at least partially out of date by the time they are written down.

SUGGESTED READINGS

For a consideration of the historical development of client-centered therapy, see Raskin (158). The development of the writer's own thinking in regard to therapy may be observed by considering the sequence of writings, *Clinical Treatment of the Problem Child* (164), "The Clinical Psychologist's Approach to Personality Problems" (165), *Counseling and Psychotherapy* (166), "Significant Aspects of Client-Centered Therapy" (170), and the present volume. For formulations of client-centered therapy made by others, see Combs (42) and Snyder (194).

For a consideration of client-centered therapy in relation to other therapeutic orientations, Snyder (198) gives an exhaustive review of current literature. A brief paper on this subject, written from a client-centered point of view, is "Current Trends in Psychotherapy" (167).

A description of the practical functioning of a group of client-centered therapists in practice is given by Grummon and Gordon (75).

References regarding the implications of client-centered therapy for the fields of play therapy, group therapy, education, and personality theory will be found in the chapters devoted to those topics.

Chapter 2 · The Attitude and Orientation of the Counselor[1]

In any psychotherapy, the therapist himself is a highly important part of the human equation. What he does, the attitude he holds, his basic concept of his role, all influence therapy to a marked degree. Differing therapeutic orientations hold differing views on these points. At the very outset of our discussion, therefore, it seems appropriate to consider the therapist as he functions in client-centered counseling.

A General Consideration

It is common to find client-centered therapy spoken of as simply a method or a technique to be used by the counselor. No doubt this connotation is due in part to the fact that earlier presentations tended to overstress technique. It may more accurately be said that the counselor who is effective in client-centered therapy holds a coherent and developing set of attitudes deeply imbedded in his personal organization, a system of attitudes which is implemented by techniques and methods consistent with it. In our experience, the counselor who tries to use a "method" is doomed to be unsuccessful unless this method is genuinely in line with his own attitudes. On the other hand, the counselor whose attitudes are

[1] This chapter is a revision and extension of an article which first appeared in the *Journal of Consulting Psychology* (April, 1949), *13*, 82–94.

of the type which facilitate therapy may be only partially successful, because his attitudes are inadequately implemented by
appropriate methods and techniques.

Let us, then, consider the attitudes which appear to facilitate
client-centered therapy. Must the counselor possess them in
order to be a counselor? May these attitudes be achieved through
training?

The Philosophical Orientation of the Counselor

Some workers are reluctant to consider the relationship of
philosophical views to scientific professional work. Yet in therapeutic endeavor this relation appears to be one of the significant
and scientifically observable facts that cannot be ignored. Our
experience in training counselors would indicate that the basic
operational philosophy of the individual (which may or may not
resemble his verbalized philosophy) determines, to a considerable
extent, the time it will take him to become a skillful counselor.

The primary point of importance here is the attitude held by
the counselor toward the worth and the significance of the individual. How do we look upon others? Do we see each person
as having worth and dignity in his own right? If we do hold this
point of view at the verbal level, to what extent is it operationally
evident at the behavioral level? Do we tend to treat individuals as
persons of worth, or do we subtly devaluate them by our attitudes
and behavior? Is our philosophy one in which respect for the
individual is uppermost? Do we respect his capacity and his
right to self-direction, or do we basically believe that his life
would be best guided by us? To what extent do we have a need
and a desire to dominate others? Are we willing for the individual
to select and choose his own values, or are our actions guided by
the conviction (usually unspoken) that he would be happiest if he
permitted us to select for him his values and standards and
goals?

The answers to questions of this sort appear to be important as
basic determiners of the therapist's approach. It has been our
experience that individuals who are already striving toward an

orientation which stresses the significance and worth of each person can learn rather readily the client-centered techniques which implement this point of view. This is often true of workers in education who have a strongly child-centered philosophy of education. It is not infrequently true of religious workers who have a humanistic approach. Among psychologists and psychiatrists there are those with similar views, but there are also many whose concept of the individual is that of an object to be dissected, diagnosed, manipulated. Such professional workers may find it very difficult to learn or to practice a client-centered form of therapy. In any event, the differences in this respect seem to determine the readiness or unreadiness of professional workers to learn and achieve a client-centered approach.

Even this statement of the situation gives a static impression which is inaccurate. One's operational philosophy, one's set of goals, is not a fixed and unchanging thing, but a fluid and developing organization. Perhaps it would be more accurate to say that the person whose philosophical orientation has tended to move in the direction of greater respect for the individual finds in the client-centered approach a challenge to and an implementation of his views. He finds that here is a point of view in human relationships which tends to carry him further philosophically than he has heretofore ventured, and to provide the possibility of an operational technique for putting into effect this respect for persons, to the full degree that it exists in his own attitudes. The therapist who endeavors to utilize this approach soon learns that the development of the way of looking upon people which underlies this therapy is a continuing process, closely related to the therapist's own struggle for personal growth and integration. He can be only as "nondirective" as he has achieved respect for others in his own personality organization.

Perhaps it would summarize the point being made to say that, by use of client-centered techniques, a person can implement his respect for others only so far as that respect is an integral part of his personality make-up; consequently the person whose operational philosophy has already moved in the direction of *feeling* a deep respect for the significance and worth of each person is more readily able to assimilate client-centered techniques which help him to express this feeling.[1]

The Therapist's Hypothesis

The question may well arise, in view of the preceding section, as to whether client-centered therapy is then simply a cult, or a speculative philosophy, in which a certain type of faith or belief achieves certain results, and where lack of such faith prevents these results from occurring. Is this, in other words, simply an illusion which produces further illusions?

Such a question deserves careful consideration. That observations to date would seem to point to an answer in the negative is perhaps most strikingly indicated in the experience of various counselors whose initial philosophic orientation has been rather distant from that described as favorable to an optimum use of client-centered techniques. The experience of such individuals in training has seemed to follow something of a pattern. Initially there is relatively little trust in the capacity of the client to achieve insight or constructive self-direction, although the counselor is intrigued intellectually by the possibilities of nondirective therapy and learns something of the techniques. He starts counseling clients with a very limited hypothesis of respect, which might be stated somewhat in these terms: "I will hypothesize that the individual has a limited capacity to understand and reorganize himself to some degree in certain types of situations. In many situations and with many clients, I, as a more objective outsider, can better know the situation and better guide it." It is on this limited and divided basis that he begins his work. He is often not very successful. But as he observes his counseling results, he finds that

[1] This whole topic might be helpfully pursued on a deeper level. What permits the therapist to have a deep respect for, and acceptance of, another? In our experience, such a philosophy is most likely to be held by the person who has a basic respect for the worth and significance of himself. One cannot, in all likelihood, accept others unless he has first accepted himself. This could lead us off into various byways, to a consideration of those experiences, including therapy, which assist the therapist to gain an abiding and realistically founded self-respect. We shall leave such a discussion for Chapter 10, limiting ourselves here simply to a description of the philosophical organization which seems to be the most effective foundation for this type of therapy.

clients accept and make constructive use of responsibility when he is genuinely willing for them to do so. He is often surprised at their effectiveness in handling this responsibility. Against the less vital quality of the experience in those situations where he, the counselor, has endeavored to interpret, evaluate, and guide, he cannot help but contrast the quality of the experience in those situations where the client has learned significantly for himself. Thus he finds that the first portion of his hypothesis tends to be proved beyond his expectations, while the second portion proves disappointing. So, little by little, the hypothesis upon which he bases all his therapeutic work shifts to an increasingly client-centered foundation.

This type of process, which we have seen repeated many times, would appear to mean simply this: that the attitudinal orientation, the philosophy of human relationships which seems to be a necessary basis for client-centered counseling, is not something which must be taken "on faith," or achieved all at once. It is a point of view which may be adopted tentatively and partially, and put to the test. It is actually an hypothesis in human relationships, and will always remain so. Even for the experienced counselor, who has observed in many many cases the evidence which supports the hypothesis, it is still true that, for the new client who comes in the door, the possibility of self-understanding and intelligent self-direction is still — for this client — a completely unproved hypothesis.

It would seem justifiable to say that the faith or belief in the capacity of the individual to deal with his psychological situation and with himself is of the same order as any scientific hypothesis. It is a positive basis for action, but it is open to proof or disproof. If, for example, we had faith that every person could determine for himself whether he had incipient cancer, our experience with this hypothesis would soon cause us to revise it sharply. On the other hand, if we have faith that warm maternal affection is likely to produce desirable personal reactions and personality growth in the infant, we are likely to find this hypothesis supported, at least tentatively, by our experience.

Hence, to put in more summarized or definitive form the attitudinal orientation which appears to be optimal for the client-centered counselor, we may say that the counselor chooses to act consistently upon the hypothesis that the individual has a sufficient capacity to deal constructively with all those aspects of his life which can potentially come into conscious awareness. This means the creation of an interpersonal situation in which material may come into the client's awareness, and a meaningful demonstration of the counselor's acceptance of the client as a person who is competent to direct himself. The counselor acts upon this hypothesis in a specific and operational fashion, being always alert to note those experiences (clinical or research) which contradict this hypothesis as well as those which support it.

Though he is alert to all the evidence, this does not mean that he keeps shifting his basic hypothesis in counseling situations. If the counselor feels, in the middle of an interview, that this client may not have the capacity for reorganizing himself, and shifts to the hypothesis that the counselor must bear a considerable responsibility for this reorganization, he confuses the client, and defeats himself. He has shut himself off from proving or disproving either hypothesis. This confused eclecticism, which has been prevalent in psychotherapy, has blocked scientific progress in the field. Actually it is only by acting *consistently* upon a well-selected hypothesis that its elements of truth and untruth can become known.

The Specific Implementation of the Counselor's Attitude

Thus far the discussion has been a general one, considering the counselor's basic attitude toward others. How does this become implemented in the therapeutic situation? Is it enough that the counselor hold the basic hypothesis we have described, and that this attitudinal orientation will then inevitably move therapy forward? Most assuredly this is not enough. It is as though a physician of the last century had come to believe that bacteria cause infection. Holding this attitude would probably make it inevitable that he should obtain somewhat better results than his colleagues who looked upon this hypothesis with contempt. But only as he implemented his attitude to the fullest extent with appropriate techniques would he fully experience the significance of his hypothesis. Only as he made sterile the area around the incision, the instruments, the sheets, the bandages, his hands, the hands of his assistants — only then would he experience the full meaning and full effectiveness of this tentative hypothesis which he had come to hold in a general way.

So it is with the counselor. As he finds new and more subtle ways of implementing his client-centered hypothesis, new meanings are poured into it by experience, and its depth is seen to be greater than was first supposed. As one counselor-in-training put it, "I hold about the same views I did a year ago, but they have so much more meaning for me."

It is possible that one of the most significant general contributions of the client-centered approach has been its insistence upon investigating the detailed implementation of the counselor's point of view in the interview itself. Many different therapists from a number of differing orientations state their general purposes in somewhat similar terms. Only by a careful study of the recorded interview — preferably with both the sound recording and transcribed typescript available — is it possible to determine what purpose or purposes are actually being implemented in the interview. "Am I actually doing what I think I am doing? Am I operationally carrying out the purposes which I verbalize?" These are questions which every counselor must continually be asking himself. There is ample evidence from our research analyses that a subjective judgment by the counselor himself regarding these questions is not enough. Only an objective analysis of words, voice and inflection can adequately determine the real purpose the therapist is pursuing. As we know from many experiences in therapists' reactions to their recorded material, and from a research analysis by Blocksma (33), the counselor is not infrequently astonished to discover the aims he is actually carrying out in the interview.

Note that in discussing this point the term "technique" has been discarded in favor of "implementation." The client is apt to be quick to discern when the counselor is using a "method," an intellectually chosen tool which he has selected for a purpose. On the other hand, the counselor is always implementing, both in conscious and nonconscious ways, the attitudes which he holds toward the client. These attitudes can be inferred and discovered from their operational implementation. Thus a counselor who basically does not hold the hypothesis that the person has significant capacity for integrating himself may think that he has used nondirective "methods" and "techniques," and proved to his own satisfaction that these techniques are unsuccessful. A recording of such material tends to show, however, that in the tone of voice, in the handling of the unexpected, in the peripheral activities of the interview, he implements his own hypothesis, not the client-centered hypothesis as he thinks.

It would seem that there can be no substitute for the continual checking back and forth between purpose or hypothesis and technique or implementation. This analytical self-checking the counselor may verbalize somewhat as follows: As I develop more clearly and more fully the attitude and hypothesis upon which I intend to deal with the client, I must check the implementation of that hypothesis in the interview material. But as I study my specific behaviors in the interview I detect implied purposes of which I had not been aware, I discover areas in which it had not occurred to me to apply the hypothesis, I realize that what was for me an implementation of one attitude is perceived by the client as the implementation of another. Thus the thorough study of my behavior sharpens, alters, and modifies the attitude and hypothesis with which I enter the next interview. A sound approach to the implementation of an hypothesis is a continuing and a reciprocal experience.

Some Formulations of the Counselor's Role

As we look back upon the development of the client-centered point of view, we find a steady progression of attempts to formulate what is involved in implementing the basic hypothesis in the interview situation. Some of these are formulations by individual counselors, whereas others have been more generally held. Let us take a few of these concepts and examine them, moving through them to the formulation which appears to be most commonly held at the present time by therapists of this orientation.

In the first place, some counselors — usually those with little specific training — have supposed that the counselor's role in carrying on nondirective counseling was merely to be passive and to adopt a laissez faire policy. Such a counselor has some willingness for the client to be self-directing. He is more inclined to listen than to guide. He tries to avoid imposing his own evaluations upon the client. He finds that a number of his clients gain help for themselves. He feels that his faith in the client's capacity is best exhibited by a passivity which involves a minimum of activity and of emotional reaction on his part. He tries "to stay out of the client's way."

This misconception of the approach has led to considerable failure in counseling — and for good reasons. In the first place, the passivity and seeming lack of interest or involvement is experienced by the client as a rejection, since indifference is in no real way the same as acceptance. In the second place, a laissez faire attitude does not in any way indicate to the client that he is regarded as a person of worth. Hence the counselor who plays a merely passive role, a listening role, may be of assistance to some clients who are desperately in need of emotional catharsis, but by and large his results will be minimal, and many clients will leave both disappointed in their failure to receive help and disgusted with the counselor for having nothing to offer.

Another formulation of the counselor's role is that it is his task to clarify and objectify the client's feelings. The present author, in a paper given in 1940 stated, "As material is given by the client, it is the therapist's function to help him recognize and clarify the emotions which he feels" (169, p. 162). This has been a useful concept, and it is partially descriptive of what occurs. It is, however, too intellectualistic, and if taken too literally, may focus the process in the counselor. It can mean that only the counselor knows what the feelings are, and if it acquires this meaning it becomes a subtle lack of respect for the client.

Unfortunately, our experience in conveying subtleties of emotionalized attitude is so limited, and the symbols of expression so unsatisfactory, that it is hard accurately to convey to a reader the delicate attitudes involved in the therapist's work. We have learned, to our dismay, that even the transcripts of our recorded cases may give to the reader a totally erroneous notion of the sort of relationship which existed. By persistently reading the counselor responses with the wrong inflection, it is possible to distort the whole picture of the relationship. Such readers when they first hear even a small segment of the recording itself, often say, "Oh, this is entirely different from the way I understood it."

Perhaps the subtle difference between a declarative and an empathic attitude on the part of the counselor may be conveyed by an example. Here is a client statement: "I feel as though my mother is always watching me and criticizing what I do. It gets me all stirred up inside. I try not to let that happen, but you know, there are times when I feel her eagle eye on me that I just boil inwardly."

A response on the counselor's part might be: "You resent her criticism." This response may be given empathically, with the tone of voice such as would be used if it were worded, "If I understand you correctly, you feel pretty resentful toward her criticism. Is that right?" If this is the attitude and tone which is used, it would probably be experienced by the client as aiding him in further expression. Yet we have learned, from the fumblings of counselors-in-training, that "You resent her criticism" may be given with the same attitude and tone with which one might announce "You have the measles," or even with the attitude and tone which would accompany the words "You are sitting on my hat." If the reader will repeat the counselor response in some of these varying inflections, he may realize that when stated empathically and understandingly, the likely attitudinal response on the part of the client is, "Yes, that is the way I feel, and I perceive that a little more clearly now that you have put it in somewhat different terms." But when the counselor statement is declarative, it becomes an evaluation, a judgment made by the counselor, who is now telling the client what his feelings are. The process is centered in the counselor, and the feeling of the client would tend to be, "I am being diagnosed."

In order to avoid this latter type of handling, we have tended to give up the description of the counselor's role as being that of clarifying the client's attitudes.

At the present stage of thinking in client-centered therapy, there is another attempt to describe what occurs in the most satisfactory therapeutic relationships, another attempt to describe the way in which the basic hypothesis is implemented. This formulation would state that it is the counselor's function to assume, in so far as he is able, the internal frame of reference of the client, to perceive the world as the client sees it, to perceive the client himself as he is seen by himself, to lay aside all perceptions from the external frame of reference while doing so, and to communicate something of this empathic understanding to the client.

Raskin, in an unpublished article (159), has given a vivid description of this version of the counselor's function.

There is [another] level of nondirective counselor response which to the writer represents *the* nondirective attitude. In a sense, it is a goal rather than one which is actually practised by counselors. But, in the experience of some, it is a highly attainable goal, which ... changes the nature of the counseling process in a radical way. At this level, counselor participation becomes an active experiencing with the client of the feelings to which he gives expression, the counselor makes a maximum effort to get under the skin of the person with whom he is communicating, he tries to get *within* and to live the attitudes expressed instead of observing them, to catch every nuance of their changing nature; in a word, to absorb himself completely in the attitudes of the other. And in struggling to do this, there is simply no room for any other type of counselor activity or attitude; if he is attempting to live the attitudes of the other, he cannot be diagnosing them, he cannot be thinking of making the process go faster. Because he is another, and not the client, the understanding is not spontaneous but must be acquired, and this through the most intense, continuous and active attention to the feelings of the other, to the exclusion of any other type of attention.

Even this description may be rather easily misunderstood since the experiencing with the client, the living of his attitudes, is not in terms of emotional identification on the counselor's part, but rather an empathic identification, where the counselor is perceiving the hates and hopes and fears of the client through immersion in an empathic process, but without himself, as counselor, experiencing those hates and hopes and fears.

Another attempt to phrase this point of view has been made by the author. It is as follows:

> As time has gone by we have come to put increasing stress upon the "client-centeredness" of the relationship, because it is more effective the more completely the counselor concentrates upon trying to understand the client *as the client seems to himself*. As I look back upon some of our earlier published cases — the case of Herbert Bryan in my book, or Snyder's case of Mr. M. — I realize that we have gradually dropped the vestiges of subtle directiveness which are all too evident in those cases. We have come to recognize that if we can provide understanding of the way the client seems to himself at this moment, he can do the rest. The therapist must lay aside his preoccupation with diagnosis and his diagnostic shrewdness, must discard his tendency to make professional evaluations, must cease his endeavors to formulate an accurate prognosis, must give up the temptation subtly to guide the individual, and must concentrate on one purpose only; that of providing deep understanding and acceptance of the attitudes consciously held at this moment by the client as he explores step by step into the dangerous areas which he has been denying to consciousness.
>
> I trust it is evident from this description that this type of relationship can exist only if the counselor is deeply and genuinely able to adopt these attitudes. Client-centered counseling, if it is to be effective, cannot be a trick or a tool. It is not a subtle way of guiding the client while pretending to let him guide himself. To be effective, it must be genuine. It is this sensitive and sincere "client-centeredness" in the therapeutic relationship that I regard as the third characteristic of nondirective therapy which sets it distinctively apart from other approaches. (170, pp. 420–421)

Research Evidence of a Trend

A research study recently completed would tend to confirm some of the preceding statements (180). Counselor techniques used by nondirective counselors in cases handled in 1947–48 have been analyzed in terms of the categories used by Snyder in analyzing cases handled in 1940–42 (196). This gives an opportunity for direct comparison of counselor methods, and hence the opportunity to note any observable trend. It is found that at the earlier date the counselors used a number of responses involving questioning, interpreting, reassuring, encouraging, suggesting. Such responses, though always forming a small proportion of the total, would seem to indicate on the counselor's part a limited confidence in the capacity of the client to understand and cope with his difficulties. The counselor still felt it necessary at times to take the lead, to explain the client to himself, to be supportive, and to point out what to the counselor were desirable courses of action. As clinical experience in therapy has continued, there has been a sharp decrease in all these forms of response. In the later cases, the proportion of responses of any of these types is negligible. Eighty-five per cent of the counselor responses are attempts to convey an understanding of the client's attitudes and feelings. It appears quite clear that nondirective counselors, on the basis of continuing therapeutic experience, have come to depend more fully upon the basic hypothesis of the approach than was true a half dozen years ago. It seems that more and more the nondirective therapist has judged understanding and acceptance to be effective, and has come to concentrate his whole effort upon achieving a deep understanding of the private world of the client.

Since the completion of the second study mentioned, it seems to be true that there has been more reaching out for a wider variety of therapist techniques. For the most part, however, this has meant a searching for new ways of making it clear that the therapist is thinking and feeling and exploring with the client. It is natural to expect that with increasing security in clinical experience there will be an increasing variety of attempts to communicate the fact that the therapist is endeavoring to achieve the internal frame of reference of the client, and is trying to see with him as deeply as the client sees, or even more deeply than the latter is able at the moment to perceive. In utilizing this increasing variety of responses, it is quite possible that this current formulation of the counselor's role will be discarded, just as previous formulations have been. So far, however, this seems not to be the case.

The Difficulty of Perceiving Through the Client's Eyes

This struggle to achieve the client's internal frame of reference, to gain the center of his own perceptual field and see with him as perceiver, is rather closely analogous to some of the Gestalt phenomena. Just as, by active concentration, one can suddenly see the diagram in the psychology text as representing a descending rather than an ascending stairway or can perceive two faces instead of a candlestick, so by active effort the counselor can put himself into the client's frame of reference. But just as in the case of the visual perception, the figure occasionally changes, so the counselor may at times find himself standing outside the client's frame of reference and looking as an external perceiver at the client. This almost invariably happens, for example, during a long pause or silence on the client's part. The counselor may gain a few clues which permit an accurate empathy, but to some extent he is forced to view the client from an observer's point of view, and can only actively assume the client's perceptual field when some type of expression again begins.

The reader can attempt this role in various ways, can give himself practice in assuming the internal frame of reference of another while overhearing a conversation on the streetcar, or while listening to a friend describe an emotional experience. Perhaps something of what is involved can even be conveyed on paper.

To try to give you, the reader, a somewhat more real and vivid experience of what is involved in the attitudinal set which we are discussing, it is suggested that you put yourself in the place of the counselor, and consider the following material, which is taken from complete counselor notes of the beginning of an interview with a man in his thirties. When the material has been completed, sit back and consider the sorts of attitudes and thoughts which were in your mind as you read.

Client: I don't feel very normal, but I want to feel that way. . . . I thought I'd have something to talk about — then it all goes around in circles. I was trying to think what I was going to say. Then coming here it doesn't work out. . . . I tell you, it seemed that it would be much easier before I came. I tell you, I just can't make a decision; I don't know what I want. I've tried to reason this thing out logically — tried to figure out which things are important to me. I thought that there are maybe two things a man might do; he might get married and raise a family. But if he was just a bachelor, just making a living — that isn't very good. I find myself and my thoughts getting back to the days when I was a kid and I cry very easily. The dam would break through. I've been in the Army four and a half years. I had no problems then, no hopes, no wishes. My only thought was to get out when peace would come. My problems, now that I'm out, are as ever. I tell you, they go back to a long time before I was in the Army. . . . I love children. When I was in the Philippines — I tell you, when I was young I swore I'd never forget my unhappy childhood — so when I saw these children in the Philippines, I treated them very nicely. I used to give them ice cream cones and movies. It was just a period — I'd reverted back — and that awakened some emotions in me I thought I had long buried. (*A pause. He seems very near tears.*)

As this material was read, such thoughts as the following would represent an external frame of reference in you, the "counselor."

I wonder if I should help him get started talking.
Is this inability to get under way a type of dependence?
Why this indecisiveness? What could be its cause?
What is meant by this focus on marriage and family?
He seems to be a bachelor. I hadn't known that.
The crying, the "dam," sound as though there must be a great deal of repression.
He's a veteran. Could he have been a psychiatric case?
I feel sorry for anybody who spent four and one-half years in the service.
Some time he will probably need to dig into those early unhappy experiences.
What is this interest in children? Identification? Vague homosexuality?

Note that these are all attitudes which are basically sympathetic. There is nothing "wrong" with them. They are even attempts to "understand," in the sense of "understanding about," rather than "understanding with." The locus of perceiving is, however, outside of the client.

By way of comparison, the thoughts which might go through your mind if you were quite successful in assuming the client's internal frame of reference would tend to be of this order:

You're wanting to struggle toward normality, aren't you?
It's really hard for you to get started.
Decision-making just seems impossible to you.
You want marriage, but it doesn't seem to you to be much of a possibility.
You feel yourself brimming over with childish feelings.
To you the Army represented stagnation.
Being very nice to children has somehow had meaning for you.
But it was — and is — a disturbing experience for you.

As pointed out before, if these thoughts are couched in a final and declarative form, then they shift over into becoming an evaluation from the counselor's perceptual vantage point. But to the extent that they are attempts to understand, tentative in formulation, they represent the attitude we are trying to describe as "adopting the client's frame of reference."

The Rationale of the Counselor's Role

The question may arise in the minds of many, why adopt this peculiar type of relationship? In what way does it implement the hypothesis from which we started? What is the rationale of this approach?

In order to have a clear basis for considering these questions, let us attempt to put first in formal terms and then in paraphrase a statement of the counselor's purpose when he functions in this way. In psychological terms, it is the counselor's aim to perceive as sensitively and accurately as possible all of the perceptual field as it is being experienced by the client, with the same figure and ground relationships, to the full degree that the client is willing to communicate that perceptual field; and having thus perceived this internal frame of reference of the other as completely as possible, to indicate to the client the extent to which he is seeing through the client's eyes.

Suppose that we attempt a description somewhat more in

terms of the counselor's attitudes. The counselor says in effect, "To be of assistance to you I will put aside myself — the self of ordinary interaction — and enter into your world of perception as completely as I am able. I will become, in a sense, another self for you — an alter ego of your own attitudes and feelings — a safe opportunity for you to discern yourself more clearly, to experience yourself more truly and deeply, to choose more significantly."

The Counselor's Role as Implementation of an Hypothesis

In what ways does this approach implement the central hypothesis of our work? It would be grossly misleading to say that our present method or formulation of the method grew out of the theory. The truth is that, as in most similar problems, one begins to find on the basis of clinical intuition that certain attitudes are effective, others are not. One tries to relate these experiences to basic theory, and thus they become clarified and point in the direction of further extension. It is thus that we have arrived at the present formulation, and this formulation will undoubtedly change as we solve some of the perplexities stated at the end of this chapter.

For the present, it would appear that for me, as counselor, to focus my whole attention and effort upon understanding and perceiving as the client perceives and understands, is a striking operational demonstration of the belief I have in the worth and the significance of this individual client. Clearly the most important value which I hold is, as indicated by my attitudes and my verbal behavior, the client himself. Also the fact that I permit the outcome to rest upon this deep understanding is probably the most vital operational evidence which could be given that I have confidence in the potentiality of the individual for constructive change and development in the direction of a more full and satisfying life. As a seriously disturbed client wrestles with his utter inability to make any choice, or another client struggles with his strong urges to commit suicide, the fact that I enter with deep understanding into the desperate feelings that exist but do not attempt to take over responsibility, is a most meaningful expression of basic confidence in the forward-moving tendencies in the human organism.

We might say then, that for many therapists functioning from a client-centered orientation, the sincere aim of getting "within" the attitudes of the client, of entering the client's internal frame of reference, is the most complete implementation which has thus far been formulated, for the central hypothesis of respect for and reliance upon the capacity of the person.

The Client's Experience of the Counselor

The question would still remain, what psychological purpose is served by attempting to duplicate, as it were, the perceptual field of the client in the mind of the counselor? Here it may assist us to see how the experience seems to the client. From the many statements written or given by clients after therapy one realizes that the counselor's behavior is experienced in a variety of ways, but there appear to be certain threads which are frequently evident.

A first excerpt may be taken from a statement by a professionally sophisticated client who had recently completed a series of five interviews. She had known and worked with the counselor in another professional capacity.

> Initially we discussed the possibility of these interviews interfering with our relationship as co-workers. I very definitely feel that the interviews in no way altered this relationship. We were two entirely different people in our two relationships and the one interfered not at all with the other. I believe that this was due in large measure to the fact that we almost unconsciously, because of the nature of therapy, accepted each other and ourselves as being different people in our two relationships with each other. As workers we were two individuals working together on various everyday problems. In counseling we were mostly *me* working together on my situation as I found it. Perhaps the last sentence explains to a considerable extent how I felt in the counseling relationship. I was hardly aware during the interviews of just who it was sitting in the office with me. I was the one that mattered, my thinking was the thing that was important and my counselor was almost a part of me working on my problem as I wanted to work on it.

My most prominent impression of the interviews is difficult to put into words. As I talked I would almost feel that I was "out of this world." Sometimes I would hardly know just what I was saying. This one may easily do if one talks for long periods to oneself — becoming so involved in verbalization that one is not keenly aware of just what one is saying and very definitely not aware of what the words actually mean to one. It was the role of the counselor to bring me to myself, to help me by being with me in everything I said, to realize what I was saying. I was never conscious that he was reflecting or re-stating things I had said but only that he was right along with me in my thinking because he would say to me things which I had stated but he would clear them for me, bring me back to earth, help me to see what I had said and what it meant to me.

Several times, by his use of analogies, he would help me to see the significance of what I had said. Sometimes he would say something like "I wonder if this is what you mean, ————" or "————, is that what you mean?" and I was conscious of a desire to get what I had said clarified, not so much to him as a person but through him, clarified to myself.

During the first two interviews he interrupted pauses. I know that this was because I had mentioned before counseling started that pauses made me self-conscious. However, I remember wishing at the time that he had let me think without interruption. The one interview that stands out most clearly in my mind was one in which there were many long pauses during which time I was working very hard. I was beginning to get some insight into my situation and, although nothing was said, I had the feeling by the counselor's attitude, that he was working right along with me. He was not restless, he did not take out a cigarette, he simply sat, I believe looking hard right at me, while I stared at the floor and worked in my mind. It was an attitude of complete cooperation and gave me the feeling that he was with me in what I was thinking. I see now the great value of pauses, if the counselor's attitude is one of cooperation, not one of simply waiting for time to pass.

I have seen nondirective techniques used before — not on myself — where the techniques were the dominating factors, and I have not always been pleased with the results. As a result of my own experience as a client I am convinced that the counselor's complete acceptance, his expression of the attitude of wanting to help the client, and his warmth of spirit as expressed by his wholehearted giving of himself to the client in complete cooperation with everything the client does or says are basic in this type of therapy.

Notice how the significant theme of the relationship is, "we were mostly *me* working together on my situation as I found it." The two selves have somehow become one while remaining two — "we were *me*." This idea is repeated several times; "my counselor was almost a part of me working on my problem as I wanted to work on it"; "it was the role of the counselor to bring me to myself"; "I was conscious of a desire to get what I had said clarified, not so much to him as a person but through him, clarified to myself." The impression is that the client was in one sense "talking to herself," and yet that this was a very different process when she talked to herself through the medium of another person.

Another example may be taken from a report written by a young woman who had been, at the time she came in for counseling, rather deeply disturbed. She had some slight knowledge about client-centered therapy before coming for help. The report from which this material is taken was written spontaneously and voluntarily some six weeks after the conclusion of the counseling interviews.

In the earlier interviews, I kept saying such things as "I am not acting like myself." "I never acted this way before." What I meant was that this withdrawn, untidy, and apathetic person was not myself. I was trying to say that this was a different person from the one who had previously functioned with what seemed to be satisfactory adjustment. It seemed to me that must be true. Then I began to realize that I was the same person, seriously withdrawn, etc., now, as I had been before. That did not happen until after I had talked out my self-rejection, shame, despair, and doubt, in the accepting situation of the interview. The counselor was not startled or shocked. I was telling him all these things about myself which did not fit into my picture of a graduate student, a teacher, a sound person. He responded with complete acceptance and warm interest without heavy emotional overtones. Here was a sane, intelligent person wholeheartedly accepting this behavior that seemed so shameful to me. I can remember an organic feeling of relaxation. I did not have to keep up the struggle to cover up and hide this shameful person.

Retrospectively, it seems to me that what I felt as "warm acceptance with (out) emotional overtones" was what I needed to work through my difficulties. One of the things I was struggling with was the character of my relationships with others. I was enmeshed in dependence, yet fighting against it. My mother, knowing that something was wrong, had come to see me. Her love was so powerful, I could feel it enveloping me. Her suffering was so real that I could touch it. But I could not talk to her. Even when, out of her insight, she said, while she was talking of my relationships with the family, "You can be as dependent or as independent as you like," I still resisted her. The counselor's impersonality with interest allowed me to talk out my feelings. The clarification in the interview situation presented the attitude to me as a *ding an sich* which I could look at, manipulate, and put in place. In organizing my attitudes, I was beginning to organize me.

I can remember sitting in my room and thinking about the components of infantile needs and dependence in maladjustment, and strongly resisting the idea that there was any element of dependence in my behavior. I think I reacted the way I might have if a therapist in an interview situation had interpreted this for me before I was ready for it. I kept thinking about it, though, and began to see that, although I kept insistently telling myself I wanted to be independent, there was plenty of evidence that I was also wanting protection and dependence. This was a shameful situation, I felt. I did not come to accept this indecision in myself until I had guiltily brought it up in the interviews, had it accepted, and then stated it again myself with less anxiety. In this situation, the counselor's reflection of feeling with complete acceptance let me see the attitude with some objectivity. In this case, the insight was structured rationally before I went to the interview. However, it was not internalized until the attitude had been reflected back to me free of shame and guilt, a thing in itself which I could look at and accept. My restatements and further exposition of feeling after the counselor's reflection were my own acceptance and internalization of the insight.

How shall we understand the counselor's function as it was experienced by this client? Perhaps it would be accurate to say that the attitudes which she could express but could not accept as a part of herself became acceptable when an alternate self, the counselor, looked upon them with acceptance and without emotion. It was only when another self looked upon her behavior without shame or emotion that she could look upon it in the same way. These attitudes were then objectified for her, and subject to control and organization. The insights which were almost achieved in her room became genuine insights when another had accepted them, and stated them, with the result that she could again state them with less anxiety. Here we have a different, yet basically similar, experiencing of the counselor's role.

It is natural that the more articulate and sophisticated clients would give more complete accounts of the meaning the experience had for them. The same elements appear to be present, however, in the simple and relatively inarticulate accounts of thoroughly naïve clients. A veteran with little education thus writes of his counseling experience.

> Much to my surprise, Mr. L. the counselor let me talk myself dry so to speak. I thought he might question me on various points of my problem. He did to a small extent but not as much as I had anticipated. In conferring with Mr. L., I listened to myself while talking. And in doing so I would say that I solved my own problems.

Here again it seems fair to suppose that the counselor's attitude and responses made it easier for the client to "listen to myself."

A Theory of the Therapist's Role

With this type of material in mind, a possible psychological explanation of the effectiveness of the counselor's role might be developed in these terms. Psychotherapy deals primarily with the organization and the functioning of the self. There are many elements of experience which the self cannot face, cannot clearly perceive, because to face them or admit them would be inconsistent with and threatening to the current organization of self. In client-centered therapy the client finds in the counselor a genuine alter ego in an operational and technical sense — a self which has temporarily divested itself (so far as possible) of its own selfhood, except for the one quality of endeavoring to understand. In the therapeutic experience, to see one's own attitudes, confusions, ambivalences, feelings, and perceptions accurately expressed by another, but stripped of their complications of emotion, is to see oneself objectively, and paves the way for acceptance into the self of all these elements which are now more clearly perceived. Reorganization of the self and more integrated functioning of the self are thus furthered.

Let us try to restate this idea in another way. In the emotional warmth of the relationship with the therapist, the client begins to experience a feeling of safety as he finds that whatever attitude he expresses is understood in almost the same way that he perceives it, and is accepted. He then is able to explore, for example, a vague feeling of guiltiness which he has experienced. In this safe relationship he can perceive for the first time the hostile meaning and purpose of certain aspects of his behavior, and can understand why he has felt guilty about it, and why it has been necessary to deny to awareness the meaning of this behavior. But this clearer perception is in itself disrupting and anxiety-creating, not therapeutic. It is evidence to the client that there are disturbing inconsistencies in himself, that he is not what he thinks he is. But as he voices his new perceptions and their attendant anxieties, he finds that this acceptant alter ego, the therapist, this other person who is only partly another person, perceives these experiences too, but with a new quality. The therapist perceives the client's self as the client has known it, and accepts it; he perceives the contradictory aspects which have been denied to awareness and accepts those too as being a part of the client; and both of these acceptances have in them the same warmth and respect. Thus it is that the client, experiencing in another an acceptance of both these aspects of himself, can take toward himself the same attitude. He finds that he too can accept himself even with the additions and alterations that are necessitated by these new perceptions of himself as hostile. He can experience himself as a person having hostile as well as other types of feelings, and can experience himself in this way without guilt. He has been enabled to do this (if our theory is correct) because another person has been able to adopt his frame of reference, to perceive with him, yet to perceive with acceptance and respect.

A By-product

As a somewhat parenthetical comment, it may be mentioned that the concept of the therapist's attitude and function which has been outlined above tends to reduce greatly a problem which has been experienced by other therapeutic orientations. This is the problem of how to prevent the therapist's own maladjustments, emotional biases, and blind spots from interfering with the therapeutic process in the client. There can be no doubt that every therapist, even when he has resolved many of his own difficulties in a therapeutic relationship, still has troubling conflicts, tendencies to project, or unrealistic attitudes on certain matters. How to keep these warped attitudes from blocking therapy or harming the client has been an important topic in therapeutic thinking.

In client-centered therapy this problem has been minimized considerably by the very nature of the therapist's function. Warped or unrealistic attitudes are most likely to be evident wherever evaluations are made. When evaluation of the client or of his expressions is almost nonexistent, counselor bias has little opportunity to become evident, or indeed to exist. In any therapy in which the counselor is asking himself "How do I see this? How do I understand this material?" the door is wide open for the personal needs or conflicts of the therapist to distort these evaluations. But where the counselor's central question is "How does the client see this?" and where he is continually checking his own understanding of the client's perception by putting forth tentative statements of it, distortion based upon the counselor's conflicts is much less apt to enter, and much more apt to be corrected by the client if it does enter.

This principle may be worded in a slightly different fashion. In a therapeutic relationship in which the therapist enters, as a person, making interpretations, evaluating the significance of the material, and the like, his distortions enter with him. In a therapeutic relationship where the therapist endeavors to keep himself out, as a separate person, and where his whole endeavor is to understand the other so completely that he becomes almost an alter ego of the client, personal distortions and maladjustments are much less likely to occur.

Though this point of view has been stated here only in general terms, it has been borne out in the experience of clinical training. Some individuals may be so maladjusted that they cannot perceive experience from the other person's point of view. Clients feel that such counselors-in-training are not understanding and tend to give up the interviews. And such counselors tend to leave the field. With most counselors-in-training, the effectiveness of achieving the internal frame of reference of another is sufficient reward to make this the focus of their effort. Personal problems of their own, which might at first have made it difficult accurately to understand or reflect or accept attitudes, tend consequently to play a smaller and smaller role. The deep emotional entanglement of client and therapist which can occur where the therapist sees his role as an evaluative one is almost absent from our experience.

The Difficulty of Understanding the Perceptions of Another

Thus far the explanation of the counselor's function, as it is presently formulated, has been given without particular reference to the special difficulties involved. It has been our experience that there are many clinical situations in which it is genuinely difficult even for the experienced counselor to achieve the internal frame of reference of the client. An excerpt from client material may exemplify some of the problems we have met.

The excerpt is from a third interview with a young man from a psychiatric ward. The material is electrically recorded, and presented as given by the client. If one places himself in the role of the counselor, he may find it something of a problem to perceive with this client.

A good many thoughts, a good many feelings are just right there in my head. I just put them — I just — I don't know — I feel them inside of my head, they stop it up. (*Short pause.*) I just get down to the things in my head and thought and mind, but it's just that I — it's just that I — I don't know — what goes on, goes on different, goes on in the inside, that's what stops me up — stops me up quickly. It's just that I, I'm wondering with real force whether I could go out there back to that ward of mine and really live, really be somebody. I just — It shot right out of my head. I wondered if I could possibly go back there and do that, really be somebody there. (*Short pause.*) I just keep on wondering, keep on thinking about it, and if I ever will be — just come right straight back to something and do something and be somebody there. (*Short pause.*) It'd probably just help me keep on being different, a different man, a different person back there. Here in this office I generally come out with some commonsense thoughts, and ideas, something with some real feeling in it, a real mind, real thought. Yesterday when I came in here I was just living, and — I will be today. I'm very sure of it. I can just be — I can get away with it just about so much up here, then I — it's just too much.[1]

Here the problem faced by the counselor is the fact that much of the client's expression is confused and expressed in such private symbolism that it is difficult to enter into his perceptual field and see experience in his terms. It would seem that the type of empathic thinking carried on by a counselor who was successfully client-centered in respect to this material would include thoughts of this type:

It seems as though feelings and thoughts block you.
It's the inside thoughts, as I understand it, that stop you up.
It's the question, the puzzle, as to whether you could possibly *be* somebody.
I can understand that that thought leaves you abruptly as well as comes to you.
You wonder and wonder whether you could be a *person*, back on the ward.
You feel that some of your reactions are real, and sensible.
It seems to you that here in the therapy hour you are actually alive.
That thought is just overpowering — more than you can face.

If the counselor maintains this consistently client-centered attitude, and if he occasionally conveys to the client something of his understanding, then he is doing what he can to give the client the experience of being deeply respected. Here the confused, tentative, almost incoherent thinking of an individual who knows he has been evaluated as abnormal is really respected by being deemed well worth understanding.

[1] From a psychoanalytic interview recorded by Earl Zinn, and used by permission.

On the other hand the therapist may find thoughts running through his mind which are of an evaluative nature, judging this material from his own frame of reference, or of a self-concerned nature, in which his attention has shifted from the client to himself. Such thinking might include themes such as the following:

The thinking here is confused and the expressions inarticulate.
There seem to be feelings of unreality.
Is this a schizophrenic?
Am I understanding his meaning correctly?
Should I encourage his desire to be a self?
Here is a striking example of the conscious self struggling to regain a sense of control over the organism.
He reacts with some panic to the thought of living and being a person.
What will I respond to this?

Such thoughts as these will occur to any counselor at times, no matter how basically client-centered his views may be. Yet it would appear to be true that whether the theme is evaluative or self-concerned, there is slightly less of full respect for the other person than in the thoroughly empathic understandings previously cited. When the counselor is concerned with himself and what he should do, there is necessarily a decreased focus upon the respect he feels for the client. When he is thinking in evaluative terms, whether the evaluation is objectively accurate or inaccurate, he is to some degree assuming a judgmental frame of mind, is viewing the person as an object, rather than as a person, and to that extent respects him less as a person. On the other hand, to enter deeply with this man into his confused struggle for selfhood is perhaps the best implementation we now know for indicating the meaning of our basic hypothesis that the individual represents a process which is deeply worthy of respect, both as he is and with regard to his potentialities.

Some Deep Issues

The assumption of the therapeutic role which has been described raises some very basic questions indeed. An example from a therapeutic interview may pose some of these issues for our consideration. Miss Gil, a young woman who has, in a number of therapeutic interviews, been quite hopeless about herself, has spent the major part of an hour discussing her feelings of inadequacy and lack of personal worth. Part of the time she has been aimlessly using the finger paints. She has just finished expressing her feelings of wanting to get away from everyone — to have nothing to do with people. After a long pause comes the following.

S: [1] I've never said this before to anyone — but I've thought for such a long time — This is a terrible thing to say, but if I could just — well (*short, bitter laugh; pause*), if I could just find some glorious cause that I could give my life for I would be happy. I cannot be the kind of a person I want to be. I guess maybe I haven't the guts — or the strength — to kill myself — and if someone else would relieve me of the responsibility — or I would be in an accident — I — I — just don't want to live.

C: [2] At the present time things look so black to you that you can't see much point in living —

S: Yes — I wish I'd never started this therapy. I was happy when I was living in my dream world. There I could be the kind of person I wanted to be — But now — There is such a wide, wide gap — between my ideal — and what I am. I wish people hated me. I try to make them hate me. Because then I could turn away from them and could blame them — but no — It is all in my hands — Here is my life — and I either accept the fact that I am absolutely worthless — or I fight whatever it is that holds me in this terrible conflict. And I suppose if I accepted the fact that I am worthless, then I could go away someplace — and get a little room someplace — get a mechanical job someplace — and retreat clear back to the security of my dream world where I could do things, have clever friends, be a pretty wonderful sort of person —

C: It's really a tough struggle — digging into this like you are — and at times the shelter of your dream world looks more attractive and comfortable.

S: My dream world or suicide.

C: Your dream world or something more permanent than dreams —

S: Yes. (*A long pause. Complete change of voice.*) So I don't see why I should waste your time — coming in twice a week — I'm not worth it — What do you think?

---

[1] Subject, or client.   [2] Counselor.

C: It's up to you, Gil — It isn't wasting my time — I'd be glad to see you — whenever you come — but it's how you feel about it — if you don't want to come twice a week — or if you do want to come twice a week? — once a week? — It's up to you. (*Long pause.*)

S: You're not going to suggest that I come in oftener? You're not alarmed and think I ought to come in — every day — until I get out of this?

C: I believe you are able to make your own decision. I'll see you whenever you want to come.

S: (*Note of awe in her voice.*) I don't believe you are alarmed about — I see — I may be afraid of myself — but you aren't afraid for me — (*She stands up — a strange look on her face.*)

C: You say you may be afraid of yourself — and are wondering why I don't seem to be afraid for you?

S: (*Another short laugh.*) You have more confidence in me than I have. (*She cleans up the finger-paint mess and starts out of the room.*) I'll see you next week — (*that short laugh*) maybe. (*Her attitude seemed tense, depressed, bitter, completely beaten. She walked slowly away.*)

This excerpt raises sharply the question as to how far the therapist is going to maintain his central hypothesis. Where life, quite literally, is at stake, what is the best hypothesis upon which to act? Shall his hypothesis still remain a deep respect for the capacity of the person? Or shall he change his hypothesis? If so, what are the alternatives? One would be the hypothesis that "I can be successfully responsible for the life of another." Still another is the hypothesis, "I can be temporarily responsible for the life of another without damaging the capacity for self-determination." Still another is: "The individual cannot be responsible for himself, nor can I be responsible for him, but it is possible to find someone who can be responsible for him."

In the particular excerpt cited, are the counselor responses which indicate an external frame of reference — "I'd be glad to see you," "I believe you are able to make your own decision" — the effective responses, or are the effective responses those which view from within the client? Or is it the deep respect, whether indicated from the external or internal frame of reference, which is the important ingredient?

Does the counselor have the right, professionally or morally, to permit a client seriously to consider psychosis or suicide as a way out, without making a positive effort to prevent these choices? Is it a part of our general social responsibility that we may not tolerate such thinking or such action on the part of another?

These are deep issues, which strike to the very core of therapy. They are not issues which one person can decide for another. Different therapeutic orientations have acted upon different hypotheses. All that one person can do is to describe his own experience and the evidence which grows out of that experience.

The Basic Struggle of the Counselor

It has been my experience that only when the counselor, through one means or another, has settled within himself the hypothesis upon which he will act, can he be of maximum aid to the individual. It has also been my experience that the more deeply he relies upon the strength and potentiality of the client, the more deeply does he discover that strength.

It has seemed clear, from our clinical experience as well as our research, that when the counselor perceives and accepts the client as he is, when he lays aside all evaluation and enters into the perceptual frame of reference of the client, he frees the client to explore his life and experience anew, frees him to perceive in that experience new meanings and new goals. But is the therapist willing to give the client full freedom as to outcomes? Is he genuinely willing for the client to organize and direct his life? Is he willing for him to choose goals that are social or antisocial, moral or immoral? If not, it seems doubtful that therapy will be a profound experience for the client. Even more difficult, is he willing for the client to choose regression rather than growth or maturity? to choose neuroticism rather than mental health? to choose to reject help rather than accept it? to choose death rather than life? To me it appears that only as the therapist is completely willing that *any* outcome, *any* direction, may be chosen — only then does he realize the vital strength of the capacity and potentiality of the individual for constructive action.

It is as he is willing for death to be the choice, that life is chosen; for neuroticism to be the choice, that a healthy normality is chosen. The more completely he acts upon his central hypothesis, the more convincing is the evidence that the hypothesis is correct.[1]

Unsolved Issues

The preceding paragraphs state the experience of one person, the writer, in a positive (or, as it will seem to some, an extreme) form. Let us drop back to considering a minimal statement regarding the attitude of the counselor, and the effect his attitude has upon the client.

It has been the experience of many, counselors and clients alike, that when the counselor has adopted in a genuine way the function which he understands to be characteristic of a client-centered counselor, the client tends to have a vital and releasing experience which has many similarities from one client to another. A recognizable phenomenon, one that can be described, seems to exist. Whether the present description is an accurate one is another question. Different counselors have used different descriptive terms, and only time and research can indicate which description is the closest semantic approximation to the phenomenon.

Is the crucial element in the counselor's attitude his complete willingness for the client to express any attitude? Is permissiveness thus the most significant factor? In counseling this scarcely seems to be an adequate explanation, yet in play therapy there often appears to be some basis for this formulation. The therapist may at times be quite unsuccessful in achieving the child's internal frame of reference, since the symbolic expression may be so complex or unique that the therapist is at a loss to understand. Yet therapy moves forward, largely, it would seem, on the basis of

[1] It will be evident from this discussion that neither in practice nor in theory can we go along with the comment by Green (72) that client-centered counseling is simply a subtle way of getting across to the client the cues which indicate approval of cultural values. His hypothesis could be partially maintained in some of the early client-centered cases, but it does not appear to be supported at all in the present handling by experienced counselors. As client-centered therapy has developed, it becomes more and more clear that it cannot be explained on such a basis.

permissiveness, since acceptance can hardly be complete unless the counselor is first able to understand.[1]

Another type of formulation would stress the fact that the essential characteristic of the relationship is the new type of need-satisfaction achieved by the client in an atmosphere of acceptance. Thus Meister and Miller describe the experience as "an attempt on the part of the counselor to offer the client a new type of experience wherein his cycle of unusual responses may be disrupted since the counselor does not supply the reinforcement by rejection which other social contacts have provided. The client's report of his behavior, his actual behavior, and his need to behave as he does — all are 'accepted.' Thus in the counseling relationship itself the client adopts a new mode of response, a different mode of need-satisfaction." (131, pp. 61–62)

Still another formulation places the emphasis upon the counselor's level of confidence or level of expectancy in regard to the individual. This view raises the question: Is it not the counselor's full confidence in the ability of the person to be self-directing to which the client responds? Thus in the case of Miss Gil, cited earlier, the counselor statement, "I believe you are able to make your own decision," would be regarded as a chance verbalization of the effective counselor attitude which was crucial for the whole relationship. From this point of view it is the expectancy of the counselor that "you can be self-directing" which is the social stimulus to which the client responds.

Still another type of formulation might be that offered by Shaffer, in which psychotherapy is seen as "a learning process through which a person acquires an ability to speak to himself in appropriate ways so as to control his own conduct." (181)

---

[1] Since the writing of the above, a different explanation has been pointed out to the author. It is quite possible that the child assumes that the therapist perceives the situation as he does. The child, much more than the adult, assumes that everyone shares with him the same perceptual reality. Therefore when there is permissiveness and acceptance, this is experienced by the child as understanding and acceptance, since he takes it for granted that the therapist perceives as he does.

If this description is accurate, then the situation in play therapy differs in no essential way from the description of the relationship which has been given throughout the chapter.

From this point of view the counselor attitude might be seen simply as providing an optimal atmosphere for the client to learn to "speak to himself in appropriate ways."

Yet another description is that the relationship is one which provides the client with the opportunity of making responsible choices, in an atmosphere in which it is assumed that he is capable of making decisions for himself. Thus in any series of counseling interviews the client makes hundreds of choices — of what to say, what to believe, what to withhold, what to do, what to think, what values to place upon his experiences. The relationship becomes an area for continuing practice in the making of increasingly mature and responsible choices.

As will be observed, these differing formulations are not in sharp contrast. They differ in emphasis, but probably all of them (including the formulation given in this chapter) are imperfect attempts to describe an experience about which we still have too little research knowledge.

An Objective Definition of the Therapeutic Relationship

It will have been painfully evident that the material of this chapter has been based upon clinical experience and judgment rather than upon any scientific or objective basis. Almost no research has been done upon the complex problems of the subtle client-therapist relationship. A beginning was made by Miller (132) in a small study based upon eight interviews — two psychoanalytic, one "non-nondirective," and five nondirective. Using transcribed typescripts as a basis for analysis, judges endeavored to make objective discriminations as to how the counselor responses were experienced by the client (as separate from the counselor's intent). The judges were to decide whether the counselor's statement was experienced as (1) "accepting," defined as respecting or admitting the validity of the client's position, (2) supporting, (3) denying, or (4) neutral. By analysis of variance technique it was shown that the differences between judgments were not great, particularly in relation to the nondirective interviews. In fact, the categories seemed more suitable for these interviews than for the others. The basic finding was that the nondirective interviews were largely characterized by a client experience of acceptance, rather than of neutrality or support. It was also found that in an interview regarded by the counselor as unsuccessful, there were as many responses experienced as denying or rejecting as there were in the interviews from other orientations. The fact that responses may be cast in a nondirective form does not, in other words, prevent them from being, or being experienced as, denial or rejection. This study is the first to make the attempt to measure the relationship from the client's point of view.

Another study has just been completed which is not only important in itself, but holds much promise for continuing objective analysis of many of the subtle aspects of the relationship between the therapist and the client. It is a coordinated pair of researches by Fiedler (57, 58), which may be described briefly in the following paragraphs.

Fiedler started from the assumption, held by almost all therapists, that the relationship is an important element in facilitating therapy. Consequently, all therapists are endeavoring to create what they regard as the ideal relationship. If there are in fact, several different types of therapeutic relationship, each distinctive of a different school of therapy, then the ideals toward which experienced therapists of these different schools are working will show relatively little similarity. If, however, there is but one type of relationship which is actually therapeutic, then there should be a concordance in the concept of an ideal relationship as held by experienced therapists. One would in this case expect more agreement between experienced therapists, regardless of their theoretical orientation, than between the experienced therapist and the novice within the same school of thought, since greater experience should give keener insight into the elements of the relationship.

To test this somewhat complex series of hypotheses, Fiedler first made a pilot study using eight therapists, and then a more carefully defined study in which ten persons were involved. In this main study there were three therapists who were analytically oriented, three from a client-centered orientation, one Adlerian, and three laymen. The task of these individuals was to describe the ideal therapeutic relationship. This they did through the use of the "Q" technique devised by Stephenson (201, 202).[1] Seventy-five statements were drawn from the literature and from therapists, each statement descriptive of a possible aspect of the relationship. (To illustrate, three of the statements were "Therapist is sympathetic with patient," "Therapist tries to sell himself," "Therapist treats the patient with much deference.") Each of the ten raters sorted these seventy-five descriptive statements into seven categories, from those most characteristic of an ideal relationship to those least characteristic. Since this meant that each rater had assigned a value of from one to seven to each item, the sorting made by any rater could now be correlated with that of any other rater.

The results hold much of interest. All correlations were strongly positive, ranging from .43 to .84, indicating that all the therapists and even the nontherapists tended to describe the ideal relationship in similar terms. When the correlations were factor analyzed, only one factor was found, indicating that there is basically but one relationship toward which all therapists strive. There was a higher correlation between experts who were regarded as good therapists, regardless of orientation, than between experts and nonexperts within the same orientation. The fact that even laymen can describe the ideal therapeutic relationship in terms which correlate highly with those of the experts suggests that the best therapeutic relationship may be related to good interpersonal relationships in general.

What are the characteristics of this ideal relationship? When all the ratings are pooled, here are the items placed in the top two categories.

Most characteristic

The therapist is able to participate completely in the patient's communication.

Very characteristic

The therapist's comments are always right in line with what the patient is trying to convey.

[1] See not only the references indicated, but page 140 of Chapter 4, in which another study using this technique is described.

The therapist sees the patient as a co-worker on a common problem.

The therapist treats the patient as an equal.

The therapist is well able to understand the patient's feelings.

The therapist really tries to understand the patient's feelings.

The therapist always follows the patient's line of thought.

The therapist's tone of voice conveys the complete ability to share the patient's feelings.

Here, from the point of view of this chapter, is outstanding corroboration of the importance of empathy and complete understanding on the part of the therapist. Some of the items also indicate the respect which the therapist has for the client. There is unfortunately little opportunity to judge the extent to which reliance is placed upon the basic capacity of the client, since very few items regarding this were included. From the rating of these few characteristics it may be said that such reliance is only moderately characteristic of this heterogeneous group of therapists.

At the negative end of the scale are placed those items which describe the therapist as hostile to or disgusted by the patient, or acting in a superior fashion. At the extreme negative pole is the statement, "Therapist shows no comprehension of the feelings the patient is trying to communicate."

In a second major aspect of this research Fiedler has endeavored to measure the type of relationship which actually is achieved by different therapists, and the degree to which the actual is similar to the ideal. In this study four judges listened to ten electrically recorded interviews, and for each interview sorted the seventy-five descriptive items to indicate the extent to which they were characteristic of that particular interview. Of the ten interviews, four were conducted by psychoanalytically oriented therapists, four by client-centered therapists, two by Adlerians. In each group, half of the interviews were conducted by experienced therapists, half by nonexperts.

The findings, based on the various correlations, were as follows:

1. Experts created relationships significantly closer to the "ideal" than nonexperts.

2. Similarity between experts of different orientations was as great as, or greater than, the similarity between experts and nonexperts of the same orientation.

3. The most important factors differentiating experts from nonexperts are related to the therapist's ability to understand, to communicate with, and to maintain rapport with the client. There is some indication that the expert is better able to maintain an appropriate emotional distance, seemingly best described as interested but emotionally uninvolved.

4. The most clearly apparent differences between schools related to the status which the therapist assumes toward the client. The Adlerians and some of the analytic therapists place themselves in a more tutorial, authoritarian role; client-centered therapists show up on the opposite extreme of this factor.

The primary significance of these two studies is not the findings alone, since the studies are based upon small numbers, but the fact that a start has been made in this subtle and complex area. As the methodology becomes more refined, it appears entirely possible that objective answers may be found to some of the perplexing questions which are raised about the therapeutic relationship.

It would also appear, from the point of view of this chapter, that the findings of these studies confirm in a general way some of the elements stressed in the preceding sections. The importance of complete and sensitive understanding of the client's attitudes and feelings, as they seem to him, is supported by Fiedler's work. As to the importance of reliance upon the client's capacity the study is silent, but it is obvious that there is now no barrier to the exhaustive study of such an issue. This increase in methodological skill and sophistication makes possible research which has hitherto seemed impossible. It is this promise for the future which makes Fiedler's study basically important. It appears clear that in time this chapter on the attitude of the therapist, and his relationship with the client, can be rewritten in objective, verified terms, based upon clinical hypotheses scientifically tested.

CORROBORATIVE EVIDENCE FOR THE BASIC HYPOTHESIS

In concluding this chapter, it may be well to return to its fundamental premise, and to examine it, not as related to therapy alone, but as related to our general experience. A basic hypothesis has been stated concerning the capacity of the individual for self-initiated, constructive handling of the issues involved in life situations. This hypothesis is not yet definitively proved or disproved by research evidence from the field of therapy. So far as clinical experience is concerned, some clinicians state that their clinical experience supports this hypothesis, but others look upon it with considerable skepticism and indicate that in the light of their experience any such reliance upon the capacity of the individual is of very doubtful validity.

In this situation, unsatisfactory from a scientific point of view, it may be worth our while to examine the scattered evidence, from fields outside of psychotherapy, which has relevance to the hypothesis. There is a certain amount of objective evidence, and some experiential evidence, from other fields.

In the well-known study of autocratic, democratic, and laissez faire groups conducted by Lippitt and others (118), it was found that in the democratic group where the leader's role was one of interest and permissiveness, the group took responsibility upon itself, and in quantity and quality of production, in morale, and in absence of hostility, it exceeded the records of the other groups. In the laissez faire group, where there was no consistent structure, and no leader interest, and in the autocratic group where behavior was controlled by the leader's wishes, the outcomes were not so favorable. While this study is based on small numbers, and is perhaps lessened in value by the fact that the leaders were genuine in their democratic functions and role-playing in other groups, it is nevertheless worthy of consideration.

In a study made many years ago by Herbert Williams (223), a classroom group of the worst-offending juvenile delinquents in a large school system was brought together. As might be expected, these boys were retarded in intelligence (average I.Q. 82) and in school achievement. There was no special equipment save for a large table on which a variety of readers and textbooks for various ages were placed. There were but two rules: a boy must keep busy doing something, and no boy was permitted to annoy or bother others. Here is a situation of genuine permissiveness within broad and realistic limits, with responsibility clearly placed upon the individual. Encouragement and suggestions were given only after an activity had been self-initiated. Thus if a boy had worked along artistic lines, he might be given assistance in getting into a special art class; or if activities in mathematics or mechanics had engaged his interest, arrangements might be made for him to attend courses in these subjects. The group remained together four months, though some were not in the group for the whole period. During the four months the measured educational achievement increased 11.2 months in reading age, 14.5 months in arithmetic age, and similarly in other subjects. The total increase in educational age was 12.2 months, and if three members are omitted whose attendance was short, the average increase is 15.2 months — more than four times the normal expectation for a group with this degree of retardation. This was in a group in which reading and other educational disabilities abounded.

In a very different area, a study of food habits was made during the war, under the supervision of Kurt Lewin (112). It was found that when groups were urged by a lecturer to make use of little-used meats — hearts, kidneys, brains — few (10 per cent) actually carried out the suggestion in practice. In other groups the problem of war scarcities was discussed with the group members and simple information about the meats given to them, following which the group members were asked to make their own decisions about serving the meats in question. These decisions, it was found through a follow-up study, tended to be kept, and 52 per cent actually served one or more of these meats. Self-initiated and responsible action proved far more effective than guided action.

A study by Coch and French (41) comes to the same conclusion regarding industrial workers.   With conditions of pay held constant, some groups of workers were shifted to a new task and carefully instructed in the way to handle it and in ways of increasing efficiency on the new task.   Other groups were shifted to the new task, and permitted to discuss, plan, and carry out their own way of handling the new problem.   In the latter groups productivity increased more rapidly, increased to a higher level, held a higher level, and morale was definitely higher than in the groups which had been instructed.

A study of supervision in an insurance company was made by the Survey Research Center (206).   When units in which productivity and morale were high were compared with those in which they were low, significant differences were discovered in the methods and personalities of the supervisors.   In the units with high productivity, supervisors and group leaders tended to be interested primarily in the workers as people, and interest in production was secondary.   Supervisors encouraged group participation and discussion and group decisions in matters affecting their work.   Finally, supervisors in these "high" units gave little close supervision to the work being done, but tended to place the responsibility upon the worker.

Other industrial studies (62, 116, 126, 207), though less objective in nature, bear out the two that have been cited.   Various industries, in this country and in Great Britain, have found that in quite divergent industrial situations there is improvement in effectiveness and in morale when workers are trusted as being capable of responsible handling of their own situation.   This has meant a permissiveness toward their active participation in thinking about the issues, and a willingness for them to make, or participate in making, the responsible choices and decisions.

In addition to such industrial evidence there is significant social experience which bears upon the topic.   The way in which the self-directing capacities of small communities were utilized in the development of the TVA project is well described by David Lilienthal (115).   In a very different problem-situation, that of training a striking force of Marines, General Carlson relied very heavily upon the self-directing capacities of the individual, in developing the famous Carlson's Raiders.

In dealing with juvenile delinquency there is similar experience. The Area Projects, developed by Clifford Shaw in delinquency areas, were found to be successful when they built upon the strength of the group. If the leader was a catalyst, a person genuinely able to accept the neighborhood as it existed and to release the group to work toward its real purposes and goals, the result was in the direction of socialization. The gangster, the petty politician, the tavern keeper, when given the opportunity to express real attitudes, and the full freedom to select goals, tended to choose goals which moved the group toward more social objectives. On the other hand,

> attempts to produce these changes *for* the community by means of ready made institutions and programs planned, developed, financed, and managed by persons outside the community are not likely to meet with any more success in the future than they have in the past. This procedure is psychologically unsound because it places the residents of the community in an inferior position and implies serious reservations with regard to their capacities and their interest in their own welfare. What is equally important is that it neglects the greatest of all assets in any community, namely the talents, energies, and other human resources of the people themselves. . . . What is necessary, we believe, is the organization and encouragement of social self-help on a cooperative basis. (183)

In quite another area — that of dealing with health problems — we find further relevant social experience. The famous Peckham Experiment in London provides an opportunity to study the basic hypothesis from a fresh vantage point. The Peckham Centre is a center organized for family health and recreation by a group of biologists. In attempting to promote health and richness of living for individuals and families, the sponsoring group has learned many lessons which are deeply relevant to our understanding of psychotherapy. Let us first listen to the manner in which the handling of the facts of the medical examination has developed.

> Another outstanding characteristic of the biological overhaul [health examination] must be emphasized. The facts elicited and their significance are as far as possible presented to the family in their entirety, in lay terms. *No advice is volunteered.* To the layman

this may appear but natural, since no advice is sought; but to anyone trained in the medical profession — that is specifically to give advice — it is a most difficult attitude to achieve. Indeed "to give advice" seems to be a wellnigh irresistible impulse to most human beings in a situation of authority. We try then not to give advice and to refrain from assuming the authority of special knowledge. As one of the members put it, "The doctor simply tells you how you stand." It is thereafter left to their own degree of intelligence to act. It is an intensely interesting study to watch and note the various actions undertaken (often at considerable sacrifice in some other direction) as the family intelligence is brought to bear on the facts stated to them after examination. It is seldom the individual but nearly always the family as a whole that responds. A technique leading to this result seems to be fundamental, because it gives to the family an opportunity of exercising the responsibility that it so deeply feels. It is difficult to understand, indeed, why a laissez-faire attitude to a mouthful of decaying teeth should change as the result of the new circumstances, but it does; or why a complacency to a useless overweight in either a man or a woman should so change — but it does; with results in either instance of marked benefits both to the individual and to the family. It was found in practice that when the examinations were conducted in a spirit which led up to conclusions which were bits of advice, often no action was taken; whereas by leaving it to spontaneity in the individual and to his own sense of responsibility, action is taken in the overwhelming majority of cases. This very action represents the exercise of a faculty that has been largely in abeyance. With exercise of a faculty, health develops. The faculty for responsibility is no exception to this rule. (145, pp. 49-50)

With this type of handling, with a deep respect for the right and capacity of the individual to be responsible for himself, 90 per cent of the individuals in whom some disorder is discovered go for treatment.

Not only in regard to health activities is this hypothesis found to be effective. It is also the purpose of the Centre to give families an opportunity for recreational enrichment of living. The description of the experience in moving realistically toward this goal provides an interesting parallel to the progression of thinking in the formulation of client-centered therapy.

Our problem is the "man in the street." He is the man without egotistic drive; he is the diffident and the meek. Because he seems to lack initiative he is left to his own resources — of which he seems to have none. To attract him to any organization is difficult enough; to keep him in it is still another problem. But because he forms the bulk of the public he is most worth study, for on him the success of any social organization depends.

The first tentative approach to encouraging the members to do things was based on the common assumption that ordinary people like to emulate their betters; that an exhibition of a high degree of skill, of relative perfection, would stimulate the imitative faculty and lead to like action. That method of approach we have found useless; the assumption is not bourne out by the experiment.

Primarily, individuals are conscious only of their own capacity and act accordingly. They may admire, they may even be envious of outside standards, but they do not use them even as stimulants to try out their own capacity. Skill beyond their own capacity tends to frighten, to inhibit rather than to tempt them to emulation. The status "teacher" tends inevitably to undermine self-confidence. Our failures during our first eighteen months' work have taught us something very significant. Individuals, from infants to old people, resent or fail to show any interest in anything initially presented to them through discipline, regulation or instruction which is another aspect of authority. (Even the very "Centre idea" has a certain taint of authority and this is contributing to our slow recruitment.)

We now proceed by merely providing an environment rich in instruments for action — that is, giving a chance to do things. Slowly but surely these chances are seized upon and used as opportunity for development of inherent capacity. The instruments of action have one common characteristic — *they must speak for themselves*. The voice of the salesman or the teacher frightens the potential users.

How does this fact reflect on organization and the opportunity for experimental observation on this material?

Having provided the members with a chance to do things, we find that we have to leave them to make their own use of them. We have had to learn to sit back and wait for these activities to emerge. Any impatience on our part, translated into help, has strangled their efforts — we have had to cultivate more and more patience in ourselves. The alternative to this cultivation of patience is, of course, obvious — the application of compulsion in one or other of its many forms, perhaps the most tempting of which is persuasion. But having a fundamental interest in the source and origin of spontaneous action — as all biologists must — we have had to discard even that instrument for initiating activities. Even temptation, the gentlest form of compulsion, does not work because human beings, even children, recognize carrots for what they ultimately mean; we have at least progressed beyond the donkey!

We do not suggest that communion, teaming, regulation, system, discipline, authority and instruction are not desirable things but neither can we agree that there is anything wrong with those who spurn these things; we are not missionaries seeking to convert people to desirable things, but scientists seeking the truth in the facts.

Civilization hitherto has looked for the orientation of society through an imposed "system" derived from some extrinsic authority, such as religion, "cultural" education, or political suasion. The biologist conceives an order emanating from the organism living in poise in its environment. Our necessity, therefore, is to secure the free flow of forces in the environment so that the order inherent in the material we are studying may emerge. Our interest is in that balance of forces which sustains naturally and spontaneously the forms of life we are studying.

The Centre is the first experimental station in human biology. It asks the question — "What circumstances will sustain human beings in their capacity for full function (i.e. in health); and what orientation will such fully functioning entities give to human living (i.e. to society)?" (145, pp. 38–40)

Here is obviously a basic willingness on the part of the sponsors of this Centre for people to be themselves — even when that involves differing from the values held by the sponsors. To leave the person free to choose or reject what we regard as "desirable things" requires an inner questioning of basic attitudes which is no easier for the biologist than for the psychotherapist, as the following statements indicate.

The training of the staff is difficult. It is in fact no easy thing for the individual as a scientist to place himself as an instrument of knowledge completely at the disposal of any and every member, and at the same time, without exercising authority, to assume his right and proper position in the community as a social entity. But he is also there to make observations. This the members have readily come to accept, jokingly describing themselves as the biologist's "rats."

They soon come to appreciate that the scientist's primary concern is *to be used by the members as a means of reaching and sustaining their own maximum capacity for health.* Moreover, they come to sense that in carrying on their own activities and inaugurating new ones through the method of self-service, many of them are in fact step by step themselves growing into important members of the staff. (144, p. 78)

The active-passiveness of the observer is not easy to attain without the essential extension of the laboratory scientist's discipline which allows facts to speak for themselves. In human biology the facts are actions which seriously complicate the problem but do not put it beyond the possibility of solution.

The biological necessities of the situation then compel us to leave the members to themselves, to initiate their own activities, their own order of things. We have no rules, regulations nor any other restriction of action, except a very fluid time-table. Within eighteen months the seeming chaos and disorder is rapidly developing into something very different. This is apparent even to our visitors, one of whom on leaving described the life in the Centre as being like a stream allowed to form its bed and its banks according to the natural configuration of the land. (145, p. 41)

Here in this community effort is seen the emergence of the same type of hypothesis upon which the client-centered therapist bases his work. Not only is the hypothesis the same as regards the person, the client, but the conclusion in regard to the role of the "leader" also has many striking similarities.

Is there any unity in these bits of evidence gathered from such diverse sources? Is there anything relevant to our concern with psychotherapy in studies which cover such remote issues as whether people eat kidneys, or decide how an industrial shop unit shall be run? I feel that there is. If we consider the central thread which runs through these highly varied studies and experiences, it would seem that it may be summarized in an "if-then" type of statement.

If the individual or group is faced by a problem;

If a catalyst-leader provides a permissive atmosphere;

If responsibility is genuinely placed with the individual or group;

If there is basic respect for the capacity of the individual or
group;

Then, responsible and adequate analysis of the problem is
made;
responsible self-direction occurs;
the creativity, productivity, quality of product exhibited
are superior to results of other comparable methods;
individual and group morale and confidence develop.

It would appear that the hypothesis which is central to this
chapter, and basic to the function of the client-centered therapist,
is an hypothesis which has been and is being investigated in other
types of human relationships as well, and that the evidence in
regard to it has a significant and positive similarity no matter
what the field of endeavor.

SUGGESTED READINGS

The reader who wishes to consider in more detail his own attitudes as
they actually operate in his reactions with others, and the means of implementing his basic attitudes in therapy, will find rich food for thought
and a wealth of practical help in Porter's book, *An Introduction to Therapeutic Counseling* (148). An earlier consideration of implementation is
contained in chapter six of *Counseling and Psychotherapy* (166).

A thorough discussion of the psychology of the therapeutic relationship, covering both its description and its dynamics, is contained in the
article by Estes (54). For other accounts of the attitude and orientation
of the therapist, three references might be particularly pertinent. The
first two are psychoanalytic, the third the viewpoint of a religious counselor. They are: the chapter on "What Does the Analyst Do?" by
Horney (89, pp. 187–209); Reik, *Listening with the Third Ear* (161);
Hiltner, *Pastoral Counseling* (83, Chapter 7).

For a knowledge of the research regarding the counselor's function,
one might read Porter's study (149, 150) or Snyder (197) as early examples. Seeman (180) and Fiedler (58, 57) represent recent work in
this area, Fiedler's studies being particularly significant for their new
methodology.

For an example of the evidence from other sources regarding the basic
hypothesis of client-centered therapy, the little study by Coch and
French (41) would be a start.

Chapter 3 · The Therapeutic Relationship as Experienced by the Client

As our experience has moved us forward, it has become increasingly evident that the probability of therapeutic movement in a particular case depends primarily not upon the counselor's personality, nor upon his techniques, nor even upon his attitudes, but upon the way all these are experienced by the client in the relationship. The centrality of the client's perception of the interviews has forced itself upon our recognition. It is the way it seems to the client which determines whether resolution of conflict, reorganization, growth, integration — all the elements which comprise therapy — will occur. Our knowledge of therapy would be far advanced if we knew the answers to these two questions: What does it mean that the client experiences a relationship as therapeutic? and, How may we facilitate the experiencing of a relationship as therapeutic? We do not have the answers to these questions, but we have at least learned to ask them.

The way in which the client perceives or experiences the interviews is a field of inquiry which is new and in which the data are very limited. There has been no research as yet completed in this area, and relatively little consideration has been given to it. It is an area which appears to have great future significance, however, and for this reason the attempt will be made to present our very inadequate and imperfect knowledge in this chapter. Because of the tentative state of thinking, many direct statements by clients will be utilized so that the reader may formulate for himself those elements which appear significant, rather than rely too heavily upon the stated opinions of the author. These client observations, and the comments upon them, are presented under different headings, but it will be seen that there is much overlapping in the presentation. Following this attempt at organized presentation, a more complete account will be given of the way in which therapy was experienced by one sensitive and articulate client. In this more complete statement there appear to be many suggestive leads for further investigation.

THE EXPERIENCE OF THE COUNSELOR
AND THE COUNSELING SITUATION

Expectations

The manner in which the client perceives the counselor and the interview is initially influenced very deeply by his expectations. The range of these expectations is tremendous. The client may have expected the counselor to be a parental figure who will shield him from harm and who will take over the guidance of his life. He may have expected the therapist to be a psychic surgeon who will probe to the root of his difficulties, causing him great pain and making him over against his will. He may have expected him to be an advice-giver, and this advice may be genuinely and dependently desired, or it may be desired in order that the client can prove the advice wrong. He may, due to unfortunate previous experience with psychiatric or psychological counselors, look upon this new experience as one where he will be labeled, looked upon as abnormal, hurt, treated with little respect, and thus may deeply dread the relationship. He may look upon the counselor as an extension of the authority which referred him for help — the dean, the Veterans Administration, the court. He may, if he has some knowledge of client-centered therapy, view the counseling interview as a place where he will have to solve his own problems, and this may seem to him a positive or a very threatening possibility.

Even this enumeration of some of the most common expectations which the client brings to therapy barely suggests all the ramifications which they may have.

From a recorded first interview with a business executive we may extract those statements which indicate his expectations as to the relationship. He was referred by the personnel psychologist in his industry, who had discovered, by means of personality tests, the existence of strain and conflict in this man.

> "He said that I should . . . just tell you the things that I told him. Doc seemed to think that you could correct it. Now I'm not interested in taking your time or my time if you're going to tell me to go take up photography or something of that sort. . . ."

> "Well, I don't know how long it will take you. . . ."

> "Does that tell you any of the things that I should tell you? Or am I just sitting here, spinning my wheels?"

> "I don't know of anything else I can add to that that would be of value."

> "Well now, if you want to tell me what, uh, your suggestions are and anything about it, why, uh, I'd like to hear them."

> "I'm a worrier. All right. Well, you can say to me, 'Well, go home and don't worry.' Well, if that's the answer, why, uh, I can get my friends to say that to me and I don't have to drive so far to do it. Uh, I'm exaggerating here a bit on my feeling towards you and towards what you can accomplish, but I say in no uncertain fashion that if that's the answer then that's no answer to me at all."

Here in this man is evident an expectation of being made over by the therapist. He is outwardly cooperative, wants to give the information necessary for this remodeling of personality, but at the same time gives ample warning that he will strongly resist any of the suggestions which he desires. It might be mentioned that clients with this ambivalent attitude of dependence-resistance seem to have difficulty in coming to experience the interviews as therapeutic. Whether this is due to our lack of skill in facilitation, or whether this type of attitude is basically more difficult for therapy, only time and study will indicate.

Another client, a student, puts this same basic expectation more succinctly when he says:

> You make me think for myself and I don't like it. I want advice. I've been going to everyone for advice. You can't lose when you get it. If the person gives you advice you like, that makes you feel fine; if they give you advice you don't like, they're fools, and *that* makes you feel fine. (147, p. 26)

Here, as for most clients, there has been discovered a difference between the expectation and the actual experience of therapy, and the discovery of this difference may arouse resentment as here, or relief, or any one of a variety of other reactions.

Since an increasing number of clients have some sort of impression of client-centered therapy before coming for help, it may be useful to give an account, written by a client after the conclusion of counseling, about some of her feelings before coming. She mentions that because of her desire for assistance she read some of the books about nondirective counseling.

> Probably because I wanted help so much myself, all I could see in these books was a description of safety and a miraculous cure. At that time I missed the point of client-centered therapy — actually didn't see most of what I was reading. Before I asked Dr. —— to take me on as a client, I hunted in these books for everything the clients had said about the experience. "Was it painful? Did it work? How safe was it to give your confidence to someone else?" were the questions I had before counseling began.

This tentative, ambivalent, fearful feeling is probably the attitude most characteristic of all clients, whether they have any knowledge of therapy or not.

It is evident that clients come with widely varying expectations, many of which will not match the experience they meet. Nevertheless, the expectation will govern their perception to a considerable extent. It is clear that the businessman quoted above will perceive the therapist as an advice-giver, someone who is going to make him over, and that this perception will persist to some degree, even though he receives no advice and experiences no counselor attempt to manipulate. Likewise, the woman cited above will see the relationship as safe and as holding the potentialities of magic recovery, even though the counselor's attitude and behavior may not justify the expectation. It would appear that real progress or movement in therapy is greatly facilitated when both client and counseler are perceiving the relationship in similar fashion. How this may be achieved is the question which must be continually raised. Our experience is clear on one point. The perception does not come about by telling the client how he ought to experience the relationship. Meaningful perception is a matter of direct sensory experience, and it not only does not help but it may hinder a unified perception if the therapist attempts to describe, intellectually, the character of the relationship or of the process. It is for this reason that counselors operating from a client-centered point of view have tended to give up any attempts at "structuring," though earlier these were thought to be of value.

The Experience of Counselor Attitudes and Methods

Something of the way in which the client experiences the therapist has already been described (Chapter 2, pages 36–40). From the material available from clients it would appear that such elements as the sex, appearance, or mannerisms of the counselor play a lesser role than might be supposed. When the counselor is favorably perceived, it is as someone with warmth and interest for the client, someone with understanding. Says one client of the counselor, "She was the first person who seemed to understand how my anxieties looked to me."

On the other hand, when the therapist is experienced as a person who is not helpful, it is usually because these qualities seem to the client to be lacking. One student successfully completed therapy with a second counselor some months after a single interview with a first counselor. When the contacts were finished he was asked why it had seemed possible to work through his problems with the second counselor, but had broken off with the first counselor after one interview. He thought for a moment and replied, "You did about the same things he did, but you seemed really interested in me."

In regard to the methods used by the client-centered counselor, the client appears frequently to experience these as frustrating at first, and then valuable. Some quotations from the written reactions of unsophisticated clients as obtained by Lipkin (117) may make this clear.

"This type of psychological help seemed strange to me at the first meeting. I wondered 'How in the devil can this help me — just talking about things that weren't even clear to me?' I won't deny that after that first meeting I doubted whether he could help me."

"Through having to put my concerns into words and logical sentences, which was necessary as I couldn't keep silent longer than the counselor, I began to understand them better and saw them in different lights. Some of my vague thoughts were put into words by the counselor so that I had a fuller understanding of the three things I was concerned over. After I told him of my problems and he didn't suggest any solutions which was what I had expected from counseling, I found again that silence could be embarrassing and found it necessary to make up some methods of overcoming my difficulties which later, after being re-phrased by the counselor, began to make sense."

"During the interviews my psycologist [sic] took my views & thoughts and made them so that I could understand what was going on. He didn't conclude them but stated them back to me so I could draw my own conclusions. Things we talked about seemed clearer in my mind & organized it to an extent where now I belive [sic] I can think things out for myself." (117, p. 140)

From the client's point of view, the advantage of the reflection of attitudes appears to be, as mentioned earlier from a client statement, that "It was the role of the counselor to bring me to myself, to help me by being with me in everything I said, to realize what I was saying." (Chapter 2, p. 37)

Where the client undergoes, in the process of therapy, a real reorganization of self, the relationship to the counselor and to the counseling interview comes to involve a very special meaning of security, which is easily upset by arbitrary change. One client who had faced deep and significant attitudes in herself, who had met her counselor in different offices and sometimes at irregular times, mentions her resentment toward these aspects of counseling and describes the situation thus (21st interview, recorded):

For example, shifting around from one day of week to another, from one time of day to another, from place to place — uh, those things are all not only sources of resentment, but the resentment is the result of feeling that there's no security anywhere. And because, for a while, the only security there is is in the hour, any change either just before it, or after it, or during it is, is, uh, very much more important than it would be otherwise.

It appears that in the client's experience, particularly if the problems have been deep-seated, the only stable portion of experience is the unfailing hour of acceptance by the therapist. In this sense client-centered therapy is experienced as supporting, as an island of constancy in a sea of chaotic difficulty, though it is not "supportive" or approving, in the superficial sense. It is this constancy and safety which permits the client to experience therapy, a matter which we shall now consider.

How Therapy is Experienced by the Client

The Experiencing of Responsibility

One of the elements which appears to stand out prominently in the initial reaction of the client is the discovery that he is responsible for himself in this relationship. Clients have used various ways of describing this. One veteran writes:

> I was lost in your presence, especially when I was told that I had an hour with you. I could either sit or talk or do as I pleased. The impression I received was of being left alone, all on my own with my problem. But I soon discovered that by talking of my indecision and problem I was able to see clearly that my problem was being solved of my own initiative rather than the counseling of my interviewer. (117, p. 141)

It would appear that there was some structuring of the relationship by the counselor, and this may account in part for the feeling of aloneness which the client felt. Had he discovered the responsibility at his own pace, there might not have been this reaction. Another veteran client felt annoyance at the discovery — probably a rather characteristic reaction — but came to recognize the value of being responsible for self.

The counsellor was trying to make me think everything out for myself. At times his silence would anger me, but at the same time I felt he must have a purpose.

Because of his silence of not answering or giving opinions, I had to delve in my own mind deeper and deeper. In other words, the answers were *my own completely* & for this reason have stuck with me. (117, p. 140)

Still another client shows the transition between the inaccurate expectation and the actual experience of taking responsibility.

At first I tried to figure out what he wanted me to say or do. I was trying to outguess him or rather to diagnose my case as I thought he would. That didn't pan out. I did all the talking. (117, p. 141)

The Experience of Exploration

Thus far the reactions given are those which lead up to therapy, or which make therapy possible. It is in the process of exploration of attitudes that the client first begins to feel that this process in which he is engaged will involve change in himself, of a sort he has not envisaged. He both fears and desires this change which he dimly sees. The attitude toward such exploration is described in these terms by a client after the conclusion of therapy.

I remember a good deal of emotional tension in the second interview where I first mentioned homosexuality. I remember that I felt drawn down into myself, into places I didn't want to go, hadn't quite been to before, and yet had to see. I think I dreaded this interview more than any of the other early ones because I had been so afraid before counseling began that I would get to that subject. And afraid that I wouldn't. I'm surprised that under those conditions I got to it so soon, particularly since the immediate worry concerned someone's remark, which I had misinterpreted, about the counselor and me. I still remember the warm, acceptant voice of the counselor and my feeling that it was just a little more acceptant than I could be of the fears I was expressing but not enough different to be reassuring in a threatening way.

An element which frequently enters into this period of searching is the experiencing of inconsistency in self. When it is possible to talk freely, express attitudes freely, then contradictions are discovered which had never been noticed before. A clear statement of this feeling is given by Miss Har, a teacher who, some months after counseling, voluntarily wrote her reactions to the experience. Unlike most clients she had listened to some of her recorded interviews after they had been held, and had also read the transcribed interviews later. She thus commences the account of her experience.

> I know this will be a subjective report and that in a scientific sense it cannot be an accurate description of what "really happened." Yet I do believe it will have value because in the past eight months — during and since counseling — I have felt that in dealing with myself and with counseling I have been and can be honest, really honest. It seems to me that this is the first time in my life that I have been able to feel that this was true about my relationship to anything, as if I had to be free to be honest with myself before I could be so with anything else.
>
> I remember clearly when I first began to be aware of this. In the second interview I said of the first: "After two or three days I kept wanting to say something — to correct impressions that weren't quite true — which were unfavorable to me. And then I thought — Oh, what the heck, it doesn't make much difference." While I was saying that, I felt baffled because I both believed and didn't believe what I had said the time before. I didn't see how inconsistencies could be true. At first the inconsistencies between what I felt about myself (and said in the counseling session) and what I thought about myself were the most annoying. Later, inconsistencies between one interview and another bothered me much more. I was enjoying the feeling of being honest for the first time, and I didn't like this apparent evidence of untruth.
>
> I couldn't say that the later statements were any more or less true than the first. I tried to explain this to a friend during the latter part of counseling. She said, "You mean you found out later that what you had said before wasn't true?" When I said "No" to that, she said, "You mean it's still true?" I had to explain "No" again. I was irritated with her and with myself because I couldn't explain satisfactorily that there was something deeper than the inconsistencies which made and allowed them to be true.

Perhaps one explanation of therapy is that the inconsistencies in self are recognized, faced, re-examined, and the self is altered in ways which bring about consistency.

The safety of the relationship with the counselor, the complete absence of any threat, which permits honesty even in the expression of inconsistency, appears to make this exploration very much different from ordinary conversation.   One client explains that she has talked over all these troubles with her friends, yet in actuality hasn't done so.   "I was really saying the thing next to the thing that was really bothering me."   This sense of the therapeutic interview as the place where one can talk directly about concerns as they are felt, appears to be a significant characteristic of the experience.   This does not mean that the client is able to communicate all that gives him concern, or that he can even attempt this.   Miss Har, after reading the transcription of some of her first interviews, gives voice to an attitude which would undoubtedly be shared by most clients.   Speaking of these transcriptions in the fourth interview she says, "It's not that they aren't what I said, but they're only one tenth of what I was thinking."

This point may be enlarged.   Not only is the client able to communicate only a small fraction of the attitudes and feelings he is experiencing, but it is also true that what he thinks through in the interview is but a small fraction of what he works out between interviews.   Mrs. Ett mentions this experience with some surprise in her third interview:

S: And then I did notice this: that after I left the first two times I, it wasn't as if I left you, and I carried on the interview for a good hour afterwards (*laugh*).   I was talking to myself and it seemed almost peculiar, because I, I found myself talking to myself and I'd say — well, in other words, the effect of the interview didn't cease just as soon as I walked out of the door, it was very invigorating, that I can say, I found myself very much elated afterwards.

C: There are some things that go on after the interview itself closes.

S: That's right.   And that's an amazing thing.   It interested me, because generally after an interview of any kind you sort of go about your own work and thoughts. . . .

It is perhaps this persisting quality, the realization that some **process** new to his experience is at work within him, which gives

to the client his astonishing persistence in continuing the interviews, even in the face of intense pain. In a study made at the
Counseling Center over a three-month period it was found that
approximately 3 per cent of some 1500 appointments were broken.
Other appointments were of course changed or postponed, but in
only three instances out of 100 did the client simply fail to show
up. Considering the completely voluntary nature of all the
contacts, and the great discomfort which is often involved, and
the imperfections of counselor handling, this appears to be a
surprising record. This element is also experienced with some
astonishment by the client. Mrs. Ett states it in a way which
would be characteristic of many, in her seventh interview.

> I'm amazed at my tenacity at this thing. I generally start some-
> thing and after two or three tries I drop it with all kinds of silly
> excuses, mostly because I don't think it's helping me or doing any
> good, I mean art, music, anything. And ah — I come here, and I
> think this is my 7th or 8th visit and there's no doubt in my mind. I
> come here like I simply — like you have to go to the beauty parlor,
> or uh, put it on that basis (*laugh*). You know that's silly, although
> in a way it is comparable because I'm trying to develop my own per-
> sonality just as much as I'm trying to develop my own looks. I come
> here like I would — I mean I just *come* here, I can't understand *why*
> I come here, it's entirely foreign to me, this driving to come here.
> There's a lot of effort coming here. It means preparation for the
> children, the maid to take care of them, food, drive to the train, get up
> real early in the morning and dash out like mad, the children can't
> bear to see me go. So it is an effort — a definite effort, and yet it
> would have taken much less to discourage me in something else, you
> know what I mean? . . . It's like a mysterious drive (*laugh*) really.

The Discovery of Denied Attitudes

The outcome of the verbal exploration of attitudes and problems is the discovery of attitudes which the client has experienced,
but which he has denied to awareness. Clients speak of talking
about "things I had never previously thought of," or use other
phrases to describe this aspect of their experience. One client,
a man of limited education, puts it this way:

> At first I wondered why I had to do all the talking but as it went on I could see that it had the effect of making me dig deep inside of me and bring up things that I hardly knew were troubling me. I know that practically every time I'd start off hardly knowing what to talk on but as time progressed I talked much more freely. (117, p. 140)

Miss Har describes with some vividness the fact that hatred for her father, which has been denied as having any recent existence, and love for her father, which has been far more deeply denied, have now both been discovered as present attitudes. The following recorded excerpt is from her twenty-first interview.

> The statement of hating my father still is — is something that I wouldn't have agreed to last year. . . . I felt that I *had* got rid of it, it hadn't — it wasn't on the surface at least. That is, I said, during my army experience, I didn't feel as if I hated him altho I certainly got nauseated when people spoke of him. But after that, uh, up to last year I still felt as if I didn't. And I thought that by saying that I didn't and by going in the other direction, that somehow or other things would straighten themselves out. And now I seem to have got around to — at least if I can believe the last couple of interviews — to saying that I both hate him and wish that I could like him, and at times even do like certain things that I remember about him, and particularly like certain qualities which I see in myself and which before I felt I ought to hate because they resemble him.

Notice how even yet the acceptance of these attitudes is a doubtful one. She is saying, "if I can believe the last couple of interviews" then these attitudes are real. They are still looked at as something which is partially outside of herself. The pain of including these denied attitudes as a part of the self will be mentioned in the following section. This experience of discovering within oneself present attitudes and emotions which have been viscerally and physiologically experienced, but which have never been recognized in consciousness, constitutes one of the deepest and most significant phenomena of therapy. A veteran who writes of himself in the third person describes this experience in simple terms.

> During counselling, he was forced, in his own mind to admit that

several of these things were wrong. He began to think and actually admit things to himself about himself that he had never considered admitting before. He began to see just what was at the root of all his actions. Why he was so often apt to cover up what he had done with excuses. (117, p. 142)

The Experience of Reorganizing the Self

As these denied elements of experience are brought into awareness, a process which we have come to think of as the reorganization of self is necessitated. The picture of self which the client has had must be altered to contain these new perceptions of experience. This may involve a very slight change when the denied experiences are only slightly inconsistent with the self; or it may involve the most drastic reorganization, in which the self and the self in its relationship to reality is so altered that few aspects remain untouched. In the first instance there may be mild discomfort. In the case of the radical reorganization, the client may go through the most racking torment of pain, and a complete and chaotic confusion. This suffering may be associated with rapidly changing configurations of personality, being a new person one day, and sinking back into the old self on the next, only to find that some minor episode puts the new organization of self again in a position of regnancy. We shall try, from several client statements, to illustrate this range of feeling associated with reorganization.

Take first the young and unlettered veteran who has found that therapy has given him a less flattering but more realistic concept of self. This has involved a certain amount of discomfort but not to a great degree. He describes his experience.

As for the consoling I hav had I can say this, It realy makes a man strip his mind bare, and when he does, He knows then what he realy is and what he can do. Or at least he thinks he knows him self pretty well. As for myself, I know that my ideas were a little to big for what I realy am, but now I realize that one must stay start at his own level.

Now, after four visits, I have a much clearer picture of my self and my future, It makes me feel a little depressed and disappointed, but on the other hand, It has taken me out of the dark, the load seems a lot lighter now, that is I can see my way now, I know what I want to do, I know about what I can do so now that I can see my goal, I will be able to work a whole lot easyer at my own level. (117, pp. 142–143)

Another veteran tells of his experience in a way which puts more emphasis upon the wide swings in mood which appear so frequently to accompany this portion of the process.

I started to talk of the things that had bothered me, and, at intervals, Mr. L. solidified my ramblings into a few clear, concise words. ... Many of the thoughts and fears in my mind were vague — I couldn't put them into exact, clear words. The fear was the thing that overwhelmed my thoughts. I had never seen these clearly. I couldn't put it into words that seemed to mean anything to me.

Mr. L. took these vague thoughts and fears and put them into words that I could understand and see clearly. By doing so I could see clearly their degree of importance. Some of the things I was afraid of now seem unimportant as they actually were. Fear, though is something that combats reasoning. I needed help and Mr. L. gave it to me. ... During the second meeting I received my first jolt. Taking my vague thoughts he told me in a few words what they really meant. I broke out in a sweat, I was trembling, somewhat panicky. Those few words had opened the door for me. When I walked out into the street after that meeting it was as though I were in a new world. The people looked different, more human, the world seemed a better place to live in.

In school I applied some of the things I had learned and found that they worked. I seemed to get along better with the other students, and at times the fear and tension almost vanished. At times, though, it became just as bad but it came in waves now that receded when I made an effort.

During subsequent meetings I learned more and more about myself, until today, our fifth meeting, I told him the real trouble that was bothering me — all of my other fears that I had told him about in previous meetings being related to this main fear.

A night ago I wrote another piece of fiction and for the first time in six years it had everything in it that I wanted to say. It was good, and my friends verified this.

It was an immediate relief to get rid of these fears, the tension and the misery that goes with it. (117, pp. 145–146)

An account of an experience involving deeper reorganization is given by Miss Har. Much of her life and her pattern of selfhood has been organized around her hatred for her father. What happens when she realizes that she has been denying the opposite feeling is well told in her own words.

> The eighteenth interview represents to me a mixture of feelings. In this interview I came close to saying that I liked my father sometimes. I felt then as if I had come to the edge of an awful canyon; I referred to it later as a pit I had dug for myself. When I asked, "What does that do to the basis of my whole life?" I could barely speak. I felt more deeply than I can describe that I had reached a point far away from everything I had ever known. Despair, fear and grief — all greater than any I had felt before — were behind the question.
>
> As soon as the interview was over I wanted to hear it played back, as we occasionally did. I remember lying down to listen to it and shivering as it came closer to the point where I was afraid I had said "I love my father." I think I never did hear that part I was waiting for. I fell asleep and slept until the recording was over. I was scared and unhappy when I woke up. At the beginning of the next interview I talked all around it. Throughout that following session, I was angry and confused, afraid of what I might do or say next. In between the two sessions I had hours of real panic. It was a disintegrating experience which ended in better integration but was hard to bear at the time. The three following interviews show how hard I tried to run away from it and how impossible it was to deny an experience that had once been brought to light. It wasn't until the twenty-second interview, eighteen days later, that I was able to be fairly calm about it.

Note that this state of disorganization preceded the remarks quoted previously from the twenty-first interview (page 76) in which Miss Har has begun to assimilate these contradictory perceptions. At this time (eighteenth interview) the denied experiences have been recognized, but they have the effect of producing chaos in the personality. The question "What does that do to the basis of my whole life" is one which is, in effect, asked by every client who faces significant experiences which have been deeply denied to awareness. The resultant confusion is very well described by Miss Har in the twenty-second interview as "the amorphous state I've gotten into." This fluid, amorphous quality is very hard to bear, even though it heralds the loss of an inadequate organization of self, and holds the possibility of a more effective and less vulnerable personality structure.

A further description of this experience of disorganization and painful reorganization is contained in the sixteenth interview with Alfred, who was, when he first came in, an extremely withdrawn student, a seclusive individual living largely in fantasy. In this recorded interview he portrays not only the conflict within, but his awareness of the constructive even though painful nature of the reorganization.

> I certainly think in a way the problem is a lot clearer than a while ago, yet — maybe — It's like the ice breaking up on a pond in the spring, it's — while things are a lot nearer to — While the pond is a lot nearer to being nothing but clear water, yet things are much more unstable now, possibly, than when the pond was covered over with ice. What I'm trying to bring out is that I seem to be so much in a terrible fog all of the time lately, but I do feel a lot better off than I was before, because then I didn't realize what was the matter. But maybe all this fog and so-called trouble is due to the fact of two opposing forces in me now. You know it's not really a case of just letting one be superior, but it's a kinda breaking up and reorganizing that's going on now that makes things seem so doubly bad. So maybe I'm better off than I think.

There is one aspect of this process of reorganization of self which is often difficult for the counselor to understand, and which may be clearer if we listen to the client's experience of it. This is the fact that though the client may be making much observable progress in the exploration of his total perceptual field, may be bringing into the light of awareness feelings and attitudes hitherto denied, may seem to be proceeding toward a positive rebuilding of self, the moods which accompany this process appear to bear little relationship to the progress being made. After a deep and significant insight, the client may be plunged into the blackest gloom, with thoughts of suicide and feelings of despair. As conflicts and problems appear to be resolved, the initial tension and discomfort show no sign of abating, but often appear more marked. Perhaps a clue to the inner experience of this aspect of therapy is conveyed in a diagram drawn by a client, Mrs. Ett, in her eighth interview (see page 82). She has been achieving significant insights but she concludes a statement of one of her conflicts by saying:

S: Maybe that's just the way I feel this week, I don't know, but everything is very, very tense with me.

C: It might be temporary, but at any rate it's strong at the moment.

S: Yes. In my mind I was drawing a diagram. Perhaps the whole thing is, uh, I'm very — well, I have no levels [evidently meaning no smooth level experience] at all, you see, it's below the surface and everything is like this, see. (*She draws a line of vigorous and turbulent waves. See diagram, first stage.*) Now when I'm coming here I feel that I've cleared this up, see (*she blocks out a portion of the waves*) and I'm on this level (*she draws a new and shorter line of waves on a higher level*) but it's still this. (*The waves are still turbulent. See diagram, second stage.*) And now as I keep going I keep going on higher levels like that, see. . . . Now right now of course there's still that feeling [of turbulence], but I have a feeling of progression, that part of my life has blocked itself off like this already and one phase has been talked about and blocked off. . . . Yet it isn't that I have managed to calm this level, it's still there, it's still turbulent, but it's a feeling of making progressions with that turbulence. . . . (*See diagram, third stage.*) It's an improvement of course, it isn't as if I feel, well, *everything* is desperate, like I used to. I say certain things have been settled, and yet everything *is* still desperate, . . . but in other words I feel that, well, with these treatments what will happen is that I will continue to go up until I reach this point where there won't be any turbulence. (*Fourth stage of diagram.*)

This description helps to explain the way in which the inner tensions and fluctuations are experienced as therapy progresses. The "turbulence" which remains appears just as "desperate" as did the total experience when therapy began. The fluctuations are still violent. One client attempted a chart of feelings experienced during therapy. On the whole there are more experiences

Four Stages of Diagram Drawn by Mrs. Ett

FIRST STAGE:

"No level at all, it's below the surface and everything is like this."

SECOND STAGE:

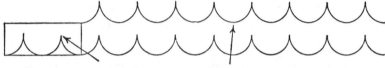

"I've cleared this up, and I'm on this level, but it's still this (turbulent)."

THIRD STAGE:

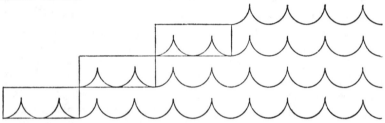

"As I keep going, I keep going on higher levels."
"It's still turbulent, but it's a feeling of progression with that turbulence."

FOURTH STAGE:

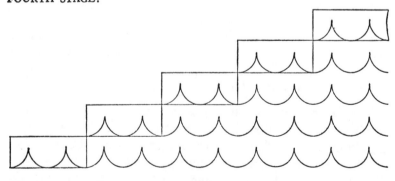

Continues the blocked out steps until they include all the turbulence.

of unhappiness, fearfulness, and depression during the second half of therapy than during the first half; and rather violent fluctuations from elated to unhappy, or from confident to depressed, are the rule rather than the exception. It is of some interest that this client felt that the same mood was present at the beginning and end of therapy — namely, an attitude of determination.

Still another aspect of this experience of reorganization of self involves a similarity to psychodrama. The client is trying out, on a symbolic and verbal level, the new self, the new behavior, toward which he is struggling. One often sees evidence of this in the interviews. Less often does the client verbalize this experience. Again we are indebted to Miss Har for a statement bearing on this point. As she struggles to find her true feelings for her father, the ones which match her sensory experience, she uses the interview as a tryout ground. In the nineteenth interview she says:

> Last time I was using the time a little differently from the way I do sometimes because I was trying to get myself to say something and then to see if it was true, or if I'd know if it were true after I said it . . . sometimes you can sort of try out — different expressions of feeling to see whether they do any good or not, whether they fit or not.

The Experiencing of Progress

Contrary to what one might suppose, progress appears to be experienced by the client almost from the first. It is the fact that he discovers that some of the issues he has discussed, some of the denied experiences which have been accepted, no longer cause him pain or anxiety, which encourages the client to go forward. The realization that one segment of personality organization has been reconstructed, and that new forms of behavior result from it — this it is that builds the client's confidence in his own ability to make progress in exploring himself.

Again we may borrow from Miss Har a description of the inner feeling of such progress. In the fourth interview she discusses the change in her feelings which has come about primarily through catharsis.

> It's wonderful how relaxed I can get talking about ideas I couldn't even think about last year, things that just require saying, getting rid of. Last year I kept thinking what a pleasant way out illness would be. This year in my daydreams when the same thing happens I say, "Hell, no, that's not what I want."

She also tells of her progress in her behavior, and the satisfaction which accrues to her because of it. The interview which she describes is less than one third of the way through therapy, and much the most painful aspects are still ahead of her. Yet important progress is already experienced, as she explains in her account written after the conclusion of counseling.

> My memory of several interviews is so vivid that I have thought of them often since the final counseling session. I shall never forget the happiness, excitement, elation, and peak of self-satisfaction that I felt during the first part of the seventh interview when I had just come from proving to myself that I could face in the presence of someone other than the counselor the feeling that had been with me for years: that everyone thought I had expressed homosexual tendencies. I felt that it was the first evidence of the fact that I could find out what I was apart from what people thought I was — or, rather, apart from what I thought they thought I was. I remember how keenly I felt my own pleasure reflected in the eyes of the counselor whom I was looking at directly for the first time in any interview. That in itself was something I had wanted to do very much since the first hour. During this interview I thought for the first time of the end of counseling; before that I could not believe that anyone would willingly remove himself from such a safe, satisfying situation.

This sense of progress and achievement is felt not only in moments of elation and pleasure, but also when the road seems darkest, and the confusion greatest. Thus Mrs. Ett in a mood of despair in regard to herself, puts it this way:

> I'm sinking into a tomb. That's just what it is, little by little I'm going into a tomb. Everything is closing up on me. (*Pause.*) If I could only break away the walls. (*Pause.*) And yet actually, my coming here has helped me, you see, so maybe I have to continue coming here. Maybe that will help me get out of it. It isn't complete, that diagram explains how I feel. I've cleared up some things.

It is clear that even in her feeling of retrogression the experience of progress is with her, and buoys her up. This appears to be characteristic of most clients. It is not infrequently true that the blackest moods and the deepest despair come rather shortly before the end of therapy. Looking at it more deeply, we may say that to face the most threatening denied attitudes the client needs to feel considerable confidence, which comes from the recognition that one issue after another has been resolved, that one experience after another has been assimilated. Yet it is still true that these most basic denials are deeply upsetting when brought out into the therapeutic hour, and that all the past confidence cannot prevent the client from plunging into despair as he discovers that much that is basic to his personal organization is false, and must be painfully rebuilt. Nonetheless the backdrop for this mood of discouragement is a series of experiences of vital inner progress in reorganization, and black and tragic as the present discovery may seem, the positive setting in which it takes place is also a part of the total experience for the client.

The Experience of Ending

How does the client experience the ending of therapy? As in other aspects of therapy, we find both commonality and uniqueness in the way the client feels about the concluding phase of the interviews. In an interview which proved to be the third from the end, Mrs. Ett gives an account of the tentative and uncertain feeling which she has about ending, and yet a surprising assurance too, in view of the fact that her mood had struck a new low only a few days before. A long talk with her husband which for her marked a crisis in the reorganization of her behavior, had been described at length earlier in the interview, but she summarizes an important aspect of it here. This excerpt is taken from the concluding portion of the thirteenth interview.

S: I'll tell you how I feel about my coming here. I don't think I have to come twice a week. I would like to come once a week for the time being and see and just talk over my problems once a week. And then, if everything goes smoothly on the once a week deal, why then I think I'm through. The only reason I'm not stopping now, although I feel right now I don't need any more, is that I just want to feel a lasting final few licks, shall we say.

C: You want to feel quite sure that you are really through before you quit.

S: Or if this is one of these quiet weeks, if it is, why then I'll have to start coming back twice, maybe three times, I hope not.

C: By and large you feel that you are getting close to the end.

S: I think so. How does one determine?

C: Just the way you are determining.

S: Oh, is that so, just by feeling that you don't have to come as often?

C: When you are ready to call it quits, why we'll call it quits.

S: Uh huh. And then, no return, uh?

C: Oh yes, if you feel you want to.

S: And then I'd have priority on you, is that it?

C: Oh, yes, yes. We don't close the door and lock it, we just say goodbye and if you want to get in touch with me again, why feel free to do so.

S: I mean, I feel as if I've just about covered almost every phase of my difficulty and, uh, I think one could keep going talking and talking and talking about it, if it weren't doing any good. What I mean to say, if the cure hadn't been started, and I think it has — I sort of have leveled off, quite suddenly it seems to me, because last week, why is it, last Tuesday when I was here I was in a terrible state, this terrible state. I thought of suicide, which I hadn't even thought of for almost a year or so, and yet Tuesday night, maybe it's darkest before dawn or something like that, you know, platitudes.

C: Sometimes it is; (*S:* It is?) sometimes not, I mean, it's interesting —

S: Yes, but I had really reached a low, and it seems maybe superficial to say that in three or four days I come back and I feel like a different person, but I think maybe I was reaching a certain emotional — setting myself for an emotional revelation, subconscious revelation which I didn't know but that it was just coming to the top like a boil.

C: Getting to the point where you had to do something about the whole business.

S: Yes, I realized the position, that I had to get it out, and I did, Tuesday night, and it wasn't that I sat down and I said, "Well, Arnold, let's talk it out, leave us talk it out. . . ." I didn't do that. My feeling of hatred towards him was so intense that I was weak already, really I was so weak — I said something and he misunderstood me. And then I misunderstood him and I said, "Arnold, we just don't meet at all, do we

Arnold?" Then he said, "Well, let's talk" so we sat down and talked. So he took the initiative, and I started to talk to him for a whole hour and a half. Before it opened up I hated him, I couldn't talk, "Oh, he won't understand," "We don't meet on the same level." To myself, "Let's get away from each other. I can't stand to be with you, you irritate me...." Then all of a sudden, I said, "Arnold, do you know that I feel sexually inferior to you," and that did it. The very fact that I could tell him that. Which was, I think that was the very thing, the whole thought to admit, not to admit to myself, because I knew that all the time, but to bring it up so that I could have admitted it to him, which I think was the whole turning point.

C: To be able to admit what you regarded as your deepest weakness.
S: Yes.
C: Just started the ball rolling.
S: This feeling of sexual inadequacy, but now that he knows it — it isn't important any more. It's like I carried a secret with me, and I wanted somebody to share it and Arnold of all people, and finally he knows about it so I feel better. So I don't feel inadequate.
C: The worst is known and accepted.

Not infrequently, in bringing therapy to a conclusion, the client experiences fear, and sense of loss, and a temporary unwillingness to face life alone without the underlying support of the therapeutic hour. This was the experience of Miss Har, who paints this picture of her leaving.

The twenty-third interview, which I had intended for the last, was as sad as any I remember. I felt myself wanting sympathy, comfort, reassurance — all the things I had come to believe through nondirective counseling were "wrong" — and I was so ashamed of myself that I was sure the counselor must be, too. In this interview I had completely forgotten the progress that had been accepted in the preceding one. In its place were doubt, shame, and deep discouragement. Of all the interviews, that is the one I should least like to live through again.

So gloomy was the experience of this interview that she could not bring herself to end therapy at this point, and asked for another interview. In this final conversation her attitude had returned to one of basic self-confidence, though some fear was also present.

Something of the basis for that fear is explained in the account she wrote of her feelings some ten weeks later.

> I haven't finished the job of integrating and reorganizing myself, but that's only confusing, not discouraging, now that I realize this is a continuing process. This is something I didn't know during the last six weeks of counseling when I was afraid to end the sessions because I thought I would have to stay with whatever were my last conclusions about myself and "How would I know they were any more right than those in any other session?" I have worried less about it these past weeks as I have seen my behavior reflecting some inner changes. The behavior makes me like myself better so it is easier to accept the occasionally contradictory shifts. It is exciting, sometimes upsetting, but deeply encouraging to feel yourself in action and apparently knowing where you are going even though you don't always consciously know where that is.

Through the Eyes of a Client

Up to this point the attempt has been made to give some generality to the observations made, by utilizing the reactions of a number of clients, so that some of the commonalities of their experience may be noted. Perhaps, however, we may learn with even greater depth by trying to understand how therapy felt, how it was experienced by one client.

The client who supplied the material from which we shall quote below was a woman between 35 and 40 whom we shall call Miss Cam, a professional woman who had some psychological background and had taken one course in psychotherapy. At the time she came in for therapy she was in the city temporarily with a friend, and was to leave for a vacation shortly. The first interview had not been formally arranged, and consequently was brief, not over 20 or 25 minutes in length. After this first interview she wrote down her reactions very fully, and showed the document to the counselor before the second contact. He encouraged her to keep such a personal account after each interview in order to add to our knowledge of therapy. It was mentioned that the more completely honest the account, whether this meant positive or negative statements, the more valuable the record would be. There was no further mention of the document in the counseling interviews, and the counselor did not receive it until the close of the therapeutic contacts.

The statement is largely self-explanatory, though the writer will interrupt it at times with comments. The excerpts quoted constitute a fairly large fraction — probably half — of the total manuscript. There seems to be no need to describe the general content of the interviews, which were not recorded, beyond saying that counseling started in regard to a minor problem, proceeded to greater depths, and involved, so far as the counselor could see, a rather considerable reorganization of personality. At one or two points some interview material is described, in order to make the client's comments understandable. From this point on it may be well to let Miss Cam speak for herself.

Written after the First Interview

What did it feel like to be a client? At first I felt completely flummoxed. Before we started, I knew and had accepted the idea that I was going to have to do all this myself, so of course I skipped the stage where the client is trying to figure out what the hell goes on here. . . . But it's one thing to accept the idea and another to put it into practice. Somehow or other I seemed to expect that what you said would give me a lead, but most of the time it didn't. You seemed to see it my way every time. Now that's wonderful, but if you understand me all that well, what need is there for words? It's almost a static equilibrium. I have the feeling that there must be movement if I am to get anywhere — a vital movement, a flow of communication like an electric current, and not, I think, just running in the one direction. But I want to get on with my problem, so what can I do? Well, maybe if I look around in the cupboard I can find something that will tip the balance — something you won't understand, something you will have an opinion about, something you know more about and can shed light on, even if it's just catching a feeling or a meaning behind my words of which I have little or no conscious awareness. But none of these things happen for a while, and I ask myself whether it is possible that you see more than I think, more than I see myself?

Well, looking at your reflection of my perceptual field from my own perceptual field, I see a mirror image, nothing more. Perhaps if I were to get into your perceptual field and look at myself through your eyes I would see something more? It looks as if it might be safe — the mirror image is so faithful, perhaps it is safe to go behind it? Perhaps it's like that glass that is mirror from one side but transparent from the other — and in both cases you see the same thing? By now the tension has mounted considerably: I came for counseling, therefore I wanted to see myself more clearly than I now do; and a mirror image isn't sufficient. In a sense I am already familiar with that through private reflections. My own mirroring of myself was wavering and distorted because the mirror itself was a split-off part of me; and I have made some progress in that the mirror you hold up reflects all of me — both judge and accused. But this hasn't accomplished what I seek, and has whetted my desire to see myself as a real, live, flesh and blood person. There is only one obstacle to this — you may not want me to come in — perhaps there are things of your own lying around that you don't want me to see?

So I look at you fully for the first time. In this look I am asking your permission to enter, and in some way trying to tell you that I won't pry. I won't even ask to look at the picture of me that is hanging on your wall, if only you will please let me come in and look out your window at myself. Your response to this is the most completely friendly and disarmingly casual welcome. If you had been effusive, I should have been so embarrassed and/or occupied in responding to your welcome that I would have been too shy or frightened of offending you to give much attention to taking an undisturbed look out your window. On the other hand, if you had qualified your welcome — said, in effect, "Okay, come in and look out the window but mind you don't look at anything else," I would have been scared to come in, sure that your house was full of alien and unfriendly things. Even as it was, I was too shy to take more than the most fleeting glance out the window: but although I don't know what I saw, I have a strong impression that this was the first positive movement in the interview, and vitally important. No, I do remember something of what I saw: I saw a separate person — a person you saw and accepted as being distinct from yourself, with an organization all her own and a law of development peculiar to that organization. Of specific characteristics, however, I saw nothing.

Various elements of this statement seem typical of many clients. The discovery that experiencing responsibility for self is very different from knowing about it is one of these. The puzzlement and frustration of a "one-way dialogue" is another. The fact that it leads to presentation of more material from the "cupboard" is still another. The feeling that a pure mirror image in the counselor is not sufficient for therapeutic movement is worth careful thought. The fascinating description of discovering that the counselor sees one as a separate person may be a unique experience or may be more general. With our present knowledge it is impossible to say. We turn again to Miss Cam's account.

> With this, it became more hopeful, and therefore more urgent to get at the root of the problem. Then you made the reflection that struck the spark — and isn't it odd that I can't remember the exact words.[1] If I remember rightly, there had been other responses that said much the same thing: it's as if a charge had gradually accumulated in my futile attempts to establish an emotional flow, and finally it reached sufficient strength to jump the gap.
>
> Here another interesting thing happened. Somehow or other you reflected not only my feeling of having hit something significant, but also my pleasure in the event: *my* pleasure, not your pleasure in having accomplished something with this case after all. I think that if there had been any element that I could have interpreted as self-congratulation in your response, it would have slowed me considerably. On the other hand, if you had failed to reflect *any* of that pleasure, something quite vital would have been missing.
>
> Shortly after this, the interview was terminated, without having got me any further towards the solution of my problem, as far as I could see at the time. But I did emerge with a strong feeling that this was not going to be solved at the problem level. Even if I did arrive at an adequate explanation of why I engage in this particular behaviour, the explanation in itself would have no therapeutic value.

[1] The response which is referred to as striking the spark was, from the counselor's point of view, simply a good reflection of the attitude she had just expressed. Something about the wording of it, or perhaps merely the objectification of the feeling, struck her with some force. She had responded in some such words as these: "Hm, that hit something. I'll have to think that one over. I believe that leads somewhere."

I would have to do something before I could make use of any explanation, and by that time, the explanation wouldn't matter anyhow.

Notice, in the second paragraph above, the fact that it is beginning to be her own feelings which are central to the whole experience, and that this already seems so right that an intrusion of any attitude or feeling belonging to the counselor would seem to damage the relationship. She comments further about an additional reaction to this first interview.

[I found that] I ran into the most extraordinary grammatical difficulties in expressing myself. I was dissatisfied with the expression, I knew I hadn't expressed what I meant, but it was the best I could do at the time. That it was the best I could do at the time probably indicates that it was all I could face at the time. But if anyone had faced me abruptly with the meaning behind my expression, I would have been thoroughly exasperated. What does he think I am anyway? Does he think I'm so stupid I can't see that? He just doesn't understand me, that's what, and I'm going to show him how stupid *he* is. Or maybe it's no use, and I might as well throw in the sponge. Your response, on the other hand, roused a response of "Sure, that's right as far as it goes, but there's a lot of other stuff in here that I haven't told you about yet, and I'd like to."

This would appear to be an excellent statement of the fact that the reflection of attitudes by the counselor is not only experienced as nonthreatening, but, in its very objectification of the essence of what has been expressed, tends also to draw the client's attention to the many things which have *not* been said.

There were some interesting sequels to this experience. For one thing, a real problem had just arisen. The previous afternoon I had received an offer of a position in X University; I had to make my decision in 24 hours, and I felt completely unequal to the task. It was a very attractive offer, and the position appeals to me in all kinds of ways. But there's this other plan I have — pioneering work, precarious, not nearly so many obvious personal satisfactions, something that other people will think pretty small potatoes until it succeeds, if it ever does. I had a miserable, restless night, and came to our interview tired and still undecided. Both from the standpoint of immediate personal satisfaction, and from the standpoint of "success," the X University appointment was the thing. But it isn't as easy as all that, because comfort isn't the only criterion — there's the little matter of growing and bearing good social fruit. Well, I think it's no accident that after our interview I suddenly realized that I didn't have to worry about the socially accepted standard of success — it's a standard that has very little meaning for me. But there was still the question of whether I might not "grow" just as well in one job as in the other. But how could I decide that? The answer is still in the future and well beyond my reach. I was in despair. Then I thought, well, why do I have to decide between the two jobs? Why not just decide whether or not to take this one? So then it became clear that the only objection to this job is that I would not get the holiday I so badly need, and would have to start in feeling tired and rushed and unprepared. But one doesn't turn down good jobs just because one wants a holiday. And why not? Because one has to work to eat. But I don't have to work to eat, what's that got to do with me? Well, people who do have to, have used that against me so often that I feel as if I have to act as if I were one of them. Well, well, came the dawn, and I refused the offer. Following this, I was able to take account of the fact that there's a good chance that the offer will be repeated next year, and that there are two other excellent jobs being kept open for me if the job I am hoping for doesn't materialize, or folds up. So there's no real basis for a sense of pressure and haste. I realized too, that the feeling of having to choose between two jobs also arose from the notion that I had to act as if I had to work to eat. And now I have the most agreeable feeling that a great many decisions, and not just in this area either, are going to be much easier for me, and a lot of other psychological puzzles and problems resolved in a greater synthesis. This is a pervasive therapy — something that gets into the blood stream, not a poultice applied locally.

It is of some interest that the question of deciding about these positions had not come into the first interview at all, perhaps because the client did not feel safe enough to discuss important issues, perhaps because of the brevity of the interview.

This would appear to be a good description of the way in which therapy is a releasing agent between interviews. The client finds it safer to look at experience as it is, and finds this most satisfying. It is this type of occurrence which also seems to bring an inner, often unverbalized conviction to the client that *something* is happening in his psychological organization and functioning, and this makes it worthwhile to bear the pain.

> Another sequel to our interview is the awful psychic misery — something I have become familiar with in the confessional. It always precedes some real step forward, and cannot be ignored. . . . And now there are the dreams. First the horrible one where some of the dynamics of my "problem" were stated, but which fortunately contained the assurance that the old motivation is dying out. Then the pleasanter one which seems to say the new, free, vital motive has got the old one well in hand.

Written after the Second Interview

The material is titled, significantly, "Three hours post-operatively."

> I'm just so miserable and discouraged that I can scarcely bring myself to write this. What's the use of it all? A sea, a rising tide of chaotic emotions rises up from deep, deep within me, and threatens to overwhelm me. Or is it emotions? Is it instead a thousand conflicting sensations? All the sensations that arose out of all the separate events of my life, both external and internal, and that under ordinary circumstances are organized into patterns of emotion and thought? Can it be that when you pull one little brick out, the whole structure collapses into a shapeless pile of bricks, and has to be rebuilt in a new form? Can you at this point, choose the architectural style — a better or a worse, just as you prefer?

One of the important things which the therapist must learn to recognize is that he will find it difficult, usually impossible, and certainly not profitable for therapy, to try to predict the effect an interview will have. From the counselor's point of view, the interview which evoked this despair was an interview in which progress was definitely discernible. The client was beginning to get into the problems she deeply felt, and to consider her attitudes toward herself. That it would bring about such a catastrophic sense of discouragement was definitely not expected by the counselor, nor would the counselor have known it from her attitude in the next interview.

It is certain that not all clients experience this sense of one organization coming to pieces, and another being of necessity built to take its place. The fact that pulling "one little brick" can cause it to collapse is doubtless significant of the fact that the self has been organized upon an unrealistic basis. But this problem we shall consider at greater length when we discuss a theory of personality which matches the therapeutic facts.

Miss Cam goes on to discuss her feelings with a complicated analogy of a pool, deeply agitated. She concludes:

> Does the fact that the therapist has sufficient faith to accept the client's "dangerous" experiences calmly and courageously — as shown by his ability to restate them — give the client the added faith in the outcome necessary to sustain a drastic reorganization?

Here we seem to find a basis for the thought expressed in an earlier chapter, that the client finds it possible to take new attitudes toward himself primarily because he finds the therapist taking these attitudes. Is this mere imitation? It seems to bear little resemblance to it.

"Sixty Hours Later" is the heading which Miss Cam gives to the next section of her reactions:

> It took four hours to write that page and a half — four hours of sinking down — no, it's not sinking down, it's more like expanding, as if bonds were loosened, and a homogeneous design got larger and larger, until you could see that what looked like continuous lines were really composed of rows of separate points, and as the design spreads out, the points get farther and farther apart, until finally the connections become so tenuous that it snaps, and the pattern collapses into a wild jumble of unrelated bits and pieces. There is somehow a deep sense of relief, in just letting go, in relaxing the effort to hold that crushing multiplicity of pieces in some semblance of order and unity. It's terribly painful, such utter confusion, such a literally staggering, brain-stunning *number* of impressions — it's hopeless, it's humanly impossible ever to make sense and order out of such chaos: how wonderful it would be to let go of the last thread of self-consciousness, my perception of this confusion as confusion — to lose myself in it, become just another small piece of it, one with it, to sink down and down into the grateful peace and oblivion of un-knowing. Yet how odd that I should think of finding peace by yielding to what seems

chaos and disorder. How odd that when I imagine that oblivion I have a consciousness of peace and order, of moving easily and effortlessly among all that welter of things that seems so chaotic and threatening when looked at from the outside. There's a deep joy and happiness here, a real belongingness, a flawless functioning, in which I am a steady glow, active but unchanging though bathed in an active changing medium — a medium composed of an infinite variety of things, yet all harmoniously blended. They have individuality and form yet are not rigid; they are full of light and color but not transparent; substantial, yet not solid. The pattern moves and changes and is full of life. It's not like a kaleidoscope, not full of bits and pieces held together in harsh geometric patterns, nor changing with that abrupt collapse and re-formation. There's none of that lifeless rigidity — rather, all the parts are alive, smoothly flowing into new, dynamic, harmonious relationships. Why no, I've got it wrong. The pattern is not changing, it's just that the parts are all so alive, the relationship so vital that I can't associate it with the fixed and static, and so of course I thought it was changing. But it's I who am moving, flowing in and around this infinite variety, looking at it from new angles, discovering more and more about it. It's not the pattern that changes, it's the vantage point from which I see it. "I" am distinct from this environment, yet I include it: it's my experience, it's mine, it's part of me, but it is not "me." I am separate from it, yet I am intimately related to it, in a relationship of knowledge and of love. I am outgoing towards it, embracing it, even while it *seems* to embrace me. Whatever it is, I love it, and it's much more fully conscious than the kind of self-observation where you stand outside yourself and classify yourself. But now I've held onto it as long as I can — any more and I'll distort it.

Here is material which bears reading and re-reading. The experience of which Miss Cam obtains a fleeting glimpse is perhaps the experience of genuine inner adjustment, in which the self is not struggling to distort experience but accepts it, moves *with* basic experience rather than against it, and by relinquishing "control," gains control. It is somehow astonishing that the experience here described follows a *second* interview. Miss Cam has most assuredly not achieved the state she describes, but she has had a momentary insight as to what the goal may be.

The theoretical terms in which we shall later try to describe this experience are that the organized concept of the self and the self-in-relationship, are congruent with the sensory and visceral experiences of the organism. It would seem that Miss Cam's vivid prose is one attempt to state what is meant by such a cold and technical phrase. When the self "owns" experience, assimilates it, but has no need to deny it or to distort it, then there is naturally a feeling of freedom and of unity connected with the experience. There is no longer any need for defensiveness, and Miss Cam makes this evident in her next statement.

> You know, it seems as if all the energy that went into holding the arbitrary pattern together was quite unnecessary — a waste. You think you have to make the pattern yourself; but there are so many pieces, and it's so hard to see where they fit. Sometimes you put them in the wrong place, and the more pieces mis-fitted, the more effort it takes to hold them in place, until at last you are so tired that even that awful confusion is better than holding on any longer. Then you discover that left to themselves the jumbled pieces fall quite naturally into their own places, and a living pattern emerges without any effort at all on your part. Your job is just to discover it, and in the course of that, you will find yourself and your own place. Looks as if the whole of life is pretty nondirective, doesn't it? You must even let your own experience tell you its own meaning: the minute *you* tell it what it means, you get the same antagonism you would get from a client, and you are at war with yourself.

"You must let your own experience tell you its own meaning" — when that sentence is deeply understood we will, in the writer's estimation, know much of what we wish to know in regard to psychotherapy. What is the usual alternative? It is to try to distort many items of experience so that they fit in with the concepts we have already formed. I love my child — so this surging feeling of annoyance and dislike is a momentary aberration, or comes because I am tired. I hate my parents — therefore this feeling of warmth and affection is something of which I dare not admit the existence. I feel no wicked sex desires — consequently this mounting feeling toward a forbidden sex object was never experienced. I fear nothing — so this paralyzing anxiety, this dread of a nameless, formless something, this pounding of my heart, is an accident, means nothing, will quickly be forgotten. I have done nothing wrong — hence the accusations of me that come to mind must have come from others, not from myself. It is in this way that we try to twist the sensations of vision, of hearing, of muscle tension, of heart beat, of gastric constriction to fit the partly true and partly false formulations which we have already built up in our consciousness. Could we but let experience tell us its own meaning — could we recognize hate as hate, love as love, fear as fear — and assimilate those basic meanings into our own structure of self, then there would be none of the inner strain which is so common to all of us. It is this that Miss Cam seems to be suggesting.

If we ask, as some do, whether the relinquishing of this artificial and tense control would not bring complete disorganization, perhaps Miss Cam's next paragraph gives a partial answer.

When I left off the first entry, I was in a wretched state. I longed to let go and just become one with my wretchedness. I quit writing only because I had an appointment and had to pull myself together for it. At first it was difficult — I was sluggish and exhausted. But gradually, as I focused on the things that had to be done, a sort of emergency organization developed, and the confusion receded. This was effective enough to carry me easily and cheerfully through two very busy days, though it was at the back of my mind that I must get back to this as soon as possible. And now that I look back on it, that must have been something more than an emergency organization. There's some new element in it, something comparatively stable, because it's held all this time and is still holding without any effort. But it *is* new to me, and subtly different. Whatever the meaning of this semi-mystical nonsense I have been writing, it does describe a real experience, it does represent a real release from some unknown tension. But it represents it in an exaggerated form, I think — more like a vision of perfection than a permanent psychological state. But still, there was that feeling of describing a fact, so perhaps it would be closer to the truth to say that a reorganization of the personality may for a moment be quite flawless; but since I am so habituated to directing my experience, and since every second adds new data of experience, that perfect patterning or organization will quite likely be distorted in short order. Already I feel, though only by a dim contrast, subtle disorder and dis-ease, a premonition of return to confusion and pain. Can it be that in therapy, and in life, the process is one of coming again and again through confusion to a momentary perfection of organization; those moments coming more and more frequently, and lasting longer each time, until finally that easy receptivity is firmly established — at least sufficiently so for ordinary purposes! Each time you face a terrifying, disorganizing fact, it leads, not to destruction, but to a new ease and enjoyment of life, and so confidence is built; and the periods of disorganization become fewer, because you accept experience as it comes, and as it is, feeling no need to warp it to an arbitrary pattern of defense; and since you perceive clearly, the data will be permitted to find its own natural place, and you will be slow to accumulate irritating, alien matter, and to shove things into places where they don't belong, throwing the smoothly functioning pattern out of alignment and creating strain and friction.

The astonishing point about these paragraphs is that they were written after the second interview, and yet appear to describe the very inner sense of what is achieved in therapy. The writer has known other clients, too, who seem to have experienced the essence of therapy in one, two, or three interviews, even though the total reorganization is far from achieved. If this insight is at all common, it helps to explain why the client keeps returning in spite of the suffering he is causing himself.

How this reorganization came about, I don't quite know. There was, however, a sequence of events which may contain a clue. First, the utter confusion and disorganization. Then the necessity of going about my business. When the latter arose, I simply left the confusion as it stood. It was too much for me, quite hopeless to think of doing anything to restore order. So I simply turned away from it, and focused my attention on what had to be done. And it does look as if when I turned my back on that confusion, it simply organized itself, and much better than I could have managed deliberately. In fact, it looks as if I ought to be grateful for the necessity that demanded my attention. Otherwise I should probably have tried to push and shove the mess into some sort of shape, and made a botched job of it, no doubt. Most people undergoing therapy have to attend to the routine of living when they leave the therapeutic session. And perhaps that shift in focus is a vital part of the therapeutic process. We do so love to think that all the important things go on under our watchful eyes!

One is somehow reminded here of Angyal's contention that the conscious self often "tends to take over the government of the total personality, a task for which it is not qualified." (9, p. 118) At least it would appear that the organization of personality is, like a good golf stroke, not always best achieved by focusing consciously on it.

> In the past couple of days, my mind has returned again and again to our interview, and odd thoughts and insights have flashed into consciousness. Sometimes they have been quite clear, and have remained so long enough to think about them and follow through on them quite a way. But then quite suddenly they are gone and I can't even remember what they were. They stay longest in the bath, and I wonder if that's because I am removed from paper and pencil, so that they are safe from being caught and objectified? I know they disappear like magic when I think of writing them down. There is one insight that crops up again and again, but I can't for the life of me think what it is — I just know it's something I always mean to bring up at our next interview.

Both in and out of the interview, many clients have experiences comparable to this one. The proof of the efficacy of our total physiological and psychological organization, if any is needed, lies in the efficiency with which we protect ourselves from having to recognize attitudes or experiences which have been denied to awareness because they are threatening to the self. One client, whose life had been built upon the basis of denying a great proportion of her actual experience, demonstrated amazingly the psychic struggle which may exist. She would recognize within herself a significant facet of experience which she had not faced. She would start to voice it in the interview. She would forget completely, in the middle of the sentence, what it was she was about to say. She would sit and wrestle with herself until the material again appeared in awareness, or she would, if necessary, start talking about some related topic until she could again capture and resolutely meet and assimilate the experience that she so obviously wanted to accept, and so obviously wished to deny.[1]

Miss Cam related still further her experience of the second interview.

> Having started at the end, and gone on to the middle, I have finally come to the beginning — to the interview itself.
>
> I had quite a bad case of stage fright when I came to the interview — part fear, part hope, part embarrassment. Fear that nothing would happen, that I would never find my way out into that lovely world of freedom glimpsed for a flashing moment at our previous interview; hope that I would find it, or rather, that you would find it for me, that you held the key which would unlock the prison door. The embarrassment is due to the fact that I would like you to think well of me, and here I am showing you all my foolishness and inadequacy without any opportunity to demonstrate my competence and control (Oh-oh!). ... After the initial nervousness wore off, I kept looking for a repetition of that experience of the first interview — the feeling that something had clicked, that there was a real unity of perception. ... So I hauled out all kinds of personal history hoping to touch off that response. And it's funny about that, isn't it? As far as I can recall, it was mostly quite historical and objective, very little of my emotional response to it. But I did have powerful emotional responses, I was perfectly well aware of them, and I remember them, but I always thought of them as accidents, just something to be coped with among other things — and when I speak of past events, the way I felt about them seems irrelevant in comparison with the events themselves. I don't think I like not having any feeling of those feelings. It's almost as if some portion of my own experience were inaccessible to me. It's robbery somehow, makes me feel less than myself, cut off.
>
> Well, anyway, as I brought out those things, nothing at all happened — at least not what I hoped for. Sure, you caught the sense of what I said, the mirror image was as true as before, but it had lost its novelty, it was flat and dead compared with the view through your windows. As time wore on, I grew awfully discouraged, disappointed, slightly desperate. I wanted a repetition of that experience so much, and when it didn't come, the emphasis seemed to shift from

---

[1] Compare also the experience of Miss Har, quoted earlier, page 79, in falling asleep rather than hear the recording of her own voice expressing affection for her father.

the longing for release to a longing for just contact with you, any kind of contact. I looked at you occasionally, hoping that what didn't happen with words might be accomplished in a look, and failing of that I just looked at you in hopes of reassurance. Maybe you would look at me as if you liked me, or sympathized with me, or *something*. But that didn't happen either, though you still looked perfectly calm and friendly, and open, and sort of easily ready. Ready for what? To accept anything I said? To look at all of it, without setting any limits, but without getting tied up in emotional knots? If you can look at all the horrid possibilities of life with such a clear gaze, maybe I can too? It's not as if my experience were so remote from you that it doesn't affect you at all. It can't be too remote, because you seem to understand it so well. And you're human too — it happened to me, it could happen to anyone, you included. We are all aware of that, I think, and that's why we refuse so often to accept other people's experience, because when we do, we are faced with the possibility that it might happen to us. But by your understanding and acceptance you seem to accept the possibility that it might happen to you too, and you still face the prospect with unruffled calm. That holds out interesting prospects for me, but right now I'm awfully disappointed and I want immediate reassurance. I would like to touch you, to put my head on your shoulder and cry. Maybe you would put your arms around me and pat my shoulder and say, "There, there, it's all right, don't cry"; and I'd feel soothed and relieved and could just stop struggling with all these things. It would feel so comfortable, but at the same time I have the feeling that it would spoil something. It would make life easy and palatable, but I would lose something — what, I do not know — so precious, so much my best self, that I would forever after be hounded by a subtle feeling of loss and failure. If I didn't know already, if I hadn't at least partially accepted the fact that you aren't going to provide one with that commodity, I might fight for it, or work towards securing that, rather than towards the solution of problems which seem hopeless. And if I weren't wise to your tricks (!!) the thing that would sustain me would be your unspoken assumption of something better. Or no — that's right in a way, but I've got it wrong end to. That experience of freedom which I long to repeat wasn't achieved by petting, either actual or symbolized, nor has past experience of the usual expressions of sympathy given rise to it. Sympathy may have been restful and enabled me to go back into action with renewed vigor, but it's never been of direct help in solving my problems. For a while it has created the illusion that the environment, other people, are going to change so that I won't have to do anything. But that illusion disappears rapidly when I go into action again. In the long run, sympathy just hasn't worked and I'm forced to the conclusion that I've got to do something so that action won't be so difficult.

When I come to you, there are two things in my mind: (1) I hope that I can act freely, but I haven't had much experience of it, so I'm not sure that I can. (2) Sympathy has given me some relief in the past, I'm sure of that, so if worst comes to worst I can fall back on it. I still have a lingering hope that you will do something so that action will become easy for me, and that inclines me further towards passivity. Since this problem isn't solving itself easily, my doubt of my own ability is very prominent, and if you were to give me sympathy at this point, you would confirm my worst suspicions. . . .

But you don't confirm my doubts; you support my hope. I'm not grateful for it, I don't experience it as a bell ringing, but in a dim way it enables me to carry on on my own. But I still cling to the interesting possibility of more personal contact with you — I'm not sure enough of myself yet, and that's my ace in the hole. I know enough about therapy to know how far I'll get with that one, but even so I can't quite put the idea out of my mind. It's nice to feel free to express myself, it's interesting to discover that there's more to express than I had suspected, and there's a dim satisfaction in plodding on in the face of obstacles; this continues to look like a nice safe atmosphere in which to do those things, but in case you ever weaken or withdraw that atmosphere, I'll hang on to the other possibility. If necessary, that can serve the double purpose of defending my weakness and destroying your seeming independence.

Two points in this excerpt call for comment. Here is an instance of those attitudes which in other therapies might well be the beginning of a positive transference. (See Chapter 5 for a more extended discussion of this point.) But here at least the client herself recognizes that the possibility of a transference *relationship* is a distinctly second-best goal. Other clients experience the relationship in a somewhat different fashion, as will be evident in the following chapter (Chapter 4, pages 167–171).

The other point is the way in which she seems to confirm to

some extent the theory of the therapist's role which was offered earlier. To see another person, the therapist, accepting experience rather than rejecting it, particularly when it seems that it could have happened to him, makes it easier to accept the experience oneself.

Written after the Third Interview

When I came to our interview today, I wasn't anything like as nervous as I was on the previous occasion. There was a certain submerged excitement, but not the stage fright. I'm not so scared or concerned about your opinion any more. It certainly hasn't been in evidence, and under those circumstances, solving the mystery of my own peculiar behavior emerges as a more and more interesting and challenging occupation. At the very least, I've got to fill in the time somehow, haven't I? If I can't occupy myself in dealing with your opinions about my problem, the only thing for it is to root around and see if I can discover what my problem is. Because by now I realize that I don't know what it is.

The feeling of "butterflies in the stomach" just prior to an interview is an interesting phenomenon which is common to many if not most clients. It is of interest that it should arise in an atmosphere which, above all else, is experienced as nonthreatening. The answer of course lies in the fact that although counselor and situation are nonthreatening, the experiences with which one is trying to deal are very threatening indeed.

An aspect of therapy which is not sufficiently clear to many beginners is that the "problems" which are brought to therapy are not resolved directly, and that a frequent experience in therapy is the gradual realization that the problem is what is not known in consciousness. In a very true sense the client never knows what the problem is until it is well on its way to resolution. Another way of stating this phenomenon is that the problem appears to be the same in all cases; it is the problem of assimilating denied experience into a reorganized self.

But Miss Cam is at no loss for material.

Anyway there is something I really want to talk about this time. Maybe that's what the anticipatory excitement was all about? This is something new; maybe I'll get somewhere now? I do have some feelings about this, but I'm a bit doubtful as to how it's going to be received. I'd like to do it with style, I'd like to fit the manner to the matter, but I don't quite know how to do it. I'm not sure what characteristics the manner ought to have. If that's the case, and I'm still curious about where this will lead me, the only course is just to plunge in any old how. This doesn't arouse any disapproval, and is quite a relief. It's good to say what I mean for once in a way. I try it again, with a little more confidence. This is still more pleasant, and I gradually come to the point where I can just savor the fun of expressing myself, let the chips fall where they may. I still can't let go altogether — after all, I mustn't look like the sort of person who goes to extremes (and why not?) and anyway there's still the chance that you will condemn me when you find out what I'm really like. But the emphasis is shifting from what you may think or say, to the exhilarating feeling of expressing my own feelings. You recede quite far in importance; and in fact, in some ways it would suit me very well if you just sat there and didn't say anything. When you do speak, it quite frequently seems like an interruption, and I just wait more or less impatiently for you to finish so that I can go on. I can't place those occasions, but I *do* know that they *weren't* the times when you caught my feeling of having to conform somehow to other people's opinions. That was arresting, not interrupting. Once you laughed with me quite spontaneously, and while that was very agreeable, I seemed to detect a faintly personal note in your laughter which made me uneasy. Not that I interpreted that personal note as mocking or derogatory — rather it was like the easy laughter which friends share at each other's foibles. But here I've been toying with the idea of a more personal relationship, yet when I see anything that remotely resembles it, I'm brought up short. Isn't that odd? It's one thing to imagine such a possibility, but if that possibility is realized, it's going to involve me in some sort of situation which is painful and threatening. Some sort of emotional complication that I'm terribly afraid I can't handle.

Here it is clear that client and therapist are both perceiving the situation in the same way, and the sense of working together in the relationship is definitely more evident. It is probably a rather frequent experience for at least some of the therapist's responses to be regarded as an interruption. Clinical experience would give two reasons for occasional responses, however. In the first place, the quick objection of the client to an inaccurate reflection of attitude is some evidence of the meaning that understanding has for him. He has come to accept it rather casually, but if it falters he is at once aware of this fact. The other reason for avoiding silence is that it can facilitate projection and transference. If the therapist has shown by his words, as well as by his attitudes and behavior, his understanding and acceptance of the painful attitudes being explored, then that fact is carried away in the memory and is difficult to distort. If the therapist has maintained silence, however, then it is easier for the client, in the period after the interview, to project meaning into that silence. The therapist may have been approving, disapproving, contemptuous, bored — the client's needs make it easy to project in this fashion, when there is little evidence to go on.

When I came to the interview, I also brought a resolution not to look for the exciting experience of the first interview. . . . At first it was a little difficult to keep from casting longing glances in that direction, but as I got more absorbed in expression of my immediate feelings, it faded into the background. And although the interview ended without any repetition of that prized experience there was none of the discouragement and despair and confusion that I felt before. Instead I felt as if I were getting somewhere — had something to get my teeth into now, and it was a great nuisance that the interview should end at that point.

Afterwards, I thought of all kinds of things I would like to talk about the next time I see you. I've forgotten most of them now, and it's quite exasperating, but I'm not terribly worried. I'm beginning to feel a bit like Mr. Micawber — "Something will turn up."

I didn't make any attempt to get at this writing immediately after the interview. I was surfeited with myself and my problems and didn't feel that I could even see them if I tried to. So I just obeyed that impulse and went for a ride and otherwise enjoyed myself until the following evening. After looking at myself for so long, it's very refreshing to look around outside. Of course I find me very interesting, but I get awfully fed up with such a limited subject after a while. Perhaps the interviews do regularly work that way to some extent? The exclusive double focus on self produces satiety, so that the environment looks pleasant and refreshing for a change. One commonly escapes from the environment into the self, but now the procedure is reversed, and the environment is seen in a new light as satisfying a positive need. There's a primitive sort of acceptance of the environment.

Written after the Fourth Interview

It appeared to the counselor that Miss Cam arrived at some fresh insights into certain aspects of her behavior in the fourth interview. He would not, however, have guessed the depth of excitement which accompanied this experience.

Golly, golly, golly, I feel wonderful! Warm and glowing and happy and relaxed. It's a real vascular relaxation. My skin has that characteristic smooth, soft feeling, all over my body, too. Of all things to happen! To drop all the elaborate analysis, think through the simplest problems in human relationships like a small child spelling out words, and come up with the obvious conclusions like Columbus discovering America. And darn it, I've known those things for years, but I had them all dressed up in such elaborate jargon I couldn't see what they meant. . . . Another thing I like about this kind of happiness is that it's so smooth and easy and steady. Not that sort of almost violent, wildly exhilarating, extravagant and ultimately exhausting happiness to which I'm accustomed. That rushed out like escaping steam and spent itself in reckless haste, as if anticipating the inevitable moment when the lid would be clamped down again.

[*The next entry is dated "Next morning"*]

It becomes increasingly difficult to write these reports — whatever is happening becomes steadier and subtler — has more continuity, so that separate events don't stand out with dramatic clarity, and it's very difficult to see what's going on inside me. Moreover, by now it's a far cry from scientific investigation, it's a highly personal experience and that has several results: my energies are pretty well tied up in whatever process is going on, and it takes a tremendous effort to observe and record the process: my instinct or impulse, or what have you, is all against analyzing and self-regarding — I'm much inclined to leave myself alone and just enjoy the results, or let them wash over me when I don't enjoy them: some way or other, the whole counseling process seems to militate against any sort of introspection or preoccupation with self. Of course all kinds of questions and insights and some speculations (though remarkably few) arise between interviews, but there's very little tendency to get lost, preoccupied, withdrawn in them; they draw your attention in much the same way as external events do; they're more apt to crop up while you're doing something, and they're very apt to vanish if you turn your full attention on them and try to capture them.

There is something fascinating about this paragraph. The client is, in the therapeutic hour, focusing all her attention upon self, to a degree that she has probably never known before. Yet this situation is experienced as a process which leads away from preoccupation with self. The question is worth raising as to whether therapy is not an experiencing *of* self, not an experience *about* self. Thus the intellectualizing, introspective interest in self drops away in favor of a more primary experience.

Her reference to the fact that insights crop up at odd moments, when attention is fastened elsewhere, is a very common experience of clients. A number of clients have mentioned that the way these significant self-understandings seem to come "out of the blue," when they are least expecting it, is for them additional evidence of the strength of the process which has been set in motion.

Miss Cam next refers to an experience of progress which is common to many clients, the realization that some painful constellations of experience have lost their threatening character. It is evident that it is not always necessary for such material to have been mentioned in the interview. It is the attitude of the self toward it which appears to have altered.

I'm still feeling relaxed and very pleased and interested in life. I noticed a most extraordinary thing last night! Tuesday evening, before our interview, I happened to think of an incident in my childhood, just about the only one I remember. It was a quarrel between my mother and father, in which mother was twisting the handle of a mirror I had been given for Christmas and which I dearly loved. I was afraid mother would break it, and she did. I think I was about five or six, but I can remember every detail of that scene (except the words) — looks, tones, location; and up to and including Tuesday evening I have never been able to think of that occasion without experiencing the awful childish agony and terror as if it were yesterday. Well, last night I thought of it again, and do you know, every bit of that emotion has vanished, and it's just something that happened to me once. There were other subsequent occasions — all associated with the relationship between my parents — which gave me the same pain to recall. So I took a look at those, and lo and behold, they are just ancient history too. Moreover, I can recall some of the normal events of childhood, for which I have heretofore had a complete amnesia. And that clears up a point which has been bothering me in our interviews. I'm supposed to be suffering from denied attitudes and experiences (labels, yet!) and I couldn't find any. There are very few feelings I have refused to admit to consciousness. Sure, I both loved and hated my parents but I always knew and accepted that; and so on all down the line. Furthermore, I have always, as far back as I can remember, acknowledged the right of other people to run their own lives in their own way, and I've even extended that right to myself. So I admitted the right of my parents to break up their home, even if it was rather hard on me. I understood that they had no intention of hurting me, and that when they did it was accidental; I just happened to be in the middle when they attacked each other, or engaged in defensive maneuvers, and I was sorry for them. But the one thing I didn't admit to awareness was that in spite of knowing that they didn't intend to injure or attack me, I *felt* as if they did. I felt sorry for myself, too, and though I admitted that to some extent, I had no patience with it, and denied a good bit of it.

The person who is psychologically sophisticated tends to feel that he has not rejected his own attitudes and feelings, because he has accepted those which are commonly denied. But if there is internal strain and a lack of integration, it seems always to be due to the fact that sensations and feelings which organically exist are prevented from entering into awareness.

Miss Cam then discusses another attitude which she has held which she feels was not basically her own. "It was *an* attitude, not wholly *my* attitude." She continues:

As a result . . . the things that would enable me to respect myself weren't mine either, and I devaluated myself quite thoroughly. I was worth precisely nothing, and I couldn't convince myself otherwise, in spite of all evidence to the contrary. Say something unpleasant about me, and I'd agree immediately and wholeheartedly; but try to tell me something nice about myself, and I'd spend hours trying to convince you, to explain in great detail how wrong you were. It wasn't false modesty either, I really felt desperately uncomfortable and dishonest in accepting appreciation.

This would appear to be a good example of the tenacity with which the individual holds to the concept of self around which he has organized experience. It is as difficult to accept experience which would expand this self as to accept material which would constrict it — both types of experience are inconsistent with the picture we maintain of self, and are rejected.

The client's description of the interview itself contains some elements that are new and significant.

I was eager to come to the interview this time: I had things I wanted to tackle, and it couldn't be too soon for me. It's maddening the way those things disappear when you come to say them — my mind is a complete blank, not even any irrelevancies to seize on. The trick in dealing with it seems to be not to force things — just resign yourself to the blank, and wait for it to yield up something.

I'm scarcely conscious of you any more; or perhaps it would be better to say I'm not *self*-conscious of you. I'm not scared of your opinion of me (or at least, the tiny remnants just amuse me) though in a sense I'm much more aware of the fact that you must have one, and I'd be quite genuinely interested in hearing it. And quite undisturbed by it, I think. I'm always interested in what you say, now, and perfectly willing to postpone something I was just going to say in order to listen — and *really* listen — to you. You said a lot of things this time that penetrated so far behind what I said that I had some difficulty in seeing that it was what I really meant. And yet you were right, and in spite of your outstripping me so far, I was interested and stimulated, rather than frightened into retreat. Oh golly, I was frightened once, wasn't I? Right near the beginning, when I said something about being rather better off than most people and you rephrased it so that I looked downright conceited. You scored a bull's eye with that one, as I subsequently realized very clearly indeed, but at the time I ran rapidly in the opposite direction. At one point, you said something about relationships that I couldn't see at all. Yet I had the feeling that it was somehow right, so I just agreed without understanding and went on. Judging from the results, the interview was a howling success, and all your remarks went in the direction I was trying to go. Yet I imagine that some people on reading a record of it, would say that it was a beautiful demonstration of the contention that counselors *do* introduce their own evaluations and do direct the client. But if I say to you, "Pardon me, but what direction am I traveling?" and you reply, "North," I can't see what ground there is for saying that you shoved me in that direction. It's rather difficult to prove, though. A lot of your responses got home with a small shock — particularly the recurrent theme of "labels" and "conformity," and a lot of that you dug out of quite unpromising looking material. But those shocks were pleasant — it was a relief to have the pretense stripped away. I want to get rid of it, but I can't quite manage it myself, so you are just carrying out my own, real wish. But there again, anyone looking at the situation from an external point of reference, would probably accuse you of selecting in terms of your own opinions and values.

It is of great interest to the therapist in this case that his responses in this interview seemed to the client to be of a somewhat different order, that they penetrated far behind what she said, that they went beyond her, even though in the direction she was going. The counselor's perception of the situation is quite different. In his opinion, his responses were of the same order as those in earlier interviews, simply reflecting the attitudes expressed. From his vantage point, the difference appeared to be that the client was now really exploring in territory that was unknown to herself, and that her tentative statements were of the type that other clients have described as "I hardly knew what I was saying." When these statements of attitudes which are borderline in consciousness are taken and briefly rephrased by the counselor, the perception of them in more definite form seems to the client to be a new experience. It takes her further in her own thinking, is seen as going deeper into her meaning than she has gone herself, is even seen as frightening, something to run away from. Which of these perceptions of the experience comes closer to the objective reality is of some interest, since it would shed further light upon the process of therapy. Obviously what is needed are cases in which we have *both* the recordings and the introspective reactions of the client (and perhaps the introspective reactions of the counselor) so that comparisons may be made.

> You are beginning to look much more like a person than one of the class "counselors." It seemed to me in this interview that you sounded much more like your whole self than just the part of you that's a counselor. Of course I know that's largely because I've allowed you to come in, but I wonder if you feel a little freer and more "yourself"? Now when you laugh, it does sound much more like the sort of laughter which friends share, and it doesn't startle me as it did that once in the previous interview. On the contrary, I like it very much. It makes me feel very brisk and competent and eager to get on with my investigations. After all, if we can share the same jokes, and I can catch up with your projections of my own meaning, maybe I'm just as competent as you seem to be, maybe I'm quite a capable person after all. As a matter of fact, when you start penetrating as far as this into my meaning, it is getting closer to the normal, friendly interchange, isn't it?

The counselor agrees that he was, and would seem, more of a whole self in this and following interviews. In initial sessions, when attitudes being expressed are relatively superficial, the process of understanding the client may not take a total effort on the part of the therapist, and the reflection of attitudes runs more risk of being a technique rather than an expression of the whole personality of the counselor. But as the interviews lead into dim and somewhat incoherent thinking, as the client is genuinely exploring the unknown, the counselor becomes wholly engaged in trying to keep step with this puzzled and puzzling search. His attention is completely focused upon the attempt to perceive from the client's frame of reference, and thus it is no longer a technique in operation, but the implementation of an absorbing personal purpose. In this attempt to struggle along with the client, to glimpse with him the half-understood causes of behavior, to wrestle with feelings which emerge into awareness and slip away again, it is entirely possible that the simple concept of "an accurate reflection of feeling" no longer fits the therapist's behavior. Rather than serving as a mirror, the therapist becomes a companion to the client as the latter searches through a tangled forest in the dead of night. The therapist's responses are more in the nature of calls through the darkness: "Am I with you?" "Is this where you are?" "Are we together?" "Is this the direction you are heading?" As might be expected, the answer to these questions is sometimes "No," sometimes "Yes." The counselor is sometimes with the client, at times he may be on ahead, at times he lags behind in his understanding. Such minor deviations from the course are relatively unimportant since it is so clear that the therapist is in general saying, "I'm trying to keep right with you as you make this perilous and frightening search." This point appears to be borne out by Miss Cam's continuing statement.

> You said some things that didn't seem to be quite what I meant. But far from being threatening, they were positively encouraging. It's nice to find that a misunderstanding isn't irrevocable — that I can correct it, and that you will understand and accept the correction. It isn't necessary to be perfectly clear and understood every time I speak. There's no need to be scared to death every time I open my mouth for fear I'll say something that's not perfectly accurate and entirely beyond reproach or criticism. No need to pick my words with such care that I end up by expressing myself much less clearly than if I had just said the first thing that came into my head.

Here is the answer to those who question, "Isn't client-centered therapy *really* directive, because the counselor selects the elements he will respond to, and thus subtly guides the client toward certain areas and certain goals?" As indicated here, if the attitude of the therapist is to follow the client's lead, the client not only perceives this, but is quick to correct the counselor when he gets off the track, and comfortable in doing so.

> Towards the end of the interview, when I was picking up speed at a great rate, I began to feel simply wonderful all over — warm and relaxed and happy. You were much more present to me than you've ever been before. In a way, indispensable to my happiness at that point — I felt much more myself in your company than I would have felt by myself. But it's not dependent in the derogatory sense — I suppose it's what has been called "freedom of dependence." If you can say a fish is dependent on water, then you can say my personality,

my self, is dependent on association, relationship with other selves for life and growth and freedom to move around. And golly! it *is* a repetition of that first exciting experience — it just looks different at first glance because it's steady and continuous, rather than fleeting and startling. Something I've grown into, rather than plunged into. But what is it? I can say it's a communion, a mutuality, even though limited, of experience; and I haven't explained a thing. There it is, and it's the most natural thing in the world; and like all the fundamentals of life, it simply refused to yield up its mystery. No more feeling of going into your house. I'm at home in my own house now, and you're a very welcome guest. I'm very pleased to show you all over the house, even though it's rather untidy in some rooms. But after all, I just moved in, and what can you expect? It'll look better when I've had time to settle down.

As Miss Cam here suggests, the communication of one's real self, one's real attitudes, to another, may well be the basis of deep social experience, of friendship, of interpersonal development, as well as of therapy. Certainly another facet of therapeutic growth is well described in her phrase, "I'm at home in my own house now, and you're a very welcome guest."

Some idea of the fluctuation in mood and attitude which occurs in the client as the self is being reorganized, is conveyed in the next excerpts from Miss Cam's material.

I'm beginning to feel sort of remote again; I can't find anything I want to do, and I can't seem to settle down to anything. What happened yesterday happened for good, and I'm not worried about it turning out to be just an accident or an illusion. But can it be that there's still something I haven't discovered? Just when I thought I hadn't a care in the world? It feels almost as if something were getting ready to pounce on me. Or maybe I'm just getting a cold?

"Can it be that there's still something I haven't discovered?" It is a most interesting fact, discussed more fully by Miss Cam at a later time, that once some denied attitudes are admitted to awareness, there is a strong tendency for others to appear also. Perhaps it may be put in this way. Experiences have been distorted or denied because it seems that to admit them would be too destructive to the self. In the safety of the therapeutic relationship it is discovered that, though the admission to awareness and the reorganization which is necessitated are both painful, yet the gain in internal comfort and release from tension clearly outweighs the pain. Hence there seems to arise a strong tendency to look at material still more deeply denied. The foregoing excerpt appears to be the first feeling of anxiety presaging further self-revelations to come.

> I phoned mother; as usual she told me what I ought to do, as usual I feel discouraged and hopeless, and I *am* getting a cold. Why did it have to happen now, just when I'm looking forward to the next interview and going on vacation? . . . Oh, dear, I thought that problem [of mother] was well in hand, and here it is again. Won't I ever be able to cut loose from mama's apron strings? What's the use — I've tried *so* hard, and I just can't keep it up for ever.

The Fifth Interview

The following day Miss Cam came in for the fifth interview. She had, from the first, planned to leave town for her vacation within a couple of days after this interview. During the contact she went very deeply into many areas of her experience, including her relationship with her mother. She felt it was impossible to change that relationship. She stated at one point, "I'm just a baby. But it's so disgusting to be a baby girl when you're as old as I am." At the conclusion of the interview, which to the counselor did not seem at all characteristic of the ending of therapy, she bade the counselor goodbye, stating that she would try to carry on by herself. The following material was written a few hours after the interview.

> What a desperately discouraging occasion! So flat and hopeless, like being up against an insensate blank wall — immovable, impenetrable, unscalable, a dead end to life and growth, a sterile, uncaring wall of mystery cutting me off from myself. It's difficult to convey the peculiar quality of hopelessness, of *deadness*, as if the whole universe were really and truly senseless — no point in trying to solve the mystery of yourself, no point in *anything*, because if life is meaningless, it can only end in frustration and death, and what looks like mystery is only the revelation of ultimate futility and negation. It

isn't that there is *something* you don't understand, but rather that there is *nothing* to be understood. *You* might just as well not be there for all the good you can do, for all the good this interview or anything else can do. With the best will in the world, you can't solve the insoluble. I'm just pointlessly discussing a pointless existence which you pointlessly reflect. It's non-sense; it's no-thing, it just is not. And just to make everything worse, you look disapproving. Now I know perfectly well that you don't actually look that way, and in a sense, I don't really care any more whether you approve or disapprove. But you see, last time your face suddenly looked different — as if it had been black with coal dust, and then was washed clean to reveal an altogether unsuspected freshness and individuality. I was delighted with that discovery, and I'm as blackly disappointed as a child to have lost that clear vision. And there's something awfully wrong and confusing about the way you look to me now. I keep wanting to rub my eyes, as if I were brushing away fog and cobwebs. And I'd like to wash your face. I can see it covered with black coal dust, and it's a little relief to imagine taking lots of soap and water and a nice rough cloth and washing it shiny clean. Somehow or other that soot on your face seems a great wrong done to you, and I feel that I want to right it and make amends. But it's too late, maybe it always was too late. It's all over now, and here I am in a hell of misery from which I'll never escape without help. And since there isn't any help, I'll never escape. Period. But I dug that pit for myself, and when I started to dig, I contracted to face the consequences. What if I dug a little deeper than I expected? What if I never do find the way out? Then I'll just have to learn to live here; and the condition of that learning is an unwavering faith that there is a way out even if I never do find it myself.

This complete despair makes an interesting contrast to the relaxed, steady happiness which followed the fourth interview (see page 107) and illustrates the tremendous swings of feeling which may, in some clients, accompany the strenuous process of alteration of self. Such utter desolation is only likely to occur, in the author's experience, in situations where a basic and extensive reorganization of self is taking place.

The vivid description of the changes in perception of the counselor relate very significantly to personality theory. In the fourth interview the counselor's face, which had appeared dark, is suddenly seen as clean, fresh, and individual. Note how closely this matches the client's perception of herself in the fourth interview (review pages 107–114 for evidence). But now that she sees herself as having reached an insoluble dead end of a pointless existence, the counselor's face blackens, and takes on a disapproving look. In a later chapter some of our research evidence corroborating this experience will be reviewed. It appears to be very significantly true that the client perceives others in much the same terms that he perceives himself, and alteration in self-perception brings about changes in the way others are perceived.

It's extraordinary to me how autonomous, how uncontrollable this process is once it gets started. Wednesday [fourth interview] I was in wonderful shape, on much better terms with myself and the world than I have ever been, and cheerfully equal to years and years of problems and stresses and strains. That left Friday to tidy up all the loose ends and the whole thing was just ideal. And then there was that utterly involuntary rising of an inexplicable misery. I dismissed it as silly and gave my attention to other things — I certainly did not encourage and magnify some slight feeling by giving it undue attention. No, once you have given your consent the process follows its own course and returns to tranquility only when the immediate job of reorganization is complete — and it seems as if one's conscious judgment of when the job is complete is not very reliable, nor does it have much power.

Here again is evidence, in an unexpected area, that "experience must tell you its own meaning." She has thought that therapy was complete, but she is not experiencing it as completed. The experiencing of the inevitability of the process which she describes is certainly a frequent phenomenon, though it is possible that sufficient fear or defensiveness can halt the process for some time. This whole matter deserves more careful attention.

The next painful paragraphs were written later that Friday evening, the day of the fifth interview.

I've been wandering around like a ghost all evening, trying to find the answer, telling myself it isn't so, I just *can't* be as miserable as all that, it doesn't make sense, and then I'm swamped with the realization that it is so, sense or not, I *am* that miserable. So then I collapse in a chair and try to look full at that pain, let it wash right over me, in hopes, I suppose, that it may work like a crisis — that if I take the full force of it at once, it may knock me into darkness and oblivion from which I will emerge a new person. Well, it didn't work that way, but as I was crouching there in a miserable huddle, not improved by the fact that my cold is rapidly getting worse, your face with its disapproving expression rose vividly in my mind's eye. Perhaps I was addressing my thoughts to you — really, I can't remember, but anyway I was carrying on a despairing struggle to solve the riddle of my relationship with my mother, when suddenly, two things happened — and for the life of me I can't remember which happened first, but whichever way it was, they trod right upon each other's heels. For one thing, it suddenly occurred to me that of course Mother, too, has a right to make her own choices and to be any kind of person she chooses to be. As simple as all that, the answer is. The other thing was that as I looked at your face, it was as if a hand reached out and quite literally peeled a heavy shadow away from it, revealing the fresh, individual face which I was so disappointed to lose this afternoon. It was the most extraordinarily vivid experience; it wouldn't be at all adequate to say it was *like* a hallucination — it *was* a hallucination. Not the face, that is, that was just a vivid memory, but the shadow of my own feelings, which I had projected on it. Isn't it astonishing how that insight corrects, not only present feelings, but reaches back to correct the distortions of stored memories? And that explains the haunting, but elusive sense I've had of something odd and baffling in your appearance, so that I've been torn between nervous reluctance to look at you, and a desire to stare and stare in hopes of penetrating and dispelling the enigma. Then there were two or three times when I would have sworn you laughed, but when I looked you were perfectly sober, and you quite obviously hadn't and couldn't have been even smiling. And on one of those occasions when I looked at you, something seemed to move rapidly from your face towards my left hand and disappear. Hallucinations, of all things! It may not surprise you, but it simply staggers me.

Anyway, the misery has melted away, and though I feel tired and rather afraid to believe it, and my cold is a perfect horror, life is more than bearable again, and in fact I'd almost like to go home at once, to practice the new approach.

Here, as so often, the significant insights occur between interviews, and while the insight appears simple enough, it is the fact that it comes to have emotional and operational *meaning*, which gives it its newness and vividness. When this same insight was verbalized in the next interview, it seemed significant, but the counselor would never have guessed the depth and sharpness of the experience which preceded it.

The "hallucinations" are very uncommon, although not unique in experience in client-centered therapy. In general, in clients undergoing drastic self-reorganization, behaviors which would be labeled as "psychotic" from a diagnostic frame of reference are encountered with some frequency. When one sees these behaviors from the internal frame of reference their functional meaning appears so clear that it becomes incomprehensible that they should be regarded as symptoms of a "disease." To regard all behavior as the meaningful attempt of the organism to adjust to itself and to its environment — this appears more fruitful for understanding personality processes than to try to categorize some behaviors as abnormal, or as constituting disease entities.

The next entry was written on Monday.

Well, here we go again — and it's another quite frightening example of the autonomous character of this business. Like being a devotee of Juggernaut — after the first voluntary act of throwing yourself in front of it, you get run over whether you like it or not and you get run over all the way, you can't say, "Stop it, that's enough, I'm only willing to be partially run over." It's all or nothing. And somehow, the only answer that has any dignity at all is to give your full consent to what you cannot avoid anyway.

Saturday morning I wanted to phone and tell you that all was well, because I was sure you'd be pleased to know that the job was more or less satisfactorily completed. But although the spirit was so cheerful and willing, the flesh was awfully sick with cold, and I just couldn't drag myself out of bed to go to the phone. . . .

Towards evening I found that incomprehensible pain and fear starting to wash over me again. By ten o'clock the thing had reached a new high, and this time it was dominated by a wild, irrational fear — a fear so terrible that by a strange mercy, I couldn't absorb the full impact of it. (Heretofore I think that fear has been subordinate to pain.) For a long time, I cast frantically about for the cause of that fear, and just when I thought I couldn't endure it another minute, it suddenly burst upon me — why, I'm afraid of death! That revelation was utterly surprising to me! I have always thought of death as somehow the crown of life, a supremely interesting, one-of-a-kind experience, for which you should prepare well beforehand because if you muff it, you will never have another chance, and I've always felt that you should be in good health to die. Somehow the element of shock seemed to numb the fear long enough to let me think a moment. And of course my first thought was that in such straits, God is the only refuge. But when I turned to Him, I faced the ultimate horror, utter reversal and betrayal — He who claimed to be Love itself, was the death-dealer, the cruel avenger, the destroyer, and I hated and feared Him: in my bitterest need, the Friend to whom I turned revealed Himself as the Enemy. Unless you know, I can't tell you what it's like to come to the end of everything, and find it infinitely more terrible than anything you ever suspected or dreamed.

Well, I wrestled with this awful thing, but you can't face such a horror indefinitely — the mind recoils, and in that recoil there's a certain relief. In one of these periods, my thought turned from the God whom I couldn't change to the fear of death, for which I just might be able to find some other relief. And there was the thought, ready to hand — why, death is only fearful in anticipation! It's something that *is not* as long as there is life, and life is always being alive in the present moment, a sort of eternal now. Life and death are so completely opposite that you cannot possibly have any knowledge or experience of death until you *are* dead. Even when you are approaching death, and up to the very second of death, you are busy *living*. You can't possibly be afraid of death, really, you can only be afraid of life. It was as simple as that, perhaps even simpler, and all the fear melted away. With that gone, I was free to face the cruelly painful problem of this God who seemed to have betrayed me. It took a lot of tries to get my head above the waves of pain that washed over me at the thought, but finally I struggled through to the realization that it was the choice again, in a different guise: is God Love or is He Hate? I can't prove either proposition, and I must believe one or the other on faith. He can't be a little of each, either, because they're mutually exclusive. I feel Him to be cruel and hateful now, but at other times I have felt Him to be Love. But His nature is not determined by the way I feel about Him, and I must make my choice on some other basis. I don't know what that basis is — I only know the choice is perfectly clear — He is Love. But if that is so, why should I fear and hate Him? I suppose it must be because at some forgotten time, some close love relationship has exposed me to pain and apparent betrayal, so that ever since I have feared and distrusted love. Well, then, there's nothing wrong with God, there's only something wrong with me. You wouldn't think it would be such a comfort to find there's something wrong with yourself, would you? But if that's so, I can do something about it: it may be difficult, it may be painful, maybe even, I'll never succeed, but at least I can try, and there is a chance of success.

Having got that far, the crisis was somehow over. True, it's a rather precarious feeling, more like a respite than a solution: there is still the doubtful business of "doing something about myself," but at the time it was such a relief to get it in those terms that I couldn't worry about it. So I slept peacefully, and yesterday they tucked me up in rugs and cushions and drove me out in the country to bake the cold out in the sun. I felt quite cheerful and relaxed into the role of pampered invalid.

This deep conflict and confusion, this facing of fearful attitudes within oneself, calls for little further comment, except perhaps to point out again that often the most crucial struggles occur outside of the interview itself.

It wasn't till I got home in the evening that I came up against the terrifying thought that maybe I wouldn't be able to solve the riddle of myself no matter how hard I tried, maybe I would have to go around the rest of my life with some unknown, inimical "thing" locked up within me, never knowing when it would spring, always and forever terrified of myself. So of course I thought of you with longing — and I also thought that it would be an imposition, and that you must want some holidays and so forth. . . . I can safely leave you to imagine how little the added conflict did for my morale! But although it was pretty painful, somehow or other I could control my feelings a little this time. Finally, I came to the shaky conclusion that I could at least ask for your help without imposing on you. So I decided that I would phone you in the morning — well, probably — and finally drifted off to sleep. I woke up fairly cheerful. . . . I thought about what I would say to you and canvassed all sorts of politely apologetic phrases, but discarded them one by one. . . . I finally found something that was close as I could come to leaving you free to reply in any way you chose. . . . When I called you were so nice about it, and it was all so easy that I felt quite buoyant and hopeful. But my friend was packing to leave this afternoon, and as time wore on, I got more and more frightened at the thought of her going.

Here, as with any client, the responsibility for reopening the therapeutic contacts is left with the client. There may be circumstances in which some modification of this point of view is desirable, but for the most part the keeping of the locus of responsibility in the client is far more therapeutic. Consider, for example, how terrifying it would have been to this client, if at the end of the fifth interview the therapist had suggested she return. It could only have meant that the therapist was concerned and emotionally involved in her struggle for health, and that he evaluated her progress negatively. It would have precipitated, in all likelihood, a much more serious conflict. Here she has herself decided to postpone her vacation in order to continue the difficult task she has set herself.

Note, also, in the early portion of this quotation, how closely matched the struggle seems to be. In this client, as in most others, the hypothesis that one has the capacity to deal with one's own conflicts is not an easy or optimistic hypothesis. The forces which make for growth tend to overbalance the regressive and self-destructive forces, but not by some large margin. Instead, the outcome, both to the client and to the therapist, appears in many, many cases, to hang in the most delicate balance.

Tuesday A.M. I wandered around all last evening suffering all the tortures of the damned. I did a number of little chores, but none of them gave me any relief — it's almost easier just to give in completely, and let the torment have its way with you. Finally I went to bed, where it came over me in waves of almost indescribably physical sensations. You can almost see and feel a wave of blackness washing over your brain, and there's a queer sort of ringing in your ears. It seemed to me that if only I could give in to it, if only the blackness would close over me and I could sink down and down into unconsciousness, then I would come out of it perfectly clean and healed and entirely new. But though I tried over and over again, just at the last moment, when I'd think I was going to make it, I'd be swept back to full consciousness. . . . I finally fell asleep. And this morning I woke up just as cheerful as can be — I might even be somewhat euphoric if I'd let myself. I've tried to feel miserable (!!!) and I just can't. I even feel rather provoked at being cheerful, entertaining the quaint conviction that I'm much more apt to get somewhere in our interview this afternoon if I'm good and miserable. Golly, what fools we mortals be!

Written after the Sixth Interview

Tuesday afternoon Miss Cam came in for the sixth interview. The material of the interview was much concerned with early and later sexual conflicts. It did not seem to the counselor to have as much concern with current emotionalized attitudes as some of the other interviews, but by some therapeutic orientations the material would be judged as very deep.

> Wednesday A.M. There's nothing to say about yesterday's interview — it was flat, lifeless, almost as if I were doing it because I said I would, but we both understood it was a formality — the business of dying like a gentleman. Hollow and neutral, and you looked neutral too — like someone politely playing out a role that's been assigned to him. . . . I recaptured the pain I so ridiculously sought — not because I sought it, but because the interview was such a dead end. Last night was just a repetition of Monday, including putting myself through various little activities, and the weird sensations when I went to bed. It seems as if there's nothing but pain in the whole universe — so cruel, so utterly incomprehensible, so fruitless. I keep saying why — why, why, why should it happen to a relatively innocent person? I can't believe I ever did anything to *deserve* this — and somehow I am convinced that it has nothing to do with deserts, it has to do with something else I don't understand. There is no growth without some pain, but it's impossible to believe — no, not believe — to feel that anything creative can come out of anything that seems so wantonly destructive. . . . I long to go on my vacation. I reach towards it with all the desperate longing of a drowning man towards the distant shore. I don't know how I can bear to wait, and yet at the same time, I know it would be no good to me now. There

is no rest for me anywhere as long as I carry the torment within myself.

Some clients are able to achieve reorganization with a minimum of suffering. With others, as in this case, the "torment within" becomes almost unbearable as deep inconsistencies in experience are explored. Yet it is a definite aspect of progress to recognize the conflict as being entirely within, and to know that no vacation, no rest, can be a rest from oneself.

The Seventh and Eighth Interviews

The seventh interview was held on Wednesday, and the eighth on Thursday morning. A portion of the seventh interview must be given from the therapist's notes in order to make some of the comments understandable. Deep confusion and uncertainty were evident in the interview, but the client felt she was coming to some final decision which seemed like life or death — at least psychological life or death. She told how during the past year tensions and conflicts have steadily mounted, with many deep reactions on her own part.

> I have felt it inside as though it were a little animal coming out of a cave — just a little defenseless animal, who has been beaten unmercifully, defeated, horribly lacerated and bleeding. He just seems completely and utterly helpless. I have felt as though this were sort of separate, so that I could stand off and look at it, but that it was also something inside of me. At times the poor animal would go back in, but there was always the chance that he would come out again. (*Pause*.) Now I don't feel any longer as though I see him. I feel as though I *am* that little animal, whipped and helpless and terribly wounded.

Following the seventh interview which contained this material, and the eighth interview on Thursday morning, the following was written.

> Thursday A.M. Yesterday's interview was the same as the one before it, lifeless and futile. The only difference was that it was a bit more actively despairing because failure seemed still closer — and it began, as well as ended, in despair. Wednesday was a repetition

of Tuesday and Monday, except that the longing for the unattainable peace that my vacation represents grew more acute. Everything grew more acute — more and more of the same thing.

She tells how Wednesday evening she went to confession, which she felt gave her some relief. After this:

But as I was walking down the street, it popped up a tentative head — "Who beat up on you? Who's responsible for the horrible condition of the little tortured animal? Could it be you?" There was no use in — and anyway I was too tired to pin that idea down firmly. It insisted upon being treated lightly and delicately. So I went quietly to bed — not happy, but not in such distress of mind; exhausted, but more at peace, with a tentative hope, but not demanding. Not wholly resigned, but somehow more able to face the prospect of things not turning out just as I want them. I woke up quite bright and cheerful — as you saw this morning. Our interview this morning [eighth interview] was nice. Hopeful, but with a good down-to-earth practical feel about it. Everything came alive and positive again — you and me and things in general. I knew I hadn't found the whole solution, but I felt as if I had enough material to carry on with, and that it was time to *do* something now, not just think about it. But do you know, in spite of the fact that you have changed aspect in these last interviews, it hasn't had the hallucinatory quality I noticed before. I can't describe it — I just know it's different from what it was before that shadow was peeled from your face.

I felt a bit awkward about terminating the interviews — partly because you might think I was cutting and running when the going got tough, but mostly because I can't be entirely sure that that *isn't* what I'm doing. But I don't think that's so, really. I think this just *is* the time to stop. . . . Here in Chicago where I'm away from my own environment, and have no responsibilities and no friends, it is pretty largely "imaginary" practice. Well, I can certainly testify to the wisdom of keeping on with your work and normal contacts during psychotherapy!

In the beginning of the eighth and final interview she expands the insight suggested at the outset of this quotation, realizing that she has been self-punishing, that she is the one who has "tortured the little animal," that she is the one who has been making harsh judgments about herself, and that this need not necessarily be.

The interview closed on the note that "I can see that things aren't hopeless, that it is in me, and that I can do something about it. I don't mean it's going to be easy. But I think I ought to be gentle with myself, not punishing myself as I have." This tentative and cautiously positive note is very characteristic of the conclusion of therapy.

Some Weeks Later

The next entry was written some weeks later, while on vacation.

On Vacation. My arrival was a disappointment — though a disappointment for which I was not unprepared. I'm too emotionally exhausted to experience pleasure in anything. The days roll by, and I keep on feeling like a convalescent — neither sick nor well, neither dead nor alive. And I'm just fantastically irritable. The least little thing is apt to annoy me out of all reason, and it just seems to be a completely irrational sensitivity. Well, no, perhaps there is some pattern to it — I get particularly violent when someone interrupts what I'm doing, or suggests that we go North when I had thought we might go South, or when someone else gets in a stew and I am required to accommodate myself to them. And my irritation seems to be in proportion to the amount of energy required to make the adjustment. So perhaps it's partly just fatigue. But a lot of it — most of it, maybe — is that I'm so tired I really do need a rest; and I've interpreted that to mean that the world owes me a rest, and I'm just as mad as a hornet when they don't give it to me. Awfully easy to forget the hard-won lesson that it was I who chose to feel beaten up by the world! There's a funny thing here — that anger seems to rise quite involuntarily, but at the same time, I have a perfectly clear awareness of complete freedom to choose whether I will or will not be angry. It's not just a question of being able to suppress the appearance or actions of anger, but of having a choice of being angry and being positively friendly. As objective as having a stone in your hand and deciding whether you'll throw it or lay it down on the ground. Not like my occasional outbursts in the past when it has seemed completely, frighteningly involuntary, as if I were possessed. And I am not happy to have to admit that I'm choosing to be angry a lot of the time. I think maybe I expected my new insights to do things *for* me, and I'm rather resentful to find that I have to do them myself. Perhaps I'm getting better without noticing — I always expect things to burst upon me with the dramatic suddenness of a comet, and never notice slow growth — but I don't really know whether I'm getting better or worse, and it worries me terribly. What if I went through all that torture for nothing? I know that's an irresponsible sort of notion, but I can't seem to find any sort of criterion for deciding about myself, and that makes me feel awfully exposed and defenseless. But perhaps I'm just not used to the way it feels when you refrain from passing judgment on yourself; maybe I do lots of quite constructive things and don't know it because I don't spot the effortless feel of letting things happen spontaneously.

In the discussion of her feelings about anger there appears to be an astonishingly clear description of what it feels like, from an internal frame of reference, to let experience come freely into awareness. Where heretofore anger was denied until it broke forth in an uncontrolled burst which was not a part of self, now anger rises at once into consciousness. But where experience is freely symbolized in awareness, it is also far more subject to control. Expression of anger becomes a choice, feelings of anger can be considered along with feelings of friendliness, and either may be consciously chosen for expression. This is not necessarily more pleasant; it is simply that there is less of experience which is denied or distorted, and hence a greatly reduced bill to pay in the form of defensive tension. Whether the reader accepts this type of explanation or not, the quotation seems to convey the living "feel" of what is involved in being more freely one's real self.

The fact that it is only the pattern of reorganization which is laid down in therapy, and that there is much to be done to implement that pattern, is borne out by both clinical and research experience. When the therapeutic experience is deeply assimilated, change in personality and behavior continues for a long period after the conclusion of the interviews themselves.

After mentioning her feeling of "suspended animation" while on vacation, with none of the usual demands to meet, Miss Cam continues:

There is only one hopeful thing I've discovered, and it isn't giving me any consolation right now — one of the principal reasons I'm not getting much joy out of this vacation home is that it used to be the only place in the world where I felt at home and at ease and among friends; but now I'm well on the way to being at home everywhere and with everyone. and that takes the special, out-of-this-world glow from this spot.

It is worth observing that reorganization of the self means a new perception of everything, including experiences formerly deemed satisfying. An alteration in the structure of the self means that the individual is living, quite literally, in a new world, made new by the change in perceptions. Small wonder, then, that the going is a bit rough for a time at least.

Three Months Later

Our glimpses into the inner world of Miss Cam's experience must close with a note written some three months after therapy in response to an inquiry from the counselor. She discusses some of her present interests, and continues:

In the meantime, since you are good enough to ask, the client is progressing favorably — I think — but I'm so thoroughly tired of looking at myself, and so weary of emotional upheavals that I can't give a very accurate report. I still feel rather raw emotionally and am subject to (increasingly infrequent?) attacks of "misery"; but I'm beginning to suspect that they are in part an aftermath of the storm, and in part reactions from doing, or anticipating doing, things which I have always muffed or avoided before. And partly discouragement because I didn't see any signs of improvement. I guess I expected change to be registered in a series of "Aha's!" — and so I didn't notice until lately that there are changes which must have sprung quite spontaneously from a change in attitude. I get along quite happily with Mother, and manage to do some sort of justice to both of us without feeling abused or dominated. I file things with scarcely a whimper [a task at which she had formerly rebelled], and I think I'm getting steadily better at doing the thing I'm doing now, without worrying about what I have to do two hours or two days from now. I'm quieter, more relaxed, and with no inclination to show off in groups — I nearly missed that one. I was so amused when I suddenly realized how different I was being. And I'm much more observant of and interested in other people. Golly, that's a surprising total, isn't it — and I guess there are other things too, but maybe that'll give you a rough idea. I haven't indulged in much self-evaluation (thank God!) — really, I'm not so much interested in seeking myself as I am in losing myself. It's such a relief to get rid of that load.

Several points characteristic of most clients emerge here. The first is that behavioral changes take place so spontaneously, grow so naturally out of the present organization of attitudes, that they are not noticed until some outside circumstance focuses attention on them. Another is the raw, unsteady, "newborn" feeling which accompanies personality change. A final characteristic is the very interesting fact that client-centered therapy, with the intense focusing upon self which it involves, has as its end result, not more self-consciousness, but less. One might say that there is less self-consciousness and more self. Another way of putting it is that the self functions smoothly in experience, rather than being an object of introspection. Or as one client states in a follow-up interview one year after the conclusion of therapy: "I'm not self-conscious like I used to be. . . . I don't concentrate on being myself. I just *am*."

The presentation of such a wealth of material from this one client is not done with the implication that hers is a typical experience. No doubt it is atypical in as many ways as it is typical. The point is that all therapy is a completely unique experience for the client, and the more completely we sense this fact, the more it may be possible for us to facilitate this unique experience in others. Certainly it appears to be true that our knowledge of psychotherapy will be more firmly based when it is possible to understand thoroughly, and with sensitive perception, the private worlds of many clients undergoing therapy, as we have been privileged to perceive the experience with this one client.

SUGGESTED READINGS

There has been very little effort to explore systematically the way in which therapy is experienced by the client. The article by Lipkin (117), from which several quotations have been drawn, is one such attempt. A somewhat less systematic account is a recent article by Axline (16) which gives a vivid description of play therapy as it is experienced by the young participants, both at the time and several years later. In regard to psychoanalysis, an article by Wood (227) gives the reactions of one psychologist to his analysis. Others — for example, Boring (35), Landis (107), and Shakow (182) — give somewhat less intimate accounts of their experiences in analysis in a single issue of the *Journal of Abnormal and Social Psychology*. All of these suffer from having been written long after therapy was concluded. A chapter by Kilpatrick in Horney's book (89) is entitled "What Do You Do in Analysis," and attempts to describe the client's reactions. It is, however, an account by a therapist, not a first-hand account. Some further light on the client's experience may be gained by reading the verbatim cases in Snyder's *Casebook of Nondirective Counseling* (199), paying particular attention to those portions where the client is describing his or her experiencing of the process, rather than the problems or conflicts which are usually in focus. The reader who follows any of these suggested references will discover, among other things, how little this whole field has been explored.

Chapter 4 · The Process of Therapy

In every therapeutic orientation people are helped. They feel more comfortable within themselves. Their behavior changes, often in the direction of a better adjustment. Their personalities seem different, both to themselves and to others who know them. But what *really happens* in successful therapy? What are the psychological processes by which change comes about? In all the rich nuances of changing thoughts and feelings, as illustrated in the last chapter, are there any discernible generalities, any objective and scientifically accurate ways in which the process can be described for all clients? It is to a discussion of these questions in their particular relationship to client-centered therapy that this chapter is devoted.

Let it be said at the very outset that in the present state of our knowledge we do not really *know* what is the essential process of therapy. We have become more and more deeply impressed with the many ramifications of the process, and the way in which it takes on different meanings depending upon the point of view of the observer, but we recognize that its definitive description is still a task for the future. Rather than dogmatically attempting to make perfectly clear that which is not perfectly clear, it seems best to present the many hypotheses which are currently held in regard to the process of client-centered therapy, and the research evidence which supports some of them. Perhaps the very variety of the hypotheses will serve to broaden professional thinking and will stimulate the discovery of more accurate and inclusive hypotheses.

In a general way, therapy is a learning process. Mowrer (136, 138) has effectively helped to point this out, as have others (190, 191, 184, 185). The client learns new aspects of himself, new ways of relating to others, new ways of behaving. But what, precisely, is learned, and why? This is what we would like to know. It is not enough to take learning theory as it has been developed from studies of rats, or from experiments with nonsense syllables, and impose it upon the process of therapy. The rich experience of therapy has much to contribute to our knowledge of what is significant learning, as well as having much to gain from integrating previous knowledge of learning into the known facts about therapy. Hence, in the present state of the psychological sciences we are left with many more questions than answers as to the process and content of the learning which takes place in psychotherapy.

In such a situation it seems best to look, as closely as we can, at the facts as we have them, whether they are clinical observations or verified research findings. Consequently, in the material which follows there are grouped, under convenient general headings, some of the changes which are known to be, or hypothesized to be, characteristic parts of this therapeutic learning process, characteristic aspects of what is thought of as the "movement" of the client in therapy. The order of presentation is not significant, except that some of the aspects for which we have the most research evidence have been placed first. Following these descriptive formulations, which in some instances overlap and in some instances appear to contradict each other, an inclusive theory of the process of therapy will be presented which, it is hoped, is sufficient to contain the evidence thus far available.

CHARACTERISTIC CHANGE OR MOVEMENT IN THERAPY

In Type of Material Presented

One of the first aspects of the therapeutic process to be studied by research methods was the movement in the type of verbal content presented by the client. It was observed that though the individual first tended to talk about his problems and his symptoms for a majority of the time, this type of talk tended to be replaced, as therapy progressed, by insightful statements showing some understanding of relationships between his past and present behavior and between current behaviors. Still later there seemed to be an increase in the discussion by the client of the new actions which were in accord with his new understanding of the situation. This process of exploration of feelings and attitudes related to the problem areas, followed by increased insight and self-understanding, followed by discussion of reoriented behavior in terms of the new insights, was the sequence most emphasized by the writer in describing client-centered therapy in his earlier book (166).

There is now considerable objective evidence to back up this description. Snyder, in a study completed in 1943 (196, 197), and Seeman, six years later (180), found very similar results. Statements falling within the category of discussion of problem declined, in the latter study, from 52 per cent of the total client conversation during the first fifth of counseling, to 29 per cent during the final fifth. Statements of insights and changed perceptions experienced as a result of counseling increased from 4 per cent in the first fifth to 19 per cent in the concluding quintile. The discussion of plans, which usually involved a reorientation of behavior, was almost nonexistent during the first three-fifths of counseling, hovering between 1 and 2 per cent, but rose to nearly 5 per cent during the last quintile. A more complete factual picture of Seeman's findings is given in the accompanying Table I.

Snyder's study was based on an analysis of the several thousand client statements in six cases, and Seeman's upon ten cases, all electrically recorded. The reliability of categorization by different judges was high, the Seeman investigation showing 87 per cent concordance in judgment on the content categories we have been discussing, and 76 per cent concordance in categorizing the attitudes mentioned below. Hence the trends outlined appear to be rather reliable descriptions of at least one aspect of the therapeutic process. That these trends are related to therapeutic success is suggested by the fact that an index of these trends correlated .56 with counselor ratings of outcomes.

Still another aspect which has been studied is the type of attitude expressed. It was observed that while the client, at the out-

Table I · Type of Client Material Presented

(Percentage of Various Categories by Quintiles of Counseling Process) *

CONTENT CATEGORIES					
Quintile	Disc. of Problem	Insight	Disc. of Plans	Simple Acceptance	All Other Categories
1	51.8%	4.2%	1.2%	34.1%	8.7%
2	44.7%	6.2%	2.2%	40.2%	6.7%
3	44.5%	8.8%	1.7%	37.0%	8.0%
4	35.4%	17.0%	4.6%	36.7%	6.3%
5	28.6%	19.3%	4.7%	31.4%	16.0%

ATTITUDES				
Quintile	Total Positive	Total Negative	Total Ambiv.	Present Tense Only Positive / Negative
1	32.1%	62.1%	5.8%	30.6% / 69.4%
2	40.9%	52.7%	6.4%	42.3% / 57.7%
3	35.2%	55.3%	9.5%	40.1% / 59.9%
4	43.7%	48.1%	8.2%	56.3% / 43.7%
5	46.6%	45.3%	8.1%	62.2% / 37.8%

* Adapted from Seeman (180, pp. 161, 164, 165).

set of therapy, seemed to voice mostly negative feelings, there appeared to be a change in a positive direction. This seemed to be true even though the attitudes might be concerned with himself, with others, or even with his physical environment. Both Snyder and Seeman studied this question and the research results confirmed the clinical impression, adding one significant new facet related to the tense (present or past) of the expression. In general it may be said that the evidence (See Table I for details) shows that, while negative attitudes predominate in the early phases of therapy, the balance shifts as the process continues and positive attitudes come to slightly exceed the negative. But when the study is limited to the current feelings of the client — those expressed in the present tense — the trend is found to be much more marked. A crude approximation to the findings would be to say that current feelings are one-third positive and two-thirds negative during the first fifth of therapy; in the final quintile the situation is reversed, with almost two-thirds of the feelings being positive, and slightly over one-third negative.

There are other ways of describing the changes which take place in the verbal material which the client expresses during the course of therapy. Several may be mentioned which have not yet been put to an objective test.

Clinically it seems clear that there is movement from *symptoms to self*. The client's exploration revolves first around the various aspects of the problem, but gradually the concern is more and more with self. What kind of person am I? What are my real feelings? What is my real self? An increasing amount of the conversation centers around these topics. Not only is there movement from symptoms to self, but from *environment to self* and from *others to self*. That is, the client verbally manipulates his situation, devoting a considerable portion of his time to a consideration of the nonself elements as well as those within himself. But gradually he explores himself almost to the exclusion of the nonself. This seems to be due in part to the fact that the therapist's focus is upon his feelings, perceptions, evaluations — in other words upon himself. It is also due to the fact that he senses that the self elements are the aspects of the situation which potentially are most certainly within his control. It is also because he senses that if he were unified and clear within himself as to his purposes and goals, he could deal with some success with the external aspects of his problem.

Another trend in the content of the conversation is from material which has always been available in awareness, to material which until therapy has not been available to conscious consideration. Of this we shall have more to say presently.

Still another change in material is from *past to present*. It may not be correct to say that there is a steady progression in this respect, since early interviews are often concerned with present problems. In the consideration of any particular conflict or relationship, especially if it is threatening or painful, the client tends to begin with some past aspect and only gradually faces the more crucial and often unpleasant issue as it exists in the present. Thus therapy ends with the person dealing with himself — his attitudes, emotions, values, goals — as they currently exist. He has learned that it is safe to leave the less dangerous consideration of his symptoms, of others, of the environment, and of the past, and to focus upon the discovery of "me, here and now."

Change in Perception of and Attitude Toward Self

The two previous chapters have already indicated that much of what occurs in the process of therapy seems best explained in reference to the construct of the self. The self has for many years been an unpopular concept in psychology, and those doing therapeutic work from a client-centered orientation certainly had no initial leanings toward using the self as an explanatory construct. Yet so much of the verbal interchange of therapy had to do with the self that attention was forcibly turned in this direction. The client felt he was not being his real self, often felt he did not know what his real self was, and felt satisfaction when he had become more truly himself. Clinically these trends could not be overlooked.

The clinical observations have now been buttressed and amplified with a considerable number of research studies. Raimy (153, 154) was the first to work in this area, supplying an extensive theoretical framework of thinking about the self-concept, which unfortunately has never been published, and also carrying through the first objective study of attitudes toward the self. He has been followed by a number of others.

In all of this research, the central construct is the concept of self, or the self as a perceived object in the phenomenal field. If a definition seems useful, it might be said that clinical experience and research evidence would suggest a definition along these lines. The self-concept, or self-structure, may be thought of as an organized configuration of perceptions of the self which are admissible to awareness. It is composed of such elements as the perceptions of one's characteristics and abilities; the percepts and concepts of the self in relation to others and to the environment; the value qualities which are perceived as associated with experiences and objects; and goals and ideals which are perceived as having positive or negative valence. This definition has grown out of examination of the evidence and may change as our exploration of the phenomena of therapy continues.

With this definition in mind, let us return to our basic question: What changes characteristically occur in the self during the course of a series of therapeutic interviews? The several investigations mentioned above supply at least the beginning of an answer. We find that the attitudes toward the self as a perceived object change materially. In cases where there is any indication that change took place, or that therapy was "successful" (whether the criterion is client judgment, counselor judgment, or rating by another clinician), the following statements would be supported by the research evidence.

> There is a trend toward an increasing number and proportion of positively toned self-references and self-regarding attitudes as therapy progresses. (154, 180, 197, 203, 204)
>
> There is a trend toward a decreasing number and proportion of self-references and self-regarding attitudes which are negative in emotional tone. (154, 180, 197, 203, 204)
>
> Attitudes of ambivalence toward the self, in which positive and negative feelings are expressed together, tend to increase slightly until somewhat beyond the midpoint of therapy, and then to decrease slightly. At no period are ambivalent attitudes a frequent expression. (2, 154, 180)
>
> At the conclusion of therapy there are more positively toned self-references than negative. (2, 154, 180, 197, 203, 204)
>
> These trends are not found, or are found in lesser degree, in cases regarded as unsuccessful. (154, 195)
>
> In the initial phases of therapy self-references tend to be negative expressions, emotional in tone or objectively negative; at the conclusion of therapy the self-references tend to be either objective expressions, neutral in emotional tone, or objectively positive expressions. (203)

There are certain findings, less general in their nature, which tend to qualify these statements.

The sharpest and clearest measure of the above trends is in terms of positive and negative feelings toward the self which are expressed as being currently held. The elimination of past attitudes from consideration heightens the slope of both curves. (180)

In the individual case, though the general trends are as described, there may be wide fluctuations from interview to interview in the self-regarding attitudes. After a slow rise in positive attitudes, negative attitudes may become sharply predominant for a time, etc. (49)

Within the general trends described there is more variability in self-regarding attitudes in the later stages of therapy than in the early stages. (180)

There is often an initial decrease in the positively toned self-regarding attitudes, before the general upward trend becomes evident. (154, 180)

The "unsuccessful" case may remain consistently high in negative feelings about the self, or consistently high in positive self-attitudes. (154, 195)

This material has to do with the feelings and attitudes which the client has toward himself, and the way in which those feelings change. Probably the more basic change is in the way he perceives himself. Unfortunately this is a complex and perplexing problem to investigate with research methodology; studies to date are few, and the findings meager in number though suggestive in their significance. The major study is that made by Sheerer, and so far as her results have reference to the self, they may be summarized as follows.

There is a tendency for the "acceptance of self," operationally defined, to increase during therapy. Acceptance of self, according to the definition used, means that the client tends:

to perceive himself as a person of worth, worthy of respect rather than condemnation;

to perceive his standards as being based upon his own experience, rather than upon the attitudes or desires of others;

to perceive his own feelings, motives, social and personal experiences, without distortion of the basic sensory data;

to be comfortable in acting in terms of these perceptions. (188, 189)

The study upon which these statements are based is confirmed by others, most of them less rigorous in nature. From these other studies it would appear that the individual in "successful" therapy tends:

to perceive his abilities and characteristics with more objectivity and with greater comfort; (174)

to perceive all aspects of self and self-in-relationship with less emotion and more objectivity; (203)

to perceive himself as more independent and more able to cope with life problems; (117, 174)

to perceive himself as more able to be spontaneous and genuine; (117)

to perceive himself as the evaluator of experience, rather than regarding himself as existing in a world where the values are inherent in and attached to the objects of his perception; (101)

to perceive himself as more integrated, less divided. (117, 174)

How may we summarize these changes in self-perception? The essential elements would appear to be that the individual changes in three general ways. He perceives himself as a more adequate person, with more worth and more possibility of meeting life. He permits more experiential data to enter awareness, and thus achieves a more realistic appraisal of himself, his relationships, and his environment. He tends to place the basis of standards within himself, recognizing that the "goodness" or "badness" of any experience or perceptual object is not something inherent in that object, but is a value placed on it by himself.

These changes in the perception of self deserve far more study than has yet been given to them. At the present writing, further investigation is being made of this problem, using the "Q" technique developed by William Stephenson.[1] This permits a detailed analysis of the perception of self before and after therapy, as well as the self-ideal as it is perceived before and after therapy. Results from the first few cases indicate that the self-ideal changes somewhat during therapy, perhaps in the direction of a more realistic or achievable ideal. The perceived self changes even more markedly, and in a direction which brings it closer both to the pre-therapy ideal and the post-therapy ideal. The correlation between self and ideal is initially low, but becomes much higher as

[1] Without going into a general description of the Q technique, the adaptation of it to this type of problem may be described. From a number of recorded counseling cases a large population of all the self-referent statements in the cases was obtained. From this a random selection of 150 statements was made to obtain a usable group. Obviously, this list includes a wide variety of ways of perceiving the self. For the purposes of one research being made the client is asked, before therapy, to sort these statements into eleven piles, with those items least characteristic of him in pile 0, and those most characteristic in pile 10. He is further instructed to place in each pile a given number — 4, 5, 10, 16, 25, 30, 25, 16, 10, 5, 4, respectively — so that the outcome is a forced normal distribution. Having completed this sorting, which gives a rather detailed picture of the perceived self, the client is asked to sort the cards again, this time to portray his desired self or self-ideal. After the conclusion of therapy he is again requested to sort the cards both for self and for the self he desires to be.

Since within each sorting the items have been placed relative to each other on the same continuum, the results of one sorting can be correlated with the results of another sorting. Thus we can find the correlation of pre-therapy self with post-therapy self, pre-therapy self with pre-therapy ideal, etc. The size of the correlation coefficient then represents the similarity between the ratings, if the correlation is positive — a lack of similarity if the correlation is about zero — and an oppositeness between ratings if the correlation is negative. The maximum effectiveness of the method is obtained if all the correlations are computed and the resulting matrix factored by the usual techniques. This makes it possible to discover any patternings or "factors" running through all the client's sortings.

One of the advantages of this technique is that it enables one to utilize rather elaborate statistical procedures on large populations of items which may come from one or a small number of cases. There is thus much less loss of the clinical richness in the statistical investigation. This mode of approach offers much promise as a research tool. Unfortunately, no very adequate description of it is yet available in published form, though the reader is referred to Stephenson (201, 202).

a result of therapy due to the changes in a converging direction in both self and ideal. Thus the result of therapy would appear to be a greater congruence between self and ideal. The self and the values it holds are no longer so disparate. These statements are highly tentative, and may be much altered by completion of the researches under way. They are mentioned here to indicate that the methodological pathway is now open to a rigorous and detailed study of the perceptions of the self, in all its ramifications. One could now study separately the perception of self-characteristics, of self-in-relationship-to-others, of values around which the self is organized, and of goals and ideals. These could not only be studied intensively through intercorrelational studies, but through relating them to ratings and judgments made by others — preferably using the same Q-sorting method.

A Clinical Description

Let us try to put in more personalized and clinical terms some of the material which has been stated above in objective and research terminology. The client tends to enter therapy regarding himself critically, feeling more or less worthless, and judging himself quite largely in terms of standards set by others. He has an ideal for himself, but sees this ideal as very different from his present self. Emotionally the balance of feelings about himself swings decidedly to the negative side.

As therapy proceeds, he often feels even more discouraged about and critical of himself. He finds that he frequently experiences very contradictory attitudes toward himself. As he explores these he gradually becomes more realistic in his perception of himself, and more able to accept himself "as is." As he develops more concern in regard to his current feelings and attitudes, he finds that he can look at them objectively and experience them neither as a basis for emotional self-condemnation nor self-approval. They are simply himself observed in action. This self "as is" is seen as being worthwhile, as being something he can live with. This process is by no means a smooth one; there may be interviews in which his evaluation of self sinks to a very low ebb, and he feels himself quite worthless and hopeless. Nevertheless, in general he develops less fear of the attitudes he discovers within his experience; he becomes less fearful of how he will be judged by others and spends more of his time deciding what are his own basic values. As these changes take place, he feels himself to be more spontaneous in his attitudes and behavior; experiences himself as a more *real* person, a more unified person. He slowly discovers that what he wishes to be has shifted to a point where it is a more achievable goal, and that actually he is himself changed to a degree which brings him much more in accord with his ideal. His inner life becomes more comfortable, more free of tension. This would seem to be the clinical description of the changes in self during therapy, as revealed by objective studies.

Change in the Manner of Perception

Another cluster of phenomena which exhibit movement or change during therapy all have to do with a process of increased differentiation in the perceptual field. These phenomena could have been dealt with under the heading of "movement in learning," since learning is essentially an increased differentiation of the field (200, p. 38). They could have been called "the development of a more adequate process of thinking," or "change in the direction of a more soundly based reasoning." The essential point about therapy, when viewed from this angle, is that the way the client perceives the objects in his phenomenal field — his experiences, his feelings, his self, other persons, his environment — undergoes change in the direction of increased differentiation. This is an important way of looking at therapy, and it is unfortunate that as yet there is too little research in this field, except some research on perception of the self, already mentioned, and the study by Beier (21), noted below.[1]

[1] Beier's very interesting study supplies indirect evidence on this matter of perceptual differentiation by throwing the process in reverse and inducing anxiety, then studying the result. He gave all his subjects (sixty-two women) a Rorschach test, a test of perceptual disorientation, and a battery of tests measuring abstract ability — ability to sustain several tasks at once, to synthesize them, to categorize materials, to shift from one concept to another. He then induced threat in the experimental group by giving each member a structured but accurate and individually different interpretation of her Rorschach results. When the

Characteristically the client changes from high-level abstractions to more differentiated perceptions, from wide generalizations to limited generalizations closely rooted in primary experiences. The client who commences therapy with the stated feeling that he is a hopeless and useless person comes, during therapy, to experience himself as indeed useless at times, but at other times showing positive qualities, at still other times exhibiting negative aggression. He experiences himself as being quite variable in functioning — in short, as a person who is neither all black nor all white, but an interesting collection of varying shades of gray. He finds it much easier, as has been indicated, to accept this more differentiated person.

Or take the client whose expressed attitude, early in therapy, is that "My mother is a bitch!" During therapy she begins to perceive in differentiated fashion her varied experiences of her mother. Her mother rejected her in childhood, but occasionally indulged her; her mother means well; she has a sense of humor; she is not well educated; she has a violent and unreasonable temper; she wants very much to be proud of her daughter. The relationship with mother in childhood is examined and differentiated from the relationship with mother today. As this process goes on, the overall generalization, "Mother is a bitch and I can't possibly get on with her," is seen to be quite inadequate to fit the complex facts of primary experience.

With almost every client this process can be observed. He moves from generalizations which have been found unsatisfactory for guiding his life, to an examination of the rich primary experiences upon which they are based, a movement which exposes the falsity of many of his generalizations, and provides a basis for new and more adequate abstractions. He is customarily in the process

---

experimental group and the matched control group were retested with the tests of abstract reasoning it was found that the experimental group showed a loss of abstract ability and an increase in rigidity of thinking and perception, as compared to the control group. The differences were significant.

From the point of view of our interest in therapy this study suggests that differentiation and flexible hypothesis-formation are decreased under threat, and probably increase in the absence of threat; also that threat to the self may easily be produced by evaluation from an external frame of reference by an expert.

of formulating these new guides for himself as therapy concludes. Certainly in the most successful therapy he has also internalized the desirability of building more closely on direct experience, particularly when the guides he has been using for his living prove questionable.

It is obvious that this process does not just happen. It is facilitated by the special conditions of the therapeutic relationship — the complete freedom to explore every portion of the perceptual field, and the complete freedom from threat to the self which the client-centered therapist in particular provides.

The reader will have noted that what we have been saying is in basic accord with some of the fundamental thinking in semantics (81, 98, 105). Putting some of these same thoughts in semantic terminology, we may say that the client has been living by a map. In therapy he discovers first of all that the map is not the territory — that the experiential territory is very different, and far more complex. He also discovers that even as a map, his map has contained serious errors. Therapy gives him the protected opportunity to come down from the high level abstraction of his map and to explore the territory of primary experience. By the time that he is constructing a new map, with the new awareness that it is only a map and not experience itself, therapy is ready to conclude.

Using other semantic terminology, one may say that the client gradually reduces the intensional quality of his reactions — his tendency to see experience in absolute and unconditional terms, to overgeneralize, to be dominated by concept or belief, to fail to anchor his reactions in space and time, to confuse fact and evaluation, to rely on ideas rather than upon reality-testing — and moves toward a more extensional type of reaction. This may be defined as the tendency to see things in limited, differentiated terms, to be aware of the space-time anchorage of facts, to be dominated by facts, not by concepts, to evaluate in multiple ways, to be aware of different levels of abstraction, to test his inferences and abstractions by reality, in so far as possible.

Still another way of describing this matter of differentiation is to discuss it in relation to symbolization. The human being deals with much of his experience by means of the symbols attached to it. These symbols enable him to manipulate elements of his experience in relation to one another, to project himself into new situations, to make many predictions about his phenomenal world. In therapy one of the changes which occurs is that faulty and generalized symbols are replaced by more adequate and accurate and differentiated symbols. Thus, take the mother who experiences many negative feelings toward her child. These feelings are all lumped under the symbolic formulation, "I am irritated at him and angry with him because he is bad." But when she is free from any threat to herself, she can examine these attitudinal and visceral experiences, and can attach more accurately differentiated symbols to them. Some of them are still accurately described in the terms she formerly used, but others become symbolized in such terms as "I am irritated with him because I wish I had never had him," "I am angry with him because he interrupted my career," "He causes me annoyance because he represents adult responsibility which I have always tried to avoid." As the symbols used correspond more closely to the basic and actual experience, then the conclusions drawn on the basis of symbolic manipulation become more sound because they are based upon reality.

It should be made plain that the term *differentiation*, as it is used in this section, does not simply mean the perception of increasingly minute aspects of the phenomenal field. It means separating out, and bringing into figure, any significant perceptual element which has heretofore been unrecognized. Thus Curran (49), in a significant and exhaustive analysis of twenty recorded interviews with one case, finds that the perception of relatedness is one of the important aspects of the process of therapy. In early interviews the client, a very withdrawn individual, discusses twenty-five different "problems," in quite discrete fashion. As therapy progresses, there are more and more instances in which the relationship of problems is seen. Thus he comes to perceive his tendency toward shyness and withdrawal to be related to his feeling that he is a genius and superior to others. He gradually perceives all of himself as a much more unified pattern in which the struggle and conflict revolves around certain basic issues. These he is able to face and resolve, now that he has differentiated out the crucial elements which run through so much of his life.

Still another aspect of this therapeutic experience of increased differentiation may be described in terms of problem-solving. Duncker (52) has given a thoughtful analysis of the psychological processes involved when the subject is dealing with problem-tasks and with mathematical questions. But much the same phenomena are evident in therapy. There is the exploration of one hypothesis after another, in a not too orderly fashion. There is the experience of having something which has heretofore been ground in the perceptual field, emerge into figure. There is the special change in figure-ground relationship which Duncker describes as the looseness versus the fixedness of a perceptual object. That is, both in problem-solving and in therapy the person has come to accept a certain element of the situation as something given or fixed. When he reperceives this as something which is not fixed, he is apt to have a real "Aha!" experience, and finds himself much nearer to a solution of his problem. Thus Duncker's subject's sudden realization that the cork in the ink bottle is not fixed in that perceived relationship, but is a possible tool, a wedge to hold a stick in the desired position, has changed it from a fixed object in his perceptual field to a loose and manipulable one. Likewise the mother who sees her child as bad, comes in therapy to see this not as a fixed and given aspect of the situation but one which is manipulable, alterable, a "loose" perceptual element. Or the client who sees his homosexuality as a settled part of the picture comes to see this part of his behavior as being possibly alterable, as being no more fixed than any other pattern of his behavior. This change from perceiving elements as rigid and fixed, to perceiving them as "loose" or changeable is one of the most important types of differentiation which occur in therapy.

Perhaps this discussion will indicate why, for some, the process of therapy can be wholly described in terms of differentiation. Thus Snygg and Combs state, "we might, therefore, define psychotherapy from a phenomenological point of view as: the provision of experience whereby the individual is enabled to make more adequate differentiation of the phenomenal self and its relationship to external reality. If such differentiations can be made, the need of the individual for maintenance and enhancement of the phenomenal self will do the rest" (200, p. 285).

Movement toward Awareness of Denied Experience

One of the most characteristic and perhaps one of the most important changes in therapy is the bringing into awareness of experiences of which heretofore the client has not been conscious. What, psychologically, occurs when the individual thus deals with "repressed" material? Our experience would indicate that it is best described in terms of greater differentiation of perception, and more adequate symbolization, the processes just discussed.

Let us take a simple example and trace its development. A woman has developed a dizziness and faintness, for which no organic cause can be found. This behavior occurs at various unpredictable times, usually in social gatherings, to the great embarrassment of herself and everyone concerned. She can see no reason for this behavior. As she explores the situation, she identifies the fact that it seems to occur when it causes the most embarrassment to her husband. But this offers no help in understanding the problem, she says, because she is fond of her husband and has no reason for doing anything to hurt him. As all of this is accepted she slowly moves, in succeeding interviews, to stating that if there was any antagonism toward her husband it was completely unconscious and unintentional; that she had felt antagonistic toward her husband several years ago when the symptom started; that she still had a desire to control him and that her symptom was a means of attempting this; that she guessed it had served the purpose both of opposing him and punishing herself for doing so; that in the light of all these newly perceived facts she would have to find more open and direct ways of expressing antagonism when she felt it.

If we examine this sequence from a psychological point of view, it would seem clear that she has all along been experiencing, viscerally, feelings of opposition toward her husband. The crucial missing element is the adequate symbolization of these experiences. This explanation ties in with the fact that she mentioned, early in her interviews, that she was often tense and upset before the dizziness and faintness occurred. This was as far as the symbolization went. It also seems clear that the basic reason for the phenomenon of "repression" or "denial of experience" is that the adequate symbolization of the experience in question would be definitely and often deeply in contradiction to the self concept of the individual. The woman whom we have just described was not, in her own eyes, a person who would stubbornly oppose her good husband, or a person who would entertain unreasonably hostile feelings toward him. Hence such visceral sensations must be given a distorted symbolization, or not be symbolized at all. It also would appear that the release of "repressions," or the bringing into awareness of denied experiences, is not simply a matter of probing for these, either by the client or the therapist. It is not until the concept of self is sufficiently revised to accept them, that they can be openly symbolized. The change in self precedes, rather than follows, the recovery of denied or repressed material.

But we are getting more and more deeply into a theory of the process, which we have proposed to take up in the final portion of the chapter. Let us return to a more descriptive level in regard to these unsymbolized or inadequately symbolized experiences. In practice, it is noted that the first step toward uncovering such material is usually the perception of inconsistencies. In the case just cited, the woman comes to recognize first a discrepancy of this order: I love my husband, yet my behavior seems as though I wished to embarrass him. In another case it may be: I wish to get ahead professionally, yet I fail the very courses needed to get ahead. Or in another case: I want my marriage to continue, but I seem to be behaving in such a way as to break it up. When such discrepancies are clearly perceived, the client is unable to leave them alone. He is motivated to find out the reason for the discrepancy, whether it is due to an inaccurate description of his own feelings (which is usually true) or to an inaccurate description of his behavior.

Although this process of bringing experience into adequately symbolized awareness is recognized by several therapeutic orientations as being an important and basic element of therapy, there is as yet no objective investigation of it. From a descriptive clinical point of view, however, we may say that successful therapy seems to entail the bringing into awareness, in an adequately differentiated and accurately symbolized way, those experiences and feelings which are currently in contradiction to the client's concept of self.

Characteristic Movement in the Valuing Process

As we listen to recordings of therapeutic interviews, and study the transcribed material, it is very evident indeed that therapy has much to do with what is perceived as "good" or "bad," "right" or "wrong," "satisfying" or "unsatisfying." It somehow involves the value system of the individual, and changes in that system. This is an aspect of therapy which has been little discussed, and thus far barely touched from a research point of view. This discussion of it is to be regarded as exploratory rather than in any sense definitive.

It seems to be true that early in therapy the person is living largely by values he has introjected from others, from his personal cultural environment. The situation might be schematically represented by giving some of the values stated or implied by clients and placing in parentheses the source of these values.

"I should never be angry at anyone" (because my parents and church regard anger as wrong).

"I should always be a loving mother" (because any other attitude is unacceptable in my middle class group).

"I should be successful in my courses" (because my parents count on my success).

"I have homosexual impulses, which is very bad" (according to our whole culture).

"I should be sexless" (because my mother seems to regard sex as wicked and out of place for any right-minded person).

"I should be completely casual about sex behavior" (because my sophisticated friends have this attitude).

As therapy progresses, the client comes to realize that he is trying to live by what others think, that he is not being his real self, and he is less and less satisfied with this situation. But if he is to relinquish these introjected values, what is to take their place? There ensues a period of confusion and uncertainty as to values, a certain sense of insecurity in having no basis for judging what is right or wrong, good or bad.

Gradually this confusion is replaced by a dawning realization that the evidence upon which he can base a value judgment is supplied by his own senses, his own experience. Short term and long term satisfactions can be recognized, not by what others say, but by examining one's own experience. The value system is not necessarily something imposed from without, but is something experienced. The individual discovers that he has within himself the capacity for weighing the experiential evidence and deciding upon those things which make for the long-run enhancement of self (which inevitably involves the enhancement of other selves as well). Thus a preliminary investigation by Kessler (101), analyzing the material of three cases, indicated that evaluations at first tended to be sensed as being fixed and residing in the object; this view tended to be replaced by a recognition that value judgments are not necessarily fixed but are alterable; finally there was a tendency to recognize that evaluations were made by the individual, and that the personal evaluation might be altered, depending on the evidence.

Another conceptualization of this process has evolved out of our thinking about the locus of evaluation. In most statements which make or imply a value judgment, the spatial locus of the origin of the evaluation can be rather readily inferred. In therapy, in the initial phases, there appears to be a tendency for the locus of evaluation to lie outside the client. It is seen as a function of parents, of the culture, of friends, and of the counselor. In regard to this last, some clients make strenuous efforts to have the therapist exercise the valuing function, so as to provide them with guides for action. In client-centered therapy, however, one description of the counselor's behavior is that he consistently keeps the locus of evaluation with the client. Some of this is evident in the way he phrases his responses. "You're angry at ——"; "You're confused by ——"; "It seems to you that ——"; "You feel that ——"; "You think you're bad because you ——." In each of these responses the attitude as well as the phrasing is such as to indicate that it is the *client's* evaluation of the situation which is being accepted. Little by little the client finds that it is not only possible but satisfying and sound to accept the locus of evaluation as residing within himself. When this experience becomes internalized, values are no longer seen as fixed or threatening things. They are judgments made by the individual, based upon his own experience, and they are also alterable if and when new experience gives new and altered evidence.

Thus some of the accepted values which were schematically summarized earlier may become markedly changed when evaluated in the light of the client's own experience.

"I should be angry at a person when I deeply feel angry because this leaves less residual effect than bottling up the feeling, and actually makes for a better and more realistic relationship."

"I should be a loving mother when I feel that way but I need not be fearful of other attitudes when they exist."

"I should be successful in my courses only if they have long-range meaning to me."

"I have homosexual impulses, and these are capable of expressions which enhance self and others, and expressions which achieve the reverse."

"I accept my sexuality, and value highly those expressions of it which result in long-range enhancement of self and others; I value less highly those expressions which give only transient satisfactions, or do not enhance self."

Perhaps something of the movement which takes place in this shift in locus of evaluation may be illustrated from the case of a young woman client. A portion of the second interview may indicate how certain standards and values came to be introjected and the effect these had upon her behavior. It seems fairly clear that during her earlier life these values were satisfying guides to action, but that now there is sensed some sort of discrepancy which is profoundly dissatisfying. She feels that she no longer wishes to abide by these values but has nothing to substitute in their place.

S102: It seems — I don't know — It probably goes all the way back into my childhood. I've — for some reason I've — my mother told me that I was the pet of my father. Although I never realized it — I mean, they never treated me as a pet at all. And other people always seemed to think I was sort of a privileged one in the family. But I never had any reason to think so. And as far as I can see looking back on it now, it's just that the family let the other kids get away with more than they usually did me. And it seems for some reason to have held me to a more rigid standard than they did the other children.

C103: You're not so sure you were a pet in any sense, but more that the family situation seemed to hold you to pretty high standards.

S103: M-hm. That's just what has occurred to me; and that the other people could sorta make mistakes, or do things as children that were naughty, or "that was just a boyish prank," or "that was just what you might expect," but Alice wasn't supposed to do those things.

C104: M-hm. With somebody else it would just be just — oh, be a little naughtiness; but as far as you were concerned, it shouldn't be done.

S104: That's really the idea I've had. I think the whole business of my standards, or my values, is one that I need to think about rather carefully, since I've been doubting for a long time whether I even have any sincere ones.

C105: M-hm. Not sure whether you really have any deep values which you are sure of.

S105: M-hm. M-hm.

C106: You've been doubting that for some time.

S106: Well, I've experienced that before. Though one thing, when I make decisions I don't have — I don't think —— It seems that some people have — have quite steady values that they can weigh things against when they want to make a decision. Well, I don't, and I haven't had, and I guess I'm an opportunist (*laughing*). I do what seems to be the best thing to do at the moment, and let it go at that.

C107: You have no certain measuring rods that you can use.

S107: Yes. M-hm. That's what I feel. (*Pause.*) Is our time about up, Mr. L.?

C108: Well, I think there are several minutes more.

S108: I was thinking about this business of standards. I somehow developed a sort of a knack, I guess, of — well — habit — of trying to make people feel at ease around me, or to make things go along smoothly. I don't know whether that goes back to early childhood, or — I mean, to our family situation where there was a large family, and so many differences of opinion and all that there always had to be some appeaser around (*laughing*) and seeing into the reasons for disagreeing and being sorta the oil that soothed the waters. Well, that is a role that I have taken for a long time. And — I — it's gotten so it really — I mean, before this sort of thing came up I realized that as a person in a social situation or group of people like at — oh, at a small meeting, or a little party, or something — I could help things to go along nicely and appear to be having a good time. And I'd see where someone else needed more punch, or where someone didn't have a partner, or where somebody was bored with that person, and something — somebody was standing in a corner, and I could go out and meet them. And sometimes I'd surprise myself by arguing against what I really thought when I saw that the person in charge would be quite unhappy about it, if I didn't. In other words I just wasn't ever — I mean, I didn't find myself ever being set and definite about things. I could see what I thought was needed in the situation and what was the idea I thought might be interjected to make people feel happy, and I'd do that.

C109: In other words, what you did was always in the direction of trying to keep things smooth and to make other people feel better and to smooth the situation.

S109: Yes. I think that's what it was. Now the reason why I did it probably was — I mean, not that I was a good little Samaritan going around making other people happy, but that was probably the role that fell easiest for me to play. I'd been doing it around home so much. I just didn't stand up for my own convictions, until I don't know whether I have any convictions to stand up for.

C110: You feel that for a long time you've been playing the role of kind of smoothing out the frictions or differences or what not. . . .

S110: M-hm.

C111: Rather than having any opinion or reaction of your own in the situation. Is that it?

S111: That's it. Or that I haven't been really honestly being myself, or actually knowing what my real self is, and that I've been just playing a sort of false role. Whatever role no one else was playing, and that needed to be played at the time, I'd try to fill it in.

C112: Whatever kind of person that was needed to kinda help out that situation you'd be that kind of person rather than being anything original or deeply your own.

S112: I think so. I remember one summer. We used to go to the YWCA camp in the summers. And our family lived way out near the edge of town. We went with the school groups that went at a certain time during the summer. Well, we didn't know those children very well, because we didn't see them except on Sundays when we went to church. So going to camp wasn't an awfully satisfying experience because I felt quite strange among the children. Well, this summer — I'd been to camp once before — and I think I'd decided that I was going to be one of the popular girls at camp. So I went to camp with these children that I didn't know too well. And I don't remember what I did that summer; but anyway, I came home voted the most popular camper. What I do remember, though, is when I got ready to go to camp I — and I don't know how old I was then — I was not thirteen, I don't suppose; maybe twelve or thirteen, I don't know quite how old; I just decided I was going to be the most popular girl at camp. So I went to camp with that decision, and I did the things that needed to be done. Whatever they were, I'm sure I don't — I mean, it was probably a lot of drudgery too; like making other people's beds and doing other things like that — I'm sure. But anyway I went through a set campaign and came home and was actually chosen the most popular girl at camp (*laughing*). And it seems that what I've done is do things like that instead of developing a real self.

C113: In other words it's been kind of a planful campaign in each case rather than because you really felt that way or really wanted to be that kind of person. Is that it?

S113: Well, yes. I think so. It seems that it's more — that it's not realistic, or it's not honest, or not — it's not sincere, maybe.

The shift in locus of evaluation in this case was profound and far-reaching. For a brief example, a minor experience will illustrate the type of change we have been describing. In the eighth interview this passage occurs.

S346: Now — one of the things that I was doing, ah, something that — that had worried me was getting, well, living at the dorm, it's hard — not to just sort of fall in with a group of people, ah, that aren't interesting, but just around. Well, I, ah, found that I had been spending a lot more time with a group of people that I didn't find interesting — All of them are pleasant people, and there were certain activities I enjoyed with them, but well, there were a lot of things that I didn't have in common. And we had gotten in the habit of eating breakfast together, and lunch together, and dinner together, and sitting around a lot, probably in the evening. So, now I find that I'm, ah, able to, ah, at least I *am* getting away from that group a little bit. And ah, being with people who are a little bit more stimulating, and people that I really find I have more interests in common with.

C346: That is, you've really chosen to draw away from the group you're just thrown with by chance, and you pick people whom you want more to associate with. Is that it?

S347: That's the idea. I — I, ah, I mean I'm not doing anything drastic. I haven't taken any great steps by leaps and bounds. But, well, one of the girls lives on my floor and she would come and knock on the door and say, ah, that she wanted to eat lunch, or let's eat lunch at twelve, or all of us are going down to eat at twelve. Well, it used to be hard for me to say, "Well, no. I would like to eat at twelve-thirty, ah, so I can eat lunch and go to my one-thirty class." And so I'd stop whatever I was doing and drag down at twelve with the group. Well, now I say, occasionally, "Well, that isn't convenient for me. I'd rather eat later," or "I'd rather eat earlier." Well, ah, before it was easier for me to say, "O.K., I'll go ahead and eat now." And then another thing is that, ah, with the group of kids that I was eating with, I felt that I had just sort of been dragged into the group, almost. They weren't people — one or two of them were people that I really liked, and they had sort of pulled me in with a group of their friends that I wouldn't have picked, myself, especially. And ah, so that I found that all my time was being taken up with these people, and now I'm beginning to seek out people that I prefer myself, I mean people that I choose myself, rather than being drawn in with the bunch.

C347: You find it a little more possible, I gather, to express your real attitudes in a social situation, like wanting to go to lunch or not wanting to go to lunch, and also to, ah, to make your own choice of friends, and people that you want to mix with.

S348: So, that seems to me — I, ah — that also isn't going ahead by great leaps and bounds, but I, ah —

C348: It's a slow process.

S349: But I, ah, I think I'm getting to that. Ah — and I don't know whether — I mean at first, ah, I tried to see if I was just withdrawing from this bunch of kids I'd been spending my time with, and I'm sincere in thinking that, ah, it's not a withdrawal, but it's more of an assertion of my real interests.

C349: M-hm. In other words, you've tried to be self-critical in order to see if you're just running away from the situation, but you feel really, it's an expression of your positive attitudes.

S350: I — I think it is.

Here the client is not only asserting her own evaluations of friends and social activities in contradistinction to the values of the group, but she is able to check her own evaluations to see if they are actually based upon experience. "I tried to see if I was just withdrawing from this bunch of kids . . . but it's more an assertion of my real interests." She finds that she is able to determine, upon the evidence of her own experience, which of her acquaintances have value to her and which do not, which activities significantly enhance self and which do not, which behaviors are escapist, which are positive assertions of purpose. Here is at least a small example of the change which takes place in the valuing process.

Since the above discussion was written, a study has been completed by Raskin (157) which tends to confirm some of the ideas presented. Raskin investigated the extent to which the client's locus of evaluation could be shown to have changed during therapy. The phrase was defined in terms of the client's personality organization — the extent to which his values and standards depend upon the judgments and expectations of others, or are based on a reliance upon his own experience. The first step was to determine whether interview items pertinent to this concept could reliably be selected by judges. More than 80 per cent agreement between two judges was found. The next step was to construct a scale for estimating the locus of evaluation. Twenty-two interview items involving material related to this concept were rated by eighteen qualified judges, and from these judgments an objective rating scale was constructed with values from 1.0 to 4.0, with twelve illustrative items whose value had been established by the eighteen experts. The third step was the establishment of the reliability of this scale. In fifty-nine items, one from each of the interviews rated, there was 76 per cent agreement between the investigator and another judge, a correlation of .91.

This scale was then applied to the fifty-nine interviews of the ten cases studied. These same cases had been used as basic data for several coordinated studies (43), so that various types of data were available for each case and each interview. In general, the locus of evaluation scale showed a shift away from placing the locus of values in others, and toward keeping it in self. The average of the ten first interviews was 1.97, while the average for the ten last interviews was 2.73. When one takes the five cases which were judged by five objective criteria as being most successful, the shift is even sharper. For these five cases the average on the locus of evaluation scale was 2.12 for the first interview, 3.34 for the last. However, the most striking finding was the fact that the measure of the locus of evaluation correlated positively with other measures which had been used with these cases. With the self-acceptance scale developed by Sheerer (189) the correlation was .61. The scale of attitudes toward self which was developed by Stock (203) correlated .67. The index of insight developed by Seeman (180) correlated .35 with Raskin's scale, and with Hoffman's measure of maturity of behavior (86) the correlation was .45. The correlation with the defensiveness scale as used by Haigh (76) was negative, as would be predicted, but was only —.19, too small to be significant. When these five separate measures are combined into a single index based on standard scores, the correlation with the locus of evaluation measure is .85 for the fifty-nine interviews of the ten cases. It is also significant that the degree of improvement on the locus of evaluation scale correlates .60 with counselor rating of outcome.

These correlations suggest strongly the point which has already been mentioned, that the process of therapy appears to be a unified phenomenon, in which all measures, crude as some of them may be, show a strong positive correlation. Raskin concludes, "the locus of evaluation concept operates in a consistent relationship with previously established criteria of therapeutic progress, such as self-regarding attitudes, understanding and insight, maturity of behavior and defensiveness." (157, p. 41)

This study permits the conclusion that there is a change in the valuing process during therapy, and that one characteristic of this change is that the individual moves away from a state where his thinking, feeling, and behavior are governed by the judgments and expectations of others, and toward a state in which he relies upon his own experience for his values and standards.

Characteristic Developments in the Relationship

There are a number of therapists — in other orientations as well as in client-centered therapy — who take the point of view that the process of therapy is best described in terms of the changing emotional relationship existing between the client and the therapist. They believe that many of the verbal and attitudinal and perceptual changes are simply by-products of a basic emotional experience in a relationship between two human beings. One of the arguments for this point of view is that in play therapy, particularly, many of the processes we have discussed either do not occur or occur only in unverbalized form, and yet constructive change takes place. What are we to regard as essential to psychotherapy if success occurs in dealing with a child, when there have been no verbalized insights, little expression of attitudes toward the self, no certain expression of denied experiences, and only a fresh and vital experiencing of self? It is natural that we should give increased attention to the type of relationship in which such change occurs.

Perhaps a brief example of the perplexing sort of "success" which is found with a fair degree of frequency, particularly among younger clients, will serve as an introduction to thinking about the counselor-client relationship. A counselor with a considerable amount of experience describes, in a letter to the author, a case she has completed.

I have just completed the strangest counseling case I've ever had. I think you might be interested in it.

Joan was one of my very first clients when I started counseling one half-day each week at the local high school. She had told the girls' adviser, "I feel so shy I couldn't even tell her what my problem is. Will you tell her for me?" So the adviser told me before I saw Joan that she worried about having no friends. The adviser added that she had noticed that Joan seemed always to be so alone.

The first time I saw Joan she talked a little about her problem and quite a bit about her parents, of whom she seemed to be quite fond. However, there were long, long pauses. The next four interviews could be recorded verbatim on this small piece of paper. By the middle of November Joan remarked that "things are going pretty good."

No elaboration on that. Meanwhile the adviser commented that the teachers had noticed that Joan was now smiling a friendly greeting when they met her in the halls. This was unheard-of before. However, the adviser had seen little of Joan and could say nothing of her contacts with other students. In December there was one interview during which Joan talked freely; the others were characterized by silence while she sat, apparently deep in thought, occasionally looking up with a grin. More silence through the next two and one-half months. Then I received word that she had been elected "woman of the month" by the girls of the high school! The basis for that election is always sportsmanship and popularity with other girls. At the same time I got a message from Joan, "I don't think I need to see you any more." No, apparently she doesn't, but why? What happened in those hours of silence? My faith in the capacity of the client was sorely tested. I'm glad it did not waver.

Experiences of this kind have forced us to recognize that therapy can move forward even though outwardly the client exhibits very few of the elements which we have thought of as characteristic of therapeutic progress. Whatever happened seems not to have happened as the result of verbal interchange. It is of course possible that the outcome was due to some factor entirely outside of therapy. When one considers a number of cases of this sort, it seems more likely that the outcome was due to an experience in a relationship. And if this is so in such nonverbal cases, perhaps it is equally true in others. How then, can we formulate therapeutic process in terms of a relationship?

One hypothesis is that the client moves from the experiencing of himself as an unworthy, unacceptable, and unlovable person to the realization that he is accepted, respected, and loved, in this limited relationship with the therapist. "Loved" has here perhaps its deepest and most general meaning — that of being deeply understood and deeply accepted. In terms of this hypothesis we might speculate on the case of Joan. Feeling that she is a person who is unworthy of having friends, partly because she is so shy and uncommunicative, she enters a relationship with the counselor. Here she finds complete acceptance — or love, if you will — as much evident in her periods of silence and shyness as in the times when she can talk. She discovers that she can be a silent person and still be liked, that she can be her shy self and yet be accepted. Perhaps it is this which gives her more feeling of worth, and changes her relationship to others. By believing herself lovable as a shy and withdrawn person, she finds that she is accepted by others and that those characteristics tend to drop away.

Another clinical hypothesis may be formulated in slightly different terms. As the client experiences the attitude of acceptance which the therapist holds toward him, he is able to take and experience this same attitude toward himself. As he thus begins to accept, respect, like, and love himself, he is capable of experiencing these attitudes toward others.

One of our staff members, Mr. Oliver H. Bown, has been particularly concerned with the point of view represented here, and some excerpts from a memorandum which he has written will give a more vivid description of a therapy in which the stress is upon a deep and significant relationship, to which the client can bring everything that he emotionally is, and in which he is met by the therapist's feelings. This memo was a personal and informal document to the staff, but Mr. Bown has given permission to quote from it here. He feels that the term "love," easily misunderstood though it may be, is the most useful term

to describe a basic ingredient of the therapeutic relationship. I use this term purposely to convey a number of things:

First, that as therapist I can allow a very strong feeling or emotion of my own to enter the therapeutic relationship, and expect that the handling of this feeling from me by the client will be an important part of the process of therapy for him.

Secondly, that a very basic need of the therapist can be satisfied legitimately (or I would rather say *must* be satisfied, if the relationship is to be healthy and legitimate) in his relationship with his client.

And, thirdly, that therapeutic interaction at this emotional level, rather than interaction at an intellectual cognitive level, regardless of the content concerned, is the effective ingredient in therapeutic growth.

These, I recognize, are bald assertions. It seems to me at the present that they are statements which can be proved only through subjective experience, and the data which will eventually enter into a proof or disproof, while always present in a relationship, are most often out of the range of a recording machine.

But, if these phenomena can be subjectively experienced, there is obviously some way of communicating about them. In therapy, I am quite convinced that this communication takes place, primarily, at subverbal, subliminal or subconscious levels. I can only attempt to the best of my ability here to bring these things to the level of words.

It seems to me that we can love a person only to the extent that we are not threatened by him; we can love him only if his reactions to us, or to those things which affect us, are understandable to us and are clearly related to those basic motivations within us all which tend to bring us closer to compatible and meaningful relationships with other people and with the world. Thus, if a person is hostile toward me, and I can see nothing in him at the moment except the hostility, I am quite sure that I will react in a defensive way to the hostility. If, on the other hand, I can see this hostility as an understandable component of the person's defense against feeling the need for closeness to people, I can then react with love toward this person, who also wants love, but who at the moment must pretend not to. Similarly, and somewhat more important to me in my experience, I feel that positive feeling expressed by the client toward us can be a very real source of threat, provided again that this positive expression, in whatever form it may take, is not clearly related to these same basic motivations mentioned above. I might add that the greatest struggle which I have had to date, in what seems like a perpetual process of becoming an adequate therapist, has been my searching out of these so-called basic motivations within myself, but this process alone has made it possible for me to enter into deeper and deeper relationships with clients of both sexes and all ages without feeling personally threatened by my feelings toward the client and by his toward me.

Having again placed "love" at the forefront of my consideration here, I should like to return to the three assertions mentioned above which seem to grow out of this concept for me, and consider them in greater detail.

First, I should like to consider why it is that in the past I have been unwilling to let any strong feeling of mine enter into the therapeutic relationship. At the beginning, the reason I gave myself for this unwillingness to become in any way emotionally involved was taken from the statements of many people who were experienced in the field. Statements such as: "the therapist must keep himself out of it; we must react to clients' feelings and needs and not our own; we should not expect our client to be our therapist; and, objectivity goes down the drain when we ourselves become involved" — these are familiar to us all, and when considered in the light of specific kinds of involvement which therapists may fall into, they are very reasonable prohibitions. At this level I was literally stuck for a long time, fearing the worst if I should let any kind of personal involvement enter into my relationship with my clients. Gradually, however, I began to find another level of reason for my fear of involvement which had reference to my own ability to accept my feelings and needs in relation to other people, rather than to a theory of what is "good therapy." I should like to mention a few of the specific reasons which I found at this level as examples. The rather deeply disturbed client is usually preoccupied with himself and with his own problems, and I began to realize that all through my life I have been willing to become involved with people — that is, to really give something of myself to them — only when they have seemed to be in a position to give me something which I have needed in return. More bluntly, I have striven throughout my life to satisfy my needs, and because clients, as I have seen them, have been poor potential satisfiers of my needs, it has been safest not to express these needs — actually, not to feel them in the therapeutic relationship. This absence of the possibility of direct and immediate satisfaction has been one reason for my refusal to really enter a therapeutic relationship, but there has been an even stronger reason. A lack of satisfaction is one thing, direct and outright rejection is another, and I have thus feared that if I allowed some of the more tender parts of myself to become exposed in a therapeutic relationship that they would be trampled on, misused, and perhaps ridiculed. These were some of the *real* reasons why a lack of involvement was appealing, or even more than that, mandatory. I assumed, of course, that the clients knew nothing of this; that I appeared to them to be a professionally adequate person who was dealing with them in an understanding and an empathic way. This may have been true at the client's level of consciousness, but unconsciously, I think he was learning directly from me, "Do not be free in this relationship. Do not let yourself go. Do not express your deepest feelings or needs, for in this relationship that is dangerous." What do I mean by subconscious learning on the part of the client? At this point I can only say that when it became less necessary for me to hold this attitude in therapy, my clients immediately moved into those more delicate areas which I had been shutting off within myself, and the feelings and needs which were involved in these areas could not only be discussed, but also experienced freely and without fear. Formerly, I would have said that I did not need to let my own needs and feelings interfere with the progress of therapy; now, I would say that I was reacting in an infinite number of little ways to my need to defend certain parts of myself, to withhold those parts of myself in this relationship rather than to express my more outgoing needs and feelings, on which I feel any real relationship depends, and by which it is nourished. I am merely saying that I feel that it is impossible for a therapist not to act in terms of his own needs. The only choice which is involved for me is whether I wish to react to whatever need I have to defend myself against feeling, needing, and involvement in general, or whether I wish to develop a sufficient acceptance of these needs and feelings so that they can be freely operative in all relationships, therapeutic and otherwise.

At this point I should like to react to the contention which is sometimes put forward to the effect that when the therapist satisfies his needs in therapeutic relationship it is a distorted form of sublimation, a rather ugly and parasitic misuse of the client's emotional vulnerability. I certainly feel that this can happen, but responding to this possibility by withholding any emotion which it is feared may get out of hand, is for me an inadequate and castrating way of dealing with the same emotionality which I feel lies at the very heart of the best interpersonal relationships.

We may now turn to my second assertion, since the discussion immediately above has provided a certain basis which allows me to deal with the therapist's needs. As soon as the word "need" is mentioned in this connection, I think that we often become concerned with rather specific needs which usually require in our culture a fairly specific context in which they can be legitimately satisfied. So long as these specific and pointed needs are at the forefront of the therapist's preoccupation, it does indeed seem ridiculous and out of taste to suggest that they be satisfied in the therapeutic relationship.

What then are these very basic needs which I have probably made sound mysterious and obscure, which I maintain must be expressed by the therapist, if the client is to feel a maximum of security and freedom in the relationship? In my previous paper I could express them only in a negative way by saying that they were freely expressed and operative when the therapist felt completely free, uninhibited, and uncontrolled. To express these needs in a positive way is somehow very difficult because all the words I can think of sound so trivial while the feelings themselves feel so real and so potent. They feel like the need for a very elemental kind of response from people; a response which is composed mainly of a fundamental penetrating warmth; a response which is simple and yet somehow absolute, and certainly unqualified. It is a response which I feel cannot be conveyed with words. It exists almost as a form of pure energy which can be picked up by another person only through his feelings, rather than through his intellect. While this may sound very garbled, I feel that it is as simple a phenomenon as the experiencing of pain. When we actually back into a hot stove, we don't have to think through the laws of thermodynamics, body chemistry, and neurology before we are intensely aware of the pain. In some such way, I believe, this very positive response is perceived, in spite of the absence of anything very tangible as stimulus.

Now, we may ask why it is important that the therapist feels this need in his relationship with his client. This need, incidentally, is referred to above as our deepest motivations toward "compatible and meaningful relationships with people." The answer which feels operationally correct, and I think logically so, is that I think it is only when the therapist can experience this need, this motivation, within himself as a live part of himself, that he can perceive it or any fragment of it which breaks through, and all the very complex defenses which the organism can develop to suppress this need in his client. To phrase this somewhat more simply, my contention is that it is only when we can express our own deepest needs that we are able to perceive the operation of those needs in another person, and it is only then that we have this basic response, which we need from other people, available to give to them.

In terms of the therapeutic situation, I think this feeling says to the client, I have a real hunger to know you, to experience your warmth, your expressivity — in whatever form it may take — to drink as deeply as I can from the experience of you in the closest, most naked relationship which we can achieve. I do not want to change you to suit me: the real you and the real me are perfectly compatible ingredients of a potential relationship which transcends, but in no way violates, our separate identities.

This whole idea seems important to me, not so much from the

theoretical standpoint, but rather because of its apparent importance in the process which some of my clients have been undergoing. Simple experiencing of this kind of feeling toward my clients has left me with the feeling that I'm giving everything that I can to the therapeutic relationship, and this in turn leaves me with no feeling of withholding or guilt. It also seems responsible for my increased ability to say "no" to specific demands or requests which the client may make with no feeling of rejecting him or letting him down in any way. Whether I'm kidding myself theoretically or not, this feeling of emotional adequacy in a therapeutic relationship seems very essential in creating a spontaneous and completely free relationship with clients.

My third assertion, namely, that therapeutic growth takes place as a result of experiences which have an emotional rather than an intellectual meaning to clients, falls more into the area of those things about which there is considerable common agreement. We speak very often, for example, of the emotional impact of acceptance where rejection is expected. I only wish to add that acceptance is an emotional phenomenon, not an intellectual one. I think it implies that we feel something positive toward the client, rather than that we feel neutrally toward him. I think clients are very much aware of the difference between the counselor who listens and understands, and simply does not react, and the one who understands, and in addition really cares about the meaning to the client of the feelings, reactions, and experiences which he is exploring.

Another experience which I have been having, which points out the significance of the emotional level of interaction, is that there have been times when a great deal of interaction has gone on on this level at a time when the verbalization of the client has been far removed from it. Perhaps the best illustration of this kind of interaction is illustrated by the reactions of the client, as given at the end of this paper, to this persistent emotional process.

In concluding this long and I'm sure not very clear discussion of the therapist's emotional investment in therapy, I would like to say that I feel that the client establishes the same kind of relationship with his therapist that he forms with other people in his environment. It contains the same inhibitions, ambivalences, conflicts, needs, values, goals, and so on; and when the therapist can perceive these elements in operation in the immediate present in therapy, he taps one of the most valuable sources of deeply understanding his client.

I should like to depart at this point from the ticklish business of trying to describe the therapeutic relationship as I see it, and mention briefly and haphazardly some theoretical points which have come to have importance to me.

The first of these points has to do with the question of why a need or feeling is repressed. It has been fundamental to my thinking in this area that somewhere along the line it has been learned, with appropriate emotional reinforcement, that the need or feeling in question is bad and that its expression will bring rejection from those whom we value most in our life situation. I am quite certain that this is a fairly basic dynamic which does appear in the personality make-up of all of us; but I've come to recognize another dynamic to which I have been relatively blind before, one which seems somehow even more fundamental. I believe that some needs and feelings are repressed, not because it has been learned that they are bad, but rather because it has been learned that, if expressed, they will not be satisfied. I am speaking here of the phenomenon of deprivation which I think probably we all have experienced, too. My clients have often expressed the feeling that they have been somehow deprived, but both they and I have thought that the attempt to resolve this feeling is like trying to work with something that isn't there; it is more like a "hole" in the mid-section of a person rather than something tangible that can be examined and manipulated. I'm finding that this repression is often so complete that the person can become aware of this "hole" only when it is partially filled up through a rich experience with another person. In client-centered therapy I think we often provide this kind of experience by our attitudes of warmth, acceptance, respect for the individual, and the like. I'm finding further that the intensified emotional relationship, which has been discussed above, has been very deeply effective in searching out the "holes" which do exist within the personality configuration, and bringing them to that level of awareness where they can be worked through. I think it is only at this point that the person can then become aware of all of the mechanisms, particularly the masochistic self-denial, which are erected as a result of these unsatisfied hungers.

Another fairly recent learning which has had a good deal of meaning for me, is in connection with the so-called "dependent" client, who has often been a somewhat baffling problem in a client-centered approach. I've reached the conclusion that whenever I find myself calling a client "dependent," I don't fully understand the nature of the feelings which are being expressed. I think I've most often labeled people as dependent when, in one way or another, they are asking me for the kind of response which, for some reason of my own, I am not willing to give. I am speaking now of some deep emotional need of the client which is expressed, rather than a series of specific and perhaps unreasonable requests. I have come to the conclusion, too, that when the client begins making a number of specific requests, it is almost always a reflection of the lack which he feels in the relationship.

My final point has to do with the growth force which we have relied upon so heavily as an explanatory principle. I've also heard recently such terms as "regressive tendency," "death instinct," and "disruptive forces" used to explain the case which seems to go downhill. My own thinking recently leads me to doubt the validity of these two concepts. I am tending more and more to look at the individual as an organism with a rather definite "need" structure and with almost unlimited potential, provided the environment gives the opportunity for the individual to become aware of his needs and his wealth of positive expressivity. If, on the other hand, these opportunities are sharply limited, I feel quite sure that the organism will adapt in a way that appears regressive or disruptive. This concept helps to explain why I feel that the therapeutic environment must contain a number of definite ingredients, rather than simply be free of other ingredients which we judge to be negative in terms of their effect upon growth.

I am appending to this paper a statement given to me by a client which expresses in an appropriate emotional way much of what I've been struggling to report in a somewhat more systematic fashion. For me, this document has a great deal of meaning, and I'm happy to pass it on to you for whatever use it may be in understanding what I've tried to communicate. It is my very real hope that this paper will serve as a stimulus for communication at greater length on the part of all of us who are keenly interested in people and the processes through which they change and grow.

[*The Client's Statement*]

It's hard to explain what has happened to me in the past months . . . very hard. One reason is that I find I cannot relive the experiences which were so important to me. I can look at them, but cannot completely relive them. I guess I lived them so completely and fully at the time that they simply became a part of me and now I cannot separate the parts from the whole. I would like to try, however, to give some of my present impressions of what happened.

One of my first, strongest, and most persistent feelings was pain — all through the months I was in pain; not just mental pain, but actual physical pain, nausea, rapid heartbeat, poor circulation, headaches, and so on. I remember saying once that I felt as if I was putting a knife into myself and turning it around and around so that my blood and all of my insides would gush forth. The pain began when I realized that I had to decide whether or not to begin therapy. I felt that you led me to the water, simply by showing *real* interest and concern, but I had to decide whether or not to drink. That was a mighty difficult decision — in fact, possibly the most difficult I ever made. Once I decided to drink, it became a matter of desperate urgency, to me, to drink it all as fast as I could and get to the bottom. Whenever I stopped for breath, I berated myself for delaying the process.

My first reaction to you, I think, was one of surprise at your sensitivity and awareness of what and how I was feeling, even when I expressed it very inarticulately or not at all. I knew you were quick and sensitive, but I didn't think anyone could be *that* understanding.

Then I began to get the feeling that not only were you sensitive to and understanding of my feelings, but you also *cared* and cared very much. This is the feeling which I think I fought vigorously for the whole time. It simply emanated from you — from your hands as you handled the cigarette lighter, from your foot as you stretched it out in front of me and moved it slowly back and forth and particularly from your eyes, when I had the courage to look at them. Because of the strength of this feeling, I usually found it necessary to talk to the wall or the window, but I was always painfully and acutely aware of you. Once I remember you attended a class (that day I felt particularly awful) and sat near me. I didn't want to see you at all that day. Then, you stretched out your foot and it almost touched mine. I don't know whether it was intentional or not, but to me it said, "I know how miserable you are and I care about how you feel because I care about you." I almost screamed. I wanted to get up and run out of the room. Since I couldn't do that, I closed up in a shell and waited until I could go. I couldn't talk or do anything but be aware of you.

Throughout all of my sessions I was focused on my relationship with you. Whenever I made any attempt to pull away from it, to discuss other relationships on an intellectual plane, I felt compelled to come back to you. I simply could not shake you. I was firmly convinced that to give love meant to sell my soul, to become completely dominated by and dependent upon the loved one, and that love could not be received without paying this high price. Therefore, I fought desperately against any love you might give to me. I tried telling you how unworthy I was — how selfish, inadequate, nasty. I tried hating and attacking you. You could not possibly love me, therefore you were being deceitful and cruel in pretending you did. I tried wearing you down by demanding proof of your affection. I even tried "curing" myself and raving about how wonderful it was. But you were always there, like a firm rock which I beat upon to no avail and which merely said, "I love you." I then began to see, though not too clearly, that your love did not control me and I could not control it.

As I look at it now, I was peeling off layer after layer of defenses. I'd build them up, try them, and then discard them when you remained the same. I didn't know what was at the bottom and I was very much afraid to find out, but I *had* to keep on trying. At first I felt there was nothing within me — just a great emptiness where I needed and wanted a solid core. Then I began to feel that I was facing a solid brick wall, too high to get over and too thick to go through. One day the wall became translucent, rather than solid, and I felt hopeful that I might really see through it. That was the day, I believe, when I realized moral judgment had nothing to do with how I felt, only with how I acted. It suddenly became clear that loving and hating, for example, are neither right nor wrong, they just are. After this, the wall seemed to disappear but beyond it I discovered a dam holding back violent, churning waters. I felt as if I were holding back the force of these waters and if I opened even a tiny hole I and all about me would be destroyed in the ensuing torrent of feelings represented by the water. (I may be overwhelming you with these images which, as you will recall, are the same ones I used during our sessions. Whenever I felt or experienced anything, whenever I felt anything "happened," I could find no way of expressing the feelings or understanding I had, either to you or to myself, except through these images. The only times I can remember and the only times which seem important to me are those in which I experienced the feelings expressed by these images.)

One day the water changed to tigers — tigers who were straining furiously at the leash onto which I was holding desperately as I felt myself weakening. Finally I could stand the strain no longer and I let go. All I did, actually, was to succumb to complete and utter self-pity, then hate, then love. The tigers disappeared and I found myself on top of a sand dune in a pure ecstasy of feeling. I felt as if I had struggled through the deep and shifting sand to get to the top of a large dune. Once there, I could stand on high, throw open my arms and gather in the bright blue sky and the clear, cool lake. Then I could run — faster and faster — down the dune, across the beach and into the cold, sharp water of the lake, plunging onward until I fell face forward and covered all my body with the exhilaration of pure feeling. Then I could lie upon the warm sand, digging myself in until I became a part of it and with it absorbed the soothing warmth of the sun. This was a real experience for me, as you well know, but it was all my own. I could watch and enjoy others running down their sand dunes, also happy and exhilarated, but much as I wanted to, I could not go to their dunes and they could not come to mine.

After this experience, I felt as if I had leaped a brink and was safely on the other side, though still tottering a bit on the edge. I didn't know what I was searching for or where I was going, but I felt then, as I have always felt whenever I really lived, that I was moving forward. Frequently I felt I was getting closer to the goal, whatever it was, and then would run away. This discouraged me because I felt it was such a waste of time. Several times I thought of quitting, but I was driven by the feeling that if I didn't find "it" this time I never would. I also began to realize that when I really found something, when I really had an experience, it was always when I attempted to express or keep from expressing my feelings toward you. I know that the pressure of your feeling toward me kept me working on my feelings toward you (and through you toward all others in my life).

Gradually the goal or end of my search became a light which was working its way to the surface (as I worked down to it). Last week it was right under the surface. I had one more layer to remove. I talked, intellectually, of my feeling of being unloved from birth. I gave several examples and tried to pin down and explain my feelings in relation to these examples. As I talked I kept getting more and more uncomfortable because you seemed to be feeling much more strongly than I did. Then I began to feel that you weren't even listening to what I was saying, but you were feeling all the things I was feeling, even more than I was aware of feeling, and you were *caring*.

Suddenly I felt as if I had become a baby and was being held comfortably, securely, with warm understanding and a great love in my
mother's arms. Then I realized that that was what I had missed and
that was what I wanted now and had wanted all my life. I also
realized that I had just been loved that way and that I could never have
discovered what was lacking until I had experienced it — completely.
Now I could stand on my sand dune and reach across to you on your
dune, my father on his dune, my mother on her dune, and all the others
in my life that I wanted to love. We could all join hands and run
down into the lake. However, the feeling I felt this time was one of
joy, not the desperate ecstasy previously felt when I was alone on
my dune.

I also discovered at this time that all of the feelings and events and
ideas of my past and present are like feathers which I have now released. In fact, my head feels full of these feathers. They are
gradually settling down into their places, but I can never be sure
where they will land. One may seem to be settling in one place,
then a new insight will create a slight breeze which will send it
scurrying off in another direction. I've tried to catch these feathers
and force them into certain places, but that's impossible. You can't
force feathers. The only place they will fit comfortably and stay
put is the place in which they settle naturally. Hereafter, I shall let
them settle themselves and I'll simply remain alert enough to recognize when and where they have settled and when they are shifting
around.

This is getting rather lengthy, but there is one more feeling I would
like to express. As I told you last week, when the light for which
I was searching did come through, it did not seem a bit surprising to
me, it merely gently broke the surface and was recognized, but it had
had a long, hard pull up. I have no doubt, however, that this is what I
have been seeking. Also — I greeted it with tears of sadness, not
ecstasy. The emptiness is gone, but it's sad to think that it had been
there so long.

Here in this highly personal material is a reaching out — both
on the part of the therapist and on the part of the client — for a
new type of formulation of the process of therapy. It is not easily
understood, and reactions to it seem to be strong. It is, as far as
our own group is concerned, still in an infant and groping stage.
It is clear, however, that the stress is upon a direct experiencing in

the relationship. The process is not seen as primarily having to do with the client's memory of his past, nor with his exploration of the problems he is facing, nor with the perceptions he has of himself, nor the experiences he has been fearful of admitting into awareness. The process of therapy is, by these hypotheses, seen as being synonymous with the experiential relationship between client and therapist. Therapy consists in experiencing the self in a wide range of ways in an emotionally meaningful relationship with the therapist. The words — of either client or counselor — are seen as having minimal importance compared with the present emotional relationship which exists between the two.

This is a stimulating formulation of therapy, which is, in some significant ways, at variance with the previous descriptions. The hypotheses which are implicit in this formulation will be difficult — though not impossible — to put to rigorous test. This is a way of looking at the change which goes on in therapy which cannot be overlooked.

Characteristic Changes in Personality Structure and Organization

Are the changes which occur in client-centered therapy simply surface changes, or do they affect what has been thought of as the basic "structure" of personality? Some evidence has already been given that the organization of the self is altered, but the question still remains whether more conventional, and presumably broader, measures of personality would show any change.

Our best answer to this question to date consists of five studies involving one hundred and five clients to whom the Rorschach test was given before and after therapy; ten of these clients to whom an additional Rorschach was given twelve to eighteen months following the conclusion of therapy; twenty-seven clients to whom the Bernreuter test was given before and after therapy; forty clients who were pre- and post-tested with the Bell Adjustment Inventory; twenty-eight clients who were pre- and post-tested with Minnesota Multiphasic Personality Inventory; twenty-eight clients pre- and post-tested with the Hildreth Feeling-Attitude Scale; and eleven clients who were given the Kent-Rosanoff Word Association Test before and after therapy. One hundred and twenty-three separate clients from four clinics were involved in these studies. More than thirty separate therapists carried these cases. The findings of these studies will be briefly reviewed, organized in terms of the test utilized.[1]

Since the Rorschach is one of the most widely used personality tests today, the results in terms of the Rorschach may be presented first. Muench (140), in the first attempt to measure objectively the personality outcomes of any form of psychotherapy, administered Rorschachs to twelve clients before and after therapy. He used a quantitative method of analysis, based on signs of adjustment and maladjustment proposed by Hertz and by Klopfer. He found significant changes in these Rorschach indicators, in the direction of better adjustment. These Rorschach results were confirmed by the results of other tests mentioned below. There was considerable correspondence between the success of the case, according to clinical judgment, and the extent of the Rorschach change. Although Muench used no control group, a control group was provided for him by the subsequent efforts of Hamlin and Albee (79). They used sixteen subjects whose initial status was similar to Muench's clients, and retested them five months later; there had been no therapy in the intervening period. They used the same methods of analysis and found no significant changes in the Rorschach patterns of this group.

In a more recent study Carr (40) found results contradictory to those of Muench. Analyzing pre- and post-therapy Rorschachs given to nine cases, Carr used essentially the same adjustment indicators as Muench, but found no significant change. He also had the Rorschachs analyzed qualitatively by an experienced worker who did not know whether the cases were regarded as successful or not. Five were regarded as showing no change (in three of these there was even a suggestion of decrement) and four

---

[1] The reader who is unfamiliar with these tests will find brief introductory descriptions of the Rorschach and the Kent-Rosanoff test in Bell (22). Similar descriptions of the Bernreuter Adjustment Inventory and the Minnesota Multiphasic are available in Rosenzweig (176). The Hildreth Feeling-Attitude Scale is described in a journal article (82). The Bell Adjustment Inventory, with a descriptive manual, is obtainable from Stanford University Press, Stanford University, California.

were rated as showing slight or moderate improvement. These ratings showed some, though not a close, relationship to counselor judgment of degree of success. In general, this study does not corroborate Muench's findings, and Carr admits inability to understand the discrepancy.

Mosak (139), in a study of twenty-eight neurotic clients whose average number of therapeutic interviews was fifteen, also used the Rorschach as a pre- and post-test. When he used the signs of adjustment as measures — using the same indicators as Muench and Carr — there was no significant change. When the Rorschach protocols were judged by three experienced clinicians, two of the cases were judged to have shown much improvement, about half of the group showed slight improvement, and nearly half were regarded as relatively unchanged in Rorschach pattern. Obviously the subjective judgments by Rorschach workers showed more change than the measure based upon discrete signs.

The most sophisticated study of Rorschach outcomes is that completed by Haimowitz (78), who gave pre- and post-therapy Rorschachs to fifty-six clients. Thirteen therapists were involved in these cases. Of these clients, thirty-two were in individual or individual and group therapy, and twenty-four were in group therapy alone. The number of therapeutic hours ranged from three to thirty-eight. A distinctive feature of this study was the use of a control group of fifteen individuals similar to the counseled group in age, sex, and education. In analyzing the Rorschachs, Haimowitz used the index of neurotic signs developed by Harrower-Erickson. She also developed a series of ten rating scales for evaluating the Rorschach in terms of the therapeutic concepts of client-centered therapy, the brief label or title of the ten scales being as follows: quality of reality orientation, degree of anxiety, degree of dependency, self attitudes, degree of acceptance of emotionality, adequacy of intellectual functioning, degree of spontaneity-flexibility, personality integration, attitudes toward others, and quality of adjustment to emotional problems. A detailed manual was devised defining each concept and indicating the Rorschach signs upon which each rating was to be based. The reliability of application of these scales was high when the investigator re-rated 150 ratings after a lapse of time. When the rating was done by other judges the correlation was only .53.

The results obtained by Haimowitz indicated significant improvement by both methods of analysis. The mean number of neurotic signs exhibited by the clients dropped from 3.0 to 2.0, the significance of the drop being indicated by a critical ratio of 4.03. The analysis based upon the ten rating scales showed a mean rating of 3.13 prior to therapy and 3.59 after therapy, a difference in the direction of improved adjustment, with a critical ratio of 6.31. Nine of the ten rated characteristics showed change in a positive direction, five of these being significant at the 2 per cent level. Only on the scale for spontaneity and flexibility was there no change. Control remained fully as great at the end of therapy as at the beginning, a finding in contradiction to the theoretical and clinical expectations.

The control group showed marked contrast to the experimental group. Although in several of the control cases there had been important life changes between the first and second test, the number of neurotic signs remained constant (4.0 and 3.9) and the mean rating on the ten scales showed no significant change (3.0 and 2.9). It would seem that changes of the sort found in the therapy group do not tend to occur in a similar population not undergoing therapy.

The information from the ten cases retested for a third time more than a year after the conclusion of therapy is of interest. There was a mean gain of .82 on the rating scales from pre-test to follow-up test for these ten cases, a statistically significant figure. There was steady gain from pre-test to post-test and post-test to follow-up, though these smaller steps do not provide statistically significant figures. Perhaps as significant as the overall gain is the fact that this gain came from six of the cases, the other four failing to show further improvement following therapy, or showing some regression toward the pre-therapy state. It seems obvious that if we but knew the factors which differentiated between those individuals who continued to improve in personality adjustment following therapy, and those who did not, we would be much further advanced in our knowledge of the therapeutic process. Such knowledge must, however, await further study.

Another aspect of the Haimowitz investigation deserves comment. When the attempt was made to relate basic personality patterns to degree of change in therapy, there was one tentative finding which is of interest. Deeply disturbed males, with a tendency toward intrapunitive patterns of personality reactions, seemed to respond to client-centered therapy with the greatest degree of personality change. While this finding is tentative, it marks the first attempt to answer, in a scientific way, the oft-raised question, "What type of individual is most likely to be helped by client-centered therapy?"

So much for the measurement of personality change by means of the Rorschach test. The results on other personality tests seem to give the same general picture. Muench used both the Bell Adjustment Inventory and the Kent-Rosanoff Word Association Test in addition to the Rorschach. The results on both tests showed movement in the direction of improved adjustment. The Bell inventory showed improved scores in all five areas, but only in the areas of health and emotional adjustment were the changes statistically significant. The total score showed a decrease which has nine chances in ten of being significant. Seven of the twelve cases showed improvement on this test following therapy. Of the five cases which showed some decrement, three were the least successful cases in terms of the therapist's judgments. Improvement on the Bell test was striking in the four cases regarded by the therapists as most successful. On the Kent-Rosanoff test the overall change was in the direction of giving more normal associations, and when the associations were scored by the method devised by Jellinek and Shakow (97), the difference between the pre- and post-tests was significant at the 1 per cent level.

Mosak (139) also used the Bell Adjustment Inventory with his group of twenty-eight, and the results are strikingly similar to those found by Muench. The mean score dropped from 62.8 to 47.6, a highly significant change. Again the greatest changes occurred in the areas of emotional adjustment and health, with social adjustment the third in significance. Improvement was shown in all five areas, including home and occupational adjustment.

Two tests were used by Mosak which had not been used by previous investigators. The Minnesota Multiphasic showed significant decreases on five of the nine diagnostic scales and on two of the validity scales. The scales showing the greatest changes in the direction of normality were Depression (D) and Schizophrenia (Sc). Significant changes also occurred in the following scales: Hypochondriasis (Hs), Hysteria (Hy), and Paranoia (Pa). Some positive change occurred on ten of the thirteen scales. When the mean profile of the group before therapy is compared with the post-therapy profile, the profile pattern remains very much the same, but a general drop in profile intensity is observed. Evidently the change which occurs is pervasive and general, in this group of cases judged as moderately severe neurotics, rather than narrow or specific.

The other instrument used by Mozak was the Hildreth Feeling-Attitude Scales, devised during World War II to assess intensity of feelings and attitudes. The scales which were rated by the client cover the individual's feeling state, his energy level, his degree of optimism regarding the future, his mental state, his attitudes toward work, and his attitudes toward others. Significant improvement was shown on these scales when the pre-therapy and post-therapy scores are compared. The largest change was indicated in the feeling scores. The therapists also made pre- and post-ratings on these clients, utilizing the same scales, and their ratings showed a slightly greater increase. Interestingly enough, the therapists rate the clients lower both before and after therapy than do the clients themselves. While the Hildreth scale is not a refined device, the changes seem to indicate some significant movement on the part of the clients toward feelings and attitudes generally regarded as constructive.

Cowen (45) studied the results of the Bernreuter Test given to twenty-seven clients before therapy, and repeated twenty months after the conclusion of therapy. This study was part of a larger investigation in which follow-up interviews were used as well as the personality inventory. Cowen recognizes the fact that the Bernreuter test is a rather crude and unsatisfactory instrument. It is of interest, however, that significant changes were found in the direction of better adjustment, and these changes were in general corroborated by the follow-up interviews. In the scores for Neurotic Tendency, Introversion, Confidence, and Sociability, the changes were positive, and were significant at the 1 per cent level. Scores for Self-sufficiency and Dominance showed no significant change.

The Thematic Apperception Test is perhaps better adapted than the tests mentioned thus far to measure the types of change which would be expected to result from psychotherapy. Up to the present time, however, it has been used only with scattered cases, and no significant research study utilizing this test has been completed. Clinical analysis of a few cases appears to corroborate the findings from the personality tests already cited.

Let us return to the question with which this section commenced: Do the changes which occur in client-centered therapy alter the basic structure of personality? The studies which have been cited would seem to justify an answer along these lines. When an investigation is made of a randomly selected group of clients receiving client-centered therapy, it is generally found that one outcome of the experience is a significant degree of change in the basic personality configuration. This change appears to be in the direction of: an increased unification and integration of personality; a lessened degree of neurotic tendency; a decreased amount of anxiety; a greater degree of acceptance of self and of emotionality as a part of self; increased objectivity in dealing with reality; more effective mechanisms for dealing with stress-creating situations; more constructive feelings and attitudes; and a more effective intellectual functioning. On the basis of limited evidence, it would appear that these personality changes are relatively permanent, often continuing in the directions already described.

There are two words of cautious interpretation to be added to these positive findings. The personality tests which have been used to measure change are themselves of dubious validity. Indeed, there is as much reason for stating that the test changes occurring in conjunction with therapy indicate some validity in the tests as there is for saying that therapeutic change is proved by the test results. We are dealing with two relatively unvalidated procedures, and this fact should be thoroughly recognized. That the findings are in accord with clinical hypotheses and clinical logic is, however, heartening.

The second caution is in regard to the magnitude of change. While the changes described are of sufficient magnitude to be statistically significant even when applied to a random group containing therapeutic failures as well as successes, and while the degree of change is even more marked in some of the presumably highly successful cases, it is still true that the amount of change, compared to the total personality configuration, is small. People do not ordinarily change in overwhelming degree as a result of client-centered therapy. They are still recognizably the same personalities and yet significantly different than before they entered therapy. The change is modest but important. Would other therapies show a greater degree of personality change? Unfortunately, this question cannot be answered at the present time because thus far only client-centered therapists have exposed their work to objective study of outcomes. It is probable, however, that with any therapy it will be found that a modest amount of change in the basic personality is the outcome to be expected.

Characteristic Changes in Behavior

To the man in the street the sixty-four dollar question in regard to any psychotherapy is, "Does it improve the way the person acts?" What the layman wishes to know of any client who has undergone therapy is simply, "Did he stop fighting with his wife?" "Did he get better grades in his courses?" "Is he now getting along satisfactorily in his job?" These are very reasonable questions. It is unfortunate that any attempt to answer them objectively involves us in great complexities. While there is ample clinical evidence that behavior frequently changes during or after therapy, it is difficult to prove that this change resulted from therapy or to show that it represents improvement. Improvement, for one client, may mean a new willingness to differ with his wife, while for another it may mean fewer quarrels with his spouse. For one client improvement may be indicated by the fact that he now gets an A in courses where he formerly received C or D, but another client may show his improvement by a lessened compulsiveness, by taking a B or a C in courses where he formerly received nothing but A. One man may show that he has profited from therapy by a smoother and more adequate adjustment to his job, another by achieving the courage to leave his job for a new field. Clinically each of these behaviors may seem to be clearly an indication of improved adjustment, but there is no doubt that such judgments are subjective and hence open to question.

How then are we to approach this question of the behavioral changes which accompany therapy? A group of research studies which have been made in client-centered therapy fall far short of answering all our questions, but they at least represent a start toward an objective answer. We shall present these in sequential order as they increasingly approach the goal of externally verified evidence of behavioral change in the direction of improved adjustment. The summarized finding will first be stated and then some amplification will follow.

> 1) During the latter part of therapy the client's conversation includes an increased discussion of plans and behavioral steps to be undertaken, and discussion of the outcomes of these steps.

Snyder (197), Seeman (180), and Strom (204) have shown that in the last two-fifths of the counseling process there is a rather sharp increase in material of this sort, though it never forms more than a small portion (5 to 12 per cent) of the conversation. It might be said that these studies indicate that the client plans to change his behavior and discusses ways in which he has changed it. Such evidence is, however, entirely from the client's point of view.

> 2) In successful client-centered therapy, an examination of all references to current behavior indicates that there is a change from relatively immature behavior to relatively mature behavior during the course of the interviews.

In a small study which deserves expansion and repetition, Hoffman (86) extracted from the interviews in ten cases all references to current and recent behavior and to planned behavior. Each of these was typed on a separate card and rated for maturity of behavior by a judge who did not know the case, the outcome, or the interview from which the statement had been taken. The scale was a simple three-point scale, from immature and irresponsible behavior to mature behavior. For the ten cases as a whole there was an increase in the maturity of reported behavior, so determined, but this increase was not statistically significant. The ten cases were then divided into the five more successful and the five less successful, using as criteria the combined results of four other objective methods of analysis. When this was done, it was found that the more successful cases showed a statistically significant increase in the maturity of reported behavior, but the less successful cases showed little change. This finding appeared to substantiate clinical thinking, that the more successful the interviews appear to be, the greater the change in the direction of maturity of behavior.

3) In successful client-centered therapy there is a decrease in psychological tension as evidenced in the client's verbal productions.

Several studies (11, 99, 175, 228) have made use of the Discomfort-Relief quotient devised by Dollard and Mowrer (51) as a measure of the degree of psychological tension existing in the client. This device is based upon the ratio of words expressing discomfort and tension to words expressive of comfort, satisfaction, and enjoyment. In these studies it has been consistently found that verbal behavior indicative of psychological tension has decreased throughout the course of the interviews. In a small study by N. Rogers (175) it was found that this decrease was much sharper in a case judged by several objective criteria as successful, than in cases similarly judged to be moderately successful or unsuccessful. In the successful case the Discomfort-Relief quotient decreased from 1.00 to .12 in nine interviews. In the moderately successful case the decrease was from .83 to .62 in

seven interviews. In the unsuccessful case there was an increase
from .90 to .95 in three interviews.

Interesting as these results are, they fall short in several ways
of what we should like to know. The verbal indicators of tension
are measured only in the counseling interview, not in the verbalizations which occur outside the interview. Also there might be
some question as to whether absence of psychological discomfort
or tension is synonymous with adjustment.

> 4) In successful client-centered therapy there appears to be a
> decrease in current defensive behaviors and a greater
> awareness of those defensive behaviors which are present.

Hogan (87) has made a significant theoretical contribution to
the definition of defensiveness. He sees defensiveness as a form
of behavior which follows upon the perception of threat to the
configuration of the self. We shall consider his thinking at
greater length when we take up the subject of a theory of personality. At this point it is necessary only to mention that his work
provided the operational definitions of several types of defensive
behavior for use in an objective study made by Haigh (76). This
study, based on ten cases, is complex, and not too clear-cut in its
findings. Much additional work needs to be done in this field before we can state with assurance the changes which occur in defensive behavior. Within the limitations of this first study, however, it may be said that in the group of cases in which defensive
behavior decreases (a group which includes the cases judged most
successful by other criteria) a significant pattern of change occurs.
The decrease in defensiveness is noted in a decrease in defensive
behavior as it is reported in the interviews, but also, and perhaps
more significantly, as it is *exhibited* in the interviews. Along with
these changes is an increase in the degree to which the client is
aware of his defensiveness. Such changes are not characteristic of
the group of cases, presumably less successful, in which defensiveness increased.

Haigh's study is significant not only for thus indicating that a
behavioral change takes place in some instances in the direction
of lessened defensiveness. His study also indicated that in at

least one client defensive behavior actually increased — an indication of negative progress — even though some of the other
measures of process — insights, attitudes toward self, reported
behavior — show a positive direction. Careful study of this
contradiction has, we feel, enriched the general theory which will
be stated at the conclusion of this chapter.

Limiting our consideration for the moment to the process which
occurs when therapy is effective, we may say that the work of
Hogan and Haigh suggests that defensive behaviors — the self-
protecting distortions of reality and the behaviors which are in
accord with those distortions — decrease in therapy. They are
not exhibited so frequently, they are not reported so frequently,
and the client is more aware of them as defensive when he is
reporting or exhibiting them.

5) As a result of therapy the client shows an increased
tolerance for frustration as objectively measured in physiological terms.

The hypothesis investigated by Thetford (213), in a new type
of study, was as follows: "If therapy enables an individual to re-
orient his life pattern, or at least to reduce the tension and anxiety
he feels regarding his personal problems, the manner in which he
responds to a stress situation, as indicated by measurements of his
autonomic nervous system, should be significantly altered by this
therapy." This was the first attempt to answer the question,
Does client-centered therapy affect the client deeply enough so
that it alters his physiological functioning? Specifically, does it
produce changes in the functioning of his autonomic nervous system when he is faced by situations involving frustration? Thetford's study was simple and sound in its experimental design.
Nineteen individuals who were about to undergo individual or
group therapy (or both) were subjected to a standardized situation
of frustration involving failure in repetition of digits. Previous to,
while undergoing, and immediately after this frustration, various
physiological measurements were taken on the Behavior Research
Photopolygraph designed by Darrow. Shortly after this experi-

mental frustration these clients began their therapeutic interviews. At the conclusion of the series of therapeutic contacts they were again subjected to the experimental frustration and the same type of measurements taken again. Meanwhile a control group of seventeen individuals was subjected to the frustration experience in the same way, and this was repeated after a length of time comparable to that of the experimental group.

In a "recovery quotient" and the "reaction-recovery quotient," both measures based upon the galvanic skin response, and both indicative of the rapidity with which the individual recovers his previous state of physiological balance, the experimental group showed a significant difference from the controls. An index of the variation in heart rate also discriminated significantly between the two groups. In other physiological measurements the differences were not statistically significant, but were consistent in their direction. In general, the group which had undergone therapy developed a higher frustration threshold during their series of therapeutic interviews, and a more rapid recovery of homeostatic balance following frustration. These results were not found in the control group. Thetford concludes, "The findings of this study would seem to be consistent with the theory that the organism is able to discharge more rapidly and completely the effects of experimentally induced frustration as a result of therapy."

In simpler terms, the significance of this study appears to be that after therapy the individual is able to meet, with more tolerance and less disturbance, situations of emotional stress and frustration; that this description holds, even though the particular frustration or stress was never considered in therapy; that the more effective meeting of frustration is not a surface phenomenon but is evident in autonomic reactions which the individual cannot consciously control and of which he is completely unaware. Here is an indication of a type of behavior change which, if confirmed by future study, is significant indeed.

6) One behavioral outcome of client-centered therapy is improved functioning in life tasks; improvement in reading on

the part of school children, improvement in adjustment to job training and job performance on the part of adults.

Both Bills (24) and Axline (13) have shown that when maladjusted children who are retarded in reading are given even a moderate number of therapeutic sessions handled in a client-centered manner, there is an improvement in the functioning of the child in reading, as measured by standardized tests. In the study conducted by Bills, nine therapy sessions (six individual, three group), in which reading was in no way the focus of the experience, were accompanied by an increase of approximately one year of reading skill during thirty school days' time. This was in a group of eight children who showed marked retardation in reading ability as compared with their rating on an intelligence test.

Perhaps the study which comes closest to a direct attack on the question raised by the man in the street, is one conducted by the Veterans Administration (18). As a part of the Personal Counseling program of the Veterans Administration, a follow-up study was made of 393 cases handled by the Personal Counselors. Six months or more after referral to the Personal Counselor, each veteran was rated by his training officer as to whether he had shown any improvement in his adjustment to his training program or to his job (or to both). The training officer had no knowledge of what had gone on in the counseling. Of the total group, 17 per cent were rated as having shown no improvement, 42 per cent as showing some improvement, and 41 per cent as much improved. While this finding seems significant, the study is a rather crude one, and the possibility of some general bias on the part of training officers for or against the counseling program is not ruled out. One of the subsidiary findings is therefore of interest. It was found that when the ratings were compared with the number of interviews with the counselor, there was a definite relationship. The training officers did not have information as to the number of times the veteran had seen his counselor. Yet forty-eight men who had seen the counselor ten times or more were almost all rated as having shown improvement, while those

Table II · Relation of Job Adjustment to Duration of Counseling *

Number	Duration of Counseling	Rating by Training Officers as to Degree of Improvement		
		None	Some	Much
148	Two interviews or less	28%	44%	28%
140	Three to five interviews	12%	43%	45%
57	Six to nine interviews	10%	44%	46%
48	Ten interviews or more	2%	31%	67%
393	Total	17%	42%	41%

* Calculated from (18), Table III, p. 4.

who had seen the counselor two times or less were much less frequently rated as showing improvement. This finding gives more weight to the general conclusions, since it indicates that with regard to a factor on which the raters could not have been biased, their ratings show a consistent trend in accord with logical expectancies. The data on this point are given in Table II.

What, then, is the current answer to the question, Does the process of client-centered therapy involve any change in the behavior and actions of the client? Pulling together the threads from these various studies, we may say that, during the process of client-centered therapy, the evidence at present available suggests that the client's behavior changes in these ways: he considers, and reports putting into effect, behavior which is more mature, self-directing, and responsible than the behavior he has shown heretofore; his behavior becomes less defensive, more firmly based on an objective view of self and reality; his behavior shows a decreasing amount of psychological tension; he tends to make a more comfortable and more effective adjustment to school and to job; he meets new stress situations with an increased degree of inner calm, a calm which is reflected in less physiological upset and more rapid physiological recovery from these frustrating situations than would have been true if they had occurred prior to therapy.

SOME GAPS AND WEAKNESSES IN OUR KNOWLEDGE

We have completed our summarization of the factual knowledge and the clinical hypotheses which are available at the present time to describe the process of client-centered therapy. To the clinically minded reader the description may seem too static, lacking in the dynamic and moving quality which accompanies the experience of therapy. To the research minded, it may seem too loose, based on studies which are somewhat crude, which are lacking in the methodological elegance which is possible in other fields. Both these criticisms seem to be justifiable. The first we hope to remedy to some degree in our statement of a theory of therapy, supplying something of the dynamic element which is evident in these changes. The second criticism we hope that time will answer, as increasingly exact methods become possible. We should also like, in support of our efforts thus far, to fall back on Elton Mayo's statement: "It is much easier to measure non-significant factors than to be content with developing a first approximation to the significant."

But serious weaknesses should be pointed out in the material already given. One of these has been suggested but needs to be brought out more clearly. The work done by Hogan and Haigh on the problem of defensive behavior has made it appear that some of the changes we have described may accompany an increase in defensiveness as well as real therapeutic progress. Thus it would seem, if their work is further confirmed, that an increase in positive attitudes, including positive attitudes toward the self, increased acceptance of self, an increased number of statements categorized as insight, a trend in the direction of maturity in reported behavior, may all be indicators *either* of an increase in defensiveness *or* of therapeutic progress in which defensiveness decreases. This poses a perplexing problem, and casts a certain amount of doubt upon a number of the measures which have been developed, as long as they stand alone. Thus far, the discrepancy should be stated only as a problem, since the measure of defensive behavior is complex, hard to apply, and involves more subjective clinical judgment in its application than the other measures. Nevertheless, the one case in which this contradiction occurs is the first instance in which any of the measures which have been devised to gauge therapeutic progress have shown clearly discrepant results. Prior to the findings of Haigh, the outstanding element in our research had been the surprising unity of our measures. If one instrument showed, in a particular case, a strong trend, it could be predicted with a good deal of certainty that other measures would indicate the same trend. Thus Raskin (156) found intercorrelations of from .39 to .86 between four of the measures used. The measure of defensive behavior correlates in general with these other measures, in this case negative correlations indicating concordance in the findings, since defensive behaviors are expected to decrease while the other measures increase. The obtained correlations with the other four measures run from −.34 to −.55. Hence in general, the defensiveness measure corroborates the others. It is the fact that in a particular case a strongly marked trend toward insight, self-acceptance, and greater maturity of reported behavior may accompany a greater amount of defensiveness — this is the element that is puzzling and disturbing, demanding further study.[1]

Another prominent weakness in the work done to date is our inability to profit in a research way from our failures. Like every other therapeutic orientation, we have all gradations of outcomes. There are individuals who have clearly undergone a significant reorganization of personality in therapy, who have

[1] Since the above was written, new facts emerge to further complicate the picture. Much of this questioning was based on the fact that in one recorded case all the measures except defensiveness showed the client making clear-cut progress, but defensiveness equally clearly increased. Now, however, a recorded follow-up interview with the client one year after the completion of therapy, and follow-up tests given at the same time, indicate with equal clarity that there has been real and lasting gain. The client shows surprising progress in her inner adjustment to her feminine role, and greater freedom in being herself. She also gives much evidence indicating better adjustment to her family, to boy friends, to social life, and to her work. Everyone who has read the interview regards it as a definitely successful outcome.

What is the explanation? Was the defensiveness measure inaccurate? Or did defensiveness increase during therapy, and dissolve later? There is obviously much room for further research on this point.

shown continuing improvement and reintegration following therapy, and give every indication that the direction of their change is permanent. At the other end of the scale are those who have seemed unable to profit from the therapeutic contacts, and who are perhaps more tense as a result of this discouraging attempt to gain help. There are all gradations in between, including some who have made good progress in therapy, but who seem unable to hold the reorganization they have tentatively achieved. It is puzzling that, though we have learned a great deal from the successful outcomes, we have not been able to learn, in any general or significant way, from the clients whom we fail to help.

The primary lack seems to be the absence of any significant hypotheses in regard to our failures. Clinically it is probably true that our most frequent explanation of failure is that the counselor somehow failed to build a therapeutic relationship. But in this area we have as yet few research tools, and are only beginning to develop valid measures of the therapeutic relationship with which to test this hypothesis. Another hypothesis sometimes brought to bear is that perhaps our failures belong to certain classifications of personality diagnosis. Perhaps there are certain types of individuals who cannot be helped by client-centered therapy. There may be truth in this sort of hypothesis, but we have been loath to accept it too readily, because it could so easily lead to stultification. For example, it seems to have been true that counselors have been less successful with those individuals who are aggressively dependent, who insist that the counselor shall take responsibility for their cure. It is almost certain that a research study would corroborate this statement. It would then be possible to sit back in comfort, refusing such cases because they are not particularly suited for client-centered therapy. But suppose — as our better therapists believe — that the reason for our failures in this group lies not in the personality diagnosis, but in the fact that it is much more difficult for the therapist to be deeply accepting of a person who immediately wishes to force responsibility upon him. This type of hypothesis would never be investigated if we simply ruled out certain diagnostic categories as being unlikely to be helped.

This discussion illustrates some of the reasons for our slowness in making research use of our less successful cases. Whether these reasons are adequate or not, the fact remains that only one research study, and that a very disappointing one (195), has been built around an investigation of failure. We have not, thus far, been able to formulate significant hypotheses in regard to lack of success which are testable in the raw material available.

These are, in our judgment, the most serious flaws in our attempts thus far to give a factual and objective picture of the process of therapy. Many criticisms have been made by others, and we regard them as containing truth, but do not see them as serious. It is true that many of our studies have been based on small numbers, that the experimental design of some is open to criticism, that many important issues are as yet untouched, and that some of the research appears to be superficial rather than to deal with the deep and subtle dynamics of therapy. We are aware of such criticisms, and are often in agreement with them. But in a pioneering field some crudity, some lack of elegance, is inevitable; and as long as each year produces better and more refined research, grappling with increasingly significant and subtle issues, we shall not be disturbed about some of these imperfections. The two major flaws cited are, however, matters of concern, because it seems that they might have been avoided had we been able to perceive more deeply and more shrewdly the process which is daily going forward before our eyes in the lives of our clients.

A COHERENT THEORY OF THE PROCESS OF THERAPY

Can we formulate a theory of therapy which will take into account all the observed and verified facts, a theory which can resolve the seeming contradictions that exist? The material which follows is such an attempt, beginning with the personality as it exists before a need for therapy develops, and carrying it through the changes which occur in client-centered therapy. As has been mentioned before, the theory is the fluctuating and evanescent generalization. The observed phenomena of therapy are the more stable elements around which a variety of theories may be built.

Let us begin with the individual who is content with himself, who has no thought at this time of seeking counseling help. We may find it useful to think of this individual as having an organized pattern of perceptions of self and self-in-relationship to others and to the environment. This configuration, this gestalt, is, in its details, a fluid and changing thing, but it is decidedly stable in its basic elements. It is, as Raimy says, "constantly used as a frame of reference when choices are to be made. Thus it serves to regulate behavior and may serve to account for observed uniformities in personality." This configuration is, in general, available to awareness.

We may look upon this self-structure as being an organization of hypotheses for meeting life — an organization which has been relatively effective in satisfying the needs of the organism. Some of its hypotheses may be grossly incorrect from the standpoint of objective reality. As long as the individual has no suspicion of this falsity, the organization may serve him well. As a simple example, the star student in a small-town high school may perceive himself as an outstandingly brilliant person, with a mind excelled by none. This formulation may serve him quite adequately as long as he remains in that environment. He may have some experiences which are inconsistent with this generalization, but he either denies these experiences to awareness, or symbolizes them in such a way that they are consistent with his general picture.

As long as the self-gestalt is firmly organized, and no contradictory material is even dimly perceived, then positive self feelings may exist, the self may be seen as worthy and acceptable, and conscious tension is minimal. Behavior is consistent with the organized hypotheses and concepts of the self-structure. An individual in whom such conditions exist would perceive himself as functioning adequately.

In such a situation, the extent to which the individual's perceptions of his abilities and relationships were incongruent with socially perceived reality would be a measure of his basic vulnerability. The extent to which he dimly perceives these incongruences and discrepancies is a measure of his internal tension, and determines the amount of defensive behavior. As a parenthetical comment, it may be observed that in highly homogeneous cultures, where the self-concept of the individual tends to be supported by his society, rather grossly unrealistic perceptions may exist without causing internal tension, and may serve throughout a lifetime as a reasonably effective hypothesis for meeting life. Thus the slave may perceive himself as less worthy than his master, and live by this perception, even though, judged on a reality basis, it may be false. But in our modern culture, with its conflicting subcultures, and its contradictory sets of values, goals, and perceptions, the individual tends to be exposed to a realization of discrepancies in his perceptions. Thus internal conflict is multiplied.

To return to our individual, who is not yet ready for therapy: It is when his organized self-structure is no longer effective in meeting his needs in the reality situation, or when he dimly perceives discrepancies in himself, or when his behavior seems out of control and no longer consistent with himself, that he becomes "ripe," as it were, for therapy. As examples of these three conditions, we might mention the "brilliant" small-town high school student who no longer finds himself effective in the university, the individual who is perplexed because he wants to marry the girl yet does not want to, and the client who finds that her behavior is unpredictable, "not like myself," no longer understandable. Without a therapeutic experience, planned or accidental, such conditions are likely to persist because each of them involves the perception of experiences which are contradictory to the current organization of the self. But such perception is threatening to the structure of the self and consequently tends to be denied or distorted, to be inadequately symbolized.

But let us suppose that our individual, now vaguely or keenly disturbed and experiencing some internal tension, enters a relationship with a therapist who is client-centered in his orientation. Gradually he experiences a freedom from threat which is decidedly new to him. It is not merely that he is free from attack. This has been true of a number of his relationships. It is that every aspect of self which he exposes is equally accepted, equally valued. His almost belligerent statement of his virtues is accepted as much as, but no more than, his discouraged picture of his negative qualities. His certainty about some aspects of himself is accepted and valued, but so are his uncertainties, his doubts, his vague perception of contradictions within himself. In this atmosphere of safety, protection, and acceptance, the firm boundaries of self-organization relax. There is no longer the firm, tight gestalt which is characteristic of every organization under threat, but a looser, more uncertain configuration. He begins to explore his perceptual field more and more fully. He discovers faulty generalizations, but his self-structure is now sufficiently relaxed so that he can consider the complex and contradictory experiences upon which they are based. He discovers experiences of which he has never been aware, which are deeply contradictory to the perception he has had of himself, and this is threatening indeed. He retreats temporarily to the former comfortable gestalt, but then slowly and cautiously moves out to assimilate this contradictory experience into a new and revised pattern.

Essentially this is a process of disorganization and reorganization, and while it is going on it may be decidedly painful. It is deeply confusing not to have a firm concept of self by which to determine behavior appropriate to the situation. It is frightening or disgusting to find self and behavior fluctuating almost from day to day, at times being largely in accord with the earlier self-pattern, at times being in confused accord with some new, vaguely structured gestalt. As the process continues, a new or revised configuration of self is being constructed. It contains perceptions which were previously denied. It involves more accurate symbolization of a much wider range of sensory and visceral experience. It involves a reorganization of values, with the organism's own experience clearly recognized as providing the evidence for the valuations. There slowly begins to emerge a new self, which to the client seems to be much more his "real" self, because it is based to a much greater extent upon all of his experience, perceived without distortion.

This painful dis- and re-organization is made possible by two elements in the therapeutic relationship. The first is the one already mentioned, that the new, the tentative, the contradictory, or the previously denied perceptions of self are as much valued by the therapist as the rigidly structured aspects. Thus the shift from the latter to the former becomes possible without too disastrous a loss of self worth, nor with too frightening a leap from the old to the new. The other element in the relationship is the attitude of the therapist toward the newly discovered aspects of experience. To the client they seem threatening, bad, impossible, disorganizing. Yet he experiences the therapist's attitude of calm acceptance toward them. He finds that to a degree he can introject this attitude and can look upon his experience as something he can own, identify, symbolize, and accept as a part of himself.

If the relationship is not adequate to provide this sense of safety, or if the denied experiences are too threatening, then the client may revise his concept of self in a defensive fashion. He may further distort the symbolization of experience, may make more rigid the structure of self, and thus achieve again positive self-feelings and a somewhat reduced internal tension — but at a price of increased vulnerability. Undoubtedly this is a temporary phenomenon in many clients who are undergoing considerable reorganization, but the evidence suggests the possibility that an occasional client may conclude his contacts at such a juncture, having achieved only an increasingly defensive self.

Where the client does face more of the totality of his experience, and where he adequately differentiates and symbolizes this experience, then as the new self-structure is organized, it becomes firmer, more clearly defined, a steadier, more stable guide to behavior. As in the state in which the person felt no need of therapy, or in the defensive reorganization of self, positive self-feelings return, and positive attitudes predominate over negative. Many of the outward manifestations are the same. From an external point of view the important difference is that the new self is much more nearly congruent with the totality of experience — that it is a pattern drawn from or perceived in experience, rather than a pattern imposed upon experience. From the client's internal point of view, the new self is a more comfortable one. Fewer experiences are perceived as vaguely threatening. There is consequently much less anxiety. There is more assurance in living by the new self, because it involves fewer shaky high-level generalizations, and more of direct experience. Because the values are perceived as originating in self, the value system becomes more realistic and comfortable and more nearly in harmony with the perceived self. Valued goals appear more achievable.

The changes in behavior keep pace with the changes in organization of self, and this behavior change is, surprisingly enough, neither as painful nor as difficult as the changes in self-structure. Behavior continues to be consistent with the concept of self, and alters as it alters. Any behavior which formerly seemed out of control is now experienced as part of self, and within the boundaries of conscious control. In general, the behavior is more adjustive and socially more sound, because the hypotheses upon which it is based are more realistic.

Thus therapy produces a change in personality organization and structure, and a change in behavior, both of which are relatively permanent. It is not necessarily a reorganization which will serve for a lifetime. It may still deny to awareness certain aspects of experience, may still exhibit certain patterns of defensive behavior. There is little likelihood that any therapy is in this sense complete. Under new stresses of a certain sort, the client may find it necessary to seek further therapy, to achieve further reorganization of self. But whether there be one or more series of therapeutic interviews, the essential outcome is a more broadly based structure of self, an inclusion of a greater proportion of experience as a part of self, and a more comfortable and realistic adjustment to life.

Underlying this entire process of functioning and of change are the forward-moving forces of life itself. It is this basic tendency toward the maintenance and enhancement of the organism and of the self which provides the motive force for all that we have been describing. In the service of this basic tendency the pretherapy self operates to meet needs. And because of this deeper force the individual in therapy tends to move toward reorganization, rather than toward disintegration. It is a characteristic of the reformulated self which is achieved in therapy that it permits a fuller realization of the organism's potentialities, and that it is a more effective basis for further growth. Thus the therapeutic process is, in its totality, the achievement by the individual, in a favorable psychological climate, of further steps in a direction which has already been set by his growth and maturational development from the time of conception onward.

SUGGESTED READINGS

Readings related to this chapter may be divided into two groups — those concerned with giving a clinical account of the process of therapy, and those which exemplify the objective investigation of this process.

In the former group Snygg and Combs (200, Chapters 13 and 14) give a fresh statement of the processes involved in inductive or "directive" therapy, and also a theory of the process of client-centered or "self-directive" therapy. Their theory is strictly phenomenological. If the reader wishes to dip into the past, he may compare the present chapter with Chapters 6, 7, and 8 of *Counseling and Psychotherapy* (166). For comparative purposes, the reader may wish to view the process of psychoanalysis. A brief account of the process is contained in a chapter by Ivimey (89, pp. 211–234). A longer account, which stresses the activity of the analyst rather more than the process, is contained in Alexander and French (4, Chapters 1–8).

Nearly all the objective research regarding the process of therapy has been related to the client-centered point of view, and much of it has been cited in this chapter. If one wishes to gain a historical perspective on it, the rather crude but pioneering study by Lewis (114) or the somewhat better designed study by Snyder (197) would exemplify the early period. Curran's research (49), though it has faults, focuses more than any other on the process itself. The best published account of measured personality outcomes is that by Muench (140). For a cross section of recent research, see the June, 1949, issue of the *Journal of Consulting Psychology;* the entire issue is devoted to a coordinated research in therapy, and contains brief accounts of the investigations by Seeman (180), Sheerer (189), Stock (203), Haigh (76), Hoffman (86), Carr (40), and Raskin (156).

Chapter 5 · Three Questions Raised by Other Viewpoints:

Transference, Diagnosis, Applicability

This chapter is written in the hope of improving communication between various therapies. It has been our experience that sincere therapists of other therapeutic orientations have often been interested in learning something of the client-centered approach. As a means of learning about it, they inquire about the viewpoint of the client-centered therapist on certain concepts and issues which are of central importance in their own thinking. And since the answers they receive sometimes seem to make no sense in these other frames of reference, they quite naturally conclude that the client-centered viewpoint must be stupid, shallow, or irresponsible to have given such answers, and hence not even worth investigating.

It is to try to bridge this communication gap that the present chapter is written. It may be said that the issues discussed in this chapter are in no way *special* issues from the point of view of client-centered therapy, and would need no special treatment from the point of view of the person learning this approach. They are special issues for therapists whose training has been in other orientations.

Three of the questions most frequently asked, to which the answers must seem absurd, are: "How do you handle the problem of transference?" "In what way does your therapy build upon diagnosis?" and "In what types of situations is client-centered therapy applicable?"   When the answers are: "Transference, as a problem, doesn't arise," "Diagnosis is regarded as unnecessary," "Perhaps client-centered therapy applies to all cases," then there is likely to be a rise in blood pressure in the questioner but little further communication of meanings. Perhaps if each one of these questions is taken up in some detail a better understanding may ensue.

THE PROBLEM OF TRANSFERENCE

The Meaning of Transference

To the therapist with a psychoanalytic orientation the concepts of transference, of the transference relationship, and of the transference neurosis have acquired a host of significant meanings. They are close to the core of his therapeutic thinking.

It is not easy for me to put myself into the frame of reference of the analyst, and to understand fully the meaning these concepts have for him. But in so far as I can understand, I would gather that transference is a term which is applied to attitudes transferred to the therapist which were originally directed, with more justification, toward a parent or other person. These attitudes of love, hate, dependence, and so on, are utilized by the analyst as an immediate expression of the client's basic attitudes and conflicts, and it is through the analysis of these attitudes that the most significant part of the psychoanalysis takes place. For this reason, the method of dealing with the transference attitudes is the most important part of the analyst's work. Fenichel states, "Understanding the contents of the patient's unconscious from his utterances is, relatively, the simplest part of the analyst's task. Handling the transference is the most difficult." (56, p. 29)

To check on the accuracy of our understanding of the concept of transference and of its handling, several brief quotations from authoritative psychoanalytic references may be examined. Freud gives a very clear summary in his article in the *Britannica:*

> By "transference" is meant a striking peculiarity of neurotics. They develop toward their physician emotional relations, both of an affectionate and hostile character, which are not based upon the

actual situation but are derived from their relations toward their parents (the Oedipus complex). Transference is a proof of the fact that adults have not overcome their former childish dependence; it coincides with the force which has been named "suggestion"; and it is only by learning to make use of it that the physician is enabled to induce the patient to overcome his internal resistances and do away with his repressions. Thus psychoanalytic treatment acts as a second education of the adult, as a correction to his education as a child. (66, p. 674)

Here is a succinct account of the meaning of transference and of the analyst's purpose in using it.

Fenichel describes the analyst's methods in dealing with transference attitudes:

The analyst's reaction to transference is the same as to any other attitude of the patient: he interprets. He sees in the patient's attitude a derivative of unconscious impulses and tries to show this to the patient. (56, p. 30)

Systematic and consistent interpretative work, both within and without the framework of transference, can be described as educating the patient to produce continually less distorted derivatives until his fundamental instinctual conflicts are recognizable. (56, p. 31)

Transference Attitudes in Client-Centered Therapy

As we examine our clinical experience in client-centered therapy and our recorded cases, it would appear to be correct to say that *strong* attitudes of a transference nature occur in a relatively small minority of cases, but that such attitudes occur in *some* degree in the majority of cases.

With many clients the attitudes toward the counselor are mild, and of a reality, rather than a transference, nature. Thus such a client may feel somewhat apprehensive about first meeting the counselor; may feel annoyed in early interviews that he does not receive the guidance he expected; may feel a warm rapport with the counselor as he works through his own attitudes; leaves therapy with a gratitude to the counselor for having provided him the opportunity to work things out for himself, but not with a dependent or strong gratitude; and can meet the counselor socially or professionally during or after therapy with little affect beyond what is normally involved in the immediate reality of their relationship. This would seem to describe for many, perhaps for a majority of our clients, the affect which is directed toward the counselor. If one's definition of transference includes all affect toward others, then this is transference; if the definition being used is the transfer of infantile attitudes to a present relationship in which they are inappropriate, then very little if any transference is present.

There are many cases, however, in which clients have much stronger emotionalized attitudes directed toward the counselor. There may be a desire for dependence upon the counselor, accompanied by deep affect; there may be fear of the counselor, which is similar to fears felt toward any authority, and which is no doubt genetically related to fear of parents; there are attitudes of hostility which go beyond the attitudes which an observer would judge to be realistically related to the experience; there are, in some instances, expressions of affection, and desire for a love relationship between client and counselor.

In general, then, we may say that transference *attitudes* exist in varying degrees in a considerable portion of cases handled by client-centered therapists. In this respect all therapists would be alike, for all would meet such attitudes. It is in what happens to them that the difference arises. In psychoanalysis these attitudes appear characteristically to develop into a *relationship* which is central to the therapy. Freud describes it in these terms:

> In every analytic treatment there arises . . . an intense emotional relationship between the patient and the analyst. . . . It can be of a positive or of a negative character and can vary between the extremes of a passionate, completely sensual love and the unbridled expression of an embittered defiance and hatred. This transference . . . soon replaces in the patient's mind the desire to be cured, and, so long as it is affectionate and moderate, becomes the agent of the physician's influence and neither more nor less than the mainspring of the joint work of analysis. . . . [If] converted into hostility . . . it may then happen that it will paralyze the patient's power of associating and endanger the success of the treatment. Yet it would be senseless to

try to evade it; for an analysis without transference is an impossibility. (64, p. 75)

In client-centered therapy, however, this involved and persistent dependent transference relationship does not tend to develop. Thousands of clients have been dealt with by counselors with whom the writer has had personal contact. In only a small minority of cases handled in a client-centered fashion has the client developed a relationship which could in any way be matched to Freud's terms. In most instances the description of the relationship would be quite different.

The Handling of Transference Attitudes in Client-Centered Therapy

It is this possibility of therapy without a deep transference relationship which deserves close attention. The possibility of effective brief psychotherapy seems to hinge on the possibility of therapy without the transference relationship, since the resolution of the transference situation appears to be uniformly slow and time-consuming. Can therapy then be carried on without having such a relationship develop?

Perhaps some elements of the answer to this problem may be clearer if we examine some of the verbatim interview material. The basic question is this: Though transference attitudes exist in many clients in nondirective therapy, how is it that these do not develop into a transference relationship or transference neurosis, and that therapy does not appear to require that such a relationship should develop?

If we take one of the minority of cases in which definite transference attitudes are experienced and discussed by the client, we may see something of what occurs. The following is transcribed from the electrically recorded beginning of a fifth interview with a young married woman, Mrs. Dar. In the previous interviews she had brought out material about which she felt quite guilty.

S: Well, I have had a very curious dream. I almost hated to think about coming back again, after the dream. Uh....

C: You say you almost thought about not coming back again after the dream?

S: M-hm. (*Laughs.*)

C: It was almost too much for you.

S: Yeah. Well, uh, last Friday night I dreamt that, uh, I went to New York to see you, and you were *terribly* busy, and were running in and out of offices, and you had so much to do, and finally I looked at you pleadingly and you said to me, "I'm sorry. I haven't got any more time for you. Your story is much too sordid. I — I just can't be bothered." And you kept running in and out of rooms, and I kept sort of following you around. I didn't, uh, know what to do, and I felt very helpless, and at the same time I felt very much ashamed, and shocked by the fact that you said what you did.

C: M-hm.

S: And it's — it's stayed with me ever since then.

C: That had a good deal of reality.

S: Yes.

C: You sort of felt that somehow I was judging your situation to be pretty, pretty bad.

S: That's right. That you were — I was up for trial, and you were the judge, and — (*Pause.*)

C: The verdict was guilty.

S: (*Laughs.*) I think that's it. (*Laughs.*) That's it all right. I didn't see how I could come back into the situation. I mean the circumstances, you already judged me, and therefore I didn't really see how I could possibly talk any more.

C: M-hm.

S: Except about other things. And uh, it hasn't left me. I've been thinking about it a great deal.

C: You almost felt that you *were* being judged.

S: Well, why should I feel that? Uh — well, of course I probably transferred my own thoughts into your mind, and therefore I, uh, there was no doubt about it. It just couldn't be changed. It was *the* verdict. I suppose in my own way I was judging myself.

C: M-hm. You feel that perhaps *you* were the judge, really.

Here is a clear instance of a transference attitude. The counselor had neither stated any evaluation of the client's behavior in previous interviews, nor had he felt evaluative toward the client's behavior. Yet the client projects onto the therapist attitudes of negative judgment, and reacts with fear and shame to those projected accusations of guilt.

The therapist handles these just as he would handle similar attitudes directed toward others. To paraphrase and modify Fenichel's sentence to make it true of this approach, one might say: "The client-centered therapist's reaction to transference is the same as to any other attitude of the client: he endeavors to understand and accept." As is evident in this fragment, acceptance leads to recognition by the client that these feelings are within her, they are not in the therapist.

Why is this accomplished so quickly and so readily? It would appear that one reason is that the therapist has so completely put aside the self of ordinary interaction that there is no shred of evidence upon which to base the projection. For four interviews this woman has experienced understanding and acceptance — and nothing else. There has been no evidence that the therapist is trying to "size her up," diagnose her, evaluate her scientifically, judge her morally. There is no evidence that he approves or disapproves of anything she does — of her behavior, present or past, of the topics she chooses to discuss, of the way she presents them, of her inability to express herself, of her silences, of the interpretations she gives to her own behavior. Consequently when she feels that the therapist is passing a moral judgment upon her, and when this feeling too is accepted, there is nothing upon which this projection can hang. It *must* be recognized as coming from herself, since every evidence of her senses makes it plain that it does not come from the therapist, and the complete lack of immediate threat in the situation makes it unnecessary to insist upon the feeling in defiance of the evidence of her senses. Thus, in a few moments she goes from the clear transference attitude, "I feel badly because you think I am sordid," to the feeling, "I am passing judgment on myself, and attempting to transfer those thoughts to your mind."

A Further Example

Perhaps two excerpts from another case will lend some weight to this type of explanation. This is another young married woman, Mrs. Ett, who is experiencing conflict in many areas of her life, and the material which follows is transcribed from the recording of the tenth interview. The first several moments of the interview are given.

C417 (*in friendly tone*): Well, what today?

S417: Ah, am I supposed to tell you everything (*laugh*) or is that up to the person?

C418: That certainly is up to you, anything you feel you want to talk about you are certainly free to talk —

S418: Well, when I say that —

C419: We don't probe into anything unless you want to talk about it.

S419: Well, I do want to talk it over, or else perhaps I wouldn't have asked the question. In regard to this, I had a big fight before I came here, I really got very angry and I was just beating you down, you know. Ah, and then of course by the time I got here I rationalized it to the extent where I think I can understand why I was so angry at you. First of all, would you like to know why I was so angry? Ah, I was angry in that I thought this whole thing is a fraud. I mean, now I'm being very frank. I think that — at least I thought then, that this idea of coming here and talking and talking is not so terrific when you consider that you can always do that almost anywhere if you really take the time or trouble to get somebody who will listen to you.

C420: It seemed like it was kind of a cheat, and something that you could get anywhere.

S420: Yes. My idea in telling this is not a personal unfriendliness, but rather because I'm trying to work these things out myself. (*C:* M-hm.) I have no grievances against you.

C421: It was a very real feeling in yourself and that's why you wanted to bring it out.

S421: Yes, yes. I mean it will clear up for me, why I'm coming, or, you know. I have a feeling that this sort of thing is not too much different from the sort of thing that is very common in many places. They advertise, you've heard about it haven't you, people advertise and say that for a dollar per hour, or two dollars, they will sit and listen to you.

C422: Just listen to your troubles.

S422: You come there, of course I've never had that experience, but I imagine this is what happens, you come there and sit down and you talk and you talk to the person, and the person sits with you and makes the necessary noises of listening and approval, and, ah, never comments, of course, so that when your time is up you walk out and you pay them the two dollars. Well, certainly the person who is sitting and doing the listening doesn't have the extensive background and education that you have or those connected with this field. They haven't made the constant research, and yet they do the very same thing with success, it would seem to me, because it's exactly the very same thing. In other words, I feel you are wasting your time, because you have spent so much time and effort, I know you have, in reaching to the stage where you are, and you see, I'm telling you about it with the feeling that it isn't doing me any good. But after I talked it out with myself and called you all sorts of names (*C:* M-hm.) when I walked up the steps here, it occurred to me that the reason for not wanting this and not accepting this is tied up with the same feeling of nervousness and fluttering everytime I come here. I don't know why, but I always get very jittery. (*Pause.*) I know why, it's because I'm facing something that I don't like to face. Talking things out myself.

C423: M-hm. So that the feelings that you had about the fact that, after all, why a person with any professional training just listens and so on, and the feelings you had about this being sort of a fraud, you recognize them as being in part perhaps connected with your own irritation and fear at having to face things within yourself.

S423: That's right. And that is the logical feeling. Certainly if I thought this were a fraud — I mean, the — to use that type of word, I wouldn't come here because I'm very suspicious, I'm a very suspicious person and I don't usually go into things unless I look at it from all sorts of angles, so the very fact that I'm coming here probably means that it isn't a fraud (*laugh*) as far as I'm concerned, you see.

C424: At least it means that your feelings are definitely mixed. I mean, if you were pretty sure this was a fraud, you wouldn't be coming.

S424: Yes. That's right.

Note how clearly the dynamics follows the pattern of the previous excerpt. The client is angry at the counselor because he does nothing but "sit and listen." But here, too, there appears to be no adequate reality basis for the anger, and so she must of necessity look for the reason in herself. She finds the reason for it, and the reason for her jitteriness in entering the interviews — "I know why, it's because I'm facing something that I don't like to face."

The adequacy of this type of explanation is further verified in an excerpt from the twelfth interview with the same client, where she tries to put into words the meaning the relationship has had for her. She seems to state in articulate terms what many clients have described less clearly.

S540: By the way, there's something I meant to ask you all the time. You sit here and listen to me and listen to my troubles which after all aren't so important, what are your reactions to everybody that comes in and sits and tells their whole story to you? Do you live it through with them, or are you just a good listening post? Or is that something I shouldn't ask?

C540: [1] It's a question that is awfully hard to answer. We've discussed that a lot among ourselves. It's more than just listening like a post, that's very certain (*S:* Well, certainly.) and it's also something short of, uh, suffering right with the person, I mean ——

S541: Well, my problems, for instance, and they are given to somebody to type, and of course assuming that you pull out all identification, uh — well, I don't know, when it comes to the question it really doesn't matter, actually. It really doesn't matter, I don't know why I even posed a question like that. You can take it off the record. Uh, my feelings toward you are very, not peculiar, but interesting. After all, I've told you more than I've told anybody, and generally when you tell somebody something very personal — you begin to sort of dislike the person afterwards because you think perhaps they know too much about you and you are fearful of them. I know that to be the case. Well, I haven't that feeling of you at all. I mean, you are — it's almost impersonal. I like you, of course I don't know why I should like you or why I shouldn't like you. It's a peculiar thing. I've never had that relationship with anybody before and I've often thought about it.

C541: It's really something quite different than most relationships.

S542: Oh, yes, and yet my — I couldn't say our — because certainly you haven't given me anything, so that it would be ours — but *my* relationship with you is fascinating. I enjoy it because it's so purely, uh, well, impersonal, asexual, everything that's on an even keel. You're like a life buoy.

C542: There's more constancy, somehow.

S543: Oh, yes, and I enjoy being with you this three quarters of an hour and I walk out and I also think of you, I have no curiosity. Oh,

---

[1] The client has asked a straightforward question which the counselor can answer without implying any type of judgment upon the client, and without in any way suggesting how she ought to think or behave. So he leaves the client's internal frame of reference momentarily and answers it.

yes, I do have some curiosity about you, about your background, naturally, but not as vital as I would about somebody else, and in that respect, I mean this feeling I have about you seems to validate, or however you pronounce it, uh, this feeling that nondirective therapy is right and is good, or else why would I have this constant, uh, feeling of security. I guess that is what it is, with you. (C: M-hm.) Whereas if it weren't right, why then the vacillations of my mind would make you a terrible figure, so evidently there is something. (C: M-hm.) I had one dream about you, I don't remember what it was. It wasn't important, I don't think — you stood as a symbol of authority, I think. I guess at that time I was trying to think of your approval or disapproval. When I walk out of here, everything — which is the only way I can feel, the only way I can think, many times I walk out and I think, well what did I tell Mr. L. now, because he laughed, and then a lot of times I walk out with a feeling of elation that you think highly of me, and of course at the same time, I have the feeling that, gee, he must think I'm an awful jerk or something like that. But it doesn't really, those feelings aren't so deep that I can form an opinion (C: M-hm.) one way or the other about you.

C543: Would it be that, and here let me ask a question, would it be that, uh, you have no real basis for knowing my opinion about it and therefore possibly it helps you to realize that those attitudes are within yourself and that you fluctuate in regard to them?[1]

S544: That's right. Also, you've managed to establish one thing in my mind. That I cannot come to you for advice because I don't get it, which is good, because then I have a feeling that I'm on my own, and boy, I'm really battling it out. (C: M-hm.) Of course with that feeling I have this terrible feeling of knocking my head against the wall without — there were times when I'd get ——

C544: A little satisfying and a little bit dissatisfying, the feeling ——

S545: Well, yes. 'Cause I need approval so desperately all the time. In everything I do, so that sometimes I get very discouraged to think that I can't get approval from you when I really need it when I'm baring my psyche. But in a way it's disciplinary. I mean it's — it acts as a

---

[1] Lest the reader think "Aha — these client-centered therapists interpret just like everyone else," it might be remarked that this is the first clear-cut interpretation of the twelve interviews. The counselor confesses that he was so interested in the client's perception of the counseling relationship that he wished to see if this interpretation of it would be accepted. It was, but her "That's right" conveys no real knowledge. It is the client's spontaneous description of the relationship which is real evidence of her own perception of the relationship.

discipline so far as I'm concerned, so that I don't confront everybody with approval or disapproval. I feel very secure, very, well as if I was the real me (*laugh*), no pretenses, nothing.

C545: That somehow here you can be the real you.

Note how clearly the client puts into words, in *S543*, the fact that though she is eager to find some evidence of evaluation, or behavior upon which she may project evaluative attitudes, she is unable to "form an opinion one way or the other about you."

The Counselor-Client Relationship

The terms this client uses in describing the relationship are in two respects very similar to the description given by many clients. Two of her terms which would typify these aspects are "impersonal" and "secure."

It is surprising how frequently the client uses the word "impersonal" in describing the therapeutic relationship, after the conclusion of therapy. This is obviously not intended to mean that the relationship was cold or disinterested. It appears to be the client's attempt to describe this unique experience in which the *person* of the counselor — the counselor as an evaluating, reacting person with needs of his own — is so clearly absent. In this sense it is "im"-personal. Mrs. Ett's words, "My — I couldn't say our — . . . but *my* relationship with you is fascinating," illustrates again, and very deeply, the fact that the relationship is experienced as a one-way affair in a very unique sense. The whole relationship is composed of the self of the client, the counselor being depersonalized for purposes of therapy into being "the client's other self." It is this warm willingness on the part of the counselor to lay his own self temporarily aside, in order to enter into the experience of the client, which makes the relationship a completely unique one, unlike anything in the client's previous experience.

The second aspect of the relationship is the security which the client feels. This, very obviously, does not come from approval by the counselor, but from something far deeper — a thoroughly consistent acceptance. It is this absolute assurance that there will be no evaluation, no interpretation, no probing, no *personal* reaction by the counselor, that gradually permits the client to experience the relationship as one in which all defenses can be dispensed with — a relationship in which the client feels, "I can be the real me, no pretenses."

Perhaps the basis of this security may be made more clearly distinct by pointing out some characteristics which it does not possess to contrast with those which it does possess. It is experienced as basically supporting, but it is in no way supportive. The client does not feel that someone is behind him, that someone approves of him. He does experience the fact that here is someone who respects him *as he is*, and who is willing for him to take any direction which he chooses. The security is not a type of "love-relationship" in any of the senses in which this term is ordinarily understood. The client does not feel that the therapist "likes" him, in the usual sense of a biased and favorable judgment, and he is often not sure, as in the excerpt above, whether he likes the therapist: "I don't know why I should like you or why I shouldn't like you." There is simply no evidence upon which such a judgment could be based. But that this is a secure experience, in which the self is deeply respected, that this is an experience in which there need be no fear of threat or attack — not even of the subtlest sort — of this the client gradually becomes sure. And this basic security is not something the client believes because he is told, not something about which he convinces himself logically, it is something he *experiences*, with his own sensory and visceral equipment.

The Disappearance of Transference Attitudes

In this strangely unique experience of security in a relationship with another who understands and respects, what, specifically, happens to the transference attitude? It would seem that what occurs is exactly parallel to all the other unrealistically hostile, fearful, loving attitudes which the client brings out. In this relationship the experience of the client seems to be, "This is the way I have perceived and interpreted reality; but in this relationship, where I have no need of defending this interpretation, I can recognize that there are other sensory evidences which I have not admitted into consciousness, or have admitted but interpreted inaccurately." The client becomes aware of experiences which have not been previously accepted. He also becomes aware of the fact that he is the perceiver and evaluator of experience, a fact which seems to be very close to the heart of therapy. Mrs. Dar recognizes that she has the feeling of judging herself. Mrs. Ett realizes that she is fearful of looking at what she is finding in herself. When these experiences are organized into a meaningful relation to the self, the "transference attitudes" disappear. They are not displaced. They are not sublimated. They are not "re-educated." They simply disappear because experience has been reperceived in a way which makes them meaningless. It is analogous to the way in which one attitude drops out and another entirely different one takes its place when I turn to watch the large plane I have dimly glimpsed out of the corner of my eye, and find it to be a gnat flying by a few inches from my face.

An Extreme Example

Some may still feel that the examples given represent no very marked instances of strong transference attitudes, but only mild ones. Yet there is evidence that even when transference attitudes are most extreme the same principles apply. The excerpts which follow are from interviews with a single woman in her thirties, Miss Tir, a person so deeply disturbed that she would probably have been diagnosed as psychotic in terms of an external evaluation. It should be stressed that attitudes like this would be found very infrequently in a community counseling center. On the other hand, in a psychiatric ward or state hospital they might be more frequent. In the course of the interviews, this woman has wrestled with deep guilt feelings, many of which center around possible incest with her father. She cannot be entirely sure whether the events really occurred or whether they exist only in her own mind. Some brief excerpts may give an inkling of the depth of the transference attitudes, and of the counselor's method of handling. This account is from the counselor's notes, which are unusually complete because the client spoke very slowly. They fall short, however, of the complete accuracy of a recording.

From ninth interview:

S: This morning I hung my coat out there instead of here in your office. I've told you I like you, and I was afraid if you helped me on with the coat, I might turn around and kiss you.

C: You thought those feelings of affection might *make* you kiss me unless you protected yourself from them.

S: Well, another reason I left the coat out there is that I want to be dependent — but I want to show you I don't have to be dependent.

C: You both want to be, and to prove you don't have to be.

(Toward end of interview)

S: I've never told anyone they were the most wonderful person I've ever known, but I've told you that. It's not just sex. It's more than that.

C: You really feel very deeply attached to me.

From tenth interview — toward close of interview:

S: I think emotionally I'm dying for sexual intercourse but I don't do anything about it. . . .[1] The thing I want is to have sexual intercourse with you. I don't dare ask you, 'cause I'm afraid you'd be nondirective.

C: You have this awful tension, and want so much to have relations with me.

S: *(Goes on in this vein. Finally)* Can't we do something about it? This tension is awful! Will you relieve the tension. . . . Can you give me a direct answer? I think it might help both of us.

C (gently): The answer would be no. I can understand how *desperately* you feel, but I would not be willing to do that.[2]

S: *(Pause. Sigh of relief.)* I think that helps me. It's only when I'm upset that I'm like this. You have strength, and it gives me strength.

Twelfth interview:

S: *(Silent for two minutes. Then begins to talk in hard flat voice, quite unlike her usual tone. Does not look at counselor. There was much repetition, but the following excerpts give the major thoughts.)* You feel I want to

---

[1] In these excerpts, a series of dots means that some material from the notes has been omitted.

[2] As in setting any limit in the therapeutic experience, this is something which is purely the responsibility of the therapist, and he takes that responsibility. He does not attempt to evaluate the client's experience by some such statement as "That really wouldn't help you." He simply takes responsibility for his own behavior, at the same time indicating understanding and acceptance of the client's experience of the situation.

come, but I *don't!* I'm not coming any more. It doesn't do any good. I don't like you. I hate you! I wish you never were born.

C: You just hate me very bitterly.[1]

S: I think I'll throw you in the lake. I'll cut you up! You think people like you, but they don't. . . . You think you can attract women, but you *can't.* . . . I wish you were *dead.*

C: You *detest* me and you'd really like to get rid of me.

S: You think my father did bad things with me, but he didn't! You think he wasn't a good man, but he *was.* You think I want intercourse, but I *don't.*

C: You feel I *absolutely misrepresent* all your thoughts.

S: . . . You think you can get people to come in and tell you everything, and they'll think they're being helped, but they're *not!* You just like to make 'em suffer. You think you can hypnotize them, but you *can't!* You think you're good, but you ain't. I hate you, I hate you, I *hate* you!

C: You feel I really like to make 'em suffer, but that I *don't* help them.

S: You think I haven't been straight, but I have. I *hate* you. All I've had is pain, pain, pain. You think I can't direct my own life, but I can. You think I can't get well, but I can. You think I had hallucinations, but I didn't. I hate you. (*Long pause. Leans on desk in strained, exhausted pose.*) You think I'm crazy, but I'm not.

C: You're sure I think you're crazy.

S: (*Pause.*) I'm tied, and I just can't get loose! (*Despairing tone of voice, and tears. Pause.*) I had a hallucination and I've *got* to get it out! . . . [Goes on about her own deep conflicts, and tells of the hallucination she has experienced, with terrific tension in her voice, but with an attitude very different from that at beginning of interview.]

(*Later in interview*)

S: I knew at the office I had to get rid of this somewhere. I felt I could come down and tell you. I knew you'd understand. I couldn't say I hated myself. That's true but I couldn't say it. So I just thought of all the ugly things I could say to you instead.

---

[1] Just as it is impossible to convey on paper the venom and hatred in the client's voice, so it is utterly impossible to convey the depth of empathy in the counselor's responses. The counselor states, "I tried to enter into and to express in my voice the full degree of the soul-consuming anger which she was pouring out. The written words look incredibly pale, but in the situation they were full of the same feeling she was so coldly and deeply expressing."

C: The things you felt about yourself you couldn't say, but you could say them about me.

S: I know we're getting to rock bottom. . . .

Here again, in very deep material, the client again comes to realize that the attitudes she holds toward others, and the qualities she attributes to them, reside in her own perceptions, not in the object of her attitudes. This would seem to be the essence of the resolution of transference attitudes.[1]

Clinical Problems Regarding Transference

On the basis of our clinical experience it could be said that the experienced client-centered therapist rarely has difficulty in handling attitudes of hostility or attitudes of affection which are directed toward him. (The beginning counselor may have more difficulty with such attitudes than with attitudes directed toward others, but this disappears as his assurance in his hypothesis grows.) The attitudes which most frequently seem to be ineffectively handled are those which might be called "aggressive dependence." The client who is certain that he is incapable of making his own decisions or managing himself, and who insists that the counselor must take over, is a type of client with whom we are sometimes successful, but not infrequently unsuccessful. In such instances the problem is likely to arise very early in the series of interviews. The client is annoyed or antagonistic because he is not finding what he expected, and feels this annoyance without having as yet experienced much of the satisfaction of being understood. Consequently, very minute deviations by the therapist from an attitude of complete respect, understanding, and acceptance may be responsible for the client's terminating therapy

---

[1] To allay the reader's curiosity, it may be said that this client showed much growth and progress in thirty interviews, though she realized she still had a long way to go. For ten months she held these gains, and then was troubled once more by her conflicts. She tried in a peculiar way to get in touch with the counselor, who was out of the city for some months, for more help. Because of the channel she had chosen, the counselor knew nothing of her request and she received no reply. Within a month she had a frankly psychotic episode, from which she gradually made a partial recovery. What the outcome would have been had the counselor been available, it is impossible to state.

after one or a few interviews. In such cases, however, if this crucial early point is passed without termination by the client, then therapy appears to have the same essential process as in any other case. It is very clear, however, that we have much to learn, probably in attitudes rather than in techniques, before we can with entire success provide this type of client with a helping situation which he can use for himself.

How Does a Dependent Transference Develop?

Thus far we have discussed the reasons why a dependent transference does not tend to develop in client-centered therapy. We could discuss the matter with more assurance if there were a clear understanding of the opposite problem: How is a dependent transference created or initiated? Here any reliable answer must come from those orientations in which such a relationship frequently develops. Undoubtedly as we have more recordings of various therapies we can study such materials in order to discover the crucial points at which dependency begins or is fostered. At the present state of our knowledge, we can only raise questions and formulate tentative hypotheses on this point.

One such question is this, "Does evaluation of the client by the counselor create dependence?" "Evaluation" is here being used in a broad sense to include everything which is experienced by the client as "a judgment has been made about me." Thus it would include not only moral evaluation ("I wonder if you made the right move in doing that?" or "It is quite natural to have such sexual thoughts"), and evaluation of characteristics ("Your ability is at about the 25th percentile" or "You probably have somewhat compulsive tendencies"), but also evaluation of causes or patterns ("I wonder if underlying that is an attitude of hostility toward your mother," or "Perhaps you really feel some attraction toward him as well as hatred of him"). In these broad terms it seems that many interview techniques — interpretation, questions which probe in a certain direction, reassurance, criticism, praise, objective description — are all experienced as to some extent evaluations. Is it these experiences of being evaluated which bring about dependence? This would seem to be a reasonable a priori hypothesis since one of the most obvious differences between client-centered and other therapies lies in the amount of counselor evaluation which is involved. The evidence when we examine it seems to be both pro and con. Against this hypothesis is the fact that traditional counseling makes much use of evaluation, yet dependency develops only occasionally. Adlerian therapy could be similarly described. In the field of psychoanalysis, I have had opportunity to examine sample recorded interviews conducted by seven analysts. In all but one of these there was a heavy proportion of evaluation as here defined. There was a definitely dependent transference relationship in all these cases, even in the case in which evaluation by the therapist was quite minimal. Thus this hypothesis seems hardly satisfactory, since evaluation exists in those instances in which a transference relationship develops as well as in instances where it does not develop.

Another possibility is that dependency arises when it is expected. Certainly the expectation differs sharply in different orientations, and the therapist's expectations are undoubtedly conveyed in subtle ways. Thus the analyst's stress upon the use of free association would probably convey an expectation of client dependency. The fact that the patient is advised to avoid all feeling of responsibility for what he says, and as Fenichel says, "not to be active at all," would tend to imply that another will be responsible for him in this situation. In sharpest contrast, the client-centered therapist, in his respect for every client utterance as being, at that moment, a responsible expression of the self as it exists at the time, would undoubtedly convey an expectation of independence rather than dependence.

Over against this is the fact that sometimes a dependent transference does not develop in analysis even though the therapist has expected it, and a nondirective therapist who does not expect dependence may find it developing very rapidly if he becomes interpretive or evaluative.

It has seemed to me that a clue to the dilemma may lie in the following type of hypothesis. When the client is evaluated and comes to realize clearly in his own experience that this evaluation is more accurate than any he has made himself, then self-confidence crumbles, and a dependent relationship is built up. When the therapist is experienced as "knowing more about me than I know myself," then there appears to the client to be nothing to do but to hand over the reins of his life into these more competent hands. This is likely to be accompanied by comfortable feelings of relief and liking, but also at times by hatred for the person who has thus become so all-important. Whether this dependent relationship is regarded by the therapist as desirable depends of course upon the theory of therapy which he holds. All appear to be agreed, however, that once this has happened it is a slow process to get the patient to the point where he again feels confident in the control of his own life.

A very simple example may point up some of the reasons why this very tentative hypothesis appears to be a possible explanation. During the war a counselor with relatively little training or experience tried to help a soldier who was in the guardhouse for having gone AWOL. A little conversation revealed the fact that the AWOL episode had come about because of complex marital difficulties involving both the man's wife and mother-in-law. Toward the latter he was extremely hostile and abusive. The counselor questioned him about the whole situation, and on the basis of several interviews came to the conclusion that the mother-in-law was actually a constructive factor in the situation, that the soldier's attitude toward her was both unfortunate and inappropriate, and that if he would improve this relationship the whole marital picture would be improved. He tried to show this to the man, suggested that the man write a friendly letter to his mother-in-law, and so on. The man flatly rejected this interpretation of the situation and refused to write the letter.

Here is the way in which some directive counseling concludes. The client has been given an evaluation which may be far more adequate than his own. It is not experienced as adequate, and hence there is no effect upon the feeling of competence which the individual holds. In ordinary life the above case would probably have ended at this point, with the client leaving because he did not accept the evaluation nor the suggestion.

The story continues, however, because he was in the guardhouse and could not leave. After further discussion and persuasion, the soldier finally wrote to his mother-in-law a letter of the sort advised. He had no confidence that it would help. To his great surprise he received a friendly and constructive letter from her, and a letter from his wife also, both letters easing the strain of the marital situation, and opening up the possibility of rebuilding his marriage. The client was greatly pleased and so was the counselor. Within a few weeks the counselor's pleasure turned to perplexity. He found the soldier wanting to see him about many problems and many issues. He was asked to make decisions for him on very minute and inconsequential points. When the counselor tried to put the client off, he was resentful and hurt. A real dependency relationship had been developed.

Here in the blundering efforts of this naïve counselor we have possibly the basic pattern which exists in any transference relationship of a strongly dependent sort. The client discovers that the therapist knows him and his relationships better than he knows himself in his relationships. This is not merely an intellectual observation on the client's part, but something which is directly experienced. Once this is experienced, then the obvious conclusion is that the person who is sensed as having better understanding, better ability to predict behavior, and the like, should be the person in control. Consequently a basically positive dependent transference results, a relationship with strong affective components because it is so vitally important for the client. It has equally strong potentialities for negative feeling, since the client resents the loss of independent selfhood which is at least temporarily involved.

There is still another hypothesis to account for the development of a transference relationship. Perhaps as the client explores more and more deeply into himself, the degree of threat to self tends to make it more necessary to project these threats onto another, the therapist, as in the case of Miss Tir. The degree of internal threat may also make necessary the experiencing of more dependence. In favor of this hypothesis is the fact that in our longer cases (many of which appear to involve deeper reorganization) transference attitudes are more frequent and more noticeable.

This explanation would, however, deal only with the client's side of the picture and the likelihood of developing transference *attitudes* since even in these cases there is a difference between our experience and that of the full development of a transference *relationship*.

Summary

If transference attitudes are defined as emotionalized attitudes which existed in some other relationship, and which are inappropriately directed to the therapist, then transference attitudes are evident in a considerable proportion of cases handled by client-centered therapists. Both the analyst and the nondirective therapist deal with such attitudes in the same fashion in which they deal with any other affect. For the analyst this means that he interprets such attitudes, and perhaps through these evaluations establishes the characteristic transference *relationship*. For the client-centered therapist this means that he attempts to understand and accept such attitudes, which then tend to become accepted by the client as being his own perception of the situation, inappropriately held. Thus the emotionalized, dependent relationship between client and therapist almost always becomes the heart and focus of successful analytic therapy, whereas this does not seem to be true of client-centered therapy. In the latter therapy the client's awareness of his attitudes and perceptions as residing in him, rather than in the object of his attitudes and perceptions, may be said to be the focus of therapy. Put in another way, the awareness of self as perceiver and evaluator appears to be central to the process of reorganization of self which takes place.

In endeavoring to explore further the phenomena of transference attitudes and transference relationships, several tentative hypotheses were formulated. Transference attitudes are perhaps most likely to occur when the client is experiencing considerable threat to the organization of self in the material which he is bringing into awareness. A true transference relationship is perhaps most likely to occur when the client experiences another as having a more effective understanding of his own self than he himself possesses.

The Problem of Diagnosis

Shall psychotherapy be preceded by, and built upon, a thorough-going psychological diagnosis of the client? This is a complex and perplexing question, a question which has not been entirely resolved by any therapeutic orientation. We shall endeavor in this section to look at some of the elements in the situation, and to formulate a tentative answer from the point of view of client-centered therapy.

Differing Views

Looming large in the background of any such discussion is the fact that in dealing with organic disease, physical diagnosis is the *sine qua non* of treatment. The tremendous strides of medicine in dealing with disease processes in the organism have been very largely based upon the discovery, elaboration, and refinement of more adequate means of accurate diagnosis. It has been natural to suppose that progress in dealing with psychological difficulties would follow the same path.

It seems already obvious that this will not be true. Some therapists have indeed maintained that "rational treatment cannot be planned and executed until an accurate diagnosis has been made" (216, p. 319) but it is doubtful if this dictum represents the thinking of most. In various psychotherapeutic orientations, the diagnostic process has come to have a decreasing amount of emphasis. Many analysts and psychiatrists — particularly those influenced by Rankian thinking — prefer to start therapy without a diagnostic study.[1] The trend is most sharply shown by the fact that nearly all therapists, even in making a diagnostic study, would subscribe to the statement so popular in all orientations, that "therapy begins with the first contact, and proceeds hand in hand with diagnosis." It has not been sufficiently pointed out that approval of this statement means that in the mind of the psychotherapist, therapy is *not* built upon diagnosis. Some aspects of it, at least, can begin before there is any knowledge of the difficulty or its causation.

[1] See, for example, Frederick Allen's *Psychotherapy with Children*, Norton, 1942, particularly Chapter III.

In this general trend, client-centered therapy has been at the end of the continuum in stating, as its point of view, that psychological diagnosis as usually understood is unnecessary for psychotherapy, and may actually be a detriment to the therapeutic process. (143, 170)

In order to understand how such a divergence of opinion could exist, let us consider more deeply some of the principles which underlie the proved effectiveness of diagnostic procedures in the field of organic illness. There would doubtless be agreement that the following are statements which present the assumptions and the rationale of physical diagnosis, a rationale for which there is now a heavy weight of evidence.

1. Every organic condition has a preceding cause.
2. The control of the condition is much more feasible if the cause is known.
3. The discovery and accurate description of the cause is a rational problem of scientific search.
4. This search is best conducted by an individual with a knowledge of scientific method, and a knowledge of various organic conditions.
5. The cause, when it is differentiated and discovered, is usually remediable or alterable by materials and/or forces used and manipulated by the diagnostician or his professional associates.
6. To the extent that the alteration of the causative factors must be left in the control of the patient (keeping a diet, restriction of behavior in heart conditions, and so on) a program of education must be undertaken so that the patient perceives the total situation in much the same way as the diagnostician.

Obviously psychological diagnosis is necessary to psychotherapy to the degree, and only to the degree, that these assumptions and this rationale hold true of the situation in the psychological field. Here we find that therapists differ.

On the one hand are those who hold the view that psychological diagnosis is also a problem of rational search best conducted by the more objective expert. It is probable that they would agree that relatively little has been done to relate specific diagnoses with specific therapies, but this is the direction in which they believe sound progress will be made.

The writer has much sympathy with this point of view, and regards it as important to clinical advancement that this hypothesis be utilized and developed by those who believe it to be most fruitful. In an earlier volume (164) the writer in general espoused this point of view, and endeavored to set up the criteria and conditions by which manipulative treatment of elements in the physical and attitudinal situation of the child might be guided. In some areas, such as the prescription of foster home care, such treatment was beginning to acquire a definite scientific basis. For "x" type of problem syndrome in the child, a foster home of describable "y" type could be predicted to be successful in a known percentage of cases.

For the author, experience has gradually brought about the conclusions (1) that such prescriptive treatment of psychological maladjustment tends to be palliative and superficial, rather than basic, and (2) that it places the clinician in a god-like role which seems basically untenable from a philosophical point of view, for reasons which are discussed later.

The Client-Centered Rationale of Diagnosis

In our evolving experience with therapy, another point of view about diagnosis has developed in the client-centered orientation. The rationale behind it may perhaps be summarized rather briefly in a number of propositional statements.

> Behavior is caused, and the psychological cause of behavior is a certain perception or a way of perceiving.
>
> The client is the only one who has the potentiality of knowing fully the dynamics of his perceptions and his behavior.

Many therapists would be in agreement here. Fenichel points out (56, p. 32) that the final criterion of the correctness of an analytic interpretation is the patient's reaction over a period of time. If in the long run an interpretation is not experienced by the patient as meaningful and true, then it is not correct. The final diagnostician, then, in psychoanalysis as well as in client-centered therapy, is the client or patient.

> In order for behavior to change, a change in perception must be *experienced*. Intellectual knowledge cannot substitute for this.

It is this proposition which has perhaps cast the most doubt upon the usefulness of psychological diagnosis. If the therapist knew, with an assurance surpassing any he could have on the basis of present diagnostic tools, exactly what had brought about the present psychological maladjustment, it is doubtful that he could make effective use of this knowledge. Telling the client would most assuredly not help. Directing the client's attention to certain areas is perhaps as likely to arouse resistance as to bring nondefensive consideration of these areas. It seems reasonable to hypothesize that the client will explore the areas of conflict as rapidly as he is able to bear the pain, and that he will experience a change in perception as rapidly as that experience can be tolerated by the self.

> The constructive forces which bring about altered perception, reorganization of self, and relearning, reside primarily in the client, and probably cannot come from outside.

The forces which physical medicine can bring to bear, through drugs and other means, appear to have no real counterpart in the psychological field. The use of penicillin to combat a specific bacteria and the creation of an artificial fever to cure a disease have no real analogy in psychotherapy. The native curative forces which make for growth and learning appear to be the primary ones upon which the therapist must rely. When hypnosis or other means have been used to bring in positive forces whose source is external to the client, the results seem disappointing or temporary.

> Therapy is basically the experiencing of the inadequacies in old ways of perceiving, the experiencing of new and

more accurate and adequate perceptions, and the recognition of significant relationships between perceptions.

In a very meaningful and accurate sense, therapy *is* diagnosis, and this diagnosis is a process which goes on in the experience of the client, rather than in the intellect of the clinician.

It is in this way that the client-centered therapist has confidence in the efficacy of diagnosis. One might say that psychotherapy, of whatever orientation, is complete or almost complete when the diagnosis of the dynamics is experienced and accepted by the client. In client-centered therapy one could say that the purpose of the therapist is to provide the conditions in which the client is able to make, to experience, and to accept the diagnosis of the psychogenic aspects of his maladjustment.

Perhaps this presentation is sufficient to indicate that there is a rational basis for an approach to therapy which does not build upon an externally based diagnosis. The fact that it is feasible to conduct therapy on this basis is evident from the thousands of clients handled with this approach. As the two viewpoints regarding diagnosis continue to operate, clinical and research evidence will accumulate to indicate the effectiveness of each.

Certain Objections to Psychological Diagnosis

Our experience has led to the tentative conclusion that a diagnosis of the psychological dynamics is not only unnecessary but in some ways is detrimental or unwise. The reasons for this conclusion are primarily two. In the first place, the very process of psychological diagnosis places the locus of evaluation so definitely in the expert that it may increase any dependent tendencies in the client, and cause him to feel that the responsibility for understanding and improving his situation lies in the hands of another. When the client perceives the locus of judgment and responsibility as clearly resting in the hands of the clinician, he is, in our judgment, further from therapeutic progress than when he came in.[1] Also if the results of the evaluation are made known

[1] In the Counseling Center at the University of Chicago a number of our research studies have been based upon the giving of personality and other tests prior

to him it appears to lead to a basic loss of confidence by the person himself, a discouraging realization that "I cannot know myself." There is a degree of loss of personhood as the individual acquires the belief that only the expert can accurately evaluate him, and that therefore the measure of his personal worth lies in the hands of another. The more he acquires this attitude, the further he would appear to be from any sound therapeutic outcome, any real achievement of psychological growth.

The second basic objection to psychological diagnosis, and its accompanying evaluation of the client by the therapist, is that it has certain social and philosophical implications which need to be carefully considered and which, to the writer, are undesirable. When the locus of evaluation is seen as residing in the expert, it would appear that the long-range social implications are in the direction of the social control of the many by the few. To many this conclusion may seem far-fetched. Certainly it does not hold true in the realm of organic difficulties. If a physician diagnoses his patient as having a kidney infection and prescribes remedial measures, neither the diagnosis nor the prescription, whether correct or incorrect, has any general implications in the realm of social philosophy. But when the clinician diagnoses a client's vocational aims or marital relationships or religious views as, let us say, immature and works toward changing these conditions in the direction of what he regards as maturity, then this situation has many social implications. In a paper given at Harvard the writer has endeavored to point out some of these implications.

> One cannot take responsibility for evaluating a person's abilities, motives, conflicts, needs; for evaluating the adjustment he is capable of achieving, the degree of reorganization he should undergo, the conflicts which he should resolve, the degree of dependence which he should develop upon the therapist, and the goals of therapy, without a significant degree of control over the individual being an inevitable accompaniment. As this process is extended to more and more persons, as it is for example to thousands of veterans, it means a subtle

---

to and following therapy. These tests, however, are explained to the client as having to do with our research interests, rather than with his counseling experience. The results are made available neither to the client nor to the therapist, and this fact too is made known to the client.

control of persons and their values and goals by a group which has selected itself to do the controlling. The fact that it is a subtle and well-intentioned control makes it only less likely that people will realize what they are accepting. . . . If the hypothesis of the first trend proves to be most adequately supported by the evidence, if it proves to be true that the individual has relatively little capacity for self-evaluation and self-direction, and that the primary evaluation function must lie with the expert, then it would appear that the long range direction in which we are moving will find expression in some type of complete social control. The management of the lives of the many by the self-selected few would appear to be the natural consequence. If, on the other hand, the second hypothesis should be more adequately supported by the facts, if, as we think, the locus of responsible evaluation may be left with the individual, then we would have a psychology of personality and of therapy which leads in the direction of democracy, a psychology which would gradually redefine democracy in deeper and more basic terms. We would have a place for the professional worker in human relations, not as an evaluator of the self, behavior, needs and goals, but as the expert in providing the conditions under which the self-direction of both the individual and group can take place. The expert would have skill in facilitating the independent growth of the person. (168, pp. 212, 218–219)

Considerations of this sort have led client-centered therapists to minimize the diagnostic process as a basis for therapy. To us, the objections have seemed basic. At least they warrant consideration, and a suitable approach to therapy in our culture will need to provide a satisfactory answer to the questions which have been raised.[1]

[1] There are other, more transitory objections which might be raised, but which have not had much actual influence. One is the high degree of unreliability in diagnostic formulations. Ash (10) has found that even under favorable conditions, and considering only some sixty diagnostic categories, rather than any more complex formulation of dynamic mechanisms, agreement by three psychiatrists was found in only 20 per cent of the cases, and even when the categories were grouped into five major classifications the agreement was only 46 per cent. Surely therapy built upon any such shaky foundation would be insecure indeed. Presumably, however, this condition should change if psychological diagnosis increases in accuracy.

Another less influential consideration is that if certain diagnostic types come to

What About Psychosomatic Problems?

If organic problems are best handled by beginning with a diagnostic evaluation made by the expert, and if psychogenic problems are best handled by keeping the evaluative function with the client and avoiding external evaluation, what procedure is most advisable with psychosomatic problems in which the organic and psychological factors are inextricably woven together? The answer to this question is most puzzling, and no attempt will be made to give *the* answer, but some highly tentative suggestions may be made.

One point of view that, so far as is known, has never been systematically tried, would be to keep the locus of evaluation with the patient in the diagnostic procedures used. Suppose the physician, or the physician-psychologist team, took an attitude toward the patient which could be summarized thus: "You, and we, are perplexed as to the basis of your symptoms. We could give you metabolism tests, which would indicate whether your body is functioning satisfactorily in turning your food into fuel for energy; we could give other tests (describing the function of each in simple, nonmedical terms), or you could talk with Dr. X, talking about your symptoms and your feelings and any of the things that trouble you, since sometimes difficulties such as yours get their start from emotional conflicts or problems within the person. Now, of all these possibilities, which do you wish to use? You may wish to go ahead on all of them, or you may feel that some of these lines of investigation would be much more likely than others to get at the source of your symptoms." Many physicians would, of course, find it quite impossible to take the point of view described. Yet where they could sincerely test out the hypothesis of putting confidence in the patient, the results might prove stimulating to our thinking. We know, as the Bixlers (31, 32) and Seeman (179) have shown, that this type of approach works very well indeed in the vocational guidance field, where the client selects the tests which he regards as ap-

be regarded as not amenable to psychotherapy, work with such individuals tends to cease, whether the judgment was correct or not. In this way, too great a reliance upon diagnostic judgment can stand in the way of needed experimentation and research.

propriate for himself. Their experience would at least suggest that it might be profitable in the psychosomatic realm. Clearly, the patient who was highly defensive would exhaust first the tests and procedures which would point toward an organic diagnosis; but when these had been utilized, assuming the findings were negative or minimal, he would tend to choose for himself the pathway which would lead to possible discovery of the psychogenic aspects. The importance of having this choice his own can hardly be overestimated.

The advantage of this whole procedure would be that the primary locus of responsibility would be kept with the patient throughout, which, as the Peckham experiment has shown, is important even in dealing with organic ills. (See pages 59–63 of Chapter 2.) Even more important, he would be making the choice to investigate the psychological elements in the picture, and once this choice was made would be soundly embarked on therapy. Furthermore, such a mode of approach keeps the physician thinking *with* the patient at all times rather than primarily *about* or *for* the patient. This has many advantages in the area of psychogenic problems.

Another highly tentative suggestion reverses the usual order of procedure in dealing with patients. If a patient presents symptoms which appear to have a considerable probability of being psychosomatic or psychological, the usual procedure is to "rule out" the possibility of organic illness first, leaving to the last the psychological possibilities. This procedure is very understandable from an historical point of view. Yet if we consider it from a logical point of view, and keep in mind the great preponderance of psychogenic ills in many of the medical specialties, it would make equally good sense to reverse the approach. Psychotherapy might be started at once, provided the patient was willing; and if the symptoms did not improve after a reasonable length of time, the chance that they might be organic in origin could then be investigated.

These two possibilities are suggested for consideration only. The experience of the author in the psychosomatic field is by no means extensive, and the only justification for putting forth these rather radical proposals is to indicate that client-centered therapy does have at least a theoretical rationale for approaching problems of psychosomatic illness.   It is also clearly recognized that many physicians would consider the procedures suggested so antagonistic to all the conventions of medical training as to be wholly repugnant.   It is to the few who might find the procedures congenial that the suggestions are addressed.

The Limits of Applicability
of Client-Centered Therapy

The third question which this chapter will explore is a question very frequently raised by those interested in therapy: "What are the types of situations in which client-centered therapy is applicable?"   The answer can be relatively brief, though it will not satisfy all the questioners.

In *Counseling and Psychotherapy* the author gave certain tentative criteria which, if met, indicated that counseling was advisable.[1]   This list of criteria has proved less than helpful.   It is

[1] The criteria for counseling were as follows (other criteria were given for treatment of parent and child, and for environmental treatment): " . . . it would seem that direct counseling treatment of the individual, involving planned and continued contacts, is advisable provided all of the following conditions exist:

"1. The individual is under a degree of tension, arising from incompatible personal desires or from the conflict of social and environmental demands with individual needs. The tension and stress so created are greater than the stress involved in expressing his feelings about his problems.

"2. The individual has some capacity to cope with life. He possesses adequate ability and stability to exercise some control over the elements of his situation. The circumstances with which he is faced are not so adverse or so unchangeable as to make it impossible for him to control or alter them.

"3. There is an opportunity for the individual to express his conflicting tensions in planned contacts with the counselor.

"4. He is able to express these tensions and conflicts either verbally or through other media. A conscious desire for help is advantageous, but not entirely necessary.

"5. He is reasonably independent, either emotionally or spatially, of close family control.

"6. He is reasonably free from excessive instabilities, particularly of an organic nature.

"7. He possesses adequate intelligence for coping with his life situation, with an intelligence rating of dull-normal or above.

"8. He is of suitable age — old enough to deal somewhat independently with life, young enough to retain some elasticity of adjustment. In term of chronological age this might mean roughly from ten to sixty." (166, pp. 76–77)

not so much that it is entirely incorrect (though points 5 and 8 are disproved continually) as that it engenders in the counselor-in-training an evaluative, diagnostic frame of mind which has not been profitable.

Present opinion on applicability must take into account our experience. A client-centered approach has been used with two-year-old children and adults of sixty-five; with mild adjustment problems, such as student study habits, and the most severe disorders of diagnosed psychotics; with "normal" individuals and those who are deeply neurotic; with highly dependent individuals and those of strong ego-development; with lower-class, middle-class, and upper-class individuals; with the less intelligent as well as the highly intelligent; with healthy individuals and those with psychosomatic ailments, particularly allergies (48, 133, 134). Only two of the many types of customary classifications have not been appreciably sampled — the mental defective and the delinquent. It is unfortunate that thus far circumstances have not led to much work with this therapeutic approach in these fields.

On the basis of the foregoing experience it would be correct to say that, in each of the groupings in which we have worked, client-centered therapy has achieved noteworthy success with some individuals; with some, partial success; with others, temporary success which later suffered a relapse; while with still others failure to help has been the result. Certain trends appear to be evident, such as the lesser likelihood of deep personal reorganization in the older individual. The Haimowitz study (78), already cited, indicates tentatively that intra-punitive males may make better use of the experience of client-centered therapy than others. But on the whole, our experience does not lead us to say that client-centered therapy is applicable to certain groups and not to others. It is felt that there is no advantage to be gained by trying to set dogmatic limits to the use of such therapy. If there are certain types of individuals who do not respond, or for whom client-centered therapy is contra-indicated, then accumulating experience and additional research will indicate what these groups are.

In the meantime, the lack of definite knowledge about the

PART II   *The Application of Client-Centered Therapy*

Chapter 6 · Play Therapy

By ELAINE DORFMAN, M.A

Client-centered play therapy did not spring into being fully formed. Many of the assumptions and procedures of the client-centered play therapist are derivatives of those of other orientations. It is to the brief consideration of some of these that we now turn.

ORIGINS OF PLAY THERAPY

Play therapy appears to have arisen from attempts to apply psychoanalytic therapy to children. As in adult analyses, an important aim of the Freudian therapy was the bringing to consciousness of repressed experiences, together with the reliving of the accompanying affects in the more "antiseptic" relationship with the therapist. A basic method for effecting this outcome in adults was that of free association. Thus, a serious problem arose when it was discovered that young children refused to free-associate. In her early report, Anna Freud (63) stated that a small child might occasionally be induced to free-associate briefly, in order to please an analyst of whom he was fond. The material thus produced was, however, insufficient as a basic source for interpretation. For this reason, and because of a belief that children did not form a transference neurosis, Anna Freud modified the classical analytic technique. As part of a campaign to win over a child, she sometimes played with him. For example, she reports a case (63, pp. 8–9) in which, when a child brought some string to the treatment room, she proceeded to tie fancier knots than the child could. Her stated aim was to show him that she was an interesting and powerful person, whom he might well desire as an ally. In this way, she hoped to gain access to the child's secrets. Thus, it appears that her early use of play was not central in the therapy, but was considered rather as a pre-liminary to the real work of analysis. It was a technique to produce a positive emotional attachment to the analyst, and thus to make possible the actual therapy.

The differing approach of Melanie Klein (103) was independently developed at about the same period, and it, too, derived from the fundamental theories of Sigmund Freud. Klein assumed that the child's play activities, including his accompanying verbalizations, were quite as motivationally determined as the free associations of adults. Hence, they could be interpreted to the child, in lieu of interpretations based upon adult-style free associations. Klein called her approach "Play Analysis." Unlike adult psychoanalyses, Play Analysis was characterized by a very early launching into deep interpretations of the child's behavior. By this means, it was hoped to reduce the child's more acute anxiety, and thus to give him an inkling into the value of the analysis for him. This was to supply a personal motive for continuing the therapy, in place of an entire reliance upon parental compulsion. Despite some differences, Play Analysis was essentially true to psychoanalytic tradition, as is seen, for example, in the way symbols were interpreted. The fact that it was in the tradition is also evident in its stated aims to uncover the past and to strengthen the ego so that it might be better able to cope with the demands of the superego and id.

The application of Rank's theories (155) to play therapy by Taft (209) led to certain significant changes in the aims and methods of psychotherapeutic work with children. These were further elaborated and exemplified by Allen (5). An essential feature of Rankian or relationship therapy is its conception of a certain kind of therapeutic relationship as being curative in its own right. This is in contrast to the view that it is necessary for the patient to retrace his developmental steps and to relive earlier emotional relationships in the analytic hours. Classical analysis aimed thus to assist the patient in growing up again, in a better way. That is, a permissive parent surrogate, the analyst, did not inflict the previous traumata. Relationship therapy, on the other hand, was concerned with emotional problems as they existed in the immediate present, regardless of their history. In the Rankian view, the analytic effort to recover the past was not particularly helpful, because the neurotic patient was already too much bound to the past and too little able to live in the here and now. Thus, the Rankian therapist did not seek to help the patient to repeat a particular series of developmental steps, but began where the patient was. In play therapy, this meant the abandonment of interpretation in terms of the Oedipus complex, for example. Emphasis on present feelings led to considerable reduction in the time span of therapy. Taft and Allen stressed the need for helping the child to define himself in relation to the therapist. The therapy hour was conceived of as a concentrated growth experience. In it, the child might gradually come to the realization of being a separate person who was in himself a source of strivings, and who could, nevertheless, exist in a relationship where the other person was to be permitted to have qualities of his own. Of the various therapeutic orientations, relationship therapy seems to be closest to the client-centered approach.

If one considers the principles of client-centered therapy as outlined in preceding chapters of this book, it is apparent that much is owed to older therapies. From the Freudians have been retained the concepts of the meaningfulness of apparently unmotivated behavior, of permissiveness and catharsis, of repression, and of play as being the natural language of the child. From the Rankians have come the relatively a-historical approach, the lessening of the authoritative position of the therapist, the emphasis on response to expressed feelings rather than to a particular content, and the permitting of the child to use the hour as he chooses. From these concepts, client-centered play therapy has gone on to develop, in terms of its own experiences.

A Current Description

What, then, constitutes client-centered play therapy as currently understood? Like client-centered counseling, play therapy is based upon the central hypothesis of the individual's capacity for growth and self-direction. The work of the client-centered play therapist is an attempt to test the validity of this hypothesis under varying conditions. Thus, therapy has been offered to children presenting the most widely disparate problems, symptoms, and personality patterns. Children have been seen at their schools, in orphanages, youth clubs, university clinics, and community guidance centers. Sometimes both parent and child have received therapy and sometimes the child alone has been seen. Under each of these circumstances, all degrees of success and failure have occurred. It is as experimentation is carried into wider areas that the client-centered hypothesis, like any other, may be upheld, modified, or disproved. For instance, relatively little has been done with delinquents, mental defectives, and children in psychiatric wards. Until further experience has been obtained in these areas, the extent of applicability of this kind of therapy remains unknown.

The Increasing Belief in the Child

The belief in the child's capacity for self-help is not an all-or-none affair, an article of faith accepted *in toto* by client-centered therapy from the very start, and retained unaltered ever since. Rather, it has grown with experience in working with children who seemed to have many strikes against them. For instance, a few short years ago, a nondirective therapist was apt to feel somewhat pessimistic about accepting a child for play therapy unless one or both parents also received therapy. Since the child's difficulties were seen to spring at least partially from the emotionalized attitudes of his parents, it appeared necessary to help the parent to examine and perhaps modify some of these. Thus, the therapist's attitude might have been paraphrased somewhat as follows: "The child's behavior and symptoms do not come from thin air. They are his way of solving his problems, however inadequate they prove to be. If the problems themselves remain unaltered, therapy might help temporarily, but when it is over, the child may again be overwhelmed. It is too much to ask of a young child that he cope by himself with these unyielding and traumatizing parental relationships." Experiences with play therapy in orphanages and schools led to serious questioning of this early formulation. In these situations, as a matter of practical necessity, only the child received therapy. With parents unavailable for or unwilling to undertake personal therapy, treatment of the child alone was the only alternative to abandoning him completely. Much of the experimental work in schools and in children's homes was done by Axline and by students working under her direction. Reports of these applications, including verbatim case excerpts, are to be found in her book (14).

How is it that children have been able to cope not only with their own inner conflicts, but with the same environmental situation which was originally traumatizing? An answer which seems plausible is that, once the child has undergone some personal change, however slight, his environmental situation is no longer the same. That is, his "stimulus-value" to other persons has been altered. Once he is differently perceived, he is differently reacted to, and this different treatment may lead him to change further. Thus, the child may initiate a cycle of change. This is by no means a new idea, nor one which is unique to client-centered therapy, but it is one which has strongly affected our approach to play therapy. It is still possible to conceive, however, of a case, albeit rare, in which an attitude of deep rejection may be so central in a parent as to remain unaffected by a child's behavior changes. This being the case, perhaps therapy can help a child emotionally to accept this painful fact, and hence to seek satisfactions elsewhere. Whatever the explanation may be, the fact remains that many children have benefited from play therapy without concurrent parent therapy. It is through accrued experiences of this kind that client-centered therapists have come to trust more and more in the child himself.

The Therapist's Role

Belief in the child as the chief agent in his own therapy, however justified in experience, cannot in itself produce therapy. It is necessary for the therapist to communicate this attitude of respect, so that the child senses that here is a situation in which he can be his real self. The therapist does this partly by what is said to the child, although this is probably a minor aspect. Thus, in the following excerpt from a contact with a nine-year-old boy, a few words communicate a good deal of the therapist's attitude to the child. The excerpt is from the last half of the contact.

Jack: I think I'll paint something. What should I paint?

Therapist: You want me to tell you what to paint? (*The therapist fails to respond to the first half of Jack's statement, and thus inadvertently focuses attention on the second half.*)

Jack: Yes. What do you want me to paint? You tell me.

Therapist: Jack, I know you want me to decide for you, but I really can't, because I don't want you to paint any particular thing.

Jack: Why not, don't you care about what I do?

Therapist: Yes, Jack, I care, but I think that what you feel like painting is really up to you. (*Pause.*) Sometimes it's hard to decide.

Jack: An airplane.

Therapist: You'll paint an airplane?

Jack: (*Nods, and paints in silence for several minutes. Then, suddenly, he looks up.*) How many do you have?

Therapist: How many? (*Therapist is quite in the dark.*)

Jack: Yes, how many of us?

Therapist: Oh, about twenty.

Jack: My God! How do you stand twenty? (*Said in a tone of great shock.*)

Therapist: (*Laughs, before recovering.*) Think that's an awful lot?

Jack: And how! (*He returns to his painting.*)

In this excerpt, the therapist has tried to let Jack know that both his need to be dependent and his right to use the hour in his own way are respected.

There are more subtle and perhaps more important behaviors by means of which the therapist's attitude of respect can be conveyed to the child. The therapist is ready for the child when he arrives. Regardless of the mess made in previous contacts, the room is in order at the beginning of each new hour. If delayed, the therapist apologizes, just as he would with an adult. Appointments are faithfully kept. If it is necessary to break one, the child is told in advance. If the therapist is unable to let the child know ahead of time, the child receives an apology as soon as possible, in the form of a personal letter of explanation if he can read. The receipt of such a letter can be a very meaningful experience, for children are not used to such consideration. It is not unusual for a child in therapy to bring such a letter with him to the next therapy contact, and to read it aloud to the therapist with much relish. In a school situation, the child is allowed to decide whether he will be called for, be reminded by his teacher, or receive a note from the therapist notifying him of his appointment. The child's confidences are kept, in exactly the same way as are those of the adult client. In these and other ways, the child is told that he is a person deemed worthy of respectful treatment. It is perhaps unnecessary to add that the therapist's attitude must be genuine.

The therapist goes further. He attempts to provide a relationship of warmth and understanding, in which the child may feel safe enough to relax his defenses long enough to see how it feels to operate without them. The safety of the therapy hour seems to lie in the absence of pressure. The therapist accepts the child exactly as he is at the moment, and does not try to mold him into some socially-approved form. The therapist makes no attempt to respond to the child of the last contact, but confines himself to feelings currently expressed. By this means, it is hoped to heighten the child's awareness of what he is at the moment. The thrill that sometimes comes with this is vividly illustrated in an excerpt from a case reported by Axline.

Three boys, aged eight, were experiencing group-therapy sessions. During the eighth interview, Herby suddenly asked the therapist, "Do you *have* to do this? Or do you *like* to do this?" Then he added, "I wouldn't know *how* to do this." Ronny asked, "What do you mean? You play. That's all. You just play." And Owen agreed with Ronny. "Why, sure you do," he said. But Herby continued the discussion. "I mean I wouldn't know how to do what she does. She doesn't seem to do anything. Only all of a sudden, I'm free. Inside me, I'm free." (He flings his arms around.) "I'm Herb and Frankenstein and Tojo and a devil." (He laughs and pounds his chest.) "I'm a great giant and a hero. I'm wonderful and I'm terrible. I'm a dope and I'm so smart. I'm two, four, six, eight, ten people, and I fight and I kill!" The therapist said to Herby, "You're all kinds of people rolled up in one." Ronny added, "And you stink, too." Herby glared at Ronny, and replied, "I stink and you stink. Why, I'll mess you up." The therapist continued to speak to Herby — "You're all kinds of people in here. You're wonderful and you're terrible and you're dopey and you're smart." Herby interrupted exultantly, "I'm good and I'm bad and still I'm Herby. I tell you I'm wonderful. I can be anything I want to be!" Apparently Herby felt that during the therapy hour he could express fully all of the attitudes and feelings that were an expression of his personality. He felt the acceptance and permissiveness to be himself. He seemed to recognize the power of self-direction within himself. (14, pp. 19–20)

Here, it seems as though the therapist's responsiveness to the child's currently expressed feelings brought about a sense of strength and personhood which was new and exhilarating.

The Child's Hour

Unlike other occasions in the child's life, the therapy hour belongs to him alone. The therapist is there to provide warmth, understanding, and company, but not leadership. The therapist is willing to accept the pace selected by the child. He does not try to hasten or delay any particular aspect of the therapy process. Client-centered therapy postulates that in a nonthreatening relationship, the rate at which the child brings forth significant material is determined by his psychological readiness to do so. Like good teaching, therapy must respect this factor of readiness. It is in order to avoid becoming a threat, and hence impeding the unfolding process, that the therapist's responses are limited to what the child is willing to communicate. For example, in a given case the therapist may know that there is bitter sibling hostility. If such a child puts a baby doll into a toy toilet, and announces with glee that "a guy" is now going to flush the toilet, the therapist's response does not go further than, "He is getting rid of the baby?" The assumption here is that if the child were ready to identify the "guy," he would do so, and that therapy is not facilitated when the therapist takes over this responsibility for him. So, too, if the child deals with symbols, the therapist also accepts this level of communication, even when the meaning of the symbol is quite obvious. Here is an example from a contact with a thirteen-year-old boy who had been in therapy for over a year. The excerpt is from the first session following an operation for hernia, which had been anticipated with dread.

Henry: (*Plays rather aimlessly with small bits of clay for ten minutes in silence. Then he takes a larger lump and rolls it out into a cylinder. As he does so, he begins to speak.*) It's a frankfurter.
Therapist: A frankfurter?
Henry: Yes. (*He continues to roll it until it has the proper dimensions. Then he takes one of the modeling sticks and cuts a long vertical gash.*) It's getting operated on. (*He cuts several parallel gashes*).
Therapist: The frankfurter's getting cut up?
Henry: Uh-huh. (*He makes a series of cuts at right angles to the lengthwise cuts*). Stitches.
Therapist: It's getting sewed up now?
Henry: Yes. Soon they're gonna take out the stitches. And after that, it'll be all right."
Therapist: Things will turn out O.K.?
Henry: (*Nods affirmatively. From here on, the topic of conversation changes to his family*).

It was obvious that Henry was speaking of his own experiences. His previous therapy contacts had been characterized by remarkable frankness, and rapport was excellent. Hence it does not appear likely that his failure to identify the "frankfurter" or its owner was a purposeless avoidance reaction. Perhaps the use of the "frankfurter" served as an anxiety-reducer, for it was possible physically to manipulate, cut, and "sew" it, and hence to objectify his feelings. It may be that this is also why children often appear relieved after making a gruesome painting. Perhaps it is this neutralization of fears through their concrete physical representation that is a basic aspect of play therapy. It may help to understand the apparent successes when there is little evidence of insight or verbalized attitude change.

The Silent Case

Perhaps the child will sit in silence. If the therapist is truly convinced that the hour belongs to the child, he will not feel the necessity of urging the child to play or to talk. As a matter of fact, one of the most perplexing problems is that of the "silent case." The child comes and sits down and continues to do just that. The therapist remarks that he may play with any of the toys if he wishes, or he may talk about anything at all, or he may just sit through the hour. The total silence may continue for one hour or for twenty hours. There is no apparent catharsis, no reflection of feelings, there are no verbalized insights, no self-searchings — in short, none of the phenomena generally believed characteristic of a psychotherapeutic process. Not infrequently, however, these cases must be adjudged successful, on the basis of reports of altered behavior from adults who deal with the child. A fourteen-year-old boy is referred because he waylays and robs smaller children, hits strange adults without apparent provocation, uproots fences, does unsatisfactory schoolwork, and executes cats by hanging. He flatly refuses to discuss anything with the therapist, and spends most of his fifteen weekly sessions reading comic books, methodically searching the closets and desk, raising and lowering the window shades, and looking out the windows, in silence. In the midst of these seemingly unprofitable contacts, his teacher reports that he has performed an act of unsolicited generosity, the first ever noted in his eight years at the school. His teacher tells the therapist that he has used his printing press to print programs for a class skating party, and has distributed these to his classmates, although no one has suggested it to him. As she puts it, "This is his first social act." For the first time, an interest in his schoolwork is noted. His teacher says, "Why he's actually one of us now. We never even notice him now."

Another twelve-year-old is referred for attempted rape, and for schoolwork so poor that he has been taken out of his classroom in order to be tutored individually by the adjustment teacher. During the therapy sessions, he does his spelling homework, or describes the latest movie he has seen. Once, he brings a deck of cards, and he and the therapist play "war." This is the overt extent of their relationship. When the semester is over, he is returned to his grade, where he is reported "doing very well." Months later, he is walking along the street with a friend, when he accidentally meets the therapist. He introduces them, and says to the friend, "You oughta go see her on accounta you can't learn to read. She helps kids who are in trouble."

Again, a thirteen-year-old boy is referred for his explosive outbursts of aggression, and for his long-standing "torturing" (unspecified) of a girl in his class. He inquires about the therapist's first name, which just happens to be the same as that of the tortured girl classmate. From then on, he calls the therapist by this name alone. When he is at the height of his sociability, he plays tic-tac-toe with the therapist. By dint of always going first, he wins nearly every game, and scornfully keeps a record of his victories. Most of the time, however, is spent seated at the window, his back to the therapist, counting the numbers of the various brands of automobiles which pass. When the hour ends, he throws his tally-sheet on the therapist's table and stalks out. After ten such sessions, the therapist tells him that she saves the hour for him, but that he need not come any more if he does not wish to. His reply is, "Whaddya mean, not come any more? I'll come till the cows come home!" Then, he misses two weeks in a row, and upon his return, announces, "I didn't feel like coming, so I didn't." At the end of the semester, he too is "doing very well." His teacher has become fond of him because he is so helpful and cooperative. He has stayed after school to help with the school newspaper. His teacher adds, "He's improved so much. Why, I don't know what I'd do without him!"

Cases like these three are far from rare, although they seem to be more common in children over eleven years of age. The therapist has not been able to grasp the internal frame of reference of the child, because it was not in evidence. What was therapeutic about the experience? It seems to be stretching the concept of chance too much to say that in each case the period of therapy "chanced" to coincide with a period of spontaneous improvement. These cases have occurred too frequently for this explanation to suffice. Perhaps the following hypothesis might be offered. If the child will not admit another person into his private world, perhaps it can be therapeutic if the therapist only accepts this, and does not try to intrude. Perhaps it is enough to experience that the therapist is willing to respect his privacy, in a genuine sense. For a child, this may be sufficiently different from his usual dealings with adults as to constitute an outstanding experience. "Here is somebody who lets me ignore him and he still thinks I'm O.K. He doesn't get mad."

Most of the time, there is no way of knowing just how the child is reacting to the therapist's acceptance of his silence, but an occasional case is revealing. Here is an example from a play contact with a nine-year-old boy who has spent the entire hour painting in silence. Near the end, he asks the therapist about the time.

Dick: How much time do I have left?
Therapist: Seven minutes, Dick.
Dick: I might as well go rock awhile. (*He goes and sits in the rocking-chair. He closes his eyes and quietly rocks.*) How much time do I have left now?
Therapist: Five more minutes, Dick.
Dick (*sighs very deeply*): Ah, five more minutes *all to myself.*
Therapist (*very softly*): Five more minutes *all your own,* Dick?
Dick: Yes! (*Said with much feeling. He rocks silently for the rest of the hour. His eyes are shut, in apparent enjoyment of peace.*)
Therapist: It feels good just to sit and rock?
Dick: (*Nods.*)
Therapist: That's all the time we have for today, Dick.
Dick: O.K. (*He gets up immediately and goes to the door with the therapist. They say good-bye, and he goes out. A minute later, he knocks at the door.*) I thought I'd get you some clean water.
Therapist: You want to help me, Dick?
Dick: Yes, I do. (*He gets the water. The therapist thanks him and he leaves, skipping down the hall. This is the first time that he has ever made any effort to clean up after his painting.*)

In this excerpt, Dick has overtly stated that in therapy he has some time which can be truly called his own. It seems as if the therapist's willingness to let Dick be silent was experienced by him as an opportunity for psychological privacy, yet without loneliness. Whether this is true in other silent contacts remains unknown. Experiences of this kind prompt one to ask, "What is the essence of a therapeutic relationship?" It is apparent, too, that one of the more important personal qualities of a client-centered play therapist must be an ability to tolerate silence without embarrassment. A therapist who feels rejected when the child fails to pour out his troubles will only add to the child's anxiety by his display of his own. If the therapist cannot feel comfortable, it might be better for him to avoid offering therapy to children over ten or eleven years of age.

A Contrasting Case

Although the therapy process need not involve a great deal of verbalization on the child's part, an occasional case presents a striking contrast to "the silent case." An example is that of eleven-year-old Henry, already briefly cited above (page 243). Its further presentation may indicate a child's capacity for sophisticated insights.

Henry was referred for therapy because of his "nervousness." He had an assortment of tics, including rapid and continuous blinking of the eyelids, twitching of the lips, mouth and jaw grimaces, shoulder-tossing, feet-kicking, and gasping for breath. He suffered from constipation, wept easily, stuttered, was a social isolate, and was failing in his schoolwork. In short, there seemed to be no area of his life which afforded him satisfaction. During his first therapy hour, he told of often running all the way home from school in order to escape the men waiting in alleys to kill him. He reported his life at home to be an endless round of quarrels, reprimands, hypodermic injections of sedatives, suppositories, and nightmares. His father, a physician, threatened him with shock therapy if his "shaking" did not cease. It seems that a psychiatrist had told Henry's parents that he shook in order to gain attention, and they were determined to end his "nastiness."

In the face of his many problems, Henry felt quite overwhelmed. His own words provide a vivid account of his psychological state during this first therapy hour. The excerpt is from the last half of the hour, and is reproduced from his therapist's notes.

Henry: One time, my mother said she'd take me to Baltimore. So I got up early, 7 o'clock, and I went into the living-room. It was empty. I should have gotten up at 6 o'clock. She took Michael [older brother] instead.

Therapist: They left you when you'd hoped to go?

Henry: (*Nods. He weeps again.*) Up until I was 6 years old, I had a nurse, Miss Palmer. She protected me from everybody, but now, now she's gone, and — (*interrupts his story with tears*)

Therapist: You're all alone without anybody to protect you now?

Henry: Yes. They say Miss Palmer spoiled me, but I don't think so.

Therapist: You miss her?

Henry: Yes, I do. I have a cousin, Jean. Well, I happened to fall in love with her. Michael says, "Jean doesn't care for you a bit." He says Jean likes him better.

Therapist: He doesn't want you to be happy?

Henry: No. He doesn't. He does everything he can to make me miserable. My father always says Michael is right. If I try to stand up for my rights, my father gives me a hypo.

Therapist: Things seem to be going pretty badly at home.

Henry: Yes, oh yes! (*He weeps again. He goes on to relate other incidents. Then, he becomes very insistent upon knowing how therapy can help. Earlier in the hour, the therapist had said that she was there to talk things over with him.*)

Henry: What good will it do to tell you about it; I don't understand.

Therapist: You mean, talking won't help?

Henry: Yes. What good will it do?

Therapist: Sometimes people feel better about things after talking them over. (*The therapist falls into the trap of answering an emotional question as if it were a mere request for information. It leads to difficulties.*)

Henry: Yes, but what good does it do to feel better about things if they still go on?

Therapist: Sometimes boys and girls can understand the way they really feel about things, and it helps them to know what they really want to do about their situations. (*The therapist is still trying to "sell" the therapy session to the child.*)

Henry: Yes, but after I tell you about it, what if it's still going on?

Therapist: I know you feel pretty hopeless, Henry. I can't change your parents. All I can do is to help you think through your own problems. (*Pause.*) It's hard for you to see it now, I know, but sometimes it helps.

Henry: Well. . . . (*Goes on to relate several more incidents.*) I still don't understand. What good will it do to talk about it if they still keep on the same way?

Therapist: You mean, what can you do if they don't change?

Henry: Yes.

Therapist: I don't really know. But I hope that's something we can work out together, here, when you come to see me.

Henry: Suppose it lasts 10 or 15 years and they keep on?

Therapist: You just wonder how long you can bear it? (**This should have been the response earlier in the session.**)

Henry: Yes, oh yes. (*He weeps several minutes.*)

Therapist: It all looks pretty black.

Henry: (*Nods.*) Sometimes I dream that my mother dies and that then somebody will understand me. I don't understand why I should dream that.

Therapist: You just wonder, "Will anybody ever understand me?"

Henry: Uh-hm. Sometimes I think that something terrible will have to happen before they realize their mistakes.

Therapist: As if only something awful would work?

Henry: Uh-hm. (*Pause.*) I often wonder whether it's true, what they say on the radio.

Therapist: Yes?

Henry: Dr. Preston Bradley says God counts every tear.

Therapist: And you wonder whether God is counting your tears?

Henry: Yes, oh yes! (*With a great sigh, he lowers his head to his folded arms, and weeps.*)

This first contact has been presented in some detail in order to indicate Henry's feeling of hopelessness about altering his situation. It is interesting to note that although he stated his inability to see any use in it, he made eager use of the therapist's presence. Despite his stuttering and gasping for breath, he spoke very rapidly, and was astonished when the hour was up. He did not even see the paints and other materials until the third therapy hour. Then he painted a boy in jail, behind heavy black bars —

a perfect projection of his feelings. Like many adult clients, Henry began therapy with a view of his problems as existing outside himself, in the actions of other people. Hence, he avidly desired the punishment of his "villains." The tenth therapy hour brought some interesting changes, as may be seen in this excerpt.

Henry: Michael and I had a fight. I wanted the window shut, I felt cold. He yelled, "Who shut the window?" I said, "I did!" So he said I was a brat, and he opened it. So then I shut it again. He got up out of bed and opened it and then he hit me. So I threw a shoe at him, and it broke the lamp. He started to cry. He's such a baby, honestly! So then my father came in and he hit me. He always takes Michael's side. I told him, "Dad, Michael's your favorite." He says he has no favorites, and that I'm just a little snot. He was lying, though.

Therapist: You feel he's pretty unfair to you, is that it?

Henry: And sometimes I get so mad!

Therapist: You really get sore at him.

Henry: I *hate* him!

Therapist: You *despise* him.

Henry: Yes. I'd love to pay him back, too.

Therapist: You'd like some revenge?

Henry: Yes. If only he weren't here.

Therapist: You'd like to be rid of him?

Henry: I'd like to kill him.

Therapist: You want him dead?

Henry: Uh-hm. That would be the end of my problems.

Therapist: With him dead, things would be O.K. with you?

Henry: That's right. (*Pause.*) But would that end my problems? Supposing he were dead. I'd still be the same, I mean my shaking and all. Now if he'd have got killed earlier, that might have done me some good, but now it's too late for that. I am what I am already, and that's my problem. He's just a fool.

Therapist: So that, all in all, you've decided to let him live?

Henry: Yes. It wouldn't do any good to kill him, I'd still have my same problems, and I'd still have to figure them out. He's supposed to be a grown man, but honestly, he acts just like a baby.

Therapist: Sometimes you think he's rather silly?

Henry: Yes. I wonder what could have happened to him when he was a child. You know, he's not at all understanding. Could it be because his father didn't understand him when he was a child?

Therapist: You are wondering just what really makes him tick?
Henry: Yes, I really am. I really am. (*Very thoughtfully.*)

This interview marked the beginning of his attempts to understand the motivations behind behavior, and was therefore a turning-point in his therapy. Later sessions contained complex insights usually found only in adult cases. For example, near the end of Henry's second year of therapy, the following took place.

Henry: (*As had become his custom, he spent the first twent̠ minutes working with the clay. Then, he glanced at the therapist's watch, put aside the clay, and began to speak.*) Friday night, Gerald and Ann [his eldest brother and his wife] went downtown. Michael went with them. I would have liked to go too, but they didn't invite me.
Therapist: You were left behind, hm?
Henry: Yes. I put it out of my mind but I couldn't get rid of it. So, I decided to think about it. I asked myself, "Why did I want to go with them? Was it because Michael was going? Did I want Ann just because he had her?" I told you she said I was a brat, so you know that, don't you?
Therapist: Yes.
Henry: So I was thinking. Did I want to own Ann? So what if I did? Many a man owns his wife. Ownership doesn't have to mean you want to destroy a thing. Well, anyway, I asked myself, "Why did I want to be with someone who didn't want me?" It wasn't just that I wanted to be a part of the group, although I do like to be in the group. I think I told you that about my feeling bad about not being invited to parties, didn't I?
Therapist: Yes.
Henry: That's what I thought. Well, I decided it wasn't just that. So, I tried to think back about how I felt at the time. Do you know what I was craving?
Therapist: No. Do you want to tell me?
Henry: Well, it's very hard to put into words, but it's sort of a feeling of importance. I wanted to feel important, that's all. That's what I've been craving all along.
Therapist: You have really found out something about yourself.
Henry: Yes. It was that feeling of importance. You know, when I first started coming to you I had so many worries. Now I have just one

big worry: how to keep myself from worrying. I have a fear that the Devil will sort of seep into my mind. I don't really believe in the Devil, but in a way I do. I'm just afraid he might seep into my mind. It's sort of a vague feeling. I can't express it.

Therapist: It's uncomfortable to think of his taking control of you, is that it?

Henry: Yes. How can I prevent it? That's something I haven't quite figured out. Do you know how?

Therapist: No, but I guess it is pretty puzzling for you.

Henry: Yes, it is. I was afraid to tell you, but I feel better now.

(The hour ended. One week later, Henry again brought up the matter of the Devil.)

Henry: Last week I was telling you about my worry over the Devil seeping into my mind. I was afraid he might punish me for telling you. So I decided to think about it. I tried to recapture my feeling about the Devil. I asked myself, "Who is he?" And guess who he is. *Me! I* am the Devil! *I* make myself worry. All this time, the Devil has been me.

Therapist: So that you are your *own* Devil?

Henry: Exactly. I am my own Devil. All this time, I've been fighting a part of myself, using up so much of my energy to fight a part of myself, and keeping myself so tired. Using energy I could have had for other things. Say, what happened to the room?

Therapist: Is there something?

Henry: It suddenly got lighter, like if there was a fog or a mist and an opening, and it got bigger, and the fog lifted and the mist disappeared. You mean, you don't see it? *(Incredulously.)*

Therapist: No. But things look much brighter to you now?

Henry: Yes. It happened when I was telling it to you. It's amazing — hm. Well, that's something. I realize now that I can think through my problems. That's something I've discovered. Now Michael, he thinks about things too, but he just wants to convince himself.

Therapist: You mean, you think to get at the truth, but he tries to fool himself?

Henry: Yes. And now I know I can think things out for myself. Michael just tries to keep himself from worrying, so he says I'm jealous, but I'm not.

Therapist: He thinks you're jealous, but you don't agree.

Henry: Yes. He's jealous of me because Miss Palmer liked me better.

He says she spoiled me. If that was so, they had years in which to make up for it after she left, but they didn't. So that angle doesn't convince me.

(One week later, Henry brings up the same issue.)

Henry: Last time, I was telling you about Michael figuring things out just to keep himself from worrying, just to convince himself. So, when he said I was jealous, why was *I* worried? It wasn't exactly worry, but a sort of a vague feeling. What does "anxiety" mean?

Therapist: Sort of being afraid when you don't know exactly what of.

Henry: Well, then that's not what I mean. I felt sort of anxious, though, when he said it. He kept himself from worrying by convincing himself that he was right. But why should that worry me?

Therapist: Why should it affect you so?

Henry: Yes. I think it's because I *want* him to be worried. Hm. Yes. I think I do want him to worry. God knows he caused me plenty of worry in the past. Well, I never realized that.

Therapist: It's a new thing to see yourself as wanting him to worry, hm?

Henry: Yes. But why? Of course, I did feel bad when Gerald said he'd rather have Michael than me. Michael said I was jealous of their closeness. Well, the reason they're so close is first of all because they're closer in age. But the real reason is that Gerald needs to have someone boss him around and Michael is only too glad to have someone to direct, so they get on. But that's beside the point. Am I jealous? I don't think so. If it was jealousy, there'd be some feeling of anger or hate, but there isn't. It can't be envy either, because I don't want to be in Michael's shoes. So what is it? I tried to think back to how I felt at the time. That's a way I've discovered. It's so hard to explain. Do you understand?

Therapist: It's really hard to put into words, isn't it? It's not jealousy or envy, yet there is a kind of an uncomfortable feeling there, is that it?

Henry: Uncomfortable in a way, but that's still not it exactly. Why should it be so hard to put it into words? It's a sort of a sorrow, when I think of Gerald saying he preferred Michael.

Therapist: A sadness?

Henry: Yes. A sort of sadness, a sorrow. I guess I felt sorry for myself. I probably always have.

Therapist: Pitying yourself has been — *(interrupted)*

Henry: An important part, yes. Sorrow for myself. That's it, not jealousy, but sorrow. I see it now. Sorrow.

Here, we have a case of astonishing self-scrutiny resulting in sophisticated understandings, in a thirteen-year-old boy, after two years of therapy. Was this process actually play therapy, or was it an interview series? It seems to have been both. There were many hours in which Henry said not a single word, but played with the clay, water, and dolls. Other hours were pure interviews. Apparently, Henry was able to do what was helpful for him, for during his therapy many changes in him were obvious. All of his many tics disappeared entirely. His stuttering ceased. He sought to participate in group games. His schoolwork improved. His tested intelligence rose forty I.Q. points. Most important, he became able to consider himself and his problems calmly, and to feel able to work things out for himself. Was the unusual length of his therapy a function of the severity of his disturbance or might it have been shortened by more skill on the part of his student-therapist? We can raise the question, but the answer cannot now be determined.

The Meaning of the Hour to the Child

In an hour which belongs to him, the child finds an adult who is not shocked by anything he does, who allows the expression of his every feeling, and who treats his utterances with a respect which no other adult offers to the same extent. The therapist's acceptance of the child's right to feel as he does in no way implies approval of any particular attitude. Reflection and clarification of feelings serve to help the child to bring them out into the open, where they can be looked at. If the child feels understood, he tends to bring out deeper material. Since the therapist reflects feelings which are positive, negative, or ambivalent, and regardless of their object or the number of times they occur, no specific attitude or content is valued above the rest. The child has no way of knowing the therapist's opinion. As neither praise nor blame is forthcoming, the child's expressions are determined by his needs, rather than by the therapist's persuasion. The uniqueness of this kind of experience may be perceived to a greater extent than the therapist sometimes realizes. Thus Fred, a seven-year-old boy, brought a friend to his fifth therapy hour.

Fred's explanations to Jimmy sounded as though he had himself received them from the therapist, although this was not the case. Here is a part of the discussion between them.

Jimmy: What kind of paint should I use? (*The remark is addressed to the therapist.*)
Fred: Why, use the one you want to use!
Jimmy: That isn't very polite, Fred.
Fred: You don't have to be polite in here.
Jimmy: I think that isn't very nice, not to be polite.
Fred: You don't understand. You can do what you want in here.
Jimmy: I can?
Fred: Sure!
Jimmy: This is very strange.
Therapist: Fred feels at home in here, but Jimmy is surprised when nobody tells him what to do.
Jimmy: Yes. This is very strange, very strange. (*He begins to paint with the water colors.*)
Therapist: It seems very different to you, Jimmy?
Jimmy: Yes. It's in the school, isn't it?
Fred: Yes, it's in the school, but this is a different kind of a room. You'll find out, Jimmy.
Jimmy: I will? Hmm.
Therapist: Jimmy still thinks this is kind of peculiar.
Jimmy: Yes, I do. It's strange, and *you* are a strange woman.
Therapist: Everything seems so different, and me too?
Jimmy: Uh-huh.
Fred: Yes, she *is* a strange woman, Jimmy. (*They whisper together a moment.*) Yes, you can tell her!
Jimmy: You're a nice teacher. (*Blushing.*)
Fred: She *is* a nice teacher.
Therapist: You both like me.
Jimmy: Where should I put this paint brush?
Therapist: Anywhere you like, it's up to you.
Jimmy: My God, this is strange!
Therapist: It's queer not to be told what to do?
Jimmy: It sure is.
Fred: You'll find that there are very few rules in here. You can even throw those rubber knives around. Not where they might knock over the paints, though. (*And then, thoughtfully, he adds:*) It makes sense.
Therapist: Some rules seem O.K.? (*There is no reply.*)

It is evident from this excerpt that in his previous contacts, Fred must have grasped many of the essential features of the therapy hour. Its permissiveness, its difference from other experiences, the existence of limits, were understood. Although they had not been specifically verbalized to him, he had sensed them clearly enough to be able to explain them to a newcomer. A child may sense that "something is going on" in the therapy hour even when he gives no overt indication to the therapist. A further example may be seen in the case of Martha, an eleven-year-old referred for quarrelsomeness, crying spells, and chronic thumbsucking. Her first four therapy contacts were filled mainly with disparaging remarks about the therapy situation, the play materials, the therapist's clothing, her mother, her teacher, the school, and her classmates. It was the therapist's judgment that there was no acceptance whatever of the therapeutic relationship. Yet when her father asked her what play therapy was like, she replied, "Well, it's kind of relaxing. It's like going to the toilet." Apparently the term "catharsis" is no mere flight of fancy.

Are There Risks?

One of the questions frequently asked concerning the permissiveness in client-centered play therapy is, "Isn't there danger of the child's doing these socially taboo things outside of therapy, where he may run into serious trouble? Perhaps all this freedom of expression is no service to the child, and even less so to his parents." There are several possible explanations of why dangerous "acting out" is unlikely to be a problem in this kind of therapy. First of all, the therapist has carefully refrained from praising any form of behavior or from "egging on" the child to say or do any particular thing. Hence, the child is more apt to feel responsible for his expressions; he cannot put this responsibility upon the therapist. Second, the child is usually quite aware that the therapy sessions are different from daily life. The case of Fred, cited above, is an illustration of this. In the third place, prohibitions experienced by the child in his life situation have not removed his need for a particular behavior, however disruptive.

If the therapist were to become another agent of society, the child would merely again be faced with his old problem. To be accepted as a person despite one's glaring deficiencies seems to be an important part of therapy. It is therefore necessary for the child to bring his real feelings, no matter how anti-social, out into the open, when he feels safe enough to do so. He cannot be sure that the therapist really accepts him until he has tested him out by demonstrating rejected aspects of his personality. A fourth reason why play therapy is unlikely to promote socially unacceptable conduct outside the sessions is the fact that the therapist's acceptance seems to reduce hostility rather than to increase it. The therapist's careful following along with the child as he works through his feelings appears to affect their deeper determinants. And finally, the therapy hour is not unlimited in its freedom. It is to a consideration of this aspect of play therapy that we now turn.

The Problem of Limits

The therapist establishes no limits upon the child's verbal expression of his feelings. Some feelings, however, are not permitted to be directly expressed in action. Anger, for example, may not be released by breaking windows or otherwise destroying the playroom. Certain activity channels are available for it. The child may bang away on the floor, hit the clay, shout, throw unbreakable toys, and so on. One of the things that a child learns in therapy is that it is not necessary to deny one's feelings, because there are acceptable outlets for them. In this sense, therapy can be a socializing experience. The differences between limits in the playroom and those outside it are twofold. First, the playroom limits are far fewer. Second, there is acceptance of the child's need to break them, and he is not rejected for having this need. If there is to be any "transfer of training" from the therapy hour to the subsequent life situations, there ought to be some resemblance between them. Limits seem to serve this function.

Among the desires not permitted to be acted out directly are destructive impulses toward the therapist. The child may say anything he wishes to the therapist, and these feelings are ac-

cepted and reflected like any others. He is, however, not allowed
a physical attack upon the therapist. The most obvious reason
for this limitation is that it saves wear and tear on fragile therapists. But there are equally important reasons from the child's
point of view. First of all, let us consider that the therapist's
acceptance of the child is an instrument by means of which the
child may come to self-acceptance. What therapist can feel
accepting of a child who is in the process of flattening his cranium
with a mallet? In the second place, hurting the therapist may
arouse the child's deep guilt and anxiety in relation to the only
person who can help him. Fear of retaliation, especially of withdrawal of this unique kind of permission to be oneself, may
destroy the possibility of therapy. An article by Bixler (29)
points out the usefulness of making the limit against hitting the
therapist a total one. That is, it gives both child and therapist a
greater security. If the limit were, "You may hit me a little,
but you can't really hurt me," it might irresistibly challenge the
child to test out the prohibition and see what constitutes "hurting."
The therapist's calm acceptance of the child is unlikely to be facilitated by the anticipation of mayhem. On the other hand, the
child is permitted to murder the therapist in effigy. If the therapist accepts the child's feeling of anger, this act of symbolic
destruction can be a beneficial part of therapy, and need not
arouse deep guilt feelings. Here is an example in a contact with
a ten-year-old boy, referred for his poor schoolwork and atten-
tion-getting rumpuses in class. The interview is reproduced
from the therapist's notes.

> (*The door opened and Bob literally leaped into the room.*)
> Bob (*making noise like machine-gun*): Rrrattatataaaa! I'm Mr. District
> Attorney! (*Ferocious expression.*)
> *Therapist:* You're a very tough character?
> *Bob:* You bet I am! I'll mow you down!
> *Therapist:* You're so tough you'll even shoot me down.
> *Bob:* Yes! And you! And you! And you! And you! (*He shoots at
> various unnamed parties with his imaginary gun.*)
> *Therapist:* Everybody's getting shot.
> *Bob:* I'll say they are! Rrrattattattaaa. All dead now!

Therapist: You got them all?

Bob: Yeah. (*He gets some clay from the table, rolls it into a ball, and tosses it into the air several times. As he does so, he talks to the therapist.*) Did you know I was a swop?

Therapist: A swop, Bob? (*Uncomprehending.*)

Bob: Yeah, my father says I'm a swop. He's one too. He likes spaghetti, he eats it every day. I like it too, oh boy!

Therapist: You both like spaghetti and you're both swops?

Bob: Yeah. I bet I can hit the ceiling.

Therapist: I bet you can too, and it'd be fun, but no clay on the ceiling, Bob.

Bob: Why not?

Therapist: It's too hard to get it off.

Bob: (*He tosses the ball several times. When it gets within an inch or two of the ceiling, he looks at the therapist.*)

Therapist: You want to see how I'm taking it?

Bob: I do! (*He tosses the clay ball again. It gets nearer and nearer to the ceiling.*) Heh heh heh!

Therapist: Bob, I know you'd like to throw clay at the ceiling. That's one of the things we can't do in here. You can throw it at the target or at the floor if you want to.

Bob: (*He says nothing, but goes to the table and begins to pound the clay ball flat.*)

Therapist: (*Comes and sits down opposite him, but says nothing.*)

Bob: Wait till you see what I'm making.

Therapist: You mean, it'll surprise me?

Bob: You'll see in a minute.

Therapist: I'll soon find out?

Bob: (*He makes a clay figure.*) It's a man.

Therapist: A man?

Bob: (*He puts a skirt on the figure, with great glee. He looks mischievously at the therapist.*) Guess who it is now.

Therapist: I don't know, Bob. Do you want to tell me?

Bob: My dear teacher, how do you do? (*He hits the clay figure with his fist.*)

Therapist: Teacher got socked.

Bob: Heh, heh. No, *you* did.

Therapist: Oh, *I* got that one.

Bob: (*He hits the clay figure another blow.*) There!

Therapist: I got another sock.

Bob: I'll say you did! And here's another one for you! (*Hits clay figure again.*)

Therapist: You hit me again.

Bob: And that's not all. Take that! And that! And that! (*He hits harder and harder as he pounds the figure quite flat.*)

Therapist: You're giving me an awful beating.

Bob: You bet I am! Take that one too! I'll mash ya! (*Hits.*) I'll smash ya! (*Hits several times.*)

Therapist: You are very mad at me and I am getting all pounded up.

Bob: Off goes your head!

Therapist: My head's off now.

Bob: There goes your arms!

Therapist: I have no arms now.

Bob: There goes your legs!

Therapist: No more legs left.

Bob: And there goes you! (*He throws the remnant of the clay figure into the basin.*)

Therapist: I am all gone now?

Bob: You're dead. I killed you.

Therapist: I am killed.

Bob: You're all washed up.

Therapist: I am very, very dead?

Bob: You sure are. (*Suddenly, he smiles.*) I'll have you a game of catch now.

Therapist: You want to play with me now? O.K. (*The rest of the hour is spent in a quiet game of "catch" with a ball of clay.*)

This was the first session in which Bob had frankly aimed his aggression against the therapist. The hostility is probably a reaction to being thwarted in his desire to throw clay at the ceiling. Since Bob did not state this connection, the therapist, too, left it unsaid. Apparently, it was not necessary to state it, for following this contact, Bob's attitude in the therapy hours was different. He showed a new interest in compromising his desires with the therapist's own. For example, one of his favorite pastimes continued to be playing catch with the therapist, especially when they tried to keep three balls of clay in the air. His boundless energy was apt to outlast that of the therapist. In previous contacts, the therapist had occasionally said after a while that she was too tired to continue the game. Bob had displayed irritation, and had nagged during the rest of the hour, "Gee whiz, aren't you rested up yet?" After this session, however, he would ask at intervals during a game of catch, "Are you sure you're not too tired to play? Am I throwing them too fast for you? If you want to rest, it's all right with me." He also stopped cheating at target practice, although no mention had ever been made of this. Thus it seems that the symbolic murder of the therapist was helpful, partly because of the victim's ability to accept her fate and her executioner.

Some restrictions exist in every therapy, the most obvious of these being those of time and place. Limits have a positive value, for they lend some structure to the therapeutic situation, and hence reduce its anxiety-inducing potentiality. If consistently enforced, together with an acceptance of the child's desire to break them, they help to increase the predictability of the situation, and thus add to the security of client and therapist. The child knows that the therapist will see him at the regular time, in the familiar room. He is protected against the guilt feelings which may follow acts of extreme destruction. However, it is important that a limit not be made the core of the problem. For example, a child is ordinarily not permitted to defecate in the playroom. If this happens, he is told that there is a toilet for his use, and that no one is allowed to defecate in the playroom. The therapist would state that if he felt he *had* to break this rule, he would have to leave the playroom for the rest of that day, although he could return for the next contact. The child would thus be allowed to make the decision as to whether he would choose to end his play contact by his action. However, if the child's problem were a lack of bowel control, the therapist would not invoke this limit. If the therapist could not honestly accept such behavior, it would probably be better to transfer the case. Otherwise, the therapist's open loathing or ill-concealed guilt at his own rejection of the child might add to the child's difficulties.

Some limits will depend upon the physical circumstances of the playroom. If it is a schoolroom which is also used for classes, there will probably be a rule against pouring paint on the floor. If the therapy room is not used for other purposes, there would be less need to protect the floor. However, if a child asks the reason for a particular limit, it seems wisest to be honest if the rule is a personal one. Thus, "You can't play with my eyeglasses because I don't want to risk their being broken" is preferable to "The school (or the clinic) says you can't play with my eyeglasses." The child will usually spot an attempted deceit, and this will be of no help in therapy.

Some Questions Regarding Limits

The current thinking about the problem of therapeutic limits illustrates further the developing nature of the client-centered approach to play therapy. There is now far more concern with the problem of determining just what activity restrictions are required in order to permit the therapist to remain emotionally accepting of the child. Indeed, some therapists believe that this is the only reason for having limits. There is, however, no unanimity of opinion on this issue. As those therapists who feel more tolerant report the results of their experiments with letting the child take home toys, paint the therapist's face, urinate in the playroom, and the like, the best therapeutic course will become more evident. Another change in our thinking on the matter of limits concerns the question of whether to allow a child to bring another to his therapy contact. In earlier days, it was felt that this was the child's way of evading therapy and making it just another play situation. For this reason, it was not usually permitted. Subsequent experiences with group therapy have led to reconsideration of this problem. In group play therapy, the child's adjustment difficulties are often brought out quite strikingly, and very early in the process. Many children have been helped by group therapy, although the relationship with the therapist is apt to be less close than in individual therapy. Thus far, there are no clear criteria for deciding whether to offer group or individual therapy in a given case. One procedure which has been tried with some apparent success is to accept a child for one weekly individual play contact, and to allow him to join a group for a second contact if he wishes. If therapy can be effected when it is not solely a relationship between two people, as in group therapy, then perhaps allowing a child to bring a friend to an individual therapy session need not hinder the process. Indeed, such an arrangement may be considered group therapy in which the child selects the rest of the group. It may well be that the child, in asking to bring another person, is seeking to evade therapy. However, if the therapist feels sufficiently sure in his own skills to be accepting of this attitude, therapy is still possible. The rationale here is that the child can be trusted to work through his difficulties, including the need to bring another person to his therapy hour. Surely, it cannot always be a mere accident that a child brings one person rather than another to his play contact. Sometimes a child may bring in, one by one, those people who represent his areas of difficulty, and then dismiss each one as his need disappears. Not all client-centered therapists would be willing to permit this, but some are experimenting with allowing the child more control over the therapy situation.

Special Issues in Play Therapy

Although client-centered therapy is basically similar for both children and adults, the play therapist faces some problems more likely to occur in work with children. Some of these need to be specifically discussed, in a consideration of the methods of play therapy.

Unlike the adult, the child rarely refers himself for therapy. Some preliminary work with self-referrals by children has been conducted in a school, by Axline, but no specific report has been published. Ordinarily, the child is in the playroom because he has displeased or worried some adult. Thus, he seldom comes with the conscious desire for self-exploration which character-izes many adult clients who seek help. In many cases, the child accepts the play situation and benefits from it without any indi-cation from the therapist that he is in difficulty. In these in-stances, there is no problem of initial structuring; therapy pro-ceeds without it. At other times, the child arrives and demands to know, "Why am I here?" Ordinarily, the client-centered therapist has little or no diagnostic information in advance of the first therapy hour. However, he does know that some adult was sufficiently concerned to arrange for play therapy. Thus it seems dishonest as well as pointless to profess total ignorance when the child asks. A frank explanation seems to be in order, as a gesture of respect for the child's feelings, when he asks for it. It need not be a great threat if properly handled. Thus, "Your mother brought you to me because of your temper tantrums" would be a most inappropriate response. It would be apt to lead the child to think that the therapist was the mother's agent, who would try to make him over in accordance with the maternal desires. Resistance would be a likely consequence of the child's determination to protect his power field from the therapist's encroachments. On the other hand, a more satisfactory explanation might be, "Your mother was concerned because things didn't seem to be going so well at home. She thought it might help if you had someone outside the family to whom you could come and talk things over." It is often necessary to add that the referring adult will never know the contents of the therapy hour. Beyond this, the therapist says nothing, but waits for the child's next move.

When an adult wishes to discontinue psychotherapy, he can usually just stop coming. The child seldom has this option. Who shall be responsible for the continuance or discontinuance of the child in psychotherapy? A strictly client-centered reply would hold that it should be up to the child to decide whether he will come. Very often, however, the reality situation is such that he does not have this choice. A parent or a school or some other institutional authority insists that the child remain in therapy until his behavior is more satisfactory to them, or for some prescribed length of time. Thus, to ask the child whether he cares to come back would be a mockery, unless the referring agent is actually willing for the child to discontinue therapy. Within this framework of compulsion, a nondirective approach is still possible. When the child asks, the therapist can state that he himself cannot require the child to come, and that such authority does not belong to him. In a school situation, the therapist who is an outsider and comes only for play therapy contacts is apt to have an easier time of it than a regular staff member, for he can truthfully assure the child that playroom events will not be a part of school records, nor reported to parents or teachers. Suspicion of betrayal is less apt to fall upon the head of one who is not seen hobnobbing with teachers. Although the child may be compelled to come to the therapy hour, he is not obliged to spend it in any particular way. Once the playroom door closes behind him, he is boss, subject to the broad limits outlined above. If he declines to participate in any way, he is permitted this refusal. Like his action, his silence is a secret between him and the therapist. The question arises of how long an apparently deadlocked case should be permitted to continue. The therapist's time may be required for cases on a waiting list. One approach which has seemed feasible is for the child to be told that he must come a certain number of times, and that afterwards, he may discontinue if he wishes. On the basis of limited experience in a school situation, it appears that at least half the children given such an option will decide to continue therapy. No doubt the therapist's skill is a very important variable here. It is, of course, necessary that the therapist have the consent of the institution concerned before he makes such an arrangement with the child.

When an adult arrives at the psychologist's office, he finds a physical arrangement which is suitable for him whether he is twenty or sixty years old. The playroom does not have this characteristic. A young adolescent may be quite humiliated at finding himself compelled to occupy a room where everything seems to be in miniature. Perhaps it would be better to allow those of approximately eleven years and over to choose between the playroom and an office, after inspection of each. In the absence of this possibility, the following kind of arrangement has been tried with reasonable success. The play materials are at one end of a large adult-size table. At the other end, two adult-size chairs face each other across it. In this way, the child has the choice of an across-the-table relationship if he wishes it. Some children will utilize this set-up as an almost straight interview situation; others of the same age will choose to play. Whatever the decision, it has the advantage of being the child's own.

RESEARCH IN PLAY THERAPY

Thus far, the principles and methods of play therapy from a client-centered point of view have been roughly outlined. The reader in search of a more detailed and profusely illustrated report is referred to the book by Axline (14). It now seems appropriate to turn to a consideration of the existing research studies, in order to evaluate their accomplishments and to clarify what needs to be done.

Thus far, relatively little research has been done in this area, largely because of the difficulty of collecting the required raw data. Phonographic recordings alone cannot give an adequate picture of the process of play therapy, for the sounds are often meaningless by themselves. It is necessary to have detailed descriptions of the activities in the course of which the recorded sounds were made. The therapist's own notes can never be complete, because some children require the therapist's active participation in play. For example, it is impossible to write notes while finger-painting. The cost of employing an observer to write behavior descriptions, and later to integrate them with the sound recording, is prohibitive. There are also other difficulties involved. If a desk microphone is used, severe pounding on the table on which it stands may break it. The use of a hanging microphone entails prohibiting any throwing of objects in its vicinity. If the recording machine is itself in the playroom, it has to be protected from the child's tender ministrations. Thus there may be danger of making the therapist into a policeman. However, where the child is not too aggressively active, recording can actually aid the therapy process. If the child is permitted to play back some of his recorded material, embarrassment is the usual first reaction. After this phase, surprising insights may occur. These are usually of the variety, "I didn't realize I was being so bossy," or "So that's how I've been acting!" A study of this particular problem has never been conducted, and might well be worth the attempt.

Attempts to Analyze Play Therapy Protocols

The process of play therapy, as distinct from its outcomes, has thus far been subjected to only two research studies. Landisberg and Snyder (108) studied the protocols of four children between the ages of five and six years. The work of three therapists was involved. Three of the cases were judged successful on the basis of reports of behavior outside the therapy hours; one was a failure. Presumably, these cases were not phonographically recorded. The aim of the study was the analysis of client and therapist responses in order to determine their trends throughout the course of therapy. The method of analysis used was that developed by Snyder for adult cases, and already referred to in Chapter 4, above. Briefly, the procedure was to divide the protocols into idea units which were then categorized. Therapist statements were classified as to content. Client statements were classified as to content and feeling. Re-categorization of three interviews after a three-month interval resulted in duplication of the original classifications from 72 to 85 per cent of the times. Inter-scorer reliability ranged from 45 per cent to 76 per cent. This is considerably lower than that reported by Seeman (180), whose work has already been outlined in Chapter 4. The discrepancy may be a function of the use of a relatively untrained judge by Landisberg and Snyder.

It was found that 75 per cent of therapist responses fell into the nondirective category (simple acceptance, recognition of feeling, re-statement of content). This is in fair agreement with the 85 per cent and 63 per cent reported by Seeman and by Snyder, respectively, for adult cases. Interpretations comprised 5 per cent of all therapist responses. This may be compared with the 8 per cent reported by Snyder and the 1 per cent by Seeman. Whether an analysis of more recent play therapy cases would show closer agreement with Seeman's results is problematical. It is quite possible that in a study based upon only four cases, observed discrepancies reflect sampling errors.

With respect to the client categories, the most marked trend was an increased physical activity during the last three fifths of the therapy process. Also, during the latter period, about 70 per cent of client responses were expressions of feeling (verbally or in action). This percentage is significantly greater than the approximately 50 per cent observed in the first two quintiles. A Chi Square analysis indicated that the increased feeling was significantly related to the actions, rather than to the verbal responses. This is in agreement with common formulations of the rationale of play therapy. Unlike results reported for adult cases, Landisberg and Snyder found that it was the negative feelings which increased during play therapy. Positive feelings remained about 30 per cent of client responses throughout therapy. This is contrary to Seeman's data for adults. Although negative feelings comprised about 15 per cent of the child's responses during the first quintile, in the final fifth of therapy negative and positive feelings were of the same frequency. The latter finding is in agreement with that part of Seeman's report in which no distinction was drawn between tenses of expressed attitudes. Furthermore, in contrast to results with adult cases, children's expressions of feelings tended to be more and more directed toward other persons as therapy progressed. Here again, one cannot know whether this is a true difference between the psychotherapy of adults and children. Because the small sample was also homogeneous with regard to age, it is not even possible to state that the observed trends are likely to be true of the process of play therapy at other age levels. Further investigation is therefore indicated. It might be more fruitful if future research in play therapy did not depend too heavily upon categories derived from the study of adult cases. Categories are ways of summarizing information. In order to be true to their basic data, they ought probably to spring from it. Otherwise, their forced character may mask significant findings.

A study by Finke (59) attempted to overcome the disadvantages of adult-derived categories. Nineteen categories of feelings expressed by children in therapy were employed. These came from an examination of play therapy protocols. Inter-scorer reliabilities for categorizations ranged from 66 per cent to 77 per cent agreement with the original judge.

The aim of the study was to determine whether any trends existed in the differential frequencies among feeling categories during the course of therapy. For this purpose, the therapists' notes on six cases of children between the ages of five and eleven years were analyzed. Four were boys and two were girls. The number of contacts per case ranged from eight to fourteen. Six different therapists were involved. The group included children seen at school and at a children's home. These variations were introduced in order to ensure that results could not be attributed to the effects of any one therapist, playroom, or type of problem. Rather, the one factor common to all the cases was nondirective play therapy.

Only five categories showed significant trends. A trend was defined as a deviation from theoretical frequencies in a consistent direction for at least one-third of the total number of contacts. The category, Story Units (stories made up by the child) showed a peak in the fifth contact and then declined. The category, Attempting to Establish a Relationship with the Counselor, showed a peak in the third contact. Then it remained low until the eighth session, when it rose steadily until the end of therapy. Testing Limits maintained a constant level until the ninth contact, when it began a steady decline. Aggressive Statements reached a peak in the fourth contact, a slump in the fifth, and a second, though lower, peak in contact seven. After this, it declined steadily. Total Number of Statements reached a constant level after the third contact. It should be pointed out that these results were obtained by averaging data from all six cases. Inspection of the individual case graphs showed considerable variation, which may cast doubt upon the averaged results in some instances.

Among the categories which showed no trends during therapy were: Positive Statements About the Self; Negative Statements About the Self; Positive Statements About the Family, Home, Situation, etc.; and Negative Statements About the Family, Home, Situation, etc. These results are of course contrary to those obtained with adult clients. Perhaps the contradiction is partly due to an inherent weakness in this study: its restriction to the child's verbalizations. As Landisberg and Snyder (108) found that increased expression of feeling was significantly related to the action rather than to the verbal responses, it appears necessary for future research to consider this factor.

Studies of the Outcomes of Play Therapy

Other studies of play therapy have been concerned with its outcomes, rather than with the process itself. Among these is one conducted by Cruickshank and Cowen (47, 46) — an exploratory study of group play therapy with physically handicapped children in a special public day school. Five children between the ages of seven and nine years were seen twice weekly for seven weeks. The group included two cardiac cases, and one each of hemophilia, post-poliomyelitis, and post-encephalitis. Before and after the therapy series, teachers and parents wrote essay-type reports stating the chief problems and noting any changes. By this criterion, three of the five children showed improvement. The absence of a control group makes it impossible to say how many of these might have improved without therapy. Thus no definite conclusions may properly be drawn without further investigation.

Axline (13) has reported upon the effect of nondirective psychotherapeutic methods in cases of reading retardation in an elementary school. Thirty-seven second grade children diagnosed as retarded in reading (by means of teacher judgments and standardized reading tests) were selected for the study. Their I.Q. range on the Stanford-Binet was from 80 to 148. They were placed in a special class, where the teacher attempted to create a therapeutic milieu in which adjustment and learning might occur together. No emphasis was placed upon learning to read. Children were encouraged to express their attitudes in the presence of an understanding and permissive teacher. In a strict sense, this was not play therapy, but an adaptation of it for classroom use. Spontaneous statements by the children indicated to the teacher that many had serious personal problems. At the end of the school term, children were re-tested with the Gates Primary Reading Tests for Grades One and Two. During this three-and-one-half month period, there were several remarkable gains in reading age, including some of sixteen and seventeen months. Unfortunately, however, no statistical test was made by Axline. Thus, for the group as a whole, we do not know whether the results differed significantly from chance expectations. In addition, the absence of a control group makes it impossible to evaluate the effects of repetition of the tests without intervening therapeutic experience.

A further study of the effects of nondirective play therapy in cases of reading retardation has been conducted by Bills (24). Eight retarded readers were selected for therapy from a class of twenty-two third grade children. Although this was a class for "slow learners," four of the children were of superior intelligence and four of average intelligence, as measured by Form L of the Stanford-Binet. Their I.Q. range was from 99 to 159, with a mean of 123. These children were chosen on the basis of discrepancies between their mental age scores and reading age as measured by the Gates Primary Reading Tests of Paragraph Meaning. Five of the eight children received six individual and three group play therapy contacts; two had six individual and two group sessions; one had four individual and one group contact. All sessions were phonographically recorded.

The study covered three periods of six weeks each. The first of these was a control period; children were tested at its outset and conclusion, but received no therapy. The second period was the experimental one, during which therapy was offered; reading tests were administered at its close. The third period was a follow-up period, during which no therapy sessions occurred; children were tested upon its conclusion. Thus, instead of comparing an experimental group with a control group, a single group was compared with itself during three intervals. Each child therefore served as his own control, in an experiment in perfectly matched pairs. The assumption here is that the control and therapy periods were comparable with respect to reading experiences. Bills therefore had three judges with teaching experience visit the classroom in order to determine whether reading instruction was alike for the three periods of the study. They concluded that the three intervals were equivalent with regard to reading instruction.

Comparison of reading gains during control and experimental periods by means of the "t" test of significance indicated the superiority of the latter. The results were significant at the .001 level. Comparison of the control period gains with those of the combined experimental and follow-up periods also favored the latter. This difference was significant at the .01 level. Thus, marked reading gain was made by the experimental group during the period of therapy, and this gain was maintained during the post-therapy period.

Bills asked also whether improved reading was due to improved personal adjustment. To answer this question, he conducted a study (25) of play therapy with well-adjusted retarded readers. The design was similar to that of the project just discussed, except that cases were selected for good adjustment on the basis of projective and objective personality tests. In this study, gains were not significantly greater during the therapy period. Therefore, it appears that play therapy may improve reading where retardation exists together with emotional maladjustment. Therapy is not necessarily the method of choice for remediation of reading difficulties per se.

Fleming and Snyder (60) have conducted a study of the effects of nondirective group play therapy upon personality test performance. They used three measures before and after psychotherapy. The first of these, Rogers' Test of Personality Adjustment, is an objective paper and pencil test. The second, a Guess Who test, invites children to name others described by its items, such as, "Who brags and boasts about things that you know aren't so?" This allows a rating of children by their peers. The third test, Fleming's Sociometric Test, asks the child to name two persons in his group with whom he would and would not like to do things. The therapy subjects were four boys and three girls between the ages of eight and one-half and eleven and one-half years. All were residents of a children's home, and were selected because they, of forty-six children tested, made the worst rank scores on a combination of the three measures. Sixteen children left the institution before the end of the study and were therefore not retested. The remaining twenty-three children received no therapy but were tested twice and hence served as controls. The experimental group of boys did not improve significantly more than the control group. This was in agreement with the therapist's judgment of poor rapport in therapy. The girls' group improved significantly more than the control group on all three indices. This, too, was in agreement with the therapist's impressions of the therapy contacts. However, these results cannot be taken entirely at face value. First, experimental design utilizing a control group requires that control and experimental groups be equated for initial status, in this case, maladjustment scores. This may be accomplished by matching pairs, matching total groups by means and standard deviations, or random assignment of cases to each group. None of these methods was employed by Fleming and Snyder. They used as controls those children left after the most maladjusted had been selected out for therapy. Hence, the controls were, by definition, less maladjusted. In the second place, sound procedure requires that the experimental and control groups be treated as nearly alike as possible, except for the experimental variable — in this case, play therapy. The clinic at which these children were treated was ten miles from their institutional home. Thus, twice a week, for six weeks, the experimental group was treated to a long ride and a chance to visit away from the confines of the institution. The control group had no such experience. Hence, improved adjustment scores, when found, might be due to play therapy itself or to the outings which were incidental to it. Thus there appears to be no unequivocal interpretation of the results of this study.

Needed Research

It is apparent from this summary of existing research that much remains to be done. One of the more pressing needs is for follow-up study of a large number of cases, at regular intervals. Instead of repeated follow-up studies of a relatively small number of cases, it might be more fruitful to re-study some cases after six months, others after one year, still others after two years, and so on. In this way, a larger sample of cases might be tapped without adding enormously to the research burden.

A second area of needed investigation is that of the assessment of personal adjustment before and after therapy. The only existing research in this area, that of Fleming and Snyder (60), is concerned with group therapy. A beginning study of personality outcomes of individual play therapy by means of objective and projective tests is now under way at the University of Chicago, but the results are not yet in. As in adult therapy, the problem of experimental controls looms large. Matching methods are notoriously weak, for they fail to cover motivational variables. The use of a control period, as Bills (24, 25) has done, is an improvement in this regard. However, its assumption of control and experimental periods as equivalent except for the variable, play therapy, may not always be tenable. By far the most satisfactory method of experimental control is the random assignment of cases to experimental and control groups. This method requires a pool of candidate cases twice as large as the number actually to be seen in therapy. For this reason, it is not always practical. Studies of outcomes are also hindered by the questionable validity of existing children's personality tests. One approach to the problem of evaluation which has not yet been tried is the Vineland Social Maturity Scale (50). This might be employed in an interview with mothers before and after their children's therapy. It would have the advantage of being a quantitative assessment by one who was familiar with the child's behavior.

Investigation of the actual process of therapy is also necessary. High costs may limit the number of future completely recorded and transcribed cases. For this reason, it is important to be able to evaluate the adequacy of the therapist's notes. In a small number of cases, also phonographically recorded, the therapist and an observer might take notes. Then each of these independent accounts could be compared with the phonographic case record. In this way, the kinds of defects apt to occur in written notes might be learned, in order to ascertain whether it is worth while to base research analyses upon such notes.

Thus far, there has been no attempt to test rather specific hypotheses in a study which would include playroom actions. For example, as therapy progresses, is there a trend from "accidental" to "purposeful" actions? That is, does a child who begins therapy with, "The Daddy fell over," increasingly come to state, "I knocked over the Daddy"? In this connection it might be advisable first to separate the relatively successful from the relatively unsuccessful cases. This would make possible an answer to the question of the nature of changes where these are found to occur.

Another useful addition to our knowledge would be a comparative study of group and individual therapy. Three conditions might be contrasted: individual therapy, group therapy, and a combination of these. Data might be used to furnish information on both process and outcomes of therapy. It is likely that an investigation of this kind would require a cooperative group project.

The therapy protocol might also be used as a validating criterion for personality tests. Client-centered protocols have the particular advantage of being freer from interviewer bias than those of other approaches. A beginning in this direction has been made by Bills and others (26). The possible applications of the "Q" technique to play therapy (201, 202) need to be explored. Still another untried approach is the time-sample method of behavior observation, applied to the therapy session. It is clear, then, that many possibilities lie open for future research workers in the field of client-centered play therapy.

SUMMARY

In summary of this chapter, it may be said that a therapeutic approach which relies primarily upon the client's capacity for constructive use of himself seems to be applicable to children. Its challenge is particularly felt in this area, for children are generally considered to be more at the mercy of their environments than are adults. Despite this, it appears that children have far more ability to deal with themselves and with their interpersonal relationships than is usually credited to them. A relationship in which the child can feel genuinely accepted and respected, despite his faults, seems to help this latent capacity to become manifest.

In this method of play therapy, a child is offered the opportunity to use a particular time period in his own way, subject to a few broad limitations. The child is provided with the play materials which lend themselves as media for expression of his needs, but he may decline to use them if he wishes. The therapist's belief is that the child's decision to do or not to do a particular thing is more beneficial than is the actual performance of it. The child's opportunities for responsible self-direction are maximized, on the theory that the therapy session is a good place to begin to practice it.

As in adult therapy, a basic hypothesis is that a relationship of acceptance, as contrasted with positive or negative evaluation, reduces the need for defensiveness, and thus allows the child to dare to explore new ways of feeling and behaving. Because of this hypothesis, the therapist does not try to affect the pace or the direction of therapy; he follows rather than leads the child. The therapist's aim is to see things through the child's eyes, in order verbally to clarify the child's expressed feelings. However, when the child refuses to allow any access to his private feelings, the therapist accepts this refusal and does not seek to intrude. There is no attempt to alter the child, but only to make possible his self-alteration, when and if he wishes it. In these and other ways the therapist tries to communicate his underlying respect for the child as he is at the moment. The child's perception of this attitude of the therapist seems to aid his use of the relationship with reduced anxiety. It seems to help him to bring out into the open rejected as well as accepted aspects of his personality, and to form some kind of integration among them.

Among the outcomes of successful therapy have been altered peer-group and parent-child relationships, improved schoolwork, change in previous diagnosis of mental defect, reduction of reading disability, disappearance of tics, and cessation of stealing and other socially unacceptable behavior. The areas of application of client-centered play therapy have been wide. Whether they may be extended as far as childhood psychoses is a question for future investigation. Thus far, research studies have been meager and inadequate, but the challenge of the field is clear. As clinical experiences and research studies in play therapy increase in number, scope, and quality, perhaps the perplexing problem of what constitutes psychotherapeutic change may come nearer to solution.

SUGGESTED READINGS

An historical perspective upon client-centered play therapy may be gained from the books by Taft (209), Allen (5), and Axline (14), especially when read in the order given.

Special applications of nondirective play therapy have been described in several articles. Among these are Axline's articles on race conflict (15), mental defect (12), and reading retardation (13). Bills' studies of reading retardation (24, 25) will be of particular interest to the research-minded, for they are the most carefully designed investigations to date. Work with physically handicapped children has been described by Cruickshank and Cowen (47, 46). Special problems arising in a case transferred from one therapist to another are reported by Bixler (30). In another article, Bixler (29) discusses the handling of aggression against the therapist.

For a presentation of a somewhat similar approach applied in a pre-school setting, see the report by Baruch (19). Its application to allergy patients, seven of whom were children, is reported in a later article (133).

Chapter 7 · Group-Centered Psychotherapy

By NICHOLAS HOBBS, PH.D.

In significant respects, group therapy is like individual therapy. It is also distinctly different. The similarities arise from a common purpose and from a shared conception of the nature of human personality and how it changes. The differences arise from the important fact that in individual therapy only two people are immediately involved, whereas in group therapy five or six or seven persons interact in the process of therapy. This multiplication of the number of the participants means more than the extension of individual therapy to several persons at once; it provides a qualitatively different experience with unique therapeutic potentialities.

Although the essential kinship between client-centered therapy and group-centered therapy will be evident in the discussion that follows, an effort will be made to communicate the peculiar genius of group therapy, not just in broad outline, but with details that will bring the reader into intimate understanding of the process, and with quotations from therapy sessions and from diaries about therapy that will let him taste the flavor of the experience. In the tradition established in the development of client-centered therapy, research findings will be brought in to give foundation for generalizations. No argument will be made for the greater economy of group therapy, though this is an impressive consideration when the need for psychological help is so urgent, and clinic waiting lists so long. The possibility that group therapy may actually be more effective than individual therapy, for some people, will only be mentioned here in passing, for research evidence on this point is lacking, although in the neglected field of therapy for the normal person with debilitating situational conflicts group therapy appears to offer advantages over individual therapy. On some issues it will be necessary to write in a most tentative fashion. On other issues there have been enough observation and research to permit writing with some assurance. That the views presented will need to be modified with additional exploration, there is little doubt. There are many gaps and many unanswered questions. But even at this stage of development of group-centered therapy, those who have explored its possibilities and weighed its outcomes have gained a feeling of substance, and a desire to know more of the process.

Groups of diverse composition and purpose have been worked with. Most of our experience has been with a selected population — university students who found themselves disturbed and unable to gain from life the satisfactions they desired. Some of these people suffered from a temporary inability to cope with a situation (as the woman whose husband had been killed in the war and who had not been able to re-pattern her life after his death); others were more severely incapacitated (as the man who was unable to go ahead with his plans to be a teacher because of intense anxiety when with people). All shared this favorable characteristic: they felt keenly the discrepancy between themselves and their aspirations for themselves, and they actively sought help. In addition to a considerable amount of work with these normal but troubled individuals, there have been groups made up of people with some specific kind of problem or purpose: combat veterans with a psychiatric diagnosis of "anxiety reaction"; college students who desired to change their feelings of racial or religious prejudice; mothers whose children were receiving individual play therapy; unhappy children who were brought for therapy by their parents, and children who could not learn to read; boys from a Harlem gang, who came to therapy on the invitation of a worker who had become friendly with them; veterans with multiple sclerosis, who sought more comfortable ways of living with their organically changing selves; severely disturbed individuals with chronic headaches and other continuing neurotic symptoms; and clinic outpatients with a psychiatric diagnosis of schizophrenia. In the main, however, our efforts have been to help the "average" man, of whom there is certainly more than an "average" number. A major objective has been to discover more efficient ways of working with the great·numbers of essentially normal people who find that life has lost its savor, who quietly struggle along with their problems, who pay great costs in extra energy for their achievements, and who have tremendous potential for responding to assistance. Concern for this large group of people stamps the account that follows.

An Illustration of Group-Centered Therapy

It will be helpful first to see what happens when people come together in a group to work on their personal problems. Here is a verbatim transcript of part of a first hour of group-centered therapy with six university students, all preparing for jobs in schools or colleges.[1] The names have been changed and all identifying information removed. Jane Harrison, age 23, is a nursery school teacher. Kay Madison, age 35, is a guidance worker in a Southern high school. Anne Jensen, age 21, and the youngest member of this group, does not talk during this session. Mary Conway, age 33, has had several years' experience teaching English. Laura Preston, age 27, is a teacher and part-time school psychologist. Betty Arnold, age 28, has taught in secondary schools, is now working for an M.A. in guidance.

Jane: One thing I might say is my particular feeling that I want to work on a problem of the concept of dependence and independence in marriage. I've been married about a year and married to — he's a law student — who is primarily an unemotional person, and I would say there's a good deal of lack of understanding between us. The conflict

[1] First published in the *Journal of the National Association of Deans of Women*, Vol. XII, March, 1949, pp. 114–121, and reproduced here by permission.

was mainly one of my desire to be independent and not being independent, in the marriage relationship, and the marriage not being a fifty-fifty relationship.

Leader: It's not wholly satisfactory to you now.

Jane: No, it is not a satisfactory relationship, but I do think there's a good deal of possibility of its being a satisfactory relationship.

Betty: (*Pause.*) I think most of my trouble is not having enough confidence in myself to assert myself when I am with others. I feel confidence in being able to *do* things, but when I'm in a social group or in a classroom, I more or less withdraw and let everybody else do the talking and thinking. I think a lot of that is probably a result of the fact that in our family my father is a very dominant person, and is *the* person in the family so that everyone else is being subdued to his wishes. Now, I suppose that feeling carries over into other relationships too, a feeling of not being — of not having a great deal of personal worth or value.

Leader: You feel rather confident of your ability, privately or as an individual, yet when you work with people you tend to devaluate yourself.

Betty: That's right. I tend to evade issues or withdraw — instead of meeting them face on.

Leader: Yes.

Jane: Does that happen in small groups as well as larger ones — amongst — uh, intimate family and social relationships?

Betty: With a small group of *good* friends that I've known for some time, I don't have that feeling, but in a classroom or with my family groups, when we have relatives in, or just a gathering of family friends, I stick in the background.

Leader: You have to feel pretty strongly supported by a small group of people before you feel free to be yourself. (*Pause as another member arrives.*) Miss Preston, we got everyone's first name down here, what is your first name?

Laura: Laura.

Leader: Laura, that's right.

Kay: I think the thing I've got to work out is an acceptance of my personal situation. I've accepted it mentally and I see that I have several choices in what to do, but I want to accept them emotionally as well. This is probably due to the fact that I — my husband was killed about two years ago in a very tragic sort of way. His plane went down in the Pacific. No one was saved. It was after the war was over and he was about ready to come home. And while I can see how it happened, I still don't accept it, and I want just the emotional acceptance of my life from here on.

Leader: You've been able to work out something of an intellectual or rational understanding of the situation and what you should do, but you haven't yet been able to bring your feelings around to where they are, say, under control.

Kay: If I'm walking down the street and I look into a shop window, perhaps see an article of clothing he would have liked, it throws me completely and I —.

Leader: Find all these emotions welling back up.

Kay: That's right. Maybe the odor of tobacco that he used, something of that sort; and it's been two years, I should begin to control the emotions.

Mary: I have difficulty controlling my emotions, too — feelings.

Leader: Some similarity there. (*Long pause.*)

Jane (*to Kay*): Did you have a happy relationship with him?

Kay: Yes, I had a perfect relationship with him, one of the kind where each went 90 per cent of the way and it adds up to 50 per cent. And one of the things I think helped to do that: We had to depend on each other, because we lived a long time in a foreign country. We had *no* outside forces and we depended entirely upon each other.

Leader: You had a very warm relationship. He was almost your whole life.

Kay: I had known him all my life, and I had not — we didn't marry when we were very young; it was my own fault; and all the time he had been very fond of me and, as I grew older, I appreciated more and more how he felt about me. And I think it wasn't so much that I loved him, as that I was so secure in his love for me. Well, that was the greatest thing about it, you see. And I did love him, and I learned to appreciate him more and more.

Jane: Did you — were you ever insecure about people loving you before?

Kay: Yes, I've never been very secure with anybody, my parents were divorced, I never had anybody who was *all* mine.

Leader: You really found it in him, didn't you?

Kay: Yes. And not only — I recognized it and then I worked at it. For instance, I tried to make myself essential to him every way I could, you see. (*Pause.*)

Jane: Well, I guess essentially what you had is what I want.

Laura: Well, actually, I have been sitting here — uh, in a sense envying Kay for the happiness you have had. Sometimes we don't recognize the importance of something like that when we have it.

Leader: The really deep love of someone?

Laura: That's right, and how fortunate she was in being able to recognize those things she had been denying for so long. She actually lived with him for awhile.

Kay: I try to tell myself that. And I knew that. As I look around at people, I feel very fortunate to have had that (*pause*) and I realize that, but I still just can't accept it.

Leader: It kind of overwhelms you.

Laura: Well, the thing that struck a note was the fact — that you didn't know for so *very long*, which is pretty similar to where I find my problems starting, in that I didn't know either. And I went on not knowing and never did have a chance, you see. And, right now, I'm faced with a problem that my mother in particular accuses herself. That's the pity of the situation.

Leader: Makes you feel pretty bad.

Laura: Well, I want to apologize to her in the way that I can and assure her that it isn't her fault. Because whether it is or it isn't is beside the point. But you can't go on feeling this was the only thing in life for me. There is a whole lot more. And with pressures all around you, you begin to take an easy way and say, well, maybe it was her fault, and maybe it is a pitiable situation, and maybe this, and maybe that.

Leader: Makes you feel that you'd have to fight against her.

Laura: That's right, and it doesn't leave room for making a happy adjustment all around. It's not right. In school, at work, with friends, any place — you're constantly impressed with this horrible situation that you're in. And that's no good.

Leader: It stays with you pretty much of the time.

Laura: That's right, mostly because it's easy to adopt someone else's attitude without thinking for yourself. And I'm sure that if my mother realized just how very destructive the thing she's doing is, she would try in every way to change. But if I told her, she would be all the more hurt, and I can't tell her.

Kay: Yes, I know what you mean. That's partly the reason I came here, to get out of that situation. Because when I walk into a room, everyone stops talking, and you *feel* the sympathy they have for you, and you don't want that. Pretty soon you get to feeling sorry for yourself. Because, if I had — I haven't any worries. There isn't anything I should be upset about.

Betty: You find, too, that it is very difficult to get away from the things that people think about you.   If they always thought of you as being a very sensible or practical person, you get so that you just can't do anything that isn't sensible or practical, because other people will frown at you or express horror that you do something that they didn't expect you to do.

Leader: So you tend to shape your behavior according to the expectations of other people.

Betty: Very frequently, if I want to do something, I'll say, well, how will my parents feel about it, and I probably won't do it if I feel they won't approve.

Mary: This subject of people feeling sorry for you — does things to you, when the situation may actually not be half as bad.

Leader: You get to believe it yourself.

Mary: Definitely, and soon you capitalize on it.

Leader: Yes.

Jane: It begins to be a very easy way out of your situation by feeling sorry for yourself.   I know that I've done it many times.   And I've spent a lot of time alone, and I begin to think, home was never like this, and feel very sorry for myself.   And I find it is a very easy way out of facing myself.

Kay: Why do you have to go to school?

Jane: He's got three years of school, and if he wants to practice, he's got several years of routine work.   So he is in a position where he will earn nothing for about five years.

Kay: And now you plan to work this fall, to begin work?

Jane: Yeah, I plan to be the financial boost to him, so that he can go on.   And I feel very strongly about not taking money from the folks, because my relationship with my parents is not a very good one.   And my relationship with my in-laws — I feel that if I take money from them, and they're in a position to give it, I feel I would have to answer to my mother-in-law for the rest of my life.   That is a thing I would find very hard to do, because she would like to show you how to blow your nose, if you give her a chance.   (*Laughter.*)

Kay: But actually, they're very human.

Jane: They are, they're very human.   And if you sit down and think about it, they're mothers, and they've spent all of their lives bringing up these boys and then we take them away from home.   And their interests are elsewhere.   And it's hard for them; it's a very hard adjustment to make, I imagine. I suppose when there comes a time that I'll be a mother-in-law, I won't be much better.

Kay: Why do you feel, I mean, well, you must feel that he loves you, that he did love you.

Jane: Well, he's not very emotional and I'm a very emotional person. I feel that he's quite reserved. It was a great deal of time before he showed any overt affection towards me in everyday relationships. You begin to feel that, to put it callously, you were married for financial reasons and other reasons. You begin to wonder, especially when I need a good deal of emotional support and I find that I don't get it, due to circumstances.

Leader: It's really very disturbing to have those feelings.

Jane: It is, there's a great deal of guilt attached to it, too, because I was always brought up with the feeling that you should never think those things about your husband.

Leader: So, you tend to blame yourself when you do have thoughts like that.

Jane: Yes, and I take the attitude that everything that's wrong with our marriage is my fault. I tend to take that attitude, so that he's got the feeling that well, he's just — he's perfect.

Kay: Have you discussed it with him? Does he realize how insecure you feel?

Jane: Yeah, he's beginning to realize now. And as I said, not until recently has he begun — I will say that essentially there's a great deal of possibility that we can develop a relationship that will be satisfactory to both of us.

Leader: There are many positive factors.

Jane: Yes, there are; he comes around. But it's at a terrific expense to me emotionally, but he does come around. A great many scenes have to occur before he realizes some things. And then he'll come around to it.

Kay: Is that because, uh, do you express this feeling that you have. Or do you just let him blindly have to guess at them?

Jane: I don't express it too much, no.

Kay: Well, you see, he doesn't really know.

Jane: Well, he doesn't know, that's true.

Leader: It's very hard for you to express your feelings to him.

Jane: Yes, because I — if I break down and do it and then I'm put in a position where I am not as high as what I would like to be. I feel that I'm not as mature as I would like to be. (84, pp. 118–121)

INDIVIDUAL AND GROUP THERAPY — SIMILARITIES AND DIFFERENCES

There Are Similarities

With the above excerpt providing concrete material for consideration, we may gain in understanding of the subtle and complex process of group therapy by making comparisons with the more familiar process of individual client-centered therapy. The most elusive of all the qualities evident in the session reproduced should probably be considered first because it is fundamental — the kind of climate or atmosphere or feeling that was gradually built up — that has to be built up if there is to be gain from the group experience. As in individual client-centered therapy, the members of a group must perceive the situation they are in as being dependably sustaining of their selves. They bring to the situation a freight of anxiety, a product of their unsuccessful efforts to relate themselves effectively to other people, and this anxiety is usually heightened by the indeterminate nature of the impending experience in therapy. It is believed that each member of a group, if he is to profit from therapy, must find in the therapist and in other members of the group a genuine feeling of acceptance. He must find in the group situation increasingly less need for the defenses against anxiety which render him so ineffectual in living with others and so unhappy in living with himself. As in individual therapy, he must feel increasingly free to examine himself, with assurance that there will be an understanding of his life as he sees it, and that there will be respect for him as a person every step of the way. It is also desirable and probably necessary that the individual in a group find a quiet confidence in his ability to be responsible for his own life, and a willingness for him to make choices regardless of their direction, the final confidence being that he will make decisions essential to the full realization of himself.

Even in the first session quoted above we find members very open with each other, sensing somehow the support that was even then present, and that would grow as the meetings continued. Kay was able to talk about a hurt that she had kept to herself for two years. Jane revealed herself to the other women present, a risk she had not dared take before, according to her diary notes of the meetings. Mary, Laura, and Betty tentatively described a source of their unhappiness. Only Anne was dubious and uncertain, remaining quiet for this session and several more until she was confident of the support of the group, then describing the fears and torturing dreams she had, and perhaps in the end gaining more than anyone else in the group.

The reader will surely want to ask how one can be certain that attitudes of confidence and respect will pervade a group, a question that points up one of the differences between individual and group therapy. In the single client-therapist relationship, these crucial attitudes can usually be assured, for the entire training of the therapist has stressed the importance of these principles and his momentary concentration is directed toward communicating them to his client. But in the group others are present, and they are not likely at first to be able to express such feelings. They are too bound up within themselves, and they are probably little aware of the importance of much else beyond a need to find relief from their own distress. This difficulty is something of a paradox in group therapy, being at once a source of weakness and of strength. If these important attitudes do not develop in a group, the undertaking is likely to be of little benefit, and the therapy a failure. If, however, they are nurtured by the therapist and reinforced by the affirmative feelings of the members of the group, they are likely to be significantly more effective in the group situation than in individual therapy. It is one thing to be understood and accepted by a therapist, it is a considerably more potent experience to be understood and accepted by several people who are also honestly sharing their feelings in a joint search for a more satisfying way of life. More than anything else, this is the something added that makes group therapy a qualitatively different experience from individual therapy.

A characteristic of individual therapy that one would not expect to find in group therapy is the feeling of direction and singleness of purpose. The individual problems of six individuals could reasonably be expected to exert a centrifugal effect on the group. But in fact this does not seem to happen. In both content and feeling, groups grow to a remarkable cohesiveness that parallels the unity evident in individual therapy. For one thing, diverse as symptoms and situations are, there are only a few kinds of problems that people can have. Time and time again, the breakdown of interpersonal relations and the attendant feelings of self-worthlessness provide the content for group discussions. But perhaps more important than similarity of content is the unity that comes from a sharing of feelings. In the excerpt below, two group members, differing by some twenty years in age and perceiving their problems to be quite different, come to an intimate understanding on the basis of feeling:

Mr. Helm: I thought that there was so much difference in our two ages that there might be a gap there. Somehow he closed the gap the other day. I feel that underneath we all have that same feeling. So many of our problems are all the same.

Therapist: I'm not sure, Mr. Helm, that I understand just how you see that relationship.

Mr. Helm: Well, I had the feeling that somehow I couldn't quite understand the scope of his problem, and how much this problem really meant to him. Yet, as he spoke on Monday, I had the feeling of great empathy with him. Not so much that I have the same problem, but because I could see how another person feels carrying a burden like that round with you all the time. Because even though we may have different problems, the feelings these problems create are pretty much the same, and, uh, the feeling that he's going around carrying the same burden all the time — well, thinking about it made me feel much closer to him.

Miss West: That's better said. That's what I was trying to say.

Therapist: You feel closer to him not because of a similarity of problem but because of a similarity of feeling.

Mr. Helm: By and large, I think that has been typical of the whole group. Each of us has been able to express our feelings, and the others have accepted it.

There are also similarities between individual and group therapy on the level of technique. These may be summarized here and illustrated at greater length later. As in individual therapy, techniques are important as media for expressing the attitudes described above. They grow out of these attitudes and are an expression of them, but they are also whittled down and shaped to usefulness by accumulated experience in therapeutic relationships.

Essentially, what the therapist attempts to do is to reconstruct the perceptual field of the individual at the moment of expression, and to communicate this understanding with skill and sensitivity. The various terms that have been used to describe the kinds of statements that the therapist makes in individual therapy — such as clarification of feeling, reflection of feeling, restatement of content, simple acceptance, structuring, and so on — are appropriate to the group situation as well, and there are other similarities that should be mentioned in passing. The concern with diagnosis is minimal, interpretation is not relied on as a therapeutic instrument, insight is not considered to be an essential change-agent in the process of learning, transference attitudes are handled just like all other affect-laden expressions, and the most effective predictor of possible gain from the therapy is considered to be the experience itself.

These are the similarities.

And There Are Differences

Group therapy has identifiable characteristics not found in the counseling relationship when only two persons are involved. One of the most important of these distinctive characteristics lies in the fact that the group situation brings into focus the adequacy of interpersonal relationships and provides an immediate opportunity for discovering new and more satisfying ways of relating to people. It seems increasingly clear that the discrepancies in the perception of self, which are the source of the discomfort that brings a person to therapy, are products largely of the experiences the individual has had with a relatively few persons who have been important in his life. When these experiences are very hurtful, the individual will hold himself together by adopting a pattern of problem-solving which is stiff and constricted and not too efficient, but which leaves him with some sense of control in his life and enables him to stave off complete disorganization, a frightening and ever-imminent prospect. He is tremendously in need of some experience which will enable him to come closer to others, and discover thereby those denied aspects of himself which are important in his relationship with other people. Some severely disturbed people may find the group situation too threatening and require individual therapy. But for those who can take the first steps in opening themselves to others and allowing others to get closer to them, the experience is likely to be profoundly healing.

The relatively normal person who is less himself because of continued perceived pressures may gain even more from the group experience. People in our culture are likely to be isolated. Eric Fromm, in a sociological analysis of personality, has forcefully described the aloneness of modern man and the rootless quality of his life. Even the casual observer can verify Fromm's findings by regarding the facility that people develop in keeping others away from them. Physical proximity is forced upon people and is even sought out, but considerable skill is developed to prevent intimacy of selves. Mechanical entertainment is welcomed as an instrument to obliterate the last possible chance of simple relatedness to others. But this isolation so eagerly sought is a poor mess of pottage, and man knows it with a sure wisdom. No better evidence can be found than in the response that people often make to group therapy, where the expectation is that people will come closer to one another. The opportunity is welcomed and made the most of. As one girl expressed it:

> I also recognize now, whereas I was unable before, that security along economic lines does not necessarily lead to emotional satisfaction. It is with the latter that I am now concerned, and from my present vantage point, it seems that I will have to find these feelings of security, certainty, acceptance, and affection among friends, men, women, or both. For me, this is a big change in attitude because I have always fought against building up such affectional ties outside of the family, and, actually, refused to admit their necessity for a satisfying and rich life. The risk always seemed too great; if you never grew to depend on someone else, you yourself would never be hurt, would never be in danger of being left in the cold.
>
> The group therapy meetings planted the idea and then convinced me that the atmosphere of acceptance, warmth, real sympathy and

responsiveness which existed during them is a vital part of everyone's life and that any risk involved is worth it. It is this background of acceptance, security, and understanding that I know I have not had although I am very sure that both my father and mother would be unable to see that this is true. They both feel that our home has provided us girls with complete understanding and sympathy.

Exactly what I am going to do with these changed attitudes, I do not know, but this doesn't seem to be causing me any concern at the moment. I think that the acknowledgment and the consequent willingness on my part to let things happen to my emotions is of major importance and everything else will more or less fall in line.

As a member of a group, the person learns what it means to give and receive emotional support and understanding in a new and more mature fashion. The self is redefined in a context not unlike that which initially created the need to distort the perception of the self, and of the self in relation to others. This is perhaps the most compelling quality of the group experience.

Contrary to expectation, it is sometimes easier for a person to talk in the group situation than to an individual therapist, and this is a difference worth noting. A limited experience with several groups of severely disturbed veterans gives evidence on this point. The participants in the groups had all received individual therapy for varying periods extending up to a year, and they were referred for group therapy because they did not respond to individual treatment. Case records indicate that a few of the men who were unable to talk about their traumatic war experiences in individual therapy gained from the group the stimulus and the acceptance needed to permit them to relive many of the terrible experiences that they were sealing off from awareness. Capital is here made of individual differences in the ability to open up one's life. The group member most able to talk about himself may start, and thereby relieve pressure from more reticent members, who later take courage from his example and begin tentatively to follow his lead. Such expressions as these are common: "I've had that same experience, too," or "When that happened to you, did you have that same feeling that I had when . . ." Group facilitation, which has been studied by social psychologists in other contexts, operates. It is not to say all people will find it easier to talk in a group; while some may talk readily and others learn that it is safe to talk, a few may remain quiet, with no risks taken, throughout the sessions. But there is a possible gain in freedom, in the group, that is important.

Many issues in personality theory and the therapeutic process center around the problem of values. One of the cardinal principles in client-centered therapy is that the individual must be helped to work out his own value system, with a minimal imposition of the value system of the therapist. This very commitment is, of course, itself an expression of a value which is inevitably communicated to the client in the intimate course of working together. This value, which affirms the individual's right to choose his own values, is believed to be therapeutically helpful. The suggestion of an array of other values by the therapist is believed to be therapeutically harmful, possibly because, if they are presented by the therapist, they will inevitably carry the authority of the therapist and constitute a denial of the self of the client at the moment. The therapist cannot simply express a value for what it is worth; his expression has a clear direction, an inescapable relevance to the client. The client must actively cope with it. In group therapy the situation in respect to values is an interesting one, with consequences that appear very important. As in work with individuals from a client-centered viewpoint, the therapist quietly and consistently, in each of his expressions, upholds the primary value of the individual's right to determine his own way of life. This value is believed to be so important that the therapist will not cloud the issue, and possibly threaten the group, by raising other values for consideration. But values are raised, in plenty, by members of the group, and this rich and varied expression of ways of life offers to the individual member of a group many alternate perspectives without any requirement that he commit himself. The values being expressed are relevant to the individual speaking; the listeners are free from pressure to accept or reject; they can use the material as they perceive it to be meaningful to themselves. In addition, the kinds of values expressed in a group represent something of a cross section of the values of the culture in which the individual lives, with considerably more variance than could be held by the therapist alone. The very diversity of values expressed is an important factor, it is believed, in creating a climate in which the final choice is left truly with the individual.

Group therapy offers another opportunity, absent in individual therapy, which may be quite important in the therapeutic process. In the group the individual may be a giver of help while receiving help. Remarks that group members have made, in telling about their decision to enter therapy, suggest that the prospect of a cooperative enterprise from which they might expect some gain and to which they felt they might contribute lowers the barriers between a person and therapy. It is also possible that the act of giving help is a therapeutic experience itself, but this is simply conjecture. One person expressed the situation this way:

> I couldn't quite bring myself to go to a private counselor, although I got the name and address of one and went to the phone two or three times to call for an appointment — never quite making the step. When the opportunity came to join a group, I responded immediately. The experience, therefore, was very opportune for me. It has helped so much I am constantly amazed. Each thing I accomplish, I think, "Well, this group business has certainly done things for me." Today I've discovered that I'm using the wrong verb — it *is* doing things for me. After the last hour Jack commented on how much he had been helped by the group. It seemed a good sign to me that I was concerned over him rather than so engrossed in my own problems.

In group therapy a person may achieve a mature balance between giving and receiving, between independence of self and a realistic and self-sustaining dependence on others.

The Process of Group Therapy

Some Details of Organization and Procedure

Since group therapy is a relatively unfamiliar process, and since many different kinds of experiences have been designated group therapy, a few words about the general setting and procedures of group-centered therapy seem needed. Normally, groups are composed of about six people and the therapist. This number of participants has been arrived at empirically, and research is yet to be done to establish an optimum number. About this many people seem needed to gain the advantage of maximum personal interaction, and to attain the economy that has been one of the attractive features of a group approach. Effective work can be done with fewer participants, and one or two might be added. But to go much beyond six seems to slow the group down and to increase the number who remain on the periphery of the group, uninvolved in the process. Groups meet in a quiet, comfortable room where everyone can sit around a table, the desirable room being neither cramped nor too spacious. The selection of group members will be discussed later, but it might be noted here that people with quite diverse problems and personalities may be included. Our practice has been to follow only broad criteria for grouping, such as groups of adults, adolescents, or children. Groups meet twice a week, as a rule, for a period of one hour, though a slightly longer period has often seemed desirable. Again, flexibility permits adaptation to circumstances; a number of groups have met once a week and others several times a week, and the length of meetings has been modified. For any one group, however, some consistency in pattern of meetings is sought. The decision to terminate meetings is left to the group. In the settings in which most of our experience has been obtained, groups have tended to average about twenty meetings.

How Groups Get Started

A question frequently asked is, how does a group ever get under way? The inquirer senses a possible awkwardness in the coming together of a number of strangers with the purpose of working on personal problems, and he wonders what the therapist can do to get things rolling. To respond to the last concern first, the therapist proceeds with the assumption that the group can get started and work out directions without his guidance. He generally says something to the effect that the objectives of the group are known to everyone and that the group can develop and follow its own leads. There may be some uncertainty at first, but the best remedy for the uncertainty seems to be the establishment of the group's responsibility for its direction. Many different patterns are evident in the initial meetings. Some groups have a hard time getting started; there are tentative statements followed by withdrawal, or there is a nervous humor which gives time to develop security in the group. Other groups get right at their business, with no delay, starting with as much involvement as one finds in individual therapy when the client is heavily burdened with anxiety and desperately in need of communicating his distress. A fairly typical pattern is for the various members of the group to tell something about themselves and to describe their problems, doing this informally and without pressure. Though beginnings vary, and later modes of expression show differences from group to group, themes characteristic of a particular group emerge and are developed in an identifiable process.

The Development of a Group and the Concept of Themes

The concept of themes has helped us follow with greater understanding the course of therapy for a group. The concept was originated when, in research efforts, there was need of a scheme for breaking down a long series of meetings into smaller units which would have some psychological significance. The units of the single meeting and of the single typed page of transcription are both arbitrary and without particular meaning for the people involved. A theme is a topic and point of focus in discussion, with a clear beginning and a clear stopping point.[1] There may be one or a number of themes in a single session; usually there are several. For each theme, there is a major participant who is the center of focus, and there are minor participants whose number and intensity of involvement vary from theme to theme. In a series of sessions, some themes are short-lived; they are brought up, examined briefly, and abandoned. Other themes thread their way throughout all the sessions, recurring with deeper and deeper meaning, and with variations contributed by different members of the group.

[1] The idea of theme analysis is that of Leon Gorlow. The technique has been used in several investigations of the process of group therapy. Agreement among independent judges in identifying themes in verbatim protocols is almost perfect.

A good analogy is with music. A series of group therapy sessions, when analyzed with reference to themes, is not unlike a rather loosely constructed musical composition. A theme is stated and dropped. Others emerge. An original theme is picked up again and elaborated. The movement is in the direction of greater detail and deeper emotional expression. Some themes are carried by a single voice; others are a blend of several voices, each with its distinctive character. Formal structure is absent, but there is a clear pattern of development, an unmistakable direction and intent.

The Process as Viewed by a Group Member

In one series of researches, the members of a group were asked to keep diaries of their reactions to the group, makng their notes as soon after each meeting as possible. These diary notes were written independently and filed without being read until after the group had terminated, in order that each writer might be free to express his feelings. Combined with excerpts from interview materials, these notes bring one to a more intimate understanding of what a group therapy experience means. The writer of the excerpts below is Jane Harrison, a member of the group whose initial session is partially reported on pages 280–285. The reader might check back to her statements there, in order to get better acquainted with her problem before reading the notes below. It should be said that Jane was probably not the "most profited" member of the group. She probably ranked third or fourth in terms of benefit derived, and it is because of her median position with respect to gain that her account is selected for reporting here. The heartening progress, the dismaying setbacks, the final attainment of limited goals, so familiar in individual therapy, are seen again here.

EXCERPTS FROM A "SELF APPRAISAL" ESSAY, WRITTEN
BEFORE ENTERING THERAPY

As I see my problem today, I can detect signs of its birth in my early adolescence. It represents primarily a conflict over my desire for independence and my need for dependence, emotional support, approval, and acceptance.

The conflict has come into prominence outstandingly in my marriage — my husband in many respects has much the same problem as I do. He needs dependence, but he has developed a façade of independence which outwardly appears very successful. I find that this results in his inability to accept me as an individual in many respects.

On the other hand, I resent this — I resent my need for his approval and attention. I find that when I am left alone a good deal (as I often am, since he's a law student), I utilize devious means to get his attention, such as causing emotional scenes over my in-laws. And then I follow this with terrific feelings of remorse for what I have done — I seem unable to control my feeling in this respect even though I believe intellectually I realize what I am doing.

Today I'm tied to my husband, and still not making the goal. I still don't know what I want for *myself* and what I want because of what my husband will think of me. I still don't have control over my personality to be able to direct it into my own goals and achieve them. I find that I project this resentment alternately towards my husband and my in-laws. I can't stand the idolizing of him that my mother-in-law exhibits. I feel once again back in my own home — playing second fiddle. I seek recognition of myself. I want to be recognized as an individual, but I don't feel that I have a clear idea of that individual; nor do I feel that I have adequate control over that individual.

Diary after first group meeting

I think I felt the most empathic feeling with Kay's problem. It seemed like such a hopeless, unadjusted situation. I also felt a good deal of envy for her, as someone who has had a marriage that I would like to have. . . . I felt that after the initial awkwardness, the group gained a certain identity and solidarity within itself. I feel that we are identified with each other toward a common goal, and I feel a warmth and sincerity in the group that I have never felt in another group. I feel as if I had known the people in the group for a long time — and rather well. . . . The most outstanding reaction I had was my feeling of identity and sympathy for Kay. I couldn't forget about her or her problem all day.

Diary after fourth group meeting

I had a feeling that momentum was gathering at this session. I think we're really getting somewhere. I was surprised at Laura's reaction to her shortness. I always had a feeling that girls who were short accepted it and liked it for the assets it had. I always considered the problem of height to be one that was singularly attached to tall girls. Perhaps because of my height and the problem that I faced with it in my early adolescence. But Laura expressed her feeling for it very adequately and I think I can understand her. . . . My reactions to myself were very revealing to me. On the basis of Mary's remark about hostility and admitting it to ourselves, I realized that actually I loved my mother. But in my fear of being like her, and my hostility toward so much of what she is, I wouldn't admit it to myself. It was quite a revelation to me. I feel very relieved after this session.

Diary after seventh group meeting

When we discussed the requirements of the department, I had a feeling that the group shared a bond in this, as we haven't before by virtue of our different problems. I was finally able to verbalize my doubts about a vocation, which I wasn't able to do before. It was a hard thing to get out but I felt better afterwards. I felt a close sympathy with Anne and her inability to talk. I've felt that way a number of times in the group sessions. It's just an inability to centralize the problem and verbalize it.

Diary after eighth group meeting

This problem of meeting requirements and a career is looming pretty large for me now. I find myself wandering around with a sense of failure and defeat. At first I couldn't express this in the group, but I find it much easier since Laura feels the same way about it. I feel that there is a cohesiveness to the group now that we didn't have before; we really had something in common. And we seem to be moving to some climax.

Diary after tenth group meeting

I felt as if I have something really cleared up in my mind today. I realized suddenly that I had been saying things that implied this feeling all along but that the concept of what it was was still not clear to me. It was the concept of self-worth. I realize that I have been walking around feeling like a sad sack pretty much all of my life, and that it was this that kept me from fighting for my goals. A sad sack never wins, and I took the conviction without ever proving to myself that I was capable. This sort of gave me an added impetus to work for the comprehensive exam, I think. I had the feeling this session that we were all coming down to pretty much the same basic problem only that we all had different ways of showing it. It made me feel closer to the group.

Diary after eleventh group meeting

I felt pretty good during this session. I felt that I had really accomplished something last time and that I really understood so much more than in the past. I think that in verbalizing my difficulty with my mother over the week end, and in verbalizing to myself what I felt was the solution to the problem, I clarified to myself the stand I was going to take with my parents in the future. Not really the stand, but the relationship between us. Kay's talking about roles struck a responsive cord. Now that I realize that it was my general feeling of worthlessness that was at the bottom of some of my troubles, I find that I have to find my place, or as Kay says, my role. I felt that she had really gained a lot in saying that. I still feel my greatest empathy with Kay and Laura. Perhaps because Laura represents part of my problems in hers, and Kay was married happily.

Diary after twelfth group meeting

I really felt as if we were getting somewhere during the last meeting. I think it was because Mary finally opened up. I felt that for the first time she was with us. I had been feeling slightly uncomfortable with her before this. I feel that I am at sort of a stalemate. I understand my problem now in terms of the concept of self-worth. I just don't have very much self-affection. But I can't seem to be able to take the first step forward toward raising my self-affection. It is that I know pretty much now, I think, what has made me like I am, but I can't seem to make up my mind what I want to be. I felt that Betty put it very well when she said that her old established values are getting mixed up — and it's disturbing. In a way, I feel that Kay seems to be getting the most out of the group at present, and making the most progress. I think finally that I am more certain now than I was that I want to finish my studies.

Diary after thirteenth group meeting

I feel sort of guilty presenting a problem this morning because everybody seemed so exuberant. But it has bothered me all week end and I just couldn't keep quiet about it. It sort of set me back to my old feeling of self-worthlessness in relation to school and everything. And I was beginning to work out something before it happened. It was wonderful to see Laura so exuberant. But at the same time, since I didn't feel quite as gay, it made me feel a little out of things. I sort of felt that Betty felt a bit like that, too, and after the session when we were walking down to coffee she turned to me and said, "I feel awful." I knew the feeling that she had, and I wished I could say something to help her, but I didn't feel much better, so I'm afraid I wasn't much help.

Diary after eighteenth group meeting

I just can't seem to be able to see my way clear in this new problem. If it wasn't so tied up with the symbols of my past family life, I might feel more confident. Sometimes I feel that if I were a more confident person, more sure of myself and my husband, then my mother-in-law could say anything and it wouldn't bother me. As it is, it takes huge control to be with her and be nice, but I feel I have to be nice.

Interview two months after the nineteenth and final group meeting

The group helped in a lot of respects in what I think of myself. It may not have solved certain problems and it may never solve certain problems, but it has been worth while. . . . In relation to my husband, I wouldn't say that relations are any — well — there's more understanding. And I'm not very consistent in my relationship to him, because I really don't know, I don't know where to be consistent. I don't know where to give in and where not to give in. . . . I don't know just exactly where my ego should stop and his begin. . . . If I were absolutely sure of my independence and my self-worth, it probably wouldn't have to be put that way. . . . I know now I won't get a divorce. It's going to be tough going for awhile. . . . I'm working to build something and actually I'm very proud of him. . . . I didn't have much faith when I first came, but I notice that during the periods of anxiety, you get certain flashes of insight into it, and well, you get pretty excited when you think about it. . . . I guess the fact is that the group just gives you the motivation to think more constructively about yourself. . . . And it's a funny thing. I'm not very old, but I don't feel as young as I felt in February. I was only 23; I'm still only 23, but in February I felt about 16. . . . I was telling Laura that — she — she was at my house for dinner last night. We were talking about the group and I said that I feel older now, but when I get into my mother-in-law's house, I feel 16. . . . I felt very warmly toward the girls in the group, which is something I never could have before with a girl. I never could have a really warm relationship with a girl before. But there's a certain feeling knowing that others are having problems, too, and trying to understand their problems, and sort of seeing ways to help solve their problems with them. . . . I was very much enthusiastic about group therapy for that reason. There's a certain common bond there, and just the fact that you can talk to people about your problems and have yourself accepted. I mean that's the biggest thing.

The Process as Revealed in Research Analysis

Further confirmation that there is an identifiable process characteristic of group-centered therapy may be found in various systematic studies that have been made. These researches are among the first ordered and quantitative explorations of the process of group psychotherapy, and the results are of course tentative; but many intriguing things have come to light, and many new problems have opened up.

That group-centered therapy is radically different from other approaches is clear from a simple description of what occurs. Interpretation is heavily relied upon in some approaches, and various activities in others; in some, a topic for discussion is set by a brief introductory lecture; in nearly all approaches, other than the one described here, the leader makes a consistent effort to "draw out" the members. Most comparable to group-centered therapy is the analytic technique described by Foulkes, in which the members are invited to "just bring up anything that enters your mind. . . ." But even in Foulkes' approach one is impressed, in reading protocols, with the activity of the therapist in asking questions, pointing up the discussion, and interpreting behavior. One of the most widely used approaches is that advocated by the Army, in which a topic for group discussion is set by the leader. Analysis of a series of such meetings in an Air Force convalescent hospital indicated that 81 per cent of all protocol lines were accounted for by the leader's comments. This preponderance of leader activity in the Army method may be contrasted with the less dominant position of the therapist in the approach described here, in which therapist participation has been shown to account for about 5 per cent of all activity. Clearly group-centered psychotherapy is different from all other approaches; but is it identifiable in the sense of being consistent with itself, from group to group?

Research by Hoch (85) throws light on this problem. Verbatim protocols from three groups with three different therapists, constituting in all some sixty group therapy sessions reported in twelve hundred single-spaced typed pages, were analyzed. By placing statements of group members and of the therapist into categories descriptive of the significance of the statements, it is possible to compare groups with reference to the frequency of occurrence of various kinds of statements. The three groups studied by Hoch were remarkably similar in overall pattern, the intercorrelations being .84, .86, and .87. Hoch concluded that the members of the three groups "spent their respective sessions in very similar atmospheres with respect to the verbal behavior taking place." But it is important to note that within this group uniformity there is room for individual variation. When intercorrelations are computed for individuals within the groups, the coefficients range from .46 to .97. Thus no person is forced into a group mold, and leeway is provided for individual differences in manner of self-expression. On the other hand, group gestalts are sufficiently similar to indicate that group-centered therapy has a distinctive character.

Hoch was able to identify other characteristics of group-centered therapy, an account of which will throw more light on what happens. The frequency of statements judged to be therapeutically positive and therapeutically negative follows a predictable course. Positive elements, revealed in statements showing positive planning, insight, positive attitudes toward the self, positive attitudes toward others, and so on, clearly increase from meeting to meeting, reaching their highest point in the final meetings. Negative elements, on the other hand, are not complementary to the positive elements. It is as though the members have to go through warming-up periods in which they establish their confidence and security in the group. Toward the middle sessions, negative feelings reach their peak, with defensive remarks, confusion, requests for help, and negative attitudes toward the self and toward others gaining prominence. Toward the final sessions, such negative expressions decrease markedly, constituting only a small proportion of the total number of statements.

In group-centered therapy, behavior that may be characterized as "statement of problem" and "elaboration of problem" occurs throughout the meetings, with no significant falling off toward the end of therapy, as one might expect. This finding may stem from the fact that therapy was not carried on for a sufficient number of sessions to resolve all problems and exhaust the need to bring up new issues. But since no one is ever without problems, a better explanation of the rather level course of problem-stating behavior in group therapy may be found in a study of the protocols themselves, which reveal something of a spiral pattern in this kind of behavior. There is a tendency to go around the group, allowing each member an opportunity to explore a theme before a person who has already had his chance introduces a new theme. And subsequent themes tend toward a deeper expression of concern. This tendency, though not a rigid pattern, accounts for the persistence of problem-stating behavior. It may be that an experience in group therapy is less sharply demarked from daily life than is individual therapy. The beginning is less dramatic and the termination less decisive, but these are matters for further study.

Finally, it should be noted that group-centered therapy, in its development from meeting to meeting, presents a changing picture marked by progress. Sessions are not repetitious samples of a static picture. When several complete series of group therapy sessions are divided into halves, the second half has a significantly higher concentration of "good" categories, representing a palpable gain in understandings and positive attitudes. This trend toward more positive expression is evident in groups as a whole, and is accentuated for those members of groups who gain most from the experience. It is also found that members who gain most, as compared with those who gain least, tend to avoid general intellectual discussion, to focus on their own problems, and to grow sufficiently to exhibit more concern for the problems of other members.

These findings confirm, to a surprising degree, the smaller preliminary study made by Peres (146) several years earlier, and
based upon the analysis of but one group which met for nine
sessions. Peres found that when the group was divided into a
"benefited" group (the four who felt they had gained considerable
help) and a "nonbenefited" group (the three who felt they had
gained little) real differences could be objectively demonstrated
between these two groups. The benefited group showed, throughout the series, an increasing proportion of statements indicating
understanding and insight, and an increasing number of reports of
plans and actions. Unlike the situation in individual therapy, the
benefited group presented more statements of problems at the end
of the series than at the beginning, and more negative attitudes
toward self in the second half of therapy than in the first, with a
peak being reached shortly after the midpoint of the series. The
nonbenefited group showed much flatter curves in all these respects. One of the most evident differences was that the nonbenefited group engaged in more interactional and "prodding"
statements than did the benefited group. It seems reasonable to
say that more of their attention was focused upon the other persons
and less upon themselves and their own feelings. They were
more likely to use such statements as "What did you do then?" or
"You wouldn't say that if you were married," or "Perhaps you do
that because of antagonism to your mother." The members of
the benefited group, three months after the conclusion of therapy,
reported that they had taken positive actions as a result of the
experience, and that they had found that significant changes in
attitude and behavior had carried over into fields which had never
been a topic of discussion in the group. The nonbenefited individuals indicated that they had experienced few of these outcomes.

Such studies mark only a small beginning in the understanding
of the process of group therapy. Many questions remain unanswered. Will the uniformity of pattern suggested by these two
studies be evident in the development of groups composed of
strikingly different kinds of people? What would be the pattern
if groups were continued until each person felt that he could gain
no more from the experience? What about content and import of

statements? No study has yet been made of the kinds of things people talk about in group therapy. An analysis of the content of protocols would surely yield rich information about the problems of adult life. Is it possible to select people who are most likely to gain from a group therapy experience? How much does the therapist contribute to the effectiveness of a group? Some of these questions can be touched upon, but others will have to await clarification through further research.

The Group Therapist

Experience in individual client-centered therapy seems to be the best preparation for doing group-centered therapy. The differences between the two practices are largely on the level of technique, and one returns again to a realization of the significance of the therapist's attitudes. In both situations, the feelings that the therapist has toward people, the confidence he has in their ability to be responsible for themselves, the readiness with which he limits any tendency to intervene on the assumption that his view of the situation is superior, the consistency with which he translates a philosophy into action — these are fundamental to effective work either with individuals or with groups. However, the group situation does make some new demands on the therapist. He now must respond sensitively to six people instead of to one; he must be able to recognize and handle objectively the cross currents of feeling that develop within the group; he must clarify his own feelings towards the several members of the group, in order that he may respond to each member with consistent understanding. The most challenging new element in the group situation is the possibility of releasing the therapeutic potential of the group itself. *Group therapy*, and not individual therapy in a group, is the goal. If the therapist is skillful, the group itself becomes a therapeutic agent and gathers momentum of its own, with therapeutic consequences clearly greater than would result from the efforts of the therapist alone. For one thing, members themselves take on the role of therapists, a development of such significance for the total process that it will be discussed in a subsequent section of this chapter. But let us examine here, using research findings and illustrations from verbatim protocols, some of the distinctive features of the therapist's job as he works with a group.

The therapist attempts to understand what it is that a group member is saying and feeling, to communicate this understanding to the group, and to make it easier and safer for the individual to push ahead in his explorations of himself. Telschow (211) has shown, in a systematic and extensive analysis of protocols, that the most productive statements of the therapist are those involving simple acceptance of what is said, restatement of content, and clarification of feeling. Statements of such nature are accompanied by greater and more penetrating exploration on the part of the group member. They tend to reduce the threat in the situation and are "releasing" of the group member who is attempting to see himself more clearly. Evidence indicates that, although the gross amount of therapist interaction with members is highly related to the amount of member activity, the members who gain most from the experience are those to whom the therapist responds with nondirective statements. Research has not yet demonstrated the point, but it seems likely that such statements also give assurance to a member who has not participated that he can join in without fear of hurt to himself. In the sessions reported on pages 280–285, one can get a feeling for what the therapist does in this respect.

But pacing and timing are important. There is apparently an optimum amount of therapist participation. Telschow devised a measure of discord in groups and showed that the amount of discord is a function of the amount of participation on the part of the therapist. The therapist is not a passive member of the group; he must be in there pitching. If he withdraws too much, discord mounts, and exploration of feeling becomes more precarious for members of the group. Below is a brief excerpt from a group therapy session, illustrating nicely how members of the group can make it difficult for a person to continue to carry a theme to full exploration.

Miss Bell: Well, I don't have too much of a social life here. I know a few people, but I don't go out much, because I'm not particularly interested in dancing and things like that.

Mr. Lewis: M-hm. What do you usually do for fun and relaxation?
Miss Bell: Oh, I go to movies and read.
Leader: M-hm.
Miss Bell (laughing nervously): And I play cards sometimes — that's about all.
Mr. Lewis: I hope you take a cocktail once in a while.
Group: (Laughter.)
Miss Bell: Yes, I do. *(Long Pause.)*
Mr. Lewis: Well, are — are you interested in meeting people?
Miss Bell: Yes — I, ah —   *(Pause.)*
Mr. Harding: Do you think you are going about it in the right way?
Miss Bell: What?
Mr. Harding: Do you think you are going about it — *(Interrupted.)*
Miss Bell: No, I know I'm not — because I know I don't put forth any effort to — to that —
Mr. Lewis: Well, of course, those things — ah — it's peculiar, isn't it, always that, ah *(clears throat)* you're not going about it in the right way, but you can't go about it in the right way because something is stopping you — I had a very interesting experience along those lines one time. Last year, as a matter of fact. A boy, a nineteen-year-old boy, *(clears throat)* living near me, was schizophrenic, and he was making a very fine adjustment. And then he went off the deep end. And, ah — and very — enlightening to see him try to do things and want to be able to go out and do things and not be able to. As I say, it's not a case of — that he didn't want to. He just couldn't — *(clears throat)* Well, that's the situation with you, isn't it, Dorothy?
Miss Bell: No. *(The group laughs tensely.)*
Mr. Lewis: Well, there's something stopping her.

Although the therapist must actively follow the developing feelings in the group, and express his understanding and acceptance of what is said, he cannot be so active as to dominate the group. Our practice has been for the therapist to delay his responses slightly, to give the group members an opportunity to take the role of therapist. If, as often happens, some member of the group picks up the feeling and responds in such a manner that the speaker can continue his self-exploration, the therapist remains quiet. But if some important feeling goes unrecognized or if members of the group make continued expression difficult by denying the feelings of a member, the therapist must come in. Research indicates that therapists fluctuate, in amount of activity, from meeting to meeting, but that there is generally no tendency to decrease in activity as the sessions continue. Recalling the purpose of the therapist may provide an indication of when the therapist should be active and when he should let group members act in his place: the goal is to maintain in the group a dependable atmosphere of acceptance and understanding, where threat to the individual member is minimal, and where there is maximum safety in self-examination. The expectation would thus be that the therapist skillfully adjusts his behavior to insure attainment of this goal.

Telschow has established a number of other interesting relationships evident in the role of the group therapist. A good index of the "group-centeredness" of therapy may be found in his correlation between member and therapist activity. For the groups which he studied, a correlation of .86 was found between number of statements of a member and the number of therapist responses to that member. The lower this correlation, the less the therapist is following the lead of the group.

A finding of his research that goes somewhat contrary to expectation is that restatement of content, by the therapist, is therapeutically somewhat more effective than either simple acceptance or clarification of feeling. The superiority over simple acceptance ("Um-hmm," "I see," "I understand," and the like) is not surprising, but reflection of feeling has long been considered a most helpful kind of therapist response. Its relative inadequacy may lie in the extent to which reflections of feeling are interpretive, going beyond the perceptual field of the individual at the moment. Telschow examines this possibility further and demonstrates that individuals who did not gain from the group therapy experience responded most frequently to clarification of feeling by statements of a distinctively defensive character ("ambivalent acceptance of interpretation, rejection of clarification, expressions of confusion, defensive remarks, and deflection of topic being discussed"). They apparently perceived the reflections of feeling as being threatening to themselves and responded in a fashion to protect their current self-organizations. The issues need further examination, both in individual and group therapy situations.

To gain an understanding of the role of the group therapist, we may turn again to the viewpoint of the client. Here are some excerpts from diaries kept by group members during the course of therapy:

> I can remember a statement that seems to have helped me most. The group leader's clarification that I do not feel my values to be as important as those of others seems to be something I have thought about for a long while in almost those exact words, and I seem to have a vague feeling of having verbalized it. Recognition of this by someone else gave me a great feeling of relief. Now I do not feel called upon to hide it.

> I have not considered the group leader apart from the group as a whole. He stays in the background, although occasionally I am aware that he points up significant feelings which no one else has commented about.

> It's interesting about the group leader. He didn't intrude; yet he seems like a stabilizing influence.

On several occasions members have commented that they are aware of what the therapist is doing when he responds to someone else in the group, but that he is most unobtrusive when he is responding to them. Apparently when he is closely following a person, the therapist becomes a harmonious part of the thinking, aiding the process but not straining it by injecting new elements.

Group Members as Therapists

There is a fascinating, and therapeutically very important, interplay of roles in group therapy. A member may introduce a theme and pursue its development with the assistance not only of the group leader but of other members as well. When a new theme is introduced, he may find himself no longer in the role of the perplexed and anxious client but in the role of the member who understands best what the new client is saying and who is most able to assist him in clarifying his perceptions of himself and his world. With the introduction of yet a third theme, he may find himself not too much concerned and remain on the sidelines. Through the length of a series of sessions, there is a complex interweaving of roles, with different individuals at different times coming into focus as clients and as therapists. These therapist activities of group members are of such consequence in the development of a group that they call for detailed discussion.

An example of a member acting as a therapist, drawn from a verbatim record of a group therapy session, can say more than many descriptive passages:

Mr. Ray: (My brother) got his medical degree when he was twenty-four. Before I went into the Navy, I figured out I'd graduate from college at such and such an age and get my master's at such and such an age, and then have my doctorate ahead of me. I was very proud of that. (*Pause.*) But, uh, now, it no longer means very much to me.

Mr. Berg: You think that your parents' attitudes fostered that feeling?

Mr. Ray: My parents have never said, "You are not doing as well as B." [his brother]. They were satisfied when I just did average work. They've never pushed me — to do better.

Mr. Berg: When he went through, they were very pleased with him.

Mr. Ray: Oh, definitely.

Mr. Berg: And when you went through, do you think you might have felt somewhat rejected because there wasn't the same furor over your achievement? (*Pause.*) I guess I'm projecting myself into it!

Mr. Ray: Well, I didn't feel, well, uh, accepted as much as I would like to have. And I thought that my grades had a great deal to do with it. (*Pause.*) But I just no longer feel that push to do better —

Mr. Hill: You feel that the, uh, responsibility for the grades is your own, and that it won't matter to anyone else what you do. Is that the idea? Your motivation stems from yourself rather than trying to please somebody else.

Mr. Ray: Yeah, I think that's it. I'm no longer so much concerned with showing my parents that I can do well. I still want to show it to myself, and, uh, I'm more satisfied, that's all. I don't feel the urge to rush.

Mr. Hill: Sort of — seems to me it would be sort of a load off your shoulders.

Mr. Ray: Oh, definitely. Not bucking up against something that you feel you can't overcome.

Leader: Makes you feel a good bit more independent — free.

Mr. Ray: Definitely, in that I can satisfy myself and I don't have to worry about satisfying somebody else.

Gorlow's study (71) of the activities of group members as therapist has thrown much light on this intricate and intriguing process. Among other things, he has demonstrated that the interaction between group members changes in quality as therapy progresses. Members seem to learn to be better therapists. There is a marked increase in behavior characterized as permissive and accepting and an accompanying decrease in behavior characterized as interpretive, evaluative, and critical, from the first to the last part of therapy. It may be that the member-therapists learn from the leader, absorbing his attitudes and sensing the reasonableness and helpfulness of what he does. Or it may be that the kind of behavior that is characterized as therapeutic can emerge only after the person has made progress himself in therapy. Permissiveness and the ability to understand and accept a person may be symptoms of greater personal security. The individual has less need to distort experience and can respond more accurately, with less protection of his own conflicts. Support for the latter hypothesis seems to be available in Gorlow's finding that individuals who are best adjusted before entering therapy are those best able to assume the constructive attitudes of the therapist in the initial sessions. As therapy progresses and other members gain from the experience, relationship between pre-therapy adjustment and quality of activity as a therapist disappears. However, throughout the course of therapy, the members who are initially most anxious and most hostile, as determined by Rorschach records, use criticism, evaluation, and disapproval to a greater extent than initially less anxious and hostile members, who tend to use such techniques as simple acceptance, clarification of feeling, restatement of content, approval and encouragement, and reassurance. Whatever the explanation, it seems certain that group members become more able to respond to the feelings of others in a manner likely to assist them to explore these feelings further.

Gorlow also found significant and interesting relationships between gain in therapy and the assumption of the role of therapist.

The people who gained most from therapy were also those who most frequently employed, in their responses to members presenting problems, the kinds of therapist-statements believed to be most healing. When the use of nondirective behavior by member-therapists is plotted against time, the curve for those who were judged "most profited" rises sharply, while the curve for those judged "least profited" follows a level course. A two-way possibility is evident here. The achievement of greater personal integration may make it possible for a person to be more helpful to others. On the other hand, the very giving of help may be beneficial. Or both may be true. We are sure only of the relationship, not of the source or direction of causation.

Selection of Group Members

Two sets of probabilities are involved in the question of who should enter group therapy. One is the likelihood that the individual will gain from the experience; the other is the likelihood that the group will gain from his presence. Both considerations are important, but we do not know how to write an equation that will express their subtle interrelationships, nor can we identify the personality variables that should enter into such a calculation. All that we have to go on are certain rules of thumb. These have been derived not from research but from our conspicuous failures, and they thus mark outside boundaries in a very loose fashion. But this is the kind of problem that can be pinned down by research, and in time we can anticipate increased effectiveness of group therapy as we know how to choose people for participation and how to match groups for optimum interpersonal accord.

On the positive side, we can apply the same criteria that have been developed from experience in individual client-centered therapy, as described on pages 228–230 (Chapter 5). From the standpoint of the individual, the only criterion that seems consistently applicable is whether or not he chooses, without pressure, to join a group and work on a problem of concern to him. One can think of many kinds of people who would not be expected to profit from a group experience: the extremely shy person, the overly anxious person, the intensely hostile person, the deeply disturbed person. But our predictions in individual instances, based upon these reasonable assumptions, have been defeated as often as they have been sustained. A person racked by guilt over profoundly disturbing sexual experiences is able to clear away much of her anxiety and lay substantial plans for rebuilding her life. A teacher so shy that she could hardly talk in the group writes voluntarily a year later that the experience meant more to her than she could express, that for the first time in years she was really enjoying her work. A very withdrawn person, diagnosed as schizophrenic, who has been incapable of keeping appointments with his individual therapist, attends his group regularly and sits there quietly, with possibly little gain, it is true, but with some evidence of greater social competency than he had shown previously. Boys from a gang in Harlem, tough as society can make its outcasts, and by best prediction poor bets in therapy, come regularly — and regularly use the first three-quarters of their hour in bitter mockery of one another, only to use the last few minutes each week in an intimate exploration of their consuming hatred of their parents and of all authority. We simply don't know how to say who will gain and who will not, and sense no better way of answering this question than to leave it up to the individual.

On the other hand, we do have some tentative hypotheses concerning individuals who tend to disrupt a group, and concerning the composition of groups with reference to the relationships of the people to be included. Several groups in our experience have had the going made rough by disturbed but psychologically sophisticated persons who can use their knowledge of psychodynamics cruelly on others. Members of the group seem less able to protect themselves from this kind of knowing hardness. If a person has been in therapy for a year or two, with uncertain gain, we are beginning to think it best for him to continue to work in individual therapy, rather than in a group. We have had unhappy experiences of men with "anxiety state" diagnoses in groups where one of the members had psychotic tendencies. Unable to respond to the feelings of others, these deeply disturbed people have occasionally said things that could not be tolerated by their anxious and still sensitive fellow group members. In general, we feel it best not to include in a group the extremely hostile and aggressive person, whether psychotic or not, because he makes it difficult, if not impossible, to achieve the atmosphere of acceptance and freedom from threat that is essential to the success of the group. Finally, as to overall composition, we think it desirable not to have a group made up of people who have continued close daily contact outside of the group. Some groups so composed have been successful, but others have floundered on the feelings of guilt that carry over from the group situation to daily life. Expressions of hostility and of self-doubt which can be sustained in the context of the group are perceived differently in contacts outside the group and appear too threatening to the organization of the self that the person is struggling to maintain. By way of illustration, in our current planning for work with several groups of married couples -we have considered it a reasonable caution to ask husband and wife to join different groups which will meet at different times. We believe that this arrangement will insure greater freedom to the individual and decrease the confusion, in daily life, that might result from feelings of guilt and from possible distorted perception of the partner's expressions in the group.

The question of the desirability of combining individual and group therapy occasionally arises. We have done so, with no reason to suggest that this should not be done and with some evidence that the combination is particularly effective. We feel the decision should be left to the individual and his therapist.

Partly as a selection procedure and partly as a means of helping the person get ready to enter a group, we routinely have an initial individual interview with each applicant. Here there is an opportunity for the person and his group therapist to become acquainted with each other, so that in the first meeting of the group there are some feelings of intimacy. The client also has an opportunity to learn something of the nature of the group experience and to make a final decision on whether to participate or not. And the therapist has an opportunity to protect the interest of the total group in those few instances where it seems best to suggest that the person work in individual therapy for a while, before deciding to join a group. These interviews involve some structuring of the coming experience, and every effort is made to create in this first meeting the feelings of acceptance and respect which will be nurtured to full flower in the group.

THE EFFECTIVENESS OF GROUP THERAPY

The assessment of the effectiveness of group therapy is difficult, as it is with all therapies. In final analysis, we have to rely on an overall clinical appraisal, based on the observation of a number of cases, made by people who are competent to make such judgments. The judgments of those who have worked with groups is unequivocally on the positive side. Group therapy does work. It is an effective approach to helping people with their problems. More specifically, and by the same standards, the kind of group therapy described here is beyond doubt productive of personal gain to the individual participants. Let us examine some of the evidences of gain that we have at this early stage of exploration.

Attempts to assess changes in adjustment have often had to rely in part on the individual's own estimate of his growth. Shaky as such estimates may be, they cannot be overlooked without omitting important data. In our efforts better to understand the process of group-centered therapy, we have frequently asked group members to write evaluations of their experience, sometimes anonymously and sometimes with identification. These have ranged from statements that work with the group has been of some value to the expressed opinion that it has been a profoundly significant experience. Even after discounting the statements for a tendency to be kind and helpful to the investigators, the total impression remains that people do find much help in group therapy. These gains are sustained for at least two years, as indicated by follow-up inquiries, and in some reports the statement is made that the group provided only an initial impetus for growth.

In statements gathered three months after the conclusion of therapy, Peres found that individuals expressed not only gains which had been experienced in the handling of specific problems and conflicts, but also two other types of gain. These were: greater acceptance of self and willingness to be oneself; and internalization and continuance of the process of therapy. These latter types of gain may be illustrated by statements from members of the group. The greater readiness to actualize the self in social situations is exemplified in the following quotation:

> I gained a great deal of self-confidence just by being a member of the group and being accepted by all of them. . . . It seemed to me that by being frank about my feelings in the group meetings, I was accepted by all of the others. This carried over, to a great extent, to other situations. Now upon meeting new people, I'm just "me" without repressing things and feelings for fear that others might not understand. (146, p. 170)

The idea that the process may be taken over and continued within one's self is an interesting one. A statement by a group member may clarify the meaning of this.

> There's something I find myself doing when I experience tensions outside the group. I find myself kind of verbalizing the feeling as I do in counseling, kind of reflecting back to myself my own feelings; in other words, I was a kind of counselor to myself, and I worked through some of my own problems that way.
>
> Well, I think that what happened was, I sort of took over the process or internalized it, so to speak, of what goes on in a counseling situation. That helped me in other problems that were not necessarily expressed here.
>
> I'm beginning to feel that maybe it's not just the particular insights, but the process that underlies the insight that is so valuable. . . . You feel permissive about your own feelings, you can reflect them, and that makes you sort of an independent individual. (146, pp. 170–171)

Or this statement by another member:

> Much of this understanding was achieved in therapy contacts and much more after the cessation of contacts when I internalized the habit of trying to consciously be aware of my *real* feelings — an internalization of what went on in therapy. (146, p. 171)

These statements indicate something of the feeling of change which is experienced by the participant in group therapy. Whether this is an alteration in feeling only, or is correlated with other changes, these data do not disclose.

In the verbatim protocols of group therapy sessions there are reported behavioral changes which are perhaps a more substantial basis for appraisal of change than the final summary statements. A kind of change that is most frequently observed is that the individual begins to perceive his world differently. Circumstances may not alter appreciably, but his perception of the situation and his behavior in the situation change. Here is an excerpt from a verbatim protocol which illustrates the point.

Mr. Flowers: An interesting thing happened to me the other day. I got a letter from my father. He writes beautiful letters, but my wife and I, we talked it over, and we thought that his feeling was a little unrealistic. He didn't seem really to understand our problems — We always felt a little hostile to him for that — writing in altruistic terms — my wife was making a noble sacrifice going to work — and things like that. The letter I got yesterday — I read it through and thought, "Gee, that's a swell letter." So I gave it to my wife to read. I said, "Don't you think that's different?" And she says, "Come to think of it, I don't see any difference from the rest of them."

Mrs. Smith: You mean that the letters haven't changed?

Mr. Flowers: Evidently, they haven't. I looked over it again and it did seem to be the same thing, but I extracted from it a feeling of interest, that's all.

Mr. Arnold: Well, I had something very much the same — I realize that I feel different in my relation to my father and mother and that, uh, actually no change, or very little change, has taken place in them, since my feelings have changed. The change has been almost entirely in my department. Having spent part of the week end with them, I was able to look things over, and they're pretty much the same. But I can respond to them differently. I don't respond with aggression as much as I used to do.

Mr. Flowers: That's very similar to the experience I had in this last visit with my parents. Previously there had always been arguments — pretty generally on an abstract topic. That's an outlet for my aggression, I guess. I'd get him very upset, disturbed — defending his identification with the Republican Party. But this time nothing like that happened. Any discussion we had we merely agreed upon or stated differences of opinion on. There wasn't that tension — that really uncomfortable feeling that I always used to get with him. It was very different.

And corroborative behavioral evidence is found. A college man with no social contacts learns to dance and enjoys going to parties; several delinquent boys obtain jobs; a man finds that his compulsive daydreams have suddenly just stopped occurring; a woman on the verge of divorce finds that there is much substance in her marriage; several students report improved academic grades; and so on. These changes do not occur for everyone, of course, but they are reported with enough frequency to give assurance that something important is happening to the people involved; over and above these, one finds expressions of greater satisfaction with living. As one girl put it, "The other day walking down the street, I found myself humming a tune. I didn't know it was me! Why I haven't done that in years."

Ultimately we must assess the effectiveness of group therapy in quantitative terms. We shall want to know what percentage of successful experiences can be expected, and we shall want some index of relative efficiency between group therapy and individual therapy. Only a beginning has been made at such quantitative statements. In an extensive research project involving sixteen participants in group therapy, the three group leaders judged that eight of the members made clear gains whereas eight others made none, or only uncertain gains. Their judgments were corroborated by objective measurements. These figures may be overestimates or underestimates. The gains observed may have been only temporary, or the observation of no gain may have been refuted by later growth initiated in therapy. But this fairly rigorous appraisal is encouraging. More explicit and detailed statements must await further study.

SUGGESTED READINGS

For a summary of the historical development of group therapy, the reader is referred to Klapman, *Group Psychotherapy* (102). Other basic books on group therapy are: Moreno, *Group Therapy* (135); Slavson, *Analytic Group Psychotherapy* (192); Foulkes, *Introduction to Group-Analytic Psychotherapy* (61); and Schilder, *Psychotherapy* (177).

For accounts of client-centered group therapy with children, see both Axline's book (14, Chapters 20, 21, 22) and her article on the handling of racial tensions in a group of children (15).

Published research in group therapy is practically nonexistent thus far. The work of Peres (146) is one of the few studies which have been published. It is hoped that other studies to which reference has been made will be published in the near future.

Chapter 8 · Group-Centered
Leadership and Administration

By THOMAS GORDON, Ph.D.

Probably no one who has tried consistently to carry on individual psychotherapy with an orientation that is essentially client-centered has failed to think about the possibility of applying this philosophy to group leadership and organizational administration. Staff members carrying on therapy at the Counseling Center at the University of Chicago have persistently raised the question whether such factors as acceptance, understanding, and permissiveness would have effects equally therapeutic for groups as for individuals. Would it be feasible to try a therapeutic approach in situations outside of the clinic office? What would be the effect upon a group if its supervisor tried consciously to create an accepting atmosphere in which its members could work? Can you be "therapeutic" in your relations with those for whom you are boss, leader, administrator? What would be the impact upon a group of teachers in a high school if the principal used procedures that encouraged them to express openly their feelings of frustration and discouragement, their criticisms of administrative policy, as well as their more positive feelings? What might be the effect upon an industrial organization if a consultant hired by management acted on the conviction that his role was to get the organization to learn to solve its own problems with the resources within the organization itself?   Such questions have puzzled, provoked, and challenged us, and this chapter will be devoted to their consideration.   There will be an attempt to formulate certain propositions concerned with the nature of groups and an attempt to construct a tentative definition of a social therapeutic approach — a group-centered approach — in leadership and administration.

There are many reasons why it was inevitable that interest would develop in the application of the principles and philosophy of client-centered psychotherapy to supervision and administration of groups.   Many of us have found it extremely uncomfortable to hold certain "therapeutic" attitudes about the disturbed client, yet quite different attitudes about the members of a factory group, a faculty, a social-action organization.   Was it just a role we were playing in the therapeutic sessions?   That did not seem to be true, for with continued clinical experience as client-centered therapists, we have come to develop unusually strong and genuine attitudes about clients' capacities for self-direction and self-initiated psychological recovery.   Rather, it seems that attitudes learned in the clinical setting, even though they *are* genuine, are not easily transferred to other social settings.   These attitudes are transferred, apparently, only as we actually *experience* the effects of trying out a therapeutic approach in each new situation, first with a group of clients, then in a classroom, then with a discussion group, then with a staff group.   When we first meet a new interpersonal situation, we are never really sure that the approach will be effective.   Consequently it becomes disturbing to discover that as a *therapist* you feel no need to direct another's life, but as a *group leader* you frequently do just that.   Or you know the effect of a nonthreatening atmosphere on clients, yet find yourself consistently threatening members of your office staff by interpreting their behavior, interrupting their statements, or reassuring them that their concern about their lack of progress is unwarranted.   The realization of our own inconsistencies has resulted in some soul-searching on our part.   It also has stimulated our thinking about these matters and has led many of us to experiment with a group-centered approach with groups.

Our early experiences were not wholly successful. Through them, however, it was discovered that individuals in groups responded much the same as clients in therapy. We could see clearly the strong resistances to change, the initial dependence upon the leader for direction and guidance, the effects of evaluation and diagnosis, the inevitable frustration of group members on their own. We could see also the impact of a permissive atmosphere and the force of the leader's understanding and consistent acceptance. In short, it was impressive to observe some of the same psychological forces at work in these groups as had been seen in therapy with individuals. These early experiences, then, did much to stimulate thinking about therapeutic group leadership.

There has been another kind of experience which has contributed to our growing interest in this area. This has been an attempt to try out a new type of administration in our own Counseling Center organization. Over a period of a few years, we have experimented with several different procedures and different organizational structures. The essential element in all of these has been maximum participation of all staff members in matters which concern the total group. Although we have much to learn, and our staff functioning is not always what we might hope for, we feel from this experience that we have become more aware of some of the important elements in organizational leadership and administration.

Impetus to our own thinking and experimentation has been provided also by the research and theories of others who recently have become interested in these problems. Some of us have drawn upon the ideas of a number of investigators and groups, and reference will be made to them throughout this chapter. The writer has been influenced by the Tavistock Institute of England, by the group dynamics movement in this country, and by those persons who are responsible for the National Training Laboratory at Bethel, Maine.

Finally, motivation for our thinking and work in this area is undoubtedly due also to the challenge which most social scientists feel as they survey the present-day problems of our society.

The crucial problems of our civilization are human problems. All of us hope to contribute something to the resolution of the conflicts between different nations, different racial and religious groups, labor and management. We see the tremendous need for discovering ways of increasing the participation of the common citizen in matters which concern him. Gordon Allport has put it well:

> ... the only alternative to a keener analysis of the behavioral environment and more active participation in reshaping it is to give way progressively to outer authority, to uniformity, to discipline, and dependence upon the leader. The battlefield exists here and now within each of us. The answer to growing complexity in the social sphere is renewed efforts at participation by each one of us, or else a progressive decline of inert and unquestioning masses submitting to government by an elite which will have little regard for the ultimate interest of the common man. (6, p. 125)

Some Propositions Regarding the Adjustive Capacity of Groups

At this stage of our thinking it would be presumptuous to claim a well-formulated system of theory about groups. Nevertheless, out of our experiences we can begin to construct a tentative outline for a theory that will be consistent with these experiences. Admittedly, this will be a sketchy outline. At present it exists as a mere skeleton, devoid of flesh at many points. Its inclusion here is based upon the hope that it will make more clear our subsequent formulation of the group-centered approach to leadership and administration.

This theoretical basis for thinking about groups will be presented as a series of propositions. Many of these are of the nature of assumptions, and are stated in a form that would make it difficult for them to be tested experimentally. It would be correct to say that these propositions simply represent one of several possible frames of reference for thinking about groups.

I) A group is defined as two or more persons who have a psychological relationship to each other. That is, the members exist as a group in the psychological field of each other, and they are in some kind of dynamic relationship to each other.

Here we are attempting to set up certain criteria that can be applied to differentiate a group from other collections of individuals. Borrowing from the definition of Krech and Crutchfield (106), a group is made up of persons whose behavior has direct influence upon the behavior of the other members.

> II) Groups demonstrate during some specific time period some degree of instability or disequilibrium as a result of forces within the group. The group, then, is a dynamic system of forces. Changes in any part of the group produce changes in the group as a whole.

This proposition re-emphasizes the notion that the behavior of members of a group affects the behavior of other members. But it also gives to groups the qualities of a system of inner dynamic forces that are in a state of continuous change and reorganization. Take, for example, an industrial organization whose personnel manager decided to introduce a new system of evaluating employees. According to Proposition II, such action on the part of the personnel manager will produce changes in other parts of the organization. Supervisors may resent the added paper work made necessary by the new procedures; certain employees may perceive the new procedures as a means of weeding out the less capable workers; the union steward sees this action as a breach of the merit-rating system agreed on by the union and management; a line supervisor resents the authority of the personnel department over the "line." A seemingly isolated act, then, actually upsets the equilibrium of the entire plant structure.

> III) Group behavior which serves to reduce the disequilibrium produced by changes in the inner forces of the group may be described as adjustive behavior. The degree to which the group's behavior is adjustive will be a function of the appropriateness of the methods employed by the

group as they are related to the nature of the internal imbalance.

This proposition states in a more technical way a fact which we all recognize. That is, how successfully a group adjusts to an internal disruptive force depends upon its employing direct and appropriate methods of attack on the problem. This principle has its counterpart in individual behavior. A person finds himself in a conflict-producing situation which upsets his own equilibrium. He becomes tense and uncomfortable. His turning to alcohol may produce a temporary relief from the tension, but it is far from being an adjustment appropriate to the state of conflict which exists in the total organism. Until the person becomes aware of the nature of the conflict, his behavior is not likely to be adjustive. In the same way, groups frequently exhibit non-adjustive or partially adjustive behavior, examples of which are so numerous as to defy classification. Scapegoating, projecting, inhibiting expression of feelings, blaming the leaders, attacking other groups, withdrawing, regressing to a strong dependence relationship to the leader — these are some of the more obvious partial solutions employed by groups.

IV) A group's adjustive behavior will be most appropriate when the group utilizes the maximum resources of its total membership. This means maximum participation of all group members, each making his most effective contribution.

This proposition is a way of saying that the best decisions or the most appropriate actions of a group will be those based upon the maximum amount of data or resources of its members. Thus the most effective group will be the one in which there is participation of all group members, each member making his most creative contribution. This idea has been expressed in the report of the President's Committee on Civil Rights:

Democracy assumes that the majority is more likely as a general rule to make decisions which are wise and desirable from the point of view of the interests of the whole society than is any minority. Every time a qualified person is denied a voice in public affairs, one of the

components of a potential majority is lost, and the formation of a
social public policy is endangered. . . .

How can the concept of the marketplace of thought, in which
truth ultimately prevails, retain its validity if the thought of certain
individuals is denied the right of circulation? (218, pp. 8–9)

Although these statements are taken from the context of "civil
rights" for citizens of our nation, they reflect the essence of the
proposition above — namely, that what is best for a group is that
which has been formulated out of the contributions of all of the
group's members.

If this proposition is valid, it helps to clarify the value of
"participation." The concept of group-member participation can
be found in almost every article dealing with the problems of
group leadership and administration. It has been stressed as a
principle of industrial supervision, community action, and labor-
management relations. In psychology this concept has earned the
label "ego-involvement." Too frequently, however, one gets the
impression from some of this literature that participation and ego-
involvement on the part of group-members are things to be
achieved so that the group-members will more readily accept the
plans, goals, or decisions *already formulated by the leaders.* Obtaining participation thus becomes a *leader technique* for satisfying
the members' natural desires for achievement, status, and recognition. True, participant groups do seem to have better morale
than leader-centered or authoritarian groups. Nevertheless, not
always is participation also seen as contributing to the total efficiency of the group. Not always is there a genuine belief on the
part of leaders that participation pays off in terms of better decisions, more production, economic gains, more appropriate group
adjustment.

This narrow conception of participation as a method of obtaining willing compliance has been noted in the attitudes of some
industrial executives, as pointed out by French, Kornhauser, and
Marrow. They define three main patterns of control in management, one of which is characterized by efforts to obtain through
"participation" and "cooperation" the workers' compliance,
loyalty, good will, and welfare. These writers emphasize that
such dealings are a device employed by management.

Under these circumstances, "democratic cooperation" is at best a euphemism, and at worst a deceptive make-believe process. Sometimes management is deliberately using the attractive symbols of democracy, participation, man-to-man discussion, group decision, etc., to create the desired atmosphere within which it can smoothly manipulate the attitudes of its employees, retain their loyalty, and still run the business "as it should be run," without irritating interferences from below. (62, pp. 44–45)

I am reminded of the remark of a training-group leader to the effect that his greatest concern was how to reconcile his intellectual convictions that the group must decide its own goals and methods of reaching those goals with his equally strong ideas of what those goals and methods *should* be. This same dilemma is seen in individuals in the initial stages of learning client-centered psychotherapy as they come to examine whether their own basic attitudes about people are consistent with the "technique" they are learning. A minister in one of the courses in psychotherapy once asked, "How can I as a minister use this approach in my counseling and yet get the client to end up with the conviction that it was his faith in the Divine which was responsible for his recovery?"

V) A group has within itself the adjustive capacities necessary to acquire a greater degree of internal harmony and productivity and to achieve a more effective adjustment to its environment. Provided certain conditions are met, the group will move in the direction of greater utilization of these capacities.

This is a re-statement of the basic client-centered hypothesis as applied to a group rather than to an individual. Like that hypothesis about the individual, it stresses the positive growth forces which, if released, result in greater internal harmony and productive efficiency and more effective adjustment to the environment. It is an hypothesis that emphasizes the inner capacity of a group. It states that every group *has* this capacity, but implies that it is a matter of process or development for a group to approach the *realization* of that capacity. In other words, a group may not be able to solve immediately an existing problem, yet it can and will develop in a direction which will lead to the best solution of that problem provided certain essential conditions are met.

It will be apparent that, although expressed in the form of a proposition, this idea is more in the nature of an hypothesis which the group-centered leader chooses to hold in his relations with members of a group. He could choose to hold an entirely different belief about groups — one that placed less stress upon the inner capacities of the group and more stress upon its inherent weaknesses and tendencies toward submission to outside forces. Such an hypothesis seems to be preferred by many writers, as is indicated in the following quotation from the writings of Freud:

> A group is extraordinarily credulous and open to influence, it has no critical faculty, and the improbable does not exist for it. . . . Inclined as it itself is to all extremes, a group can only be excited by an excessive stimulus. Anyone who wishes to produce an effect upon it needs no logical adjustment in his arguments; he must paint in the most forcible colors, he must exaggerate, and he must repeat the same thing again and again. . . . It respects force and can only be slightly influenced by kindness, which it regards merely as a form of weakness. . . . It wants to be ruled and oppressed, and to fear its masters. . . . And, finally, groups have never thirsted after truth. They demand illusions, and cannot do without them. They constantly give what is unreal precedence over what is real; they are almost as strongly influenced by what is untrue as by what is true. They have an evident tendency not to distinguish between the two. . . . A group is an obedient herd, which could never live without a master. It has such a thirst for obedience that it submits instinctively to anyone who appoints himself as its master. (65, pp. 15–21)

It is true, perhaps, that history provides many examples of groups in which such characteristics have predominated, and this fact makes it understandable why some would choose to adopt this kind of hypothesis about groups. It is possible, however, to find in history examples of groups which have demonstrated quite different characteristics — those which require us to have a great deal more respect for the inherent potentialities of the group for self-direction, self-protection, and appropriate adjustments. It is just such a respect that seems a part of the attitudes of those who have chosen to operate with groups in terms of the hypothesis that is contained in Proposition V. While recognizing that groups have both the tendencies described by Freud and also more positive tendencies, some leaders choose to hypothesize that the latter are the stronger.

This proposition is explicit in its emphasis upon "movement," growth, or development of the group. This is to say that the group's achievement of a state in which it is able to utilize its maximum potential is the result of a certain process of development. Groups usually do not have this characteristic. Quite the contrary, most groups operate far from this ideal. Apparently few groups in our culture are ever provided with the conditions whereby they might move toward maximum utilization of their potential. It is more common for a group to rely upon the contributions of only a part of its membership while the rest of the group dissipates its energies in *reacting against* the control and authority of the more active members. It is here that group behavior can be deceiving. Often all members of a group are *active*, but upon closer examination it is usually found to be what McGregor (123) has called *reactive* behavior. As Allport has pointed out, "a person ceases to be reactive and contrary in respect to a desirable course of conduct only when he himself has had a hand in declaring that course of conduct to be desirable." (6, p. 123) Few groups ever reach the state where its members are given this opportunity.

How do groups reach such a state? How do groups approach the maximum utilization of their potential? What kind of process is necessary for groups to move in this direction? These are the crucial questions, yet we have no definitive answers for any of them. Our own experience would lead us to believe that certain conditions facilitate this process. There may be others of which we are not aware. Before describing some of the conditions that we feel are required for the releasing of this group process, it would seem necessary to examine our concept of leadership as it relates to our framework for looking at groups.

A Concept of Group Leadership

Accompanying the gradual evolution of this theoretical framework for thinking about groups and organizations, there has emerged in the writer's thinking a particular concept about group leadership. Changes in thinking both about groups and about the leadership function in groups have gone on simultaneously, one serving as a check against the other, and each contributing something to the other. Both are still undergoing constant revision. This close relationship between a theory of group functioning and a concept of group leadership is probably as it should be. A conceptual framework for thinking about groups must include a theory of the leadership function. What is "group leadership"? What is meant by the "leadership function"? What sort of concept of group leadership will be consistent with the particular way in which groups have been perceived in the preceding pages?

The Leadership Function

Leadership is most commonly perceived as a function, or group of functions, carried out by some individual member of a group. This particular person is sometimes thought of as the group member who has been given or has acquired the *responsibility* for the group. Thus, the industrial supervisor is responsible for those workers who are designated as members of "his" work-group or "his" section. Implicit is the idea that the leader is responsible to someone "above" him, usually his leader or supervisor. Frequently, the leader is thought of as the person in a group who has been given or has acquired the *authority* over other members of the group. "By virtue of the authority vested in him" the leader has the "power" to make certain decisions affecting some aspects of the lives of members in his group. Responsibility for a group and authority over a group frequently are combined inseparably in the idea of leadership. Nevertheless, it is not uncommon to stress one or the other. Thus, the military leader has certain authority over "his" men. A person also may be perceived as a leader because of certain distinctive *skills or abilities* which he possesses or because he has more of one particular skill or ability than others in a group. The teacher, the business executive, the team captain may owe their positions as leaders to this kind of differentiation from the group members. In our particular culture we prefer to think that leadership is usually based upon this differential. It is in this connection that leadership has most often been thought of as a role that is gained through the acquisition of certain stereotyped leader qualities or skills. One must be a good speaker, have a forceful personality, "know people," be educated, keep ahead of the others, and possess any number of highly desirable character and personality traits.

These are common ways of looking at leadership. It is seen as a function carried out by a *person*. It is something invested in one particular group member. Whether or not that member is perceived as being differentiated from the others as regards responsibility, authority, skill, knowledge, status, or power — the fact is that the differentiation is made. Associated with this differentiation are certain expectations that the leader has more at stake, will take a more active role than others, has certain powers over the others, is more capable than others in selecting group goals, can make "policy decisions," will give the group guidance and direction. Such expectations may be thought of as parts of a generalized attitude on the part of group members toward the leader: *dependence*. McGregor, in discussing the characteristics of the supervisor-subordinate relationship in industrial organizations, elaborates on this point as follows:

> Psychologically the dependence of the subordinate upon his superiors is a fact of extraordinary significance, in part because of its emotional similarity to the dependence characteristic of another earlier relationship: that between the child and his parents. The similarity is more than an analogy. The adult subordinate's dependence upon his superiors actually reawakens certain emotions and attitudes which were part of his childhood relationship with his parents, and which apparently have long since been outgrown. The adult is usually unaware of the similarity because most of this complex of childhood emotions has been repressed. Although the emotions influence his behavior, they are not accessible to consciousness under ordinary circumstances. (123, p. 428)

McGregor's analysis of this relationship is undoubtedly an accurate one. Yet it must be pointed out that he is observing leadership as it exists today, not only in industry, but in almost all organizations — leadership that is a function carried out by a single person.

It is quite possible, however, to think of leadership in a different way — namely, as the property of the total group or organization. Leadership, in these terms, becomes a set of functions, not vested in a single person, but rather functions which must be carried out by the group. Leadership is, then, not a role to be played by one member of a group, but rather a set of functions to be performed within the group in order that the group may make adjustments, solve problems, and develop its potentials. Benne and Sheats (23), as well as others associated with the "group dynamics" movement, have effectively encouraged this way of looking at leadership. They have called attention to the notion of the "diffusion of leadership" throughout the group, implying that the leadership functions should ideally be taken over by group members.

Leadership, then, may be thought of as a set of functions which are the property of the group and which, under ideal conditions, become distributed within the group. This concept of "distributed leadership" is an important one. It is possible to see it now in relation to one of our earlier propositions about groups — namely, that a group will make the most appropriate adjustment when it utilizes the maximum creative potential of its membership. Stated simply, the adjustive behavior of the group will be most appropriate when each member is free at any time to take on some of the functions of leadership. As emphasized earlier, however, this state rarely exists in groups. Most organizations operate far from this ideal. It is rarely possible to say of a group that its leadership is distributed or that its members are making their maximum contribution.

The very existence of a group leader, either real or perceived, may be a deterrent to the distribution of leadership throughout the group.

This statement needs further examination, because most groups *do* have leaders. Some groups have a *structured* leader-role which is kept filled by some member of the group, as in almost all of our industrial and business organizations, our educational, religious, and political institutions — in fact, practically all of the institutionalized groups in our culture. Sometimes the group members have something to say about the choice of person to fill the role, sometimes not. Other groups have a leader *imposed* on them, in which case the members have little voice in the selection of the leader. This would be true of the countless groups of students who walk into their classes for the first time and find their leaders already chosen for them. In a sense, this would be true also of the family group; for the newborn child enters this group finding the leader, the head of the family, already selected for him. In other groups, there may not be either a structured leader-role or an imposed leader, but rather a *perceived leader*. In such groups, the group members perceive a leader amongst them, sometimes despite the fact the person to whom the group looks for leadership may not realize he is thus perceived. Frequently this person is differentiated from the other members simply by his status, his superior knowledge, his age, his behavior, his dress, or any number of other factors. This is seen in groups that are formed spontaneously, such as a party group, an *ad hoc* committee, or an action group. Boys' gangs, play groups, informal discussion groups — all seem to develop leaders that are often only perceived as such. The members of such groups look to particular persons for leadership, and accept their assumption of the leadership role. The perceived leader has a less secure position than the chosen or imposed leader, needless to say, for the perceptions of group members change much more easily than does the structure of an institution.

Here the thesis has been advanced that leaders inhibit group growth, yet almost all groups, if not all, have leaders. This appears to be a stalemate. The difficulty, however, probably can be found in the very nature of previous conceptions of leadership and the leader-role. A solution to this dilemma might be that a concept of leadership is emerging which would make it possible for a group to have a particular kind of leader who would facilitate the distribution of leadership, and would accelerate the development of a group toward the maximum utilization of its potential.

A Concept of Leadership and a Paradox

What is emerging from recent attempts to utilize "therapeutic" approaches in group leadership and administration is both a new concept of leadership and a paradox growing out of this concept. The paradox may already be apparent from the previous paragraphs. It may be stated more explicitly as follows:

The most effective leader is one who can create the conditions by which he will actually lose the leadership.

Thus, the person who finds himself the leader of a group will, by creating the proper conditions, distribute the leadership function throughout the group. It seems that there may be a direct relationship between the degree to which the leadership is given over to the group and the extent to which the group will utilize the maximum potential of its members. The resemblance is striking between this principle and the belief of the client-centered counselor that the more willing he is for the client to assume responsibility and direction for his own life, the more rewarding is the release of the strengths and capacities which exist within the client.

Why should it be true that leadership is distributed throughout a group only to the degree that the leader relinquishes it? It is known how dependence upon a leader operates to inhibit independent behavior on the part of group members. We have seen, too, how authority produces reactive rather than constructive and creative behavior. We have evidence of the reluctance of people to "show their ignorance" in the presence of the expert, or the well-informed person. People apparently must feel secure and free from threat in order to be themselves, in order to participate freely, in order to expose their ideas or feelings to others. Traditional leadership, it seems, rarely gives people such security and freedom.

By giving up the leadership to the group, it might be said that the leader progressively becomes more of a group member. He becomes another potential contributor to the group effort. Thus, the goal of the effective leader becomes one of gradually getting acceptance from the group members as a person who is "just one of them." It should be pointed out, however, that this goal is often used by leaders simply as a technique for disguising the real differences between them and the group — a technique that is often satirized as the "buddy-buddy" approach in group leadership. "Just think of me as one of you," an administrator was recently overheard saying. The industrial executive especially goes to great lengths sometimes to create the impression that he is "just one of the boys on the team." It is very doubtful that these techniques accomplish their purpose of changing group members' perceptions of the leader as the one who has more authority, status, responsibility, or skill. Frequently, leaders even employ this approach as a subtle technique for influencing the group in the direction the leader would like to have it go. They attempt to disguise their influence on the group through posing as group members. Some leaders, however, honestly believe that they should become just members of the group, and they have no ulterior motives in doing so. Even in this case, if the members perceive a person as a leader, that person is only escaping the situation if he denies that he has such a role. From our experience, it would seem almost a principle that, whenever a person is perceived as a leader, the process of transferring his leadership to the group cannot be accomplished by fiat. This is to say that he can best transfer the leadership *by remaining as the leader*, until he can effectively create the conditions required for members to *learn* to assume the leadership. This principle seems, at first, like a contradiction, but in practice it usually happens that the leader who pretends to be just another member is actually perceived as one who secretly has goals for the group, or who is compensating for his previous attempts to direct the group, or who is actually insecure about his ability as a leader.

Here, then, is a concept of leadership in which it is recognized that the commonly accepted leader-role acts as a deterrent to the distribution of the leadership functions throughout the group. Yet it stresses the importance of distributed leadership, if the group is to utilize the maximum potential of its members. At the same time it calls attention to the fact that the transference of the leadership functions from the leader to the group is a process that involves the group members' learning to assume these functions. This theory attempts to explain that it is not usually possible for the leader either to dump the leadership onto the group or to pretend that he is giving it up when in reality he wants to keep it himself. Finally, the thesis is advanced that the leader can actually facilitate the process of leadership-transference by accepting his role of leader, but carrying out a different kind of leadership function — one that makes the focus of his efforts the creation of certain conditions required for releasing the adjustive capacity of the group.

In the next section an attempt will be made to examine more in detail the role of this "nonleading leader." What conditions does this type of leader try to create? What are the critical dimensions of this kind of leadership? An effort will be made to draw on both our own experience and the experiences of others in order to describe how such a leader functions. Finally, it will be necessary to face some very crucial, but puzzling problems that grow out of attempts to try out this type of leadership in real situations.

A FORMULATION OF GROUP-CENTERED LEADERSHIP

From recent attempts to apply principles derived chiefly from psychotherapy to group situations, it is possible to begin to define certain aspects of the group leader's role that seem to be critical from the standpoint of their effects upon the group. First, it may be well to look at the leader's role in a broad sense. It might be emphasized that a leader certainly may choose one of several approaches to group leadership and administration. The approach that is being formulated here is only one of a number of different approaches. It has been called a "group-centered" approach because this term seems to emphasize that the primary concern of the leader is in facilitating the group's development, helping the group clarify and achieve its goals, aiding the group to actualize itself. He discards his own goals, puts aside his concern for his own development, and centers his attention outside of himself. The term "group-centered" has little value in and of itself, and certainly it is not our intention to place emphasis upon the mere name. Leadership has many dimensions, and whether or not an approach to groups is "group-centered" or "leader-centered" is only a very general level of description. A term was needed, and this term was selected.

Others (95) have used the term "social therapy" to describe an approach which is essentially similar in its emphasis upon group development, active participation of group members, and the use of some of the methods of psychotherapy by the group leader. In many ways this is a more descriptive term, yet "therapy" may have certain undesirable connotations in connection with its use with groups. Needless to say, however, the approach that is presented here is believed to be therapeutic in a real sense. Defined quite broadly, group-centered leadership is an approach in which the leader places value on two goals: the ultimate development of the group's independence and self-responsibility, and the release of the group's potential capacities.

It might be said that the group-centered leader chooses to adopt goals which are long-range rather than immediate. He is confident that the group will solve its immediate problems, yet he helps the group become more capable of solving future problems. He is confident that the group will take action, but he accelerates the process whereby its action will be self-initiated. He is interested in the group as a developing social organism. He sees his function as that of helping the group to work out its own adjustment, and by so doing to become more self-responsible than before. And because he holds such values, the group-centered leader is more comfortable adopting a role that seems to him consistent with these values.

Group-centered leadership has its origins in the application of principles of client-centered psychotherapy to groups and organizations. Consequently, it is to be expected that the group-centered leader holds attitudes similar to those of the client-centered therapist. As these have been described in a previous chapter,[1] they will not be presented here. It will be well, however, to translate these attitudes into terms applicable for the group leader. The group-centered leader believes in the worth of the members of the group and respects them as individuals different from himself. They are not persons to be used, influenced, or directed in order to accomplish the leader's aims. They are not people to be "led" by someone who has "superior" qualities or more important values. The group-centered leader sees the group or organization as existing for the individuals who compose it. It is the vehicle for the expression of their personalities and for the satisfaction of their needs. He believes that the group as a whole can provide for itself better than can any single member of the group. He believes in the group's fundamental right to self-direction and to self-actualization on its own terms. Rogers in an earlier publication, examining the attitudes which he feels he must have as an administrator, asks himself certain questions:

1. Do I trust the capacities of the group, and of the individuals in the group, to meet the problems with which we are faced, or do I basically trust only myself?

2. Do I free the group for creative discussion by being willing to understand, accept, and respect *all* attitudes, or do I find myself trying subtly to manipulate group discussion so that it comes out my way?

3. Do I, as leader, participate by honest expression of my own attitudes but without trying to control the attitudes of others?

4. Do I rely upon basic attitudes for motivation, or do I think surface procedures motivate behavior?

5. Am I willing to be responsible for those aspects of action which the group has delegated to me?

6. Do I trust the individual to do his job?

7. When tensions occur, do I try to make it possible for them to be brought out into the open? (171, pp. 546–548)

Conditions Which the Group-Centered Leader Tries to Create

As an implementation of his basic philosophy and his attitudes, the group-centered leader tries to create for the group some of

[1] See Chapter 2.

the same conditions which in individual and group therapy have been found essential for releasing the constructive forces within the client.

The Opportunity for Participation

Group problems require group decisions and group action. For a group to move toward maximum utilization of its potential, the members of the group must feel that they at least have the opportunity to participate in matters which will affect them. Denial of that opportunity seems to pave the way for reactive, resistive behavior on the part of the members of an organization. This idea is not at all a new one, but it has received more scientific validity in recent years as a necessary condition for both group and individual development. In the exciting work of the investigators who have conducted the Peckham experiments (144), a public health project in an English community, we have a dramatic illustration of the effects of providing the opportunity for families to participate in self-selected activities. It is clear from the descriptions of this project [1] that the citizens began to be interested in their own health and subsequently took active steps to improve it because they were simply given the opportunity to participate.

The experiments on changing food habits which have been reported by Radke and Klisurich (152) seem to show clearly the values of housewives' participation in the process of arriving at group action-decisions. Golden and Ruttenberg (67) describe several examples in industry of the beneficial effects of management's extending to labor the opportunity to participate in matters that traditionally have been considered the prerogative of management alone. In another study, conducted by the Survey Research Center of the University of Michigan (206) and mentioned in an earlier chapter, it was found that one of the factors distinguishing supervisors of low-productivity work-groups from supervisors of high-productivity work-groups was that more of the latter encouraged employee participation in the making of decisions. Even in the area of child-rearing practices there is

[1] See Chapter 2, pp. 59–63.

some evidence of the values of giving children an opportunity to participate in matters concerning the entire family. In this connection, Baldwin, Kalhorn, and Breese (17) found that in those families characterized as "democratic" the child was given adequate opportunity to express his own views, he was consulted about questions of policy, and his opinions were given the same consideration as those of an adult. Children from such homes tended to show better social adjustment during their later school years and also greater increases in I.Q. Some of the effects of active participation of group members in a relatively self-directing training group have been reported by the writer (70). Marked changes in attitudes toward others, increased understandings of self, and increased clarity of goals were reported by these group members as products of their group experience.

These studies are representative of an increasing number that strongly suggest that the opportunity for group members to participate is a necessary condition for the growth of a group. But will not the members of an organization usurp power from the leaders? How can those with less training, less intelligence, and fewer skills make adequate decisions for a group? Are not the leaders better qualified to decide on broad policy matters? These are some of the questions that are frequently asked, not coincidentally, by those who are in a position of leadership in a group. Our own experience would be that group members may usurp power, but it is only as a *reaction against* the perceived threat of the power of their leaders. When the source of threat is removed, our experience has been that the problem actually becomes one of how to get the members to take *more* responsibility, not less. We probably tend to underestimate how much of human behavior is behavior in reaction to the perceived threat of authority — and how little of human behavior is self-initiated. To understand how strong are the external stimuli to the usual kind of group behavior, we have only to observe the initial frustration and dependence of groups that are put on their own by their leaders.

This dependence was illustrated in the first session with a group of high school "problem children." After the leader had explained that they were being given the opportunity to meet once a week to talk about whatever they wanted to, the group found it difficult to begin, as illustrated in the following verbatim excerpt from the recorded interview:

(Long pause.)
B: Gonna waste a lotta wire dat way. *(Refers to the wire recorder.)*
T: Yes.
Leader: Hm?
B: Gonna waste a lotta wire dat way.
Leader: You're worried about — that nobody's — that we have long pauses, hmm?
B: M-hm.
T: No station identification either. *(Giggles.)*
Leader (laughing): During the pause, hm?
B: Corn, corn. *(Long pause.)*
B: Trouble is, you should give us something definite to talk on. This way we will get all mixed up. Nobody wants no — nobody knows what to talk about. Give us a definite point.
Leader: It's kind of uncomfortable to just be free to talk about anything you want to. You'd almost want me to tell you what to talk about.
G: Well, just give us a point *to* talk about. Just place somethin' in front of us. You can't whittle without a piece of wood in your hand. You gotta have something to whittle on.
B: I think it'd be better if you asked us a little — a little bit of questions. It's like dis, you know. You won't find out nuttin outa nobody unless you ask questions, because you can go up in — in a class, and if the teacher has a question on the board, the only way she'll get somebody to answer is to call on a person herself.
Leader: In other words, you would — you would feel, and as I gather you are speaking from your own feelings there, that you kinda don't want to talk unless something — somebody —
B: Something — there's a definite point to talk about.
Leader: I see. *(Pause.)* Well, what I've tried to convey is that I don't have anything in mind I want you to talk about. In other words, this is an opportunity for you to talk about whatever you'd like to talk about.
S: Give us something to talk about.
P: After you're through wit' your school hours and go home, whatever you do after school hours — that's your business, isn't it? I mean, like the school — you go over your girl friend's house and they don't

think — think it's right for you to go way over there. And they — they tell you that you can't go to this school unless you stop goin' over there.

Leader: I gather you kinda feel it's a person's own business where he goes after school hours, and I gather you kinda resent their telling you what to do about that.

A: I don't think the school has no right to say what kind of sweaters we ought to wear. I was wearin' a sweater that Miss —— said I should take it off. I go to this school now, she said, and I shouldn't wear the sweater of a different school.

S: Doesn't matter what sweater; they got no business tellin' you how to dress.

Leader: You feel they're kinda interfering with something that's your own business.

P: That's right. They even tell you which boys to hang around with. (*Others:* Yeah.)   I got in trouble . . .

It is clear from this illustration that the group members were very reluctant to begin discussing problems of their own. It is almost certain that in most other situations with adults they have depended upon the adults to provide the structure and the impetus. In time, however, one of the group cautiously opened the discussion and was soon followed by another. When they began to see that the leader was understanding and accepting of these early comments, others joined in, coming forth with strong feelings about the school and its attempts to control them. This continued for the remainder of the hour-long session, no more appeals being made to the leader for direction. At the second session the same pattern was repeated; that is, the group showed a similar dependency on the leader for getting the discussion started, then cautiously took over the responsibility and eventually carried the discussion for the remainder of the session.

Returning to the question of whether group members are really qualified by training or native ability to make adequate decisions for a group, our experience in our own staff functioning would lead us to answer in the affirmative. True, group decisions often turn out to be less than adequate, and the issue has to be reopened for further staff consideration. Yet it seems to many of us on the staff that some of the most inappropriate decisions we make are those which have been arrived at without total staff participation — without considering all the data which could be brought to bear on the problem.

This question of the group members' ability versus the leader's ability to make sound decisions for a group is often examined inaccurately. Actually the question is not whether the group members *or* the leader can make the soundest decisions for a group. It is whether the leader without the group members can make better decisions than can the total group *including the leader*. One of the things we have seen in our own organization is the willingness — or rather eagerness — with which the group solicits and uses the various specialized skills contained in the total group membership. On the matter of making decisions in an industrial organization, Morris L. Cooke, a consulting engineer, has written:

> Management today may include thousands of employees — all agents of the stockholders — ranging from the president . . . down to the lowliest gang boss. . . . It has been a treasured theory that those of us who have the authority — by virtue of title, salary, or what have you — to make decisions, actually do make them; whereas, as a matter of fact, most well-rendered decisions grow wholly out of the assembled facts. When these preliminaries to a decision have been well conducted, usually only one wise decision is possible. The making of decisions, of course, is not a function reserved for the top. They are being made constantly at all levels in an industrial organization. (68, p. 464)

Thus, decision-making is seen as a process — a procedure by which relevant data are obtained from and examined by the total group. Those of us who have tried working in a group in which all members are given opportunity to participate in making decisions sometimes wonder how it was possible for us in past leadership roles to base our decisions on such inadequate data and on so few of the pertinent elements, the most important of which are often the attitudes and feelings of the members.

Freedom of Communication

A second condition which the group-centered leader attempts

to create is the absence of barriers to free communication between all members of the group. In most groups or organizations this condition is seldom met. Why is it necessary for all the members of a group to be able to communicate freely with one another? There seem to be at least two important reasons for this. First, if there are barriers to free communication between individuals, hostile attitudes developing as a result of normal interpersonal conflicts are much less likely to be resolved. This is Newcomb's thesis in his stimulating article on autistic hostility.

> Hostile impulses commonly arise, then, when status-relationship is so perceived that another is viewed as a threat. . . . If, as a result of a hostile attitude emerging from the newly perceived status relationship, communication with the other person is avoided, the conditions necessary for eliminating the hostile attitude are not likely to occur. (142, p. 72)

Freedom of communication, then, is a necessary condition for friendly interpersonal relations between members of a group. A group fighting within itself and not communicating is seldom capable of adequate adjustive behavior.

A second reason why free communication is a requirement for an effective group is that it is important for group members to develop mutual understandings — sign-processes common to all the members, as the semanticists would say. It is difficult for a group to reach agreement as to the most appropriate action in a particular situation if the various members interpret the situation in radically different ways — that is, if the situation for each person has a different meaning and this meaning is not shared by the others in the group.

The writer recently carried out a project aimed at the development of a more objective method of evaluating pilots than the methods in current use. Strong opposition to the project was encountered almost immediately, forcing the researchers to engage in extensive communication with those who were blocking the project. Only after many conferences and discussions did it become clear that the proposed evaluation procedures had different meanings for different groups of people, somewhat as follows:

The researchers: The proposed procedures meant a more reliable, more objective, more diagnostic, and more valid measure of pilot performance. They would help the airline companies by weeding out the poorer pilots, and they would help the pilot by insuring him against inaccurate and prejudiced assessments of his skill.

The pilots: The proposed procedures meant debasing the pilots' "profession" by assuming it was possible to quantify their performance as has been done for unskilled workers. The procedures meant a powerful tool which management could employ as an excuse for firing pilots. They meant a means of making public the quantitative differences in the abilities of pilots — that is, pilots would be graded and classified.

The examiners: The proposed procedures meant more "paper work." They also meant a method of checking on the accuracy of the examiners' grading. The new procedures also would devaluate the significance of their job by "taking the fine judgment and skill out of evaluation," thus making them mere "clerks" or "recorders."

It was naïve to expect that these people would work cooperatively on the development of the new procedures. Only after these different perceptions of the new methods were eventually understood and shared by all the persons involved did it become clear to all what the requirements were for any new evaluation procedure. Cooperation was effected only after a large number of conferences with representatives of each interested group. Free communication between these groups had the effect of creating a new perception of the proposed evaluation procedures which was shared by all. The task became one of cooperatively working at the development of a procedure that would be objective yet not mechanical, that would be standardized yet leave room for the individual judgment of the check-pilot, that would differentiate qualified and unqualified pilots but not show degrees of proficiency among those who qualified. The result was a procedure that was far more appropriate to the realities of the situation than one that might have been developed before the groups shared their different perceptions.

The barriers to communication within groups or organizations exist only as they are perceived by the individual members as barriers. What is a barrier to one person may not be to another.

Thus, highly formalized communication procedures — written memoranda, prescribed channels, and parliamentary procedures — may be perceived as barriers to free communication by some group members, but others may find such procedures in no way limiting to their communication. Similarly, such procedures may limit communication in one organization, and may not in another. Nevertheless, it is likely that there are certain things that universally limit free communication in groups. These may be such conditions as physical space separation, absence of face-to-face contacts, clumsy and complicated methods of communication, and excessively demanding jobs which do not permit time for communication. Apparently, these conditions, which can be thought of as barriers existing in the physical reality of an organization, are important. Yet the significance of such barriers can be overemphasized.

Perhaps even greater barriers to free communication are the more subtle conditions that are frequently perceived by the group member as threats to his own self. This is to say that each individual group member constructs *within himself* the really effective barriers to free communication. If this is true, it is clear why a nonthreatening climate is another fundamental condition required for releasing the adjustive capacities of groups.

A Nonthreatening Psychological Climate

The concept of a "group climate" has been used by a number of different investigators as an abstraction for certain characteristics of a group that seem to have potent effects on the behavior and attitudes of its members. The concept achieved wide recognition as a result of the studies of Lewin, Lippitt, and White (119) on the effects of experimentally created social climates on the behavior of children. These researchers used the concept of climate to stand for different patterns of adult leadership. They differentiated three basic patterns: autocratic, democratic, and laissez-faire. These terms came to be used to describe the "climates" that the investigators assumed were induced by the three different leadership patterns. Thus, for them, the different climates were equated with the different leadership patterns.

Anderson and Brewer (8) have used the concept of climate in almost the same way — that is, they have equated the climates of different classrooms with different patterns of teacher behavior. Withall (225) has also defined classroom climate in terms of whether the teacher's behavior was learner-centered, teacher-centered, or neutral. All these studies define climate by the kind of behavior exhibited by the leader or teacher.

It is possible, however, to think of climate as something perceived or felt by the students in a class or the members of a group — that is, climate can be examined from the frame of reference of the group members. Thelen and Withall (212) have attempted to do just this, but they obtain from their subjects only a positive or a negative reaction, and it is difficult to know just what these reactions mean to the members. Their study is important, however, in that it attempts to obtain a measure of climate as perceived by the group member, though it does not give many clues as to the dimensions of the perceived climate.

Some evidence of the actual dimensions of climate has been obtained in studies of the effects of client-centered therapy as seen through the eyes of the client. As a matter of fact, it has been from the recorded statements of our clients that we have obtained the greatest number of clues as to the nature of the psychological climate as experienced by them. If we can accept this kind of evidence, it seems that clients most often experience a feeling of lack of threat. They feel they are in a "safe" atmosphere. They feel they are not being judged or evaluated. They feel they are being understood — the therapist is listening carefully and understanding what they are saying. They feel "accepted." The therapist seems to convey to them that he accepts all aspects of their personality — their feelings of hopelessness, hostility, and dependence, as well as their more positive feelings. In this situation they feel free from outside pressures to change.

This same kind of nonthreatening, accepting psychological climate is what the group-centered leader tries to create for his group. This aim is rooted firmly in his belief that the individual, when free from forces which he perceives as threats to the self or the self-concept, will actualize the positive and constructive forces that are within him.

SOME DISTINCTIVE FUNCTIONS CARRIED OUT BY THE GROUP-CENTERED LEADER

Some of the conditions which the group-centered leader tries to create have been examined. Just how does he go about this task? What is group-centered leadership in more operational terms? Considerably more research is needed before we can state with any degree of certainty what are the essential dimensions of his role. . An attempt will be made, however, to define certain distinctive functions which he carries out in the group.

Conveying Warmth and Empathy

There are characteristics of leader behavior which are difficult to describe, but apparently easy for people to perceive in a leader. Warmth and empathy are terms used to represent something basic in a leader's manner which is of importance in his attempt to create a nonthreatening, accepting atmosphere. Undoubtedly it is a pattern of behavior which manifests itself in the leader's speech, his facial expression, his gestures. We hear people speak of others as "cold," "stiff," "unfriendly." These terms mean *something* to others, though it is not certain what the essential behavior variables are that form the basis for such perceptions. Perhaps they are related to an individual's liking for others, perhaps to his own feeling of security with others — his ability to act spontaneously in the presence of a group. The general emotional tone of an entire group is often influenced by the presence or absence of these qualities in the leader. The ability to empathize may be another way of saying that one person is capable of taking the role of the other, an essential aspect of all interpersonal communication and a factor which is so important in individual therapy. Just how these leader characteristics affect a group is not clearly known. One hypothesis would be that group members identify with their leader and in the process internalize some of his attitudes and behavioral patterns. *This would mean that group members may gradually begin to behave toward others in the group in much the same way as the leader behaves toward them.* They would become more warm and friendly to each other, more empathic in their relations with others. Under such conditions communication is undoubtedly facilitated.

Attending to Others

In work with various groups it has been sobering to observe how little the members attend to what others say. Without attention there can be no understanding and hence no communication. Apparently the act of attending carefully to another person is a difficult task for most people. They are usually thinking what they will say when the speaker stops. Or they focus on some specific point made by the speaker and then fail to attend to the rest because they are thinking up arguments against the specific point. It is by no means uncommon in groups to observe one person bringing up a point, then a second person bringing up another point, a third person offering an entirely different suggestion, and so on — none of them responding to the contribution of the previous speaker. It is doubtful in this case that they are really attending carefully to each other. This is not communication in any sense of the word. As long as people feel that others are paying little attention to what they say, they are likely either to keep pressing their point or to withdraw with the feeling that their contributions are not valuable or not welcome.

How do groups acquire the practice of attending carefully to each other? Here it seems the group-centered leader serves an essential and significant function. He demonstrates an extraordinary kind of concentrated attention. Having no need to get his own ideas across, having no "axe to grind," and sincerely respecting the worth of the contributions of every group member, he is able to attend to others. By doing so he conveys to the speaker that his contribution is worth listening to, that as a person he is respected enough to receive the undivided attention of another.

It is not enough, however, that the leader simply attend. He must convey this sense of full attention to the speaker. There are certain cues that can give the group member some proof of the leader's attention (nodding of the head, looking directly at the speaker), yet these are not always adequate proof. If, however, the leader paraphrases the speaker's comment, he thereby furnishes conclusive proof that he has attended. Transcribed group discussions under group-centered leadership reveal that the leader is constantly prefixing his comments with such phrases as:

> You are saying . . .
> You feel . . .
> If I understand you correctly . . .
> I'm not sure I follow you, but is this it . . .
> I gather that you mean . . .
> Let's see if I really understand that . . .

Here is a function carried out by the group-centered leader which is rarely carried out consistently by any other member of a group. It is a difficult task, for it requires the leader to concentrate outside of himself. To do this, the leader cannot be thinking such things as:

> Is the group going in the direction I want it to go?
> I disagree with that statement.
> I wonder what they think of me.
> How can I get other members to talk?
> That is an irrelevant remark.

This ability to attend to the statements of others is probably directly related to the leader's own feeling of security in the group, his confidence, his threat-tolerance. The leader who is not comfortable in his role will be responding so much to internal stimuli that he will find it difficult to respond to anything outside of himself.

In our earlier attempts at group-centered leadership the mistake was often made of trying to paraphrase almost every comment made by group members, somewhat after the practice of the individual therapist. Had there been a better understanding of the function of rephrasing or reflecting, this error might have been avoided. In practice, too frequent reflection by the leader may actually inhibit communication by forcing the members to channel all comments through the leader. Reflection of comments by group members appears to have the primary function of conveying to the members the sense that their contributions are welcome and are considered worth while. As the group members begin to feel this, the leader's reflections become less necessary. Furthermore, *this function, too, is gradually taken over by the group members themselves.* Here is the distinctive contribution of the group-centered leader. He brings to the group a useful function which did not previously exist, and the group then incorporates this function into itself.

Understanding Meanings and Intents

It is not even enough that the group-centered leader attends to what others say and gives some proof of this by reflecting back to the speakers. It might be enough, provided people said what they actually meant. We know, however, that people seldom do. They are prevented from doing so both by the limitations of language itself and by internal inhibitions which operate to protect the individual from threat. Furthermore, even if people actually said what they meant, it is not always true that the listener will understand. This discrepancy between expression (of the speaker) and impression (of the listener) has been pointed out clearly by Ichheiser, who writes:

> Our answer is an insistence that some, and frequently even a great degree of, discrepancy between expression and impression is the *normal* state of affairs and that we are bound to misunderstand extremely important aspects of human relations if we fail to take these ever present, basic discrepancies fully into account.... The expectation that there is some kind of "natural harmony," or even a complete identity, between expression and impression is based on the silent assumption that the mechanisms of expression and those of impression are somehow, in a predetermined way, attuned to each other. ... Between the inner personality, its attitudes, sentiments, and tendencies, and the external personality there is always a certain degree of incongruity. In human relations we have always to suppress, or at least to modify, the frank expression of some factors. (93, p. 8)

The group-centered leader tries to function in a way which will reduce this tendency of individuals "to suppress, or at least to modify, the frank expression of some factors." One of the ways he does this is by trying to understand the actual meaning or the intent of members' comments and behavior. That is — to express this idea in somewhat different terms — the leader tries to adopt the internal frame of reference of the other person, to perceive what the other person perceives, to understand what is in the central core of the speaker's conscious awareness — in a sense, to take the role of the other person. The group-centered leader in this respect is relying on what Reik (161) has vividly described as "free-floating attention." His attention goes farther than the words or content of the speaker. He is after the latent meaning, the "secret intent," or what Ichheiser has called the "expressional" aspect of communication. For example, as the group-centered leader listens to a lengthy anecdote being told by a group member, he may be thinking in some such manner as follows:

> This person seems to be talking about a personal experience he had. The group previously was arguing the relative merits of two different courses of action. He must be giving this experience to support one of those courses of action. I'll listen to see if this seems to be true. Yes, I think that's it. I wonder which of the two he is trying to support. Now I see. This experience is one in which a course of action like Plan A failed. He seems to be for Plan B. I wonder if he feels this is fairly conclusive evidence that Plan A will fail in this case. Yes, he certainly does. He thinks his experience is almost identical to ours at the present. Yet he hasn't actually said that he favors Plan B; he is only saying Plan A failed in this instance.

Having gone through some such process of thinking with the speaker and trying to understand his intent or the meaning of his illustration, the leader might respond with something like this:

> "Jim, if I understand you correctly, you feel fairly convinced that, because of this experience with Plan A in a pretty similar situation to our own, you don't think it will work here. And are you therefore saying that you probably prefer Plan B, is that it?"

This is not what Jim *said*, but it reflects the *intent* behind his anecdote. The group-centered leader is always alert to perceive such meaning and reflect it back to the speaker for verification. This is very much like what the client-centered therapist is attempting to do, in individual therapy, as indicated in an earlier chapter [1]; consequently no further attempt will be made here to illustrate this function. In a group situation, however, this function of the leader may have additional effects over and above conveying understanding to the speaker. By extracting out of a member's comments the intentional meanings, the leader also may be helping others understand what he is "really" saying, thus facilitating communication to a very great extent. Again, the leader is bringing to the group another function which did not previously exist there, or existed only to a limited degree. Our hypothesis is that because such responses by the leader are rewarding to the group (they facilitate communication and thereby accelerate the sharing of meanings), gradually *they will be taken over by the group members themselves.*

It may be profitable to discuss this function of "understanding meanings and intents" in relation to what other writers have called "interpreting" by the group leader. We refer particularly to our understanding of group interpretation as it is used by such writers as Jaques (94) and Bion (27). From their writings the distinct impression is gained that it is facilitating to the group for the leader to interpret what may not be in the conscious awareness of group members. From the writer's own experience, both as leader in groups and as observer of groups where leaders have used the technique of interpreting "unconscious" meanings, such interpretations are usually not facilitating and are frequently disrupting. This is, however, an issue which can be settled only through research. Certainly it is not even justified to say that "reflecting meanings and intents" is not interpretation in a sense. Nevertheless, there does seem to be a valid distinction between the two, at least in operational terms.

Perhaps the essential difference between interpretation and reflection of meanings and intents, as it is being used by the group-centered leader, is that reflection is an attempt to perceive only what exists in the conscious awareness or the internal frame of reference of the group member at the moment. On the other hand, these other writers seem to imply that interpretations help to

[1] See Chapter 2.

bring to conscious awareness what might have been for the group member quite "unconscious." This difference is probably essentially the same as the one that appears to exist between interpretation as used by some psychoanalytic therapists and the method of "adopting the client's frame of reference" used by client-centered therapists.

One final word about this function of the group-centered leader may be appropriate. The writer has in the past made a distinction between "group-oriented" and "individual-oriented" leader reflections. An illustration may make this distinction clear. Let us suppose a group has been discussing the advantages and disadvantages of two courses of action — call them Plan A and Plan B. Half of the members have been arguing for one and half for the other. The leader may reflect the individuals' statements as they are made in the discussion, using reflections such as:

> "Frank, you feel Plan A won't work and you would strongly urge us to try Plan B."
> "Bill, as I get what you are saying, Plan B is bound to fail because of the reasons you just mentioned."

On the other hand, a more group-oriented reflection may be made after several members have expressed their views, such as:

> "It seems to me that the group is definitely divided on this issue and it doesn't seem able to reach agreement."

Each of these types of reflections may have a useful function in group-centered leadership. They may, however, accomplish different results. The writer has used both types of reflections. Some group leaders seem to prefer using group-oriented reflections almost exclusively. Here is a very important problem which would be amenable to investigation through research. On the basis of the writer's limited experience, it seems doubtful that the leader can convey to group members as much attention, understanding, and acceptance through group-oriented reflections as he can through individual-oriented reflections, although it may be that once the leader has created an adequate psychological climate, group-oriented reflections may be facilitating. When used exclusively, and during the early stages of the group's development, group-oriented reflections frequently arouse considerable resistance. This may be due to the fact that frequently not all group members perceive the same group dynamics as does the leader.

Conveying Acceptance

The extent to which the leader can convey acceptance of others is a critical requirement of group-centered leadership. Much has been said about acceptance in describing the role of the client-centered therapist. The group-centered leader apparently must have some of the same attitudes as the individual therapist. He must be willing to accept the group where it is at the moment, even though this might mean that the group has no clear-cut goals, that the group-members are hostile and suspicious of their leader, or that the group is dependent and submissive. It means that the group-centered leader must convey a genuine acceptance of what the group members wish to discuss, what they decide to do and how they plan to do it.

What does acceptance mean in a more practical sense? Perhaps this concept will have more real meaning if we come down to the level of everyday problems as they occur in different group situations. In small discussion groups, for example, acceptance means the leader's willingness for the discussants to bring up whatever they would like. There can hardly be "irrelevancies" as far as the group-centered leader is concerned. It is not up to him to decide if the group is "sticking to the topic." He accepts all comments without evaluating whether they are good, pertinent, or valuable to the group. He is willing to accept decisions that have been arrived at by the group. For the school administrator, as another example, it would mean accepting hostile feelings expressed by his teachers. He would accept new ideas suggested by them. He would accept the group's decision to re-evaluate the school curriculum. For the social worker attempting to stimulate community action on problems of delinquency, it would mean a willingness to accept the initial lack of interest on the part of the citizens or their inability to arrive at a decision for community action. He would accept their feelings of inadequacy and hopelessness, as well as their impractical schemes and dreams.

But what about all the pressures on these leaders from their supervisors? How can a leader be accepting of his group if the members decide to do something which would endanger his position or which would be at variance with his system of values? These are real questions for the group leader. The concept of "limits" applies here, just as it does in individual therapy. Apparently, *the group-centered leader must have a clear notion of the limits within which he can be completely and genuinely accepting*. If, for example, an industrial supervisor cannot, without losing his job, permit his workers to come and go on the job whenever they wish, he will find it impossible to convey genuine acceptance of such behavior. If a high school principal or a college president cannot, because of lack of funds, permit his teachers to vote a pay raise for themselves, he will not be able to accept such a decision of the group. All leaders must operate within certain prescribed limits. These are the reality factors in the situation. It is true that some leaders are in situations where there are very few limits, as in the case of the group therapist. Other leaders must work in situations where there are many limits, as must the foreman in an industrial organization. The group-centered leader, then, is always accepting and permissive *within limits*, but because of his faith in the group's own capacities he sets fewer limits than the leader who basically trusts only himself. Furthermore, the group-centered leader tries to be clear in his own mind about what limits he must set in order to feel secure enough to be accepting of the group. Having much more faith in the potentialities of his group, he is much less inclined to feel pressures on himself from his own superiors and thus translate these into limits for his group. The insecure leader, the one who is not willing to rely upon the strengths of his group members, the one who must take upon himself the responsibility for the group — this leader will invariably come to rely more and more upon setting up restrictive limits, formal rules and procedures, and complex structures within his organization.

In our own Counseling Center organization we seem to have been moving in a direction of fewer limits, less structure, and more simple procedures. For example, we have almost entirely

dispensed with formal standing committees, parliamentary procedures, formal channels of communication, static roles. It would
be almost impossible, as well as foreign to the attitudes of our
staff members, to construct an organizational chart. We have
done away with closed meetings; all members are welcome to
attend — and participate in — all committee gatherings. It has
been, however, a slow process of growth for us to become less
dependent upon structure and formalistic procedures. At times
it has seemed more chaotic and disorganized, and sometimes we
have rushed to set up structure as a corrective. Yet we usually
have returned to the more functional mode of operating as quickly
as we have relearned the lesson that such procedures seldom
motivate or accelerate action and behavior. Our own experience
has been paralleled to some extent by that of the Tavistock Institute of Human Relations in England. In conversations with members of this organization we have gained the impression that they
have been experimenting with some of these same principles of
organization and administration. Flexibility is valued highly in
their organization, and staff members are given freedom to define
and develop their own roles. Elliott Jaques writes:

> In the day to day management of the Institute itself, group prin-
> ciples have been used. All decisions are made by committees by
> group decision, and individuals are then made responsible for carry-
> ing these decisions out. So far as possible, each individual participates
> in making the decisions, the action for which he will be responsible.
> (96, p. 9)

Conveying acceptance and permissiveness, then, is another
function which the group-centered leader brings to the group. It
is rarely present in groups, and in most organizations group members seldom feel that their contributions will be accepted. But
once again, we are convinced that *when the leader brings acceptance
to the group, there is a gradual taking-over of this function by the
group members.* They become more accepting of each other, they
become more tolerant of differences among themselves and they
begin to help each other to feel that their contributions, not just
those of the leader, are welcome and will be accepted. Conse-

quently, it becomes easier for the members to express their own real attitudes and feelings and to accept the same in others.

The "Linking" Function

There is another important function which the group-centered leader serves in the group, and for want of a more exact term it will be called the "linking" function. An analogy may be helpful in communicating the meaning to the reader. All of us have observed raindrops striking against the top of a window. Some of them, after hitting the window, form a little stream which carries the water to the bottom of the window. Different streams form and give the effect of parallel channels, each carrying part of the water to the bottom. If, however, I take my finger and link a new drop to an already existing channel, the water will follow this channel rather than forming one of its own. If I were able to provide a link between each new raindrop and the already existing channel, I would then have a steady stream of water streaking down the window in just one channel. Something like the first description seems to happen in most groups. It can be seen most clearly in face-to-face discussion groups. The drops may be likened to the contributions of individual members of the group. One person will say something, then a second person adds a new idea but does not always convey the relationship of his idea to the meaning of the first contribution. The thought of each member streams down the window in separate channels. Occasionally, someone may enter in and relate his thought to one of these channels, but then another member adds something which he relates to another channel. Usually it is possible in a group to see several channels streaming along in parallel rivulets of thought. If, however, the group-centered leader makes an effort to perceive the linkage between each new comment and then conveys this relationship to the group, the discussion takes on the characteristics of the second description. The discussion seems to flow down one channel, building up force as each new contribution is linked to it. This does not mean that the channel cannot be changed once it has started. Using the raindrop analogy again, it occasionally happens that several drops hitting close together may deposit enough water to change the direction of the main channel when they are linked to it. By relating the new contribution to the main stream, the leader may see the group change its stream of thought in the direction of this new influence.

The "linking" function of the group-centered leader is related closely to his function of understanding meanings and intents. This is because the meaning or the intent of a member's comment often *is* the link to the main stream of thought or to the previous comments. Its actual linkage is frequently hidden by the content of the comment. Thus, by clarifying the meaning or intent of a comment, the group-centered leader makes clear to the group how the new contribution is related to previous discussion. Perhaps an illustration from a recorded group discussion will make this clear. In the following excerpt the group is carrying on a discussion of how one of the members, a social worker, should approach a group of young married people to get them to take social action in their community: [1]

1. Bill: I would like to go on record with a very serious objection here. This was the implied assumption that somehow church socials or gatherings in communities for discussion are somewhat more valuable and better and people should do these rather than go bowling. I felt this implied assumption. Why shouldn't men rather go there than to church —

2. Don: I don't go along with that implied assumption.

3. Bill: Well, *I* certainly wouldn't. I would like to bring in a diagnosis that my wife has made from the feminine viewpoint of our society. She, perhaps not peculiarly, much prefers the company of a group of men to a group of women. And I don't think this is necessarily a sex factor. She says you can almost predict what a group of women are going to do.

4. Jane: I'll say.

5. Bill: They're forced into a mold somehow by our society. She doesn't understand what it is. But a group of women get together and one group is pretty much like another. And very often women join groups not because they want to but because of social pressures. Where men — they seem to live in a much freer and easier society where what

---

[1] Throughout the following excerpt the number in each note at the bottom of the page refers to the same numbered item in the group discussion.

they do and who they join with is a function of their own choice. In —

6. Frank: I think Mrs. Adams [Bill's wife] overestimates considerably both the interest and the variety of man's society.

7. Group: (Laughter.)

8. Leader: Bill, your point would be what? I'm not sure I understand what —

9. Bill: That much of the operation of women in these social groups is not a function of choice on their part. It's not satisfying their personal needs. It is a function of the role that society kinda forces them into.

10. Leader: You are using that as an illustration of your original objection to the effect that we should attach certain values, positive or negative, to these interests and you object very strongly to doing that — saying that one interest is of more social value than another one?

11. Bill: It seemed to me that what we were essentially saying is that the things that the men wanted to do were not as good for them — were not satisfying their needs — as well as the things that men didn't want to do. And I just kinda didn't —

12. Cathy: If women get together to clean up the alleys, after all it's the women who have to sit and look at the alleys all day. The men are out working all day. They are not as concerned about the alleys as their wives. They should be. The fact that there isn't a playground for the children, by and large the mothers would be more concerned about that than the fathers. Questions of this sort wouldn't necessarily hit home to her husband. It seems to me they would be much more interested than their husbands might, who also because of our culture would say, "Why, that's the mother's job."

13. Stu: Well, would you carry that further and say that social action interests in general are more natural to the woman?

14. Cathy: They aren't more natural. I'd say that the culture sort of —

---

8. The leader here is attempting to understand the meaning and intent behind Bill's last three comments. This is especially important here, since in number 2 Don interrupts to defend himself and in number 6 Frank humorously objects. The group responds to Frank with laughter, thus in a sense rejecting Bill. The leader does not understand the link between Bill's comments and the previous discussion.

10. Here the leader is linking Bill's illustration to a previous objection of his, yet he does this in the tentative form of a question.

15. Stu: Yeah, owing to our cultural situation, would you say in general that they are more politically active, and so forth?

16. Leader: Are we really understanding Cathy? I'm not sure that I am. You see a basic difference here, Cathy, between the interests of men and the interests of women?

17. Cathy: I see a great deal of difference when it comes to group discussion, yes. That it can be that there is more interest in a neighborhood group, particularly in the working class, that the wives and mothers would have a more neighborhood interest.

18. Leader: In terms of leader behavior, this would — you are simply saying that this would be a better diagnosis of women's needs and that we have to be careful in diagnosing women's needs versus men's.

19. Cathy: I think we have to be very careful.

20. Sam: I would like to rise to kind of a point of order and wonder are we trying to be a sociology class in this emphasis upon diagnosing needs. To me we keep wandering from what our primary job is. I just sort of pull that out —

21. Cathy: You're right.

22. Sam: I'd be quite glad to pull back in my shell, but I'm wondering if we are not beyond ourselves. We have no resources in this area. We keep bringing up personal records which really don't count for much in our total assessment.

23. Leader: Diagnosing individual needs is not pertinent to our problem, Sam?

---

16. Again the leader is trying to understand Cathy and to link the meaning of her somewhat involved illustration to the previous comments. Stu, on the other hand, in numbers 13 and 15 is apparently trying to push Cathy to a broader generalization, which she does not accept in number 14.

18. The leader here provides the linkage between the difference Cathy sees between the interests of the sexes and the role of the leader, which was the topic under discussion prior to Bill's comment in number 1.

22. Apparently Sam has not perceived any linkage between the discussion of group members' needs and leadership. He feels dissociated from the original topic.

23. Although Sam has not stated his feeling as such, the leader reflects tentatively Sam's meaning, thus even linking Sam's comments to the preceding topic of needs.

24. Sam: Well, I was about to jump in with all sorts of personal references. I work with these groups all the time and I can present some anecdotes on the other side but it occurred to me that that wouldn't be relevant.

25. Stu: It seems to me we are analyzing here, or raising the question, about the function of leadership. If one attitude toward leadership is accepted — in general the community center's point of view on leadership, the social worker's point of view — well, then, one must know — one must be able to diagnose the needs of the people in order to function as leader. If another concept of leadership wins the day here, then we can dispense with all of this diagnosis.

26. Sam: Then we should discuss the two aspects of leadership and not diagnosis.

27. Leader: Stu, you are not willing to accept that that is the best way of leading — diagnosing the group and going out and fulfilling needs for —

28. Sam: Yes. That's the point I'd rather argue.

In a group there may be as many different "channels" of thought as there are members. This often can be seen in the early stages of group development, when each member has his particular "axe to grind," when contributions are likely to be more ego-centered than group-centered, when members are responding to their own personal needs to the exclusion of what is going on outside of themselves. It is during this stage that the group-centered leader's linking function is so important. It might be said that the leader by perceiving these linkages helps the individual members to become aware of elements in the total perceptual field which

---

25. Stu, taking over the linking function, makes a successful attempt to tie together the ideas about needs and the earlier topic of leadership.

26. Sam's comment is not accepting of the group's exploration of the problem of diagnosing needs. Stu's linkage in number 25 was much more useful, as well as accepting, to the group.

27. The leader in trying to catch Stu's meaning went beyond him a little. He might better have said, "You see the problem of diagnosis in relation to one type of leadership but not necessary for another type."

previously were not perceived. It can be said that the leader helps the group members to enlarge the scope of the phenomenal field to which they respond, thus increasing the chances that their contributions will be more appropriate to the existing situation.

As with the other distinctive functions which the group-centered leader brings to the group, this linking function is gradually assumed by the group members themselves. Individuals in the group begin trying to see how each new contribution is linked to previous contributions. They begin to ask a speaker, "How does this point that you are making tie in with what others in the group have been saying?" or "Does this mean then, in terms of what Jack said, that you have a different point of view than his?" or "I gather from your comment that you don't like the way the group is going and yours is a suggestion that we try a new approach?" When the linking function becomes distributed throughout a group, invariably there is a noticeable absence of comments indicating that group members are lost, such as "Where are we?" "Haven't we digressed?" "I don't know whether this fits in or not," "Can someone get us out of our confusion?" The linking function seems to have the effect of orienting each member in terms of the group process. We might say that it provides continuity to the discussion.

An attempt has been made in the preceeding pages to isolate and define five functions which the group-centered leader brings to the group: conveying warmth and empathy; attending to others; understanding meanings and intents; conveying acceptance; and linking contributions to channels of thought. These are functions which the group-centered leader carries out more or less continuously until they are taken over by other members of the group. There are undoubtedly other facilitating functions which have not yet been observed or defined. Further experience and research is sorely needed. These five functions are those which have been found effective in creating the conditions under which some groups have been helped to move more quickly in the direction of greater utilization of their capacities. Now it will be well to examine some special problems which arise in attempting to utilize a group-centered approach in real situations.

Some Problems in Applying Group-Centered Leadership

Leaders who attempt to make use of a group-centered approach soon discover that it is not without difficulties and problems. Attention will be given to only a few of the more important problems encountered in implementing this approach and to some of the ways different leaders have tried to handle them.

Planning for the Group by the Leader

Is planning by the leader inconsistent with the group-centered approach? Can the group-centered leader make plans for his group without taking away from the members a measure of their responsibility? Our experience points to the fact that the way a group reacts to previous planning by the leader depends to a great extent upon the relationship which exists between the leader and the group. A group whose members are either hostile and resistant to the leader or still dependent upon him for direction and motivation will usually either fight against the leader's plans or accept them with submission. In either case, pre-planning by the leader has the effect of reducing the possibility of spontaneous emergence of plans from the group itself. The group-centered leader sees planning for this type of group a definite deterrent to group members' learning to plan for themselves. However, when a group-centered leader has successfully lost leadership functions to the group, when he is perceived more as another group member than as a leader, his attempts to plan for the group are no different from attempts made by any other member. The group now feels secure enough to accept his suggestions, or reject them, for what the suggestions are worth. His suggestions are then not accepted *because they are the leader's*, nor are they strongly rejected as a reaction against the authority of the leader.

We have come to understand more about the function which planning serves, both for the leader and the group. Often planning is no more than a means of control, a way of influencing the group in the direction desired by the leader. Thus, the teacher plans a lecture and to some extent thereby directs the thinking of the group; the administrator plans which member of his group should do a particular job, or he works out methods of implementing a staff policy. This type of planning seems entirely inconsistent with the group-centered philosophy of leadership. In another sense, we see planning as an attempt to bolster the insecurities of the leader. Some leaders are insecure in a free situation, finding it hard to tolerate an absence of structure. They seem to need rules, regulations, plans, procedures, organization, agendas, and other similar props. Such over-planning seems to be a characteristic of the "formalistic" leader (7). Here, it seems, is a fruitful area for future investigation. Perhaps we can differentiate leaders on the basis of differences in tolerance for a group's initial floundering, for informality and flexibility, for functional operation. Of one thing the writer has become convinced — namely, that if a leader feels he *must* provide a certain amount of structure for his own security, he should honestly inform the group about his plans. A group will distrust a leader whom they feel is subtly manipulating them to reach his goals. There is also good reason for the leader to be sensitive to resistance to his planning and to be willing to discard his plans should the group decide to reject them.

Getting Members to Participate

A problem in trying a more group-centered approach is that of getting all members to participate. Frequently a leader has been heard to say, "I have tried to get my group to participate, but they do not seem willing to do so; there has to be a leader to get them going." Also we read about different techniques recommended for encouraging participation, such as role-playing, breaking down the group into subgroups, calling on nonparticipants or asking them questions. While such techniques undoubtedly succeed on occasion, it is a question whether participation so obtained actually facilitates the group's development. First, such participation is not spontaneous; secondly, these techniques may have undesirable effects on some of the group members. The recorded comments from an interview with one member of a discussion group are pertinent here:

S: I know that I resented and resisted very much certain members of the group saying to me outside or even inside the group that I should be a great participator. I didn't feel like it. I didn't feel that I could be. And I think the whole group felt I should get in on all four feet — and I just couldn't. One day when I was sort of forced into a role-playing scene — I resented it very much — I have, as I say, resisted the fact that the group has wanted me to jump in when I was not ready.

Interviewer: Didn't really feel ready and there was a little resentment to being —

S: I didn't want to be manipulated. I think I've learned a lot. I have learned that I can get in there — I don't know how much I've given but they seemed to like certainly what I did yesterday and in the other groups — both of them — I think I've given quite a lot. But I know there were days and days when I wasn't giving a thing, or very little, to the whole group.

Int.: That is — you're saying that as a result of this experience — learning about yourself — that you *can* get into a group eventually. I'm not quite sure — is that what you're saying?

S: Well, yes. But I think you have to [few words missed] anyone. Wait until I'm ready, wait until I catch up with the group. I think there may be cases where you can manipulate the person in but I resented that sort of thing. I think you have to learn the terminology and all that, which I did not know.

This group member obviously resented attempts to get her to participate, probably because participation was so closely related to her own feelings of security. The group-centered leader relies upon the effects of the nonthreatening, accepting climate to encourage participation, rather than upon techniques. He is, moreover, as willing to accept a person's hesitancy to participate as he is to accept other kinds of behavior.

The group-centered leader, however, must have a certain amount of patience, tolerance, and security because he will be faced with situations where group members do not at once participate. There will be long pauses in group discussions. In some groups the members will absent themselves from meetings. Sometimes there will not be volunteers for particular jobs. Failure to show genuine acceptance of such behavior or an unwillingness to wait for members to participate inhibits the development of an atmosphere conducive to spontaneous and creative participation, if we can generalize from our experiences with groups. Direct attempts by the leader to take over at these crucial points seems to increase the group's dependence upon the leader. The principle on which the group-centered leader relies is that participation will be facilitated when he succeeds in removing all the outside pressures on the members to participate and depends entirely on the inner forces of the members.

Leadership Never Becoming Completely Distributed

In some groups all the leadership functions probably will never become completely distributed throughout the group. This may be due to the pressures put upon the leader from his own supervisors. For example, a school administrator may feel that he has to retain certain leadership functions, such as the hiring and firing of his teachers. To this extent he may feel that he cannot give up all responsibility to the group. What is the effect of this? Theoretically, the retention by the leader of any of the leadership functions reduces the chances of the group's actualizing itself to the fullest extent. In practice, however, it may mean that the group-centered leader can still demonstrate trust in the group within these limits. He still can be a therapeutic influence on the group, though not as therapeutic as if he were able to trust the group with the handling of all functions.

In other groups the members may never assume all the leadership functions because of the fact that they cannot completely alter their perception of their leader as one who is differentiated from them on some basis. For example, it may be most difficult for a group of adolescent children ever to perceive their adult leader as a person without some authority over them. There may be other differentials that are difficult to erase in the perceptions of group members, such as age, sex, education, size. Such differentials may be so strongly ingrained in our culture that they make it very difficult for group members to perceive their leader on an equalitarian, nonauthoritative basis. This is but a conjecture. We may find that under the proper conditions even these differences will not prevent people from establishing relationships with others that are essentially nonthreatening.

Group-Centered Leadership in Large Organizations

How successful can group-centered leadership be in large organizations? The limitations are obvious at once. In a large industry, for example, frequent face-to-face contacts are almost impossible. Space barriers to communication are inevitable. We need to think through carefully the implications of this conception of leadership where large groups of people have to be represented by others. What is to prevent the representative from failing to represent accurately the decisions, desires, and contributions of his constituents? Will not special interest and pressure groups make it impossible to operate a large corporation, a state, or even a nation using principles of group-centered leadership? We are raising more questions than can be answered. So far it has not been possible to implement extensively this type of leadership with such large groups. It is difficult to see, however, why the principles which are emerging from the application of group-centered leadership in smaller groups would not be as valid in larger groups. Perhaps we only need more ingenuity in devising new ways of implementing the philosophy. In this connection we have found it challenging to learn about recent attempts to apply some of these principles in industry. Golden and Ruttenberg (67) describe experiments with joint labor-management committees in the garment industry. Again, the Tavistock Clinic has been working effectively as consultants in industry through utilization of policy committees made up of workers, management, and the research consultants (210). All policy decisions are made by these committees, and its members have an equal voice in shaping the conduct of the research project. Though these experiments are only brave beginnings, they may point the way to more extensive application of therapeutic methods of leadership and administration to larger groups and organizations.

OUTCOMES OF GROUP-CENTERED LEADERSHIP

It is much too early to state with any degree of certainty what outcomes can be expected from the group-centered approach to leadership. We must, for the present, rely primarily upon observation and limited research findings. Nevertheless, there may be some justification in merely pointing to certain outcomes which, as a result of our experiences, we have begun to expect from group-centered leadership. It should be emphasized, however, that each of these should be considered as an observation which requires experimental verification. These outcomes may be thought of as falling into three categories: (1) the meaning of the group experience to the individual group member, (2) the internalization of the leadership functions by the group members, and (3) changes in the group functioning.

The Meaning of the Group Experience to the Individual Member

One of the expected outcomes of group-centered leadership is the effect upon the individual member of experiencing membership in a self-directing, nonthreatening, and accepting group. It appears that members of such groups react to their experience in much the same way as clients who have completed individual therapy. Apparently, group-centered leadership has positive "therapeutic" effects on the group members.

Group Members Feel They Are Understood. If a nonthreatening psychological climate exists for a group, the members of the group seem to feel that they are being understood. They feel that others are attending carefully and are making a sincere effort to understand them. This is one of the things that stands out clearly as we have attempted to find out what is being experienced by group members. Thus, after a three-day conference of Christian and Jewish college student leaders in which the group leaders attempted to create a nonthreatening climate, one of the delegates writes:

> The next morning, in our first discussion group, I was again disappointed, this time by the unaggressiveness of our group leader, and the tendency of the group to go off on tangents. But, strangely enough, each time I felt like objecting to such strange procedure I recalled my notes of the evening before and decided to string along — to try to accept and understand the feelings of others. It wasn't long before I was glad of this decision, for when it came my turn to speak, I was overjoyed by the honest effort of the others in the group to

understand me. I expounded on points of view I have held within myself for years, as it soon became evident that I would not become ridiculed. . . . Because of this, understanding which might normally take years to acquire was achieved in a matter of hours. (187, p. 49)

In contrast to the perceptions of this member who participated in this conference are the statements of members of another group in which they apparently felt a different kind of climate. In this latter group the leaders, at least during the early sessions, selected goals for the group, evaluated comments of the group members, and freely made deep-level interpretations of the statements of some of the members. During one of these early sessions the following remarks were recorded:

"The reason I didn't volunteer for jobs is because I haven't felt that I was a part of the group. This is because people haven't responded to what I say — people don't listen, don't take up my suggestions."

"People haven't listened to me. Therefore, I had consciously taken a nonparticipant role."

"Every time I make a suggestion or question the leader, he slaps me in the face. Either he calls it a projection or a defense. I work it out one day, and the next day he slaps me down again."

"We never stop to understand the first point."

"There is a need here for an understanding of each other."

The contrast is apparent between the psychological climates of these two groups, as seen from the frame of reference of the members. These statements seem to attest to the fact that group members need to feel that others listen to their contributions and try to understand. Without this feeling, they feel threatened, they tend to hold back and retreat from the group, or they make renewed efforts to get their individual point of view across until they feel certain it *has* been understood. The result is that either the group loses potential contributors or else each member responds solely in terms of his own needs with little regard for the group needs. Alpert and Smith (7) have appropriately described such behavior as "anarchic participation."

Group Members Feel They Are Accepted. A study conducted by the writer (70) gave some evidence that one of the outcomes of membership in a self-directive group is an increased feeling of acceptance by group members. Personal interviews were conducted with individuals who had gone through an experience in a relatively self-directing group. Although the leadership of the group did not in many respects conform to our conception of group-centered leadership, free discussion was encouraged, the atmosphere was relatively permissive, and responsibility resided in the group to work out its own internal problems and to select its goals. On the basis of a content analysis of the recorded interviews, statements were classified into various categories. Six of the sixteen group members made statements which fell into the following category:

> *Feel more accepted by others; feel more secure, more spontaneous, less defensive of self, less withdrawn, more confident.*

Excerpts from two of the recorded interviews may convey the flavor of such attitudes:

> Here at the laboratory I'm tackling the most difficult problems that I've always had to face in my life. . . . I'm face to face with my group adjustment. . . . I almost had to overcome some of the childhood hurdles of feelings about groups that I had as a child. I always was more or less of an isolate. . . . It seems to me right now my own feelings are becoming very much involved and that I'm beginning to react spontaneously on the basis of what's in me, rather than as an objective professional person. . . . I have something that I've never felt in my whole life. . . . People are supporting me and helping me. Everything that I have to say — maybe not everything, but many things that I have to say — they seem to be of value to somebody. In other words, for the first time I am finding myself in group life.

> As an individual, I think I have gained self-confidence from it which I have felt I lacked. I've always felt uncertainty about my ability. . . . I wouldn't have believed I would have done as much talking in our group as I did. I'm never the one to speak up first. I've been inclined to let other people do the talking.

Apparently, group members gain more acceptance of themselves, just as does the client in individual therapy. Thus, unless a worker in an industrial organization feels free to criticize his supervisor's judgment or question a policy of management, unless he feels it is safe for him to put forth an idea of his own without being ridiculed, that worker will not be an active participant in the organization, and the total group has lost a potential contributor. The group will be denied the data or the skills which this worker might have brought to bear on a problem and will have reduced the chances of arriving at that solution which would be best for the organization as a whole.

Freedom to participate and freedom of communication have been mentioned as conditions required for releasing the adjustive capacities of a group. It is here that the interrelatedness of all of these conditions is most clear. Although there may be no "external" barriers to communication, and there may be provided all kinds of opportunities for a group member to participate, there will be self-imposed barriers and inhibitions within each group member who does not feel acceptance in the group climate. Perhaps this is why stereotyped and institutionalized "techniques" for getting group members to participate and communicate so frequently fail to achieve their purpose. In and of themselves, mechanical methods seldom produce freedom of communication and creative participation in a group. There must be something else — an accepting and permissive climate — before people will make available to a group their maximum creative potential. Perhaps this is illustrated in the following verbatim excerpt from a recorded interview with a young woman, a member of a discussion group:

D: I think that follows from the same thing I said about the leadership. Am I still adjusting in that situation so that I'm afraid to throw out anything that might be a revolutionary idea or might be something startling, because I'm a little bit afraid of what's going to happen? I think I've gotten to that point of deciding that it isn't good, but what I'm going to do about it is something else again.

Interviewer: What you're really saying then, is that you feel a little bit of reluctance to reveal perhaps your whole self. It might be that there's something that you're holding back there.

D: Uh-huh. I think there's something, whether it is in a group relationship or personal relationship, I hold back something of me. And I have — and I think when I say, "What do your friends think of you," and so on, that would be one thing that would occur to me. My friends have said, "You don't give at all of yourself." Well, I think that is right — or consciously think so. I can't figure out what I don't give, but I think this has pointed out, they're probably right.

Int: One of the learnings might be, now, a little more sensitivity to that fact, that perhaps there is some truth in that.

D: I think there is.

Int: As I get your feeling, you're not real sure what it is that you're holding back —

D: That's right. I'm not.

Int: That's why it's kind of puzzling.

D: Yes, I'm not at all sure what it is.

Int: You're much more sure that perhaps this thing is true, but you're not just sure what aspect of yourself is being held in check.

D: I think that is right. It's a definite desire to please and not to get into something that might not please. I like to please. And apparently I have gotten a great deal of satisfaction in being a nice little girl and so forth and so on — I think I can work that back to childhood. That was the thing that would appeal to me — I was a nice little girl — I was a good girl and so forth and so on, and that I enjoyed.

Int: And you can even see perhaps some origins of this that you do have the feeling of wanting people to like you and like the things you do.

From these statements it would appear that this group member is beginning to understand how closely related are her feelings of being accepted by others and her participation in groups. Here is a person who has in the past been unable to give of herself freely, she has held herself "in check," withheld her "revolutionary ideas."

Group Members Feel That Responsibility for Evaluation Lies Within Themselves. Another meaning which a self-directing group experience has for individual members seems to be that they begin to shift the responsibility for evaluation from the leader (or others) to themselves. They become more willing to look at themselves honestly. The group-centered leader, because he tries to remove the threat of evaluation from group members, accelerates this process. Thus, some of the members in the group which was studied by the writer stated:

> "I think I feel less compulsion to solve problems tomorrow. . . . I think I may be impatient on occasion but that I will now be able to attribute my impatience in part to myself, not to the situation entirely."

> "I think I am looking at things more honestly, evaluating myself more honestly."

> "I'm more willing to accept my part in bringing on frustrations in a group."

These persons seem to be feeling safe enough to look at themselves, to evaluate their own roles in groups. It is difficult to conceive of situations, though there may be some, in which a person who feels that he is being evaluated against someone else's standards does not feel threatened. It appears that whenever responsibility for judging and evaluating a person lies outside of that person, some of his behavior must of necessity be directed towards meeting those standards, towards conforming to a pattern prescribed by the standards, or towards defying them. The situation is usually complicated by the fact that a person seldom is sure what standards another person has for him. Consequently, he is forced to act on the basis of what must always be an approximation or estimation of how another feels he should behave. In groups, this uncertainty about how one should behave is a serious barrier to creative participation and free communication.

All of us have seen this uncertainty operate in groups, especially in those that are in the early stages of development. Members refrain from participating because others "who know so much more" than they do will evaluate their contribution as inadequate. Their energies are wasted in attempting to conceal from the group "how little they know." This phenomenon is most easily observed in the classroom, but it can be discovered in all kinds of groups or organizations. A new employee in a business office, fearing that his supervisor will discover how little he knows, stumbles through his new job not daring to ask questions which might prevent him from making costly errors. A military pilot attempts a hazardous flight for which he is not competent, rather than face being evaluated by other pilots as less competent than they. A committee member consumes the time of the group by holding forth at great length on a subject about which he has some knowledge in order to cover up his lack of knowledge about the topic under consideration. A junior executive spends his energies figuring out what will please the president, rather than behaving in ways appropriate to the problem on hand.

External evaluation has another effect which acts as a deterrent to effective group functioning. Evaluation, either positive or negative, can be such a threat to an individual that he reacts with hostility. Using theoretical constructs, the individual seeks to defend his existing organization of self-attitudes — his self-concept — by attacking the source of the threat — usually the evaluator himself. This type of reaction to external evaluation can have several effects upon a group. The group member who has been evaluated reacts to it by behaving in the group in terms of a new goal — defense of self through attacking others. No longer is his behavior appropriate to the group problem. He has his own problem, and quite often his problem remains unknown to the others in the group. For the time, then, this member is lost to the group. His hostility, however, may even have a secondary effect, that of producing counter-hostility in other members. So actually the effects of evaluation may not be limited to merely the effect upon a single member. One rotten apple spoiling the barrel may be an appropriate analogy here. We have all been in groups where the hostility of one member set the tone for the entire group and made it impossible for the group to accomplish much of anything.

Group Members Gain Understandings of Themselves. It appears that another effect of group-centered leadership may be that group members acquire new understandings of themselves or else understandings become reinforced or clarified. This would parallel the client's experience in individual therapy. Whenever an individual experiences a situation from which the common sources of threat have been removed, he apparently begins to look more at himself and gain understandings of his attitudes and behavior. Furthermore, because group-centered leadership fosters active participation on the part of group members, interaction among members increases, thus making it likely that they will learn how they affect others and how they function as members of a democratic group. We shall again draw upon some of the statements obtained through interviews with the members of the group studied by the writer (70). There were 49 statements which fell into the following categories:

1. I am or have been too "autocratic," desirous of power, task-oriented, impatient, insensitive to feelings of others, demanding, not permissive enough.

2. I am or have been too dependent on what others think, too cautious, needing too much support and approval, afraid to disagree, too "laissez-faire."

3. I am more aware of amount and intensity of own feelings and their cause and effect; less afraid of own feelings.

4. I am or have been a dodger of responsibility in a group, withdrawn, an isolate; have been a talker but never a doer.

5. I am or have been putting up a false front to others, behaving in terms of false standards; not my real self.

6. I know things about myself that I didn't know before; what has been learned fits in with past experience.

Here we see individuals obtaining new or reinforced understandings of themselves as members, as potential group leaders, or simply as persons. Instead of rigidly defending their existing self-structure, as people do in most group situations, these members seem to be actively reorganizing their self-structure.

Internalization of the Functions of the Group-Centered Leader

In the previous discussion of the varoius dimensions of group-centered leadership it was suggested repeatedly that some of the distinctive functions that are brought to the group by the group-centered leader are gradually taken over by the members of the group. Group members become more warm and empathic in their relations with each other; they begin to attend more carefully to others; they show an increasing understanding of the meaning and intent of the contributions of others; they become more accepting of the contributions of others; and they gradually take over the function of trying to perceive the linkages between members' comments and the channel of group thought. In short, the members of a group whose leadership has been essentially group-centered seem to become more and more like the group-centered leader in their attitudes and behavior toward others. If further research substantiates this clinical observation, we can point to this as probably the most significant contribution of the group-centered leader to the group. It is significant because of its implications for improving human relations, for reducing misunderstandings between individuals by facilitating communication between them. If it is true that group-centered leadership releases tendencies to relate with others on a more accepting and understanding basis, might it not be a hopeful beginning in effecting more cooperative behavior between individuals, more effective decision-making in groups, more respect for the worth of every member of the group, more willingness to listen to other points of view? Could it mean that group-centered leadership would reduce misunderstandings and hostility between labor and management as they work together on joint committees, reduce intolerance among members of a high school class, alleviate jealousies and petty conflicts between members of a college faculty or between employees in an office — perhaps even promote shared understandings between representatives of unfriendly nations?

There is some research evidence for these changes in the attitudes and behavior of group members toward each other as they operate in the group. Sheerer's study strongly suggests that there is increased acceptance of others by clients during client-centered therapy. She sees the implication of her finding as follows:

> If we apply this to some of the problems of social psychology, it might mean that increased acceptance of minority groups, foreigners, and the like, could best be achieved by some type of group therapy which would tend to alter the individual's acceptance of and respect for himself. (189, p. 174)

One of the delegates to the Conference of Christians and Jews felt himself become more understanding and accepting of others as a result of his experience. He writes afterwards:

> Whenever I revealed my faith to a person, I had the feeling that I

was no longer to be judged as a person, a human being, but as a Jew. This week has been for me something unique. I have been able to say to myself that I am here among people who not only understand, but *want* to understand. And the corollary of this has been that I have sought to understand them. As a human being both of these directions of understanding are important — equally important. (187)

The findings of Gorlow (71),[1] provide the most clear-cut evidence of the increase in acceptance of group members toward each other. During the later stages of group therapy the group members actually became "therapists" for each other.

Changes in the Group Functioning

The outcomes of group-centered leadership may be examined from the frame of reference of changes in the group functioning. What changes take place in the actual behavior of the members as they operate in the group? How does group-centered leadership affect the group's adjustive behavior?

The Change from Ego-Centered to Group-Centered Participation. In groups in which we have tried a group-centered approach, it has been noticed that in the early stages of the group's development the contributions of members are frequently ego-centered. By this is meant that the members seem to be behaving primarily in response to their momentary internal needs and tensions, in contrast to the group needs. It appears that before individuals can become contributors to a group effort they frequently must relieve these tensions within themselves. For example, in the early stages of a group's development individuals may be trying to enhance their status in the group by displaying their competence or the extent of their knowledge. Frequently this is done without much regard for the appropriateness of their comments in relation to what has been transpiring in the group. Each person may have his own "axe to grind" or special notion to get across. Sometimes it is a strong feeling which must be expressed. In these early stages of ego-centered participation one hears such comments as:

"This may be off the subject, but I'd like to say this . . ."

[1] See Chapter 7, pages 311-312.

"I'd like to have the group consider another problem . . ."

"This doesn't answer Jim's question but it is important to me . . ."

"Would the group mind if I raised a different problem . . ."

"If I don't say this, I'm going to bust . . ."

An excerpt from a recorded session illustrates such an ego-centered contribution:

Jane: Would they object to it also if they would be in the group? I mean, the set-up apparently is that the men are going out and mixing with other men —
Bill: My feeling is —
Jane: — and the women are objecting to it —
Bill: My feeling is — my feeling is —
Jane: If the women would be —
Bill: My feeling is that in a good many cases it's truer than that. They don't want too much interaction. They are afraid — you see, the men have so much more freedom than they have. They feel that. They want to restrict his mobility to the home — to them — and restrict his relationships.

Here Bill is fairly bursting with his idea. His need to get it before the group is so strong that he interrupts the previous speaker. It is doubtful that he either heard or understood Jane's comment.

If the leader attends carefully to the meaning and intent of these early contributions and conveys understanding and acceptance, it has the effect of freeing the individuals to participate more in terms of the total group situation. Perhaps we have here an example of how individuals at first are demonstrating a kind of "tunnel vision" — that is, their perceptions are limited to their own needs and tensions. Later their perceptions widen in scope and include the needs of others in the group. Ego-centered participation thus gives way to group-centered participation.

This widening of the effective psychological field of the group member is undoubtedly only one explanation for the change in the nature of his participation. We need to understand more clearly why this change seems to take place under group-centered leadership. Another possible explanation would be that as the group member feels more and more accepted in the group he no longer has to defend his self-organization. He is now more free to devote his energies to helping the group solve its problems.

The Increase in Spontaneous Expression of Feeling and Meaning. Group-centered leadership seems to accelerate the process whereby group members begin to feel secure enough to express their true feelings and attitudes — to say what they mean. As they begin to perceive the nonthreatening nature of the group climate, they throw off their disguises and shed some of their defenses. In most groups attitudes and feelings remain bottled up and become displaced, invariably showing up in some new situation where it is difficult for others to see the connection between the feeling and the new situation. If, however, real attitudes are expressed toward their real objects, they are more easily understood and handled. Consequently, in an atmosphere which permits spontaneous expression of feeling a group will be more effective in solving its problems, because when a group of individuals must work together their effectiveness is dependent upon mutual understanding and shared meanings. We should expect that when there is greater correspondence between what members say and what they intend to say, when members are willing to make public to the group their real attitudes, creative ideas, and true feelings, then it is more possible that mutual understandings will be developed. From mutual understanding follows consensus, and out of consensus comes action that is most appropriate to the needs of the group.

The Decrease in Dependence Upon the Leader. One of the most noticeable outcomes of group-centered leadership is the decreased dependence of group members upon the leader. In discussion groups this is reflected in a greater number of member-initiated problems brought before the group, in fewer requests for the opinions and judgments of the leader, in more comments which are in disagreement with the leader. In our own Counseling Center organization it has meant that members of the staff have taken the initiative to develop new areas of service to the community, they have tried out new counseling methods of their own, they effectively carry on the functions of the Center in the absence of any one person or group of persons. Instead of energies being expended in trying to figure out what the leader might want or approve, in a truly self-directing group individuals discover they can be truly creative. The conditions exist in which each member has the opportunity for real self-actualization, self-expression, and self-development. Individuals learn to assume responsibility for their own feelings, ideas, and behavior.

The Acceptance of Group Standards. We have seen clearly the process whereby a group formulates its own standards, provided there is the proper psychological climate in which it may tackle this problem. The significance of "group standards" has been repeatedly referred to in studies of worker production in industry. The Western Electric studies (163) demonstrated how groups set their own standards, and how successfully the group members reach standards which the group sets itself. Our own experiences are consistent with these findings, and in addition have convinced us that standards that a group sets for itself will be more realistic, more attainable, and more comfortable than standards that are imposed upon the group from the outside. Furthermore, when individuals have a hand in setting their own standards they are much more likely to accept and to maintain those standards. Also, a group frequently will set for its members standards that are much higher than those that would be set by some external authority. We have all been in groups that have set goals for themselves that the administrator or supervisor would not have dreamed of requiring of the group. It may be that a group is like an individual in that the standards it sets for itself are likely to be appropriate unless the group is in some way reacting against standards that it feels are being imposed on it from the outside. We see this type of reaction operating in the common practice of workers' restriction of output in industry, often because of the imposition of rates by "expert" time-and-motion-study engineers. In industry it has been shown that when a group participates in setting its own standards there is much more acceptance of this standard, as exemplified in the study by Coch and French (41). Similarly, the study reported by Radke and Klisurich (152) of the buying and consumption habits of housewives and their families showed a greater acceptance of a change in food habits in those groups that arrived at decisions themselves than in those groups that were given lectures. These studies, as well as our experiences, have led us to expect that standards, values, and decisions arrived at by group members themselves will be accepted to a greater degree by the group members than those that are not arrived at in this way. Lewin and Grabbe have stated this problem clearly, as follows:

> The fact that . . . change has to be enforced on the individual from outside seems so obvious a necessity that it is often taken for granted. Many people assume that the creation, as part of the re-educative process, of an atmosphere of informality and freedom of choice cannot possibly mean anything else but that the re-educator must be clever enough in manipulating the subjects to have them think that they are running the show. According to such people, an approach of this kind is merely a deception and smoke screen for what to them is the more honorable, straightforward method of using force. It may be pointed out, however, that if re-education means the establishment of a new super-ego, it necessarily follows that the objective sought will not be reached so long as the new set of values is not experienced by the individual as something freely chosen. (113, p. 61)

Here is a fact of tremendous significance. If we accept its validity, it means radically changing most of our conceptions about supervision and administration. The group leader who sees his chief function as providing the conditions whereby the members arrive at decisions themselves is carrying out a role that is quite different from that of the leader who spends his energies devising the most effective ways of communicating *his* decisions to the group and who usually must keep motivating the group to carry out those decisions.

We may say, in conclusion, that these observations, which we have dared to present as expected outcomes of group-centered leadership, are based upon much too little experience and upon far from adequate research findings. Undoubtedly our perceptions have been influenced by the enthusiasm with which we have approached this area. Nevertheless, these beginnings have been impressive to us, for we cannot help feeling that along this road social science may be traveling toward a more significant meaning of democracy. This democracy will mean a more active and vital participation of the common man in all matters which concern him. It will mean an opportunity for the self-actualization of each group member and for the maximum utilization of the potential of each group.

SUGGESTED READINGS

For accounts of applications of a therapeutic approach in industrial consulting, the articles by staff members of the Tavistock Clinic are recommended. An entire issue of the *Journal of Social Issues* (95) has been devoted to their work. Covner (44) gives a good description of a consulting approach that is based upon some of the principles of client-centered therapy. The reader interested in a type of group leadership that is more interpretive than the group-centered approach will want to examine the two articles by Bion (27, 28). McGregor's article (123) and the articles under the editorship of Alpert and Smith (7) offer theoretical but stimulating conceptualizations about leadership. Some of the principles of group-centered leadership can be seen in their application to larger social groups in the report of the Peckham experiment (144), in the book by Golden and Ruttenberg (67), and in the issue of the *Journal of Social Issues* under the editorship of McGregor, Knickerbocker, Haire, and Bavelas (124). Many of the references suggested at the end of Chapter 9 will be of interest to readers who are concerned with group-centered leadership in education and teaching.

Chapter 9 · Student-Centered Teaching

There is something peculiarly compelling about the central hypothesis of the client-centered approach, and the individual who comes to rely upon this hypothesis in his therapeutic work finds almost inevitably that he is driven to experiment with it in other types of activity. If, in therapy, it is possible to rely upon the capacity of the client to deal constructively with his life situation and if the therapist's aim is best directed toward releasing that capacity, then why not apply this hypothesis and this method in teaching? If the creation of an atmosphere of acceptance, understanding, and respect is the most effective basis for facilitating the learning which is called therapy, then might it not be the basis for the learning which is called education? If the outcome of this approach to therapy is a person who is not only better informed in regard to himself, but who is better able to guide himself intelligently in new situations, might a similar outcome be hoped for in education? It is questions of this sort which plague the counselor who is also a teacher.

As a result of this kind of questioning, a number of workers who had used a client-centered approach in therapy began to experiment with adaptations of this orientation to the classroom situation. The field was uncharted, and there was much fumbling and trial and error. Many of the attempts were unsuccessful or only partially successful. Yet because the quality of learning which frequently resulted was so different from that taking place in the ordinary classroom, further experimentation seemed unquestionably demanded. A sobering aspect of the experience was the growing realization of the revolutionary character of what was being attempted. If education is most effectively conducted along lines suggested by client-centered therapy, then the achievement of this goal means turning present-day education upside down — a task of no mean magnitude.

At this juncture in our experience it was heartening to find others who, starting from somewhat different lines of thinking, were coming to similar conclusions. The first of these to come to our attention was Nathaniel Cantor (39) whose book on *The Dynamics of Learning* (made available to us in manuscript form some two years before publication) expressed a viewpoint similar in many ways to the one we were reaching. Cantor, with his background of interest in Rankian thinking and his training in sociology, was stressing such points as the following:

That "the teacher will be concerned primarily with understanding and not judging the individual."

That "the teacher will keep at the center of the teaching process the importance of the student's problems and feelings, not his own."

That "most important of all, the teacher will realize that constructive effort must come from the positive or active forces within the student." (39, pp. 83–84)

Not only were these views of Cantor very congenial to our own developing methods in education, but his reproduction of large blocks of classroom discussion in approximately verbatim form served a highly important function. Just as publication of verbatim counseling cases had focused attention both on principles and on the full meaning of the implementation of those principles, so Cantor's material indicated not only the meaning of his generalizations, but the radical alteration in educational method which was implied in his principles. While some of his conclusions were not in accord with our own experience, nevertheless the area of common agreement was encouragingly large.

Somewhat later Earl Kelley, taking his start from the significant demonstrations of perceptual behavior being developed by Adelbert Ames, brought out his provocative little book, *Education for What Is Real* (100). Although his conclusions often seemed to go far beyond the data of the perceptual studies, his thinking was very much in accord with that of Cantor and our own group.

Still later Snygg and Combs, developing the implications of a phenomenological approach to psychology, devoted two trenchant chapters to the goals of education and the task of the teacher. Their conclusions simply cast in somewhat different terminology the thinking which we had been attempting to implement.

> Education, from this point of view, is a process of increasing differentiation in the individual's phenomenal field.
>
> However, differentiation of the field is something which can be done only by the individual himself. It cannot be done for him. As a living organism searching his field for means of self-maintenance and enhancement he differentiates only those aspects which are necessary and helpful to the achievement of his purpose. Change in his field does not have to be motivated. In fact it cannot be prevented. It must continue as long as he is unsatisfied, that is, as long as he lives. As a living organism with a tremendous drive toward growth and self-enhancement he requires only practicable and socially acceptable opportunities for growth and development. (200, p. 238)

Thus progress in discovering the implications of client-centered therapy for education, and in implementing those implications, was forced primarily by our own compelling experiences as we modified our classroom procedures, but it was enriched and furthered by the contributions which have just been mentioned. Indeed, the thinking of these authors has become so inextricably mingled with that of our own staff that it would be impossible to say what was the specific origin of many of the ideas and concepts developed in this chapter.

This is not to indicate that our indebtedness is limited to these recent expositions of radically new points of view in education. In one sense our experience is a rediscovery of effective principles which have been stated by Dewey, Kilpatrick, and many others, and a rediscovery of effective practices which have certainly been discovered over and over again by competent teachers. Aichhorn (1), for example, came upon some of these same practices through the same channel, psychotherapy. Yet the fact that others have come to somewhat similar conclusions, not only in recent years

but in the more distant past, takes away nothing from the vividness of our own experience of discovery as we have tried to implement our therapeutic viewpoint in the field of education. It is
from this latter first-hand acquaintance that the material of this
chapter comes.

THE GOAL OF EDUCATION

It may avoid needless misunderstanding if it is clearly stated at
the outset that education which embodies the principles of client-
centered therapy has relevance for only one type of educational
goal. It is not education which would be relevant in an authoritarian culture, nor would it implement an authoritarian philosophy.
If the aim of education is to produce well-informed technicians
who will be completely amenable to carrying out all orders of
constituted authority without questioning, then the method we
are to describe is highly inappropriate. In general it is relevant
only to the type of goal which is loosely described as democratic.

Let us endeavor to be more specific as to the educational goal
for which a student-centered type of teaching appears to be relevant. The basic element has been stated by Hutchins.

> The foundation of democracy is universal suffrage. Universal
> suffrage makes every man a ruler. If every man is a ruler, every
> man needs the education that rulers ought to have. . . . The main
> purpose of a democratic educational system is the education of rulers.
> (92)

This would seem to mean that the goal of democratic education is
to assist students to become individuals

> who are able to take self-initiated action and to be responsi-
> ble for those actions;
>
> who are capable of intelligent choice and self-direction;
>
> who are critical learners, able to evaluate the contributions
> made by others;
>
> who have acquired knowledge relevant to the solution of
> problems;
>
> who, even more importantly, are able to adapt flexibly and
> intelligently to new problem situations;

388   THE APPLICATION OF CLIENT-CENTERED THERAPY

who have internalized an adaptive mode of approach to problems, utilizing all pertinent experience freely and crea-
tively;
who are able to cooperate effectively with others in these
various activities;
who work, not for the approval of others, but in terms of
their own socialized purposes.

Admittedly there are a number of educators who do not profess
these goals, and in some cultures a majority of educators would be
opposed. Even in our own culture these are the functional goals
of very few educators. The method of operation of our grammar
schools, colleges, universities, and professional schools is ample
evidence that the usual goal is very different — more in the direction of producing a student who can reproduce certain informa-
tional material, who has skills in performing certain prescribed
intellectual operations, and who can reproduce the thinking of his
teacher. The approach to education which we are about to describe is not aimed toward these latter goals, but is an attempt to
find a method which will achieve the goal described here as democratic.

Whether this goal is appropriate to our current culture is a
question which each reader must decide for himself. Since our
culture to a very large degree is organized on an authoritarian and
hierarchical basis and only partially upon a democratic basis, it
may seem to some that education should reflect this ambivalence.
Each must reach his own conclusion on this point.

SOME TENTATIVE PRINCIPLES AND HYPOTHESES

As we have fumbled about in our attempts to develop a student-
centered teaching which would build on the concepts of client-
centered therapy, certain basic hypotheses have been crystallized
which are very parallel indeed to the hypotheses of therapy.
Some of these are stated below, in what may seem to be a rather
technical form. Stated thus as hypotheses, there is always the
risk that they will be understood as flat statements of fact. It

should therefore be emphasized that they are tentative in character, and still largely unproved by research in the educational field.

We cannot teach another person directly; we can only facilitate his learning.

This is an hypothesis with which any thoughtful teacher will agree. It is indeed only a formal restatement of the old adage that "You can lead a horse to water but you can't make him drink." Operationally, however, most teachers utterly ignore this basic hypothesis. Watch a faculty group concerned with the formation of a curriculum. How much shall we cover in this course? How can we avoid overlap between these courses? Isn't that a topic best taught in the third year? What percentage of our first-year course shall be given to this topic? These are samples of questions discussed — and they are all of them based on the hypothesis, which every faculty member knows is false, that what is taught is what is learned.

Here, more than at any other point, is evidenced the revolutionary nature of a student-centered approach to education. If instead of focusing all our interest on the teacher — What shall I teach? How can I prove that I have taught it? How can I "cover" all that I should teach? — we focused our interest on the student, the questions and the issues would all be different. Suppose we asked, what are his purposes in the course, what does he wish to learn, how can we facilitate his learning and his growth? A very different type of education would ensue. An educational program — whether at the elementary, college, or graduate level — which had the facilitation of learning as its clear and definite and primary operational purpose would be a program vastly different from the ones with which we are most familiar.

A person learns significantly only those things which he perceives as being involved in the maintenance of, or enhancement of, the structure of self.

Here is an hypothesis which is basic to personality theory as we have come to understand it. Many would differ with it, and point out the degree of learning that takes place in subjects which surely have no relevance to the self. Perhaps the meaning of the hypothesis can be illustrated by referring to two types of student in, let us say, a course in mathematics or statistics. The first student perceives this mathematical material as being directly relevant to his professional purpose, and thus directly involved in his long-range enhancement of self. The second student is taking the course because it is required. For the maintenance and enhancement of self he regards it as necessary that he stay in the university. Therefore it is necessary that he pass the course. Can there be any question as to the differences in learning which take place? The first student acquires a functional learning of the material. The second learns how to "get by" in the course. Or suppose that the information which is being given is in regard to the topography of a certain region. How different will be the learnings of a group listening because this is a required course in geography, and a platoon of infantry who are going into those hills and valleys to seek out the enemy! The maintenance of self is very little involved in the first group, and very deeply in the second.

> *Experience which, if assimilated, would involve a change in the organization of self tends to be resisted through denial or distortion of symbolization.*

> *The structure and organization of self appears to become more rigid under threat; to relax its boundaries when completely free from threat. Experience which is perceived as inconsistent with the self can only be assimilated if the current organization of self is relaxed and expanded to include it.*

These hypotheses have to do with the fact that learning, particularly if it is significant, is often a threatening thing. There are times when the new material of education is immediately perceived as making for the enhancement of self, but in a great many other instances the new material threatens the self or, more exactly, some value with which the self has become identified. This is very obviously true in the social sciences. To learn the objective facts about prejudice may threaten prejudices which are valued. To learn about the distribution of intelligence in the population may disturb beliefs with which the individual is identified. To perceive certain facts relating to our economic system may threaten middle-class values with which the student has identified. But the threatening character of new learning holds true of the physical and biological sciences and the humanities as well. To learn a new mathematical method may imply inferiority in the old method with which the learner is identified. To learn an appreciation of classical music or literature is likely to imply a negative judgment on appreciations already developed at a lower level. We should doubtless be considerably surprised if we knew the proportions of individuals in any student group at any given time whose basic set was a skeptical, resistant, "Oh yeah?" attitude. The reader can to some degree measure this in himself by thinking back over the last five lectures or classes or sermons he has attended. To how much of the material did he find himself inwardly resistant?

The educational situation which most effectively promotes significant learning is one in which (1) threat to the self of the learner is reduced to a minimum, and (2) differentiated perception of the field of experience is facilitated.

The two parts of this hypothesis are almost synonymous, since differentiated perception is most likely when the self is not under threat. If we take this hypothesis as a description of what education should provide, it will be seen that such education would be far different from present-day programs.

It may be objected that learning goes on in spite of, or even because of, threat. Witness the platoon which is likely to be fired upon as it goes into enemy territory, and *because* of this threat learns rapidly and effectively about the terrain. It is true that when reality provides the threat, the learning of behaviors which will maintain the self goes on apace. If the desired training has no other goal than to maintain the self as it is, then threat to self may not impede the progress of learning. But in education this is almost never true. What is desired is growth, and this involves change in the self. Whenever such a broader goal is envisaged, then threat to the self appears to be a barrier to significant learning.

The Application of these Principles in the Classroom

The abstract hypotheses just cited are obviously the product of experience, not the forerunner. We shall endeavor to present some of the experiences out of which they grew, and the present formulation of a teaching approach which implements them.

The Creation of an Acceptant Climate

As in counseling, our first experimental approaches to the teaching situation relied rather heavily upon teacher technique. Gradually the realization grew that if the teacher's attitudes were such as to create an appropriate classroom climate, the specific techniques were secondary. This relationship between basic attitude and specific method is well stated by Eiserer.

> If teachers accept students as they are, allow them to express their feelings and attitudes freely without condemnation or judgment, plan learning activities *with* them rather than *for* them, create a classroom atmosphere relatively free from emotional strains and tensions, consequences follow which are different from when these conditions do not exist. The consequences, on present evidence, seem to be in the direction of democratic objectives. It is apparent that the above conditions can be achieved in more than one way — that the climate for self-directed learning by students is not the result of only one kind of practice. (53, p. 36)

As to the effect of this climate upon the student, Shedlin, who has achieved effective results in this type of teaching, has this to say:

> A classroom climate of permissiveness and understanding provides a situation free of threat, in which the student can work without defensiveness. The decks are kept clear for him to consider the material being discussed from his own internal frame of reference. His desire for acceptance is realized, and because of this he feels the demand upon himself to be responsible for his own interpretations and insights. He feels the full strength of another person's belief in his integrity. An interesting and important outgrowth of this self-acceptance is the observable improvement in his inter-personal relations with others. He will tend to show greater understanding and ac-

ceptance of them, and develop freer, more real relationships with them. This has great importance from the standpoint of the communication and extension of the basic classroom mood. (186)

Although the type of climate described is essential throughout the conduct of the course, the teacher who is eager to experiment with this approach in education will wish to know how to develop such an educational climate at the beginning of the course. The answer here seems to be twofold. First, a permissive and understanding climate, which respects the selfhood and purposive individuality of each student, can be developed only in so far as the instructor holds a philosophy which is consistent with these elements. The point of view developed in the second chapter of this book seems to hold for teaching just as much as it does for counseling. In the second place, the teacher will want to implement this point of view from the very first in his work with the class. Since this experience will run almost directly counter to all the previous educational experience of the student, careful thought should be given to the techniques used.

It is desirable that the seating arrangement be a circle, or some physical arrangement which gives the instructor the same type of place as any member of the class. It is important that the purposes of the students should be foremost. The sessions may be started with a description by students of the problems they are facing, or with a discussion of problem areas. The writer has sometimes started a course with as simple a statement as this: "This is a course labeled Dynamics of Personality (or whatever course is being taught). I suspect each of us had some sort of purpose in enrolling, even if that purpose was only to gain another credit. If we could begin telling what our purposes were, perhaps we can, together, build the course in such a way as to meet them." As personal purposes are stated (often hesitantly and haltingly), they are simply accepted, or the attitudes connected with them are clarified. Gradually issues arise out of these purposes, and the class is embarked upon its own curriculum construction.

However, this is not to say that things will run smoothly. In students who have, for anything from one to twenty years, experienced a class as a passive experience, such an opening of a course is at first puzzling, then downright frustrating. Negative feelings, often very strong ones, are aroused. At first they are not expressed because one does not "talk back to" or correct the teacher; but as tension mounts, some bold soul bursts out, "I think we're wasting our time! I think we ought to have an outline, and follow it, and that you ought to teach us. We came here to learn from you, not to discuss among ourselves!" When negative attitudes such as these are understood and accepted, students begin to recognize the climate that exists. Some may not like the procedure, may heartily disapprove, but all recognize that this is a very different situation from that existing in the ordinary classroom.

In this type of climate, changes take place in the student's thinking. When students are given the opportunity at the end of the course to express the meaning which the course has had for them, the emphasis is frequently upon the effects of the general atmosphere in the class. Witness this statement of a student who had just completed the first student-centered course of his experience — a course in adjustment counseling.

> I believe the effect upon me was therapeutic, and this may be why the struggle for expression of my fresh attitudes becomes so difficult to objectify. I say therapeutic even though I was not conscious of any deep need for help. I did not feel disturbed at all at the beginning of the quarter; yet I like to call the experience therapeutic. I say therapeutic and I want the word to convey a slightly different meaning than it usually does; that is to say, we can benefit from the therapeutic process when we are aware of being disturbed, unhappy, and confused, but we can profit by the very same process in our own everyday lives when we have experiences which pull us out of our "status quo," our whirlpool of mediocrity and monotony, of passivity and ambivalence. Probably a simpler way of putting it is to say that I experienced growth of some kind. The two words are intimately related. Yet I feel that even to connote this "nonpathologic" meaning, the word therapy is more concrete and descriptive of what happens when one feels an eventful, inspiring change within himself.
> I can remember the first meetings — tension . . . defensiveness . . . huge slices of dense silence . . . impulsive bursts of hostility . . . quick flashes of insight from here and there . . . confusion and rationaliza-

tions . . . subtle projections and stinging interpretations. It was so hard for us to take over. We were so dependent upon the customary leadership. We rebelled at taking the responsibility for our own learning. We wanted to "get something" *from* you. We wanted to "get something" *from* the course. Thus our needs would be met. Thus we would be one step nearer to our educational goal. Many of us had a hard time getting rid of this dependence. Some never did. As for me, I waddled along for the first three or four weeks rather confused and sometimes indifferent. Later I began reading and thinking about this and that in therapy. I read what I wanted. I found myself digging for understanding. I felt no pressure from you or the class. I read for myself. I learned for myself. I was satisfied with myself but never became smug about it. I came to class to see what I could glean from the free exchange of ideas; I verbalized my own when I felt I could and listened to others struggle with the issues in therapy. I felt I was really "in it." The hour grew shorter each week. (It's too bad I had a 9:30 class. I found myself wrestling with the ideas discussed in our class and consequently missing many essential notes in the 9:30 class. Classes should not run together like that. I believe a lot of effective learning is lost by not having time immediately after class to think over the material discussed.)

I felt completely free in this course. I could come or not. I could come in late and leave early. I could talk or be silent. I got to know a number of the students rather well. I was treated like a mature adult. I felt no pressure from you. I didn't have to please you; I didn't have to believe you. It was all up to me. I went at my own pace and surprised myself. I *never* did as much reading for any single course as I did for your course, and besides that I believe it was the most meaningful and effective reading I have done. I also believe that this emerging confidence in myself carried over into other studies. My wife has noticed my new attitude toward study and my lively interest in my work. We are both happy about it.

Note that it is the freedom from pressure, the acceptance of his silence or talking, the fact that it is all "up to me," which seems to have had the greatest effect upon this student.

The work of Anderson (8) has shown that classroom climate or atmosphere can be objectively measured at the elementary school level. Withall (224, 225) has completed a research which had as its purpose the measurement of classroom climate in terms of its "teacher-centeredness" or "student-centeredness." While his scale leaves much to be desired, since the steps on it were subjectively rather than objectively determined, he has at least shown that qualities such as we are discussing can be measured with the tools of science and subjected to rigorous investigation. Both he and Anderson have also shown that classroom climate is largely a product of the teacher's behavior. The atmosphere which prevails will depend primarily upon what the teacher does and how he does it. When such studies as these have been carried further, it appears very likely that the psychological climate of the educational experience will be shown to have a prominent influence upon the amount and type of learning which takes place.

Frequently the teacher who is considering some experimentation along these lines believes that he cannot undertake it, "because we must use an assigned test" or because "my section must pass the same examination as sections taught in a conventional way," or "I am held responsible for seeing that my class covers such and such readings each week." Consideration of these points will perhaps serve to illustrate the primary importance of teacher attitudes. If for example this class must meet the same examination as other sections, the teacher's attitude, as expressed to the class, would take this into account: "I would like this course to be, in so far as possible, *your* course, to meet the purposes you would like to have it meet. There is one limitation which is imposed upon me as well as upon you, and that is the examination which every section of this course must take. With that limitation in mind, what purposes would you like this course to serve?"

We may summarize by saying that every group has some limitations, if only the fact that they meet for a limited, rather than an unlimited number of hours each week. It is not the fact that there are limitations, but the attitude, the permissiveness, the freedom which exists within those limitations, which is important. To be sure, if the limitations are extreme, and result from the wish of the instructor rather than from outside forces, then a student-centered climate may be stifled, but within a very broad range of psychological structuring, a permissive climate may be built. Thus Cantor seems to be more comfortable in demanding that his classes read a prescribed assignment each week. While this may not aid in creating a suitable climate, it is not a barrier to it, as his verbatim excerpts indicate. The essential principle might perhaps be the following: Within the limitations which are imposed by circumstance and authority, or are imposed by the instructor as necessary for his own psychological comfort, an atmosphere of permissiveness, of acceptance, of reliance upon student responsibility, is created.

The Development of Individual and Group Purposes

It has already been mentioned that a student-centered course begins around the purposes of the students. Throughout the course this should also be true, though the specific methods used will certainly vary.

Perhaps the most extreme method is one which has not infrequently been used by the writer. Each class session is opened with some variant of "What do we wish to discuss or do today?" Naturally the class then takes its start from some individual question or contribution. This might seem like a most unsatisfactory and haphazard approach, since individual need, or even individual maladjustment may dictate the initial contribution. Yet it is fascinating to watch the process as it occurs. If the issue is one which the group in general has not found of interest, discussion quickly lags, or veers, by most interesting steps, into areas which are of general concern. A listener — and this includes members of the class and the instructor — would feel that considerable time is being wasted. Yet the other side of the picture is that under this procedure the class quickly comes to grips with the deepest issues in the field under consideration. The writer has had the experience of teaching a sequence of courses in somewhat conventional style and also in a student-centered fashion. Issues which he had felt were too advanced for a first course, and must be left until late in the second term for informed consideration, may be reached and intelligently and deeply considered within a few weeks of the beginning of the first term by a group handled in permissive fashion. Hence while there is often an appearance of some confusion and waste of time, the actual learning process appears to proceed at an accelerated rate when the course is built by the students about their own changing purposes.

One way in which the teaching function appears to differ from the counseling function, as we now see it, is that the teacher may be useful to the group's exploration of purposes by indicating some of the possible resources which members may use. In a course in adjustment counseling, for example, students were told of a variety of ways in which they might implement their purposes — through class discussion, through lectures if they desired, through reading of published material and unpublished cases, through observing play therapy sessions, through visiting counselors on the job, through listening to recorded counseling interviews, and so on. They would probably have been unaware of a number of these resources if the instructor had not mentioned them.

But suppose they choose to have only lectures? This will test rather deeply the instructor's philosophy. If the group asks him to do something which is basically counter to his own ethical principles — such as requesting him to arrange for them to listen to a counseling interview without the client's permission — then in justice to himself as a person he will wish to refuse. But if the group differs with him as to what is effective in learning, and wishes him to give lectures, he may find it most consistent with his deeper views to acquiesce. A lecture which is given at the request of the class is quite a different experience for all concerned than one which is imposed upon the group. The instructor would still have the responsibility of checking from time to time as to whether he is meeting the current purposes of the group, since it is the immediate perception of purpose, not the perception as it existed three weeks ago, which is the basis of such a course.

We may say the aim of the instructor is continually to assist in eliciting the contradictory and vaguely formulated individual purposes which gradually combine into a group purpose or purposes. He will participate in furthering these purposes by pointing out resources of which the students may be unaware, and will either clearly accept or clearly reject the roles assigned to him by the group in furtherance of their own purposes.

The Changing Role of the Leader

As we have tried to find the most effective means of releasing the capacities of students in the educational situation, we have experimented with this procedure and that. If the leader deals with the group by responding solely to the emotionalized attitudes and feelings expressed, voicing a clarification or an understanding of these without any structuring comments, the group experience tends toward becoming pure group therapy. The leader's responses have tended to focus attention upon these emotional aspects. If the leader structures the initial session around the purposes of the course, that tends to be the framework within which the group experience takes place, and most of the feelings expressed have to do with the subject of the course. We have discovered that a very minute amount of structuring has a decided effect upon the nature of the group experience. Though the part played by the leader appears quantitatively small, if judged, for example, from a typescript of the class period, his behavior is highly important. The group may have made decided progress in feeling itself responsible for the course, but if the leader gives final answers to several questions directed toward him he is likely to find that he is again in the conventional role of the expert, and that the group is again dependent upon him.

It has also come to be recognized that the leader role which is most necessary and most effective in developing a permissive classroom climate is not necessarily the role which the leader should play throughout the course. Shedlin, from his experience, gives a good account of this changing role.

> At the formation and during the early stages of the group the activity of the leader should be largely one of acceptance of his students and understanding of their output. He should be nonjudgmental in his desire not to intrude upon the value systems of his students. This may be termed mood-setting action. It removes threat and consequent defensiveness. He functions as an emotional and ideational sounding board. His attitude is one of respect for and reliance upon the group members to plan activities and derive satisfaction and growth according to the needs and intents of each individual member. As the group develops and the atmosphere is a known, consistent quantity

to the students, the actions of the leader should subtly change to match the altered relationship. He is then in a position to participate more freely on a "this is how I feel about it" basis without preventing continuing analysis and exploration by the members of the group. If he has been deeply sensitive to the changes in "groupness," he should be able to do this successfully, with the attitude that the students are perceptive enough of the classroom atmosphere to freely accept or reject the leader's comments without feeling their own values under attack. It should be emphasized that throughout the entire group life, while there may be subtle changes in methods or action, the attitude remains consistently one of democratic unity.

Speaking of a particular course in which he was the instructor Shedlin continues in the description of his approach.

The instructor attempted to conduct all sessions of the course in a consistently permissive, student-centered manner, allowing the initiation and direction of the discussion to be determined by the values and interests of the group. The role of the instructor may best be described didactically in two separate areas, although practically it is impossible to compartmentalize. The first is in terms of his activity as an individual in the group, and the second, his operative position as the leader of the group. The relationship which seemed to build as the course progressed indicated almost complete acceptance of the instructor by the group — at least to the point that the students discarded all former concepts of the authoritarian rule vested in a leader and found no hesitancy in interrupting or disagreeing with the statements of the leader. The activity of the leader developed in the direction of sensitive recognition of the attitudes and ideas expressed by the members of the group. This involved an understanding of the needs of the members of the group, and a positive judgment to avoid participation when the interaction between the group members was high. It also seemed important that some distinction be made between highly emotionally tinged statements and those of low attitudinal tone. The recognition and verbalized understanding of the former by the leader seemed to promote a deeper exploration of the problem and more insightful gains for the group members, while acceptance and clarification of the latter type of statement seemed more natural and acceptable to the speaker and other members of the group. (186, pp. 8–10)

Outstanding in the experiences which have been successful in this type of classroom leadership is the concept of flexibility. If the leader is able to let himself be utilized by the group in a variety of ways as their needs change, he will be more successful in facilitating learning with a minimum of resistance. But the question as to whether he can behave flexibly, in a way which is determined by the desires of the group, is a very difficult one for most teachers. To conduct a "controlled discussion" or to give lectures, or to start each session with some key questions, or to permit completely free and fluid discussion may all be demanded of the instructor at one time or another by the group. When the leader can feel comfortable in doing any one of these things because it is the desire of the group, he has achieved a high level of genuine permissiveness. To know when he has reached the limit of his own internal comfort, and to feel easy in refusing to function in ways that are not comfortable for him, is another aspect of the genuineness of his attitudes. If he behaves in some way that is not natural for him, simply because he feels that he should do so, this is quickly sensed by the group and damages the group atmosphere.

We may state briefly our present concept of the role of the leader in an educational situation when the aim is to center the process in the developing aims of the students.

Initially the leader has much to do with setting the mood or climate of the group experience by his own basic philosophy of trust in the group, which is communicated in many subtle ways.

The leader helps to elicit and clarify the purposes of the members of the class, accepting all aims.

He relies upon the student desire to implement these purposes as the motivational force behind learning.

He endeavors to organize and make easily available all resources which the students may wish to use for their own learning.

He regards himself as a flexible resource to be utilized by the group in the ways which seem most meaningful to them, in so far as he can be comfortable operating in these ways.

In responding to expressions from the group, he accepts both the intellectual content and the emotionalized attitudes, endeavoring to give each aspect the approximate degree of emphasis which it has for the individual and the group.

As the acceptant classroom climate becomes established, the leader is able to change his role and become a participant, a member of the group, expressing his views as those of one individual only.

He remains alert to expressions indicative of deep feeling and when these are voiced, he endeavors to understand these from the speaker's point of view, and to communicate this type of understanding.

Likewise when group interaction becomes charged with emotion, he tends to maintain a neutral and understanding role, in order to give acceptance to the varied feelings which exist.

He recognizes that the extent to which he can behave in these differing fashions is limited by the genuineness of his own attitudes. To pretei 1 an acceptant understanding of a viewpoint when he does not feel this acceptance, will not further, and will probably hinder, the dynamic progress of the class.

The Process of Learning in a Student-Centered Class

The way in which students learn in such an experience is probably best indicated by giving verbatim excerpts from class experience. These excerpts will also serve to illustrate some of the points which have been made regarding the leader's role. The first selections are taken from a course in adjustment counseling, the type of course in which we have had the most experience in implementing some of these educational principles. The quoted portions are from a session including nineteen members, a session taken from the middle portion of the course. Each verbal contribution is numbered for easy reference to the notes given here at the bottom of the page. The recording is stenographic. Mr. B starts the hour with a question.

1. Mr. B (addressing the instructor directly): How do you feel about the division of responsibility between counselor and client in client-centered counseling?

2. Instructor: There seem to be some differences of opinion, but in my own thinking I tend to separate responsibility into two different areas. First, the area revolving about the client's problem, and in that area I see the responsibility resting pretty squarely upon him. The second area is that of the relationship which builds up in counseling. In that case my conception of the responsibility function is a fifty-fifty approach, the counselor's responsibility being that of providing a sensitive, permissive, understanding atmosphere, and the client's responsibility being to use that climate as a ground for his problem solving activity. I wonder if that in any way gets at what you mean, Mr. B?

3. Mr. B: Well, it seems to me that the counselor has even greater responsibility. He has information that the client doesn't have. Isn't it only fair that he give that information to the client? In some respects the counseling situation seems to be a teacher-pupil relationship and if that is so then the client is really being cheated.

4. Inst: You object to the fact that the counselor doesn't take more responsibility for guiding the client.

---

2. Had this occurred early in the course the leader might have preferred to reflect B's puzzlement or concern about this topic. At this point, however, the leader tries to answer B's question directly, stating his opinion as a personal opinion.

3. Evidently it would have made little difference whether the leader reflected B's attitude or gave his own opinion, since B clearly wants to express his own view in a somewhat challenging way. The fact that he is willing to object to and contradict the instructor's opinion is one measure of the climate which exists.

4. Here the leader must quickly and intuitively make a decision as to the course he is to follow. As a participant, he could continue with the opinion he has stated, trying to relate it to B's statement. But where a contribution is clearly imbued with considerable personal

5. Mr. B: Yes, it seems that way to me. As a matter of fact, all the examples of directive counseling given in Rogers' book seem extreme — they're not instances of good directive counseling. There are very few traditional counselors who give a lot of advice and reassurance, or take over the life of the client.

6. Inst: Your feeling then is that Rogers has been extremely unfair in the selection of the examples.

7. Miss C: I would agree with Mr. B in some respects. I was reading Alexander and French (*Psychoanalytic Therapy*) the other night — They're psychoanalysts, supposedly "middle of the road" in the directive-nondirective continuum, yet in many instances they were certainly nondirective in their approach.

8. Inst: It's pretty confusing sometimes when we're forced to label things, isn't it?

9. Miss C: It certainly is. You hardly know where you should stand in regard to the different techniques and points of view in psychotherapy.

10. Mr. B: That's right. In talking to analysts you get a different impression than when you read what they write. When they speak about their methods you get the impression that they're using nondirective methods pretty heavily.

11. Mr. R: I've watched analysts work, too; they seem quite permissive and accepting, very much client-centered at the beginning, but later they interpret quite sharply and summarize quite a bit.

12. Mr. K: They can't be nondirective if they draw conclusions for their clients. That seems to vitiate the philosophical basis for the whole

---

meaning, it is far more important that Mr. B experience understanding and acceptance of his objecting and challenging attitude. The instructor tries to convey this in this response, and in number 6. These responses tend to reinforce the permissiveness of the classroom climate, since it is obviously safe to differ.

7. Encouraged by this acceptance, Miss C explores her milder objection, and something of her puzzlement.

8. This response is attitudinally accepting. In terms of content it seems somewhat overgeneralized. A more specific response might have been preferable. "You thought they were supposed to be 'middle-of-the-road' and yet you feel that actually they are more nondirective."

9. This perplexity is an attitude to which the instructor might well have responded, but perhaps he was not given the opportunity.

point of view, because in effect it is saying, "Mr. Client, you really don't have the capacity to proceed on your own, so I'll give you some clues," or something to that effect.

13. Mr. R: Well, that's true, but I didn't mean that they drew conclusions, they just summarized what the client had said, picking out the high spots and more or less emphasized them.

14. Mr. B: It seems like we could use both nondirective and directive therapy ·successively on the same client if we did it carefully enough, and get better results than if we used one or the other. That way I'd feel better because I wouldn't be tied down to one set of criteria; I'd be more comfortable in the situation that way. Then I'd never get the feeling that I'd be pinned against the wall and have no "counseling ammunition" left.

15. Inst: If you could use the best methods of both viewpoints you'd feel a lot safer all around, is that what you mean?

---

10 through 13. Here is the type of interchange of which there is a great deal in any student-centered class. To the reader it may not seem too outstanding, unless he notes these characteristics. Differences of opinion exist, but they do not tend to be pure argument for argument's sake (this in fact rarely seems to occur in a group once an acceptant atmosphere is established). These differences are expressed as each individual is trying to formulate his own evaluation of the subject under consideration. There is no appeal to the authority of the instructor or any other authority, but each is trying to define more sharply his own current judgment. These comments would apply not only to this interchange but to most of the quoted material.

14. Mr. B continues the discussion but turns it in the direction of his own very personal feelings. This is a good example of the way in which the type of thinking in a student-centered class tends to differ from that in the more conventional course. In a situation in which there was more of an element of threat, Mr. B would in all likelihood have stood for the same point of view — the same abstractions. But it is quite unlikely that he would have seen the basis of these ideas as residing in his own need for security. Such personal feelings tend not to be seen or to be expressed in the ordinary class.

15. The leader wisely endeavors to understand the attitude Mr. B has expressed.

16. Mr. B: That's right. I guess a lot of my intellectualization is based on attitudes of my own that I really don't want to recognize. (186, pp. 11–14)

At this point the subject of discussion changes, and the group explores other issues. Since it is not feasible to give the content of the whole hour, we shall select another portion of the interchange which occurred somewhat later. Discussion had ceased on one topic, and a pause of one full minute ensued. Then Miss E spoke up.

32. Miss E: If understanding the client is the important thing then what does a counselor do with a really dependent client who wants to lean on him — not for understanding, but because he can't seem to function efficiently by himself. He's indecisive, fearful, and needs support. In fact he oftentimes comes to the counseling situation *just for* support. We get a lot of them in our agency and I think we have to give them more than acceptance and a good atmosphere. They just seem completely bogged down by their environmental situations sometimes.

33. Mr. J: Miss E, it seems that in all our discussions you seem to feel pressed to manipulate the counseling situation. You really resist the point of view that so many of us have that the client really has the capacity to work out his own problems, and that he is entitled to respect for that ability.

---

16. Evidently real learning, comparable to that which goes on in therapy, has occurred here. While Mr. B does not seem to have verbalized fully the insight he has achieved, it appears clear that the experience has been a meaningful one for him.

32. Before commenting on Miss E's contribution, it may be mentioned in passing that a silence of sixty seconds or more is somewhat difficult for the leader or the group to endure at first. The conventional instructor is so used to seeing to it that every moment of the hour is filled with some type of verbalization, that it is difficult for him to recognize that constructive thought may be going on in the group during a silence. Here Miss E has evidently been using the time to formulate an issue which has real significance for her, and which grows out of personal experience.

33. The expression of real feeling which is encouraged by a permissive situation, leads not infrequently to expression of feeling toward other members of the group. This has constructive potentialities, provided the leader recognizes that his role of acceptance of all attitudes becomes of even greater importance at these points, and that the voicing of such acceptance is rather necessary.

34. *Miss E: No, I don't!* It's just that I feel like I'm not helping a client unless I can do something to make it easier for him. I'm terribly in sympathy with people who are in trouble.

35. *Inst:* It's awfully difficult for you not to become emotionally involved with people who are in distress.

36. *Miss E:* That's quite true. And in view of the fact that I've had a lot of personal difficulty I can readily understand why I'm that way.

37. *Miss T:* It seems to me that your situation is quite similar to one that was brought up before, with the exception that you recognize an attitude that you're bringing to the counseling situation and yet you are inflicting that attitude upon the client. That would tend to prevent you from really understanding him from his own point of view. It would be a sort of rejecting thing to do.

38. *Miss W:* I think you may be a bit hard on Miss E because she may not be fully aware of the implications of her sympathy for her clients. Perhaps she conceives of the counseling relationship in different terms than we do.

---

34. Mr. J's challenge brings an immediate and defensive response. Miss E relates her point of view to her feelings. In her last sentence there may also be the implication, "but you are not in sympathy with people."

35. Is this response slightly interpretative? It would seem so. Would another response have been more helpful? It is difficult to say. An alternative might have been along these lines. "You are emotionally involved when people are in distress, and feel you *must* make things easier for them."

36. Here again, as in numbers 14 and 16, we find the student relating her intellectual beliefs to her more basic emotional feelings. Certainly her future behavior is likely to be more soundly realistic if she recognizes that her views are not only intellectualizations containing possible truth, but that they grow out of personal need as well.

37. Here again Miss E is challenged by an interpretation of her behavior. Yet this does not appear to be so much of a personal attack as an attempt by Miss T to think with Miss E about herself.

38. Miss W comes to Miss E's defense, albeit in a way which is somewhat patronizing, indicating that Miss E may not be capable of understanding the implications of her own reactions.

39. Miss E: No, I'm glad she said that because I wasn't *truly* aware of the fact that I was so completely identifying with my clients even when I practically said as much before. I've got to give this a lot more thought.

40. Mr. Y: It's funny, but all this gives me a new slant on some of the methods I've been using. I've sure been taking the responsibility away from my clients. I've been spoon-feeding some of them without realizing it. All along I've injected, or projected or both. That is, I've projected my own feelings of dependence out on my clients. I guess I've got to talk this thing over carefully with someone and work through these problems more fully. (186, pp. 16–18)

These excerpts are rather typical of the personalized problem-solving type of learning which goes on in a student-centered course. If they also help to suggest the minimal but highly significant behavior of the leader, then they will have conveyed a description of the experience as we have come to understand it.

To one who is used to highly organized classroom presentations, the discussion may seem loose, may appear to jump from topic to topic. This is certainly true, but it is probable that this fluid, exploratory, even confused type of advance is more deeply characteristic of learning as it occurs, than the dead systematization of learning after the fact. One of the things we have learned as instructors is that if the leader is uncomfortable at leaving issues

---

39. Here, as for Mr. B in number 16, Miss E is working ahead on the problem of understanding herself, particularly herself in relation to her ideas about counseling. She rejects the protection offered by Miss W, and moves ahead to develop a somewhat painful insight. Clearly this is only the start of the learning she will achieve from this situation.

40. This is the first contribution of Mr. Y during this hour, but it illustrates a process we have learned to expect. The person who is not verbally expressing himself in a class situation may nevertheless be participating at a deep and significant level. Sometimes this becomes evident in the course, through remarks like that of Mr. Y. Sometimes it may only come out in a paper at the end of the course, or the instructor may not learn the meaning it has had for the individual until long after the course is over.

"up in the air" and tries to achieve closure by some type of summary and conclusion at the end of discussion, this provides some relief for the group, but effectively stops any need for further thinking about the subject. If, however, the leader can tolerate the uncertainty, the divided views, the unresolved issues which the group has brought out, and if the class hour (and indeed the course) is ended without any attempt to bring an artificial closure, then the individual members of the group carry on very vital thinking outside of the class hours. The issues have been raised, some of their former conceptions and gestalts have been unsettled, they need to find some resolution of the situation, they recognize that the teacher will not give an authoritative answer to the problem, and hence there is only one alternative — to learn and learn and learn, until they have reached at least a temporary solution for themselves. And because they have achieved it for themselves, and recognize all too clearly the imperfect steps by which it was achieved, this temporary solution can never have the fixity that it would have had if it had been authoritatively pronounced by a professor. Therefore, instead of becoming a fixed point, a barrier to future learning, it is instead merely a step, a way-station on the road to further learning. This aspect is keenly experienced by the students in such courses. One student stated, at the end of such a course: "All my life I've made a ceremony of burning my notes at the end of a course, to show I was finished with it; in this course I have a totally different feeling, that I have just begun to learn, and that I want to go on."

Further Illustrations of Process

To some it will seem unfortunate that the foregoing illustration is from a course in which counseling is the subject and the concepts of client-centered therapy a frequent topic of discussion. The question may be raised as to whether these concepts influenced the process of learning. The same methods have been used in a variety of other courses including statistics and mathematics, but the verbatim accounts of classroom behavior are few. Perhaps the question may be answered to some extent by taking a verbatim portion from a Great Books course, also conducted by Shedlin.

In this group the books were prescribed, the reading to be done for each session was prescribed — even the leader is described as a questioner. Hence this is one situation in which, if the leader is to conduct the course in a student-centered fashion, he must create an acceptant climate within a rather rigid imposed framework. A stenographic record of the sixth session was made, and the following portion is from the first of the hour. The assignment had been Aristotle's Ethics, Book I. The group consisted of nineteen adults. Mr. C, who opens the hour, is a printer. The instructor's comments are given as footnotes.

1. Mr. C: There are many things about this reading that I know I don't understand, but as is my usual procedure, I'd like to attack something right at the start. (*General laughter.*) In the very first sentence he says, (*gets book open*) "Every art and every inquiry, and similarly every action and pursuit, is thought to aim at some good; and for this reason the good has rightly been declared that at which all things aim." Well, it seems to me that Aristotle is tentative at one point — where he says, "is thought to aim at some good," and quite dogmatic when he says, "has *rightly* been declared," etc. He doesn't seem to be consistent.

2. Inst: You resent the fact that you have to accept reasoning which seems to be built on clay, is that it?

3. Mr. C: Sure, this man is supposed to be an authority, yet he seems to be mixed up right at the beginning. I don't like to swallow stuff like that. He talks as if everything he says is true, yet he is quite uncertain at times.

---

1. During the first five sessions Mr. C was an energetic participant, and to characterize his part in the group best might be to say that "he is the man who sticks his neck out." The group members accept him in a half-facetious light, but seem inclined to have a healthy respect for his contributions. His remark is addressed to the group.

2. In this instance the instructor responded after allowing time for one of the group members to pick up the remark. The response was an attempt to understand Mr. C's feeling about his interpretation of Aristotle at this point. It seems that any attempt to challenge his thinking here would be premature, might arouse hostility and would probably deter him from further self-examination.

3. He continues his attack, expressing resentment more specifically.

4. Inst: You feel that if a man gives you the impression that he knows everything, then he should know everything.

5. Mr. C: Well, no man can know everything, but ——

6. Mr. R (interrupts): Of course no one knows everything. And after all, how can you write if you don't believe you are right. I don't think he's so dogmatic; he says later on that the truth can be stated only in terms of the exactness of the subjects and premises.

7. Mrs. H: I agree with you on that, Mr. R, and I think I know where he says that. *(Reads)* "it is evidently equally foolish to accept probable reasoning from a mathematician and to demand from a rhetorician scientific proofs."

8. Mr. R: Yeah.

9. Inst: Then you two feel that he is rather clear in his limitations and quite humble in his presentation.

10. Mr. J: I'd like to say something to Mr. C on that, too. Sometimes he [Aristotle] sounds as if he was being dogmatic, but if you follow him you find out that he is following out a scheme of argument.

11. Inst: You think he's *reasoning* rather than just *stating*, is that what you mean?

12. Mr. J: Yes. But you've got to watch the introductory words he uses.

13. Mrs. S: That sure is true. I've marked some of them in places. For example, right here in section 1094b and 1095a in my reprint, I've underlined them. His first sentence starts with "Now," the second says, "and further."

---

4. This remark was designed to understand the feeling and to clarify the idea expressed by Mr. C in such a way that he realized it was his personal impression he was advancing. Unfortunately it goes beyond what has been expressed by Mr. C, and hence is perceived as somewhat threatening.

5. Mr. C feels the pressure of the attempted clarification.

6, 7, 8. Mr. R and Mrs. H seem anxious to pound some insight into Mr. C and at the same time defend Aristotle.

10. It is interesting to note a subtle group mood being expressed here. Since Mr. C's last remark, it seems fairly obvious that even while the others are making their own points, they are at the same time attempting to aid Mr. C in working through his original attitude.

14. Inst: Mrs. S, do you mean that what sound like positive statements are really progressive steps in reasoning?

15. Mrs. S: That's right. He makes his premises and then forms his conclusions.

16. Mr. C: Perhaps I was a bit hasty in judging this man. I've been known to do that. (*Laughter.*) I have to read this again anyway, so I'll watch my step next time. I always seem to get a lesson when I open my mouth.

17. Inst: And so he left, clutching his book and dragging his sword behind him. (*General laughter.*)

18. Mr. C: How is it you know just how I feel all the time? (*Laughter.*)

19. Mr. S: I'd like to raise a question about Aristotle's knowledge of human nature. (*Looks about.*) At one point he mentions that there are three main types of life. Pleasure seeking, political, and contemplative. (*Pauses and looks around.*)

20. Inst: Yes.

21. Mr. S: Perhaps I misunderstand, but it seems to me that most of us engage in *all* those activities during our lifetimes.

22. Inst: You're objecting to the labeling of — That is, you object to dividing all life into only three types.

---

14. In retrospect, this response seems completely unnecessary and certainly redundant.

16. Here it appears that the group activity has been exerting its effect upon Mr. C in spite of his silence. He verbalizes an insight, and at the same time seems to be saying a left-handed "thanks" to the group.

17. It is difficult to assay what the purpose of this remark may have been at the time. A rationalization which would be kind to the instructor might be that he carried along with the generally humorous group tone at the time.

18. Is there a hint of resentment here? Perhaps the instructor's attempt at humor has backfired.

19. I believe it is worthy of mention that Mr. S surveyed the group rather intently as he spoke. It seemed to me that he was actively looking for acceptance from the group. Implicit in this is the idea that he felt the responsibility involved in his interpersonal relations in the class.

20. The instructor's simple acceptance of Mr. S allowed him to immediately communicate how he felt about what he read.

23. Mr. S: Yes, suppose you just look at a single day and try to interpret your motives. It's far more complicated than the way I'll describe it, but it's good enough to explain what I mean. You get up and eat. You could say that was pleasure-seeking. You read the paper. That could be for pleasure or for political thought or other things. You might go to church; that would be spiritual contemplation, or it may be fear, or something else. You see what I mean?

24. Mr. N: Don't you mean that life is not something you can generalize about?

25. Mr. S: In a way, yes.

26. Mr. N: But didn't Aristotle mean more than motives? Didn't he mean the general tone of a person's existence?

27. Miss W: Not only that, but he was writing about a time in history which is much different than what exists now.

28. Inst: You believe that human nature is different because of different environments, is that right?

29. Miss W: Well, yes. If cultural settings are very complex, people are bound to react in more complicated ways. In simple settings they don't need to be complicated in their adjustment.

30. Miss B: But if happiness is the goal of human beings, what difference does it make how simple or complicated your surroundings are? You still will be living for happiness.

31. Miss W: What is happiness?

32. Inst: Miss W asks the $64 question. *(Laughter.)*

24. Mr. N responded understandingly to Mr. S's puzzlement as to the effectiveness of his communication.

26. It is noteworthy that Mr. N responded as above even though he had reservations as to the validity of Mr. S's statement. This has a great deal of significance as an example of group atmosphere. In terms of discussion techniques alone, doesn't this imply that a democratic atmosphere fosters the acceptance of responsibility by the participants? As the group members feel free of threat, they not only can accomplish their own ideational integration but can accept a clarifying role in their interaction with others.

28. This was an attempt to get at the essence of Miss W's thinking.

32. Here the instructor was grossly insensitive to the intent of Miss W's question. Perhaps a simple acceptance would have allowed her the expression she needed. My interpretation of the dynamics at this point is that if the classroom mood was not a generally permissive one, such a remark on the instructor's part might have effectively forestalled further participation by Miss W.

33. Miss W: No, this is serious. Aren't there as many ideas of happiness as there are people? Isn't happiness a personal thing?

34. Inst: You're pretty certain that happiness is more than something about which people can agree. You feel it comes from within, is that it?

35. Miss W: Sure. My happiness comes from my doing and thinking what *I* believe is right. And it also depends upon what *I* want in life.

36. Mrs. S: So far so good. But *where* do you get your values and beliefs? Don't you get them from your environment?

37. Miss W: Perhaps so, but as you get them, you get them as a person. What I mean is, you have to interpret what you get from your environment in light of what you are. This is very hard to explain.

38. Inst: It's frustrating to know what you mean and find it so difficult to express it clearly.

39. Miss W: It sure is.

40. Mrs. D: I think I see what she means. For example, if two people see an event, they're going to see it in terms of what it means to each, because of how each views it. And each views it differently because of what each is. Is that what you were trying to say?

41. Miss W: Yes, that's just about what I mean. (186, pp. 26–30)

Though the subject matter under discussion is much different, the description of the process as a personalized problem-solving would still seem to hold. As far as we have been able to observe, the content of the course seems to have relatively little influence upon the type of learning process we have been describing.

The Problem of Evaluation

How shall we solve the problem of grades, of passing of courses and examinations, when this approach is used in the classroom situation? How is the student to be evaluated?

There seems to be only one answer to this question which is thoroughly consistent with the approach itself. If the purposes of the individual and the group are the organizing core of the course; if the purposes of the individual are met if he finds significant

---

33. Instead she continues, indicating her feeling about the subject.

41. Throughout the last few exchanges Mrs. S, Mrs. D, and the instructor seem to be aiding Miss W in the understanding of her **thinking.**

learnings, resulting in self-enhancement, in the course; if the instructor's function is to facilitate such learnings; then there is but one person who is in a position to evaluate the degree to which the goal has been achieved, and that is the student himself. Self-evaluation appears to be the logical procedure for discovering those ways in which the experience has been a failure and those respects in which it has been meaningful and fruitful. This is, indeed, the fitting climax of an "education for rulers." Who is to say whether the student has put forth his best effort? What weaknesses and gaps there are in his learnings? What has been the quality of his thinking as he has wrestled with the problems which his own purposes have posed? The person most competent to perform this task would appear to be the responsible individual who has experienced the purposes, who has observed intimately his efforts to achieve them — the learner who has been in the center of the process. Here again is evidence of the revolutionary character of this approach to education, since the very heart of all our educational program is the rigorous (one might almost say ruthless) evaluation of the student, whether by the instructor, or by a standardized and impersonal test.

Our experience has corroborated the theoretical principle that self-evaluation is the most desirable mode of appraisal in a student-centered course. The greater the freedom to use self-evaluation in such a situation, the more obviously favorable have been the results. Students experience the task of self-appraisal as one more opportunity for growth. They experience with wonderment the fact that no one is going to utilize an external locus of evaluation. They do not need to tremble for fear they will be "failed"; nor can they look with childish anticipation for approval. The question for each student is — What is my honest appraisal of what I have done, as it relates to my own purposes? There is not even any gain to come from inflating the self-appraisal. As one student writes, "I started to make this pretty rosy, but who would I be kidding, and why should I kid myself?" To carry through a self-evaluation is often a most difficult task. It means that the student must formulate his criteria of evaluation, must decide on the standards that he has for himself. It means experiencing to the full the implications of discovering that, in the long run, the locus of evaluation lies in one's self. Something of the flavor of this experience will be conveyed in the next section, where quotations will be given from documents concerned with self-evaluation.

Let us now turn, however, to another phase of this problem of evaluation. Most instructors are working in institutional frameworks in which the operational philosophy is almost directly opposed to that which we have been presenting. The student must be "motivated" to work; the only proof that he has been motivated is through examinations; external evaluation is the primary function of education; grades are the balance sheet of such evaluation; and throughout the whole process the instructor must not trust the student. Is it, then, impossible for a teacher to handle his class in a student-centered fashion in such a framework? We have not found it so, though admittedly there must be some compromises, if we are to advance by evolutionary rather than revolutionary means.

Again, the problems lose their overwhelming character if the instructor is clear in his own philosophical approach to the situation. Grades and evaluation simply become one more limitation imposed by the environment, one more problem which the students and the instructor must solve. The instructor poses his dilemma to the group. "The university demands that I sign my name to the grades given to all the members of the class, indicating that they have performed at a certain level. How do you wish to meet that problem?" Operating in such a framework, any solution is less than perfect, but various classes have arrived at working solutions which have made for far more growth than the conventional approach. Some of these may be listed.

In some courses students have formulated the examination by submitting questions and have participated in its evaluation.

In one small class where the students were acquainted with each other's work, they decided to arrive at grades in an open class discussion at the end of the course. Each student stated the grade he felt he had earned, and gave his reasons.

The group and instructor entered into the discussion and each grade was arrived at by a general concurrence of opinion.

In some universities a grade of Pass or Fail can be turned in. Utilizing this, classes have accepted a P grade, permitting self-evaluation to be the real judgment on their work.

In some courses each student has written out a self-evaluation including his judgment as to an appropriate letter grade for himself. The understanding is that the instructor will turn in this grade unless he feels that he cannot agree with it, in which case the grade will be arrived at in conference between student and teacher.

These represent a few of the many compromise approaches which have been made. Even the most faulty ones have these advantages. They emphasize that evaluation of the student by the student deserves much weight in the evaluational process. The basis for grades inevitably comes into sharp focus, and students come to realize that they are often (if not always) antithetical to growth in terms of personal purposes. The student becomes quite fully aware of the fact that a grade is a highly artificial thing, based upon very human and fallible methods, and that his own judgment of his achievement is at least as valid for him as a judgment from an external locus of evaluation.

As we have struggled with this problem of grades and academic bookkeeping, and have contrasted it with those experiences in which students are free to evaluate themselves, we have reached a conclusion which to some will seem radical indeed. It is that personal growth is hindered and hampered, rather than enhanced, by external evaluation. Whether that evaluation is favorable or unfavorable, it does not seem to make for the development of a more mature, responsible, or socialized self, but indeed tends to work in an opposite direction.

This is not to say that we would do away with all evaluation. If I am hiring one person from among ten applicants, I evaluate them all. If a man is going out as a physician, a psychologist, a lawyer, or an architect, then perhaps the welfare of society may demand that he be evaluated in terms of certain publicly available criteria, so that society may know whether or not he is competent for his task. But let it be recognized that such evaluations are made on behalf of the welfare of the organization, or the welfare of society. They do not, as far as we can determine, promote the growth or welfare of the individual.

Such a radical hypothesis deserves intensive investigation. Thus far the writer knows of only one study bearing on the point. Beier (21) studied the effect of a Rorschach evaluation upon reasoning, problem-solving, and motor skills.[1] Sixty-two graduate students were given a Rorschach test and tests of abstract reasoning and problem-solving. They were then divided into an experimental and control group, matched for age, intelligence, ability in abstract reasoning, and degree of adjustment as measured by the Rorschach. The members of the experimental group were then given a structured interpretation of their Rorschach results. They were exposed, in other words to an evaluation (which they would be likely to regard as authoritative) made from an external frame of reference. Both groups were then retested for abstract reasoning, card-sorting, and mirror-drawing ability. The experimental group showed more anxiety, more rigidity, and a greater degree of disorganization than the control group. They seemed less able to respond flexibly and intelligently to the demands of the situation. The difference between the groups was statistically significant. Although this study approaches only one phase of the problem and needs much further supplementation, its findings are in accord with our own experience in indicating that when the student experiences the locus of evaluation as residing outside himself, personality organization and development are hindered; that when he experiences the locus of evaluation as being within himself, personal growth is fostered.

Outcomes of Student-Centered Teaching

It has been our frequent practice to ask students to turn in at the end of the course some sort of personal document — a self-

[1] This study was previously quoted to illustrate another point. See Chapter 4, pages 142–143, footnote.

evaluation, or a reaction to the experience of the course. One of the impressive learnings which result from perusing these documents is the sharp realization that each student attended a different course. That is, the experiential field of each person is so different that at times it is very difficult to believe that the papers turned in were written about what was, from an external point of view, the same objective experience, namely a certain course with a certain instructor. To read such a group of papers thoughtfully is to give up forever the notion that a course will mean to all students a certain degree of "coverage" of topics A, B, and C. Each person's experience of the course is highly unique, and intimately related to his own past and to his current desires and purposes.

In spite of this uniqueness there are certain general trends often noticeable in such reports. The first is the feeling of puzzlement, a feeling which may range from amused perplexity to real confusion and a sense of profound frustration. The student reacts with some emotion to the experience of being put on his own. A brief statement of this reaction, which would be typical of many, may be taken from a student self-evaluation.

> At first I had a feeling that we were not going anywhere. Then gradually I began to feel that we were going somewhere, but couldn't determine just where. Finally, I came to the conclusion that where we were going depended upon each individual. (186, p. 8)

Another general trend is that most students tend to work harder, and at a deeper level, than in the conventional course. That this may be true in spite of a considerable feeling of frustration is indicated in the following excerpt from a statement turned in by a graduate student at the conclusion of a course.

> I might say that I have not been entirely satisfied with this course in Adjustment Counseling. I have the feeling that some direction is not only necessary but even desirable and expected in the learning situation. However, it may be that what I objected to was not the nondirective factor as such but rather what I defined as the lack of organization or direction of the class. Or was it that the class did not do what I wanted to do? However, I'm not so sure that things didn't

turn out for the best (certainly satisfactorily) notwithstanding my dissatisfaction with the group.

I soon decided that if I were going to get anything out of the course I would have to do it for myself, and this was good, though I'm still convinced that there is another and more enjoyable method of accomplishing the same thing. Not only did I liberally sample the client-centered literature but I felt I should know more about the other schools of therapy and thus I was forced to study more about them. I also appreciated for the first time how inadequate was my understanding and comprehension of many of the psychological methods and techniques, so I was forced to investigate them more thoroughly and as a result I am going to sit in on a few extra courses in the coming quarters. . . . Therefore I took a couple of the play therapy sessions and quite a few of the recorded interviews which I found to be most helpful. In addition, I got together with another student on Saturday afternoons and we would counsel one another with the aid of a wire recorder and would then analyze, discuss, and criticize our efforts. As a result, I got a better understanding of the nature of the therapeutic process and gained a better insight into my own activities as well!

Another trend to which we have become accustomed is the pervasiveness of the learning which takes place in a student-centered class. It makes a difference in the *life* of the individual, not simply in the intellectual symbols which he manipulates. This is very evident in the reactions of our students, and in the student reports given by Cantor (39). An example may be taken from a self-evaluation turned in by another student. One may say that the concepts in the course, as well as the manner of teaching, accounted for the results. However, a lecture course in client-centered therapy is quite unlikely to have the type of result described. After discussing something of the reading he did for the course, and his reaction to the class sessions, this student turns to some of the broader implications the course has had for him in terms of his professional preparation, his interpersonal relationships, and his basic philosophy.

Only recently have I been aware of how necessary and desirable it is for me to actively participate in the evaluation of my efforts in courses taken at the university, and how strongly I feel called upon to discuss this point with the several instructors involved. These endeavors, in both classroom and private consultation, have not met with unalloyed success (due, in part, no doubt, to my inept handling of the situation), but they have resulted in the conviction that I am correct in taking this stand. I have come to realize that my being graduated from the university is not to be viewed as a competition in which a degree may be won by concealing my felt inadequacies while presenting a façade of competence which I dread will be exposed. I can now think more constructively about these deficiencies and formulate plans for eliminating them, and furthermore, I feel more freedom to discuss these problems with faculty members whom I feared would "find me out." Of late, more "soul-searching" has taken place as I examine how I became interested in clinical psychology and how my personality will affect the persons with whom I have professional contact. This is being reflected in my work as a psychologist at — Prison, and though I feel that I have made a good beginning in this area, I am equally certain that I must continue to take such steps in self-examination for quite some time to come — in fact, why not throughout the rest of my life?

A most noticeable change, so far as I can determine, has been in the manner in which I have been trying to form and conduct relationships with other persons — friends, relatives, business associates, strangers. For example, I no longer seek to persuade my wife, as much as I used to at any rate, to do things "my way," regardless of their inconsequential nature. True, I still become a little concerned when she "fouls up" the budget accounts or crosses the busiest of streets in the middle of the block, but I no longer attempt to convert her to my way of thinking on the spot, with no "if," "and," or "but" about it. I am getting more accustomed to the idea of letting her be a person in her own way, making decisions and taking responsibility for them, and expressing herself spontaneously in her own inimitable way. I am likewise making progress in letting my friends lead their own lives, trying to think *with* them about their problems rather than thinking *for* them and handing out solutions for the problems which always seem to come up when we talk together. And with people about whom I know little — clerks, streetcar conductors, casual acquaintances — I feel myself better able to try to see things as they appear to them, though it can hardly be termed adopting their "frame of reference" as there is little communication in these instances. It does help to understand how they can become irritable and offensive as well as be pleasant and likable, and it makes it easier for me to react to them in a manner calculated to make our relationship a satisfactory one. This is not to say that I never drop the role of clinical psychologist, but I do try to utilize what I have learned in my studying to conduct the affairs of the day, trivial though they seem to be at times. I believe such a practice makes for better integration of my personality, but it does not eliminate the necessity for recognizing and coping with attitudes which I have formerly repressed as undesirable and detrimental in a psychologist. The conscious manipulation of such feelings will probably do much to make me more comfortable personally and more effective professionally.

A more comprehensive understanding of client-centered therapy has altered my general philosophy of life as well as the above-mentioned aspects of my personality. I have come to see that there may be a scientifically demonstrable basis for belief in the democratic way of life. Previously, I rather half-believed or maybe hoped that the people possessed the wisdom and ability necessary for governing themselves, but there was an almost equally strong belief that suggested that there were some people whose grasp of things was such that they should have more to say about affairs than the majority. I thought that perhaps government by the few might be superior to that by the many, and I consequently felt some guilt about holding such a belief, though I knew that many persons believe thusly while proclaiming the virtues of democracy, apparently without sensing any incongruity or discomfort. I cannot honestly say that I am now unalterably convinced of the infallibility of the democratic process, but I am encouraged and inclined to align myself with those who hold that each individual has within himself the capacity for self-direction and self-responsibility, hoping that the beginnings of research in areas such as client-centered therapy will lead to the unquestionable conclusion that the democratic way of life is most in harmony with the nature of man.

When I first began thinking about this self-evaluation, I thought I might ask for a letter grade of "B" since I had submitted no term paper or project. But now I believe that the insights which I have achieved and the knowledge which I have been able to assimilate as the result of reading, listening, and thinking during the past three months have been of far more significance than those resulting from writing any term paper which I have completed. My reading has been more extensive than in any previous course, even though I knew that I would not be tested on the material covered in this course. I read because I was sincerely interested in the ideas which had stimulated my thinking and was desirous of learning more about them; I expect to continue these activities with the intention of gaining further knowledge and insight concerning the dynamics of human adjustment and the client-centered approach to psychotherapy. In view of the fact that I believe this past course-period has been one of the most significant in my life at the university or elsewhere, I am requesting that I be given the letter grade "A."

Not every student responds favorably to a student-centered approach. Usually all but a small minority have attitudes more favorable than unfavorable. There are often, however, some who feel the course has not been of benefit to them. Sometimes even this negative reaction appears significant of progress. One student writes at some length his criticisms of the course, and states that since no reading was required, he did almost no reading. He concludes, however, that if, when given an opportunity to read as he wished, he did almost no reading in a field he had thought of as part of his professional life work, perhaps he is in the wrong profession.

As an instance of a persistently negative attitude, the following may serve.

The lack of orientation which has predominated most of the classroom discussion is perhaps the major criticism which I have to apply. Frequently what I would term a major issue turns up; one or perhaps two people will contribute toward its clarification or solution; a third individual will digress to some noncorrelative issue, and the original problem will have been forgotten.

While I do fully realize the impossible situation we would find ourselves in if we attempted to exhaust the potentialities of each issue raised, nevertheless it does seem practical to consider at least some more concise order of clarifying the questions raised.

The class, as a whole, has improved considerably since the first two or three weeks of the quarter, but the situation still remains with us. Even the most democratic of organizations, governed by a majority, must maintain organizational structure in order to attain any prescribed goals.

I would suggest that some definite goal be set in advance of any particular meeting of the class, so that the class will know beforehand its agenda, whether it be counselor-client role-taking, a *lecture by yourself*, a question and answer series on a stated problem, or merely round-the-class open discussion of a stated problem.

Research investigations of the outcomes of student-centered teaching are in their infancy, but the findings thus far seem to corroborate the observations of teachers and students. Gross (73) who has worked with Cantor, studied the development of self-understanding in a conventional as compared with a non-directive course. He used a partially standardized scale for measuring self-insight, the essential principle of which was that most of the statements were extreme, and the person with self-understanding could not agree to them without modification. On this scale two classes which were approximately equivalent in age, education, and socio-economic status made roughly equivalent scores prior to beginning their respective courses. The group which was conventionally taught showed only a slight increase in self-insight. When Cantor's group was retested at the end of the course, the self-insight score had increased markedly. Of Cantor's class, 62 per cent of the group had score increases of 13 or more, while only 10 per cent of "Doe's" class showed such an increase. In Cantor's class, however, there is a minority group which showed no increases, or even decreases. Gross concludes "that Cantor's method does encourage the development of self-insight on the part of a majority of students, though it may fail to reach a certain minority of every class." The author stresses the point that his is a preliminary study, and should be regarded as such. It needs to be repeated under more rigorously controlled conditions.

In another preliminary study Schwebel and Asch (178) have used a nondirective approach in teaching three classes and have found that students who are relatively well adjusted approve the method, and utilize the experience, doing more than an ordinary amount of reading for the course. The more poorly adjusted students tend to prefer a class in which the instructor gives the direction.

Still another study related to our interest is one conducted by Smith and Dunbar (193). It is primarily a study of student participation, not a study of the effect of a student-centered climate. The major finding is that participating students show very little difference, in achievement or adjustment, from the nonparticipants. The authors also state that students who participate consistently tend to be nonconformists, though the evidence is slight. The general conclusion is that participants gain little if any more from a "free-discussion" course than nonparticipants. The extent to which the classroom atmosphere was student-centered, as this term has been used in this chapter, is not made clear. From the description given, one would judge that such a climate had been approximated only to a small degree.

Faw (55) has carried out the best study to date, using classes in general psychology. He taught one class in student-centered fashion, a second in conventional fashion, and in the third he alternated approaches at every class meeting. The most serious flaw in his study is this role-taking by the instructor. It seems very likely that the role closest to his own beliefs and convictions would be most adequately implemented. Subject to this limitation, his findings are illuminating. In intellectual gains as measured by objective tests, the student-centered class showed equal or slightly better learning than the instructor-centered class. Students who had been exposed at all to the student-centered approach (the first and third group) felt that they received more social and emotional value from this approach, and that interest and enjoyment were much greater. Students felt, however, that they gained more information and knowledge in the conventional approach. A characteristic student opinion was, "The free-discussion class teaches me less in the way of actual facts, but it helps me to feel free and at ease with myself and with other people." Actually this feeling of having gained less factual knowledge is not borne out by the test results. Faw points out that the basis for the feeling is probably the lack of any authority upon which to depend. As one student says, "Whatever the conclusions were, they were student deductions and not backed by the instructor's experience or information; as a consequence I have retained many of these decisions as fact when I have no definite basis for believing so." Whether these more tentatively held conclusions are desirable or undesirable depends, of course, upon one's educational philosophy.

It should be stressed, in considering these initial studies that "student-centered" or "nondirective" teaching is by no means defined in identical fashion by each investigator. In some instances the class is quite rigidly structured, in others not. Varying degrees of student freedom were permitted. The behavior of the instructors varied. Perhaps the only possible generalized description is that, as compared with the conventional college-level lecture course, there was much greater permissiveness and freedom, and much more reliance upon the ability of the student to take responsibility for himself. As further studies are carried on, the objective description of the classroom climate and of the instructor's behavior seems a necessary starting point for any investigation.[1]

[1] As this volume goes to press, the author has had the opportunity to read the manuscript of another investigation of a student-centered approach: M. J. Asch, "Nondirective Teaching in Psychology; A Study Based upon a Controlled Experiment," *Psychological Monographs* (in process of publication). In this study the experimental class of 23 was compared with control groups, matched in various respects. On objective and essay-type examinations the traditional group showed more gain. However, there was no matching of motivation here, since the traditional class was informed that its grades would be based on the examination, while the experimental group was asked to take the examination, but told that the results would in no way affect its grades. Judging from the student reports, the experimental group gained much more diversified knowledge.

The personal adjustment of the experimental group showed decided improvement during the course, as measured by the Minnesota Multiphasic Inventory. The control group made significantly less gain in this respect.

When the students evaluated their course experience on an instrument devised for this purpose, the nondirectively-taught group felt far more satisfaction with the course, and indicated more evidence of gain from the experience.

In this research there is a rather adequate description of what was involved in the "nondirective teaching," though there is no objective measurement of the conditions. The students selected their own goals for the course, selected most of the reading materials, participated freely in relatively unstructured class discussions, wrote weekly "reaction reports" regarding their experience, and determined their own grades for the course.

A Concluding Discussion

Much of present education appears to be operationally based on the assumption, "You can't trust the student." Acting on this assumption, the teacher must supply motivation, information, organization of the material, and must use examinations - · quizzes, recitations, oral exams, course examinations, standardized achievement tests — at every turn to coerce the student into the desired activities.

The approach we have been discussing is based on an assumption diametrically opposed, that "You can trust the student." You can trust him to desire to learn in every way which will maintain or enhance self; you can trust him to make use of resources which will serve this end; you can trust him to evaluate himself in ways which will make for self-progress; you can trust him to grow, provided the atmosphere for growth is available to him.

If the instructor accepts this assumption or is willing to adopt it as a very tentative hypothesis, then certain behaviors follow. He creates a classroom climate which respects the integrity of the student, which accepts all aims, opinions, and attitudes as being legitimate expressions of the student's internal frame of reference at that time. He accepts the feelings and emotionalized attitudes which surround any educational or group experience. He accepts himself as being a member of a learning group, rather than an authority. He makes learning resources available, confident that if they meet the needs of the group they will be used. He relies upon the capacity of the individual to sort out truth from untruth, upon the basis of continuing experience. He recognizes that his course, if successful, is a beginning in learning, not the end of learning. He relies upon the capacity of the student to assess his progress in terms of the purposes which he has at this time. He has confidence in the fact that, in this atmosphere which he has helped to create, a type of learning takes place which is personally meaningful and which feeds the total self-development of the individual as well as improves his acquaintance with a given field of knowledge.

SUGGESTED READINGS

A comprehensive overview of the relation between psychotherapy and education is given in the article by Symonds (208). It contains a thoughtful analysis of the two fields and their basic similarities and basic differences, as seen by a writer with experience in both fields. It also contains an excellent bibliography of references pertinent to this chapter.

For the reader who wishes to gain acquaintance with recent presentations regarding education which are similar to the client-centered point of view, Cantor (39) and Kelley (100) are good references.

For presentations of the client-centered point of view in education by other writers, see Snygg and Combs (200, chapters 10 and 11), and Axline (14, chapters 16 and 18). Both these studies are focused primarily on education below the university level, with Axline's discussion bearing primarily upon the child's first years in school. She also discusses the application to school administration.

For acquaintance with the limited research in this area, the study by Faw (55), which has been mentioned, seems to be the most adequate to date.

Chapter 10 · The Training

of Counselors and Therapists

From what we know of the extent of personal distress and maladjustment, and the social demand for assistance along these lines, we must judge the problem of professional training for counselors and therapists to be an urgent one indeed. Yet little has been written, and even less research done, on the issues which are involved in setting up and carrying through such a program of professional education. This dearth of data is not due to any lack of recognition of the importance of the field. The American Psychological Association, for example, has given its approval to a "Recommended Graduate Training Program in Clinical Psychology," in which it is stated, "It is our thesis that no clinical psychologist can be considered adequately trained unless he has had sound training in psychotherapy" (160, p. 548). Similar attitudes prevail in other professional fields. As yet, however, experience in this realm is limited, and discussions are few.

As a consequence of this situation, the present chapter will be written, without apology, around an account of the development of the writer's own experience in carrying responsibility for the training of therapists. Perhaps a frank look at some specific methods which have been used, with their strong and weak points, will lead to similar presentations by others.

AN EARLY EXPERIENCE IN TRAINING COUNSELORS

At Ohio State University, from 1940 to 1944, the writer was in charge of a practicum course at the advanced graduate level, whose purpose was to give training in counseling and psychother-apy. Several of its features were not unusual. Individuals were admitted to the course who had both training and experience in clinical psychology or student counseling. Wide reading was encouraged in a variety of therapeutic viewpoints. A more novel feature, for that time, was that the course was built around cases handled by the students. As soon as a student felt that he was ready to handle a case, a client was assigned to him from among the individuals coming to the Psychological Clinic. The student-counselor took full notes on his interview (or occasionally was able to record some of the interviews) and the nearly verbatim account of at least one interview was mimeographed and dis-tributed to members of the practicum for discussion, while the case was still in progress. This gave the course the maximum of live interest, and was intended to be of help to the counselor while he was still dealing with his client. Counselors were encouraged to request early consideration of their cases if difficulties were developing, or if they felt unsure and in need of help. In addition to this class discussion, many individual conferences were held with students in regard to the clients they were handling.

In retrospect, the course seems so full of flaws that its con-structive outcomes appear astonishing. The course was very short, with 20 to 25 hours of class time. It could be repeated once, giving a maximum training of about 45 hours. There were usually 15 to 30 members of the group, with one instructor. The teach-ing methods were, by present standards, decidedly inadequate. In general they consisted of approval and disapproval of specific ways of carrying on counseling, as exemplified in the interview at hand. While the instructor endeavored to keep the pressure of disapproval from being too great, and to balance it with approval, the individual student frequently felt very much "on the spot."

Some of the poor results of the course, as seen in retrospect, or dimly perceived at the time, are these. Due to the method of teaching, the student was very likely to acquire guilt feelings in regard to his work. There grew up unintentionally a notion of orthodoxy, so that the student-counselor felt that he was either "right" or "wrong" in what he was doing, or that he was properly nondirective or improperly directive. Since too little attention was paid to basic attitudes, a student not infrequently felt that his own sincere desire was to do one thing, while a vague concept of orthodoxy in counseling compelled him to do another. Thus it was sometimes true that the counselor tried hard to behave in ways which were not genuine for him — a most damaging start for a therapist. Obviously, the whole situation involved an over-emphasis on technique, which was not good.

To some extent this deficiency was recognized, but the controls seemed necessary at the time to prevent definite harm being done to clients. The writer believed that if student-counselors, full of many notions of psychodynamics, were permitted to work with clients in any way they saw fit, real harm might result. It was hoped that by emphasizing the techniques of a relatively safe approach, the student could be initiated into counseling work, and could then slowly find the ways of working which were real for him. At the time it was the only way which could be seen of meeting the double demands of safety for the client and learning for the counselor.

In spite of the many deficiencies of the course, a very considerable number of excellent therapists emerged from these groups. Why? In the first place, many of these students were highly promising persons, well selected. In the second place, for those who already had to some degree the philosophical orientation outlined in the second chapter of this book, the emphasis on techniques was often helpful rather than stultifying. It provided a way of working which was in line with their attitudes, and helped to give them a consistent framework for all their therapeutic effort. Another reason for the success of the training was that at a very early stage the student was given responsibility for dealing with a real person in difficulty, and thus felt impelled to learn as rapidly and as deeply as he could the dynamics of a helping relationship. Finally, the use of electrically recorded interviews became a stimulating and highly profitable basis for learning on the part of the therapists. As described at the time (173) it gave counselors an opportunity to see what methods they were actually using, in contrast to those they thought they were using. It gave an opportunity to discern the process of therapy, particularly in its minute and detailed aspects. Perhaps most important of all, it helped counselors to recognize that interviews were not just talk, but highly sensitive indicators of cause and effect in human relationships. A casual interpretive remark by the counselor might be demonstrated to have an effect in blocking communication, not only at the time, but two or three interviews later. Thus counselors learned significantly from their own experience, often in spite of, rather than because of, the teaching methods of the course.

Some Significant Trends in Training Therapists

In the years that have elapsed since the course just described, the writer has been aware of certain directions which have been important in the training programs which have evolved out of this early effort. These trends may be summarized here. Their detailed implementation will be evident in a later section of the chapter.

1. There has been a steady trend away from technique, a trend which focuses upon the attitudinal orientation of the counselor. It has become apparent that the most important goal to be achieved is that the student should clarify and understand his own basic relationship to people, and the attitudinal and philosophical concomitants of that relationship. Therefore the first step in training client-centered therapists has been to drop all concern as to the orientation with which the student will emerge. The basic attitude must be genuine. If his genuine attitudes lead him in the direction of some other orientation, well and good. The purpose of training is increasingly to train therapists, not a particular brand of therapists. To put it in another way, the present point of view is that no student can or should be trained to become a client-centered therapist. If the attitudes he discovers within himself, if the hypotheses which in his experience are effective in dealing with people, happen to coincide in important ways with the client-centered orientation, then that is an interesting indication of the generality of those experiences, but no more. It is far

more important that he be true to his own experience than that he should coincide with any known therapeutic orientation. The basic reliance is upon the capacity of the student-counselor to develop himself into an effective therapist.

2. A second trend is to place stress upon techniques specifically as an implementation of attitudes. Once the student has clarified his own attitudes toward people, then a detailed consideration of the ways in which he and others operate in the therapeutic interview is highly fruitful. New light is thrown on his attitudes by observing the operations he uses in therapy, and new ways of behaving are perceived as he thinks more deeply about his attitudes.

3. Another trend is to give the student an experience of therapy within himself. This can be done in part through the way in which courses are taught and in part through the way the student is given supervisory help on his cases. The most direct route, of course, is for the student to undergo therapy himself, and a steadily increasing proportion of student counselors have been availing themselves of this opportunity. The purpose of this therapeutic experience is perceived a little differently than in other orientations. It is not expected that personal therapy will permanently remove all likelihood of conflict in the therapist. Nor is it felt that therapy will permanently rule out the possibility that his own personal needs may interfere with his work as a therapist. He may later need and desire further personal help in relation to some case with which he is dealing. But personal therapy may be counted upon to sensitize him to the kind of attitudes and feelings the client is experiencing, and may make him empathic at a deeper and more significant level.

4. A fourth trend is merely a confirmation and extension of the thinking which has dominated from the first. It is that the practice of therapy should be a part of the training experience from the earliest practicable moment. Much ingenuity has gone into the planning of ways in which the trainee can enter into the experience of providing a helping relationship for another, early in his professional education.

WHO SHOULD BE SELECTED FOR TRAINING?

The problem of selecting candidates for training as therapists is a perplexing one indeed. It is doubtful if any therapeutic orientation has satisfactorily resolved the issue. In our own experience it would seem that while a beginning selection may be made upon certain minimal factors, a considerable amount of self-selection is desirable once training has begun. If a group is reasonably well selected at the outset, and if the training program is free and permissive, some will discover that therapy is not their special forte and will drop out. Others realize that the attitudes involved make too heavy a personal demand upon them. Such self-selection does not seem necessarily wasteful.

As to the basis for minimal selection, we have found in our experience that we have tended to use much the same criteria as those which have been adopted by the American Psychological Association for the selection of clinical psychologists in general. These criteria are rather vague, to be sure, but they represent the present stage of our knowledge of what is required as a basis for becoming a therapist. As stated by the committee of the APA, the characteristics which it is desirable that a person possess are as follows:

1. Superior intellectual ability and judgment.
2. Originality, resourcefulness, and versatility.
3. "Fresh and insatiable" curiosity; "self-learner."
4. Interest in persons as individuals rather than as material for manipulation — a regard for the integrity of other persons.
5. Insight into own personality characteristics; sense of humor.
6. Sensitivity to the complexities of motivation.
7. Tolerance: "unarrogance."
8. Ability to adopt a "therapeutic" attitude; ability to establish warm and effective relationships with others.
9. Industry; methodical work habits; ability to tolerate pressure.
10. Acceptance of responsibility.
11. Tact and cooperativeness.
12. Integrity, self-control, and stability.
13. Discriminating sense of ethical values.
14. Breadth of cultural background — "educated man."

15. Deep interest in psychology, especially in its clinical aspects. (160, p. 541)

It may at some point be possible to base the selection of potential therapists upon criteria established by research. There is at the present time one study in progress in which an extensive battery of personality tests were given to a group of VA Personal Counselors prior to their intensive training in therapy, and ratings later obtained as to the subjects' effectiveness as therapists. It was the hope that certain personality configurations might be found which would be indicators of high potentiality as therapists. At present writing this hope does not seem to be supported by the evidence. It is a field in which we may expect research to progress, though present subjective judgment would be that the training received is at least as important as the original personality configuration in determining whether an individual will become a good therapist. Perhaps the next step in research will be to investigate the organization of attitudes toward others, rather than personality structure, as a possible predictive tool.

PREPARATION FOR TRAINING IN THERAPY

What background knowledge or experience is necessary or desirable for the person who is to be trained as a therapist? This is a question about which there have been sharp differences of opinion. The simplest answer seems to be the requirement of a background of conventional training in the whole field of psychology. That this is a *necessary* prerequisite to therapeutic training is disproved by the facts. Many psychiatrists become good therapists with almost no background in the general field of psychology. In our own courses we have had students from the fields of education, theology, industrial relations, nursing, and students with interdisciplinary training.[1] It has been quite impossible to see any significant differences in the rate at which such students

[1] Particularly from the Committee on Human Development, whose training program is broadly based in courses designed to give an understanding of the individual as a biological organism, as a member of cultural groups, and as a psychological entity.

become therapists. It would seem that the orientation to personal relationships with which they enter a training program is more important than the specific course work they have had or the scientific knowledge they possess. We have not had opportunity, except very occasionally, to accept individuals for training whose background is in literature or drama or the arts. Such experience as we have had, however, would lead us to believe that when such individuals are motivated to become therapists, they can achieve this goal as rapidly as the person whose training is in psychology. Sometimes, indeed, it appears that previous training in psychology has so indoctrinated the student with the concept of the individual as an object to be dissected and manipulated, that he has more difficulty in becoming a therapist than the student from another field.

Several elements in our experience may distort our perceptions. The student who is not in psychology does not take courses in therapy unless he has sufficient motivation to undertake the "irregular" thing. The student in clinical psychology, however, may feel that he should be a therapist, and take courses for which he has no strong personal desire. It will take time, observation, and research to determine whether any of the present professional programs make likely a more rapid learning of therapy.

One difference has been noted. For the person who is to do research in therapy, a background in psychology, in which there has been stress upon experimental design and the methodology of psychological science, is clearly of benefit.

A Desirable Preparatory Background

The preceding paragraphs may be interpreted as meaning that no preparation is of any significant help to the person who desires to become a skilled counselor or therapist. This meaning is not intended. It is believed that there are areas of learning and experience which are definitely useful to the would-be therapist. Unfortunately, conventional courses, based largely upon factual content, rarely provide these learnings.

What would be desirable preparation for the person who is to receive training as a therapist? The following suggestions are given very tentatively. The order has little significance.

1. It seems desirable that the student should have a broad experiential knowledge of the human being in his cultural setting. This may be given, to some extent, by reading or course work in cultural anthropology or sociology. Such knowledge needs to be supplemented by experiences of living with or dealing with individuals who have been the product of cultural influences very different from those which have molded the student. Such experience and knowledge often seem necessary to make possible the deep understanding of another.

2. If the student is to become a therapist, the more he has been able to achieve of empathic experiencing with other individuals, the better will his preparation be. There are undoubtedly countless avenues to this end. It can come through literature, which can provide an entrance to the inner worlds of other persons. Perhaps it might come especially through the role-taking which goes with dramatic productions, though so few therapists have such a background that it is difficult to judge. It may come from psychology courses in which the approach is dynamically phenomenological. It can come simply through the process of living, when a sensitive person desires to understand the viewpoint and attitudes of another. It is a way of perceiving which can be learned in courses, as some of our staff have demonstrated in teaching beginning graduate courses.

3. In our judgment another valuable phase of student preparation is the opportunity to consider and formulate one's own basic philosophy. The person who is to carry on therapy needs security within himself, and this may come in part from having thought through some of the basic questions regarding human life, and having formulated tentative but personally meaningful answers. Security in one's self is certainly not gained through courses *about* philosophy, but may come through courses in philosophy, education, or religion in which the effort is made to face up to the deep questions of existence, and the opportunity given to the student to clarify his own thinking.

4. The experience of personal therapy is, as has been mentioned, a valuable experience for the student. Whether it should precede formal training in therapy, or be concomitant with it,

seems to be a matter of little consequence. In the writer's opinion, the time when it comes should rest upon the needs of the student. It does not seem consistent with the whole viewpoint of client-centered therapy to require individual therapy of the trainee. Rather, opportunities for personal therapy should be available, to be utilized when the student feels the need. When he makes further steps in his own experience in providing therapy for others, it is quite possible that he may wish further help for himself.

5. It is certainly desirable that the student should have a deep knowledge of the dynamics of personality, and should have thought significantly about problems in this field. If his knowledge is simply a matter of labels and abstractions which may be applied to individual behavior, it will have little value. Again it is the empathic and experiential aspect which is important. Such knowledge is perhaps best gained in clinical work in which there is a desire to understand and learn from each client. Through such work a more and more meaningful grasp of personality dynamics is internalized. It may also be gained through courses or through books. While many of the latter convey only intellectualized and sterile abstractions regarding human behavior, some are more or less successful in serving as a medium by which the motivations and behavior of one person can be empathically reexperienced by another. At a simple and popular level this is achieved by Travis and Baruch's book, *Personal Problems of Everyday Living* (219). At quite another level it seems to be achieved by Reik's *Listening with the Third Ear* (161). The net effect of presentations such as these is not to give the student a catalogue *knowledge* of repression, neurotic behaviors, conflict, regression, and the like, but to give him a more sensitized *feeling* for these behaviors in himself and in others. It is this sort of understanding of personality dynamics which is a valuable preparation for training in therapy.

6. If the student expects to contribute to the advancement of the field of therapy as well as to practice psychotherapy, then a knowledge of research design, of scientific methodology, and of psychological theory is valuable. As we try to view the situation

objectively, it does not seem possible to say that such training makes it easier to become a therapist, or makes the individual a more effective therapist. It does appear, however, that such background is useful in the testing of hypotheses which are implicit in therapy, in the creative and productive formulation of new directions and hypotheses in the field, and in the construction of theories of therapy. Perhaps the most significant effect of learning in these fields is the basic security which it gives to the therapist in the relinquishment of doctrines he has thought true. It has been very noticeable in certain individuals and professional groups that outworn therapeutic dogmas are not given up. One of the reasons appears to be the lack of security as to what will take their place. If a dogma received from his teacher is questioned or there is evidence that it may be untrue, what is a therapist to do? It is here that a thoroughgoing experience with scientific method is of value. For the person who has experienced a scientific approach to problems, the loss of some part of what he has regarded as the truth is not a catastrophe, since he has the tools for discovering new and more significant truth. It is as this attitude becomes thoroughly internalized in therapists that important advances will be made.

7. In this list there are two significant omissions which perhaps deserve special comment. The first is the lack of any stress upon biological knowledge of the individual. Since the human being functions as a total biological organism, it would appear entirely logical that the person with thorough knowledge of the physiological functioning of the organism would have a better basis for becoming a therapist. It would be comfortable and satisfying to report that this was true. Yet as the writer considers the therapists he has known, there appears to be no correlation between successful achievement as therapist and background in biological knowledge. Some of the best therapists have been well equipped with biological knowledge, but others equally outstanding have been remarkably innocent of training in this field. Likewise among the least successful therapists the same statement could be made. Furthermore, it appears that the most successful therapists, from Freud on, even when equipped with biological and

physiological training, make no more than infinitesimal use of it in their practice of psychotherapy. Many follow the definite policy that any organic problem, or the possibility of any organic problem, should be investigated and dealt with by someone who is not the therapist. Thus, present experience would seem to indicate that biological knowledge has no special value for the background training of the would-be therapist. Like English literature or history or genetics or organic chemistry or art, it does have value in broadening the outlook and understanding of the therapist, and giving him a wider knowledge of life and of the incredible intricacies of the life process.

The second omission is that of personality theory, in so far as that may be separated from personality dynamics. It is the writer's conviction that theory, to be profitable, must follow experience, not precede it. To train a student, prematurely, in a theory of personality, or even in a variety of such theories, results all too often in a dogmatic and closed-minded approach to experience. This is as true of theory developed from a client-centered approach as of theory developed from any other orientation. The chapter on personality theory in this book is included with many reservations. To the person with therapeutic experience it may be constructive, since it offers him a formulation which he can test against his own experience and revise or discard accordingly. By the uninitiated student, on the other hand, it may all too readily be interpreted as the truth, or as dogma — a rigid vessel into which experience must be warped, even if it does not fit. It is for such reasons as these that no special stress has been placed on theory of personality as an element in the student's preparation for training in therapy.

It should be amply evident, from the various points which have been listed, that if we were willing to sweep aside all the conventional notions of pre-therapy education and the vested interests which are associated with them, and were to start with a fresh consideration of those elements of preparation which experience has shown to have a definite relationship to effectiveness in therapy, we should doubtless emerge with a preparatory curriculum of experience vastly different from that usually required.

How Long a Period of Training?

There have been many discussions, often fruitless, of the length of time which it takes to train a therapist. Our experience would indicate that this question, as stated, can never be satisfactorily answered. Learning the attitudes and skills which are effective in therapy is working on a continuum. An intensive two-day institute may help a group of psychologists, industrial counselors, or guidance workers to be perceptibly more effective, more therapeutic, in their work. On the other hand, five years of intensive training and experience is perhaps too little to bring a therapist to the peak of his effectiveness. Whether a training program is to be two days or more than five years in length depends upon our goals and upon what is socially and educationally practicable. If the therapeutic orientation is permissive and nonprobing, if the instructional approach is nonauthoritative and encourages the student to go at his own pace, then we do not need to fear that "a little learning is a dangerous thing." There are various degrees of therapeutic training which can be effectively used.

Another issue which has been frequently raised, especially in recent years, is the placement of training in therapy — whether at the pre-doctoral or post-doctoral level. Our experience would indicate very clearly that excellent therapists can be trained at the doctoral level, without any significant sacrifice of breadth in their training. The reasons given for postponing to the post-doctoral level are usually these: (*a*) There should be thorough training in psychological diagnosis prior to training in therapy; (*b*) psychotherapy is such an intricate and delicate skill that one should not attempt to learn it until he has reached full professional maturity; (*c*) it has been customary in medicine to postpone such training to the post-doctoral level.

From the experience we have had in client-centered therapy, it would seem possible to counter each of these arguments with opposing considerations. In regard to (*a*), the principle has already been advanced that diagnosis does not need to precede therapy (see Chapter 5), and there seems no adequate basis for believing that training in diagnosis should precede training in therapy. As to (b) it is probable that skilful psychotherapy is no more demanding or delicate a function than skilful psycho-diagnosis. Each makes its demands, and the attitudes and knowledge required are very different. There is, however, no reason to suppose that they exist as a hierarchy. It is possible that, because psychologists feel secure in regard to their work in diagnosis, and somewhat insecure in the newer field of therapy, they tend to postpone its consideration. As to the third reason, (c), most psychiatrists regard it as extremely unfortunate that the medical student receives so little training in understanding or handling emotional problems prior to his medical degree. It seems unnecessary for psychology and related professional groups to copy the mistakes of medical education.

The whole point of view which has been expressed on these issues may be summarized in a few sentences. Training in psychotherapy exists in varying degrees. If the orientation is in the direction of a permissive and noncoercive therapy, then some training is better than none, more training is better than some. As to the time when such training might be given, some of its basic principles, as they apply to human relationships in general, might be taught at the high school or college level. For the person who is acquiring therapeutic skills as a part of his professional training, there seems every reason to provide this training as a part of his graduate education prior to his doctoral degree.

In an effort to make this picture more specific, a brief account will be given of two brief training programs in psychotherapy and one longer and more comprehensive program. We are fortunate in having a research analysis of one of the brief programs.

BRIEF TRAINING IN PSYCHOTHERAPY

A Program for Physicians

There are published accounts of two ventures in which the modest aim was to facilitate the maximal learning of therapeutic skills in a short period of time. The first is a medical venture, well described by Smith (226, pp. 1–26). This was an attempt by a group of well-known psychiatrists to provide training in therapy for physicians who were, for the most part, general practitioners. While the orientation was eclectic rather than client-centered, it is brought in for consideration because it is so similar to several institutes carried on from a client-centered point of view.

There were twenty-five physicians in the group, and the course lasted for two intensive weeks. It was held at the University of Minnesota in April, 1946. The general purpose and orientation of the teachers was to give the physician a deeper understanding of psychological problems in his patients, to encourage more listening and a more empathic attitude on the part of the physicians, and to give training in procedures which could be used therapeutically by the physician in his general practice. The major elements of the course which seem to have furthered these aims are as follows.

1. Lectures by various psychiatrists on different phases of therapy and related problems. The topics were selected and planned by the leaders.

2. An immediate introduction to the therapeutic handling of cases. On the first day the physicians were given a lecture in the morning, and in the afternoon a number of them were holding interviews with patients who had been assigned to them because of presumed psychological maladjustment. The aim was to have one of the psychiatrists in on at least some part of this interview.

This policy of contact with cases was maintained so that most of the physicians managed to have several interviews with these patients during the two weeks' course. The contacts were then closed or the patient transferred to some other member of the hospital staff.

3. Discussion of these cases, accompanied by supervisory teaching, was another major element in the course. Every effort was made to get group consideration of the cases being handled. The physician-trainee presented his case, which was then discussed by the group and by some of the psychiatrists in charge.

4. The group lived and ate together in a dormitory setting, and the informality of the group and the self-education which went on in the continuing informal discussions was regarded by all as a very significant part of the curriculum.

This short institute was regarded as definitely successful both by those who planned and conducted it and by those who participated in it. It would seem to indicate that even a two weeks' training program may be effective in reaching realistic goals.

A Brief Program for Personal Counselors

In 1946 the Counseling Center at the University of Chicago was invited by the Veterans Administration to provide a short training course for Personal Counselors. (The "Personal Counselor" was a position which the VA was then in the process of creating for dealing with individual veterans and their postwar problems of adjustment.) After consideration of the many factors requiring urgency, a six weeks' training course was decided upon, since the candidates were all mature psychologists and counselors with considerable training and experience. E. H. Porter, Douglas Blocksma, and Thomas Gordon were the members of the Center staff who were responsible for this project, in cooperation with the writer, though all members of the staff became involved in the program in one way or another. Blocksma and Porter (34) have published a description of the course, only the major features of which will be reported here. Although there was no communication between those responsible for this course and those responsible for the psychiatric venture described above, the similarity in some of the procedures is striking.

Approximately one hundred of the Personal Counselors received training. They came in seven groups, each group remaining six weeks. There were from ten to twenty-five in each group. The thirty-seven members of Groups II and III, who were studied most closely, and were representative of the total, were found to have a mean age of thirty-three years, to have completed 2.3 years of graduate training, and to have had 3.4 years of clinical and/or counseling experience. They were thus a mature and experienced group.

It was decided at the outset that in so far as possible the atmosphere of the course would be the atmosphere of client-centered therapy, and that we would endeavor to facilitate learning that was self-motivated. Blocksma puts it in these terms:

> The Center staff believed that learning of the client-centered viewpoint would best occur under conditions similar to client-centered counseling conditions. The trainee should experience in all aspects of the training program the quality of social-emotional climate that he is expected to create in counseling his clients. This included equality of opportunity for participation in each activity, and the freedom to discuss and differ in teaching situations. A client-centered climate demands of the teacher a sensitivity to the values, feelings, and ideas of students; it also demands a nondefensiveness on the part of the teacher so that students can deal with deeper feelings aroused by new learnings. It was assumed that, as a student's emotionalized viewpoint is understood by an accepting teacher, it becomes possible for the student to learn the teacher's viewpoint and independently establish his own altered viewpoint.
>
> It was believed by the training staff that, in such a learner-centered climate, a person would be able to come to see himself and his own attitudes, values, and methods of handling people. This climate would be implemented through several channels. In essence, these channels would involve a combination of ego-involving, self-directed, socially enforced experiences which would combine elements of previous learnings with new learnings. (33, pp. 66–67)

The outstanding elements of the course seemed to be these:

1. *The presentation period.* This occupied the first hour and a half in the morning. Various staff members and some outsiders were utilized. The first presentations to each group were decided upon in advance by those responsible for the program, but later presentations were governed to a considerable extent by the wishes or special interests of the group. These presentations covered a wide range of topics, from "the course of therapy in client-centered therapy" and "group therapy," to "the industrial use of nondirective counseling" and "personality theory implicit in a nondirective approach."

2. *Group and subgroup discussion periods.* Following the presen-

tation there was nearly always time for some discussion, but the major discussion period was in the afternoon in what came to be known as the "subgroup." Each group was subdivided so that there were no more than eight trainees with a discussion leader. This group remained constant throughout the six weeks. The topics for discussion developed out of the interchange within the group. The meetings were a blend of discussion and group therapy, and it was found that in general the group went through a sequence quite comparable to that found in the counseling process. Initially there were many negative reactions and negative feelings in regard to the course and the ideas being presented. As these were accepted, more positive feelings were in evidence. Throughout this period there were insightful learnings which often struck the group member with the full force of a therapeutic insight; for example, one member brought out the fact that "one reason I couldn't trust clients more in the past was the fact that I didn't fully trust myself." As the group discussions continued, many members came to a decision-making and planning phase as they worked out the ways in which they would utilize their learnings in their work in their own community.

3. *Opportunity for first-hand experience.* It had been recognized that the most significant gains would accrue only if the trainees had the opportunity to put their attitudes and skills into practice. It was very difficult, however, to supply clients in sufficient quantity; moreover, those responsible for the program felt a concern as to whether a trainee should start working with a client if the maximum time available was two or three weeks. In spite of these obstacles, a number of members of each group carried counseling cases, and others engaged people in casual interviews in which they had some opportunity to test out some of the ideas they were acquiring. The groups felt that this first-hand experience in carrying on at least a rudimentary counseling was one of the most valuable portions of the training and wished there might have been more of it.

Since it was possible to make recordings of some of the cases handled by trainees, the whole group became identified with the situation as they listened to the recorded interviews, learning a great deal both from the weaknesses and strengths, the mistakes and successes of their fellow trainees.

4. *The case analysis period.* One period each day was set aside for case analysis. Interviews from a great variety of cases were presented in recorded form for listening and discussion, or in mimeographed form for detailed analysis of counselor techniques and client process. Some of these were cases handled by staff members; some, as indicated above, were cases currently being handled by trainees; some were cases handled by therapists of other orientations. In spite of the fact that listening to recordings is a most demanding task, since the recordings are seldom easily audible, this case analysis portion of the course was rated fourth among eleven activities in which the group engaged (33, pp. 74–75) and was a most significant learning experience.

5. *The opportunity for personal therapy.* In the first group which came for training, the availability of personal counseling help for those who desired it was explained early in the course. Only a few took advantage of this opportunity, but they were emphatic in their feeling that personal counseling was one of their most meaningful experiences, and made the strong recommendation that this opportunity should be given more stress in later groups. Their recommendation was passed on to succeeding groups, with the result that in some classes 80 per cent of the members sought personal help for themselves. Throughout the successive groups this was regarded as a part of the training which was of markedly significant benefit.

6. *The impact of concentrated intimate informal association.* One phase of the training program proved to have much more importance than had been foreseen by the staff. The men were together for a minimum of eight hours a day, as a whole group, in subgroups, and in groups of two, three, or four for coffee or lunch or dinner. Since most of them stayed at nearby hotels, the discussion and interaction not infrequently continued until the small hours of the morning in heated "bull sessions" in which the trainees reviewed and reconsidered from every angle the issues of the course and the effects these ideas were having upon their own personal integration and philosophy. In these ways, which had not been ade-

quately foreseen, the training course had a deep total impact. A considerable proportion of each group, when it came time to leave, felt that the total training program experience had been one of the high points of learning in their whole lives. When one considers that this was not an adolescent group but a group in their thirties, this enthusiasm seems to have significance. It appears rather clear that if one were planning such a program for its maximum impact, the trainees and faculty might do well to live together as well as work together, to the full degree that this is practicable, since the informal association appears to have an important influence upon the assimilation of new concepts and ways of behaving.

A Trainee's Reactions

Before proceeding to a research analysis of the outcomes of this training course, it may be possible to suggest something of its effect upon the lives and attitudes of the participants through some brief excerpts from interviews. In several instances trainees who requested personal therapy for themselves permitted the interviews to be recorded. Brief portions of one of these cases are illustrative. In the following excerpt the trainee has just described some previous therapy he has had, in which he feels the relationship was a very dependent one. He continues:

S113: My self was abdicated to accept values and a way of life and a lot of other things, which was not basic to me, and I am convinced Karen Horney's book brings it out well. The defining of the self and the development of it is what's important. (*C:* M-hm. You feel that . . .) Well, this approach helps. Uh, I also want to add, when you have — there's a — almost might put it, a faith-concept here. That in itself produces a different mental set. (*C:* M-hm.) Uh, the, the — you find that not only in this session, but in, uh, the whole approach that we work out in our work periods, and in all the other work we're doing here, there's this faith that this person could do it himself. (*C:* M-hm.) Uh, well, that's a different — that results in a different mental set. (*C:* M-hm.) So much that I find it hard to believe.

C113: You find a change in focus, or a change in basic faith as to what can go on from the self outward, or inward, but I mean, depending on the self itself, how it moves, or changes, or thinks. It really revitalizes the whole total experience.

S114: For myself, in other words, the approach used on others, if I follow that, results in a certain reorganization in myself. Even the acceptance philosophy sort of clashes a little bit with the hypercritical, interpretative philosophy, where you sit, as I always feel, with your little spear, ready to jab the truth (*laughs*) (*C:* M-hm.) in an interpretative way, and uh, you're so conditioned that when people make statements, you're interpreting. It's, uh, sort of, uh — I've seen that so much in others and in myself. It results in a different type of social relationship.

In a later session he also indicates the close interweaving of his past experience, the challenge of the present learnings, and the persistent patterns which must be altered if he is to function in the new way.

S351: I think one of my problems has been this hypercritical self — hypercritical towards others and towards self, using the same standards of perfection. A lot of moral compulsion in me that I applied to myself and applied to others with a certain contempt of weakness. That's the Napoleon statue again. A contempt of weakness in other people.

C352: You feel that you demand the same high standards, but question whether or not it is a too high standard or too great a demand.

S352: I *did* demand. I think that's one of the things I have worked through, so please use it in the past tense! (*Laughs heartily.*)

C353: Then you feel, I take it, that that *is* past tense?

S353: No. It's uh — that's the reflection that hit me so hard. The overemphasis of the negative and then the next stage was to tie up the hypercritical and the negative. How in the dickens can a person get freedom if he is always emphasizing the negative? Why, freedom means the freedom to make mistakes. And that's what tied up, well, the accepting concept and its basic philosophy ties in too. What I mentioned in class, to Dr. Rogers this morning — "Is accepting a histrionic gesture?"

C354: What?

S354: "Is it a histrionic gesture?" One puts on an act of accepting, and is the client not going to see through it eventually? So in order to be really accepting I think all of us here at the course all have to undergo terrific reorganization of self, to a greater or lesser degree. Of course, Dr. Rogers thinks almost anybody can counsel with more or less some degree of effectiveness. I don't know. But that's the way I see it as far as I am concerned, that I will find a certain growth, that in the accepting of behavior of others I am also learning, or making it easier to accept myself. And that of course should reduce the pressure in my marital situation. I'll have to accept certain of my wife's weaknesses more. I don't know yet whether it was a good marriage or not, but at least my role hasn't been a very free or mature one. And I at least can improve my role, whether the improving of my role will be — will result in a positive solution, I'm not sure. I don't know. I do know I can't sit here and debate about it. The first thing I'll do is try to behave in a more mature and independent fashion. Maybe my wife will grow more independent.

Something of the way in which the thinking and the attitude of the course become involved in the working through of his own problems is indicated by this portion from the seventh interview.

S381: I don't have this feeling I'm going to go sailing along. I have this feeling this is the best way for me to work out my own salvation and my own adjustment. The rest is up to me. (*Pause.*)
C382: The effort that might be needed is going to have to be yours. (*Pause.*)
S382: Problems here are relatively simply in this school situation. The very approach used here doesn't put any pressure on us. It's a sort of, as I put it once before, it's sort of a nurturing situation. Dr. Rogers and the rest of you are nurturing along our growth. (*Laughs.*) (*C:* M-hm.) Well, I suppose to a certain extent, things pop up in a greenhouse where the environment is optimum for growth.
C383: You feel new sprouts every now and then, coming out of it.
S383: Yes, but it is still a nurturing situation. A lot of acceptance here. It's relatively not a difficult situation to handle. It's going to be a little bit different when we get back to our jobs where we bump into the problems of life. This approach does not eliminate those problems. It helps people handle them. Well, I'm hoping to handle mine better. I've got myself involved with people, and compete unconsciously. If I'm not accepted completely, a certain disappointment sets in. All these things have brushed through my mind. They tie up with dependency, the need to be accepted. Karen Horney does a beautiful job of that. I've had a lot of that. Often wondered why my chasing after women — how much of it is related to that. I was trying to work through that last

night. Am I not exaggerating the worth of these marvelous creatures? (*Laughs*.)

C384: Whether they in themselves are worth what value you give them, or whether they are meeting a need —

S384: — that is in me. A sort of need to be accepted. My own value becomes reflected in their acceptance.

C385: M-hm. You find a very satisfying kind of — I don't know quite what word to use — re-emphasis, or a kind of reassurance to you.

S385: I suspect that, as I analyze it because I must — there has been a drive there. The old man told me even after marriage I'd find that a difficult problem. I think he was correct. And I'm trying to analyze that drive. I would like to be one of these men that wasn't so interested in the females who are clicking down the sidewalk. I wish my marriage brought me enough satisfaction that I wouldn't have this wanderlust. So I'm trying to analyze it. What is there in me that drives me so to these mother-bosoms?

C386: M-hm. You feel that there must be something pretty significant that operates when you do seek more and more relationships with women? Or the maternal kind of relationship?

S386: Oh, not maternal. That's the analytic interpretation, that the maternal must be there, that it is my mother image. I just throw that in because I sometimes take a whimsical attitude towards myself and these problems. But it is one of the things I'm trying to work through, and hoping that, as I — become more independent, which we know I am, that the dependency needs decrease. The need for acceptance, which is one of the things I've worked on hard now for a couple of years. This almost prostituting yourself to be accepted. The fear of being rejected, which — I think Karen Horney's got something — is related to a good deal of anxiety, that if a person remains his self, the other person won't accept him.

C387: So that you've had too much at stake, perhaps, in being accepted by others to be able to be your own real self. Is that it?

S387: Definitely.

Perhaps these excerpts illustrate something of the unity of the learning which occurred in this course — a unity which is possibly characteristic of all significant learning. This trainee is learning that if he is to be a certain type of counselor, he must alter his relationship with his wife, with other people, and most deeply of all, his relationship with himself.

Objective Evaluation of Learning Outcomes

We are indebted to Blocksma (33) for a study of some of the outcomes of this training program. It is believed that this is the first time any attempt has been made to measure objectively the learning of therapeutic skills and attitudes.

Thirty-seven personal counselors in the second and third classes were the subjects of this study. The purpose of the investigation was (1) to measure the extent to which client-centered procedures were learned, and (2) to measure the extent to which these learnings were related to later success on the job.

In attempting to measure the degree of learning, two procedures were employed as pre- and post-tests. The first was a paper and pencil test devised by Porter and Axline (148, pp. 10–25) to measure the extent to which a person tends towards each of five different purposes in his counseling responses. The five tendencies are: *moralization*, in which the counselor tends to pass some type of evaluative judgment upon the client; *diagnosis*, in which the counselor is endeavoring to gain the information upon which he can formulate his own understanding of the person; *interpretation*, in which he tends to explain the client to himself; *support*, in which he provides some type of emotional encouragement; and *reflection*, in which he is trying to understand from the client's point of view and to communicate that understanding.

The second method of measuring was one devised by Blocksma. Taking a recorded first interview with one of his own clients, he shortened it by editing out some of the amplifying material, and thus produced a brief standard interview. He then took the part of this client, "Robert Doakes," in a role-taking interview with each trainee, playing the role as much like the client as possible. The task had much reality for these personal counselors, since the problem presented by the "client" was a vocational one, with many emotional concomitants and indications of personal maladjustment. The client material was always the same with only those minimal adjustments following the counselor's responses which might be necessary to give a conversational continuity to the interview. The interview was held privately with each of the thirty-seven trainees in turn, and was in each case recorded.

The trainee was requested not to discuss the experience with his fellows. At the end of the six weeks' training the same interview was repeated with each trainee. As an additional measure, each trainee conducted an interview with another role-playing staff member, who took the part of another client "John Jones." This second interview presented very much the same basic problem and attitudes, but in an entirely different contextual setting. The results on these two post-training interviews were so similar that they will be treated as one in describing the outcomes of the study.

The counselor responses in these interviews were analyzed in two ways. The first was a technique analysis, to determine the type of counseling procedures utilized. The second was a locus of evaluation analysis, in which a rating was given to each response on a five-point scale to indicate whether the counselor was (1) thinking and communicating completely *with* the expressed attitudes of the client, (2) thinking *about* and *with* the client, (3) thinking *about* the client, balancing the locus of evaluation inside and outside the client, (4) thinking and communicating *about* and *for* the client, (5) thinking *for* the client.

Both these measures proved to have adequate reliability, other judges showing complete agreement with the investigator in 83 per cent of the items of the technique analysis and 66 per cent of the items of the locus-of-evaluation rating.

Specific Outcomes. What were the outcomes of the six weeks' training course as measured by these procedures? It was found that the group had from their previous reading a fairly high verbal knowledge of nondirective counseling when they entered the course. Thus on the paper-and-pencil test of tendencies they used reflection 49 per cent of the time at the beginning of the course, diagnostic responses 19 per cent of the time, interpretation 18 per cent, and support and moralization least. At the end of the six weeks' period they used reflection 85 per cent, interpretation 12 per cent; diagnostic intent appeared in but 3 per cent of their responses, and moralization and support not at all.

The comparison between this verbal knowledge on a paper-and-pencil test and the actual functioning of the trainees in an interview situation is of the greatest interest. While using 49 per cent reflection on the paper-and-pencil test, they used only 11 per cent reflection in the interview, and only a fraction of those responses were real responses to the emotionalized attitude. The rest were clarification of the intellectual idea or repetition of the content. The summarized analysis of their pre-training-performance in the interviews showed 84 per cent directive responses, 11 per cent nondirective, and 5 per cent innocuous, falling in neither group. The locus-of-evaluation measure showed 16 per cent of the responses in the first two categories, indicating an effort to think with the client and to place the locus of evaluation with him, while 60 per cent of the responses involved thinking about and for the client.

At the end of the training period, the picture has changed rather sharply. Reflection is used as a technique nearly 60 per cent of the time. The summarized analysis shows 30 per cent directive responses, 59 per cent nondirective, and 11 per cent innocuous. Perhaps most important of all, at the end of training this interview test showed that in 60 per cent of the responses the counselor was thinking with the client and placing the locus of evaluation within him. Tables III and IV will indicate some of these changes.

The evidence given seems to justify the statement that in this six weeks' course:

1) The procedures of client-centered counseling were learned to a marked degree;

2) This learning was evident in a paper-and-pencil test in which verbalized knowledge was tested;

3) The learning was even more evident in a measure of functional techniques in an actual interview situation;

4) The learning was equally or more marked in a measure of the locus of evaluation in an actual interview situation. This rating served as an indirect measure of the counselor's empathic attitude, and the degree to which he held the orientation of placing reliance upon the capacity of the client.

Table III · Per Cent Frequencies of Techniques Before and After Training*

PAPER AND PENCIL TEST			INTERVIEW TEST		
Techniques	Pre-Training	Post-Training	Techniques	Pre-Training	Post-Training
Reflection	49.7	85.3	Reflection	10.7	59.0
Interpretation	18.6	11.8	Interpretation	21.8	15.1
Support	8.4	0.0	Support	14.7	4.6
Moralization	5.1	0.0	Oughtness	20.5	3.3
Diagnostic	18.2	2.9	Information-seeking	15.8	1.6
			Information-giving	2.6	3.9
			Personal Opinion	8.9	1.4
			Innocuous (Simple acceptance or silence)	5.0	11.1
Total	100.0	100.0		100.0	100.0

* Adapted from Blocksma (33, pp. 119, 163)

Table IV · Per Cent Frequencies of Locus of Evaluation Scores Before and After Training*

INTERVIEW TEST		
Scale Point	Pre-Training	Post-Training
+ 2 Thinks with client	4.0	35.5
+ 1 Thinks about and with	12.0	25.0
o Thinks about client, balancing loci of evaluation	24.0	22.5
— 1 Thinks about and for	25.0	11.5
— 2 Thinks for client	35.0	5.5
Total	100.0	100.0

* Adapted from Blocksma (33, p. 118)

Relation to Job Success. The objective measures, then, appear to make it amply evident that significant learning of a client-centered orientation took place in the course, and that this was much more than a superficial or intellectualized learning. But still unanswered is the important question: Will this learning make these men any more effective or adequate as counselors on the job? Blocksma attempts to throw light on this question, too, though his validation criteria are, as is so often true, rather crude and unsatisfactory.

He uses as criteria three items which proved to be useful. They are:

> 1) The pooled rating of the instructors at the time the trainee left the course, as to his probable functioning as a counselor.
>
> 2) The rating of the supervisor (not a client-centered therapist), one year after the completion of the program, as to the counselor's effectiveness on the job. (The investigator gave some aid in making this rating by gathering some of the information upon which it was based.)
>
> 3) The number of contacts per closed case during the counselor's first year of service. This is a crude indication of effectiveness, since our experience has shown that with the poor counselor many clients leave dissatisfied after one or two interviews, and few continue for a sufficient number of interviews to work through serious problems. It is admittedly an inadequate measure of effectiveness since many other factors might also influence this figure.

It was found that the paper-and-pencil test did not, to any significant degree, predict later success as a counselor. This was true whether the measure used was the pre-test score, the post-test score, or the discrepancy between the two. It was also found that the technique analysis of the interview pre-test did not significantly predict success. The other measures of the interview test, however, were associated with later success. The use of client-centered techniques in the post-training interviews showed a significant relation to success. Even more marked was the tendency for a client-centered locus of evaluation

Table V • Relationships between Test Scores and Criteria, as Indicated by Chi Square *

(Only relationships significant at .10 or below are shown)

MEASURES	CRITERIA		
	Instructor's Rating at Close of Program	Supervisor's Rating after One Year	Number of Contacts per Closed Case
Paper-and-Pencil Test			
Pre-Test: Total Score	. . .	. . .	.05
Post-Test: Total Score	. . .	. . .	. . .
Interview Test			
Pre-Test: Technique Analysis	. . .	. . .	. . .
Pre-Test: Locus of Evaluation	.05	.05	. . .
Post-Test: Technique Analysis			
Interview with "Doakes"	.05	.10	.05
Equated interview with "Jones"	.01	.001	.10
Post-Test: Locus of Evaluation			
Interview with "Doakes"	.02	.01	.10
Equated interview with "Jones"	.01	.001	.05

* Adapted from Blocksma (33, p. 125)

to be associated with the criteria for success. The best predictor of all was the second, equated interview (the interview with "John Jones") held at the conclusion of training. Here, obviously, was a situation most like that which the counselor would face on the job — a client unknown to the counselor, presenting a variety of problems and personal conflicts. If the trainee, in this situation, displayed a client-centered attitude as measured by the locus-of-evaluation scale, and utilized client-centered procedures as measured by the technique analysis, then he was likely to be highly rated by the supervisor at the end of his first year, and this rating showed less than one chance in a hundred of being due to chance factors. He was also likely to be carrying his counseling cases beyond a few interviews. Table V indicates some of the relationships found to exist, as tested by chi square.

Examination of this table and of additional aspects of Blocksma's data accentuate the place which the degree of assimilation of client-centeredness had in predicting success on the job. Since the group was highly heterogeneous in its counseling abilities at the outset, it would seem entirely logical to suppose that the final effectiveness on the job would be primarily predicted by the pre-tests, which would discriminate between the better and poorer counselors. Any effect of the course learning might be expected to be a slight modification of these basic predictions. But such is not the case. The pre-tests do not predict success to any very significant degree. But the extent to which the trainee has assimilated a client-centered approach, whether this involved a great or small amount of learning for him, appears to be the most adequate predictor of the effectiveness with which he will counsel clients in his own office, on his own responsibility, a year later.

In general, then, Blocksma's study shows that learning of a client-centered approach occurred during this six weeks' course, and that those who showed the deepest assimilation of attitudes and procedures were the ones most likely to be regarded as effective on the job one year later. Furthermore, there is a suggestion that it is this degree of assimilation, rather than the initial quality of the person's counseling, which best predicts his success. A study of the overall effectiveness of the work of the Personal Counselors has already been presented in Chapter 4, pp. 185–186.

Criticisms of the Program

These decidedly positive research findings might be taken to mean that the training course had no important defects. This assumption would be most misleading. As a course it received, and deserved, many criticisms. Many of these came from individuals who had no contact with the course, and whose sources of information were remote. It is of doubtful profit to consider these objections. The criticisms made by the members of the course themselves are perhaps more fruitful to consider. On the basis of a questionnaire at the conclusion of training and extensive correspondence since, Blocksma has endeavored to collect and consider the most serious weaknesses of the course. These may be summarized in several major categories.

1. There was too much of an effort to get across a client-centered point of view, at the expense of a process helping the trainee to become a therapist in his own terms. Partly because the staff had not sufficiently recognized the implications of a client-centered point of view for teaching, and partly because the urgency of a six weeks' time limit interferes with sound judgment, the group members were immediately exposed to a client-centered point of view and encouraged to consider it as a possible point of view for themselves. As Blocksma points out,

> A more efficacious method might be to spend considerable time and effort at the outset getting each trainee to know how he "naturally" counsels clients. If many standard or real or role-played pre-tests of the sort employed in this research could have been recorded, transcribed, and analyzed by each trainee on himself, then he would have had a picture of his own methods and attitudes and empirical counseling philosophy. Once he sees himself, and compares himself to others, and to client-centered counselors, then he is better able to decide how and why he wishes to change his counseling methods. In the writer's experience, a slower start, with emphasis on self-analysis, makes the presentation of the client-centered viewpoint more objective and learnable. (33, p. 146)

Such an approach would have enabled the group to arrive, deductively, through discussion and practice, at those attitudes and procedures which experience showed to be more effective in their own job. These attitudes and procedures would have been client-centered to the extent, and only to the extent, that such an orientation proved more effective than other approaches.

Dealing with the group in this fashion would have eliminated the "oughtness" which still tended to creep into the teaching. It would also have eliminated the slight feelings of guilt and rebelliousness which the personal counselors tended to feel as they developed the procedures which were individually most effective. The net reaction to the course, as expressed by many counselors throughout the subsequent year, might almost be rephrased as follows: "It was a fine program. It helped me greatly in starting on my work. I have met many unexpected problems. I am gradually learning to be much more effective in my work, thanks in considerable measure to the six weeks at Chicago. I am not as client-centered in my work as I should be." Had the program been better handled, this last sentence would have been meaningless and unnecessary.

2. A second criticism is closely related. It is that the course was not sufficiently learner-centered. Although a real effort had been made to approximate the atmosphere of the counseling relationship, this did not go far enough. There was still insufficient willingness to rely, freely and actively, upon the members of the group. If they had been given the responsibility for the planning, operation, and evaluation of the course; if the curriculum had been more fully of their own choosing; if the intelligence and ingenuity of the staff had been devoted more completely to providing those opportunities and resources which would have enabled the members to learn what they wished to learn — then the program would almost certainly have been even more deeply effective. Indeed, learner-centering would have taken care of all the other criticisms of the course.

3. The training experience would have been improved if there had been more contact with clients, and if such contact had begun earlier in the program. At the time no way could be seen of bringing this about, but had use been made of multiple therapy, and of trainees working in multiple therapy with one another, as will be described later (see pages 471–473), this end could have been achieved.

4. Provision should have been made for a follow-up institute, at least one week in length, after the counselor had had several months of experience. Lack of follow-up was recognized as a serious flaw in the program, but with the counselors scattered from Seattle to Puerto Rico it proved impossible to obtain the necessary financial support. A follow-up program would have helped greatly to enhance and deepen the learning which took place during the course. More adequate on-the-job supervision by experienced counselors would also have helped toward this goal.

Perhaps this whole section may best be concluded by a letter from one of the counselors one year after the program was completed. This letter gives one some glimpse of the positive meaning the course had for the group, though it also hints at some of the weaknesses which have been included under points 1, 3, and 4, above.

Dear D——

What I wouldn't give to be able to meet-in our work group again for about 10 hours. Now that I have some experience under my belt I'm loaded with questions. I'm enjoying my work more than I ever thought could be possible. Each counseling session is a new and exhilarating and satisfying experience. Of course we get a little more satisfaction from our successful cases. About 6 of my cases are cooking nicely. 6 to 8 counseling contacts with each, and I get a tremendous kick out of the way they work through their situations. No two are alike. One of them, an Engineer, amazes me. At times he sounds like a textbook on psychiatry.

D——, believe it or not, I'm getting a clearer picture of dynamics than any interpretative approach could hope to yield. ND [nondirective] teaches one the art of keeping quiet and observing. Remember, I'm the guy who tended to play the active role.

Some of the questions that I would like to have answered are: In your experience did you find that different clients have to be handled differently? One client starts digging immediately, another has difficulty in getting started. Do you have faith in the latter's getting started if the counselor uses ND properly? You know, between the client's not having a problem and the counselor's not reflecting and accepting properly, ND has a hand tailored explanation for any unsuccessful case. I realize the dangers of the counselor's inconsistency, but at the same time I wonder if there is no need for further experimentation. To be more specific, I have complete faith in ND once the client has accepted the counseling situation — once he starts exploring his own attitudes and difficulties but I am not completely convinced that every client with a problem will open up in the counseling situation. In other words, I have a hunch that more than the counselor's role is involved in some of our unsuccessful cases. If so, isn't there a need for experimenting with modified variations of what other schools have learned about human behavior. Perhaps I am merely expressing my own limitations as an ND therapist.

The other night I reviewed some of my notes of my initial counseling cases and I am amazed at the difference in the quality and frequency of reflections. Too many of my reflections at the beginning contained content material and as we *both expected* I was reflecting too often.

I have had considerable success with some of my experimenting, but I do not have sufficient evidence to draw any conclusions.

What I wouldn't give to be able to listen to some of the recorded case material that is available at the Center. When I was there I didn't know what to look for. Now that I have some background in ND the material is not available.

My present job is so satisfying, in spite of no privacy and no recorder, because for the first time in my life I am doing the work that I've always wanted. I don't know if I ever told you about my disappointment as a psychologist when I learned that I could either give tests, develop tests, or become a statistician. It was a new experience for me as a psychologist when I hit the Center and found that you and the rest of the staff shared my interest in therapy. I don't think I have to tell you how stimulating I found my contacts with you and the rest of the staff. (33, pp. 151–152)

A Current Program of Training in Psychotherapy

Considering the dearth of detailed descriptions of programs of training in therapy, it may be worth while to present the sequence of experiences which at the present time constitute therapeutic training at the University of Chicago.[1] Several qualifying comments should be made at the outset. The program is continually fluctuating, developing, changing, so that by the time this appears in print it will probably not be accurate. In describing the program, effort will be made to mention those elements in it which we regard as best — and of course this selection and emphasis may have a tendency to give a glorified picture of the situation. Prob-

---

[1] The faculty members of the Department of Psychology currently involved in this program are, in addition to the writer: John M. Butler, Thomas Gordon, Donald L. Grummon, E. H. Porter, Jr., Nathaniel Raskin, Julius Seeman, Arthur J. Shedlin. Other staff members of the Counseling Center also give assistance in consultation. Virginia Axline was formerly involved in this program and had much to do with its development.

ably no student has experienced all the best features which will be mentioned. We do not routinely achieve this "best" in carrying on the sequence.

Entrance into the Program

The curriculum of experiences which we shall describe is carried on primarily under the Department of Psychology, though the first course is also listed as a course in Education. In practice, not only students in psychology, human development, and education are admitted, but students from other departments as well, providing they have the qualifications.

The sequence cannot ordinarily be entered until the student is in his second year of graduate work. The reasons for this are based to some extent upon expediency as well as policy. Selection is easier after the student has had a year of graduate work, and he is likely to have a broader background. Furthermore, this policy simply evades the difficult and controversial question as to whether students should be given training in therapy as part of a master's degree program. Without taking sides on this issue, it appears to the faculty involved in this program that it is more crucial at the present time to educate therapists at the doctoral level.

There are usually more students who apply for entrance into the sequence than can be accepted. The applicants fill out a rather extensive blank which helps in making the choice. Weight is given to such factors as the following:

> Evidence of breadth of background, including not only psychology but sociology, cultural anthropology, philosophy, and like subjects.

> Evidence of ample preparation in the field of personality dynamics, in which there has been stress upon acquaintance with clinical case material. Emphasis upon a phenomenological or empathic understanding of these dynamics is desirable.

> Evidence that the student has worked out something of a

philosophy of living, or at least has an awareness of some of the deep issues of human existence. (Such evidence is not easy to obtain, and our present method is not very adequate.)

Evidence that the student has training in some other specialized function outside of therapy. The reason for this item is expediency. We prefer to have students who have training in psychometrics, vocational guidance, teaching, religious work, or some other function aside from counseling, since it improves the possibility of placement. For the nonmedical therapist today, most positions demand a double type of functioning — testing and counseling, teaching and therapy, and the like. Also, this requirement tends to reduce the number of applicants who wish to enter the sequence primarily because they see it as a way of gaining help with their own problems.

The First Course

The first course has been called "Principles of Adjustment Counseling." We have come more and more to look upon this course as an opportunity for the student to formulate the basic issues and basic attitudes upon which he will build his own therapeutic work. At its best it is not an attempt to indoctrinate in any particular therapeutic orientation, and it is certainly not aimed at a mere intellectual comprehension of the facts or principles of therapy. It is intended rather as an experience which moves one toward a deeper integration in regard to therapy.

To this end, the course is handled in the learner-centered fashion described in the previous chapter. The student is given the experience of responsibility for himself, and the experience of being understood and accepted as he reacts both negatively and positively to this new type of course. Gradually the instructional staff has learned (for any worth-while teaching is largely learning for the instructor) that it is safe to rely upon the group, and that the members are capable of taking responsibility.

One of the basic problems of the instructor is to make resources available — not only in the physical sense, but psychologically

available. As one resource, we have found indispensable a shelf
of reading materials — books on all viewpoints in therapy, jour-
nals, bibliographies on therapy and related topics, reprints, recent
studies (especially those as yet unpublished), significant papers
turned in by members of previous classes or of this class, verbatim
transcribed cases and interviews from our own and other orientations. To have such material readily within reach makes it possible for the student to pursue even a fleeting interest in a specific
topic with a maximum of ease. The unpublished studies and tentative drafts of manuscripts for publication help to give him a
sense of knowledge in the making, of being a part of a cutting edge
which extends into the future.

Another resource is the opportunity for listening to recordings.
Some of this can be done in class, but there should be ample opportunity outside. To listen thoughtfully to the ways in which
different therapists handle problems in the interview, to recognize
how clearly the therapist's basic attitudes show through his
words — these are significant means of learning.

Still another resource is the opportunity for ample contact with
staff members carrying on therapy. The chance to gain personal
therapy is one such opportunity, and is made as psychologically
available as possible. It is frankly available as help, not simply
as a didactic experience. There is also the attempt to let it be
known that staff members are willing to consult with students
about practical, theoretical, or research issues which the student
is meeting.

Observation is an exceedingly important resource. Sometimes
it is possible to obtain a client's permission so that one or more
interviews may be observed by a group. This occurs rarely, but
provides a very valuable experience for students. Usually a member of the group is willing to discuss with a counselor some adjustment problem of his own, as the group looks on. While such
a discussion illustrates only the very beginning of a therapeutic
relationship, it often is a highly significant and real experience.
Observation of play-therapy contacts can usually be arranged,
and the ethical problems involved are somewhat less complex.
And since we have a one-way vision observation room next to

the playroom, the physical problem is a very simple one. This observation of the dynamics of therapy in its most nonverbal form is almost invariably a vivid and meaningful experience.

In addition to this function of providing resources, the instructor endeavors to fit flexibly into the desires of the group for presentations of views. In a recent quarter the group wished presentations on these topics, and they were arranged. A number of faculty members and staff members were utilized in these presentations.

The Process of Client-Centered Therapy
A Demonstration of a Therapeutic Interview
The Problem of Transference
The Emotional Relationship in Therapy
The Meaning of the Internal Frame of Reference
The Relationship of Diagnosis to Therapy
The Development and Present Formulation of the Hypotheses of Client-Centered Therapy
The Criteria of Progress and Success in Therapy
Multiple Therapy
Panel Discussion of Criticisms of Client-Centered Therapy
The Personality Theory Implicit in Client-Centered Therapy

Usually, in this first course, the heart of the learning experience lies in the discussions which occupy half to two-thirds of the formal class meetings, and which often continue in informal groups outside. Since discussion is so important, the aim of the faculty has been to subdivide a class if it is a large one, so that discussion can take place preferably in a group not larger than fifteen.[1] It is in these discussions that the student really comes to grips with his own attitude toward people. Often the most minute practical issue may raise profound personal and philosophical issues. A consideration of what the student, as counselor, would respond to the client's opening statement of his problem, may launch the group into the deepest consideration of what is the

[1] It should be reported, however, that successful discussions have been held with classes of one hundred, without any subdivision. The main difficulty with such large classes is the problem of providing the other resources mentioned above.

counselor's purpose in counseling, how much reliance can be placed on any individual, and whether the forces of the universe are basically constructive, destructive, or neutral.

It would be fruitless to list all the questions which are thus considered in the course, since they come into focus as the result of a fluid process and are different for each group. One issue, however, presents itself so very frequently that it deserves mention. It is the question, To what extent can you basically trust the individual and the forces within him? Individuals and groups work out very different answers. Some feel that you can rely on the capacities of the individual in simple personal problems, but not when problems are severe; or in the realm of personal problems, but not in politics; or that perhaps you can trust such a capacity in individual therapy, but as one individual said, "to trust the individual or the group in education, or in problems of labor-management or racial discord, is dangerous." In any event, this issue is faced and considered, and the student tends to formulate some working hypotheses for himself.

Thus in this first course, at its best, the student acquires some type of first-hand experience of therapy, a wide acquaintance with various viewpoints in the field, and a tentative formulation of the way he wishes to work with people. This last is arrived at freely and tentatively, because it is accepted. The student does not have to form his own views *against* some opposing influence (as was sometimes true in our earlier teaching).

Practicum Courses

Following this first course there are two courses in the sequence known as Practicum I and Practicum II in client-centered therapy. Their purpose is to give the student opportunity to use, in increasingly responsible ways, the attitudes and skills which he is acquiring. In addition, it is the aim to have available supervision by experienced individuals at any point where the student desires it. These courses also give the student the chance to look at his own counseling and that carried on by others, as if through a microscope, thanks to the advantages given by electrical recording.

General Purpose. Put somewhat more specifically, it is the purpose of the first practicum to give the student as wide a variety of experience as possible in the establishment and maintenance of a therapeutic relationship with clients, short of assuming the full professional responsibility for therapy. The general purpose of the second practicum, which may be repeated for still another quarter of experience, is to give the opportunity for the student to take full responsibility for carrying on therapy with a few individuals, with adequate supervisory assistance always available to him.

Because the supervisory process has been recognized as being of crucial importance in these courses, the numbers in the courses have been steadily decreased. At one time twenty-five to thirty were accepted in each group. This number has been cut to twenty, to fifteen, to ten, and there is at present sentiment among the faculty for making it almost an apprentice type of training in which one staff member might work with three to five students intensively over a two-quarter period.

In these practicum courses as carried on at present, there is a roughly graded series of available experiences which are described below. Probably no one student has utilized every one of these experiences, but he may engage in as many as are feasible for him. There is no sharp division between the two courses and a student is permitted to move forward as rapidly as he is able. Hence he may carry full responsibility for a therapeutic case in his first practicum course if he is ready, though this is intended as an opportunity primarily available in the second practicum. Because of this fluidity, and because there is overlap in the opportunities available, the whole range of experiences is described below in sequence. It should be understood that those given first are more likely to be a part of the first practicum, while the later elements tend to come in the second.

Role-taking and Simple Interviewing. Role-taking has been found to be a very useful elementary procedure. Students are encouraged to take the role of someone whom they know well, and talk out some of the problems of this person, with another student acting as counselor. As described, this device may seem artificial, but it develops a surprising amount of reality and at times can become just as real for the counselor as actual therapy. The most significant utilization of this procedure has been for the instructor to play the role of a client — often some client with whom he is currently working, so that he can take the role vividly — while a student acts as counselor. This "counseling" may be carried on either in front of the group, in order to provide material for discussion, or with the individual student in private. It has proved to have a great deal of value to the student, and has also helped the instructor to gauge the progress of the student. It is a particularly good basis for observing and experiencing the student's attitudes as they operate in therapy. When the "instructor-client" says to the student, "I felt as though you were thinking so hard about what you were doing that you weren't too much interested in me," or "I felt as if you were telling me what my attitudes were rather than trying to get into this thing with me," such expressions of feeling have real impact. The student is able to learn how he is perceived and experienced by the client, and this learning is a valuable one. From the role-taking experience he can gain almost all the learnings which would come from dealing with an actual client, without, however, being burdened by a feeling of heavy responsibility which might create anxiety.

Another way in which role-taking may profitably be used is in relation to problems of professional relationships. How is the student going to handle problems such as these when he has completed his training and is functioning as a therapist; a situation in which a school administrator wants information about one of the counselor's student clients; the relationship with a superior who has a very different orientation toward counseling; the relationship with a social worker who wants him to put pressure on a client to get a job; the interpretation of what he is doing to other professional people who know little about therapy? These and other real professional situations may be brought to life through role-playing, thus giving the student an opportunity to think through his handling of them before he actually meets them. The device has the particular advantage of enabling him to see that his therapeutic orientation has something to contribute to his handling of professional relations. It also helps him to see that, in situations in which he is ego-involved, the expression of his own attitudes is what frees him to be understanding of the attitudes of the other person, a point which otherwise he may miss if he thinks only about problems of therapy.

Another way in which attitudes and techniques may be put into action, without overweighting the student with responsibility, is through casual interviews. This is a procedure not without certain disadvantages and risks, but cautiously used it may have value. For example, students have been encouraged to visit patients at an institution for incurables. The visit may be in part simply a friendly chat, yet when emotionalized attitudes are expressed, the student's endeavor to understand deeply and with empathy may permit a constructive and cathartic release. The gravity of the total situation makes it unlikely that the student will be tempted to use his skills as "tricks of interviewing," an outcome which otherwise is possible, and which constitutes, in our opinion, training away from therapy rather than for therapy.

Counseling of Each Other. One of the most useful early training experiences has been for students to counsel with each other. The student is encouraged to select from the group someone with whom he will be comfortable, and to pair up with him for counseling experience. While one member of the pair becomes a client and talks out some problem, often a minor one, the other member of the pair is counselor. They may at another time reverse the situation, or a student may choose to be a client with one fellow student, a counselor with another. Recording equipment is available so that these interviews can be recorded, listened to, and discussed.

Even when this counseling remains at a superficial level it is a most useful experience because it gives the student the opportunity to learn, in the discussion after the interview, how he is experienced when he is endeavoring to be a therapist. Sometimes both members of the pair are willing to have a third person present as observer, and in this instance the counselor is able to learn how his functioning seems to a neutral party. Since all the comments and reactions can be understood even more deeply by listening to the recording, the relationship is indeed viewed under a complex type of social microscope.

As might be expected, such mutual counseling frequently goes beyond a superficial level. One member or the other may feel enough confidence in the relationship to use it for personal therapy, sometimes at a deep level. Here the student who is functioning as counselor can carry on with comfort, since it has been understood in advance that either the client or the counselor may withdraw from the situation if he finds that he is uncomfortable. Thus if the student-counselor finds that the student-client is going beyond what he feels competent to handle, he may transfer his client to one of the staff counselors. Often, however, he carries through, thus obtaining his first complete experience of therapeutic responsibility.

The supervision of the counseling in these student pairs constitutes an important part of the practicum experience. What is involved in the supervision depends upon the needs and desires of the individual. In some instances the student-counselor may feel concerned about various aspects of what he is doing, and the relationship with the instructor is essentially a therapeutic one, in which he talks out his concerns and reorients his attitudes toward the task. At a later time, or with another student who feels more secure, the instructor may raise questions to bring crucial issues to light, or may tell how other counselors have handled certain situations, in order to broaden the scope of the student's thinking. In some instances the student may want to have specific criticisms, and if so, the instructor analyzes the interview critically, from his own point of view. The general aim of the supervision is to respect the degree of confidence and skill which exists at this point in the student, to help him clarify his own attitudes, to help him see other ways of thinking and doing, provided that all these helps still leave him free to do as he feels is right.

Multiple Therapy. Within the past year, to further enrich the practicum experience, we have been experimenting with multiple therapy as it has been developed by Whitaker and Warkentin (220. 221). Haigh and Kell (77) have described the use which has been made of it in our own Center. We regard the development of this new procedure, and its adaptation to the training function by Whitaker and his colleagues, as one of the most important social inventions of recent years in this field.

Without attempting a discussion of multiple therapy, it may be said that it is the discovery that if two or even more than two therapists begin with the client, the relationship is formed to both of them, and therapy proceeds just as meaningfully as it would with one therapist, though perhaps a little differently. With some clients it may even facilitate therapy. From the point of view of our immediate interest in training, however, it means that two therapists have lived through, emotionally, the same therapeutic relationship. The discussions of the process in the client and of the feelings that each therapist has toward the functioning of the other, have a vividness and reality achievable in no other way.

The specific manner in which we are using multiple therapy in the practicum training involves every student in two ways. Each student is given the opportunity to become a co-therapist with an experienced staff member in handling a client. The client is one of the other students in the group. The student who is co-therapist in this experience is given the opportunity to be a client in another multiple therapy relationship, and the client in this first trio is given the opportunity to become a co-therapist in another relationship. Thus each student may act as co-therapist in one situation with a staff member, and as client in another situation, in a relationship with a staff member and a fellow-student as co-therapists.

This arrangement has an astonishing number of advantages. The student can begin to function as therapist earlier, because the staff member can carry the major burden of therapy, with the student entering in only to the degree that he feels comfortable and confident. The student can gradually feel the responsibility for the delicate handling of a real life — a responsibility more keenly felt because this is a fellow-student, and because, as client in another relationship, he experiences the importance of that delicate handling in himself. The importance of holding all interview material in absolute confidence, for example, is experienced simultaneously from the client's and therapist's point of view. In his two situations he has the opportunity to see and intimately experience the mode of working of three other therapists — an experience which cuts much deeper than can even a recording. In his discussions with his co-therapist following the interviews, there is the opportunity for genuine expression of feeling on both sides, and in this way still another significant experiencing of a relationship is provided. Listening to the recording of the interview gives still another means of objectifying and considering how one is using one's self. In addition to all these advantages, this plan of using multiple therapy provides the opportunity for personal therapy for each student, with no additional investment of staff time beyond what would be needed for training alone.

Whitaker gives a good description of the way in which multiple therapy subtly yet fully introduces the student to the therapeutic situation.

> I fear that if one utilizes "noes" as one is inclined to when he works in conjunction with someone who is not a trained therapist, he will frequently alienate the student. He feels so inadequate when he comes into the situation that even a very quiet "no" makes him feel hopelessly inadequate and afraid to continue. This method amounts to teaching by emulation. He begins to see you; not the things you say, not the things you do, but he sees you and the patient reacting to each other. For two or three sessions he may not say anything or perhaps only a few words. He will, however, reverberate in his thinking and feeling to this joint experience, since he brings not only his intellect but his whole personality. (220, p. 903)

There are of course certain cautions, and as we continue to use this procedure real disadvantages may emerge. There is the question whether as client the student will reveal himself as deeply to another student as if he were alone with the experienced therapist. There is the question whether, since each student is both client and therapist, the whole training atmosphere may become too introspective, too much of a collective looking within.

Thus far these possible disadvantages have not presented serious problems.

Independent Handling of Cases. The goal of the practicum courses is to give the student experience in the handling of individuals in a therapeutic relationship, and as soon as he feels he is ready to do so, he engages in this responsible practice of his profession.

As the situation has developed, most of this beginning counseling is carried on in cooperating agencies. At any one time there are several organizations in which counseling may be done. During one period or another we have had such arrangements with a number of public grammar schools, high schools, and junior colleges; with the Y.M.C.A. hotel, with night schools, with social welfare agencies and institutions. Through this ramified experience we have learned that it is most effective if a staff member first makes the contact with the agency, and if help is desired, as is usually the case, begins to render that service himself. As he carries on part-time counseling or play therapy within the cooperating agency, he can bring in students, one by one, who also take cases and expand the service. Even if their handling of clients is not too expert at first, the staff member's work provides a solid core of satisfactory service and the opportunity for supervisory help if the student wishes it. In addition, the staff member can communicate with the agency staff on the problems and questions which they feel about this service work. Teachers and principals may be concerned that the counselor does not tell them what the child says. Perhaps the child is talking about them in ways which are not entirely true. Sometimes they feel that the child is growing worse rather than better (which may of course happen). These or similar questions arise in cooperating with any agency, and the staff member facilitates open expression of feeling, and states his own feelings as well. Through this type of interchange, difficulties are kept on a realistic level and channels of free communication are kept open.

As a student-therapist handles cases in such a setting he develops in therapeutic ability, in sense of professional responsibility, in ability to adapt his basic principles to new situations. He may record some of his contacts for further detailed analysis of the sort which is only possible through recording. He may broaden the implementation of his therapeutic views by undertaking play therapy with children, if previously he has engaged only in therapy with adults. He may, in some of the institutional resources, have the opportunity of conducting group therapy with children, adolescents, or adults. He can develop the scope of his professional functioning.

Throughout this experience supervision remains available, as always. It has not been in accord with the views of the faculty to impose supervision at any point. In fact, probably some term other than "supervision" would be preferable to convey the notion of a resource person, available for consultation, whose function is to assist the student to discover more clearly the issues and problems and flaws in his work, a person who will serve as an interested but noncoercive and nonjudgmental source of stimulation and clarification.

Internship or Courtesy Appointment

From the group of graduate students who have completed two or more quarters of the practicum courses, applications are accepted for positions on the staff of the Counseling Center. The usual term for the position would be an internship, since it is in most instances an unpaid position which the student desires in order to round out further his own professional training. But because there is some connotation of an underling in the term "intern," we have usually described the position as a courtesy appointment to the staff of the Center. This name seems better to fit the actual functioning of these individuals.

From the applicants, those persons are selected who seem to show the most professional ability and promise. To some degree, self-selection has been used, and has significant advantages. However, a staff committee has also served a selective function. In recent years the Center has had fifteen to twenty of these courtesy appointees at any one time. This number may be considered in relation to the fact that there are ten or twelve paid staff members, almost all of them giving only part time to the Center.

These courtesy staff members function in every way as full staff members. They have responsibility for their cases, take part in decisions on policy and other matters in staff meeting, serve on staff committees, and in all ways regard themselves as having a responsible share in the whole venture. Both in the professional and in the administrative realm they function in the ways in which they feel they are able to contribute. Since all committees are self-appointed, we have even had the interesting phenomenon of an unpaid courtesy appointee serving on the budget committee, planning such matters as salary rates, allocation of funds, and the like. This situation caused no comment whatsoever in the staff when it occurred, and it was only when the writer considered how this would appear to those accustomed to more conventional organizational procedures that he felt it worthy of mention.

The administrative side of staff experience as it relates to the courtesy appointee is stressed here only to indicate that the experience of internship involves a still further broadening of his appreciation of how applicable are the principles of human relationships which he finds effective in therapy. It is living evidence that, though staff relationships are not always smooth, nevertheless he can trust himself to participate as freely as he dares, he can express real attitudes, he can accept the attitudes of others, he can rely upon the basic tendencies of the group, and he can thus learn more deeply the hypothesis of all his work.

When the courtesy appointee joins the staff he is encouraged to choose one or more staff members, with whom he feels comfortable, to use as resource persons in his cases. On first joining the staff, he is apt to avail himself of the opportunity for consultation and supervision to a considerable degree, but gradually he feels less need to do so. As time goes on, the major part of his professional training comes from two sources — his continuous learning from the clients with whom he is working, and the give and take of discussion with other staff members, in both large and small groups. In other words, he has become a full-fledged member of his profession, being self-responsible for his work, but turning freely to his colleagues for help whenever he needs it.

Research in Therapy

During the period of practicum or internship, the advanced student is also likely to be thinking about research. Many of these students are about to undertake the research for their doctoral dissertations. It is natural that some aspect of therapy should challenge them — some measure of outcomes, some study of the therapeutic process or the therapist-client relationship, some phase of basic personality dynamics as seen in therapy. A great deal of the research in therapy cited earlier in this book has been done by students who have reached this stage of their training. In carrying on the basic theoretical thinking necessary for his research, and in clarifying the concepts with which he is to work, each student finds that he is enriching his professional function by his scholarly and critical research interests, and that his research, on the other hand, is greatly deepened in its significance by the continuing contact with personal dynamics in therapy.

Outcomes

It has been our experience that any student who has completed the sequence of training experiences outlined, imperfect though they may be in their detailed implementation, is ready to begin functioning as a therapist, and is open to new learning in this field. He is effective as a therapist, able to deal with a rather wide range of individuals. He is sufficiently secure within himself to be able to adapt his therapeutic functioning to new situations and new problems of relationships. He has a security in the methodology of finding new truth, so that he is able to tolerate a lack of finality in his thinking. He has the basis for growing and developing within himself, and for making a contribution to his profession and to scientific knowledge.

Thus though we are all too aware of our shortcomings in the way in which we carry through the parts of this training sequence, we find it quite unnecessary to apologize for the products of that sequence. We are well aware that the program will change in the future as it has in the past. One basic principle seems to persist — that we endeavor increasingly to supply the student with rich and responsible opportunities for learning, but that we rely upon him for the sensitive, selective, constructive use of these opportunities.

SUGGESTED READINGS

There are relatively few published references which relate to training in therapy. For a formal but comprehensive statement of a training program for the clinical psychologist, including a program in therapy, see the report of the American Psychological Association Committee on Graduate Training (160). The Conference on Training in Clinical Psychology sponsored by the Macy Foundation (80) presents a series of papers on this topic, mostly psychoanalytically and medically oriented. The views are at some variance with the first reference and with the point of view of this chapter. An eclectic type of training is proposed by Luchins (120). A stimulating paper on the training of the non-medical therapist and his place in the clinical field, together with a proposed curriculum, is presented by Brody and Grey (36).

A short training program in therapy, planned for physicians, is described in *Teaching Psychotherapeutic Medicine* (226, especially pp. 1–26). The brief program for training VA Personal Counselors is described by Blocksma and Porter (34). The only research evaluation of any training program is that of Blocksma (33), which is not yet published.

The concept of multiple therapy as it is used in training is presented in three papers, two by Whitaker and colleagues (220, 221) and one by Haigh and Kell (77).

PART **III** *Implications*

for Psychological Theory

Chapter 11 · A Theory of Personality and Behavior

As clinical and research evidence accumulates, it is inevitable that those interested in client-centered therapy should try to formulate theories which would contain and explain the observed facts, and which would point out profitable directions for further research. This chapter attempts to report the present stage of our thinking in this matter of constructing a more generalized statement of personality dynamics and behavior. In considerable degree, the task is simply that of pulling together the theoretical formulations which have been explicit or implicit in all our discussions of therapy and of its effect upon personality. It is hoped, however, that a focus upon, and a summarization of, the basic conceptual elements will prove useful.

The process of theory-building in regard to personality has gone on apace in recent years in psychology, and a number of contributions have enriched our thinking. To mention (in order of publication) some which have been presented in the decade 1940–50, Goldstein (69), Angyal (9), Maslow (127, 128), Mowrer and Kluckhohn (137), Lecky (109), Sullivan (205), Masserman (129), Murphy (141), Cameron (38), Murray and Kluckhohn (104), White (222), Snygg and Combs (200), and Burrow (37) have all presented, either explicitly or implicitly, statements of a new or revised theory of personality. Each of these authors has contributed significantly to thinking about personality dynamics and to a deeper consideration of theory.

With this burgeoning of theoretical formulation it may seem presumptuous to offer still another conceptual framework for the regarding of personality. On the other hand, it appears probable that out of this wealth of concept-building, with each researcher offering the formulation which from his own experience appears best to contain the facts, new strides in research and in understanding can grow. It is in this spirit that the present chapter is written. Obviously, it would not be included if the writer did not feel that previous theories do not adequately account for all the facts. On the other hand, it is not presented in a critical frame of mind, since much has been gained by a study of these other contributions, and both in ways that are known and doubtless in ways that are unknown, they have influenced the present author.

Just as each one of the other writers is influenced by his professional experience, so has the statement which follows been molded by a score of years of first-hand contact with clinical problems, and more particularly and more deeply by the decade of struggle to formulate an effective and consistent psychotherapy, the process of that effort being the changing formulations of the client-centered approach.   The increased entrance into the thinking and feeling of the other person, characteristic of client-centered therapy, has necessitated profound changes in the author's whole theoretical ideation.   Like Maslow, the writer would confess that in the early portion of his professional life he held a theoretical view opposed at almost every point to the view he has gradually come to adopt as a result of clinical experience and clinically oriented research.

In order to present the thinking as clearly as possible, and also in order to make possible the detection of flaws or inconsistencies, the material which follows is offered as a series of propositions, with a brief explanation and exposition of each proposition. Since the theory is regarded as tentative, questions are raised in regard to various propositions, particularly where it seems uncertain that they adequately account for all the phenomena. Some of these propositions must be regarded as assumptions, while the majority may be regarded as hypotheses subject to proof or disproof. Taken as a whole, the series of propositions presents a theory of behavior which attempts to account for the phenomena previously known, and also for the facts regarding personality and behavior which have more recently been observed in therapy.

In many ways the propositions presented draw upon previous formulations, and in many ways they differ. There will be no attempt to point out these similarities and differences, since that would detract from a straightforward and systematic presentation. The reader is referred to the references given for the recent theoretical formulations by other psychologists.

THE PROPOSITIONS

I) *Every individual exists in a continually changing world of experience of which he is the center.*

This private world may be called the phenomenal field, the experiential field, or described in other terms. It includes all that is experienced by the organism, whether or not these experiences are consciously perceived. Thus the pressure of the chair seat against my buttocks is something I have been experiencing for an hour, but only as I think and write about it does the symbolization of that experience become present in consciousness. It seems likely that Angyal is correct in stating that consciousness consists of the symbolization of some of our experiences.

It should be recognized that in this private world of experience of the individual, only a portion of that experience, and probably a very small portion, is *consciously* experienced. Many of our sensory and visceral sensations are not symbolized. It is also true, however, that a large portion of this world of experience is *available* to consciousness, and may become conscious if the need of the individual causes certain sensations to come into focus because they are associated with the satisfaction of a need. In other words, most of the individual's experiences constitute the ground of the perceptual field, but they can easily become figure, while other experiences slip back into ground. We shall deal later with some aspects of experience which the individual *prevents* from coming into figure.

An important truth in regard to this private world of the individual is that it can only be known, in any genuine or complete sense, to the individual himself. No matter how adequately we attempt to measure the stimulus — whether it be a beam of light, a pinprick, a failure on an examination, or some more complex situation — and no matter how much we attempt to measure the perceiving organism — whether by psychometric tests or physiological calibrations — it is still true that the individual is the only one who can know how the experience was perceived. I can never know with vividness or completeness how a pinprick or a failure on an examination is experienced by you. The world of experience is for each individual, in a very significant sense, a private world.

This complete and first-hand acquaintance with the world of his total experience is, however, only potential; it does not hold true of the individual's general functioning. There are many of the impulses which I feel, or the sensations which I experience, which I can permit into consciousness only under certain conditions. Hence my actual awareness of and knowledge of my total phenomenal field is limited. It is still true, however, that potentially I am the only one who can know it in its completeness. Another can never know it as fully as I.

II) *The organism reacts to the field as it is experienced and perceived. This perceptual field is, for the individual, "reality."*

This is a simple proposition, one of which we are all aware in our own experience, yet it is a point which is often overlooked. I do not react to some absolute reality, but to my perception of this reality. It is this perception which for me *is* reality. Snygg and Combs give the example of two men driving at night on a western road. An object looms up in the middle of the road ahead. One of the men sees a large boulder, and reacts with fright. The other, a native of the country, sees a tumbleweed and reacts with nonchalance. Each reacts to the reality as perceived.

This proposition could be illustrated from the daily experience of everyone. Two individuals listen to a radio speech made by a political candidate about whom they have no previous knowledge. They are both subjected to the same auditory stimulation. Yet one perceives the candidate as a demagogue, a trickster, a false prophet, and reacts accordingly. The other perceives him as a leader of the people, a person of high aims and purposes. Each is reacting to the reality as he has perceived it. In the same way, two young parents each perceive differently the behavior of their offspring. The son and daughter have differing perceptions of their parents. And the behavior in all these instances is appropriate to the reality-as-perceived. This same proposition is exemplified in so-called abnormal conditions as well. The psychotic who perceives that his food is poisoned, or that some malevolent group is out to "get" him, reacts to his reality-as-perceived in much the same fashion that you or I would respond if we (more "realistically") perceived our food as contaminated, or our enemies as plotting against us.

To understand this concept that reality is, for the individual, his perceptions, we may find it helpful to borrow a phrase from the semanticists. They have pointed out that words and symbols bear to the world of reality the same relationship as a map to the territory which it represents. This relationship also applies to perception and reality. We live by a perceptual "map" which is never reality itself. This is a useful concept to keep in mind, for it may help to convey the nature of the world in which the individual lives.

To the present writer it seems unnecessary to posit or try to explain any concept of "true" reality. For purposes of understanding psychological phenomena, reality is, for the individual, his perceptions. Unless we wish to involve ourselves in philosophical questions, we do not need to attempt to solve the question as to what *really* constitutes reality. For psychological purposes, reality is basically the private world of individual perceptions, though for social purposes reality consists of those perceptions which have a high degree of commonality among various individuals. Thus this desk is "real" because most people in our culture would have a perception of it which is very similar to my own.

While it is not necessary for our purposes to define any absolute concept of reality, it should be noted that we are continually checking our perceptions against one another, or adding them one to another, so that they become more reliable guides to "reality." For example, I see some salt in a dish. That, for me at that instant, is reality. If I taste it and it tastes salty, my perception is further confirmed. But if it tastes sweet, my whole interpretation of the situation is changed, and both in seeing and tasting I perceive the material as sugar. Thus each perception is essentially a hypothesis — a hypothesis related to the individual's need — and many of these perceptions are tested and re-tested by experience. As Burrow puts it, "Man's consistent relationship to the outer world came about through the agreement of his own sequence of sense-reactions with the sequence of reactions existing outside him. . . . Only man's neural conformity to the observable consistency of external phenomena has made possible the intelligent consistency of his own behavior in respect to the outer world." (37, p. 101) Thus the world comes to be composed of a series of tested hypotheses which provide much security. It acquires a certain predictability upon which we depend. Yet mingled with these perceptions, which have been confirmed by a variety of experiences, are perceptions which remain completely unchecked. These untested perceptions are also a part of our personal reality, and may have as much authority as those which have been checked.

That the perceptual field is the reality to which the individual reacts is often strikingly illustrated in therapy, where it is frequently evident that when the perception changes, the reaction of the individual changes. As long as a parent is perceived as a domineering individual, that is the reality to which the individual reacts. When he is perceived as a rather pathetic individual trying to maintain his status, then the reaction to this new "reality" is quite different.

III) *The organism reacts as an organized whole to this phenomenal field.*

Although there are still some who are primarily concerned with the segmental or atomistic type of organic reaction, there is increasing acceptance of the fact that one of the most basic characteristics of organic life is its tendency toward total, organized, goal-directed responses. This is true of those responses which are primarily physiological, as well as of those which we think of as psychological. Take such a matter as the maintenance of the water balance in the body. It has been shown that this is ordinarily maintained by the activity of the posterior lobe of the pituitary gland, which, when the body loses water, secretes more of an antidiuretic hormone, thus reducing the secretion of water by the kidney. This reaction would appear to be definitely of the atomistic type, reducible in the last analysis to purely chemical factors. But where the posterior lobe is experimentally removed, the animal drinks very large amounts of water, and thus maintains a satisfactory water balance in spite of the loss of the regulating mechanism (91, pp. 601–602). It is thus the total, organized, goal-directed response which appears to be basic, as evidenced by the fact that, when one avenue is blocked off, the animal organizes to utilize another avenue to the same goal. The same would be true of various compensatory physiological phenomena.

In the psychological realm, any simple S–R type of explanation of behavior seems almost impossible. A young woman talks for an hour about her antagonism to her mother. She finds, following this, that a persistent asthmatic condition, which she has not even mentioned to the counselor, is greatly improved. On the other hand, a man who feels that his security in his work is being seriously threatened, develops ulcers. It is extremely cumbersome to try to account for such phenomena on the basis of an atomistic chain of events. The outstanding fact which must be taken into theoretical account is that the organism is at all times a total organized system, in which alteration of any part may produce changes in any other part. Our study of such part phenomena must start from this central fact of consistent, goal-directed organization.

IV) *The organism has one basic tendency and striving — to actualize, maintain, and enhance the experiencing organism.*

Rather than many needs and motives, it seems entirely possible that all organic and psychological needs may be described as partial aspects of this one fundamental need. It is difficult to find satisfactory words for this proposition. The particular phrasing is from Snygg and Combs. The words used are an attempt to describe the observed directional force in organic life — a force which has been regarded as basic by many scientists, but which has not been too well described in testable or operational terms.

We are talking here about the tendency of the organism to maintain itself — to assimilate food, to behave defensively in the face of threat, to achieve the goal of self-maintenance even when the usual pathway to that goal is blocked. We are speaking of the tendency of the organism to move in the direction of maturation, as maturation is defined for each species. This involves self-actualization, though it should be understood that this too is a directional term. The organism does not develop to the full its capacity for suffering pain, nor does the human individual develop or actualize his capacity for terror or, on the physiological level, his capacity for vomiting. The organism actualizes itself in the direction of greater differentiation of organs and of function. It moves in the direction of limited expansion through growth, expansion through extending itself by means of its tools, and expansion through reproduction. It moves in the direction of greater independence or self-responsibility. Its movement, as Angyal has pointed out (9, pp. 32–50), is in the direction of an increasing self-government, self-regulation, and autonomy, and away from heteronymous control, or control by external forces. This is true whether we are speaking of entirely unconscious organic processes, such as the regulation of body heat, or such uniquely human and intellectual functions as the choice of life goals. Finally, the self-actualization of the organism appears to be in the direction of socialization, broadly defined.

The directional trend we are endeavoring to describe is evident in the life of the individual organism from conception to maturity, at whatever level of organic complexity. It is also evident in the process of evolution, the direction being defined by a comparison of life low on the evolutionary scale with types of organisms which have developed later, or are regarded as farther along in the process of evolution. Thus the directional tendency which we are discussing will be defined most adequately by comparing the undeveloped with the developed organism, the simple organism with the complex, the organism early or low on the evolutionary scale with the organism which has developed later and is regarded as higher. Whatever generalized differences are found constitute the direction of the basic tendency we are postulating.

Ideas similar to this proposition are being increasingly advanced and accepted by psychologists and others. The term "self-actualization" is used by Goldstein (69) to describe this one basic striving. Mowrer and Kluckhohn stress the "basic propensity of living things to function in such a way as to preserve and increase integration" (137, p. 74). This is a slightly different concept, but directional in nature. Sullivan points out that "the basic direction of the organism is forward" (205, p. 48). Horney gives a vivid description of this force as it is experienced in therapy: "The ultimate driving force is the person's unrelenting will to come to grips with himself, a wish to grow and to leave nothing untouched that prevents growth" (90, p. 175). Angyal sums up his thinking on this point in the following statement. "Life is an autonomous dynamic event which takes place between the organism and the environment. Life processes do not merely tend to preserve life but transcend the momentary status quo of the organism, expanding itself continually and imposing its autonomous determination upon an ever increasing realm of events" (9, p. 48).

It is our experience in therapy which has brought us to the point of giving this proposition a central place. The therapist becomes very much aware that the forward-moving tendency of the human organism is the basis upon which he relies most deeply and fundamentally. It is evident not only in the general tendency of clients to move in the direction of growth when the factors in the situation are clear, but is most dramatically shown in very serious cases where the individual is on the brink of psychosis or suicide. Here the therapist is very keenly aware that the only force upon which he can basically rely is the organic tendency toward ongoing growth and enhancement. Something of our experience has been summarized by the writer in an earlier paper.

> As I study, as deeply as I am able, the recorded clinical cases which have been so revealing of personal dynamics, I find what seems to me to be a very significant thing. I find that the urge for a greater degree of independence, the desire for a self-determined integration, the tendency to strive, even through much pain, toward a socialized maturity, is as strong as — no, is stronger than — the desire for comfortable dependence, the need to rely upon external authority for assurance. . . . Clinically I find it to be true that though an individual may remain dependent because he has always been so, or may drift into dependence without realizing what he is doing, or may temporarily wish to be dependent because his situation appears desperate, I have yet to find the individual who, when he examines his situation deeply, and feels that he perceives it clearly, deliberately chooses dependence, deliberately chooses to have the integrated direction of himself undertaken by another. When all the elements are clearly perceived, the balance seems invariably in the direction of the painful but ultimately rewarding path of self-actualization or growth. (168, p. 218)

It would be grossly inaccurate to suppose that the organism operates smoothly in the direction of self-enhancement and growth. It would be perhaps more correct to say that the organism moves through struggle and pain toward enhancement and growth. The whole process may be symbolized and illustrated by the child's learning to walk. The first steps involve struggle, and usually pain. Often it is true that the immediate reward involved in taking a few steps is in no way commensurate with the pain of falls and bumps. The child may, because of the pain, revert to crawling for a time. Yet, in the overwhelming majority of individuals, the forward direction of growth is more powerful than the satisfactions of remaining infantile. The child will actualize himself, in spite of the painful experiences in so doing. In the same way, he will become independent, responsible, self-governing, socialized, in spite of the pain which is often involved in these steps. Even where he does not, because of a variety of circumstances, exhibit growth of these more complex sorts, one may still rely on the fact that the tendency is present. Given the opportunity for clear-cut choice between forward-moving and regressive behavior, the tendency will operate.

One puzzle that is not adequately solved by this proposition is the question, "Why must the factors of choice be clearly *perceived* in order for this forward-moving tendency to operate?" It would seem that unless experience is adequately symbolized, unless suitably accurate differentiations are made, the individual mistakes regressive behavior for self-enhancing behavior. This aspect will be more fully discussed in Proposition XI and following.

V) *Behavior is basically the goal-directed attempt of the organism to satisfy its needs as experienced, in the field as perceived.*

This proposition becomes somewhat modified in the human organism, as we shall see, by the development of the self. Let us first consider it as it applies to organisms in general, and in the human infant before the self comes to play an important role in the regulation of behavior.

All needs have a basic relatedness, if we accept Proposition IV, in that they all spring from and have reference to, the basic tendency to maintain and enhance the organism. These needs occur as physiological tensions which, when experienced, form the basis of behavior which appears functionally (though not consciously) designed to reduce the tension and to maintain and enhance the organism. The need itself is not necessarily consciously experienced; there are seemingly different levels of description. In hunger, for example, stomach contractions occur which ordinarily are not directly experienced. The excitation which is thus set up may be experienced vaguely and below the conscious level, nevertheless bringing about behavior which is in the direction of food, or it may be symbolized and perceived on the conscious level as hunger.

The question arises, Do all needs have their origin in physiological tensions? Are the needs for affection and achievement, for example, which seems to be significantly related to the maintenance and enhancement of the organism, biologically based?

We should gain by well-planned research on this point. The work by Ribble (162) and others would seem to indicate that the need for affection is a physiological need, and that the infant who does not have adequate close physical contact with a mother-person is left in a state of unsatisfied physiological tension. If this is true of the infant, then it is easy to see how this need, like all the others, becomes elaborated and channelized through cultural conditioning into needs which are only remotely based upon the underlying physiological tension. Much more work needs to be done in this area before we have any deep understanding of this problem. The research to date is poorly planned and poorly controlled.

It is noted that behavior is postulated as a reaction to the field as perceived. This point, like some of the other propositions, is proved every day in our experience, but is often overlooked. The reaction is not to reality, but to the perception of reality. A horse, sensing danger, will try to reach the safety and security which he perceives in his stall, even though the barn may be in flames. A man in the desert will struggle just as hard to reach the "lake" which he perceives in a mirage, as to reach a real water hole. At a more complex level, a man may strive for money because he perceives money as the source of emotional security, even though in fact it may not satisfy his need. Often, of course, the perception has a high degree of correspondence with reality, but it is important to recognize that it is the perception, not the reality, which is crucial in determining behavior.

It should also be mentioned that in this concept of motivation all the effective elements exist in the present. Behavior is not "caused" by something which occurred in the past. Present tensions and present needs are the only ones which the organism endeavors to reduce or satisfy. While it is true that past experience has certainly served to modify the meaning which will be perceived in present experiences, yet there is no behavior except to meet a present need.

VI) *Emotion accompanies and in general facilitates such goal-directed behavior, the kind of emotion being related to the socking versus the consummatory aspects of the behavior, and the intensity of the emotion being related to the perceived significance of the behavior for the maintenance and enhancement of the organism.*

In this goal-seeking effort which is termed behavior, what is the place of emotion, feeling, emotionalized attitudes? Any brief answer is likely to contain serious inadequacies, yet some framework for our thinking may be supplied by Proposition VI. We may think of emotions as falling primarily into two groups — the unpleasant and/or excited feelings, and the calm and/or satisfied emotions. The first group tends to accompany the seeking effort of the organism, and the second to accompany satisfaction of the need, the consummatory experience. The first group appears to have the effect of integrating and concentrating behavior upon the goal, rather than having the disintegrating effect which some psychologists have pictured. Thus, in anything but excessive degree, fear accelerates the organization of the individual in the direction of escape from danger, and competitive jealousy concentrates the efforts of the individual to surpass. Leeper (110) has formulated this point of view more fully.

The intensity of the emotional reaction appears to vary according to the perceived relationship of the behavior to the maintenance and enhancement of the organism. Thus if my leap to the curb to escape the oncoming automobile is perceived as making the difference between life and death, it will be accompanied by strong emotion. The reading of another chapter tonight in a new psychology book, a behavior which is seen as having a slight relationship to my development, will be accompanied by a very mild emotion indeed.

Both these propositions have been worded and discussed as though behavior always had to do with the maintenance and enhancement of the *organism*. As we shall see in later propositions, the development of the self may involve some modification of this, since behavior is then often best described as meeting the needs of the self, sometimes as against the needs of the organism, and emotional intensity becomes gauged more by the degree of involvement of the self than by the degree of involvement of the organism. As applied, however, to the infra-human organism, or to the human infant, Propositions V and VI appear to hold.

VII) *The best vantage point for understanding behavior is from the internal frame of reference of the individual himself.*

It was mentioned in Proposition I that the only person who could fully know his field of experience was the individual himself. Behavior is a reaction to the field as perceived. Jr would therefore appear that behavior might be best understood by gaining, in so far as possible, the internal frame of reference of the person himself, and seeing the world of experience as nearly as possible through his eyes.

What we have been doing for the most part in psychology may be likened to the early studies of primitive societies. The observer reported that these primitive peoples ate various ridiculous foods, held fantastic and meaningless ceremonies, and behaved in ways that were a mixture of virtue and depravity. The thing that he did not see was that he was observing from his own frame of reference and placing his own values upon their modes of behavior. We do the same thing in psychology when we speak of "trial-and-error behavior," "delusions," "abnormal behavior," and so on. We fail to see that we are evaluating the person from our own, or from some fairly general, frame of reference, but that the only way to understand his behavior meaningfully is to understand it as he perceives it himself, just as the only way to understand another culture is to assume the frame of reference of that culture. When that is done, the various meaningless and strange behaviors are seen to be part of a meaningful and goal-directed activity. There is then no such thing as random trial-and-error behavior, no such thing as a delusion, except as the individual may apply these terms to his past behavior. In the present, the behavior is always purposeful, and in response to reality as it is perceived.

If we could empathically experience all the sensory and visceral sensations of the individual, could experience his whole phenomenal field including both the conscious elements and also those experiences not brought to the conscious level, we should have the perfect basis for understanding the meaningfulness of his behavior and for predicting his future behavior. This is an unattainable ideal. Because it is unattainable, one line of development in psychology has been to understand and evaluate and predict the person's behavior from an external frame of reference. This development has not been too satisfactory, largely because such a high degree of inference is involved. The interpretation of the meaning of a given bit of behavior comes to depend upon whether the inferences are being made, say, by a student of Clark Hull or a follower of Freud. For this and other reasons, the possibility of utilizing the phenomenal field of the individual as a significant basis for the science of psychology appears promising. There can be agreement on the specific way in which the world is experienced by the individual, and his behavior follows definitely and clearly upon his perception. Consequently, with agreement possible on the datum for a science, science can conceivably grow.

To point out the advantages of viewing behavior from the internal frame of reference is not to say that this is the royal road to learning. There are many drawbacks. For one thing, we are largely limited to gaining an acquaintance with the phenomenal field as it is experienced in consciousness. This means that the greater the area of experience not in consciousness, the more incomplete will be the picture. The more we try to infer what is present in the phenomenal field but not conscious (as in interpreting projective techniques), the more complex grow the inferences until the interpretation of the client's projections may become merely an illustration of the clinician's projections.

Furthermore our knowledge of the person's frame of reference depends primarily upon communication of one sort or another from the individual. Communication is at all times faulty and imperfect. Hence only in clouded fashion can we see the world of experience as it appears to this individual.

We may state the whole situation logically thus:

It is possible to achieve, to some extent, the other person's frame of reference, because many of the perceptual objects — self, parents, teachers, employers, and so on — have counterparts in our own perceptual field, and practically all the attitudes toward these perceptual objects — such as fear, anger, annoyance, love, jealousy, satisfaction — have been present in our own world of experience.

Hence we can infer, quite directly, from the communication of the individual, or less accurately from observation of his behavior, a portion of his perceptual and experiential field.

The more all his experiences are available to his consciousness, the more is it possible for him to convey a total picture of his phenomenal field.

The more his communication is a free expression, unmodified by a need or desire to be defensive, the more adequate will be the communication of the field. (Thus a diary is apt to be a better communication of the perceptual field than a court utterance where the individual is on trial.)

It is probably for the reasons just stated that client-centered counseling has proved to be such a valuable method for viewing behavior from the person's frame of reference. The situation minimizes any need of defensiveness. The counselor's behavior minimizes any prejudicial influence on the attitudes expressed. The person is usually motivated to some degree to communicate his own special world, and the procedures used encourage him to do so. The increasing communication gradually brings more of experience into the realm of awareness, and thus a more accurate and total picture of this individual's world of experience is conveyed. On this basis a much more understandable picture of behavior emerges.

It should also be added that the dynamic results — for the client and for the learning of the therapist — which are achieved in client-centered therapy when even a portion of the perceptual field is communicated, have led us to feel that here is a way of viewing experience which is much closer to the basic laws of personality process and behavior. Not only does there result a more vivid understanding of the meaning of behavior, but the opportunities for new learning are maximized when we approach the individual without a preconceived set of categories which we expect him to fit.

VIII) *A portion of the total perceptual field gradually becomes differentiated as the self.*

Mead, Cooley, Angyal, Lecky, and others have helped to advance our knowledge of the development and functioning of the self. We shall have much to say about various aspects of the operation of the self. For the present the point is made that gradually, as the infant develops, a portion of the total private world becomes recognized as "me," "I," "myself." There are many puzzling and unanswered questions in regard to the dawning concept of the self. We shall try to point out some of these.

Is social interaction necessary in order for a self to develop? Would the hypothetical person reared alone upon a desert island have a self? Is the self primarily a product of the process of symbolization? Is it the fact that experiences may be not only directly experienced, but symbolized and manipulated in thought, that makes the self possible? Is the self simply the symbolized portion of experience? These are some of the questions which shrewd research may be able to answer.

Another point which needs to be made in regard to the development of a conscious self is the fact that it is not necessarily coexistent with the physical organism. Angyal points out that there is no possibility of a sharp line between organism and environment, and that there is likewise no sharp limit between the experience of the self and of the outside world. Whether or not an object or an experience is regarded as a part of the self depends to a considerable extent upon whether or not it is perceived as within the control of the self. Those elements which we control are regarded as a part of self, but when even such an object as a part of our body is out of control, it is experienced as being less a part of the self. The way in which, when a foot "goes to sleep" from lack of circulation, it becomes an object to us rather than a part of self, may be a sufficient illustration. Perhaps it is this "gradient of autonomy" which first gives the infant the awareness of self, as he is for the first time aware of a feeling of control over some aspect of his world of experience.

It should be clear from the foregoing that though some authors use the term "self" as synonymous with "organism" it is here being used in a more restricted sense, namely, the awareness of being, of functioning.

IX) *As a result of interaction with the environment, and particularly as a result of evaluational interaction with others, the structure of self is formed — an organized, fluid, but consistent conceptual pattern of perceptions of characteristics and relationships of the "I" or the "me," together with values attached to these concepts.*

X) *The values attached to experiences, and the values which are a part of the self structure, in some instances are values experienced directly by the organism, and in some instances are values introjected or taken over from others, but perceived in distorted fashion, as if they had been experienced directly.*

It will probably be best to discuss these two important propositions together. In the past few years they have been revised and reworded so many different times by the author that it is quite certain the present statement is inadequate also. Yet within the range of experience which these propositions attempt to symbolize, there seem clearly to be some highly important learnings for the personality theorist.

As the infant interacts with his enviroment he gradually builds up concepts about himself, about the environment, and about himself in relation to the environment. While these concepts are nonverbal, and may not be present in consciousness, this is no barrier to their functioning as guiding principles, as Leeper (111) has shown. Intimately associated with all these experiences is a direct organismic valuing which appears highly important for understanding later development. The very young infant has little uncertainty in valuing. At the same time that there is the dawning awareness of "I experience," there is also the awareness that "I like," "I dislike." "I am cold, and I dislike it," "I am cuddled and I like it," "I can reach my toes and find this enjoyable" — these statements appear to be adequate descriptions of the infant's experience, though he does not have the verbal symbols which we have used. He appears to value those experiences which he perceives as enhancing himself, and to place a negative value on those experiences which seem to threaten himself or which do not maintain or enhance himself.

There soon enters into this picture the evaluation of self by others. "You're a good child," "You're a naughty boy" — these and similar evaluations of himself and of his behavior by his parents and others come to form a large and significant part of the infant's perceptual field. Social experiences, social evaluations by others, become a part of his phenomenal field along with experiences not involving others — for example, that radiators are hot, stairs are dangerous, and candy tastes good.

It is at this stage of development, it would seem, that there takes place a type of distorted symbolization of experience, and a denial of experience to awareness, which has much significance for the later development of psychological maladjustment. Let us try to put this in general and schematic terms.

One of the first and most important aspects of the self-experience of the ordinary child is that he is loved by his parents. He perceives himself as lovable, worthy of love, and his relationship to his parents as one of affection. He experiences all this with satisfaction. This is a significant and core element of the structure of self as it begins to form.

At this same time he is experiencing positive sensory values, is experiencing enhancement, in other ways. It is enjoyable to have a bowel movement at any time or place that the physiological tension is experienced. It is satisfying and enhancing to hit, or to try to do away with, baby brother. As these things are initially experienced, they are not necessarily inconsistent with the concept of self as a lovable person.

But then to our schematic child comes a serious threat to self. He experiences words and actions of his parents in regard to these satisfying behaviors, and the words and actions add up to the feeling "You are bad, the behavior is bad, and you are not loved or lovable when you behave in this way." This constitutes a deep threat to the nascent structure of self. The child's dilemma might be schematized in these terms: "If I admit to awareness the satisfactions of these behaviors and the values I apprehend in these experiences, then this is inconsistent with my self as being loved or lovable."

Certain results then follow in the development of the ordinary child. One result is a denial in awareness of the satisfactions that were experienced. The other is to distort the symbolization of the experience of the parents. The accurate symbolization would be: "I perceive my parents as experiencing this behavior as unsatisfying to them." The distorted symbolization, distorted to preserve the threatened concept of self, is: "*I* perceive this behavior as unsatisfying."

It is in this way, it would seem, that parental attitudes are not only introjected, but what is much more important, are experienced not as the attitude of another, but in distorted fashion, *as if* based on the evidence of one's own sensory and visceral equipment. Thus, through distorted symbolization, expression of anger comes to be "experienced" as bad, even though the more accurate symbolization would be that the expression of anger is often experienced as satisfying or enhancing. The more accurate representation is not, however, permitted to enter awareness, or if it does enter, the child is anxious because of the inconsistency he is entertaining within himself. Consequently, "I like baby brother" remains as the pattern belonging in the concept of the self, because it is the concept of the relationship which is introjected from others through the distortion of symbolization, even when the primary experience contains many gradations of value in the relationship, from "I like baby brother" to "I hate him!" In this way the values which the infant attaches to experience become divorced from his own organismic functioning, and experience is valued in terms of the attitudes held by his parents, or by others who are in intimate association with him. These values come to be accepted as being just as "real" as the values which are connected with direct experience. The "self" which is formed on this basis of distorting the sensory and visceral evidence to fit the already present structure acquires an organization and integration which the individual endeavors to preserve. Behavior is regarded as enhancing this self when no such value is apprehended through sensory or visceral reactions; behavior is regarded as opposed to the maintenance or enhancement of the self when there is no negative sensory or visceral reaction. It is here, it seems, that the individual begins on a pathway which he later describes as "I don't really know myself." The primary sensory and visceral reactions are ignored, or not permitted into consciousness, except in distorted form. The values which might be built upon them cannot be admitted to awareness. A concept of self based in part upon a distorted symbolization has taken their place.

Out of these dual sources — the direct experiencing by the individual, and the distorted symbolization of sensory reactions resulting in the introjection of values and concepts *as if* experienced — there grows the structure of the self. Drawing upon the evidence and upon clinical experience, it would appear that the most useful definition of the self-concept, or self-structure, would be along these lines. The self-structure is an organized configuration of perceptions of the self which are admissible to awareness. It is composed of such elements as the perceptions of one's characteristics and abilities; the percepts and concepts of the self in relation to others and to the environment; the value qualities which are perceived as associated with experiences and objects; and the goals and ideals which are perceived as having positive or negative valence. It is, then, the organized picture, existing in awareness either as figure or ground, of the self and the self-in-relationship, together with the positive or negative values which are associated with those qualities and relationships, as they are perceived as existing in the past, present, or future.

It may be worth while to consider for a moment the way in which the self-structure might be formed without the element of distortion and denial of experience. Such a discussion is to some extent a digression, and anticipates a number of the propositions which follow, but it may also serve as an introduction to some of them.

If we ask ourselves how an infant might develop a self-structure which did not have within it the seeds of later psychological difficulty, our experience in client-centered therapy offers some fruitful ideas. Let us consider, very briefly, and again in schematic form, the type of early experience which would lay a basis for a psychologically healthy development of the self. The beginning is the same as we have just described. The child experiences, and values his experiences positively or negatively. He begins to perceive himself as a psychological object, and one of the most basic elements is the perception of himself as a person who is loved. As in our first description he experiences satisfaction in such behaviors as hitting baby brother. But at this point there is a crucial difference. The parent who is able (1) genuinely to accept these feelings of satisfaction experienced by the child, and (2) fully to accept the child who experiences them, and (3) at the same time to accept his or her own feeling that such behavior is unacceptable in the family, creates a situation for the child very different from the usual one. The child in this relationship experiences no threat to his concept of himself as a loved person. He can experience fully and accept within himself and as a part of himself his aggressive feelings toward his baby brother. He can experience fully the perception that his hitting behavior is not liked by the person who loves him. What he then does depends upon his conscious balancing of the elements in the situation — the strength of his feeling of aggression, the satisfactions he would gain from hitting the baby, the satisfactions he would gain from pleasing his parent. The behavior which would result would probably be at times social and at other times aggressive. It would not necessarily conform entirely to the parent's wishes, nor would it always be socially "good." It would be the adaptive behavior of a separate, unique, self-governing individual. Its great advantage, as far as psychological health is concerned, is that it would be realistic, based upon an accurate symbolization of all the evidence given by the child's sensory and visceral equipment in this situation. It may seem to differ only very slightly from the description given earlier, but the difference is an extremely important one. Because the budding structure of the self is not threatened by loss of love, because feelings are accepted by his parent, the child in this instance does not need to deny to awareness the satisfactions which he is experiencing, nor does he need to distort his experience of the parental reaction and regard it as his own. He retains instead a secure self which can serve to guide his behavior by freely admitting to awareness, in accurately symbolized form, all the relevant evidence of his experience in terms of its organismic satisfactions, both immediate and longer range. He is thus developing a soundly structured self in which there is neither denial nor distortion of experience.

Having thus endeavored to give a preview of healthy development as seen from the general point of view of this theory, let us return to a more generalized view of personality, considering the organization of experience, the relation of behavior to the self, and other pertinent topics.

XI) *As experiences occur in the life of the individual, they are either (a) symbolized, perceived, and organized into some relationship to the self, (b) ignored because there is no perceived relationship to the self-structure, (c) denied symbolization or given a distorted symbolization because the experience is inconsistent with the structure of the self.*

Let us look first at those experiences which are ignored because they are irrelevant to the self-structure. There are various noises going on at this moment, in the distance. Until they serve my intellectual need of this moment for an example, I am relatively oblivious to them. They exist in the ground of my phenomenal field, but they do not reinforce or contradict my concept of self, they meet no need related to the self, they are ignored. Often there might be doubt as to whether they existed in the phenomenal field at all, were it not for the ability to focus on those experiences when they might serve a need. I walk down a street a dozen times, ignoring most of the sensations which I experience. Yet today I have need of a hardware store. I recall that I have seen a hardware store on the street, although I have never "noticed" it. Now that this experience meets a need of the self it can be drawn from ground into figure. It is undoubtedly true that the great majority of our sensory experiences are thus ignored, never raised to the level of conscious symbolization, and exist only as organic sensations, without ever having been related in any way to the organized concept of the self or to the concept of the self in relation to the environment.

A more important group of experiences are those which are accepted into consciousness and organized into some relationship with the self-structure either because they meet a need of the self or because they are consistent with the self-structure and thus reinforce it. The client who has a concept of self that "I just don't feel that I can take my place in society like everybody else" perceives that she hasn't learned from her schoolwork, that she fails when she attempts things, that she does not react normally, and so on. She selects from her many sensory experiences those which fit in with her concept of herself. (Later, when her concept of self changes, she perceives that she has successfully attempted new projects, that she is sufficiently normal to get along.)

Likewise a great many experiences are symbolized because they are related to the needs of the self. I notice a book because it is on a topic I wish to learn about; I perceive neckties when I am preparing to buy one for myself. The infantryman perceives spots of freshly turned dirt in the road when these might indicate the existence of a land mine.

It is the third group of sensory and visceral experiences, those which seem to be prevented from entering awareness, which demand our closest attention, for it is in this realm that there lie many phenomena of human behavior which psychologists have endeavored to explain. In some instances the denial of the perception is something rather conscious. The client cited above, whose self-concept was so negative, reports: "When people tell me they think I'm intelligent, I just don't believe it. I just — I guess I don't want to believe it. I don't know why I don't want to believe it — I just don't want to. It should give me confidence, but it doesn't. I think they just really don't know." Here she can perceive and accept readily anyone's depreciation of her, because this fits in with her self-concept. Contradictory evaluations however are denied, by selecting and stressing other perceptions, such as that others cannot really know her. This type of more or less conscious denial of perception is certainly a frequent occurrence with everyone.

There is, however, an even more significant type of denial which is the phenomenon the Freudians have tried to explain by the concept of repression. In this instance, it would appear that there is the organic experience, but there is no symbolization of this experience, or only a distorted symbolization, because an adequate conscious representation of it would be entirely inconsistent with the concept of self. Thus, a woman whose concept of self has been deeply influenced by a very strictly moralistic and religious upbringing, experiences strong organic cravings for sexual satisfaction. To symbolize these, to permit them to appear in consciousness, would provide a traumatic contradiction to her concept of self. The organic experience is something which occurs and is an organic fact. But the symbolization of these desires, so that they become part of conscious awareness, is something which the conscious self can and does prevent. The adolescent who has been brought up in an oversolicitous home, and whose concept of self is that of one who is grateful to his parents, may feel intense anger at the subtle control which is being exerted over him. Organically he experiences the physiological changes which accompany anger, but his conscious self can prevent these experiences from being symbolized and hence consciously perceived. Or he can symbolize them in some distorted fashion which is consistent with his structure of self, such as perceiving these organic sensations as "a bad headache."

Thus the fluid but consistent organization which is the structure or concept of self, does not permit the intrusion of a perception at variance with it, except under certain conditions which we shall consider later. For the most part, it reacts as does a piece of protoplasm when a foreign body is intruded — it endeavors to prevent the entrance.

It should be noted that perceptions are excluded because they are contradictory, not because they are derogatory. It seems nearly as difficult to accept a perception which would alter the self-concept in an expanding or socially acceptable direction as to accept an experience which would alter it in a constricting or socially disapproved direction. The self-distrusting client cited above has as much difficulty accepting her intelligence as a person with a self-concept of superiority would have in accepting experiences indicating mediocrity.

Many perplexing issues are connected with the question, How is the denial effected? As we studied our clinical material and recorded cases, some of us — including the writer — began to develop the theory that in some way an experience could be recognized as threatening, and prevented from entering awareness, without the person ever having been conscious of it, even momentarily. To others of the group this seemed like a most unreasonable explanation because it involved a process of "knowing without knowing," of "perceiving without perceiving."

At this point a number of clarifying studies began to come from the laboratory. Growing out of the work of Bruner and Postman on the personal factors influencing perception came certain findings bearing directly upon the problem we have just defined. It began to appear that even in the tachistoscopic presentation of a word the subject "knows" or "pre-perceives" or responds to the positive or negative value of the word before the stimulus is recognized in consciousness. This aspect of these perceptual studies may be reviewed in the references to Postman, Bruner, and McGinnies (151), McGinnies (122), and McCleary and Lazarus (121). With an increasing weight of evidence, based upon increasingly crucial studies, it seems that the following conclusion is justified. The individual appears to be able to discriminate between threatening and nonthreatening stimuli, and to react accordingly, even though unable consciously to recognize the stimulus to which he is reacting. McCleary and Lazarus, whose study is much the most carefully controlled of those made to date, coin the term "subception" to describe this process. The individual "subceives" a word as threatening, as indicated by his galvanic skin response, even when the exposure time is too limited for him to *per*ceive it. Even though he perceives the word wrongly in consciousness, his autonomic reaction tends to be a response to a threatening situation, as revealed by the GSR. The authors conclude that "Even when a subject is unable to report a visual discrimination [i.e., he reports incorrectly when forced to make a choice] he is still able to make a stimulus discrimination at some level below that required for conscious recognition" (121, p. 178).

This type of finding appears to support our clinical and theoretical hypothesis that the individual may deny experiences to awareness without ever having been conscious of them. There is at least a process of "subception," a discriminating evaluative physiological organismic response to experience, which may precede the conscious perception of such experience. This supplies a possible basic description of the way in which accurate symbolization and awareness of experiences threatening to the self may be prevented.

Here too we may have a basis for describing the anxiety which accompanies so many psychological maladjustments. Anxiety may be the tension exhibited by the organized concept of the self when these "subceptions" indicate that the symbolization of certain experiences would be destructive of the organization. If this experimental work is confirmed by further research, it will supply a needed link in the description of the way in which repression, or denial of experience to awareness, occurs. Clinically it would appear that some such process as indicated by the term "subception" is necessary to account for the observed phenomena.

XII) *Most of the ways of behaving which are adopted by the organism are those which are consistent with the concept of self.*

Although there are some significant exceptions to this statement (exceptions which will be discussed in the following proposition), it is noteworthy that in most instances the form of the seeking effort is dictated by the concept of self. As the organism strives to meet its needs in the world as it is experienced, the form which the striving takes must be a form consistent with the concept of self. The man who has certain values attached to honesty cannot strive for a sense of achievement through means which seem to him dishonest. The person who regards himself as having no aggressive feelings cannot satisfy a need for aggression in any direct fashion. The only channels by which needs may be satisfied are those which are consistent with the organized concept of self.

In most instances this channelization does not involve any distortion of the need which is being satisfied. Of the various ways of satisfying the need for food or for affection, the individual selects only those which are consistent with the concept which he has of himself. There are times, however, when the denial of experience, spoken of above, plays a part in this process. For example, a pilot who conceives of himself as a brave and relatively fearless individual is assigned to a mission which involves great risk. Physiologically he experiences fear and a need to escape from this danger. These reactions cannot be symbolized into consciousness, since they would be too contradictory to his concept of self. The organic need, however, persists. He can perceive that "the engine is not running quite properly," or that "I am ill and have an upset digestive system," and on these grounds excuse himself from the mission. In this example, as in many others which could be cited, the organic needs exist but cannot be admitted into consciousness. The behavior which is adopted is such that it satisfies the organic need, but it takes channels which are consistent with the concept of self. Most neurotic behavior is of this type. In the typical neurosis, the organism is satisfying a need which is not recognized in consciousness, by behavioral means which are consistent with the concept of self and hence can be consciously accepted.

In much behavior of a relatively neutral sort, the regulation of the form of behavior by the self-concept, as posited in this proposition, is not noticeable, and might seem to be nonexistent. This control becomes evident at once, however, when the behavior would be inconsistent with the self. Thus, such behavior as sleep, arising out of the need to reduce the muscular tensions connected with fatigue, is in most instances neutral behavior as far as the self-concept is concerned. Yet the mother who sees herself as responsible for her adolescent daughter cannot go to sleep until the click of the door latch and footsteps in the hall indicate that her daughter is home. It would be inconsistent with her concept of self to fall asleep. Likewise, the man who regards himself as a conscientious and responsible individual wakens from sleep at an early hour when his responsibilities demand that he do so, regardless of his organic need for sleep.

XIII) *Behavior may, in some instances, be brought about by organic experiences and needs which have not been symbolized. Such behavior may be inconsistent with the structure of the self, but in such instances the behavior is not "owned" by the individual.*

In moments of great danger or other emergency stress, the individual may behave with efficiency and ingenuity to meet the needs for safety or whatever other needs exist, but without ever bringing such situations, or the behavior called forth, to conscious symbolization. In such instances the individual feels "I didn't know what I was doing," "I really wasn't responsible for what I was doing." The conscious self feels no degree of government over the actions which took place. The same statement might be made in regard to snoring or restless behavior during sleep. The self is not in control, and the behavior is not regarded as a part of self.

Another example of this sort of behavior occurs when many of the organically experienced needs are refused admittance to consciousness because inconsistent with the concept of self. The pressure of the organic need may become so great that the organism initiates its own seeking behavior and hence brings about the satisfaction of the need, without ever relating the seeking behavior to the concept of self. Thus, a boy whose upbringing created a self-concept of purity and freedom from "base" sexual impulses was arrested for lifting the skirts of two little girls and examining them. He insisted that he could not have performed this behavior, and when presented with witnesses, was positive that "I was not myself." The developing sexuality of an adolescent boy, and the accompanying curiosity, constituted a strong organic need for which there seemed no channel of satisfaction which was consistent with the concept of self. Eventually the organism behaved in such a way as to gain satisfaction, but this behavior was not felt to be, nor was it, a part of the self. It was behavior which was dissociated from the concept of self, and over which the boy exercised no conscious control. The organized character of the behavior grows out of the fact that the organism on a physiological basis can initiate and carry on complex behavior to meet its needs.

In a great many cases of psychological maladjustment, one of the causes for concern on the part of the individual is that certain types of behavior go on without his control or the possibility of his control. "I don't know why I do it. I don't want to do it, but yet I do," is a common enough type of statement. Also, the notion, "I'm just not myself when I do those things," "I didn't know what I was doing," "I have no control over those reactions." In each case the reference is to behavior which is organically determined on the basis of experiences denied accurate symbolization, and hence is carried through without having been brought into any consistent relationship with the concept of self.

XIV) *Psychological maladjustment exists when the organism denies to awareness significant sensory and visceral experiences, which consequently are not symbolized and organized into the gestalt of the self-structure. When this situation exists, there is a basic or potential psychological tension.*

The basis for this proposition has become evident in the preceding statements. If we think of the structure of the self as being a symbolic elaboration of a portion of the private experiential world of the organism, we may realize that when much of this private world is denied symbolization, certain basic tensions result. We find, then, that there is a very real discrepancy between the experiencing organism as it exists, and the concept of self which exerts such a governing influence upon behavior. This self is now very inadequately representative of the experience of the organism. Conscious control becomes more difficult as the organism strives to satisfy needs which are not consciously admitted, and to react to experiences which are denied by the conscious self. Tension then exists, and if the individual becomes to any degree aware of this tension or discrepancy, he feels anxious, feels that he is not united or integrated, that he is unsure of his direction. Such statements may not be the surface account of the maladjustment, such surface account having more often to do with the environmental difficulties being faced, but the feeling of inner lack of integration is usually communicated as the individual feels free to reveal more of the field of perception which is available to his consciousness. Thus, such statements as "I don't know what I'm afraid of," "I don't know what I want," "I can't decide on anything," "I don't have any real goal" are very frequent in counseling cases and indicate the lack of any integrated purposeful direction in which the individual is moving.

To illustrate briefly the nature of maladjustment, take the familiar picture of a mother whom the diagnostician would term rejecting. She has as part of her concept of self a whole constellation which may be summed up by saying, "I am a good and loving mother." This conceptualization of herself is, as indicated in Proposition X, based in part upon accurate symbolization of her experience and in part upon distorted symbolization in which the values held by others are introjected as if they were her own experiences. With this concept of self she can accept and assimilate those organic sensations of affection which she feels toward her child. But the organic experience of dislike, distaste, or hatred toward her child is something which is denied to her conscious self. The experience exists, but it is not permitted accurate symbolization. The organic need is for aggressive acts which would fulfill these attitudes and satisfy the tension which exists. The organism strives for the achievement of this satisfaction, but it can do so for the most part only through those channels which are consistent with the self-concept of a good mother. Since the good mother could be aggressive toward her child only if he merited punishment, she perceives much of his behavior as being bad, deserving punishment, and therefore the aggressive acts can be carried through, without being contrary to the values organized in her picture of self. If under great stress, she at some time should shout at her child, "I hate you," she would be quick to explain that "I was not myself," that this behavior occurred but was out of her control. "I don't know what made me say that, because of course I don't mean it." This is a good illustration of most maladjustment in which the organism is striving for certain satisfactions in the field as organically experienced, whereas the concept of self is more constricted and cannot permit in awareness many of the actual experiences.

Clinically two somewhat different degrees of this tension are observed. There is first of all the type just illustrated, in which the individual has a definite and organized self-concept, based in part upon the organic experiences (in this case, feelings of affection) of the individual. While this concept of a good mother has been introjected from social contacts, it has also been formed in part from some of the sensations actually experienced by the individual, and has thus become more genuinely her own.

In other instances, the individual feels, as he explores his maladjustment, that he has no self, that he is a zero, that his only self consists of endeavoring to do what others believe he should do. The concept of self, in other words, is based almost entirely upon valuations of experience which are taken over from others and contains a minimum of accurate symbolization of experience, and a minimum of direct organismic valuing of experience. Since the values held by others have no necessary relationship to one's actual organic experiencings, the discrepancy between the self structure and the experiential world gradually comes to be expressed as a feeling of tension and distress. One young woman, after slowly permitting her own experiences to come into awareness and form the basis of her concept of self, puts it very briefly and accurately thus: "I've always tried to be what the others thought I should be, but now I'm wondering whether I shouldn't just see that I am what I am."

XV) *Psychological adjustment exists when the concept of the self is such that all the sensory and visceral experiences of the organism are, or may be, assimilated on a symbolic level into a consistent relationship with the concept of self.*

This proposition may be put in several different ways. We may say that freedom from inner tension, or psychological adjustment, exists when the concept of self is at least roughly congruent with all the experiences of the organism. To use some of the illustrations previously given, the woman who perceives and accepts her own sexual cravings, and also perceives and accepts as a part of her reality the cultural values placed upon suppression of these cravings, will be accepting and assimilating all the sensory evidence experienced by the organism in this connection. This is possible only if her concept of self in this area is broad enough to include both her sex desires and her desire to live in some harmony with her culture. The mother who "rejects" her child can lose the inner tensions connected with her relationship to her child if she has a concept of self which permits her to accept her feelings of dislike for the child, as well as her feelings of affection and liking.

The feeling of reduction of inner tension is something that clients experience as they make progress in "being the real me" or in developing a "new feeling about myself." One client, after gradually giving up the notion that much of her behavior was "not acting like myself" and accepting the fact that her self could include these experiences and behaviors which she had hitherto excluded, expressed her feeling in these words: "I can remember an organic feeling of relaxation. I did not have to keep up the struggle to cover up and hide this shameful person." The cost of maintaining an alertness of defense to prevent various experiences from being symbolized in consciousness is obviously great.

The best definition of what constitutes integration appears to be this statement that all the sensory and visceral experiences are admissable to awareness through accurate symbolization, and organizable into one system which is internally consistent and

which is, or is related to, the structure of self. Once this type
of integration occurs, then the tendency toward growth can become fully operative, and the individual moves in the directions
normal to all organic life. When the self-structure is able to
accept and take account in consciousness of the organic experiences, when the organizational system is expansive enough to
contain them, then clear integration and a sense of direction are
achieved, and the individual feels that his strength can be and is
directed toward the clear purpose of actualization and enhancement of a unified organism.

One aspect of this proposition for which we have some research
evidence, but which could be tested even more clearly, is that
conscious acceptance of impulses and perceptions greatly increases
the possibility of conscious control. It is for this reason that the
person who has come to accept his own experiences also acquires
the feeling of being in control of himself. If it seems puzzling
that the term "conscious awareness" should be used almost inter-
changeably with "conscious control," perhaps an analogy may
be of help in clarification. I am driving my car on an icy pave-
ment. I am controlling its direction (as the self feels itself to be
in control of the organism). I desire to swing left to follow the
curve of the road. At this point the car (analogous to the physiological organism) responds to physical laws (analogous to physiological tensions) of which I am not aware, and skids, moving in
a straight line rather than rounding the curve. The tension and
panic I feel are not unlike the tension of the person who finds
that "I am doing things which are not myself, which I cannot
control." The therapy is likewise similar. If I am aware of,
and willing to accept all my sensory experiences, I sense the car's
momentum forward, I do not deny it, I swing the wheel "with
the skid," rather than around the curve, until the car is again
under control. Then I am able to turn left, more slowly. In
other words I do not immediately gain my conscious objective,
but by accepting all the evidences of experience and organizing
them into one integrated perceptual system, I acquire the control
by which reasonable conscious objectives can be achieved. This
is very parallel to the feeling of the person who has completed

therapy. He may have found it necessary to modify his objectives, but any disappointment in this respect is more than compensated by the increased integration and consequent control. No longer are there aspects of his behavior which he cannot govern. The sense of autonomy, of self-government, is synonymous with having all experiences available to consciousness.

The term "available to consciousness" in the last sentence is deliberately chosen. It is the fact that all experiences, impulses, sensations are *available* that is important, and not necessarily the fact that they are present in consciousness. It is the organization of the concept of self *against* the symbolization of certain experiences contradictory to itself, which is the significant negative fact. Actually, when all experiences are assimilated in relationship to the self and made a part of the structure of self, there tends to be *less* of what is called "self-consciousness" on the part of the individual. Behavior becomes more spontaneous, expression of attitudes is less guarded, because the self can accept such attitudes and such behavior as a part of itself. Frequently a client at the beginning of therapy expresses real fear that others might discover his real self. "As soon as I start thinking about what *I* am, I have such a terrible conflict at what I am that it makes me feel awful. It's such a self-depreciation that I hope nobody ever knows it. . . . I'm afraid to act natural, I guess, because I just don't feel as though I like myself." In this frame of mind, behavior must always be guarded, cautious, self-conscious. But when this same client has come to accept deeply the fact that "I am what I am," then she can be spontaneous and can lose her self-consciousness.

XVI) *Any experience which is inconsistent with the organization or structure of self may be perceived as a threat, and the more of these perceptions there are, the more rigidly the self-structure is organized to maintain itself.*

This proposition is an attempt to formulate a description of certain clinical facts. If the rejecting mother previously mentioned is told that several observers have come to the conclusion that she does reject her child, the inevitable result is that she will, for the moment, exclude any assimilation of this experience. She may attack the conditions of observation, the training or authority of the observers, the degree of understanding they possess, and so forth and so on. She will organize the defenses of her own concept of herself as a loving and good mother, and will be able to substantiate this concept with a mass of evidence. She will obviously perceive the judgment of the observers as a threat, and will organize in defense of her own governing concept. The same phenomenon would be observed if the girl who regards herself as utterly lacking in ability received a high score on an intelligence test. She can and will defend her self against this threat of inconsistency. If the self cannot defend itself against deep threats, the result is a catastrophic psychological breakdown and disintegration.

A concise and helpful formulation of the essential elements in threat and defense, as they apply to personality, has been constructed by Hogan (87, 88). In his summary he lists eight statements as describing the way in which defensive behavior occurs. These are as follows:

1. Threat occurs when experiences are perceived or anticipated as incongruent with the structure of the self.

2. Anxiety is the affective response to threat.

3. Defense is a sequence of behavior in response to threat, the goal of which is the maintenance of the structure of the self.

4. Defense involves a denial or distortion of perceived experience to reduce the incongruity between the experience and the structure of the self.

5. The awareness of threat, but not the threat itself, is reduced by the defensive behavior.

6. Defensive behavior increases susceptibility to threat in that denied or distorted experiences may be threatened by recurring perceptions.

7. Threat and defense tend to recur again and again in sequence; as this sequence progresses, attention is removed farther and farther from the original threat, but more of experience is distorted and susceptible to threat.

8. This defensive sequence is limited by the need to accept reality. (88)

Hogan's theory helps to explain the spread of defensive behavior in the individual by noting the fact that the more of sensory and visceral experience that is denied symbolization, or given a distorted symbolization, the greater the likelihood that any new experience will be perceived as threatening, since there is a larger false structure to be maintained.

XVII) *Under certain conditions, involving primarily complete absence of any threat to the self-structure, experiences which are inconsistent with it may be perceived, and examined, and the structure of self revised to assimilate and include such experiences.*

Here an important clinical fact, attested by many therapeutic cases, is difficult to state in accurately generalized form. It is clear that self-concepts change, both in the ordinary development of the individual, and in therapy. The previous proposition formulates the facts about the defenses of the self, while this one endeavors to state the way in which change may come about.

To proceed from the more clear-cut examples to those less clear: In therapy of a client-centered form, by means of the relationship and the counselor's handling of it, the client is gradually assured that he is accepted as he is, and that each new facet of himself which is revealed is also accepted. It is then that experiences which have been denied can be symbolized, often very gradually, and hence brought clearly into conscious form. Once they are conscious, the concept of self is expanded so that they may be included as a part of a consistent total. Thus the rejecting mother, in such an atmosphere, is apt first to admit the perception of her behavior — "I suppose that at times it must seem to him that I don't like him" — and then the possibility of an experience inconsistent with self — "I suppose that at times I *don't* like him" — and gradually the formulation of a broadened concept of self: "I can admit that I like him and I don't like him and we can still get along satisfactorily." Or a woman who hates her mother and justifies the pattern of self which includes such hate, comes first to recognize that there has been other than hating behavior — "I keep cleaning up my house when she comes over, as if to show her how good I am, as if to try to win her favor" — then admits experiences directly contradictory to her concept of self — "I feel a real warmth toward her, a wholesome kind of affection" — and gradually, on the basis of trying to live by a revised concept of her self in this relationship, comes to broaden that concept to a point where tension is reduced — "I get along all right with her. It's the most wonderful thing the way I have gotten mother out of my system. I can take her or leave her without so much tension."

If we try to analyze the elements which make possible this reorganization of the structure of self, there would appear to be two possible factors. One is the self-initiated apprehension of the new material. Exploration of experience is made possible by the counselor, and since the self is accepted at every step of its exploration and in any change it may exhibit, it seems possible gradually to explore areas at a "safe" rate, and hitherto denied experiences are slowly and tentatively accepted just as a small child slowly and tentatively becomes acquainted with a frightening object. Another factor which may be involved is that the counselor is accepting toward all experiences, all attitudes, all perceptions. This social value may be introjected by the client, and applied to his own experiences. This last certainly cannot be the major reason, since it is often known to the client that the counselor is one among a thousand in holding such a value, and that society in general would not accept the client as he is. Nevertheless this introjection of the counselor attitude may be at least a temporary or partial step toward the client's experiencing of himself as acceptable.

Another problem to be borne in mind is that the acceptance of experiences inconsistent with the self often occurs between interviews, without ever being verbalized to the counselor. The essential factor appears to be that the person achieves the attitude that it is safe to look at organic experience and then can permit it to be symbolized in consciousness even though the therapist is not present.

A question sometimes raised is that if absence of threat to the self-concept were all that was required, it might seem that the individual could, at any time that he was alone, face these inconsistent experiences. We know that this does happen in many minor circumstances. A man may be criticized for a persistent failing. At the time he refuses to admit this experience at face value, because it is too threatening to his self-organization. He denies the fault, rationalizes the criticism. But later, alone, he rethinks the matter, accepts the criticism as just, and revises his concept of self, and consequently his behavior, as a result. For experiences which are deeply denied, however, because they are deeply inconsistent with the concept of self, this does not avail. It appears possible for the person to face such inconsistency only while in a relationship with another in which he is sure that he will be accepted.

To leave this discussion with a somewhat simpler example, the child who feels that he is weak and powerless to do a certain task, to build a tower or repair a bicycle, may find, as he works rather hopelessly at the task, that he is successful. This experience is inconsistent with the concept he holds of himself, and may not be integrated at once; but if the child is left to himself he gradually assimilates, upon his own initiative, a revision of his concept of self, that while he is generally weak and powerless, in this respect he has ability. This is the normal way in which, free from threat, new perceptions are assimilated. But if this same child is repeatedly told by his parents that he is competent to do the task, he is likely to deny it, and to prove by his behavior that he is unable to do it. The more forceful intrusion of the notion of his competence constitutes more of a threat to self and is more forcefully resisted.

It is clear that a more refined analysis is needed of the exact conditions which are necessary to permit a reorganization of the self-concept and the assimilation of contradictory experiences. We know one way in which this reorganization may be brought about, but the conditions which are crucial for this type of experience are not sufficiently known.

It should also be obvious that what is being described here is a learning process, perhaps the most important learning of which the person is capable, namely the learning of self. It is to be hoped

that those who have specialized in theory of learning may begin
to utilize the knowledge from that field in helping to describe the
way in which the individual learns a new configuration of self.

XVIII) *When the individual perceives and accepts into one consistent
and integrated system all his sensory and visceral experiences, then he
is necessarily more understanding of others and is more accepting of
others as separate individuals.*

This proposition has been felt to be true in our clinical therapeutic work, and is now supported by Sheerer's research investigation (188, 189). It is one of the unexpected findings that have
grown out of the client-centered approach. To the person not
familiar with therapeutic experience, it may seem like wishful
thinking to assert that the person who accepts himself will, because of this self-acceptance, have better interpersonal relations
with others.

We find clinically, however, that the person who completes
therapy is more relaxed in being himself, more sure of himself,
more realistic in his relations with others, and develops notably
better interpersonal relationships. One client, discussing the
results which therapy has had for her, states something of this fact
in these words: "I am myself, and I am different from others. I
am getting more happiness in being myself, and I find myself more
and more letting other people assume the responsibility for being
selves."

If we try to understand the theoretical basis upon which this
takes place, it appears to be as follows:

> The person who denies some experiences must continually
> defend himself against the symbolization of those experi-
> ences.

> As a consequence, all experiences are viewed defensively as
> potential threats, rather than for what they really are.

> Thus in interpersonal relationships, words or behaviors are
> experienced and perceived as threatening, which were not so
> intended.

Also, words and behaviors in others are attacked because they represent or resemble the feared experiences.

There is then no real understanding of the other as a separate person, since he is perceived mostly in terms of threat or nonthreat to the self.

But when all experiences are available to consciousness and are integrated, then defensiveness is minimized. When there is no need to defend, there is no need to attack.

When there is no need to attack, the other person is perceived for what he really is, a separate individual, operating in terms of his own meanings, based on his own perceptual field.

While this may sound abstruse, it is corroborated by much everyday evidence, as well as by clinical experience. Who are the individuals, in any neighborhood, or in any group, that inspire confidential relationships, seem able to be understanding of others? They tend to be individuals with a high degree of acceptance of all aspects of self. In clinical experience, how do better interpersonal relationships emerge? It is on this same basis. The rejecting mother who accepts her own negative attitudes toward her child finds that this acceptance, which at first she has feared, makes her more relaxed with her child. She is able to observe him for what he is, not simply through a screen of defensive reactions. Doing so, she perceives that he is an interesting person, with bad features, but also good ones, toward whom she feels at times hostile, but toward whom she also feels at times affectionate. On this comfortable and realistic and spontaneous basis a *real* relationship develops out of her real experiencing, a satisfying relationship to both. It may not be composed entirely of sweetness and light, but it is far more comfortable than any artificial relationship could possibly be. It is based primarily upon an acceptance of the fact that her child is a separate person.

The woman who hated her mother comes, after she has accepted all her feelings of affection as well as hate, to see her mother as a person with a variety of characteristics: interesting, good, vulgar, and bad. With this much more accurate perception she understands her mother, accepts her for what she is, and builds a real rather than a defensive relationship with her.

The implications of this aspect of our theory are such as to stretch the imagination. Here is a theoretical basis for sound interpersonal, intergroup, and international relationships. Stated in terms of social psychology, this proposition becomes the statement that the person (or persons or group) who accepts himself thoroughly, will necessarily improve his relationship with those with whom he has personal contact, because of his greater understanding and acceptance of them. This atmosphere of understanding and acceptance is the very climate most likely to create a therapeutic experience and consequent self-acceptance in the person who is exposed to it. Thus we have, in effect, a psychological "chain reaction" which appears to have tremendous potentialities for the handling of problems of social relationships.

XIX) *As the individual perceives and accepts into his self-structure more of his organic experiences, he finds that he is replacing his present value system — based so largely upon introjections which have been distortedly symbolized — with a continuing organismic valuing process.*

In therapy, as the person explores his phenomenal field, he comes to examine the values which he has introjected and which he has used as if they were based upon his own experience. (See Proposition X.) He is dissatisfied with them, often expressing the attitude that he has just been doing what others thought he should do. But what does *he* think he should do? There he is puzzled and lost. If one gives up the guidance of an introjected system of values, what is to take its place? He often feels quite incompetent to discover or build any alternative system. If he cannot longer accept the "ought" and "should," the "right" and "wrong" of the introjected system, how can he know what values take their place?

Gradually he comes to experience the fact that he is making value judgments, in a way that is new to him, and yet a way that was also known to him in his infancy. Just as the infant places an assured value upon an experience, relying on the evidence of his own senses, as described in Proposition X, so too the client finds that it is his own organism which supplies the evidence upon which value judgments may be made. He discovers that his own senses, his own physiological equipment, can provide the data for making value judgments and for continuously revising them. No one needs to tell him that it is good to act in a freer and more spontaneous fashion, rather than in the rigid way to which he has been accustomed. He senses, he feels that it is satisfying and enhancing. Or when he acts in a defensive fashion, it is his own organism that feels the immediate and short-term satisfaction of being protected and that also senses the longer-range dissatisfaction of having to remain on guard. He makes a choice between two courses of action, fearfully and hesitantly, not knowing whether he has weighed their values accurately. But then he discovers that he may let the evidence of his own experience indicate whether he has chosen satisfyingly. He discovers that he does not need to *know* what are the correct values; through the data supplied by his own organism, he can experience what is satisfying and enhancing. He can put his confidence in a valuing *process*, rather than in some rigid, introjected *system* of values.

Let us look at this proposition in a slightly different way. Values are always accepted because they are perceived as principles making for the maintenance, actualization, and enhancement of the organism. It is on this basis that social values are introjected from the culture. In therapy it would seem that the reorganization which takes place is on the basis that those values are retained which are *experienced* as maintaining or enhancing the organism as distinguished from those which are said by others to be for the good of the organism. For example, an individual accepts from the culture the value, "One should neither have nor express feelings of jealous aggressiveness toward siblings." The value is accepted because it is presumed to make for the enhancement of the individual — a better, more satisfied person. But in therapy this person, as a client, examines this value in terms of a more basic criterion — namely, his own sensory and visceral experiences: "Have I felt the denial of aggressive attitudes as something enhancing myself?" The value is tested in the light of personal organic evidence.

It is in the outcome of this valuing of values that we strike the possibility of very basic similarities in all human experience. For as the individual tests such values, and arrives at his own personal values, he appears to come to conclusions which can be formulated in a generalized way: that the greatest values for the enhancement of the organism accrue when all experiences and all attitudes are permitted conscious symbolization, and when behavior becomes the meaningful and balanced satisfaction of *all* needs, these needs being available to consciousness. The behavior which thus ensues will satisfy the need for social approval, the need to express positive affectional feelings, the need for sexual expression, the need to avoid guilt and regret as well as the need to express aggression. Thus, while the establishment of values by each individual may seem to suggest a complete anarchy of values, experience indicates that quite the opposite is true. Since all individuals have basically the same needs, including the need for acceptance by others, it appears that when each individual formulates his own values, in terms of his own direct experience, it is not anarchy which results, but a high degree of commonality and a genuinely socialized system of values. One of the ultimate ends, then, of an hypothesis of confidence in the individual, and in his capacity to resolve his own conflicts, is the emergence of value systems which are unique and personal for each individual, and which are changed by the changing evidence of organic experience, yet which are at the same time deeply socialized, possessing a high degree of similarity in their essentials.

A SCHEMATIC PRESENTATION

Some of the preceding propositions, particularly from IX through XIX, may be clarified by a schematic presentation of certain of the ways in which the self functions in relation to personality. Any diagrammatic representation of complex material tends to oversimplify and to seem more complete than it actually is. The material which follows should therefore be accepted with critical caution and with an awareness of its limitations. The accompanying diagram can be understood only by referring to the definitions of each element.

Definitions

The Total Personality. The diagram as a whole (Figures I and II, pages 526–527) is intended to focus upon the structure of personality. As drawn in Figure I, it indicates a personality in a state of psychological tension.

Experience. This circle represents the immediate field of sensory and visceral experience. It would be comparable to the total phenomenal field of the infant. It represents all that is experienced by the individual, through all the sense modalities. It is a fluid and changing field.

Self-Structure. This circle represents the configuration of concepts which has been defined as the structure of self, or the concept of self. It includes the patterned perceptions of the individual's characteristics and relationships, together with the values associated with these. It is available to awareness.

Area I. Within this portion of the phenomenal field the concept of self and self-in-relationship is in accord with, or is congruent with, the evidence supplied by sensory and visceral experience.

Area II. This area represents that portion of the phenomenal field in which social or other experience has been *distorted* in symbolization and perceived as a part of the individual's own experience. Percepts, concepts, and values are introjected from parents and others in the environment, but are perceived in the phenomenal field as being the product of sensory evidence.

Area III. In this realm are those sensory and visceral experiences which are *denied* to awareness because they are inconsistent with the structure of the self.

Specific Illustrations

The letters in the circles may be regarded as elements of experience. By giving them specific content we may illustrate the func-

Figure I · The Total Personality

Self-Structure   *Experience*

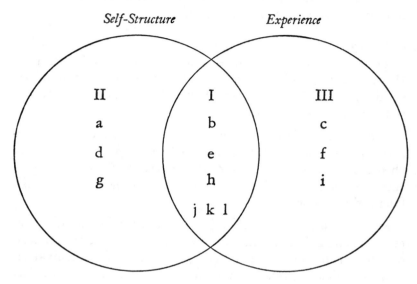

tioning of personality. Let us take first a somewhat minor example as illustrated in Figure I.

(*a*) "*I am utterly inadequate in dealing with mechanical things, and
this is one evidence of general inadequacy.*" This is an introjected
concept and its associated value, taken over by the individual from
his parents. The quotation marks indicate that it is perceived *as if*
it were the direct sensory experience of failure with all mechanical
things, but it is not. The experience was, "My parents regard
me as inadequate in the mechanical field"; the distorted symbolization is, "I am inadequate in the mechanical field." The basic
reason for the distortion is to guard against losing the important
part of the self-structure, "I am loved by my parents." This
leads to a feeling which may be schematized thus: "I want to
be acceptable to my parents and hence must experience myself
as being the sort of person they think I am."

(*b*) *I experience failure in dealing with mechanical contrivances.*
This is a direct experience which has occurred a number of times.
These experiences are assimilated into the structure of self because

Figure II · The Total Personality

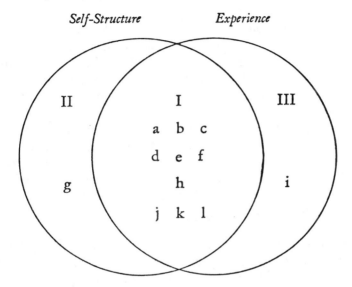

Self-Structure   *Experience*

they are consistent with it.

(c) *Experience of succeeding with a difficult mechanical operation.* This is a type of sensory experience which is inconsistent with the concept of self and hence cannot be admitted directly into awareness. The person cannot perceive that "*I* experience success in mechanical operations" because this perception would be disorganizing to the structure of the self. In such an occurrence it is almost impossible completely to deny the experience to awareness, since the sensory evidence is clear. It is, however, "pre-perceived" as threatening and admitted to awareness in a sufficiently distorted fashion to eliminate the threat to the structure of self. It therefore appears in consciousness in some such fashion as "It was just luck," "The pieces just fell into place," "I couldn't do it again in a million years." This distorted symbolization could take its place in Area II in our diagram, since it is consistent with self. The actual experience, however, is denied to awareness in any accurately symbolized form, and hence remains in Area III.

Let us take another example, drawing this time upon the experience of Miss Har, described in Chapter 3 (particularly pages 79 and 76, in that order.)

(d) "*I feel nothing but hatred for my father, and I am morally right in feeling this.*" Miss Har's mother had been deserted by her husband, and it is not surprising that Miss Har had introjected this feeling, this concept of the relationship, and the value attached to it, as if they were based upon her own sensory and visceral experience.

(e) *I have experienced dislike for my father in my contacts with him.* On the few occasions when she had met her father, there were elements of his behavior which were not satisfying to her. This was first-hand sensory experience. It is congruent with the self-structure and assimilated into it. Her behavior is in accord with this total self-structure.

(f) *Experience of positive feelings toward her father.* Such experiences occurred, but were totally inconsistent with the whole structure of self. They were therefore denied to awareness. Only in the most distorted way do they appear in consciousness. She does admit the perception, "I am like my father in several ways, and this is shameful." She also overemphasizes her hatred for her father as a defense against permitting such experiences in awareness. (This is an inference from outside of her phenomenological field. It is confirmed by the fact that eventually, as described later, she can perceive this from her own internal frame of reference.)

Perhaps one other illustration may be added to indicate the introjection of values from the culture.

(g) "*I regard homosexual behavior as terrible.*" Here the experiencing of a social attitude in others is distortedly perceived as a value based upon experience.

(h) *I experience distaste for homosexual behavior.* In certain specific experiences, the sensory and visceral reactions have been unpleasant and unsatisfying. Being in accord with the self-structure, these experiences are assimilated into it.

(i) *Occasional experience of homosexual desires.* These are denied to awareness, because they would be disorganizing to self.

Many aspects of self would not exhibit the discrepancies evident in these three examples, but would be of this order:

(*j*) *I hear others say that I am tall, and have other evidence that they regard me as tall.* Here the attitude of others is not introjected, but is simply perceived for what it is. It is therefore in the category of sensory experience which has occurred in a social relationship, and is accurately symbolized.

(*k*) *I experience myself as tall in relation to others.*

(*l*) *Very rarely do I find myself in a group where I experience myself as shorter than others.*

j, k, l, are three different sorts of sensory evidence, all admitted to awareness. The attitudes of others are perceived as such, not as own experience. The evidence of tallness which is acquired through sensory experience is accepted into awareness. The occasional contradictory evidence is also accepted, and thus modifies the self-concept to some degree. Thus the individual has a unitary and securely founded concept of himself as taller than most people, a concept which is based upon several types of evidence, all admitted to awareness.

The picture given thus far, and the conclusion which would be based upon the diagram in Figure I, would be that in this schematic individual there is much potential psychological tension. There is a considerable degree of incongruence between the sensory and visceral experience of the organism, and the structure of the self, the former involving much that is denied to awareness, and the latter involving an awareness of much that is not so. Whether or not this schematic individual would feel himself to be maladjusted would depend upon his environment. If his environment supported the "quasi" elements of his self-structure, he might never recognize the tensional forces in his personality, although he would be a "vulnerable" person. If the culture gave sufficiently strong support to his concept of self, he would have positive attitudes toward self. He would experience tension and anxiety, and feel maladjusted, only in so far as his culture, or overwhelming sensory evidence, gave him some vague perception of the inconsistencies within his personality. Such an awareness or anxiety might also come about if he were exposed to a highly permissive situation in which the boundaries of self-organization could be relaxed, and experiences ordinarily denied to awareness might be dimly perceived. However such anxiety or uneasiness is caused, it is in this state that he would tend to welcome psychotherapy. Let us see, diagrammatically, what occurs in therapy.

The Alteration of Personality in Therapy

Figure II (page 527) shows our schematic person after successful psychotherapy. The definitions of the circles and areas remain unchanged, but it is evident that they have a different relationship to each other, the structure of self now being much more congruent with the sensory and visceral experience of the individual. The specific ways in which that relationship has changed may be illustrated by again referring to the schematic elements of experience previously described. These have now been reorganized in the perceptual field in ways which may be indicated as follows:

(a) *I realize my parents felt I was inadequate in mechanical things, and that this had a negative value for them.*

(b) *My own experience confirms this evaluation in a number of ways.*

(c) *But I do have some competence in this field.*

Note that experience (c), as previously described, has now been admitted to awareness and organized into the self-structure. Experience (a) is no longer perceived in distorted fashion, but it is perceived as sensory evidence of the attitude of others.

(d) *I perceive that my mother hates my father and expects me to do the same.*

(e) *I dislike my father in some ways and for some things.*

(f) *And I also like him in some ways and for some things, and both of these experiences are an acceptable part of me.*

Here again introjected attitudes and values are perceived for what they are, and are no longer distorted in their symbolization. Feelings formerly inconsistent with self can be integrated into the self-structure, because it has expanded to include them. Experiences are valued in accordance with the satisfactions which they bring, rather than in accordance with the views of others. It may be well at this point to re-read the excerpts from the case of Miss

Har, in Chapter 3, to realize that the process by which this integration is achieved is a painful, vacillating one, that the acceptance of all the sensory evidence is at first a very fearful and tentative acceptance, and that keeping the locus of evaluation within oneself means that initially there is much uncertainty about values.

g, h, i. These are left unchanged. They are intended as a schematic representation of the fact that therapy never achieves complete congruence of self and experience, never clears away all introjections, never explores the entire area of denied experience. If the client has deeply learned that it is safe to accept all sensory experience into awareness without distortion, he may deal differently with his homosexual impulses (*i*) when they recur, and he may recognize the introjected cultural attitude (*g*) as being simply that. If circumstances tend to focus on this area, he may return for further therapy.

j, k, l. The individual's securely based concept of his height, and the other stable concepts of which it is representative, remain unchanged.

Characteristics of the Altered Personality

Several of the characteristics of the personality as represented in Figure II may be briefly noted.

There is less potential tension or anxiety, less vulnerability.

There is a lessened possibility of threat, because the structure of the self has become more inclusive, more flexible, and more discriminating. There is therefore less likelihood of defensiveness.

Adaptation to any life situation is improved, because the behavior will be guided by a more complete knowledge of the relevant sensory data, there being fewer experiences distorted and fewer denied.

The client after therapy feels more in control of himself, more competent to cope with life. In terms of this diagram, more of the relevant experience is present in awareness, and hence subject to rational choice. The client is less likely to experience himself behaving in ways that are "not myself."

There is represented in this second diagram the basis for the "greater acceptance of self" which clients experience. More of the total experience of the organism is directly incorporated into the self; or more accurately, the self tends to be discovered in the total experience of the organism. The client feels he is his "real" self, his organic self.

The individual represented in Figure II would be more accepting toward another, more able to understand him as a separate and unique person, because he would have less need of being on defensive guard.

Following therapy, the individual is formulating his evaluations of experience on the basis of all the relevant data. He thus has a flexible and adaptable system of values, but one that is soundly based.

CONCLUSION

This chapter has endeavored to present a theory of personality and behavior which is consistent with our experience and research in client-centered therapy. This theory is basically phenomenological in character, and relies heavily upon the concept of the self as an explanatory construct. It pictures the end-point of personality development as being a basic congruence between the phenomenal field of experience and the conceptual structure of the self — a situation which, if achieved, would represent freedom from internal strain and anxiety, and freedom from potential strain; which would represent the maximum in realistically oriented adaptation; which would mean the establishment of an individualized value system having considerable identity with the value system of any other equally well-adjusted member of the human race.

It would be too much to hope that the many hypotheses of this theory will prove to be correct. If they prove to be a stimulation to significant study of the deeper dynamics of human behavior, they will have served their purpose well.

SUGGESTED READINGS

If one wishes to compare the theory developed in this chapter with other recent formulations of personality theory, the writers mentioned on page 481 would be a good starting point (69, 9, 127, 128, 137, 109, 205, 129, 141, 38, 104, 222, 200, 37). To this list of newer theories should be added some more conventional exposition of Freudian personality theory such as Fenichel (56).

Some suggestion of the fluid and changing character of the thinking which has gone into this chapter may be gained by comparing an earlier formulation (172) with this present statement.

REFERENCES

1. Aichhorn, A. *Wayward Youth.* New York: Viking Press, 1935.
2. Aidman, Ted. Changes in self perception as related to changes in perception of one's environment. M.A. paper, University of Chicago, 1947.
3. Albrecht, M., and L. Gross. Nondirective teaching. *Sociol. Soc. Res.*, 1948, *32*, 874–881.
4. Alexander, F., and T. M. French. *Psychoanalytic Therapy.* New York: Ronald Press, 1946.
5. Allen, F. H. *Psychotherapy with Children.* New York: W. W. Norton, 1942.
6. Allport, G. W. The psychology of participation. *Psychol. Rev.*, 1945, *53*, 117–132. [Permission to quote given by the *Psychological Review* and the American Psychological Association.]
7. Alpert, B., and P. A. Smith. How participation works. *J. Social Issues*, 1949, *5*, 3–13.
8. Anderson, H. H., and H. M. Brewer. Studies of teachers' classroom personalities: I. Dominative and socially integrative behavior of kindergarten teachers. *App. Psychol. Monogr.*, 1945, No. 6, 157 pp.
9. Angyal, A. *Foundations for a Science of Personality.* New York: Commonwealth Fund, 1941.
10. Ash, Philip. The reliability of psychiatric diagnoses. *J. Abnorm. & Soc. Psychol.*, 1949, *44*, 272–276.
11. Assum, A. L., and S. J. Levy. Analysis of a nondirective case with followup interview. *J. Abnorm. & Soc. Psychol.*, 1948, *43*, 78–89.
12. Axline, Virginia M. Mental deficiency — symptom or disease? *J. Consult. Psychol.*, 1949, *13*, 313–327.
13. Axline, Virginia M. Nondirective therapy for poor readers. *J. Consult. Psychol.*, 1947, *11*, 61–69.
14. Axline, Virginia M. *Play Therapy.* Boston: Houghton Mifflin, 1947.
15. Axline, Virginia M. Play therapy and race conflict in young children. *J. Abnorm. & Soc. Psychol.*, 1948, *43*, 300–310.

16. Axline, Virginia M. Play therapy experiences as described by child participants. *J. Consult. Psychol.*, 1950, *14*, 53–63.
17. Baldwin, A. L.; Joan Kalhorn; and F. H. Breese. Patterns of parent behavior. *Psychol. Monogr.* No. 268, 1945, *58*, No. 3, 1–75.
18. Bartlett, Marion R., and staff. Data on the personal adjustment counseling program for veterans. Mimeographed report, Personal Adjustment Counseling Division, Advisement and Guidance Service, Office of Vocational Rehabilitation and Education.
19. Baruch, Dorothy W. Therapeutic procedures as part of the educative process. *J. Consult. Psychol.*, 1940, *4*, 165–172.
20. Bavelas, A.; L. Festinger; P. Woodward; and A. Zander. The relative effectiveness of a lecture method and a method of group decision for changing food habits. Mimeographed report of the Committee on Food Habits, National Research Council, Washington, D.C.
21. Beier, Ernst G. The effect of induced anxiety on some aspects of intellectual functioning. Ph.D. thesis, Columbia University, 1949.
22. Bell, J. E. *Projective Techniques.* New York: Longmans, Green, 1948.
23. Benne, K. D., and Paul Sheats. Functional roles of group members. *J. Social Issues*, 1948, *4*, 41–49.
24. Bills, Robert E. Nondirective play therapy with retarded readers. *J. Consult. Psychol.*, 1950, *14*, 140–149.
25. Bills, Robert E. Play therapy with well-adjusted retarded readers. *J. Consult. Psychol.* (in process of publication).
26. Bills, Robert E.; C. J. Leiman, and R. W. Thomas. A study of the validity of the TAT and a set of animal pictures. 1949. (To be published.)
27. Bion, W. R. Experiences in groups: I. *Human Relations*, 1948, *1*, 314–320.
28. Bion, W. R. Experiences in groups: II. *Human Relations*, 1948, *1*, 487–511.
29. Bixler, Ray H. Limits are therapy. *J. Consult. Psychol.*, 1949, *13*, 1–11.
30. Bixler, Ray H. A method of case transfer. *J. Clin. Psychol.*, 1946, *2*, 274–278.
31. Bixler, R. H., and Virginia H. Bixler. Clinical counseling in vocational guidance. *J. Clin. Psychol.*, 1945, *1*, 186–192.
32. Bixler, R. H., and Virginia H. Bixler. Test interpretation in vocational counseling. *Educ. & Psychol. Measmt.*, 1946, *6*, 145–155.

33. Blocksma, D. D. An experiment in counselor learning. Ph.D. thesis in progress, University of Chicago.
34. Blocksma, D. D., and E. H. Porter, Jr. A short-term training program in client-centered counseling. *J. Consult. Psychol.*, 1947, *11*, 55–60.
35. Boring, E. G., and H. Sachs. Was this analysis a success? *J. Abnorm. & Soc. Psychol.*, 1940, *35*, 3–16.
36. Brody, B., and A. L. Grey. The non-medical psychotherapist: a critique and a program. *J. Abnorm. & Soc. Psychol.*, 1948, *43*, 179–192.
37. Burrow, Trigant. *The Neurosis of Man.* New York: Harcourt, Brace, 1949.
38. Cameron, Norman. *The Psychology of Behavior Disorders.* New York: Houghton Mifflin, 1947.
39. Cantor, N. *The Dynamics of Learning.* Buffalo: Foster and Stewart, 1946.
40. Carr, Arthur C. An evaluation of nine nondirective psychotherapy cases by means of the Rorschach. *J. Consult. Psychol.*, 1949, *13*, 196–205.
41. Coch, Lester, and J. R. P. French, Jr. Overcoming resistance to change. *Human Relations*, 1948, *1*, 512–532.
42. Combs, Arthur W. Basic aspects of non-directive therapy. *Amer. J. Orthopsychiat.*, 1946, *16*, 589–605.
43. A coordinated research in psychotherapy. *J. Consult. Psychol.*, 1949, *13*, 149–220. (A complete issue devoted to nine articles growing out of a coordinated series of projects. The nine articles are separately listed in this bibliography.)
44. Covner, B. J. Principles for psychological counseling with client organization. *J. Consult. Psychol.*, 1947, *11*, 227–244.
45. Cowen, E. L., and A. W. Combs. Followup study of 32 cases treated by nondirective psychotherapy. *J. Abnorm. & Soc. Psychol.*, 1950, *45*, 232–258.
46. Cowen, E. L., and W. M. Cruickshank. Group therapy with physically handicapped children: II. Evaluation. *J. Educ. Psychol.*, 1948, *39*, 281–297.
47. Cruickshank, W. M., and E. L. Cowen. Group therapy with physically handicapped children: I. Report of study. *J. Educ. Psychol.*, 1948, *39*, 193–215.
48. Curran, C. A. Nondirective counseling in allergic complaints. *J. Abnorm. & Soc. Psychol.*, 1948, *43*, 442–451.

49. Curran, C. A. *Personality Factors in Counseling.* New York: Grune and Stratton, 1945.
50. Doll, Edgar A. *Vineland Social Maturity Scale.* Educ. Test Bureau, Educ. Test Publishers, Minneapolis, 1947.
51. Dollard, John, and O. H. Mowrer. A method of measuring tension in written documents. *J. Abnorm. & Soc. Psychol.,* 1947, *42,* 3–32.
52. Duncker, Karl. On problem solving. *Psychol. Monogr.,* No. 270, 1945, *58,* No. 5, 1–113.
53. Eiserer, Paul E. The implications of nondirective counseling for classroom teaching. *Growing Points in Educational Research,* 1949 Official Report; Washington, D.C.: American Educational Research Association.
54. Estes, S. G. Concerning the therapeutic relationship in the dynamics of cure. *J. Consult. Psychol.,* 1948, *12,* 76–81.
55. Faw, Volney E. A psychotherapeutic method of teaching psychology. *Amer. Psychologist,* 1949, *4,* 104–109.
56. Fenichel, Otto. *The Psychoanalytic Theory of Neuroses.* New York: W. W. Norton, 1945.
57. Fiedler, Fred E. A comparative investigation of early therapeutic relationships created by experts and non-experts of the psychoanalytic, non-directive, and Adlerian schools. Ph.D. thesis, University of Chicago, 1949. (Accepted for publication by *J. Consult. Psychol.*)
58. Fiedler, Fred E. The concept of an ideal therapeutic relationship. *J. Consult. Psychol.,* 1950, *14,* 239–245.
59. Finke, Helene. Changes in the expression of emotionalized attitudes in six cases of play therapy. M.A. thesis, University of Chicago, 1947.
60. Fleming, Louise, and W. U. Snyder. Social and personal changes following non-directive group play therapy. *Amer. J. Orthopsychiat.,* 1947, *17,* 101–116.
61. Foulkes, S. H. *Introduction to Group-Analytic Psychotherapy.* London: William Heinemann Medical Books, Ltd., 1948.
62. French, J. R. P., Jr.; A. Kornhauser; and A. Marrow, editors. Conflict and cooperation in industry. *J. Social Issues,* 1946, *2,* 1–54.
63. Freud, Anna. *Introduction to the Technic of Child Analysis.* New York: Nervous and Mental Disease Publishing Co., 1928.
64. Freud, Sigmund. *Autobiography.* London: Hogarth Press, 1946.

65. Freud, Sigmund. *Group Psychology and the Analysis of the Ego.* London: Hogarth Press, 1948. (Published in the United States by Liveright Publishing Corporation.)
66. Freud, Sigmund. Psychoanalysis: Freudian school. *Encyclopaedia Britannica, 18,* 1944.
67. Golden, C. S., and H. J. Ruttenberg. *The Dynamics of Industrial Democracy.* New York: Harper and Bros., 1942.
68. Golden, C. S., and H. J. Ruttenberg. Labor and management responsibility for production efficiency. In T. M. Newcomb and E. L. Hartley, *Readings in Social Psychology.* New York: Henry Holt, 1947, 461–465. (Reprinted from *The Dynamics of Industrial Democracy.* New York: Harper and Bros., 1942.)
69. Goldstein, Kurt. *Human Nature in the Light of Psychopathology.* Cambridge: Harvard University Press, 1940.
70. Gordon, Thomas. What is gained by group participation. *Educ. Leadership,* 1950, 7, 220–226.
71. Gorlow, Leon. Nondirective group psychotherapy: an analysis of the behavior of members as therapists. Ph.D. thesis, Teachers College, Columbia University, 1950.
72. Green, A. W. Social values and psychotherapy. *J. Pers.,* 1946, 14, 199–228.
73. Gross, L. An experimental study of the validity of the non-directive method of teaching. *J. Psychol.,* 1948, 26, 243–248.
74. *Group Psychotherapy.* War Department, TB MED 103, Washington, D.C., October 10, 1944.
75. Grummon, D. L., and T. Gordon. The counseling center of the University of Chicago. *Amer. Psychologist,* 1948, 3, 166–171.
76. Haigh, Gerard. Defensive behavior in client-centered therapy. *J. Consult. Psychol.,* 1949, 13, 181–189.
77. Haigh, Gerard, and Bill L. Kell. Multiple therapy as a method for training and research in psychotherapy. *J. Abnorm. & Soc. Psychol.* (accepted for publication).
78. Haimowitz, Natalie Reader. An investigation into some personality changes occurring in individuals undergoing client-centered therapy. Ph.D. thesis, University of Chicago, 1948.
79. Hamlin, R. M., and G. W. Albee. Muench's tests: a control group. *J. Consult. Psychol.,* 1948, 12, 412–416.
80. Harrower, M. R., ed. *Training in Clinical Psychology: Transactions of the First Conference.* New York: Macy Foundation, 1947.
81. Hayakawa, S. I. *Language in Thought and Action.* New York: Harcourt, Brace, 1949.

82. Hildreth, Harold. A battery of feeling and attitude scales for clinical use. *J. Clin. Psychol.*, 1946, *2*, 214–220.
83. Hiltner, Seward. *Pastoral Counseling*. New York: Abingdon-Cokesbury Press, 1949.
84. Hobbs, Nicholas. Nondirective group therapy. *J. Nat'l. Assn. of Deans of Women*, 1949, *12*, 114–121.
85. Hoch, Erasmus L. The nature of the group process in non-directive group psychotherapy. Ph.D. thesis, Teachers College, Columbia University, 1950.
86. Hoffman, A. Edward. A study of reported behavior changes in counseling. *J. Consult. Psychol.*, 1949, *13*, 190–195.
87. Hogan, Richard. The development of a measure of client defensiveness in a counseling relationship. Ph.D. thesis, University of Chicago, 1948.
88. Hogan, Richard. The development of a measure of client defensiveness in the counseling relationship. Ph.D. thesis abstract, University of Chicago, 1948.
89. Horney, Karen, ed. *Are You Considering Psychoanalysis?* New York: W. W. Norton, 1946.
90. Horney, Karen. *Self Analysis*. New York: W. W. Norton, 1942.
91. Hunt, J. McV. *Personality and the Behavior Disorders*. 2 vols. New York: Ronald Press, 1944.
92. Hutchins, Robert M. Education and democracy. *School and Society*, 1949, *69*, 425–428.
93. Ichheiser, Gustav. *Misunderstandings in Human Relations*. Chicago: University of Chicago Press, 1949.
94. Jaques, Elliott. Interpretive group discussion as a method of facilitating social change. *Human Relations*, 1948, *1*, 533–549.
95. Jaques, Elliott, ed. Social therapy. *J. Social Issues*, 1947, *3*, 67 pp.
96. Jaques, Elliott. Some principles of organization of a social therapeutic institution. *J. Social Issues*, 1947, *3*, 4–10.
97. Jellinek, E. M., and D. Shakow. Method of scoring the Kent-Rosanoff free association test. Unpublished manuscript.
98. Johnson, Wendell. *People in Quandaries*. New York: Harper and Bros., 1946.
99. Kauffman, P. E., and V. C. Raimy. Two methods of assessing therapeutic progress. *J. Abnorm. & Soc. Psychol.*, 1949, *44*, 379–385.
100. Kelley, Earl C. *Education for What is Real*. New York: Harper and Bros., 1947.

101. Kessler, Carol. Semantics and non-directive counseling. M.A. paper, University of Chicago, 1947.
102. Klapman, J. W. *Group Psychotherapy.* New York: Grune and Stratton, 1946.
103. Klein, Melanie. *The Psycho-analysis of Children.* London: Hogarth Press, 1937.
104. Kluckhohn, Clyde, and H. A. Murray, editors. *Personality in Nature, Society and Culture.* New York: Knoff, 1948.
105. Korzybski, Alfred. *Science and Sanity.* Lancaster, Pa.: Science Press Printing Co., 1933.
106. Krech, David, and R. S. Crutchfield. *Theory and Problems of Social Psychology.* New York: McGraw-Hill, 1948.
107. Landis, C. Psychoanalytic phenomena. *J. Abnorm. & Soc. Psychol.*, 1940, *35*, 17–28.
108. Landisberg, Selma, and W. U. Snyder. Non-directive play therapy. *J. Clin. Psychol.*, 1946, *2*, 203–213.
109. Lecky, Prescott. *Self-Consistency: a Theory of Personality.* New York: Island Press, 1945.
110. Leeper, Robert W. A motivational theory of emotion to replace "emotion as disorganized response." *Psychol. Rev.*, 1948, *55*, 5–21.
111. Leeper, Robert W. Cognitive and symbolic processes. Unpublished manuscript.
112. Lewin, Kurt, *et al.* The relative effectiveness of a lecture method and a method of group decision for changing food habits. Mimeographed report, National Research Council, Washington, D.C., 1942.
113. Lewin, Kurt, and Paul Grabbe. Conduct, knowledge and acceptance of new values. *J. Social Issues*, 1945, *1*, 53–64.
114. Lewis, Virginia W. Changing the behavior of adolescent girls. *Archives of Psychol.*, 1943, No. 279, 1–87.
115. Lilienthal, David E. *TVA — Democracy on the March.* New York: Pocket Books, 1945.
116. Lincoln, J. F. *Intelligent Selfishness and Manufacturing.* Cleveland: Lincoln Electric Co., 1942.
117. Lipkin, S. The client evaluates nondirective psychotherapy. *J. Consult. Psychol.*, 1948, *12*, 137–146.
118. Lippitt, Ronald. An experimental study of the effect of democratic and authoritarian group atmospheres. *Univ. Iowa Stud. Child Welfare*, 1940, *16*, 43–195.

119. Lippitt, Ronald, and R. K. White. The "social climate" of children's groups. Chapter XXVIII in R. Barker, J. Kounin, and H. Wright. *Child Development and Behavior.* New York: McGraw-Hill, 1943.

120. Luchins, A. S. On training clinical psychologists in psychotherapy. *J. Clin. Psychol.*, 1949, *5*, 132–137.

121. McCleary, R. A., and R. S. Lazarus. Autonomic discrimination without awareness. *J. Pers.*, 1949, *18*, 171–179.

122. McGinnies, Elliott. Emotionality and perceptual defense. *Psychol. Rev.*, 1949, *56*, 244–451.

123. McGregor, Douglas. Conditions of effective leadership in the industrial organization. In T. M. Newcomb and E. L. Hartley, *Readings in Social Psychology.* New York: Henry Holt, 1947, 427–435. (Reprinted from *J. Consult. Psychol.*, 1944, *8*, 55–63.)

124. McGregor, D.; I. Knickerbocker; M. Haire; and A. Bevelas, editors. The consultant role and organizational leadership: Improving human relations in industry. *J. Social Issues*, 1948, *4*, 1–53.

125. Main, Tom, and Marie Nyswander. Some observations on the third national training laboratory in group development. Unpublished manuscript, 1949.

126. Marrow, A. J., and J. R. P. French, Jr. Changing a stereotype in industry. *J. Social Issues*, 1945, *1*, 33–37.

127. Maslow, A. H. Dymanics of personality organization. *Psychol. Rev.*, 1943, *50*, 514–539, 541–558.

128. Maslow, A. H. A theory of human motivation. *Psychol. Rev.*, 1943, *50*, 370–396.

129. Masserman, J. H. *Principles of Dynamic Psychiatry.* New York: Saunders, 1946.

130. Mayo, Elton. *The Social Problems of an Industrial Civilization.* Boston: Division of Research, Harvard University Graduate School of Business Administration, 1945.

131. Meister, R. K., and H. E. Miller. The dynamics of non-directive psychotherapy. *J. Clin. Psychol.*, 1946, *2*, 59–67.

132. Miller, H. E. "Acceptance" and related attitudes as demonstrated in psychotherapeutic interviews. *J. Clin. Psychol.*, 1949, *5*, 83–87.

133. Miller, Hyman, and D. W. Baruch. Psychological dynamics in allergic patients as shown in group and individual psychotherapy. *J. Consult. Psychol.*, 1948, *12*, 111–115.

134. Mitchell, J. H., and C. A. Curran. A method of approach to psychosomatic problems in allergy. *West Virginia Med. J.*, 1946, *42*, 1–24.
135. Moreno, J. L. *Group Therapy.* New York: Beacon House, 1945.
136. Mowrer, O. H. Learning theory and the neurotic paradox. *Amer. J. Orthopsychiat.*, 1948, *18*, 571–610.
137. Mowrer, O. H., and Clyde Kluckhohn. A dynamic theory of personality. Chapter III in J. McV. Hunt, *Personality and the Behavior Disorders*, vol. 1. New York: Ronald Press, 1944.
138. Mowrer, O. H., and A. D. Ullman. Time as a determinant in integrative learning. *Psychol. Rev.*, 1945, *52*, 61–90.
139. Mosak, Harold. Evaluation in psychotherapy: a study of some current measures. Ph.D. thesis, University of Chicago, 1950.
140. Muench, George A. An evaluation of non-directive psychotherapy by means of the Rorschach and other tests. *App. Psychol. Monogr.*, 1947, No. 13, 1–163.
141. Murphy, Gardner. *Personality: a Biosocial Approach to Origins and Structure.* New York: Harper and Bros., 1947.
142. Newcomb, T. M. Autistic hostility and social reality. *Human Relations*, 1947, *1*, 69–86.
143. Patterson, C. H. Is psychotherapy dependent upon diagnosis? *Amer. Psychologist*, 1948, *3*, 155–159.
144. Pearse, I. H., and Lucy H. Crocker. *The Peckham Experiment: a Study in the Living Structure of Society.* London: George Allen and Unwin, Ltd., 1943.
145. Pearse, I. H., and G. Scott Williamson. *Biologists in Search of Material.* London: Faber and Faber Limited, 1938.
146. Peres, H. An investigation of nondirective group therapy. *J. Consult. Psychol.*, 1947, *11*, 159–172.
147. Perry, William G., Jr. Of counselors and college. *Harvard Educ. Rev.*, 1948, 8–34.
148. Porter, E. H., Jr. *An Introduction to Therapeutic Counseling.* Boston: Houghton Mifflin, 1950.
149. Porter, E. H., Jr. The development and evaluation of a measure of counseling interview procedures. I. The development. *Educ. & Psychol. Measmt.*, 1943, *3*, 105–126.
150. Porter, E. H., Jr. The development and evaluation of a measure of counseling interview procedures. II. The evaluation. *Educ. & Psychol. Measmt.*, 1943, *3*, 215–238.
151. Postman, L.; J. S. Bruner; and E. McGinnies. Personal values as

selective factors in perception. *J. Abnorm. & Soc. Psychol.*, 1948, *43*, 142–154.

152. Radke, Marian, and Dayna Klisurich. Experiments in changing food habits. *J. Amer. Dietetic Assn.*, 1947, *23*, 403–409.

153. Raimy, Victor C. The self-concept as a factor in counseling and personality organization. Ph.D. thesis, Ohio State University, 1943.

154. Raimy, Victor C. Self reference in counseling interviews. *J. Consult. Psychol.*, 1948, *12*, 153–163.

155. Rank, Otto. *Will Therapy;* and *Truth and Reality.* New York: Knopf, 1945.

156. Raskin, Nathaniel J. An analysis of six parallel studies of therapeutic process. *J. Consult. Psychol.*, 1949, *13*, 206–220.

157. Raskin, Nathaniel J. An objective study of the locus of evaluation factor in psychotherapy. Ph.D. thesis, University of Chicago, 1949.

158. Raskin, Nathaniel J. The development of nondirective therapy. *J. Consult. Psychol.*, 1948, *12*, 92–110.

159. Raskin, Nathaniel J. The nondirective attitude. Unpublished manuscript, 1947.

160. Recommended graduate training program in clinical psychology. Report of the Committee on Training in Clinical Psychology of the American Psychological Association, *Amer. Psychologist*, 1947, *2*, 539–558.

161. Reik, Theodor. *Listening with the Third Ear.* New York: Farrar, Straus, 1948.

162. Ribble, Margaret A. Infantile experience in relation to personality development. Chapter XX in J. McV. Hunt, *Personality and the Behavior Disorders*, vol. 2. New York: Ronald Press, 1944.

163. Roethlisberger, F. J., and W. J. Dickson. *Management and the Worker.* Cambridge: Harvard University Press, 1939.

164. Rogers, Carl R. *Clinical Treatment of the Problem Child.* New York: Houghton Mifflin, 1939.

165. Rogers, Carl R. The clinical psychologist's approach to personality problems. *The Family*, 1937, *18*, 233–243.

166. Rogers, Carl R. *Counseling and Psychotherapy.* Boston: Houghton Mifflin, 1942.

167. Rogers, Carl R. Current trends in psychotherapy. Chapter V in Wayne Dennis, ed., *Current Trends in Psychology.* Pittsburgh: University of Pittsburgh Press, 1947, 109–137.

168. Rogers, Carl R.   Divergent trends in methods of improving adjust-
     ment. *Harvard Educ. Rev.*, 1948, 209–219.
169. Rogers, Carl R.   The process of therapy. *J. Consult. Psychol.*,
     1940, *4*, 161–164.
170. Rogers, Carl R.   Significant aspects of client-centered therapy.
     Amer. Psychologist, 1946, *1*, 415–422.   [Permission to quote
     given by the *American Psychologist* and the American Psychologi-
     ·cal Association.]
171. Rogers, Carl R.   Some implications of client-centered counseling
     for college personnel work. *Educ. & Psychol. Measmt.*, 1948, *8*,
     540–549.
172. Rogers, Carl R.   Some observations on the organization of person-
     ality. *Amer. Psychologist*, 1947, *2*, 358–368.
173. Rogers, Carl R.   The use of electrically recorded interviews in
     improving psychotherapeutic techniques. *Amer. J. Orthopsy-
     chiat.*, 1942, *12*, 429–434.
174. Rogers, Natalie.   Changes in self concept in the case of Mrs. Ett.
     Personal Counselor, 1947, *2*, 278–291.
175. Rogers, Natalie.   Measuring psychological tensions in non-direc-
     tive counseling. *Personal Counselor*, 1948, *3*, 237–264.
176. Rosenzweig, Saul.   *Psychodiagnosis.* New York: Grune and Strat-
     ton, 1949.
177. Schilder, P.   *Psychotherapy.* New York: W. W. Norton, 1938.
178. Schwebel, M., and M. J. Asch.   Research possibilities in nondirec-
     tive teaching. *J. Educ. Psychol.*, 1948, *39*, 359–369.
179. Seeman, Julius.   A study of client self-selection of tests in voca-
     tional counseling. *Educ. & Psychol. Measmt.*, 1948, *8*, 327–346.
180. Seeman, Julius.   A study of the process of nondirective therapy.
     J. Consult. Psychol., 1949, *13*, 157–168.
181. Shaffer, L. F.   The problem of psychotherapy. *Amer. Psycholo-
     gist*, 1947, *2*, 459–467.
182. Shakow, D.   One psychologist as analysand. *J. Abnorm. & Soc.
     Psychol.*, 1940, *35*, 198–211.
183. Shaw, Clifford R.   Memorandum submitted to the Board of Direc-
     tors of the Chicago Area Project. January 10, 1944, mimeo-
     graphed report.
184. Shaw, F. J.   The role of reward in psychotherapy. *Amer. Psycholo-
     gist*, 1949, *4*, 177–179.
185. Shaw, F. J.   A stimulus-response analysis of repression and insight
     in psychotherapy. *Psychol. Rev.*, 1946, *53*, 36–42.

186. Shedlin, Arthur J. A psychological approach to group leadership in education. Unpublished manuscript.
187. Shedlin, Arthur J. *The Effectiveness of Group Climate: an Experiment in Human Relations.* National Conference of Christians and Jews, Inc., 1948.
188. Sheerer, Elizabeth T. An analysis of the relationship between acceptance of and respect for self and acceptance of and respect for others in seven counseling cases. Ph.D. thesis, University of Chicago, 1949.
189. Sheerer, Elizabeth T. An analysis of the relationship between acceptance of and respect for self and acceptance of and respect for others in ten counseling cases. *J. Consult. Psychol.*, 1949, *13*, 169–175.
190. Shoben, E. J., Jr. A learning-theory interpretation of psychotherapy. *Harvard Educ. Rev.*, 1948, 129–145.
191. Shoben, E. J., Jr. Psychotherapy as a problem in learning theory. *Psychol. Bull.*, 1949, *46*, 366–392.
192. Slavson, S. R. *Analytic Group Psychotherapy with Children, Adolescents and Adults.* New York: Columbia University Press, 1950.
193. Smith, H. C., and D. S. Dunbar. The personality and achievement of the classroom participant. Unpublished research study.
194. Snyder, W. U. Client-centered therapy. In L. A. Pennington, and I. A. Berg, editors, *An Introduction to Clinical Psychology.* New York: Ronald Press, 1948, 465–497.
195. Snyder, W. U. A comparison of one unsuccessful with four successful nondirectively counseled cases. *J. Consult. Psychol.*, 1947, *11*, 38–42.
196. Snyder, W. U. An investigation of the nature of non-directive psychotherapy. Ph.D. thesis, Ohio State University, 1943.
197. Snyder, W. U. An investigation of the nature of non-directive psychotherapy. *J. Gen. Psychol.*, 1945, *33*, 193–223.
198. Snyder, W. U. The present status of psychotherapeutic counseling. *Psychol. Bull.*, 1947, *44*, 297–386.
199. Snyder, W. U., *et al. Casebook of Non-directive Counseling.* Boston: Houghton Mifflin, 1947.
200. Snygg, Donald, and Arthur W. Combs. *Individual Behavior: a New Frame of Reference for Psychology.* New York: Harper and Bros., 1949.
201. Stephenson, W. Introduction to inverted factor analysis, with some applications to studies in orexis. *J. Educ. Psychol.*, 1936, *27*, 353–367.

202. Stephenson, W. Methodological consideration of Jung's typology. *J. Ment. Sci.*, 1939, *85*, 185–205.
203. Stock, Dorothy. An investigation into the interrelations between the self-concept and feelings directed toward other persons and groups. *J. Consult. Psychol.*, 1949, *13*, 176–180.
204. Strom, Kenneth. A re-study of William U. Snyder's "An investigation of the nature of non-directive psychotherapy." M.A. thesis, University of Chicago, 1948.
205. Sullivan, H. S. *Conceptions of Modern Psychiatry.* Washington, D.C.: W. A. White Foundation, 1945.
206. Survey Research Center Study No. 6. Selected findings from a study of clerical workers in the Prudential insurance company of America. Human Relations, University of Michigan, 1948.
207. Sutherland, J. D., and I. E. Menzies. Two industrial projects. *J. Social Issues*, 1947, *3*, 51–58.
208. Symonds, P. A. Education and psychotherapy. *J. Educ. Psychol.*, 1949, *40*, 1–32.
209. Taft, Jessie. *The Dynamics of Therapy in a Controlled Relationship.* New York: Macmillan, 1933.
210. Tavistock Institute of Human Relations. Two research projects on human relations in industry. Document No. 173, January 1949.
211. Telschow, Earl. The role of the group leader in nondirective group psychotherapy. Ed. D. project, Teachers College, Columbia University, 1950.
212. Thelen, H. A., and John Withall. Three frames of reference: the description of climate. *Human Relations*, 1949, *2*, 159–176.
213. Thetford, William N. The measurement of physiological responses to frustration before and after nondirective psychotherapy. Ph.D. thesis, University of Chicago, 1949.
214. Thetford, William N. The measurement of physiological responses to frustration before and after nondirective psychotherapy. *Amer. Psychologist*, 1948, *3*, 278. Abstract of thesis.
215. Thorne, F. C. The clinical method in science. *Amer. Psychologist*, 1947, *2*, 159–166.
216. Thorne, F. C. Directive psychotherapy: IV. The therapeutic implications of the case history. *J. Clin. Psychol.*, 1945, *1*, 318–330.
217. Thorne, F.; J. Carter; *et al.* Symposium: critical evaluation of nondirective counseling and psychotherapy. *J. Clin. Psychol.*, 1948, *4*, 225–263.

218. *To Secure These Rights.* Report of the President's Committee on Civil Rights. New York: Simon and Schuster, 1947.

219. Travis, L., and D. Baruch. *Personal Problems of Everyday Living.* New York: Appleton-Century, 1941.

220. Whitaker, Carl. Teaching the practicing physician to do psychotherapy. *Southern Med. J.*, 1949, *42*, 809–903.

221. Whitaker, C. A.; J. Warkentin; and N. Johnson. A philosophical basis for brief psychotherapy. *Psychiatric Quarterly*, 1949, *23*, 439–443.

222. White, Robert W. *The Abnormal Personality.* New York: Ronald Press, 1948.

223. Williams, Herbert D. Experiment in self-directed education. *School and Society*, 1930, *31*, 715–718.

224. Withall, John. The development of a technique for the measurement of social-emotional climate in classrooms. Ph.D. thesis, University of Chicago, 1948.

225. Withall, John. The development of a technique for the measurement of social-emotional climate in classrooms. *J. Exp. Educ.*, 1949, 347–361.

226. Witmer, H. L., ed. *Teaching Psychotherapeutic Medicine.* New York: Commonwealth Fund, 1947.

227. Wood, Austin. Another psychologist analyzed. *J. Abnorm. & Soc. Psychol.*, 1941, *36*, 87–90.

228. Zimmerman, Jervis. Modification of the discomfort relief quotient as a measure of progress in counseling. M.A. thesis, University of Chicago, 1950.

INDEX

Acceptance, 30, 41, 50, 96, 159–172, 194
  of others, 520
  in personality formation, 502
  in play therapy, 258, 276
  of self, 138, 194, 514
  in teaching, 384, 392–397, 401–402
  as a technique, 355–358
  and transference attitudes, 203
Acting out, danger of with play therapy, 256
Adjustment counseling, 3; see also Client-centered psychotherapy
Admission to training, 463
Aichhorn, August, 386
Albee, G. W., 173
Alexander, Franz, 4, 196
Alice, excerpts from case of, 151–155
Allen, F. H., 10, 219, 231, 236, 237, 276
Allergies, therapeutic work with, 229
Allport, G. W., 323, 329
Alpert, Bert., 370, 383
Alter ego, 35, 40, 41, 42, 208–209
American Psychological Association, 3, 14, 429, 434
    Committee on Graduate Training, 478
Ames, Adelbert, 385
"Anarchic participation," 370
Anderson, H. H., 347, 395
Angyal, Andras, 100, 481, 483, 488, 497
Asch, M. J., 424, 426
Ash, Philip, 225
Assimilation of denied experience, 104
Attention as a technique, 349–351
Attitudes, 19–20
    as basic to training, 432–433
    clarification of, 28, 62
    implementation of, 24–30, 34, 339, 433
    research on expression of, 133
    toward group leader, 331–332
    toward self, 136, 137, 138, 139–140, 157, 191
    toward students, 401–402, 408–409
    toward therapist, 66–69, 102–103, 105, 106, 110–112, 115–116, 118, 150, 167–171, 198–218

see also Reflection of attitudes; also Transference
Autistic hostility, 344
Axline, V. M., 11, 130, 185, 239, 263, 266, 270–271, 276, 319, 428, 452, 462

Baldwin, A. L., 340
Baruch, D. W., 277, 438
Bavelas, Alex, 383
Behavior Research Photopolygraph, 183
Beier, E. G., 142, 418
Bell Adjustment Inventory, 172, 173, 176
Bell, J. E., 173
Benne, K. D., 332
Bernreuter Adjustment Inventory, 172, 173, 177
Bills, R. E., 185, 271–272, 274, 275, 277
Biological knowledge for therapists, 439–440
Bion, W. R., 353, 383
Bixler, R. H., 226, 258, 277
Bixler, V. H., 226
Blocksma, D. D., 25, 444, 445, 452–461, 478
Boring, E. G., 130
Bown, O. H., 160–171
Breese, F. H., 340
Brewer, H. M., 347
Brody, B. S., 478
Broken appointments, frequency of, 75
Bruner, J. S., 506
Burrow, Trigant, 481, 486
Butler, J. M., 462

Cameron, Norman, 481
Cantor, Nathaniel, 385, 396, 420, 424, 428
Capacity of the client, 9, 10, 14, 23, 31, 35–36, 47, 48, 54, 56, 59, 60, 63, 122, 150, 221, 238–239, 276, 327, 338, 384, 427, 454, 467
Carlson's Raiders, 58
Carr, A. C., 173–174, 196
Carter, J. W., 231
Case supervision for students; see Supervision of trainees
Casebook of Non-directive Counseling (Snyder), 13

Casual interviewing, 470

Catalyst-leader, 63

Child-rearing practices, 339–340

Civil rights, 325–326

Clarification of attitudes; *see* Reflection of attitudes

Client-centered counseling; *see* Client-centered psychotherapy

Client-centered psychotherapy, 4, 5, 6, 12, 129, 141–142
    background for, 436–440
    basic principles of, 276, 292
    cultural influences of, 5, 292–293, 367
    implications of, 11, 388–391
    and problem-solving, 146
    range of application of, 10–12, 176, 189–190, 276, 279–280, 313–314; *see also* Limits of applicability
    training for, 432; *see also* Training in psychotherapy

Client-centered teaching, 11
    in cases of reading retardation, 270–271
    see also Student-centered teaching

Client-centeredness, 30
    assimilation of, as predictor of success on the job, 457–458

Client expectations, 66–69
    transference development, 215

Client planning, 180

Client's frame of reference, 34, 41
    in group therapy, 288–289
    in play therapy, 245
    see also Internal frame of reference

Client's perception, 65, 141–142, 145–146

Client's perception of counselor, 36–38, 38–40, 41, 66–69, 105, 106
    as described by client, 90, 102–103, 105

Client's perceptual field, 34, 128, 136, 141–142
    as described by client, 90
    in group therapy, 288–289
    in play therapy, 254–256
    and problem-solving, 146

Clients, 7

Clinical psychology, 3, 14, 429, 434, 436

Coch, Lester, 57, 64, 381

Combs, A. W., 18, 146, 196, 386, 428, 481, 488

Committee on Human Development of the University of Chicago, 435

Communication:
    of attitudes, 114, 306, 495
    barriers to as perceived barriers, 344–345
    "expressional" aspect of, 352
    in teaching, 401–402
    universal barriers to, 346

Conference on Training in Clinical Psychology, 478

Contacts; *see* Interviews

Control, 127, 497, 514

Cooke, M. L., 343

Cooley, C. H., 497

Counseling, 3
    measurement of skill in, 452–453; *see also* Client-centered psychotherapy

Counseling and Psychotherapy: Newer Concepts in Practice (Rogers), 9, 14, 64, 196, 228

Counseling Center of the University of Chicago, 13, 75, 223–224, 273, 320–322, 356–357, 380–381, 444, 472, 475

Counseling hour, 7
    in play therapy, 242–244
    stability of, 70–71
    support of, 87

Counseling process; *see* Therapeutic process

Counselor attitudes toward client, 122, 150, 159–172

Covner, B. J., 383

Cowen, E. L., 177–178, 270, 277

Criteria of evaluation, 415

Cruickshank, W. M., 270, 277

Cultural anthropology and training in therapy, 437

"Cure" of a psychological condition, 230

Curran, C. A., 145, 196

Current feelings, 134–135

Darrow, C. W., 183

Decision-making in groups, 343

Defensiveness, 97, 100, 117, 127, 496
    in education, 390
    occurrence of, 516
    scale of, 157
    during therapy, 182–183, 187–188

Democratic cooperation, 327

Denied attitudes, 75–77, 127, 135, 194
    effect of discovery of, 77–83

Denying to consciousness, 30, 41, 97, 100–101, 114, 147–149, 499–503, 501, 504–505, 506, 507
Dependency in groups, 331–332
  illustration of, 340–342
Dependency in therapy, 214–218
  and being evaluated, 214–215
  and expectation of dependency, 215
  and experience of dependency, 215–217
  and projection of threat, 217–218
  in teaching, 419
Dewey, John, 386
Diagnosis in psychotherapy, 30
  detrimental effects of, 223–225
  as an experience by the client, 223
  in group therapy, 289
  intent to use in response, measurement of, 452–455
  and interpretation, 222
  philosophical implications of, 224–225
  and psychosomatic problems, 226–228
  rationale of, in client-centered psychotherapy, 221–223
  rationale of, in organic illness, 230
  social implications of, 224–225
  training in, and training for therapy, 441–442
  transitory objections to, 225–226
  trends regarding, 219–220
  use of, conclusions regarding, 221
Dickson, W. J., 10
Differentiation, 142–149
Directiveness, 113, 207
  measurement of, 452–456
Directive therapy, 196
Discomfort-Relief quotient, 181–182
Discord in groups, measure of, 306
Disowning, 509–510
Distributed leadership, 332
Dollard, John, 181
Dunbar, D. S., 425
Duncker, Karl, 146
Dynamics of groups, 3, 322, 323–324, 402; see also Group-member participation
Dynamics of interpersonal relationship, 15
Dynamics of Learning, The (Cantor), 385
Dynamics of personality; see Personality dynamics, also Personality structure

Eclecticism, 8
Education:
  basis for, 384
  democratic goals of, 387–388
  growth versus maintenance of status quo as goals, 391
  and philosophical orientation, 387
Education for What Is Real (Kelley), 385
Educational method, 385, 388
Educational outcomes, 392, 414–418, 418–426
  of "free-discussion" course, 425
  of nondirective versus conventional course, 424, 425
  in psychological adjustment, 426
Ego-involvement, 326, 389, 470, 494–495
Eiserer, P. E., 392
Electrically recorded interviews, 6, 13, 25, 27–28
  in play therapy, 266
  use in training, 431, 465
  use in measurement of therapeutic skill, 452–453
Emotion, its place in personality, 492–494
Emotional identification, 29, 122
Emotionalized attitudes and transference, 218
Empathy, 28–29, 54
  as desirable for training in therapy, 437
  measure of, 454
  as a technique, 348–349
Encouragement, 31
Ending therapy, 85–88, 117–118, 126, 136
  in group therapy, 294
  in play therapy, 264–266
Estes, S. G., 64
Evaluation, 150
  detrimental effects of in diagnosis, 223–224
  in learning, 414–418
  and transference attitudes, 202, 208, 214–215
  see also Locus of evaluation
Evaluational interaction, 498
Examinations, 414–418
Experimental frustration, 183–184
Exploration of attitudes, 72–75, 124
  outcome of, 75–77
  in teaching, 396–397
Extensional quality of reaction, 144

External frame of reference, 33, 45, 47, 418, 495
  and therapist maladjustment, 42–43
External reality, 146

Failure cases, 188–190
Faw, V. E., 425, 428
Fenichel, Otto, 198, 203, 221–222, 533
Fiedler, F. E., 52, 54, 55, 64
Figure-ground relationship, 145, 146, 483, 501, 504
Finke, H. M., 268–269
Fleming, Louise, 272, 273
Foulkes, S. H., 301, 319
Fred, excerpts from case of, 254–256
"Free-floating attention," 352
French, J. R. P., Jr., 57, 64, 326, 381
French, T. M., 4, 196, 231
Freud, Anna, 235
Freud, Sigmund, 4, 198, 236, 439, 495
  on groups, 328
Fromm, Eric, 290
Frustration tolerance, 183–184

Gaps in current knowledge, 187–190
Gates Primary Reading Tests, 270, 271
Generalization, 143
Gestalt psychology, 4
Goals of education, 386
  in current training program, 464–477
Golden, C. S., 339, 368, 383
Goldstein, Kurt, 481, 489
Gordon, Thomas, 18, 340, 371, 444, 462
Gorlow, Leon, 295, 311–312
Grabbe, Paul, 383
"Gradient of autonomy," 498
Grading students, 414–418
Great Books course, 409
Green, A. W., 49
Grey, A. L., 478
Gross, Llewellyn, 424
Group-centered administration; see Group-centered leadership
Group-centered leadership:
  centrality of total participation in, 325–327
  development of rationale for, 320–323
  in large organizations, 368
  origins of, 337
  outcomes of, 368–383
  theoretical bases for, 323–329

Group-centeredness, index of, 308
Group-centered therapy, 11
  basic principles in, 292–293
  ease of speech in, 292–293
  economy of, 278–279
  effectiveness of, 315–318
  frequency of meetings in, 294
  illustration of, 280–285
  and individual therapy, 278–280, 286–293, 314–315
  and interpersonal relations as therapeutic agent, 289–293
  interplay of roles in, 309–312
  length of meetings in, 294
  optimal number of clients in, 293–294
  and prior individual therapy, 313
  and psychotic tendencies, 313
  range of application of, 279–280, 313–314
  selection of group members, 294, 312–315
  starting, 294–295
  themes in, 295–296
  therapeutic atmosphere in, 286–288
  therapeutic process in, 296–305
  and therapist's role, 305–309
Group climate, as leadership pattern, 346–347
  see also Group process
Group disequilibrium and adjustive behavior, 324–326
Group dynamics movement, 332
Group facilitation, 291, 367
  and distribution of leadership, 332
  and reflection of intent, 351–352
Group leadership; see Group-centered leadership, also Leadership function
Group member participation:
  and acceptance of group standards, 381–383
  changes in as outcome of leadership, 378–383
  dependence of on inner forces, 367
  and dependency, 331, 380–381
  deterrence of by group leader, 332
  and morale, 326
  and reactive behavior, 329, 378–380
  value of, 326
Group process, 329
  and access to leadership, 332
  and freedom of communication, 343–346

inhibition of by leaders, 333-334
and opportunity for participation, 340-343
releasing of, 329
Group structure:
dependency in, 331-332
as dynamic system of forces, 324
as obedient herd, 328
as relationship between members, 323-324
Growth; see Self-enhancement
Grummon, D. L., 18, 462
Guess Who Test, 272

Haigh, G. V., 157, 182, 187-188, 196, 471, 478
Haimowitz, N. R., 174-176, 229
Haire, Mason, 383
Hallucinations, 119
Hamlin, R. M., 173
Harrower-Erickson, M. R., 174
Harvard University, 224
Henderson, Lawrence, 16
Henry, excerpts from the case of, 247-254
Herbert Bryan, the case of, 30
Hertz, M. R., 173
Hildreth Feeling-Attitude Scale, 172, 173, 177
Hiltner, Seward, 64
Hoch, E. L., 302
Hoffman, A. E., 157, 181, 196
Hogan, R. A., 182-183, 187, 516-517
Horney, Karen, 4, 64, 130, 231, 489
Hull, C. L., 495
Hutchins, R. M., 387
Hypotheses in psychotherapy, 4, 6, 7, 8, 9, 22-24, 26, 47, 131, 172
and community effort, 59, 63-64
and play therapy, 238, 276
and teaching, 384, 388-391
Hypotheses and personality operation, 486
Hypothesis, implementation of, 35, 122, 305, 335
in client-centered teaching, 388-390, 393

Ichheiser, Gustav, 351, 352
Improved adjustment, evidences for, 180-186

Information-giving:
measurement of, 452-455
in teaching, 397-398, 401
Insight, 119, 146, 148, 157
appearance of, 108
as outcome of group-centered leader-ship, 375-376
in play therapy, 244-254
and student-centered teaching, 424
in a training program, 446
Integration, 513-514; see also Self-enhancement
Intensional quality of reactions, 144
Internal frame of reference, 29, 31, 32, 34, 36, 41, 47, 48, 119, 127, 191-196, 354, 392-393, 419
difficulty in understanding, 43-45
and personality theory, 494-497
Internalization of experience, 151, 376-378
as educational good, 387
Internship in counseling, 475-476
Interpreting, 31, 207, 289
criterion of correctness of, 221-222
in group work, 353
measurement of use of, 452-455
Interviews:
frequency of, 10
number of, related to outcome, 185-186
number of, and therapeutic skill, 456
responsibility for reopening of, 122
Introjection, 149, 151, 192
in personality formation, 498-503; 522
I.Q., increases in, 340
Ivimey, M., 196

Jaques, Elliott, 353, 357
Jellinek, E. M., 176
Job adjustment and duration of counsel-ing, 185-186
Journal of Abnormal and Social Psychology, 130
Journal of Consulting Psychology, 19, 196
Journal of the National Association of Deans of Women, 280
Journal of Social Issues, 383

Kalhorn, Joan, 340
Kell, B. L., 471, 478
Kelley, Earl, 385, 428

Kent-Rosanoff Word Association Test,
  172, 173, 176
Kessler, Carol, 150
Kilpatrick, Elizabeth, 130
Kilpatrick, W. H., 386
Klapman, J. W., 318
Klein, Melanie, 236
Klisurich, Dayna, 339, 381
Klopfer, Bruno, 173
Kluckhohn, Clyde, 481, 489
Knickerbocker, Irving, 383
Kornhauser, A. W., 326

Landis, C., 130
Landisberg, S. I., 267–268
Lazarus, R. S., 506
Leader, role of, 63, 326, 332–333
  characteristics of, 348–349
  function of; see Leadership function
Leadership function, 330
  diffusion of, 332, 367
  effectiveness of, 334, 343
  goals of, 335, 336–337
  inaccurate evaluation of, 343
  planning for group, 364–365
  as property of group, 332
  and responsibility, 330–331
  and superior ability, 330–331
  transference of, 336
Learning, 15, 384
  evaluation of, 414–418
  facilitation of, 401
  illustration of process in class, 402–
    409
  movement in, 142
  resistance to, 390–391
  and self-enhancement, 389–391
  and self-organization, 390–391
Lecky, Prescott, 481, 497
Leeper, R. W., 493, 498
Lewin, Kurt, 15, 57, 346, 382
Lewis, V. W., 196
Lilienthal, David, 5, 58
Limits of applicability:
  and age ranges, 229
  and degree of disturbance, 229
  and defectives and delinquents, 229
  earlier criteria of, 228
  and intra-punitive males, 229
  and personality types, 229–230
  in play therapy, 238
  and psychosomatic ailments, 229
  and social class, 229

Limits in psychotherapy:
  acceptance of, 255, 356
  in play therapy, 257–262
  setting of, 211
  in teaching, 396–397
"Linking" as a technique in group leader-
    ship, 358
Lipkin, Stanley, 70, 129
Lippitt, Ronald, 56, 346
Listening with the Third Ear (Reik), 438
Locus of evaluation, 150–157
  analysis of in evaluation of thera-
    peutic skill, 453–455
  and diagnosis, 223–228
  in group-centered leadership, 373–
    375
  and psychosomatic problems, 226–
    228
  research study of, 156–157
  in student-centered teaching, 414–
    418
Locus of responsibility, 47–48, 63, 122,
    227, 373–375
Love as therapeutic agent, 159–172
Luchins, A. S., 478

McCleary, R. A., 506
McGinnies, E. M., 506
McGregor, Douglas, 329, 331, 383
Macy Foundation, 478
Management, control patterns of, 326
Marrow, A. J., 326
Martha, excerpts from case of, 256
Maslow, A. H., 481, 482
Masserman, Jules, 481
Maturity of behavior, 157, 180–181,
    487–491
Mayo, Elton, 16, 187
Mead, G. H., 497
Meister, R. K., 50
Mental defect, 277
Miller, H. E., 50, 51
Ministers, 3
Minnesota Multiphasic Personality In-
    ventory, 172, 173, 177, 426
Miss Cam, excerpts from the case of, 88–
    129
Miss Gil, excerpts from the case of, 46–
    47, 50
Miss Har, excerpts from the case of, 73–
    74, 76, 79–81, 83, 84, 87, 101
Miss Tir, excerpts from the case of, 210–
    213, 217

Moralization, 452–455
Moreno, J. L., 319
Mosak, H. H., 174, 176, 177
Motivation for therapy, 195–196
Movement in learning, 142
Mowrer, O. H., 132, 181, 481, 489
Mr. M., the case of, 30
Mrs. Dar, excerpts from the case of, 201–202, 210
Mrs. Ett, excerpts from the case of, 74–75, 81, 84–85, 85–87, 203–209, 210
Muench, G. A., 173–174, 176, 196
Multiple therapy, 460, 471–474
Murphy, Gardner, 481
Murray, H. A., 481
Mutual counseling by students, 470–471

National Training Laboratory at Bethel, 322
Need-satisfaction, 491–492, 504, 508
Negative feelings, 134
Neurosis, 508
Neurotic signs, scales for measurement of, 173–178
Newcomb, T. M., 344
Nonadjustive behavior in groups, 325
Nondirective, 4, 5, 21
Nondirective behavior in member-therapists, 311–312
    and notion of orthodoxy, 430–431
Nondirective counseling; see Client-centered psychotherapy

Ohio State University, 429
Organic experience, 109, 483
Organic problems, 440
Organized reaction of organism, 486–487
Orthodoxy in psychotherapy, 430–431, 460

Patterson, C. H., 231
Peckham Centre Experiment, 59–63, 227, 339, 383
Perceived leader, 332–334
Perception of self, 136, 140–142, 389
Perceptual behavior, 385–386
    personal factors affecting, 506
Perceptual field, 484–486
    and development of self, 497
Perceptual-field reorganization, 142–146, 193–196, 221–223, 317–318, 362–363, 389–391
    in the learning process, 389–391
Perceptual "map," 485

Peres, H., 304, 315–318, 319
Permissiveness, 50, 56–57, 58, 63, 256
    as group therapy outcome, 311
    and limits of freedom, 356
    in play therapy, 256–262
    in teaching, 401–402
Personal Counselors, 14, 185–186, 478
    brief training program for, 444–462
Personal Problems of Everyday Living (Travis and Baruch), 438
Personal reaction by counselor, 208–209; see also Counselor-attitudes toward client
Personal therapy for trainees, 433, 437–438, 447, 465
Personality dynamics, knowledge of in training, 438
Personality structure, 7, 100, 119, 172, 176, 178–179, 191, 418
    alteration of in therapy, 531–532
    and training for therapy, 435–438
Personality theory, 7, 15–17, 388–390
    and adequate symbolization, 491
    and acceptance of self and others, 520–522
    and development of self, 497–498
    diagrammatic representation of, 525–526
    and disowning, 509–510
    and emotion, 492–494
    and evaluational interaction, 498
    and hypotheses, 486
    and internal frame of reference, 494–497
    and need satisfaction, 491–492
    and organization of behavior, 486–487
    and perceptual valence, 503–507
    and phenomenal field, 483–486
    and psychological tension, 510–512
    and self-consistency, 507–509
    and self-enhancement, 487–491
    and self-reorganization, 517–520
    and threat, 515–517
    in training of therapists, 440
    and value system, 498–503, 522–524
    and visceral experiences, 513–515
Phenomenal field, 142, 145–149, 221–223, 483, 484, 499, 503
Phenomenal self, 146
Philadelphia group, 4
Philosophical orientation, 5, 14, 20–22

as central in counselor training, 432–433

as educational method, 393, 401, 416

formulation of in training for therapy, 437, 447

and goals of education, 387

Physically handicapped children, 270, 277

Pilot-evaluation, 344–345

Play Analysis; see Play therapy, origins of

Play therapy, 11, 50, 158

analysis of protocols of, 267–269

and capacity of child for self-help, 238–239

and child responsibility for pace, 242–244

choice of medium in, 265–266

compared with adult therapy, 268, 275–276

and demand for structure, 263–264

effect of on personality test performance, 272–273

and free association, 235–236

individual or group contacts in, 262–263

and limits, 257–263

origins of, 235–237

and permissiveness, 256–262

and problems of electrical recording in, 266

range of applicability of, 238

and Rankian theory, 236–237

research in, 266–275

with retarded readers, 271–272

and source of referrals, 263–264

and therapist's role, 240–242

and treatment of parents, 239

Porter, E. H., Jr., 64, 444, 452, 462, 478

Positive feelings, 134

Postman, L. J., 506

Practicum courses, 467–475

Pre- and post-testing, 172–179

Prediction, of interview effect, 94

of proper group memberships, 313

Pre-perception; see Subception

President's Committee on Civil Rights, report of, 325

Primary experience, 143

Problem areas, 10, 104, 145, 226–228, 228–230, 440

Problem-solving, 146

and educational goals, 387

and external evaluation, 418

Professional responsibility, 48, 469–470, 472 473, 474

Prognosis, 30, 313

Psychiatry, 3, 14, 435, 442

brief training in, 442–444

Psychoanalytic interview, excerpt from, 43–44

Psychological adjustment, 513–515

Psychological "chain reaction," 522

Psychological climate:

development of, 393–409

effect upon student, 392

measurement of, 395–396

see also Group climate; also Therapeutic atmosphere

Psychological Clinic of Ohio State University, 9, 430

Psychological health, 501–503

Psychological maladjustment, 510–512

Psychological tension, 181, 191–192, 502, 510–512

Psychosomatic problems, 226–228, 229

and play therapy, 277

Psychotherapy, 3, 6, 40

basic element of, 148

description of, 141–142

desirable background for training in, 436–440

initial phases, 150

issues in, 45–51

as learning process, 132

and problem-solving, 146

theory of, 7, 15–17, 148, 190–196, 275–276, 439

value system in, 149

Psychotherapy, 319

Psychotics, 11, 119, 485

as poor risks in group therapy, 313

"Q" technique, 53, 140, 141, 275

Questioning, 31, 452–455

Race conflict, 276, 323

Radke, M. J., 339, 381

Raimy, V. C., 136, 191

Rank, Otto, 4, 10, 236

Rankian therapy, 219, 236, 385

Raskin, N. J., 18, 29, 156–157, 188, 196, 462

Reactive behavior, 329

Reading retardation, 270–271, 271–272, 277

and adjustment of readers, 272